Down to Earth Sociology

Introductory Readings

SEVENTH EDITION

JAMES M. HENSLIN, Editor

THE FREE PRESS
A Division of Macmillan, Inc.
NEW YORK

Maxwell Macmillan Canada
TORONTO

Maxwell Macmillan International
NEW YORK   OXFORD   SINGAPORE   SYDNEY

The Free Press
A Division of Macmillan, Inc.
866 Third Avenue, New York, N.Y. 10022

Maxwell Macmillan Canada, Inc.
1200 Eglinton Avenue East
Suite 200
Don Mills, Ontario M3C 3N1

Macmillan, Inc. is part of the Maxwell Communication
Group of Companies.

Printed in the United States of America

printing number

   3 4 5 6 7 8 9 10

Library of Congress Cataloging-in-Publication Data

Down to earth sociology: introductory readings / James M. Henslin,
   editor.—7th ed.
      p.   cm.
   Includes indexes.
   ISBN 0–02–914665–8
   1. Sociology.   2. United States—Social conditions.   I. Henslin,
James M.
HM51.D68   1993
301—dc20   92–30262
                                                              CIP

Credits
and Acknowledgments

Grateful acknowledgment is made to the authors and publishers who have granted permission to reprint these selections:

ARTICLE
NUMBER

1   Excerpts from *Invitation to Sociology* by Peter L. Berger. Copyright © 1963 by Peter L. Berger. Reprinted by permission of Doubleday Publishing, a division of Bantam Doubleday Dell Publishing Group, Inc.

2   Copyright © 1985 by James M. Henslin.

3   From *The Sociological Imagination* by C. Wright Mills. Copyright © 1959 by Oxford University Press, Inc.: renewed 1987 by Yaraslava Mills. Reprinted by permission of Oxford University Press, Inc.

4   Copyright © 1991 by James M. Henslin.

5   Copyright © 1985 by the Society for the Study of Social Problems. Reprinted from *Social Problems*, Vol. 32, No. 3, February 1985, pp. 251–263, by permission.

6   Excerpts from *The Yąnomamö: The Fierce People*, 2nd Edition, by Napoleon A. Chagnon, copyright © 1977 by Holt, Rinehart and Winston, Inc. Reproduced by permission of the publisher.

7   Reproduced by permission of the American Anthropological Association from *American Anthropologist*, 58:3, June 1956. Not for further reproduction.

8   "The Sounds of Silence" by Edward T. Hall and Mildred R. Hall. Reprinted by permission of the authors from *Playboy*, June 1971, pp. 139–40, 204, 206. Copyright © by Edward T. Hall and Mildred Reed Hall.

9   Reprinted by permission of Doubleday & Co., Inc., and Penguin Books Ltd., London, from *The Presentation of Self in Everyday Life*, pp. 1–15. Copyright © 1959 by Erving Goffman.

10   Reprinted by permission of the author.

33   Reprinted by permission of the author.

34   From *The Second Shift* by Arlie Hochschild and Ann Machung. Copyright © 1989 by Arlie Hochschild. Used by permission of Viking Penguin, a division of Penguin Books USA Inc.

35   Lawrence K. Hong and Marion V. Dearman, *Urban Life*, Vol. 6, No. 1, pp. 53–68. Copyright © 1977 by Sage Publications, Inc. Reprinted by permission of Sage Publications, Inc.

36   Adapted from "The Great American Football Ritual: Reproducing Race, Class and Gender Inequality" by D. E. Foley, 1990, *Sociology of Sport Journal*, (Vol. 7, No. 2), pp. 111–135. Copyright © 1990 by Human Kinetics Publishers, Inc. Reprinted by permission.

37   Reprinted by prmission of the authors and publisher from *Symbolic Interaction*, Vol. 1 (1978)

38   Jennifer Hunt, *Urban Life*, Vol. 13, No. 4 (January 1985) Copyright © 1985 by Sage Publications, Inc. Reprinted by permission of Sage Pubications, Inc.

39   From *Power, Politics and People: The Collected Essays of C. Wright Mills,* edited by Irving Louis Horowitz. Copyright © 1963 by the Estate of C. Wright Mills. Reprinted by permission of Oxford University Press, Inc.

40   Copyright © 1989 by the New York Times Company. Reprinted by permission.

41   Reprinted by permission of the authors and publisher from *American Journal of Sociology*, 97, September 1991. Copyright © 1991 by the University of Chicago. All rights reserved.

42   Abridged from "The Abolition of *El Cortito*" by Douglas L. Murray. Copyright © 1982 by the Society for the Study of Social Problems. Reprinted from *Social Problems*, Vol. 30, No. 1, October 1982, pp. 26–39, by permission.

43   From William Ouchi, *Theory Z,* © 1981 by Addison-Wesley Publishing Co. Reprinted by permission of Addison-Wesley Publishing Co., Inc., Reading, MA.

44   Reprinted by permission of the publisher from *Saturday Review*, February 8, 1975, pp. 147–149. Copyright © by *Saturday Review*. All rights reserved.

In Memory of Erving Goffman
1922–1982
Whose Example Is Our Legacy

Contents

Preface to the
Seventh Edition

Ⓘ IT IS WITH PLEASURE that I introduce the seventh edition
of *Down to Earth Sociology*, a pleasure akin to seeing a dear friend reach
another cheerful milestone in his or her life. Adopters of earlier editions
will find themselves at home, I believe, in this latest edition. They will see
many selections they have already successfully used in the classroom, and
I trust they will welcome the many newcomers.

Following the suggestions of those who have used the earlier editions
of *Down to Earth Sociology*, I have strived to continue to present down-to-
earth articles in order to make the student's introduction to sociology enjoyable as well as meaningful. These selections reflect the experiences of
people who have "been there" and who, with a minimum of jargon and
quantification, insightfully share those experiences with the reader.

Focusing on social interaction in everyday activities and situations, these
selections share some of the fascination of sociology. They reflect both the
individualistic and the structural emphases of our discipline. Social structure
is not simply an abstract fact of life; rather, it vitally affects our lives. The
decisions of the rich, the politically powerful, and the bureaucrats provide
social constraints that augment those dictated by birth, social class, and other
circumstances. By social structure our vision of life is lifted or limited, our
chances of success closed or opened. Social structure brings tears and laughter, hopes and despair.

Yet so much of sociology goes about its business as though data were
unconnected to people, as though the world consisted of abstract social facts.
From my own experiences I know that these suppositions are far from the
truth—divorced from real life—and so I have sought authors who are able
to share the realities that people directly experience. At least as I see it,

sociology is the most fascinating of the social sciences, and it is this fascination that these selections are designed to convey.

It is my hope that I have succeeded in accomplishing this goal, because I believe sociology is able to open new windows of perception that can touch every aspect of the individual's world. If these readings even come close to this goal, I owe a great debt to the many who adopted the earlier editions, and especially to those whose reactions and suggestions have helped give shape to this one.

I wish to acknowledge the help provided by the following sociologists: Richard Ambler, Herbert Aurbach, Alfred Aversa, Jr., David Ayers, Roger Baldwin, Anthony Balzano, Ralph Bishop, Phillip D. Blood, Vincent Bolduc, John Bowman, Tom Boyd, Lori Brown, Brian Byers, Jill M. Bystydzienski, Judith Coady, Gaylan Corbin, Lou Corsino, Marie Tobia Deem, Melissa Deller, Dorothy D. Delman, René M. Descartes, M. G. Dunn, Jeff Ferrell, Tanice G. Foltz, Timothy J. Frederiks, David O. Friedrichs, John R. Fuller, Robert Girvan, George Gonos, W. H. Gordon, Michael Greenhouse, Brian Harrison, C. Larry Heck, Wendel J. Hunigan, Charles E. Hurst, Donna J. Jones, Phil Kayal, Sunil Kukreja, Jeffrey A. Leavey, Janet Lohmann, Stephan L. Markson, Katherine McDade, Dennis K. Nelson, Carolyn Egan Pesackis, Diane Pike, Randolph Quaye, Carol Axtell Ray, Keith A. Roberts, Ed Royce, Allen Scarboro, Eldon E. Snyder, Barbara Stenross, Mark Templeman, Edward A. Thibault, Irene Taviss Thomson, Elizabeth Vance, Carol Warner, Margaret R. Wilhite, and Stephen Zehr. Suggestions from these individuals, who shared with me their experiences teaching from earlier editions of this book, proved invaluable in shaping this present version. It is to them, as well as to the many colleagues who gave more casual counsel, and to the students who shared with me their candid comments, that I owe a debt of guidance.

One of the more interesting tasks in preparing this edition was to gather information on the contributors' backgrounds. In addition to biographical data concerning the authors' education, teaching, and publishing, that section also contains their statements telling us why they like sociology or became sociologists. Assigning that section with the articles helps to personalize the readings and increase the student's awareness of biographical factors that go into the choice to become a sociologist.

The selections continue to be organized to make them compatible with most introductory textbooks. Through subjects inherently interesting, we cover the major substantive areas of sociology, Part I is an introduction to the sociological perspective; it invites students to view the world in a new way by participating in the exciting enterprise we call sociology. Part II, new to this edition, is designed to answer the basic question of how sociologists do research. Part III examines the cultural underpinnings of social life, those taken-for-granted assumptions and contexts that provide the contours of our everyday lives. In Part IV that essential component of our beings—sexuality and gender—is the focus. There we look at both the process by which we assume the social identity of male or female and how those identities provide the basis for interaction among adults.

Part V examines social groups and social structure, looking behind the scenes to see how people's assumptions, their location on social hierarchies, and the features of social settings establish both constraints and freedoms on human relationships and expressions of the self. The process of becoming deviant, the social context that shapes deviance, and social control are the subjects of Part VI. We examine social stratification in Part VII, looking at power, wealth, gender, occupation, education, and race as dimensions of social inequality in our society. In Part VIII, we analyze the social institutions of education, family, religion, sports, medicine, law, as well as our intertwining political, military, and economic interests. Social change is the focus of Part IX, wherein we look at the intrusion of technology on a preliterate society, changing views of the Vietnam War, workers' struggles against oppression, international economic competition, and the search for personal roots in a rapidly changing social world.

These selections bring the reader face-to-face with the dual emphases of contemporary sociological research: the focus on the individual's experiences, and the analysis of social structure. Uncovering the basic expectations that underlie routine social interactions, these articles emphasize the ways in which social institutions are interrelated. It is to their authors' credit that we lose sight of neither the people who are interacting nor the structural base that so directly influences the form and content of their interactions.

About the Contributors

Elijah Anderson (article 16) received his Ph.D. in Sociology at Northwestern University and is the Charles and William Day Professor of Social Sciences at the University of Pennsylvania. He is the author of *A Place on the Corner: Identity and Rank Among Black Streetcorner Men* and *Streetwise: Race, Class, and Change in an Urban Community*, the book from which his selection is taken.

Anderson says, "I have always been interested in how individuals relate to society and how society relates to the individual. My interest in the social conditions that people experience—especially the marginality that so many blacks feel and how they relate to the wider social system—motivated me to go into sociology to look for some of the answers. I also had good teachers who inspired me. Later I found myself wanting to contribute in a meaningful way to correcting what I saw to be misrepresentations of reality in the academic literature about people who live in ghettos."

Nijole V. Benokraitis (article 29) received her Ph.D. in Sociology at the University of Texas at Austin. She is Professor of Sociology at the University of Baltimore and has published *Affirmative Action and Equal Opportunity: Action, Reaction, and Inaction* (with Joe Feagin), *Marriages and Families: Change, Choices, and Constraints, Modern Sexism: Blatant, Subtle, and Covert Discrimination* (with Joe Feagin), from which her selection in this book is taken.

Benokraitis, who came to the United States during World War II as a political refugee from Lithuania, says, "I became a sociologist because I grew up in the slums of South Boston, watched my parents work double shifts in factories and sweatshops most of their lives, and lived in abject poverty for many years. I was determined to save America from poverty, injustice, inequality, discrimination, and other social problems. So I majored in sociology as an undergraduate and for graduate school chose sociology rather than law, social work, or business. But instead of changing the world, I became a sociology professor—and am almost as poor as my parents!"

Peter L. Berger (article 1) received his Ph.D. in Sociology from the New School for Social Research. He is Professor of Sociology at Boston University and the author of numerous books, including *The Capitalist Revolution, A Far Glory: The Quest for Faith in an Age of Credulity,* and *Invitation to Sociology,* from which his selection in this book is taken.

Berger says, "I was born in Austria and came to the United States with my parents after the war. You might say that I became a sociologist by accident. I took some courses in sociology and liked them. I have always been curious about what makes people tick, and that is what sociology is all about."

Mae A. Biggs (article 21) earned her M.A. in Sociology at Southern Illinois University Edwardsville and is an associate of the Masters-Johnson Institute (Biological Research Institute) in St. Louis, Missouri.

Clifton D. Bryant (article 19) received his Ph.D. in Sociology at Louisiana State University. He is Professor of Sociology at Virginia Polytechnic Institute and State University. He is a former President of the Southern Sociological Society and the Mid-South Sociological Association and the founding editor of two journals, *Deviant Behavior* and *Centaur: The Journal of Human/Animal Interface.* His books include *Khaki-Collar Crime: Deviant Behavior in Military Context, Sexual Deviancy and Social Proscription,* and *Deviant Behavior: Occupational and Organizational Bases.*

Bryant says, "I selected sociology as a career because sociology permits the most insightful understanding of the social world in which we live. I believe that a career should be both rewarding and entertaining—and sociology is both."

Napoleon A. Chagnon (article 6) earned his Ph.D. in Anthropology at the University of Michigan. He is Professor of Anthropology at the University of California at Santa Barbara and the author of *Yąnomamö: The Last Days of Eden, Yąnomamö Warfare, Social Organization and Marriage Alliances,* and the book from which his selection in this book is taken, *Yąnomamö: The Fierce People.*

William J. Chambliss (article 23) received his Ph.D. in Sociology at Indiana University and is Professor of Sociology at George Washington University. His books include *On the Take: From Petty Crooks to Presidents, Law,*

Order and Power, and *Exploring Criminology*. Professor Chambliss is a past President of the American Society of Criminology (1987–88) and President of the Society for the Study of Social Problems (1992–93).

Chambliss says, "I became a sociologist out of an interest in doing something about crime. I remained a sociologist because it became clear to me that until we have a greater understanding of the political and economic conditions that lead some societies to have excessive amounts of crime we will never be able to do anything about the problem. Sociology is a beautiful discipline that affords an opportunity to investigate just about anything connected with human behavior and still claim an identity with a discipline. This is its strength, its promise, and why I find it thoroughly engaging, enjoyable, and fulfilling."

John R. Coleman (article 18) was the President of Haverford College from 1967 to 1977 and then President of the Edna McConnell Clark Foundation in New York City. He has decided to try his hand at business and now runs "The Inn at Long Last" in Chester, Vermont.

Kingsley Davis (article 10) received his Ph.D. in Sociology at Harvard University and is Distinguished Professor of Sociology at the University of Southern California and Senior Research Fellow at the Hoover Institution on War, Revolution and Peace at Stanford University. His books include *Human Society*, *The Population of India and Pakistan*, and *Contemporary Marriage*.

Davis, who often travels to remote places on the globe, likes sociology because "first, sociology deals with all aspects of society, not just economic behavior or political matters; second, in regard to social change, sociology takes a longer view than most other social science fields. I became a sociologist because I wanted to write and decided that I had better learn something to write, so I elected to learn sociology. Also, I wanted to know how the social system works. We were in the Great Depression at the time, so a social science should be able to analyze and explain that terrible catastrophe."

Marion V. Dearman (article 35) received his Ph.D. in Sociology from the University of Oregon. He is Professor of Sociology at California State University at Los Angeles. He publishes in the sociology of knowledge, belief, and religion.

Dearman says, "I became a sociologist because I wanted to find out why people think and believe the way they do. There is no belief too far out for human beings to share. Focusing on this in sociology has been fun. The most interesting thing about me is that I never finished high school. After working as a printer for twenty-five years, I went to college, got my B.A. when I was forty-one, the M.A. at forty-three, and the Ph.D. at forty-five. In most of my classes, I was older than my professors."

G. William Domhoff (article 27) earned his Ph.D. in Sociology at the University of Miami. He is Professor of Psychology and Sociology at the University of California, Santa Cruz. Among his books are *Blacks in the White Establishment: A Study of Race and Class in America, The Power Elite and the State: How Policy Is Made in America,* and the book from which his selection is taken, *The Bohemian Grove and Other Retreats: A Study in Ruling-Class Cohesiveness.*

Domhoff says, "I feel an attraction to sociology because I like anything that has to do with people and what makes them tick. I especially would like to understand how to bring about greater equality and freedom in all societies." He counts sports and his work among his hobbies.

Joe R. Feagin (article 29) received his Ph.D. in Sociology from Harvard University and is Graduate Research Professor of Sociology at the University of Florida. His books include *Building American Cities: The Urban Real Estate Game* (with Robert Parker), *Racial and Ethnic Relations,* and *The Elusive Dream: Racism and the Black Middle Class.*

Feagin says, "I became interested in sociology because of an interest in racial and ethnic relations and the sociology of religion. I was inspired by great teachers at Harvard University, particularly Thomas Pettigrew, Gordon Allport, and Charles Tilly."

Douglas E. Foley (article 36) received his Ph.D. in Anthropology of Education at Stanford University and is Professor of Anthropology at the University of Texas. He is the author of *From Peones to Politicos: Class and Ethnicity in a South Texas Town, 1900–1987* and *Learning Capitalist Culture: Deep in the Heart of Tejas.*

Foley says that he likes to write cultural critiques of American society, with the hope of changing it, of helping to make it more egalitarian and humane.

Herbert J. Gans (article 28) received his Ph.D. in City Planning and Sociology from the University of Pennsylvania. He is Robert S. Lynd Professor of Sociology at Columbia University and has written such books as *The Urban Villagers, Middle American Individualism: The Future of Liberal Democracy,* and *People, Plans, and Policies: Essays on Poverty, Racism, and Other National Urban Problems.* Professor Gans is a past President of the American Sociological Association (1987–88).

Gans "finds sociology more interesting than hobbies." He says: "When I was in high school, I thought I would become a journalist, but then when I got to college I discovered that the articles I enjoyed writing most were sociology. From then on I was pretty sure I would become a sociologist." He adds, "the deeper reason I became a sociologist is because I am a refugee from Nazi Germany, and ever since I came to the United States as a teenager in 1940, I have been trying to understand the country which took me in." Whenever possible—and his family agrees—Gans rents an apartment for a month in a European city or medieval town and "explores it, living in it fully."

Erving Goffman (article 9) earned his Ph.D. in Sociology at the University of Chicago and at the time of his death in 1982 was Director of the Center for Urban Ethnography at the University of Pennsylvania. His many books include *Stigma, Behavior in Public Places*, and the book from which his selection is taken, *The Presentation of Self in Everyday Life*.

Harry L. Gracey (article 33) received his Ph.D. in Sociology at the New School for Social Research. He is in private practice in organizational development in Cambridge, Massachusetts, and has published *Curriculum or Craftsmanship?: The Dilemma of the Teacher in the Bureaucratic System* and *Readings in Introductory Sociology* (with Dennis H. Wrong).

Gracey says, "What led me to study sociology was a curiosity about how things work, which in my case got focused on the world of social life, rather than on the physical or biological world. Sociology, uniquely among the social sciences, I think, 'lifts the veil of ideology' on the working of society to see what is really going on—and who is doing it and how it is being done."

Jack Haas (article 37) received his Ph.D. in Sociology from Syracuse University and is Professor of Sociology at McMaster University. With William Shaffir, he is the author of *Decency and Deviance, Shaping Identity in Canadian Society*, and *Becoming Doctors: The Adoption of a Cloak of Competence*.

Haas says, "I became a sociologist in order to get paid for watching and talking to people and to avoid bosses and repetitive work."

Edward T. Hall (article 8) was awarded his Ph.D. at Columbia University. He is Emeritus Professor of Anthropology at Northwestern University. His books include *The Silent Language, The Hidden Dimension*, and *An Anthropology of Everyday Life: An Autobiography*.

Mildred R. Hall (article 8) received her B.A. from Barnard College and (with Edward T. Hall) has written *The Fourth Dimension in Architecture, Hidden Differences: Studies in International Communication*, and *Understanding Cultural Differences*.

Mykol Hamilton (article 13) earned her Ph.D. in Psychology at the University of California at Los Angeles. She is Assistant Professor in the Department of Psychology at Centre College in Danville, Kentucky.

Hamilton, a social psychologist, says, "I like an approach that looks at the greater social issues and causes of human behavior, rather than seeing the individual as the cause. When we look at situational or social factors, we get away from blaming the victim."

Nancy Henley (article 13) received her Ph.D. in Psychology at Johns Hopkins University and is Professor of Psychology at the University of California at Los Angeles. Her books include *Body Politics: Power, Sex, and Nonverbal Communication, Language and Sex: Difference and Dominance* (with Barrie Thorne), and *Gender and Nonverbal Behavior* (with Clara Mayo).

Henley says, "Although I am a psychologist, one of my specialties is social psychology; thus I feel close ties to sociology. One reason social psychology fascinates me is that it addresses some of the key concerns of our time, such as prejudice, conformity, social power, and cooperation. To understand human behavior, we need both psychological and sociological facts and insights."

James M. Henslin (articles 2, 4, 11, 17, 21 and 22) earned his Ph.D. in Sociology at Washington University in St. Louis. He is Professor of Sociology at Southern Illinois University Edwardsville. His books include *Marriage and Family in a Changing Society, Social Problems*, and *Sociology: A Down-to-Earth Approach.*

Henslin says, "My early childhood was marked by poverty. I was born in a rented room in a minister's parsonage. Then my parents made a leap in their economic status—we moved into our own home, a converted garage, with no running water or indoor plumbing! My parents continued their upward status, and when I was thirteen they built one of the nicest houses in town. These experiences helped make me keenly aware of the significance of 'place' and opportunity in social life." He adds, "I like sociology because of its tremendous breadth—from social class and international stratification to the self and internal conflicts. No matter how diverse your curiosities, you can follow them and they are still part of sociology. Everything that is part of the landscape of human behavior comes under the lens of sociology."

Arlie Hochschild (article 34) received her Ph.D. in Sociology from the University of California, Berkeley, where she is now Professor of Sociology. She has published *The Managed Heart: Communication of Human Feeling, The Unexpected Community: Portrait of an Old Age Subculture*, and *The Second Shift: Inside the Two-Job Marriage*, the book from which her selection is taken.

Hochschild says, "I majored in international relations at Swarthmore College (a combination of history, economics, and political science) in the early sixties when my college had no sociology department. By chance I discovered David Riesman's *The Lonely Crowd*, his *Individualism Recon-*

sidered, and C. Wright Mills' *People, Politics and Power.* It was between the covers of these exciting books that I decided that there was a powerful lens through which to see the world—and I wanted to get on the other side of it.

Lawrence K. Hong (article 35) earned his Ph.D. in Sociology at the University of Notre Dame. He is Professor of Sociology at California State University at Los Angeles and has written articles on sex, religion, family, popular culture, computer applications, and Asian Americans.

Hong says, "I became a sociologist because I'm curious about the flux, the diversity, and the complexity of social phenomena. They keep me intellectually stimulated."

Everett C. Hughes (article 32) received his Ph.D. in Sociology at the University of Chicago. At the time of his death in 1983, he was Professor Emeritus of Sociology at Boston College. He wrote such books as *French Canada in Transition*, *Collective Behavior*, and *The Sociological Eye.*

Jennifer Hunt (article 38) received her Ph.D. in Sociology from the City University of New York and is Associate Professor of Sociology at Montclair State College. She is also a research candidate in the clinical training program at the Psychoanalytic Institute at the New York University Medical Center.

Hunt has written *Psychoanalytic Aspects of Fieldwork.* She likes sociology because "it provides an unusual opportunity to explore other cultural worlds by doing in-depth field work."

Jonathan Kozol (article 30) received a B.A. at Harvard University. After teaching in the public schools for several years, he became a professional author. His books include *Death at an Early Age*, *Rachel and Her Children*, and *Savage Inequalities*, the book from which his selection is adapted.

He says that he is interested in exposing the injustices that affect children.

Elliot Liebow (article 31) earned his Ph.D. in Sociology at the Catholic University of America. Until his retirement in 1985, he was a social anthropologist with the National Institute of Mental Health. He is the author of *Tally's Corner*, the book from which his selection is taken.

Zella Luria (article 12) received her Ph.D. in Psychology at Indiana University and is Professor of Psychology at Tufts University. She is the author of *The Psychology of Human Sexuality* (with Mitchel D. Rose) and *Human Sexuality* (with S. Friedman and Mitchel D. Rose).

Luria says, "What I appreciate about sociology is its exquisite attention to the group context for explanations of behavior."

Anne Machung (article 34), who works as an editor for a publishing firm, also does free-lance writing.

Joseph Marolla (article 5) earned his Ph.D. in Sociology at the University of Denver. He is Associate Professor of Sociology at Virginia Commonwealth University. He has published articles in social psychology, criminology, sociology of education, symbolic interaction, and self-esteem.

Marolla says, "I suppose, as much as anything else, I became a sociologist because my draft lottery number was 315 in the winter of 1969—which meant that I would not be going to Vietnam. At the time, I had given very little thought to life beyond the war. Once handed the option, school seemed the reasonable thing to do since I had been doing it for a while. I was an English major, and I moved to sociology because I thought it would broaden my creative writing. . . . What I most like about sociology is that it provides a broad picture and helps us see through the facade of life as we live it. This was appealing to me, and still is. Our research on rape is an example. Psychologists are convinced that rape is due to psychological dysfunction. We have demonstrated that rape is dramatically embedded in the culture."

Gary T. Marx (article 24) earned his Ph.D. in Sociology at the University of California, Berkeley, and is Professor of Sociology at Massachusetts Institute of Technology. His books include *Protest and Prejudice*, *Sociology: Classic and Popular Approaches* (with Norman Goodman), and the book from which his selection is taken, *Undercover: Police Surveillance in America*.

Marx says, "I was drawn into sociology as a result of an exciting class at UCLA on deviance and social control. I backed into a career in sociology. Upon graduation from college, I was not ready to go to work. The University of California had no tuition, and it seemed natural to continue to study. The fact that I would have been drafted if I had stopped going to school was also a factor. Once in graduate school, the momentum carried me along. I loved the subject matter, my professors served as role models, and it simply seemed natural to become a sociologist."

Philip Meyer (article 15) earned an M.A. in Journalism at the University of North Carolina, where he is now Professor of Journalism. His books include *Precision Journalism*, *To Keep the Republic* (with David Olson), and *Editors, Publishers, and Newspaper Ethics*.

C. Wright Mills (articles 3 and 39) received his Ph.D. in Sociology from the University of Wisconsin. His scathing criticisms of American society in such books as *White Collar, The Causes of World War III*, as well as the book from which article 3 is taken, *The Sociological Imagination*, made him one of the most controversial sociologists in the United States. At the time of his death in 1962, he was Professor of Sociology at Columbia University.

Horace Miner (article 7) earned his Ph.D. in Social Anthropology at the University of Chicago. He is Professor Emeritus of Anthropology at the University of Michigan. His books include *The Primitive City in Timbuctoo, St. Denis: a French Canadian Parish*, and *The City in Modern Africa*.

Miner says, "It was by accident that I became a sociologist. Having received my degree in social anthropology, it was easy to teach sociology when I received an offer. My courses were listed in both anthropology and sociology."

Douglas L. Murray (article 42) received his Ph.D. in Sociology from the University of California, Santa Cruz. He is Research Associate at the Institute of Latin American Studies at the University of Texas at Austin, where he is also a Lecturer in Sociology.

Murray says, "My interest in sociology grew out of a life-long interest in human efforts to resolve social problems. From growing up around farm workers in rural California during the days of the Civil Rights Movement, to the social unrest of the Vietnam War era, the world around me seems to have always been buffeted by powerful demands for change and an urgent need for the resolution of social problems. Sociology has provided useful analytical tools to complement and inform my participation in this most fundamental effort at social change and social problem-solving. I am now working on pesticide-related problems."

William Ouchi (article 43) earned his Ph.D. at the University of Chicago. He is Professor in the Graduate School of Management at the University of California at Los Angeles. He has published *The M-Form Society: How American Teamwork Can Recapture the Competitive Edge* and the book from which his selection is taken, *Theory Z: How American Business Can Meet the Japanese Challenge*.

Richard Rodriguez wrote article 44 while he was a Ph.D. candidate in the Department of English at the University of California at Berkeley. Since then he has written *Hunger of Memory: The Education of Richard Rodriguez*.

David L. Rosenhan (article 26) received his Ph.D. in Psychology from Columbia University. His books include *Foundations of Abnormal Psychology* (with P. London), *Theory and Research in Abnormal Psychology*, and *Ab-*

normal Psychology (with Martin E. P. Seligman). He is Professor of Psychology and Law at Stanford University.

Barry Schwartz (article 41) was awarded his Ph.D. in Sociology at the University of Pennsylvania. He is Professor of Sociology at the University of Georgia. He has written *George Washington: The Making of an American Symbol* and *The Battle for Human Nature: Science, Modernity, and Modern Life*.

Schwartz says, "Sociology is very relevant to my own life. The more I learn about society, the more I learn about myself—and what I learn alternately inflates and deflates my ego."

Diana Scully (article 5) earned her Ph.D. in Sociology at the University of Illinois. She is Associate Professor of Sociology and Coordinator of Women's Studies at Virginia Commonwealth University. She has written *Understanding Sexual Violence: A Study of Convicted Rapists* and *Men Who Control Women's Health: The Miseducation of Obstetrician Gynecologists*.

Scully says, "I changed my undergraduate major to sociology on the day that Martin Luther King was assassinated. I felt then and continue to believe that because of its focus on social structure sociology has a greater potential than other disciplines for understanding complex problems, such as racism and sexism, and therefore can be used as a tool for accomplishing change that is meaningful collectively and individually."

William Shaffir (article 37) received his Ph.D. in Sociology from McGill University and is Professor of Sociology at McMaster University. His books include *Life in a Religious Community: The Lubavitcher Chassidim of Montreal, Experiencing Fieldwork: An Inside View of Qualitative Research* (with Robert A. Stebbins), and the book from which his selection is taken, *Becoming Doctors: The Adoption of a Cloak of Competence* (with Jack Haas).

Shaffir says, "My attraction to sociology came through the classroom. The reason I became a sociologist is that many of my best undergraduate teachers were sociologists."

Marlise Simons (article 40) is a free-lance writer specializing in magazine articles dealing with popular culture.

Mark Snyder (article 14) received his Ph.D. in Psychology at Stanford University and is Professor of Psychology at the University of Minnesota. He has written *Public Appearances/Private Realities: The Psychology of Self-Monitoring*.

Snyder says, "I was a sociology major before I became a psychology major, and a lot of the themes in my research in pschology are actually sociological themes—such as the power of roles and labels to affect people's identities and their realities with others. I work with sociological themes, but I use psychological methods to address them. The reason I like those themes is because they deal with some of the most powerful forces that affect people's lives."

William E. Thompson (article 20) earned his Ph.D. in Sociology at Oklahoma State University and is Professor of Sociology at Emporia State University and Chair of the Division of Sociology, Family Sciences, and Anthropology. He has written (with Jack E. Bynum) *Juvenile Delinquency: A Sociological Approach.*

Coming from a working class background, Thompson is the first in his immediate family to graduate from high school. He says that he is attracted to sociology because "sociology makes the entire world your laboratory."

Barrie Thorne (articles 12 and 13) earned her Ph.D. in Sociology at Brandeis University. She is Professor in the Department of Sociology and the Program for the Study of Women and Men at the University of Southern California. Her books include *Rethinking the Family: Some Feminist Questions* and (with Cheris Kramarae and Nancy Henley) *Language, Gender and Society.*

Thorne says, "A major reason I became a sociologist is that Everett C. Hughes, one of my teachers, used to observe that sociology continually shows us that 'It could be otherwise.' That is, social life—the way school, work, families, daily experience are organized—may *feel* permanent and given, but the arrangements are socially constructed, have changed over time, and can be changed. This perspective provides wonderful insights into everything from daily life to crucial social issues. It also provides impetus for making social change. If institutions seem unjust—for example, if they foster poverty and gender and racial inequality—they can be changed. I have always tried to unite my search for sociological understanding with working for social change."

Robin E. Wagner-Pacifici (article 41) earned her Ph.D. in Sociology at the University of Pennsylvania and is Associate Professor of Sociology at Swarthmore College. She is the author of *The Moro Morality Play: Terrorism as Social Drama* and *Discourse and Destruction: The City of Phila. vs. MOVE.*

Wagner-Pacifici says that she became a sociologist through a series of accidents. She says, "I like sociology because it is the original interdisciplinary discipline and because it allows me to put my imagination to work on the wide variety of subjects that I find instinctively interesting."

Philip G. Zimbardo (article 25) earned his Ph.D. in Social Psychology at Yale University and is Professor of Social Psychology at Stanford University.

His books include *Psychology and Life, Shyness,* and (with Michael R. Leippe) *The Psychology of Attitude Change.*

Zimbardo, who has taught in Italy and enjoys collecting and studying the art and crafts of the American Indians of the Northwest and Southwest, says that he likes sociology because of "the scope of the significant questions it raises about human behavior."

PART I The Sociological Perspective

Iwould like to begin this first introduction on a personal note. Since my early school days, I have immensely enjoyed reading. I used to read almost anything I could lay my hands on and was especially fascinated by books that helped me understand people better—books that described people's life situations, thoughts, relationships, hopes and dreams, challenges and obstacles. Without knowing it, I was gaining an appreciation for understanding the context in which people live out their lives—for seeing how important that context is in determining what people are like.

When I went to college, I discovered that there was a name for my interests: *sociology*. What an exciting revelation: I had found an entire academic discipline centered on understanding the general context in which people live and analyzing how their lives are influenced by it! I could not help wanting to read sociology, to take more courses, to immerse myself in it. I was hooked.

The intention of this book is threefold: to share some of the excitement and fascination of sociology, to make more visible the context of social life that affects us all—and to whet the appetite for more sociology. You will find herein an invitation to look behind the scenes—a passport, as it were, to a different way of viewing life.

As Peter L. Berger says in the opening selection, the discovery of sociology can change your life. It can help you to understand better the social forces you confront, the forces that constrain and free. This understanding has a liberating potential: By examining these forces you can stand somewhat apart from at least some aspect of society, and thereby exert more creative control over your own life.

1

But just what *is* sociology? In my teaching I have found that, initially, introductory students sometimes find this a vexing question. To provide a better grasp of what sociology is, then, in the second selection James M. Henslin compares sociology with the other social sciences, showing how sociology casts an intellectual net that provides an unparalleled approach to understanding social life.

In the third article, C. Wright Mills focuses on the liberating potential offered by sociology. As he points out, this capacity centers on understanding three main issues: (1) the structure of society—that is, how the essential components of society are interrelated; (2) where one's society stands in human history and what changes are occurring in it; and (3) what type of people prevail in one's society, how they are selected for prevalence, and what types are coming to prevail.

Thinking of life in these terms, says Mills, is a quality of mind worth striving for. It is this "sociological imagination," to use his term for sociological perspective, that allows us to see beyond our immediate confines, to seek out and understand the broader social and historical forces at work in our lives. The consequence of gaining this renewing and challenging perspective, he says, is that we are enabled to see ourselves in a different light.

It is the goal of this first Part, then, to let you dip your feet in the sociological waters, so to speak—to challenge you to venture into sociology and, while venturing, to stimulate your sociological imagination.

1 Invitation to Sociology

PETER L. BERGER

Motivated by an intense desire to know what is "really happening," what goes on "behind the scenes," sociologists study almost every aspect of life in society. As Berger indicates, nothing is too sacred or too profane to be spared the sociologist's scrutiny. But when you penetrate the surface and peer behind the masks that individuals and organizations wear, you find a reality quite unlike the one that is so carefully devised and, just as carefully, put forward for public consumption.

It is this changed angle of vision that Berger says is so dangerous, for once you have peered behind the scenes and viewed life in a new light, it is nearly impossible to revert to complacent assumptions. The old, familiar, and so very comfortable ways of looking at life become upset when your angle of vision changes. This potential of sociology is, of course, also part of its excitement.

THE SOCIOLOGIST (that is, the one we would really like to invite to our game) is a person intensively, endlessly, shamelessly interested in the doings of men. His* natural habitat is all the human gathering places of the world, wherever men come together. The sociologist may be interested in many other things. But his consuming interest remains in the world of men, their institutions, their history, their passions. And since he is interested in men, nothing that men do can be altogether tedious for him. He will naturally be interested in the events that engage men's ultimate beliefs, their moments of tragedy and grandeur and ecstasy. But he will also be fascinated by the commonplace, the everyday. He will know reverence, but this reverence will not prevent him from wanting to see and to understand. He may sometimes feel revulsion or contempt. But this also will not deter him from wanting to have his questions answered. The sociologist, in his quest for understanding, moves through the world of men without respect for the usual lines of demarcation. Nobility and degradation, power and obscurity, intelligence and folly—these are equally *interesting* to him,

---

*In this and a couple of other selections written before stylistic changes occurred in our language, "he," "his," and "him" are generic, referring to both males and females. Although the style is outdated, the ideas are not.—Ed.

however unequal they may be in his personal values or tastes. Thus his questions may lead him to all possible levels of society, the best and the least known places, the most respected and the most despised. And, if he is a good sociologist, he will find himself in all these places because his own questions have so taken possession of him that he has little choice but to seek for answers.

It would be possible to say the same things in a lower key. We could say that the sociologist, but for the grace of his academic title, is the man who must listen to gossip despite himself, who is tempted to look through keyholes, to read other people's mail, to open cabinets. Before some otherwise unoccupied psychologist sets out now to construct an aptitude test for sociologists on the basis of sublimated voyeurism, let us quickly say that we are speaking merely by way of analogy. Perhaps some little boys consumed with curiosity to watch their maiden aunts in the bathroom later become inveterate sociologists. This is quite uninteresting. What interests us is the curiosity that grips any sociologist in front of a closed door behind which there are human voices. If he is a good sociologist he will want to open that door, to understand these voices. Behind each closed door he will anticipate some new facet of human life not yet perceived and understood.

The sociologist will occupy himself with matters that others regard as too sacred or as too distasteful for dispassionate investigation. He will find rewarding the company of priests or of prostitutes, depending not on his personal preferences but on the questions he happens to be asking at the moment. He will also concern himself with matters that others may find much too boring. He will be interested in the human interaction that goes with warfare or with great intellectual discoveries, but also in the relations between people employed in a restaurant or between a group of little girls playing with their dolls. His main focus of attention is not the ultimate significance of what men do, but the action in itself, as another example of the infinite richness of human conduct. So much for the image of our playmate.

In these journeys through the world of men the sociologist will inevitably encounter other professional Peeping Toms. Sometimes these will resent his presence, feeling that he is poaching on their preserves. In some places the sociologist will meet up with the economist, in others with the political scientist, in yet others with the psychologist or the ethnologist. Yet chances are that the questions that have brought him to these places are different from the ones that propelled his fellow-trespassers. The sociologist's questions always remain essentially the same: "What are people doing with each other here?" "What are their relationships to each other?" "How are these relationships organized in institutions?" "What are the collective ideas that move men and institutions?" In trying to answer these questions in specific instances, the sociologist will, of course, have to deal with economic or political matters, but he will do so in a way rather different from that of the economist or the political scientist. The scene that he contemplates is the same human scene that these other scientists concern themselves with. But the sociologist's angle of vision is different. When this is understood, it becomes clear that it makes little sense to try to stake out a special enclave within which the sociologist will carry on business in his own right. Like Wesley the sociologist will have to confess that his parish is the world. But unlike some latter-day Wesleyans he will gladly share this parish with others. There is, however, one traveler whose path the sociologist will cross more often than anyone else's on his journeys. This is the historian. Indeed, as soon as the sociologist turns from the present to the past, his preoccupations are very hard indeed to distinguish from those of the historian. [T]he sociological journey will be much impoverished unless it is punctuated frequently by conversation with that other particular traveler.

Any intellectual activity derives excitement from the moment it becomes a trail of discovery. . . . The excitement of sociology is [not always to penetrate] into worlds that had previously been quite unknown . . . for instance, the world of crime, or the world of some bizarre religious sect, or the world fashioned by the exclusive concerns of some group such as medical specialists or military leaders or advertising executives. [M]uch of the time the sociologist moves in sectors of experience that are familiar to him and to most people in his society. He investigates communities, institutions and activities that one can read about every day in the newspapers. Yet there is another excitement of discovery beckoning in his investigations. It is not the excitement of finding the familiar becoming transformed in its meaning. The fascination of sociology lies in the fact that its perspective makes us see in a new light the very world in which we have lived all of our lives. This also constitutes a transformation of consciousness. Moreover, this transformation is more relevant existentially than that of many other intellectual disciplines, because it is more difficult to segregate in some special compartment of the mind. The astronomer does not live in the remote galaxies, and the nuclear physicist can, outside his laboratory, eat, and laugh and marry and vote without thinking about the insides of the atom. The geologist looks at rocks only at appropriate times, and the linguist speaks English with his wife. The sociologist lives in society, on the job and off it. His own life, inevitably, is part of his subject matter. Men being what they are, sociologists too manage to segregate their professional insights from their everyday affairs. But it is a rather difficult feat to perform in good faith.

The sociologist moves in the common world of men, close to what most of them would call real. The categories he employs in his analyses are only refinements of the categories by which other men live—power, class, status, race, ethnicity. As a result, there is a deceptive simplicity and obviousness about some sociological investigations. One reads them, nods at the familiar scene, remarks that one has heard all this before and don't people have better things to do than to waste their time on truisms—until one is suddenly brought up against an insight that radically questions everything one had previously assumed about this familiar scene. This is the point at which one begins to sense the excitement of sociology.

Let us take a specific example. Imagine a sociology class in a Southern college where almost all the students are white Southerners. Imagine a lecture on the subject of the racial system of the South. The lecturer is talking here of matters that have been familiar to his students from the time of their infancy. Indeed, it may be that they are much more familiar with the minutiae of this system than he is. They are quite bored as a result. It seems to them that he is only using more pretentious words to describe what they already know. Thus he may use the term "caste," one commonly used now by American sociologists to describe the Southern racial system. But in explaining the term he shifts to traditional Hindu society, to make it clearer. He then goes on to analyze the magical beliefs inherent in caste tabus, the social dynamics of commensalism and connubium, the economic interests concealed within the system, the way in which religious beliefs relate to the tabus, the effects of the caste system upon the industrial development of the society and vice versa—all in India. But suddenly India is not very far away at all. The lecture then goes back to its Southern theme. The familiar now seems not quite so familiar any more. Questions are raised that are new, perhaps raised angrily, but raised all the same. And at least some of the students have begun to understand that there are functions involved in this business of race that they have not read about in the newspapers (at least not those in their hometowns) and that their parents have not told them—partly, at least, because neither the newspapers nor the parents knew about them.

It can be said that the first wisdom of sociology is this—things are not what they seem. This too is a deceptively simple statement. It ceases to be simple after a while. Social reality turns out to have many layers of meaning. The discovery of each new layer changes the perception of the whole.

Anthropologists use the term "culture shock" to describe impact of a totally new culture upon a newcomer. In an extreme instance such shock will be experienced by the Western explorer who is told, halfway through dinner, that he is eating the nice old lady he had been chatting with the previous day—a shock with predictable physiological if not moral consequences. Most explorers no longer encounter cannibalism in their travels today. However, the first encounters with polygamy or with puberty rites or even with the way some nations drive their automobiles can be quite a shock to an American visitor. With the shock may go not only disapproval or disgust but a sense of excitement that things can *really* be that different from what they are at home. To some extent, at least, this is the excitement of any first travel abroad. The experience of sociological discovery could be described as "culture shock" minus geographical displacement. In other words, the sociologist travels at home—with shocking results. He is unlikely to find that he is eating a nice old lady for dinner. But the discovery, for instance, that his own church has considerable money invested in the missile industry or that a few blocks from his home there are people who engage in cultic orgies may not be drastically different in emotional impact. Yet we would not want to imply that sociological discoveries are always or even usually outrageous to moral sentiment. Not at all. What they have in common with exploration in distant lands, however, is the sudden illumination of new and unsuspected facets of human existence in society. . . .

People who like to avoid shocking discoveries, who prefer to believe that society is just what they were taught in Sunday School, who like the safety of the rules and the maxims of what Alfred Schutz has called the "world-taken-for-granted," should stay away from sociology. People who feel no temptation before closed doors, who have no curiosity about human beings, who are content to admire scenery without wondering about the people who live in those houses on the other side of that river, should probably stay away from sociology. They will find it unpleasant or, at any rate, unrewarding. People who are interested in human beings only if they can change, convert or reform them should also be warned, for they will find sociology much less useful than they hoped. And people whose interest is mainly in their own conceptual constructions will do just as well to turn to the study of little white mice. Sociology will be satisfying, in the long run, only to those who can think of nothing more entrancing than to watch men and to understand things human.

It may now be clear that we have, albeit deliberately, understated the case in the title of this chapter. [The chapter title from which this selection is taken is "Sociology as an Individual Pastime."] To be sure, sociology is an individual pastime in the sense that it interests some men and bores others. Some like to observe human beings, others to experiment with mice. The world is big enough to hold all kinds and there is no logical priority for one interest as against another. But the word "pastime" is weak in describing what we mean. Sociology is more like a passion. The sociological perspective is more like a demon that possesses one, that drives one compellingly, again and again, to the questions that are its own. An introduction to sociology is, therefore, an invitation to a very special kind of passion.

2 Sociology and the Social Sciences

JAMES M. HENSLIN

Introductory students often wrestle with the question of what sociology is. If you continue your sociological studies, however, that vagueness of definition—"Sociology is the study of society" or "Sociology is the study of social groups"—that frequently so bothers introductory students will come to be appreciated as one of sociology's strengths and one of its essential attractions. That sociology encompasses almost all human behavior is, indeed, precisely the appeal that draws many to sociology.

To help make clearer at the outset what sociology is, however, Henslin compares and contrasts sociology with the other social sciences. After examining the salient similarities and differences in their approaches to understanding human beahvior, he looks at how social scientists from these related academic disciplines would approach the study of juvenile delinquency.

Science and the Human Desire for Explanation

HUMAN BEINGS ARE FASCINATED with the world in which they live. And they aspire to develop ways to explain their experiences satisfactorily. People appear to have always felt that fascination—along with the intense desire to unravel the world's mysteries—for people in ancient times also attempted to understand their world. Despite the severe limitations that confronted them, the ancients explored the natural or physical world, constructing explanations that satsified them. They also developed an understanding of their social world, the world of people with all their activities and myriad ways of dealing with one another. The explanations of the ancients, however, mixed magic and superstition with their naturalistic observations.

We contemporary people are no less fascinated with the world within which we live out our lives. We also continuously investigate both the mundane and the esoteric. We cast a quizzical eye at the common rocks we find embedded in the earth, as well as at some rare variety of insect found only in an almost inaccessible region of remote Tibet. We subject our contemporary world to the constant probings of the instruments and machines we have developed to extend our senses. In our attempts to decipher our observations, we no longer are satisfied with traditional explanations of origins or of relationships. No longer do we unquestioningly accept explanations that earlier generations took for granted. Utilizing observations derived through such technical aids as electronic microscopes and the latest generation of computers and software, we derive testable conclusions concerning the nature of our world.

As the ancients could only wish to do, we have been able to expand our objective study of the world beyond the confines of this planet. In our relentless pursuit after knowledge, we are no longer limited to speculation concerning the nature of the stars and planets. In the last couple of centuries the telescope has enabled us to make detailed and repetitive observations of the planets and other heavenly bodies. From those observations we have been able to reach conclusions startlingly different from those which people traditionally drew concerning the relative place of the earth in our galaxy and the universe. In just the past few years, by means of space technology, we have been able to extend our senses, as it were, beyond anything we had before dreamed possible. We are now able to reach out by means of our spaceships, observational satellites, and space platforms to record data from distant planets and—by means of computer-enhanced graphics—to gain a changing vision of our physical world. We have also been able to dig up and return to the earth samplings of soil from the surface of the moon as well as to send spaceships to the radiation and magnetic belts of Jupiter, over a distance so great (or, we could say, with our technology still so limited) that they must travel eighteen months before they can send reports back to earth.

A generation or so ago such feats existed only in the minds of "mad" scientists, who at that time seemed irrelevant to the public but whose ideas today are producing fascinating and frequently fearful consequences for our life on earth. Some of those scientists are now giving serious thought to plans for colonizing space, opening still another area of exciting exploration, but one whose consequences probably will be only inadequately anticipated. Others are drawing plans for real space wars, with potential outcomes so terrifying we can barely imagine them. For good and evil, science directly impinges on our contemporary life in society, leaving none of us unaffected.

The Natural and the Social Sciences

In satisfying our basic curiosities about the world, we have developed two parallel sets of sciences, each identified by its distinct subject matter. The first are called the *natural sciences*, the intellectual–academic endeavors designed to comprehend, explain, and predict the events in our *natural environment*. The endeavors of the natural scientists are divided into specialized fields of research and are given names on the basis of their particular subject matter—such as biology, geology, chemistry, and physics. Those fields of knowledge are further subdivided into even more highly specialized areas, each with a further narrowing of content—biology into botany and zoology, geology into mineralogy and geomorphology, chemistry into its organic and inorganic branches, and physics into biophysics and quantum mechanics. Each of those divisions, in turn, is subdivided into further specialized areas. Each specialized area of investigation examines a particular "slice" of the natural world.

In their pursuit of a more adequate understanding of their world, people have not limited themselves to investigating nature. They also have developed a second primary area of science that focuses on the social world. These, the *social sciences*, examine human relationships. Just as the natural sciences are an attempt to understand objectively the world of nature, so the social sciences are an attempt to understand objectively the social world. Just as the world of nature contains ordered (or lawful) relationships that are not obvious but must be abstracted from nature through controlled observations, so the ordered relationships of the human or social world also are not obvious but must be abstracted by means of controlled and repeated observations.

Like the natural sciences, the social sciences also are divided into specialized fields based on their subject matter. The usual or typical divisions of the social sciences are anthropology, economics, political science, psychology, and sociology, with history sometimes included in the enumeration, depending primarily on the preference of the person drawing the list. To be inclusive, I shall count history as a social science.

Like the natural sciences, the social sciences are also divided into further specialized fields, with these branches being named on the basis of their particular focus. Anthropology is divided into cultural and physical anthropology, economics into its macro and micro specialties, history into ancient and modern, political science into theoretical and applied, psychology into clinical and experimental, while sociology has its quantitative and qualitative branches. Except for sociology, we shall not be concerned with these finer divisions.

Sociology Contrasted with the Other Social Sciences

Since our focus is sociology, we shall take a brief look at each of the social sciences and contrast each with sociology. I should point out that the differences I shall elaborate are not always so clear in actual practice, for much that social scientists do as they practice their crafts greatly blurs the distinctions I am making.

Let us begin with *history*, the social science focusing on past events. Historians attempt to unearth the facts surrounding some event that they feel is of social significance. They attempt to establish the context, or social milieu, of the event—the important persons, ideas, institutions, social movements, or preceding events that appear in some way to have influenced the outcome they desire to explain. From this context, which they reconstruct from records of the past, they abstract what they consider to be the most important elements, or *variables*, that caused the event. By means of those "causal" factors or variables, historians "explain" the past.

Political science focuses on politics or government. The political scientist studies the ways people govern themselves—the various forms of government, their structures, and their relationships to other institutions of society. The political scientist is especially interested in how people attain ruling positions in their society, how they maintain those positions once they secure them, and the consequences of the activities of rulers for those who are governed. In studying a government that has a constitutional electorate, such as ours, the political scientist is especially concerned with voting behavior.

Economics is another discipline in the social sciences that concentrates on a single social institution. Economists study the production, distribution, and allocation of the material goods and services of a society. They want to know what goods are being produced at what rate at what cost, and the variables that determine who gets what. They are also interested in the choices that underlie production—for example, why with limited resources a certain item is being produced instead of another. Some economists, but not nearly enough in my judgment, also are interested in the consequences for human life of the facts of production, distribution, and allocation of goods and services.

Anthropology primarily focuses on preliterate and peasant peoples. Although there are other emphases, the primary concern of anthropologists is to understand *culture*, the total way of life of a group of people. Culture includes (1) the artifacts people produce, such as their tools, art, and weapons; (2) the group's structure, that is, the hierarchy and other group patterns that determine people's relationships to their fellow members; (3) ideas and values, especially the belief system of a people, and their effects on the people's lives; and (4) their forms of communication, especially their language. The anthropologists' traditional focus on past societies and contemporary preliterate peoples is now widening, as some anthropologists turn to the study of groups in industrialized settings. Anthropologists who focus on modern societies are practically indistinguishable from sociologists.

Psychology concentrates on processes occurring within the individual, within what they call the "skin-bound organism." The psychologist is primarily concerned with what is sometimes referred to as the "mind." Although still regularly used by the public, this term is used with increasing reservation by psychologists, probably, among other reasons, because no physical entity can be located that exactly corresponds to "mind." Psychologists typically study such phenomena as perception, attitudes, and values. They are also especially interested in personality, in mental aberration (or illness), and in how individuals cope with the problems they face.

Sociology is like history in that sociologists also attempt to establish the social contexts that influence people. Sociology is also similar to political science in that sociologists, too, study how people govern one another, especially the consequences for people's lives of various forms of government. Sociology is like economics in that sociologists are also highly interested in what happens to the goods and services of a society, especially the social consequences of production and distribution. Sociology is similar to anthropology in that sociologists also study culture and are particularly interested in the social consequences of material goods, group structure, and belief systems, as well as how people communicate with one another. Sociology is like psychology in that sociologists also are very much concerned with how people adjust to the various contingencies they confront in life.

With those overall similarities, then, where are the differences? Unlike historians, sociologists are primarily concerned with events in the present. Unlike political scientists and economists, sociologists do not concentrate on only a single social institution. Unlike anthropologists, sociologists primarily focus on industrialized societies. And unlike psychologists, to determine what influences people sociologists stress variables external to the individual.

The Example of Juvenile Delinquency

Because all the social sciences study human behavior, they differ from one another not so much in the content of what each studies but, rather, in what the social scientists look for when they conduct their studies. It is basically their approaches, their orientations, or their emphases that differentiate the social sciences. Accordingly, to make clearer the differences between them, it might be helpful to look at how different social scientists might approach the same topic. We shall use juvenile delinquency as our example.

Historians interested in juvenile delinquency would examine juvenile delinquency in some particular past setting, such as New York City in the 1920s or Los Angeles in the 1950s. The historian would try to interpret the delinquency by stressing the social context (or social milieu) of the period. For example, if delinquent gangs in New York City in the 1920s were the focus, historians would especially emphasize the social disruption caused by World War I; the problems of unassimilated, recently arrived ethnic groups; competition and rivalry for social standing among those ethnic groups; intergenerational conflict; the national, state, and local political and economic situation; and so on. The historian might also document the number of gangs, as well as their ethnic makeup. He or she would then produce a history of juvenile delinquency in New York City in the 1920s.

Political scientists are less likely to be interested in juvenile delinquency. But if they were, they would want to know if the existence of juvenile gangs was somehow related to politics. For example, is delinquency more likely if people have less access to political leaders? Or political scientists might study the power structure within one particular gang by identifying its leaders and followers. They might then compare one gang with another, perhaps even drawing analogies with the political structure of some legitimate group.

Economists also are not likely to study delinquent gangs or juvenile delinquency. But if they did, they, of course, would emphasize the economic aspects of delinquency. They might determine how material goods, such as "loot," are allocated within a gang. But they would be more inclined to focus on delinquency in general, emphasizing the relationship of gangs to economic factors in the country. Economists might wish to examine the effects of economic conditions, such as booms and busts, on the formation of gangs or on the incidence or prevalence of delinquency. They might also wish to determine the cost of juvenile delinquency to the nation in terms of property stolen and destroyed and wages paid to police and social workers.

Anthropologists are likely to be highly interested in studying juvenile delinquency and the formation of juvenile gangs. If anthropologists were to study a particular gang, they would probably examine the implements of delinquency, such as tools used in car theft or in burglary. They would focus on the social organization of the gang, perhaps looking at its power structure. They would study the belief system of the group to see how it supports the group's delinquent activities. They would also concentrate on the ways in which group members communicate with one another, especially their *argot*, or special language. Anthropologists would stress the larger cultural context in order to see what it is about the culture that leads to the formation of such groups. They would compare their findings with what anthropologists have discovered about delinquency in other cultures. In making such a *cross-cultural comparison*, they probably would note that juvenile delinquency is not a universal phenomenon but is largely a characteristic of industrialized nations. They would point out that industrialized societies extend formal education, especially for males. This postpones the age at which males are allowed to assume the role of manhood, and it is during this "in-between status," this literal "no-man's-land," that delinquency occurs. The emphasis given by anthropologists in such a study, then, would be true to their calling: That is, anthropologists would be focusing on culture.

Psychologists also exhibit high interest in juvenile delinquency. When psychologists approach the subject, however, they tend to focus on what exists *within* the delinquent. They might test the assumption (or *hypothesis*) that, compared with their followers, gang leaders have more outgoing personality traits, or greater hostility and aggressiveness. Psychologists might also compare the personality traits of adolescent males who join gangs with boys in the general population who do not become gang members. They might give a series of tests to determine whether gang members are more insecure, dominant, hostile, or aggressive than nonmembers.

Sociologists are also interested in most of the aspects emphasized by the other social scientists. Sociologists, however, ordinarily are not concerned with a particular gang from some past period, as historians might be, although they, too, try to identify the relevant social context. Sociologists focus on the power structure of gangs, as would political scientists, and they are also interested in certain aspects of property, as an economist might be. But sociologists would be more interested in the gang members' attitudes toward property, why delinquents feel it is legitimate to steal and vandalize, and how they divide up the property they steal.

Sociologists would also approach delinquency in a way quite similar to that of anthropologists and be interested in the same sorts of things. But sociologists would place strong emphasis on *social class* (which is based on occupation, income, and education). They would want to know if there is greater likelihood that a person will join a gang if his or her parents have little education, and how gang membership varies with income. If sociologists found that delinquency varies with education, age, sex, religion, income, or race, they would want to know the reasons for this. Do children of unskilled laborers have a greater chance of becoming delinquent than the children of doctors and lawyers? If so, what factors create the differences?

The sociologists' emphases also separate them from psychologists. Sociologists are inclined simply to ignore personality and instead to stress the effects of social class on recruitment into delinquency. Sociologists also examine group structure and interaction. For example, both sociologists and psychologists would be interested in differences between a gang's leaders and followers. To discover these, however, sociologists are less inclined to give paper-and-pencil tests and more inclined to observe *face-to-face interaction* among gang members (what they do in each other's presence). Sociologists would want to see if leaders and followers uphold the group's values differently; who suggests their activities; who does what when they carry out their activities; whether the activity be simply some form of recreation or a criminal act. For example, do leaders maintain their leadership by committing more acts of daring and bravery than their followers?

Compared with other social scientists, sociologists are more likely to emphasize the routine activities of the police, the judicial process, and changing norms. The police approach their job with preconceived ideas about who is likely to commit crimes and who is not. Those ideas are based on what they have experienced "on the streets," as well as on a stereotypical belief system nurtured within their occupation. The police typically view some people (usually lower-class males living in some particular area of the city) to be more apt to commit crimes than males from other areas of the city, males from a higher social class, or females in general. How do the police develop these ideas? How are such stereotypes supported in their subculture? What effects do they have on the police and on those whom they encounter? In other words, sociologists are deeply interested in finding out how the police define people and how those definitions help to determine whom the police arrest.

Sociologists are also interested in what occurs following an arrest. Prosecutors wield much discretion. For the same act they can level a variety of charges. They can charge an individual with first degree burglary, second degree burglary, breaking and entering, or merely trespassing. Sociologists want to know how such decisions are made, as well as their effects on the lives of those charged with crimes. Sociologists also study what happens when an individual comes before a judge, especially the outcome of the trial by the type of offense and the sex, age, or race of the offender. They also focus on the effects of detention and incarceration, as well as the reactions of others when an offender is released back into the community.

Norms, the behaviors that people expect of others, obviously change over time. What was considered proper behavior a generation ago is certainly not the same as what is considered proper today. Consequently, the law changes, and acts considered to be law violations at one time are not necessarily considered criminal at another time. Similarly, acts not now considered criminal may become law violations at a later date. For example, at one point in our history drinking alcohol in public at age sixteen was within the law in many communities, while today that would be an act of delinquency. In the same way, a person under sixteen who is on the streets after 10 P.M. unaccompanied by an adult is breaking the law in some communities. But if the law is changed or if the sixteen-year-old moves to a different community, the same act is not a violation of the law. With marijuana the case is similar. Millions of Americans break the law when they smoke grass, but for several years Alaska allowed possession of marijuana for personal use, a legal right only recently removed.

Perhaps more than any of the other social scientists, the sociologist maintains a critical interest in the effects of changing legal definitions in determining what people are arrested for and charged with. In effect, sociologists are interested in what juvenile delinquency is in the first place. They take the definition of delinquency not as obvious but as problematic, something to be studied in the context of lawmaking, lawbreaking, and the workaday world of the judicial system.

By means of this example of juvenile delinquency, it is easy to see that the social sciences greatly overlap one another. Sociology, however, is an *overarching* social science, because sociologists are, for the most part, interested in the same things that other social scientists are interested in. They are, however, not as limited in their scope or focus as are the others. Except for its traditional concerns with preliterate societies, anthropology is similarly broad in its treatment of human behavior.

Types of Sociology: Structural and Interactional

As sociologists study human behavior, they focus on people's *patterned* relationships; that is, sociologists study the recurring aspects of human behavior. This leads them to focus on two principal aspects of life in society: (1) *group membership* (including the *institutions* of society, the customary arrangements by which humans attempt to solve their perennial problems, such as the need for social order or dealing with sickness and death) and (2) *face-to-face interaction*, that is, what people do when they are in one another's presence. These twin foci lead to two principal forms of sociology, the structural and the interactional.

In the first type of sociology, *structural*, focus is placed on the *group*. Structural sociologists are interested in determining how membership in a group, such as a religion, influences people's behavior and attitudes, such as how they vote, or perhaps how education affects the stand they take on social issues. For example, are there voting differences among Roman Catholics, Lutherans, Jews, and Baptists? If so, on what issues? And within the same religion, do people's voting patterns differ according to their income and education?

Also of interest to sociologists who focus on group memberships would be how people's attitudes toward social issues (or their voting) differ according to their age, sex, occupation, race or ethnicity, or even geographical residence—both by region of the country and by urban or rural setting. As you have probably gathered, the term "group" is being used in an extended sense. People do not have to belong to an actual group to be counted; sociologists simply "group" together people who have similar characteristics, such as age, height, weight, education, or, if it is thought relevant, even those who take their vacations in the winter versus those who take them during the summer. These are known as *aggregates*, people grouped together for the purpose of social research because of characteristics they have in common.

Note that sociologists with this first orientation concentrate on how group memberships affect people's attitudes and behavior. They attempt to determine the relationships between groups and then try to trace out the significance that such memberships hold for people. Ordinarily they do not simply want to know the proportion of Roman Catholics who vote Democratic (or, in sociological jargon, "the correlation between religious-group membership and voting behavior") but may try to determine what difference being a Roman Catholic makes in people's dating practices, in their participation in premarital sex, in what they do for recreation, in how they treat their spouses, or in what their goals and dreams are and how they rear their children.

In the second type of sociology, the *interactional,* greater emphasis is placed on individuals. Some sociologists with this orientation focus on what people do when they are in the presence of one another. They directly observe their behavior, recording the interaction by taking notes or by using tape, video, or film. Other sociologists tap people's attitudes and behaviors more indirectly by interviewing them. Still others examine social records—from diaries and letters to court transcripts, from memorabilia of pop culture such as *Playboy* and *Playgirl* to science fiction and comic books. They may systematically observe soap operas, children's cartoons, police dramas, and situation comedies. Sociologists who focus on interaction develop ways of classifying the *data*—what they have observed, read, recorded, or been told. From those direct and indirect observations of people's interactions, they draw conclusions about people's attitudes and what significantly affects their lives.

Types of Sociology: Qualitative and Quantitative

Another important division among sociologists is based on the *approach* (or method) they use in their research. Some sociologists are statistically oriented, attempting to determine *numbers* to represent the behavioral patterns of people. They stress that proper measurement by the use of statistical techniques is necessary if one is to understand human behavior. Many refer to this emphasis as *quantitative* sociology.

A group of sociologists who strongly disagree with this position concentrate instead on the *meaning* of what is happening to people. They focus on how people construct their worlds, how they develop their ideas and attitudes, and how they communicate with one another. They attempt to determine how people's meanings (called symbols, mental constructs, ideas, and stereotypes) affect their ideas about the self and their relationships to one another. Many refer to this emphasis as *qualitative* sociology.

Conclusion

From chicken to sociology, there are many ways of dividing up anything in life. And just as those most familiar with chicken may disagree about the proper way of cutting up a chicken, so those most familiar with sociology will disagree about how to slice up sociology. From my experiences, however, the divisions I have presented here appear to reflect accurately what is taking place in sociology today. Inevitably, however, other sociologists would disagree with this classification and would probably present another way of looking at our discipline. Nonetheless, I think you will find this presentation helpful for visualizing sociology.

It is similarly the case when it comes to evaluating the divisions within sociology. These are *not* neutral matters. For example, almost all sociologists *feel strongly* about whether a qualitative or quantitative approach is the *proper* way to study humanity.

Certainly my own biases strongly favor qualitative sociology. For me, there simply is no contest. I see qualitative sociology as more accurately reflecting people's lives, as being more closely tied into the realities that people experience—how they make sense of their worlds, how they cope with their problems, and how they try to maintain some semblance of order in their lives. I find this approach fascinatingly worthwhile.

Wherever and whenever people come into one another's presence, there are potential data for the sociologist. The street, the bar, the classroom, or even the bedroom—all provide material for sociologists to observe and analyze. Nothing is really taboo for them. Sociologists are probably right now raising questions about most aspects of social life. Sociologists can whet their curiosity simply by overhearing a conversation or by catching a glimpse of some unusual happening. In following that curiosity, they can simply continue to "overhear" conversations, but this time purposely, or they can conduct an elaborate study with a scientifically selected random sample backed by huge fundings from some agency. What sociologists study can be as socially significant as an urban riot or as common but personally significant as two people greeting with a handshake or parting with a kiss.

In that sense, then, the world belongs to the sociologist—for to the sociologist everything is fair game. The all-inclusiveness of sociology, indeed, is what makes sociology so intrinsically fascinating for many: Sociology offers a framework that provides a penetrating perspective on almost everything in which people are interested.

Some of you who are being introduced to sociology through this essay may find the sociological approach to understanding human life rewarding enough to take other courses in sociology and, after college, to be attracted to books of sociological interest. A few, perhaps, may even make sociology your life's vocation and thus embark on a lifelong journey that takes you to the far corners of human endeavor, as well as to the more familiar pursuits. Certainly some of us, already captivated by sociology's enchantment, have experienced an unfolding panorama of intellectual delight in the midst of an intriguing exploration of the social world. And, in this enticing process, we have the added pleasure of constantly discovering and rediscovering ourselves.

3 The Promise

C. WRIGHT MILLS

The "sociological imagination" is seeing how the unique historical circumstances of a particular society affect people and, at the same time, seeing how people affect history. Every individual lives out his or her life in a particular society, with the historical circumstances of that society greatly influencing what that individual becomes. People who have been shaped by their society contribute, in turn, to the formation of that society and to the course of its history.

It is this quality of mind (termed the "sociological imagination" by Mills and the "sociological perspective" by others) that is presented for exploration in the readings of this book. As this intersection of biography and history becomes more apparent to you, your own sociological imagination will bring you a deepened and broadened understanding of social life—and of your own place within it.

NOWADAYS, MEN OFTEN FEEL that their private lives are a series of traps. They sense that, within their everyday worlds, they cannot overcome their troubles, and, in this feeling, they are quite correct: What ordinary men are directly aware of and what they try to do are bounded by the private orbits in which they live; their visions and their powers are limited to the close-up scenes of job, family, neighborhood; in other milieux, they move vicariously and remain spectators. And the more aware they become, however vaguely, of ambitions and of threats that transcend their immediate locales, the more trapped they seem to feel.

Underlying this sense of being trapped are seemingly impersonal changes in the very structure of continent-wide societies. The facts of contemporary history are also facts about the success and the failure of individual men and women. When a society is industrialized, a peasant becomes a worker; a feudal lord is liquidated or becomes a businessman. When classes rise or fall, a man is employed or unemployed; when the rate of investment goes up or down, a man takes new heart or goes broke. When wars happen, an insurance salesman becomes a rocket launcher; a store clerk, a radar man; a wife lives alone; a child grows up without a father. Neither the life of an individual nor the history of a society can be understood without understanding both.

Yet, men do not usually define the troubles they endure in terms of historical change and institutional contradiction. The well-being they enjoy, they do not usually impute to the big ups and downs of the societies in which they live. Seldom aware of the intricate connection between the patterns of their own lives and the course of world history, ordinary men do not usually know what this connection means for the kinds of men they are becoming and for the kinds of history-making in which they might take part. They do not possess the quality of mind essential to grasp the interplay of man and society, of biography and history, of self and world. They cannot cope with their personal troubles in such ways as to control the structural transformations that usually lie behind them.

Surely, it is no wonder. In what period have so many men been so totally exposed at so fast a pace to such earthquakes of change? That Americans have not known such catastrophic changes as have the men and women of other societies is due to historical facts that are now quickly becoming "merely history." The history that now affects every man is world history. Within this scene and this period, in the course of a single generation, one-sixth of mankind is transformed from all that is feudal and backward into all that is modern, advanced, and fearful. Political colonies are freed; new and less visible forms of imperialism, installed. Revolutions occur; men feel the intimate grip of new kinds of authority. Totalitarian societies rise, and are smashed to bits—or succeed fabulously. After two centuries of ascendancy, capitalism is shown up as only one way to make society into an industrial apparatus. After two centuries of hope, even formal democracy is restricted to a quite small portion of mankind. Everywhere in the underdeveloped world, ancient ways of life are broken up and vague expectations become urgent demands. Everywhere in the overdeveloped world, the means of authority and of violence become total in scope and bureaucratic in form. Humanity itself now lies before us, the supernation at either pole concentrating its most coordinated and massive efforts upon the preparation of World War III.

The very shaping of history now outpaces the ability of men to orient themselves in accordance with cherished values. And which values? Even when they do not panic, men often sense that older ways of feeling and thinking have collapsed, and that newer beginnings are ambiguous to the point of moral stasis. Is it any wonder that ordinary men feel they cannot cope with the larger worlds with which they are so suddenly confronted? That they cannot understand the meaning of their epoch for their own lives? That—in defense of selfhood—they become morally insensible, trying to remain altogether private men? Is it any wonder that they come to be possessed by a sense of the trap?

It is not only information that they need—in this Age of Fact, information often dominates their attention and overwhelms their capacities to assimilate it. It is not only the skills of reason that they need—although their struggles to acquire these often exhaust their limited moral energy.

What they need, and what they feel they need, is a quality of mind that will help them to use information and to develop reason in order to achieve lucid summations of what is going on in the world and of what may be happening within themselves. It is this quality, I am going to contend, that journalists and scholars, artists and publics, scientists and editors are coming to expect of what may be called the sociological imagination.

The sociological imagination enables its possessor to understand the larger historical scene in terms of its meaning for the inner life and the external career of a variety of individuals. It enables him to take into account how individuals, in the welter of their daily experience, often become falsely conscious of their social positions. Within that welter, the framework of modern society is sought, and within that framework the psychologies of a variety of men and women are formulated. By such means, the personal uneasiness of individuals is focused upon explicit troubles, and the indifference of publics is transformed into involvement with public issues.

The first fruit of this imagination—and the first lesson of the social science that embodies it—is the idea that the individual can understand his own experience and gauge his own fate only by locating himself within his period, that he can know his own chances in life only by becoming aware of those of all individuals in his circumstances. In many ways, it is a terrible lesson; in many ways, a magnificent one. We do not know the limits of man's capacities for supreme effort or willing degradation, for agony or glee, for pleasurable brutality or the sweetness of reason. But in our time we have come to know that the limits of "human nature" are frighteningly broad. We have come to know that every individual lives, from one generation to the next, in some society; that he lives out a biography, and that he lives it out within some historical sequence. By the fact of his living he contributes, however minutely, to the shaping of this society and to the course of its history, even as he is made by society and by its historical push and shove.

The sociological imagination enables us to grasp history and biography and the relations between the two within society. That is its task and its promise. To recognize this task and this promise is the mark of the classic social analyst. It is characteristic of Herbert Spencer—turgid, polysyllabic, comprehensive; of E. A. Ross—graceful, muckraking, upright; of Auguste Comte and Emile Durkheim; of the intricate and subtle Karl Mannheim. It is the quality of all that is intellectually excellent in Karl Marx; it is the clue to Thorstein Veblen's brilliant and ironic insight, to Joseph Schumpeter's many-sided constructions of reality; it is the basis of the psychological sweep of W. E. H. Lecky no less than of the profundity and clarity of Max Weber. And it is the signal of what is best in contemporary studies of man and society.

No social study that does not come back to the problems of biography, of history, and of their intersections within a society has completed its intellectual journey. Whatever the specific problems of the classic social analysts, however limited or however broad the features of social reality they have examined, those who have been imaginatively aware of the promise of their work have consistently asked three sorts of questions:

1. What is the structure of this particular society as a whole? What are its essential components, and how are they related to one another? How does it differ from other varieties of social order? Within it, what is the meaning of any particular feature for its continuance and for its change?

2. Where does this society stand in human history? What are the mechanics by which it is changing? What is its place within, and its meaning for, the development of humanity as a whole? How does any particular feature we are examining affect, and how is it affected by, the historical period in which it moves? And this period—what are its essential features? How does it differ from other periods? What are its characteristic ways of history-making?

3. What varieties of men and women now prevail in this society and in this period? And what varieties are coming to prevail? In what ways are they selected and formed, liberated and repressed, made sensitive and blunted? What kinds of "human nature" are revealed in the conduct and character we observe in this society in this period? And what is the meaning for "human nature" of each and every feature of the society we are examining?

Whether the point of interest is a great power state or a minor literary mood, a family, a prison, a creed—these are the kinds of questions the best social analysts have asked. They are the intellectual pivots of classic studies of man in society—and they are the questions inevitably raised by any mind possessing the sociological imagination. For that imagination is the capacity to shift from one perspective to another—from the political to the psychological; from examination of a single family to comparative assessment of the national budgets of the world; from the theological school to the military establishment; from considerations of an oil industry to studies of contemporary poetry. It is the capacity to range from the most impersonal and remote transformations to the most intimate features of the human self—and to see the relations between the two. Back of its use, there is always the urge to know the social and historical meaning of the individual in the society and in the period in which he has his quality and his being.

That, in brief, is why it is by means of the sociological imagination that men now hope to grasp what is going on in the world, and to understand what is happening in themselves as minute points of the intersections of biography and history within society. In large part, contemporary man's self-conscious view of himself as at least an outsider, if not a permanent stranger, rests upon an absorbed realization of social relativity and of the transformative power of history. The sociological imagination is the most fruitful form of this self-consciousness. By its use, men whose mentalities have swept only a series of limited orbits often come to feel as if suddenly awakened in a house with which they had only supposed themselves to be familiar. Correctly or incorrectly, they often come to feel that they can now provide themselves with adequate summations, cohesive assessments, comprehensive orientations. Older decisions that once appeared sound now seem to them products of a mind unaccountably dense. Their capacity for astonishment is made lively again. They acquire a new way of thinking, they experience a transvaluation of values: In a word, by their reflection and by their sensibility, they realize the cultural meaning of the social sciences.

Perhaps the most fruitful distinction with which the sociological imagination works is between the "personal troubles of milieu" and the "public issues of social structure." This distinction is an essential tool of the sociological imagination and a feature of all classic work in social science.

Troubles occur within the character of the individual and within the range of his immediate relations with others; they have to do with his self and with those limited areas of social life of which he is directly and personally aware. Accordingly, the statement and the resolution of troubles properly lie within the individual as a biographical entity and within the scope of his immediate milieu—the social setting that is directly open to his personal experience and, to some extent, his willful activity. A trouble is a private matter: Values cherished by an individual are felt by him to be threatened.

Issues have to do with matters that transcend these local environments of the individual and the range of his inner life. They have to do with the organization of many such milieux into the institutions of a historical society as a whole, with the ways in which various milieux overlap and interpenetrate to form the larger structure of social and historical life. An issue is a public matter: Some value cherished by publics is felt to be threatened. Often, there is a debate about what that value really is and about what it is that really threatens it. This debate is often without focus, if only because it is the very nature of an issue, unlike even widespread trouble, that it cannot very well be defined in terms of the immediate and everyday environments of ordinary men. An issue, in fact, often involves a crisis in institutional arrangements, and often, too, it involves what Marxists call "contradictions" or "antagonisms."

In these terms, consider unemployment. When, in a city of 100,000, only one man is unemployed, that is his personal trouble, and for its relief we properly look to the character of the man, his skills, and his immediate opportunities. But when, in a nation of 50 million employees, 15 million men are unemployed, that is an issue, and we may not hope to find its solution within the range of opportunities open to any one individual. The very structure of opportunities has collapsed. Both the correct statement of the problem and range of possible solutions require us to consider the economic and political institutions of the society, and not merely the personal situation and character of a scatter of individuals.

Consider war. The personal problem of war, when it occurs, may be how to survive it or how to die in it with honor; how to make money out of it; how to climb into the higher safety of the military apparatus; or how to contribute to the war's termination. In short, according to one's values, to find a set of milieux and within it to survive the war or make one's death in it meaningful. But the structural issues of war have to do with its causes; with what types of men it throws up into command; with its effects upon economic and political, family and religious institutions, with the unorganized irresponsibility of a world of nation-states.

Consider marriage. Inside a marriage, a man and a woman may experience personal troubles; but, when the divorce rate during the first four years of marriage is 250 out of every 1,000 attempts, this is an indication of a structural issue having to do with the institutions of marriage and the family and other institutions that bear upon them.

Or consider the metropolis—the horrible, beautiful, ugly, magnificent sprawl of the great city. For many upper-class people, the personal solution to the problem of the city is to have an apartment with private garage under it in the heart of the city, and forty miles out, a house by Henry Hill, garden by Garrett Eckbo, on a hundred acres of private land. In these two controlled environments—with a small staff at each end and a private helicopter connection—most people could solve many of the problems of personal milieux caused by the facts of the city. But all this, however splendid, does not solve the public issues that the structural fact of the city poses. What should be done with this wonderful monstrosity? Break it all up into scattered units, combining residence and work? Refurbish it as it stands? Or, after evacuation, dynamite it and build new cities according to new plans in new places? What should those plans be? And who is to decide and to accomplish whatever choice is made? These are structural issues; to confront them and to solve them requires us to consider political and economic issues that affect innumerable milieux.

Insofar as an economy is so arranged that slumps occur, the problem of unemployment becomes incapable of personal solution. Insofar as war is inherent in the nation-state system and in the uneven industrialization of the world, the ordinary individual in his restricted milieu will be powerless—with or without psychiatric aid—to solve the troubles this system or lack of system imposes upon him. Insofar as the family as an institution turns women into darling little slaves and men into their chief providers and unweaned dependents, the problem of a satisfactory marriage remains incapable of purely private solution. Insofar as the overdeveloped megalopolis and the overdeveloped automobile are built-in features of the overdeveloped society, the issues of urban living will not be solved by personal ingenuity and private wealth.

What we experience in various and specific milieux, I have noted, is often caused by structural changes. Accordingly, to understand the changes of many personal milieux, we are required to look beyond them. And the number and variety of such structural changes increase as the institutions within which we live become more embracing and more intricately connected with one another. To be aware of the idea of social structure and to use it with sensibility is to be capable of tracing such linkages among a great variety of milieux. To be able to do that is to possess the sociological imagination.

What are the major issues for publics and the key troubles of private individuals in our time? To formulate issues and troubles, we must ask what values are cherished yet threatened, and what values are cherished and supported, by the characterizing trends of our period. In the case both of threat and of support, we must ask what salient contradictions of structure may be involved.

When people cherish some set of values and do not feel any threat to them, they experience *well-being*. When they cherish values but *do* feel them to be threatened, they experience a crisis—either as a personal trouble or as a public issue. And, if all their values seem involved, they feel the total threat of panic.

But suppose people are neither aware of any cherished values nor experience any threat? That is the experience of *indifference*, which, if it seems to involve all their values, becomes apathy. Suppose, finally, they are unaware of any cherished values, but still are very much aware of a threat? That is the experience of *uneasiness*, of anxiety, which, if it is total enough, becomes a deadly, unspecified malaise.

Ours is a time of uneasiness and indifference—not yet formulated in such ways as to permit the work of reason and the play of sensibility. Instead of troubles—defined in terms of values and threats—there is often the misery of vague uneasiness; instead of explicit issues, there is often merely the beat feeling that all is somehow not right. Neither the values threatened nor whatever threatens them has been stated; in short, they have not been carried to the point of decision. Much less have they been formulated as problems of social science.

In the 1930s, there was little doubt—except among certain deluded business circles—that there was an economic issue that was also a pack of personal troubles. In these arguments about the "crisis of capitalism," the formulations of Marx and the many unacknowledged reformulations of his work probably set the leading terms of the issue, and some men came to understand their personal troubles in these terms. The values threatened were plain to see and cherished by all; the structural contradictions that threatened them also seemed plain. Both were widely and deeply experienced. It was a political age.

But the values threatened in the era after World War II are often neither widely acknowledged as values nor widely felt to be threatened. Much private uneasiness goes unformulated; much public malaise and many decisions of enormous structural relevance never become public issues.

For those who accept such inherited values as reason and freedom, it is the uneasiness itself that is the trouble; it is the indifference itself that is the issue. And it is the condition, of uneasiness and indifference, that is the signal feature of our period.

All this is so striking that it is often interpreted by observers as a shift in the very kinds of problems that need now to be formulated. We are frequently told that the problems of our decade, or even the crises of our period, have shifted from the external realm of economics and now have to do with the quality of individual life—in fact, with the question of whether there is soon going to be anything that can properly be called individual life. Not child labor but comic books, not poverty but mass leisure, are at the center of concern. Many great public issues as well as many private troubles are described in terms of "psychiatric"—often, it seems in a pathetic attempt to avoid the large issues and problems of modern society. Often, this statement seems to rest upon a provincial narrowing of interest to the Western societies, or even to the United States—thus ignoring two-thirds of mankind; often, too, it arbitrarily divorces the individual life from the larger institutions within which that life is enacted, and which on occasion bear upon it more grievously than do the intimate environments of childhood.

Problems of leisure, for example, cannot even be stated without considering problems of work. Family troubles over comic books cannot be formulated as problems without considering the plight of the contemporary family in its new relations with the newer institutions of the social structure. Neither leisure nor its debilitating uses can be understood as problems without recognition of the extent to which malaise and indifference now form the social and personal climate of contemporary American society. In this climate, no problems of the "private life" can be stated and solved without recognition of the crisis of ambition that is part of the very career of men at work in the incorporated economy.

It is true, as psychoanalysts continually point out, that people do often have the "increasing sense of being moved by obscure forces within themselves that they are unable to define." But it is *not* true, as Ernest Jones asserted, that "man's chief enemy and danger is his own unruly nature and the dark forces pent up within him." On the contrary: "Man's chief danger" today lies in the unruly forces of contemporary society itself, with its alienating methods of production, its enveloping techniques of political domination, its international anarchy—in a word, its pervasive transformations of the very "nature" of man and the conditions and aims of his life.

It is now the social scientist's foremost political and intellectual task—for here the two coincide—to make clear the elements of contemporary uneasiness and indifference. It is the central demand made upon him by other cultural workmen—by physical scientists and artists, by the intellectual community in general. It is because of this task and these demands, I believe, that the social sciences are becoming the common denominator of our cultural period, and the sociological imagination, our most needed quality of mind.

PART II Doing Sociological Research

Iᴺ ᴛʜᴇ ɪɴᴛʀᴏᴅᴜᴄᴛɪᴏɴ ᴛᴏ Pᴀʀᴛ I, you learned that sociologists are fascinated with the unknown—how we constantly want to peer behind locked doors to better understand social life. In this second Part we will unlock two doors to give you a glimpse of what goes on behind them: You will better understand why men rape, and what life is like in a group of primitive, violent people.

Although these readings will help you to better understand certain forms of violence, they have a purpose beyond that. They are also intended to introduce you to the two major activities of science: (1) constructing a theoretical base and (2) conducting empirical research. Let us look at each of these activities.

These tasks are so joined to one another that neither is more important than the other—nor does one necessarily come before the other. When scientists do their craft, these twin tasks merge during their endeavors. For the sake of presentation, however, let us say that the *first* task of science is to conduct empirical research. *Empirical* means "based on objective observations." Sociologists cannot simply draw conclusions based on guesswork, hunches, custom, superstition, or common sense. They must conduct studies to gather information that accurately represents people's attitudes and behaviors, and they must report their observations openly, spelling out in detail how they conducted their studies so that others can test their conclusions. I have written the first selection in this Part in order to acquaint you with how sociologists do their research, which goes under the shorthand term *research methods*.

Because no specific reading summarizes the *second* task of science, constructing a theoretical base, I shall provide an overview at this point.

29

A theoretical base is necessary, for facts never interpret themselves. They must always be interpreted from within a conceptual framework—an explanation of how pertinent "facts" are related to one another—called a *theory*. By providing a framework in which to fit observations, each theory offers a unique interpretation of reality. Sociology has three dominant theories, each of which reveals a contrasting picture of social life.

The first theory is called *symbolic interaction* (or symbolic interactionism). It stresses what you already know quite well: that you live in a world filled with meaning. You are surrounded by *people* who mean something to you (from your parents to your friends), by *objects* that represent something special (your clothing, your pet, your car, your room), and by *events* that are filled with meaning (first kiss, first date, first job, birthdays, holidays, anniversaries). The term *symbol* refers to the meanings that something has for us, and symbolic interactionists focus on symbols—how we construct meanings, how we use symbols to communicate with one another, and how symbols are the foundation of our social world.

Symbolic interaction has three major themes: (1) human beings have a self, (2) people construct meaning, and act on the basis of that meaning, and (3) people take into account the possible reactions of others. Let us look at each of these points.

1. *Human beings have a self*. This means that we have the capacity to think and to talk about ourselves. We are able to reflect on our own actions, about what we have done or what we will do, or even what we hope to do or regret having done. We are even able to tell others what was going on in our mind when we did something. That is, we can reflect on our own person (self), analyzing our actions and motives, just as we can reflect on the actions and motives of others. (This is called "making the self an object.") We are aware of things in our environment, and we think about their possible effects on us.

2. *People construct meaning, and act on the basis of that meaning*. As we interact with one another, we reflect on our situation and interpret (or give meaning) to what we experience. As we recall our experiences and discuss them with others, we further refine those meanings. The significance of this human trait is that the meanings we give to our experiences (the objects, events, and so on) become the basis for how we act. For example, if someone makes physical contact with us, we want to know what it means. If we interpret it as an "accidental bump," it requires nothing but a mumbled apology—but if we interpret it as a "push," our reactions are quite different. As far as we are concerned, those are two entirely different acts. The basis for their being different, however, lies in the symbols we apply—that is, in our interpretation (or definition) of the acts.

3. *People take into account the possible reactions of others*. To anticipate how others might react to something we are thinking about doing, we *take the role of others*; that is, we think about how others might react if we do so and so, and we adjust our behavior accordingly. We take the role of indi-

viduals (specific others), as well as groups of people (the generalized other). For example, if we are tempted to steal, we might think, "What would my friend think if I took this?" (a specific other). A professional baseball player tempted to accept a bribe might think, "What would other players and the American public think of me if they found out?" (a generalized other).

In sum: Central to symbolic interaction is the principle that to understand people's behavior we must understand their symbolic worlds. Accordingly, sociologists study the meanings that people give things, for symbols hold the key to understanding both our attitudes and our behavior.

The second theory is called *functionalism*. Functionalists stress that society is an integrated system made up of various parts. When working properly, each part contributes to the stability of society: Each part fulfills a function that contributes to society's equilibrium. At times, however, a part may be dysfunctional—that is, it may fail to work correctly—which creates problems for other parts of the system. In short, functionalists stress how the parts of society are interrelated, and how change in one part of society affects its other parts.

To illustrate functionalism, let us consider why divorce is so prevalent in American society. Functionalists first point out that the family performs functions for the entire society. Over the millennia, the family's traditional functions have been economic production, the socialization of children, reproduction, recreation, sexual control of its members, and taking care of its sick, injured, and aged. During the past couple of hundred years (especially the last hundred), however, society industrialized—bringing about profound changes that have left no aspect of social life untouched.

The consequences for the family have been especially remarkable: Industrialization has eroded its traditional functions. For example, medical personnel now take care of the sick and injured, many elderly are placed in homes for the aged, and almost all economic production has moved to factories. As its basic functions were at least partially taken over by other units of society, the family weakened. Simply put, the "ties that bind" became fewer—and with fewer functions holding them together, husbands and wives became more prone to break up.

The third dominant theory is *conflict theory*. From this perspective, society is viewed as a system in which the various parts are in conflict. Each part competes for a larger share of resources—and there are not enough to go around to satisfy each group. Each group seems to want more power, more wealth, more prestige, and so on. And those groups that already have more than their share are not about to willingly redistribute it. Instead, they hold on for dear life, while trying to enlarge what they already have. As a consequence, say conflict theorists, society is not like a smoothly running machine, as the functionalists picture it, with each part contributing to the well-being of the other parts, but more like a machine running wildly out of kilter and ready to break apart. The results of this inherent conflict show up as racism, with one racial group pitted against another; sexism, with males and females squared off in the struggle for dominance; and so on.

Due to space limitations, I can only provide this brief sketch of the theories. However, each has had numerous books written about it. Among the many examples of *symbolic interaction* (the dominant orientation) of *this* book, you might look at selections by Anderson, Foley, Henslin and Biggs, and Thorne and Luria. The readings by Gans and Ouchi provide examples of *functionalism,* while the ones by Gracey, Kozol, Murray, and Mills (on the structure of power in American society), are examples of *conflict theory.* You may also want to check the references listed at the end of this introduction.

This Part of the book, then, builds upon the first Part. I hope that it will help you to better appreciate how sociologists do their research.

Suggestions for Further Reading

Babbie, Earl R. *The Practice of Social Research.* Belmont, CA: Wadsworth, 1985. A "how-to" book of sociological research; describes the major ways sociologists gather data and the logic underlying each method.

Burgess, Robert G. (ed.). *Studies in Qualitative Methodology II* .Greenwich, CT: JAI Press, 1990. Understanding the problems and rewards of field work is provided by these first-person accounts by sociologists.

Charon, Joel M. *Symbolic Interactionism: An Introduction, an Interpretation, an Integration.* Englewood Cliffs, NJ: Prentice-Hall, 1985. Provides an overview of symbolic interaction, laying out its main points. This book can help you better understand what symbolic interaction is and why it is important in sociology.

Hunt, Morton M. *Profiles of Social Research: The Scientific Study of Human Interaction.* New York: Russell Sage/Basic Books, 1986. An easy-to-understand introduction to research methods.

Merton, Robert K. *Social Theory and Social Structure.* New York: Free Press, 1968. This is the classic work on functionalism.

Mills, C. Wright. *The Sociological Imagination.* New York: Oxford University Press, 1959. Provides an overview of sociology from the framework of conflict theory.

Sociology Writing Group. *A Guide to Writing Sociology Papers,* 2nd ed. New York: St. Martin's, 1991.

Straus, Roger (ed.). *Using Sociology.* Bayside, NY: General Hall, 1985. An examination of applied and clinical sociology that provides an understanding of how sociology is used in the practical world.

4 How Sociologists Do Research

JAMES M. HENSLIN

Guesswork does not go very far in helping us to understand the social world. Our guesses, hunches, and the ideas that pass for common sense may or may not be correct. Sociolgists must gather data in such a way that what they report is objective—presenting information that represents what is really "out there." To do so, they must use methods that other researchers can repeat (replicate) to check their findings. They also must tie their findings into both theory and what other researchers have already reported. In this overview of *research methods,* Henslin outlines the procedures that sociologists use to gather data.

Renée had never felt fear before—at least not like this. It had begun as a vague feeling that something was out of place. Then she felt it creep up her spine, slowly tightening as it clawed its way upwards. Now it was like a fist pounding inside her skull.

Renée never went anywhere with strangers. Hadn't her parents hammered that into her head since she was a child? And now, at 19, she wasn't about to start breaking *that* rule.

And yet here she was, in a car with a stranger. He seemed nice enough. And it wasn't as though he were some strange guy on the side of the road or anything. She had met George at Patricia's party, and. . . .

Renée had first been attracted by his dark eyes. They seemed to light up his entire face when he smiled. And when he asked her to dance, Renée felt flattered. He was a little older, a little more sure of himself than most of the guys she knew. Renée liked that: It was a sign of maturity.

As the evening wore on and he continued to be attentive to her, it seemed natural to accept his offer to take her home.

But then they passed the turn to her dorm. She didn't understand his mumbled reply about "getting something." And as he turned off on the country road, that clawing at the back of her neck had begun.

As he looked at her, his eyes almost pierced the darkness. "It's time to pay, Babe," he said, as he clawed at her blouse.

Renée won't talk about that night. She doesn't want to recall anything that happened then.

IN THIS PAPER we examine how sociologists do research. As we look at how they gather data, we focus on this basic question: How can we gather reliable information on rape—which is to say on both rapists *and* their victims?

Sociology and Common Sense

Common sense will give us some information. From common sense (a kind of knowledge not based on formal investigation, but on ideas that we pick up from our groups, mixed with abstractions from our own experiences) we know that her rape was a significant event in Renée's life. And from common sense we know that rape has ongoing effects, that it can trigger fears and anxieties, and that it can make women distrust men.

It so happens that those ideas are true. But many other common-sense ideas, even though glaringly obvious to us, are *not* true, and so we need research to test the validity and accuracy of our ideas. For example, common sense also tells us that one reason men rape is the revealing clothing that some women wear. And common sense tells us that men who rape are sexually deprived. These common-sense ideas, however, are not on target. Researchers have found that men who rape don't care what a woman is wearing; most don't even care who the woman is. She is simply an object for their drives for power, exploitation, and sexual satisfaction. Researchers have also found that rapists may or may not be sexually deprived—the same as with men who do not rape. For example, many rapists have wives or girl friends with whom they have an ongoing sexual relationship.

If it is neither provocative clothing nor sexual deprivation, then, what *does* cause rape? And what different effects does rape have on victims? Phrasing the matter this way—instead of assuming that we know the answers—not only opens up our minds but also underscores the pressing need for sociological research, the need to search for empirical findings that will take us completely out of the realm of guesswork and well beyond common sense.

Let us see now how sociologists do their research. We shall look first at a research model, and then at the research methods used in sociology.

A Research Model

As shown in Figure 4.1, eight basic steps are involved in social research. As you look at each of these steps, be aware that this is an ideal model. In some research these steps are collapsed, in others their order may be rearranged, while in still others one or more steps may be omitted.

1. SELECTING A TOPIC

The first step is to select a topic. What is it that you want to know more about? Many sociologists simply follow their curiosity, their drive to know. They become interested in a particular topic, and they pursue it. Sometimes sociologists choose a topic simply because funds are available. At other times, some social problem, such as rape, has become a pressing issue and the sociologist wants to gather data that will help people better understand—and perhaps help solve it.

2. DEFINING THE PROBLEM

The second step is to define the problem, to determine what you want to learn about the topic. To develop a researchable question, you need to focus on a specific area or problem. For example, you may want to determine the education and work experiences of rapists, or the average age of victims.

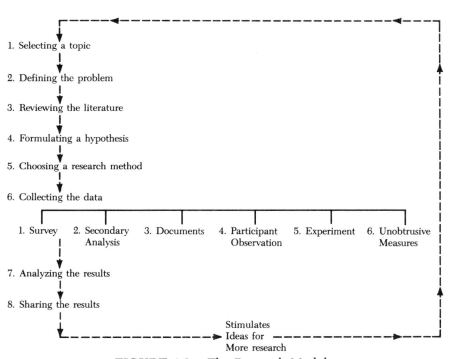

FIGURE 4.1. The Research Model

Modification of Fig. 2.2 from Schaefer 1989.

3. REVIEWING THE LITERATURE

The third step is to review the literature. Nobody wants to rediscover the wheel. If the question has already been answered, you want to know that. In addition, a review of what has been written on the topic can stir your ideas and help sharpen your questions.

4. FORMULATING A HYPOTHESIS

The fourth step is to formulate a *hypothesis*, a statement of what you expect to find according to predictions from a theory. A hypothesis predicts a relationship between or among *variables* (factors thought to be significant). For example, the statement "Men who are more socially isolated are more likely to rape than are men who are more socially integrated" is an example of a hypothesis. Hypotheses (the plural) need *operational definitions*—that is, precise ways to measure their concepts. In this example, you would need operational definitions for three concepts: social integration, social isolation, and rape.

5. CHOOSING A RESEARCH METHOD

The ways by which sociologists collect data are called *research methods*. You need to select a method that will answer the questions you have formulated. (In the next section, I go into detail concerning the six research methods used by sociologists.)

6. COLLECTING THE DATA

The next step is to gather the data. Great care needs to be taken to assure that the data are both valid and reliable. *Validity* means the extent to which the operational definitions measure what you intend to measure. In other words, do your definitions or measures of social isolation and integration *really* measure those concepts and not something else?

The concept of rape is not as simple to define (or operationalize) as it may sound. For example, there are various degrees of sexual assault. Look at Table 4.1, which depicts a variety of forced sexual activities. Deciding which of these constitute rape for the purposes of your reseach project is an example of the difficulties of developing operational definitions. Certainly not all of these acts are rape—and, therefore, not all of those who did them are rapists.

Reliability refers to the extent to which your measures and studies give consistent results. Inadequate operational definitions and sampling (covered below) will prevent reliability. For example, if your measure of rape

TABLE 4.1 Date Rape and Other Unwanted Sexual Activities
Experienced by College Undergraduates

UNWANTED SEXUAL ACTIVITY	WOMEN WHO REPORTED THIS HAD HAPPENED TO THEM (%)	MEN WHO REPORTED THEY HAD DONE THIS (%)
He kissed without tongue contact	3.7	2.2
He kissed with tongue contact	12.3	0.7
He touched/kissed her breasts through her clothes	24.7	7.3
He touched/kissed her breasts under her clothes	22.6	13.1
He touched her genitals through her clothes	28.8	15.3
He touched her genitals under her clothes	28.4	13.9
He performed oral sex on her	9.9	8.8
He forced her to touch his genitals through his clothes	2.9	0.7
He forced her to touch his genitals under his clothes	5.8	2.2
He forced her to perform oral sex on him	2.5	4.4
He forced her to have sexual intercourse	20.6	15.3

These are the results of a survey of 380 women and 368 men enrolled in introductory psychology courses at Texas A&M University. Percentages add up to more than 100 because often more than one unwanted sexual activity occurred on one date.

Source: Based on Muehlenhard and Linton 1987:190.

is inadequate, other researchers will exclude acts that you included, and include acts that you excluded. In that case, how can you compare the results?

7. ANALYZING THE RESULTS

After the data are gathered, it is time to analyze them. Sociologists have specific techniques for doing this, each of which requires special training. They range from statistical tests (of which there are many, each with its own rules for application) to *content analysis* (examining the content of something in order to identify its themes—in this case perhaps magazine articles and television reports about rape, or even diaries kept by women who have been raped). If a hypothesis has been part of the research (and not all social research has hypotheses), it is during this step that it is tested.

8. SHARING THE RESULTS

Now it is time to wrap up the research. In this step you write a report that shares your findings with the scientific community. You relate your findings to the literature, to show how they are connected to what has previously been discovered. You carefully review your research procedures so others can *replicate* it—i.e., can repeat the study to test its findings. In this way science slowly builds, adding finding to finding.

Now let us look in greater detail at the fifth step to examine the research methods that sociologists use.

Six Research Methods

Sociologists use six *research methods* (also called research designs). These *procedures for gathering data* are surveys, secondary analysis, documents, experiments, unobtrusive measures, and participant observation.

SURVEYS

Let us suppose that you want to know how many women are raped each year. The *survey*—having people answer a series of questions—would be an appropriate method to use.

Before using this method, however, you have to decide whom you will survey. What is your *population;* that is, what is the target group that you want to learn about? Is it all females in the world? Only American females? The females in a particular state, county, or city? Or only those on your college campus?

Let us suppose that your research interest is modest—that you want only to know the extent of rape on your campus. Ideally, you would survey all female students. But let us also suppose that your college enrollment is large, making this impractical. To get at the answer, then, you must select a smaller group, a *sample* of individuals, from whom you can generalize to the entire campus. Choosing a sample is critical, for it will affect the results of your study. For example, you will get different results if you survey only freshmen or seniors—or only females taking introductory sociology or advanced physics classes.

What kind of sample will allow you to generalize to the entire campus? The best is a *random* sample. This does *not* mean that you stand on some campus corner and ask questions of whomever happens to walk by. *In a random sample everyone in the population has the same chance of being included in the study.* In this case, since the population is all females taking classes at your college, all such females must have the same chance of being included in your study—whether they are freshmen, sophomores, juniors, seniors, or graduate students. It also means that such factors (*vari-*

ables) as a woman's choice of major, her grade point average, or whether she is a day or evening student cannot affect her chances of being a part of your sample.

To use a random sample, you would need a list of all currently enrolled female students. To determine which students become part of the sample, you might assign a number of each name on the list and then use random numbers to determine which particular persons become part of the sample. (Random numbers are availabe on tables in statistics books, and can be generated by computer.)

Because a random sample represents the population (in this case female students at your college), you can generalize your findings to all the female students on your campus, whether they were part of the sample or not.

In some surveys, *questionnaires*, a list of questions, are mailed to people. Although such *self-administered questionnaires* allow a large number of people to be sampled at a lower cost, control is lost. For example, under what conditions did people (*respondents*) fill them out? Who influenced their answers?

Other surveys use *interviews:* Respondents are asked questions directly. This is usually done on a face-to-face basis, although some interviews are conducted over the telephone. The advantage of this type of survey is that the researchers bring control to the situation. They know the conditions under which the interview took place and that each question was asked in precisely the same way. Its disadvantages include not only the more limited number of questionnaires that can be completed, and the increased cost, but also *interview bias*, the effects that interviewers can have on respondents that lead to biased answers. For example, although respondents may be willing to write an anonymous answer, they may not want to express their opinions to another person directly. Instead, they sometimes try to make their answers match what they think the interviewer wants to hear.

Sociologists sometimes use *closed-ended questions*, called *structured interviews*. Each question is followed by a list of possible answers. The advantages are that these are faster to administer, and make it easier for the answers to be *coded* (categorized) so they can be fed into a computer for analysis. If you use closed-ended questions, you will have to be careful to make sure that they represent people's opinions. For example, if you were to ask "What do you think should be done to rapists?" and the only choices you provide are to castrate or kill them, you would not be taking accurate measurements of people's opinions. Similarly, if you begin a question with, "Don't you agree that" ("rapists should be locked up for life"— or whatever you want to add), you would tilt the results toward agreement with a particular position.

Questions, then, must be carefully worded so they do not slant answers— because biased findings are worthless. It takes a great deal of training to construct questions that are free of bias, and sociologists are extremely critical of both how questions are worded and how they are administered (given).

To better tap the depth and diversity of people's experiences and attitudes, you may wish to use *open-ended questions*, called *unstructured interviews*, that allow people to answer in their own words. The primary advantage of this type of interview is that it allows people to express their full range of opinions. The major disadvantage is that it is difficult to compare people's answers. For example, how would you compare these answers to the question "What do you think causes rape?"

"They haven't been raised right."
"I think they must have had problems with their mother."
"We ought to kill every one!"
"They're all sick."
"I don't want to talk about it."

The research topic we are considering also brings up another significant item. Let us suppose that you want to interview rape victims. Would they really give honest answers? Will a woman even admit to a stranger that she has been raped, much less talk about it? Wouldn't all your efforts be futile?

If you were to simply walk up to a stranger on the street and ask if she had ever been raped, you can guess the results—and they certainly would give little basis for placing confidence in your findings. Researchers must establish *rapport*, a feeling of trust, with their respondents. When it comes to sensitive topics, areas about which people may feel embarrassment, shame, hostility, or other deep emotions, rapport is all the more important.

Once rapport is gained (often through building trust by explaining the significance of the research, assuring anonymity, and first asking nonsensitive questions), victims usually will talk about rape. For example, each year researchers conduct a national crime survey in which they interview a random sample of 49,000 households—about 90,000 Americans. They find that most rape victims do share their experiences with them (Shim and DeBerry 1988), and the results closely match the statistics reported by the police.

SECONDARY ANALYSIS

In *secondary analysis*, the second research method we shall consider, the researcher analyzes data already collected by others. For example, if you were to examine the basic data gathered by the interviewers who did the national crime survey just mentioned, you would be doing secondary analysis.

Ordinarily, researchers prefer to gather their own data, but lack of resources, especially time and money, may make this preference impossible to fulfill. In addition, data already gathered may contain a wealth of information not pertinent to the purposes of those who did the original study. It simply lies there, waiting to be analyzed.

While this approach can solve problems of access, it also poses its own problems. Not having directly carried out the research, how can you be sure that the data were systematically gathered and accurately recorded, and biases avoided? That may not be an easy task, especially when the original data were gathered by numerous researchers, not all of whom were equally qualified.

DOCUMENTS

The use of *documents*, written sources, is a third research method employed by sociologists. To investigate social life, sociologists examine such diverse sources as books, newspapers, diaries, bank records, police reports, immigration records, household accounts, and records kept by various organizations. (Although they are not commonly called documents, movies, television, and videotapes would also be included here.)

To apply this method to the study of rape, you might examine police reports. They may reveal what proportion of all arrests are for rape; how many of the men arrested go to trial; what proportion is convicted, put on probation, sent to prison; and so forth. If these are your questions, police statistics could be valuable.

But for other questions, police records would be useless. For example, if you want to know about the adjustment of rape victims, they would tell you nothing. Other documents, however, may lend themselves to this question. If your campus has a rape crisis center, for example, it might have records that would provide key information. Or you may obtain diaries kept by victims, and search them for clues to their reactions—especially how their orientations change over time. If you couldn't find such diaries, you might contact a sample of rape victims and ask them to keep diaries. Locating that sample is extremely difficult—but, again, the rape crisis center could be the key. Their personnel might ask victims to keep the diaries. (To my knowledge, however, no sociologist has yet studied rape in this way.)

I am writing, of course, about an ideal case, as though the rape crisis center is opening its arms to you. In actual fact it may not cooperate at all, refusing to ask victims to keep diaries and not even letting you near their records. Access, then, is another problem researchers constantly face. Simply put, you can't study something unless you can gain access to it.

EXPERIMENTS

A fourth research method is the experiment. This is the classic method of the natural sciences. Sociologists seldom use it, however, because they are more likely to be interested in broad features of society and social behavior, or in studying a social group in a natural setting, neither of which lends itself to an experiment.

The basic purpose of an experiment is to identify cause-and-effect relationships—to find out what causes what. Ordinarily, experiments are used to test a hypothesis. Experiments involve *independent variables* (those factors that cause a change in something) and *dependent variables* (those factors that are changed). Before the experiment you must accurately measure the dependent variable. Then, after introducing the independent variable, you again measure the dependent variable in order to see what change has occurred.

Let us assume, for example, that you want to test the hypothesis that pornography creates attitudes that favor rape. The independent variable would be pornography, the dependent variable attitudes toward rape. You can measure a group of men's attitudes toward rape and then use random numbers to divide the men into two subgroups. To one group, the *experimental group*, you introduce the independent variable (such as violent pornographic movies). The other group, the *control group*, is not exposed to the independent variable (that is, they are not shown these movies). You then measure the dependent variable in both groups. Changes in the dependent variable (attitudes toward rape) are due to what only the experimental group received, the independent variable (in this case, the pornography).

Because there is always some chance that unknown third variables have not been evenly divided among the groups, you would need to retest your results by repeating the experiment with other groups of men.

UNOBTRUSIVE MEASURES

The fifth method we shall consider is *unobtrusive measures:* observing social behavior when people do not know they are being studied. For example, social researchers have studied the level of whiskey consumption in a "dry" town by counting empty bottles in trash cans; the degree of fear induced through telling ghost stories by measuring the shrinking diameter of a circle of seated children; and the popularity of exhibits at Chicago's Museum of Science and Industry by the wear upon tiles in front of the various displays (Webb et al., 1966).

Unobtrusive measures could also be used to study rape. For example, you could observe rapists in prison when they do not know they are being watched. You might arrange for the leader of a therapy group for rapists to be called out of the room. During his absence, you could use a one-way mirror to observe the men's interactions, and tape recorders to preserve what they say. Such an approach would probably tell you more about their real attitudes than most other techniques.

Professional ethics, however, might disallow such a study. And I know of no research that has applied this method to the study of rape.

PARTICIPANT OBSERVATION (FIELD WORK)

Let's turn to my favorite method, one that involves the researcher in the most direct way. In *participant observation* (or field work) the researcher *participates* in a research setting while *observing* what is happening in that setting.

How is it possible to study rape by participant observation? It would seem that this method would not apply. If one considers being present during rape, it certainly does not. But there are many other questions about rape that can be answered by participant observation, answers that cannot be gained as adequately by any other method.

Let us suppose that your interest is the adjustment of rape victims. You would like to learn how the rape has affected their behavior and their orientations to the world. For example, how has their victimization affected their hopes and goals, their dating patterns, their ideas about men and intimacy? Participant observation can provide detailed answers to such questions.

Let's go back to your campus again. Assume that, like mine, your campus has a rape crisis intervention center. This setting lends itself to participant observation, for here you can observe rape victims from the time they first report the attack to their later participation in individual and group counseling. With good rapport, you can even spend time with victims outside this setting, observing how it affects other aspects of their lives.

Participant observation has the added benefit of allowing you to study whatever happens to occur while you are in the setting. In this instance, you would also be able to study the operation of the rape crisis center. As you observe counselors at work, you could also study *their* attitudes and behaviors.

As you may have noticed, in participant observation personal characteristics of the researcher become highly important. Could a male researcher, for example, conduct such research? Technically, the answer is yes. Properly introduced and with the right demeanor, male sociologists could do this research. But granted the topic, and especially the emotional states of females who have been brutally victimized by males, it may be more appropriate for female sociologists to conduct their research. Their chances of success are likely to be higher.

In conducting research, then, sociologists must be aware of such variables as the sex, age, race, personality, and even height and weight of the researcher (Henslin 1990). While important in all research methods (for example, male respondents to a survey may be more talkative to young, shapely female researchers than to obese males), these variables are especially important in participant observation (Snyder 1982).

Participant observers face a problem with generalizability. Although they look for principles of human behavior, it is difficult to know the extent to which their findings apply beyond the setting in which they occur. Consequently, most participant observation is exploratory in nature: The findings document in detail what people in a particular setting are experiencing and how they are reacting to those experiences, suggesting that other people who face similar situations will react in similar ways.

I find participant observation the most exciting of the methods. It is the type of sociology that I like to do and the type I like to read about. From these studies, I gain a depth of understanding of settings that I want to know more about but for whatever reason am not able to study, and in some cases am not even able to enter. If I were female, for example, I might have volunteered for work in my campus's rape crisis center—a technique often used by sociologists to solve the problem of access.

Conclusion: A Note on Choosing Research Methods

As you have seen, a critical factor in choosing a research method is the questions you wish to answer. Each method lends itself much better to answering particular interests or questions than do other methods. You have also seen that access to subjects is critical in deciding which research method to use. Two other factors are significant in this choice: the resources available to the researcher, and the researcher's background or training. For example, a researcher who prefers to conduct a survey may find that finances will not permit it, and instead turn to the study of documents. The researcher's background is similarly significant in this choice. Researchers who have been trained in *quantitative techniques* (an emphasis on precise measurement, numbers, statistics) are more likely to use surveys, while researchers who have been trained in *qualitative techniques* (generally, making direct observations of what people do and say) lean toward participant observation. The particular training that sociologists receive in graduate school, which sometimes depends on capricious events, orients them toward certain research methods. They feel comfortable with those, and tend to continue to use them throughout their careers.

References

Henslin, James M. (1990). "It's not a lovely place to visit, and I wouldn't want to live there." In Robert G. Burgess (ed.), *Studies in Qualitative Methodology II:* 51–76. Greenwich, CT: JAI Press.

Muehlenhard, Charlene L., and Melaney A. Linton (1987)."Date rape: Familiar strangers." *Journal of Counseling Psychology 34:* 186–96.

Schaefer, Richard T. (1989). *Sociology*. 3d ed. New York: McGraw–Hill.

Shim, Kelly H., and Marshall DeBerry (August 1988). *Criminal Victimization in the United States, 1986*. Washington, D.C.: U.S. Dept. of Justice, Bureau of Justice Statistics.

Snyder, Mark. (1982). "Self-Fulfilling Stereotypes." *Psychology Today*, July: 60, 65, 67–68.

Webb, Eugene J., Donald T. Campbell, Richard D. Schwartz, and Lee Sechrest (1966). *Unobtrusive Measures: Nonreactive Research in the Social Sciences*. Chicago: Rand McNally.

5 "Riding the Bull at Gilley's": Convicted Rapists Describe the Rewards of Rape

DIANA SCULLY
JOSEPH MAROLLA

As we saw in the previous reading, sociologists can choose from a variety of research methods. Rape was used as the example to illustrate the various ways in which sociologists collect data. In this selection, you can see how two sociologists used the research method known as *unstructured interviewing* to gather data on rape. What prompted their research was a question that many people wonder about: "Just why do men rape?"

Scully and Marolla interviewed a sample of men who had been sent to prison for rape. In what was a difficult situation, they established enough rapport that the men felt free to talk about their motives. From this selection you should gain an understanding of the reasons why men commit this violent act.

To determine how widespread (representative) these motives are, we need more studies, preferably with both convicted and unconvicted rapists. Perhaps you, now a student reading this book in the introductory course, will become a sociologist who will build on this study.

OVER THE PAST SEVERAL DECADES, rape has become a "medicalized" social problem. That is to say, the theories used to explain rape are predicated on psychopathological models. They have been generated from clinical experiences with small samples of rapists, often the therapists' own clients. Although these psychiatric explanations are most appropriately applied to the atypical rapist, they have been generalized to all men who rape and have come to inform the public's view on the topic.

Two assumptions are at the core of the psychopathological model; that rape is the result of idiosyncratic mental disease and that it often includes an uncontrollable sexual impulse (Scully & Marolla, 1985). For example, the presumption of psychopathology is evident in the often cited work of Nicholas Groth (1979). While Groth emphasizes the nonsexual nature of rape (power, anger, sadism), he also concludes, "Rape is always a symptom of some psychological dysfunction, either temporary and transient or chronic and repetitive" (Groth, 1979:5). Thus, in the psychopathological view, rapists lack the ability to control their behavior; they are "sick" individuals from the "lunatic fringe" of society.

In contradiction to this model, empirical research has repeatedly failed to find a consistent pattern of personality type or character disorder that reliably discriminates rapists from other groups of men (Fisher & Rivlin, 1971; Hammer & Jacks, 1955; Rada, 1978). Indeed, other research has found that fewer than 5 percent of men were psychotic when they raped (Abel et al., 1980).

Evidence indicates that rape is not a behavior confined to a few "sick" men, but many men have the attitudes and beliefs necessary to commit a sexually aggressive act. In research conducted at a midwestern university, Koss and her coworkers reported that 85 percent of men defined as highly sexually aggressive had victimized women with whom they were romantically involved (Koss & Leonard, 1984). A recent survey quoted in *The Chronicle of Higher Education* estimates that more than 20 percent of college women are the victims of rape and attempted rape (Meyer, 1984). These findings mirror research published several decades earlier which also concluded that sexual aggression was commonplace in dating relationships (Kanin, 1957, 1965, 1967, 1969; Kirkpatrick & Kanin, 1957). In their study of 53 college males, Malamuth, Haber and Feshback (1980) found that 51 percent indicated a likelihood that they, themselves, would rape if assured of not being punished.

In addition, the frequency of rape in the United States makes it unlikely that responsibility rests solely with a small lunatic fringe of psychopathic men. Johnson (1980), calculating the lifetime risk of rape to girls and women aged twelve and over, makes a similar observation. Using Law Enforcement Assistance Association and Bureau of Census Crime Victimization Studies, he calculated that, excluding sexual abuse in marriage and assuming equal risk to all women, 20 to 30 percent of girls now 12 years old will suffer a violent sexual attack during the remainder of their lives. Interestingly, the lack of empirical support for the psychopathological model has not resulted in the de-medicalization of rape, nor does it appear to have diminished the belief that rapists are "sick" aberrations in their own culture. This is significant because of the implications and consequences of the model.

A central assumption in the psychopathological model is that male sexual aggression is unusual or strange. This assumption removes rape from the realm of the everyday or "normal" world and places it in the category of "special" or "sick" behavior. As a consequence, men who rape are cast in the role of outsider and a connection with normative male behavior is avoided. Since, in this view, the source of the behavior is thought to be within the psychology of the individual, attention is diverted away from culture or social structure as contributing factors. Thus, the psychopathological model ignores evidence which links sexual aggression to environmental variables and which suggests that rape, like all behavior, is learned.

Cultural Factors in Rape

Culture is a factor in rape, but the precise nature of the relationship between culture and sexual violence remains a topic of discussion. Ethnographic data from pre-industrial societies show the existence of rape-free cultures (Broude & Green, 1976; Sanday, 1979), although explanations for the phenomenon differ. Sanday (1979) relates sexual violence to contempt for female qualities and suggests that rape is part of a culture of violence and an expression of male dominance. In contrast, Blumberg (1979) argues that in pre-industrial societies women are more likely to lack important life options and to be physically and politically oppressed where they lack economic power relative to men. That is, in pre-industrial societies relative economic power enables women to win some immunity from men's use of force against them.

Among modern societies, the frequency of rape varies dramatically, and the United States is among the most rape-prone of all. In 1980, for example, the rate of reported rape and attempted rape for the United States was eighteen times higher than the corresponding rate for England and Wales (West, 1983). Spurred by the Women's Movement, feminists have generated an impressive body of theory regarding the cultural etiology of rape in the United States. Representative of the feminist view, Griffin (1971) called rape "The All American Crime."

The feminist perspective views rape as an act of violence and social control which functions to "keep women in their place" (Brownmiller, 1975; Kasinsky, 1975; Russell, 1975). Feminists see rape as an extension of normative male behavior, the result of conformity or overconformity to the values and prerogatives which define the traditional male sex role. That is, traditional socialization encourages males to associate power, dominance, strength, virility and superiority with masculinity, and submissiveness, passivity, weakness, and inferiority with femininity. Furthermore, males are taught to have expectations about their level of sexual needs and expectations for corresponding female accessibility which function to justify forcing sexual access. The justification for forced sexual access is buttressed by legal, social, and religious definitions of women as male property and sex as an exchange of goods (Bart, 1979). Socialization prepares women to be "legitimate" victims and men to be potential offenders (Weis & Borges, 1973). Herman (1984) concludes that the United States is a rape culture because both genders are socialized to regard male aggression as a natural and normal part of sexual intercourse.

Feminists view pornography as an important element in a larger system of sexual violence; they see pornography as an expression of a rape-prone culture where women are seen as objects available for use by men (Morgan, 1980; Wheeler, 1985). Based on his content analysis of 428 "adults only" books, Smith (1976) makes a similar observation. He notes that, not only is rape presented as part of normal male/female sexual relations, but the woman, despite her terror, is always depicted as sexually aroused to the point of cooperation. In the end, she is ashamed but physically gratified. The message—women desire and enjoy rape—has more potential for damage than the image of the violence *per se*.

The fusion of these themes—sex as an impersonal act, the victim's uncontrollable orgasm, and the violent infliction of pain—is commonplace in the actual accounts of rapists. Scully and Marolla (1984) demonstrated that many convicted rapists denied their crime and attempted to justify their rapes by arguing that their victim enjoyed herself despite the use of a weapon and the infliction of serious injuries, or even death. In fact, many argued, they had been instrumental in making *her* fantasy come true.

The images projected in pornography contribute to a vocabulary of motive which trivializes and neutralizes rape and which might lessen the internal controls that otherwise would prevent sexually aggressive behavior. Men who rape use this culturally acquired vocabulary to justify their sexual violence.

Another consequence of the application of psychopathology to rape is that it leads one to view sexual violence as a special type of crime in which the motivations are subconscious and uncontrollable rather than overt and deliberate as with other criminal behavior. Black (1983) offers an approach to the analysis of criminal and/or violent behavior which, when applied to rape, avoids this bias. Black suggests that it is theoretically useful to ignore that crime is criminal in order to discover what such behavior has in common with other kinds of conduct. From his perspective, much of the crime in modern societies, as in pre-industrial societies, can be interpreted as a form of "self help" in which the actor is expressing a grievance through aggression and violence. From the actor's perspective, the victim is deviant and his own behavior is a form of social control in which the objective may be conflict management, punishment, or revenge. For example, in societies where women are considered the property of men, rape is some-times used as a means of avenging the victim's husband or father (Black,

1983). In some cultures rape is used as a form of punishment. Such was the tradition among the puritanical, patriarchal Cheyenne, where men were valued for their ability as warriors. It was Cheyenne custom that a wife suspected of being unfaithful could be "put on the prairie" by her husband. Military confreres then were invited to "feast" on the prairie (Hoebel, 1954; Llewellyn & Hoebel, 1941). The ensuing mass rape was a husband's method of punishing his wife.

Black's (1983) approach is helpful in understanding rape because it forces one to examine the goals that some men have learned to achieve through sexually violent means. Thus, one approach to understanding why some men rape is to shift attention from individual psychopathology to the important question of what rapists gain from sexual aggression and violence in a culture seemingly prone to rape. In this paper, we address this question using data from interviews conducted with 114 convicted, incarcerated rapists.

Methods

SAMPLE

During 1980 and 1981 we interviewed 114 convicted rapists. All of the men had been convicted of the rape or attempted rape (n = 8) of an adult woman and subsequently incarcerated in a Virginia prison. Men convicted of other types of sexual offense were omitted from the sample.

In addition to their convictions for rape, 39 percent of the men also had convictions for burglary or robbery, 29 percent for abduction, 25 percent for sodomy, 11 percent for first or second degree murder, and 12 percent had been convicted of more than one rape. The majority of the men had previous criminal histories, but only 23 percent had a record of past sex offenses and only 26 percent had a history of emotional problems. Their sentences for rape and accompanying crimes ranged from ten years to seven life sentences plus 380 years for one man. Twenty-two percent of the rapists were serving at least one life sentence. Forty-six percent of the rapists were white, 54 percent black. In age, they ranged from 18 to 60 years, but the majority were between 18 and 35 years. Based on a statistical profile of felons in all Virginia prisons prepared by the Virginia Department of Corrections, it appears that this sample of rapists was disproportionately white and, at the time of the research, somewhat better educated and younger than the average inmate.

All participants in this research were volunteers. In constructing the sample, age, education, race, severity of current offense and past criminal record were balanced within the limitations imposed by the characteristics of the volunteer pool. Obviously the sample was not random and thus may not be typical of all rapists, imprisoned or otherwise.

How Offenders View the Rewards of Rape

REVENGE AND PUNISHMENT

As noted earlier, Black's (1983) perspective suggests that a rapist might see his act as a legitimized form of revenge or punishment. Additionally, he asserts that the idea of "collective liability" accounts for much seemingly random violence. "Collective liability" suggests that all people in a particular category are held accountable for the conduct of each of their counterparts. Thus, the victim of a violent act may merely represent the category of individual being punished.

These factors—revenge, punishment, and the collective liability of women—can be used to explain a number of rapes in our research. Several cases will illustrate ways in which these factors combined in various types of rape. Revenge-rapes were among the most brutal and often included beatings, serious injuries, and even murder.

Typically, revenge-rapes included the element of collective liability. That is, from the rapist's perspective, the victim was a substitute for the woman he wanted to avenge. As explained elsewhere (Scully & Marolla, 1984), an upsetting event, involving a woman, preceded a significant number of rapes. When they raped, these men were angry because of a perceived indiscretion, typically related to a rigid, moralistic standard of sexual conduct, which they required from "their woman" but, in most cases, did not abide by themselves. Over and over these rapists talked about using rape "to get even" with their wives or other significant woman. Typical is a young man who, prior to the rape, had a violent argument with his wife over what eventually proved to be her misdiagnosed case of venereal disease. She assumed the disease had been contracted through him, an accusation that infuriated him. After fighting with his wife, he explained that he drove around "thinking about hurting someone." He encountered his victim, a stranger, on the road where her car had broken down. It appears she accepted his offered ride because her car was out of commission. When she realized that rape was pending, she called him "a son of a bitch," and attempted to resist. He reported flying into a rage and beating her, and he confided,

> I have never felt that much anger before. If she had resisted, I would have killed her. . . . The rape was for revenge. I didn't have an orgasm. She was there to get my hostile feelings off on.

Although not the most common form of revenge rape, sexual assault continues to be used in retaliation against the victim's male partner. In one such case, the offender, angry because the victim's husband owed him money, went to the victim's home to collect. He confided, "I was going to get it one way or another." Finding the victim alone, he explained, they started to argue about the money and,

> I grabbed her and started beating the hell out of her. Then I committed the act. I knew what I was doing. I was mad. I could have stopped but I didn't. I did it to get even with her and her husband.

Griffin (1971) points out that when women are viewed as commodities, "In raping another man's woman, a man may aggrandize his own manhood and concurrently reduce that of the other man" (p. 33).

Revenge-rapes often contained an element of punishment. In some cases, while the victim was not the initial object of the revenge, the intent was to punish her because of something that transpired after the decision to rape had been made or during the course of the rape itself. This was the case with a young man whose wife had recently left him. Although they were in the process of reconciliation, he remained angry and upset over the separation. The night of the rape, he met the victim and her friend in a bar where he had gone to watch a fight on TV. The two women apparently accepted a ride from him, but after taking her friend home, he drove the victim to his apartment. At his apartment, he found a note from his wife indicating she had stopped by to watch the fight with him. This increased his anger because he preferred his wife's company. Inside his apartment, the victim allegedly remarked that she was sexually interested in his dog, which he reported, put him in a rage. In the ensuing attack, he raped and pistol-whipped the victim. Then he forced a vacuum cleaner hose, switched on suction, into her vagina and bit her breast, severing the nipple. He stated:

> I hated at the time, but I don't know if it was her (the victim). (Who could it have been?) My wife? Even though we were getting back together, I still didn't trust her.

During his interview, it became clear that this offender, like many of the men, believed men have the right to discipline and punish women. In fact, he argued that most of the men he knew would also have beaten the victim because "that kind of thing (referring to the dog) is not acceptable among my friends."

Finally, in some rapes, both revenge and punishment were directed at victims because they represented women whom these offenders perceived as collectively responsible and liable for their problems. Rape was used "to put women in their place" and as a method of proving their "manhood" by displaying dominance over a female. For example, one multiple rapist believed his actions were related to the feeling that women thought they were better than he was.

Rape was a feeling of total dominance. Before the rapes, I would always get a feeling of power and anger. I would degrade women so I could feel there was a person of less worth than me.

Another, especially brutal, case involved a young man from an upper middle class background, who spilled out his story in a seven-hour interview conducted in his solitary confinement cell. He described himself as tremendously angry, at the time, with his girlfriend, who he believed was involved with him in a "storybook romance," and from whom he expected complete fidelity. When she went away to college and became involved with another man, his revenge lasted eighteen months and involved the rape and murder of five women, all strangers who lived in his community. Explaining his rape-murders, he stated:

> I wanted to take my anger and frustration out on a stranger, to be in control, to do what I wanted to do. I wanted to use and abuse someone as I felt used and abused. I was killing my girl friend. During the rapes and murders, I would think about my girl friend. I hated the victims because they probably messed men over. I hated women because they were deceitful and I was getting revenge for what happened to me.

AN ADDED BONUS

Burglary and robbery commonly accompany rape. Among our sample, 39 percent of the rapists had also been convicted of one or the other of these crimes committed in connection with rape. In some cases, the original intent was rape and robbery was an afterthought. However, a number of men indicated that the reverse was true in their situation. That is, the decision to rape was made subsequent to their original intent, which was burglary or robbery.

This was the case with a young offender who stated that he originally intended only to rob the store in which the victim happened to be working. He explained that when he found the victim alone,

> I decided to rape her to prove I had guts. She was just there. It could have been anybody.

Similarly, another offender indicated that he initially broke into his victim's home to burglarize it. When he discovered the victim asleep, he decided to seize the opportunity "to satisfy an urge to go to bed with a white woman, to see if it was different." Indeed a number of men indicated that the decision to rape had been made after they realized they were in control of the situation. This was also true of an unemployed offender who confided that his practice was to steal whenever he needed money. On the day of the rape, he drove to a local supermarket and paced the parking lot, "staking out the situation." His pregnant victim was the first person to come along alone and "she was an easy target." Threatening her with a knife, he reported the victim as saying she would do anything if he didn't harm her. At that point, he decided to force her to drive to a deserted area, where he raped her. He explained:

> I wasn't thinking about sex. But when she said she would do anything not to get hurt, probably because she was pregnant, I thought, "why not?"

The attitude of these men toward rape was similar to their attitude toward burglary and robbery. Quite simply, if the situation is right, "why not?" From the perspective of these rapists, rape was just another part of the crime—an added bonus.

SEXUAL ACCESS

In an effort to change public attitudes that are damaging to the victims of rape and to reform laws seemingly premised on the assumption that women both ask for and enjoy rape, many writers emphasize the violent and aggressive character of rape. Often such arguments appear to discount the part that sex plays in the crime. The data clearly indicate that from the rapists' point of view, rape is in part sexually motivated. Indeed, it is the sexual aspect of rape that distinguishes it from other forms of assault.

Rape as a means of sexual access also shows the deliberate nature of this crime. When a woman is unwilling or seems unavailable for sex, the rapist can seize what isn't volunteered. In discussing his decision to rape, one man made this clear.

> . . . a real fox, beautiful shape. She was a beautiful woman and I wanted to see what she had.

The attitude that sex is a male entitlement suggests that when a woman says "no," rape is a suitable method of conquering the "offending" object. If, for example, a woman is picked up at a party or in a bar or while hitchhiking (behavior which a number of the rapists saw as a signal of sexual availability), and the woman later resists sexual advances, rape is presumed to be justified. The same justification operates in what is popularly called "date rape." The belief that sex was their just compensation compelled a number of rapists to insist they had not raped. Such was the case of an offender who raped and seriously beat his victim when, on their second date, she refused his sexual advances.

> I think I was really pissed off at her because it didn't go as planned. I could have been with someone else. She led me on but wouldn't deliver. . . . I have a male ego that must be fed.

The purpose of such rapes was conquest, to seize what was not offered.

Despite the cultural belief that young women are the most sexually desirable, several rapes involved the deliberate choice of a victim relatively older than the assailant. Since the rapists were themselves rather young (26 to 30 years of age on the average), they were expressing a preference for sexually experienced, rather than elderly, women. Men who chose victims older than themselves often said they did so because they believed that sexually experienced women were more desirable partners. They raped because they also believed that these women would not be sexually attracted to them.

Finally, sexual access emerged as a factor in the accounts of black men who consciously chose to rape white women. The majority of rapes in the United States are intraracial. However, for the past 20 years, according to national data based on reported rapes as well as victimization studies, which include unreported rapes, the rate of black on white (B/W) rape has significantly exceeded the rate of white on black (W/B) rape (La Free, 1982). Indeed, we may be experiencing a historical anomaly, since, as Brownmiller (1975) has documented, white men have freely raped women of color in the past. The current structure of interracial rape, however, reflects contemporary racism and race relations in several ways.

First, the status of black women in the United States today is relatively lower than the status of white women. Further, prejudice, segregation and other factors continue to militate against interracial coupling. Thus, the desire for sexual access to higher status, unavailable women, an important function in B/W rape, does not motivate white men to rape black women. Equally important, demographic and geographic barriers interact to lower the incidence of W/B rape. Segregation as well as the poverty expected in black neighborhoods undoubtedly discourages many whites from choosing such areas as a target for housebreaking or robbery. Thus, the number of rapes that would occur in conjunction with these crimes is reduced.

Reflecting in part the standards of sexual desirability set by the dominant white society, a number of black rapists indicated they had been curious about white women. Blocked by racial barriers from legitimate sexual relations with white women, they raped to gain access to them. They described raping white women as "the ultimate experience" and "high status among my friends. It gave me a feeling of status, power, macho." For another man, raping a white woman had a special appeal because it violated a "known taboo," making it more dangerous and, thus more exciting, to him than raping a black woman.

IMPERSONAL SEX AND POWER

The idea that rape is an impersonal rather than an intimate or mutual experience appealed to a number of rapists, some of whom suggested it was their preferred form of sex. The fact that rape allowed them to control rather than care encouraged some to act on this preference. For example, one man explained,

> Rape gave me the power to do what I wanted to do without feeling I had to please a partner or respond to a partner. I felt in control, dominant. Rape was the ability to have sex without caring about the woman's response. I was totally dominant.

Another rapist commented:

> Seeing them laying there helpless gave me the confidence that I could do it. . . . With rape, I felt totally in charge. I'm bashful, timid. When a woman wanted to give in normal sex, I was intimidated. In the rapes, I was totally in command, she totally submissive.

During his interview, another rapist confided that he had been fantasizing about rape for several weeks before committing his offense. His belief was that it would be "an exciting experience—a new high." Most appealing to him was the idea that he could make his victim "do it all for him" and that he would be in control. He fantasized that she "would submit totally and that I could have anything I wanted." Eventually, he decided to act because his older brother told him, "forced sex is great, I wouldn't get caught and, besides, women love it." Though now he admits to his crime, he continues to believe his victim "enjoyed it." Perhaps we should note here that the appeal of impersonal sex is not limited to convicted rapists. The amount of male sexual activity that occurs in homosexual meeting places as well as the widespread use of prostitutes suggests that avoidance of intimacy appeals to a large segment of the male population. Through rape men can experience power and avoid the emotions related to intimacy and tenderness. Further, the popularity of violent pornography suggests that a wide variety of men in this culture have learned to be aroused by sex fused with violence (Smith, 1976). Consistent with this observation, experimental research conducted by Malamuth et al. (1980) demonstrates that men are aroused by images that depict women as orgasmic under conditions of violence and pain. They found that, for female students, arousal was high when the victim experienced an orgasm and *no* pain, whereas male students were highly aroused when the victim experienced an orgasm and pain. On the basis of their results, Malamuth et al. suggest that forcing a woman to climax despite her pain and abhorrence of the assailant makes the rapist feel powerful, he has gained control over the only source of power historically associated with women, their bodies. In the final analysis, dominance was the objective of most rapists.

RECREATION AND ADVENTURE

Among gang rapists, most of whom were in their late teens or early twenties when convicted, rape represented recreation and adventure, another form of delinquent activity. Part of rape's appeal was the sense of male camaraderie engendered by participating collectively in a dangerous activity. To prove one's self capable of "performing" under these circumstances was a substantial challenge and also a source of reward. One gang rapist articulated this feeling very clearly,

> We felt powerful, we were in control. I wanted sex and there was peer pressure. She wasn't like a person, no personality, just domination on my part. Just to show I could do it—you know, macho.

Our research revealed several forms of gang rape. A common pattern was hitchhike-abduction for the purpose of having sex. Though the intent was rape, a number of men did not view it as such because they were convinced that women hitchhiked primarily to signal sexual availability and only secondarily as a form of transportation. In these cases, the unsuspecting victim was driven to a deserted area, raped, and in the majority of cases physically injured. Sometimes, the victim was not hitchhiking; she was abducted at knife or gun point from the street, usually at night. Some of these men did not view this type of attack as rape either, because they believed a woman walking alone at night to be a prostitute. In addition, they were often convinced "she enjoyed it."

"Gang date" rape was another popular variation. In this pattern, one member of the gang would make a date with the victim. Then, without her knowledge or consent, she would be driven to a predetermined location and forcibly raped by each member of the group. One young man revealed this practice was so much a part of his group's recreational routine, they had rented a house for the purpose. From his perspective, the rape was justified because "usually the girl had a bad reputation, or we knew it was what she liked."

During his interview, another offender confessed to participating in twenty or thirty such "gang date" rapes because his driver's license had been revoked, making it difficult for him to "get girls." Sixty percent of the time, he claimed, "they were girls known to do this kind of thing," but "frequently, the girls didn't want to have sex with all of us." In such cases, he said, "It might start out as rape, but, then, they (the women) would quiet down and none ever reported it to the police." He was convicted for a gang rape, which he described as "the ultimate thing I ever did," because unlike his other rapes, the victim, in this case, was a stranger whom the group abducted as she walked home from the library. He felt the group's past experience with "gang date" rape had prepared them for this crime in which the victim was blindfolded and driven to the mountains where, though it was winter, she was forced to remove her clothing. Lying on the snow, she was raped by each of the four men several times before being abandoned near a farm house. This young man continued to believe that if he had spent the night with her, rather than abandoning her, she would not have reported it to the police.

Solitary rapists also used terms like "exciting," "a challenge," "an adventure" to describe their feelings about rape. Like the gang rapists, these men found the element of danger made rape all the more exciting. Typifying this attitude was one man who described his rape as intentional. He reported:

> It was exciting to get away with it (rape), just being able to beat the system, not women. It was like doing something illegal and getting away with it.

Another rapist confided that for him "rape was just more exciting and compelling" than a normal sexual encounter because it involved forcing a stranger. A multiple rapist asserted, "it was the excitement and fear and the drama that made rape a big kick."

FEELING GOOD

When the men were asked to recall their feelings immediately following the rape, only eight percent indicated that guilt or feeling bad was part of their emotional response. The majority said they felt good, relieved, or simply nothing at all. Some indicated they had been afraid of being caught or felt sorry for themselves. Only two men out of 114 expressed any concern or feeling for the victim. Feeling good or nothing at all about raping women is not an aberration limited to men in prison. Smithyman (1978), in his study of "undetected rapists"—rapists outside of prison—found that raping women had no impact on their lives, nor did it have a negative effect on their self-image.

Significantly, a number of men volunteered the information that raping had a positive impact on their feelings. For some, the satisfaction was in revenge. For example, the man who had raped and murdered five women:

> It seems like so much bitterness and tension had built up and this released it. I felt like I had just climbed a mountain and now I could look back.

Another offender characterized rape as habit forming: "Rape is like smoking. You can't stop once you start." Finally one man expressed the sentiments of many rapists when he stated,

> After rape, I always felt like I had just conquered something, like I had just ridden the bull at Gilley's.

Conclusions

This paper has explored rape from the perspective of a group of convicted, incarcerated rapists. The purpose was to discover how these men viewed sexual violence and what they gained from their behavior.

We found that rape was frequently a means of revenge and punishment. Implicit in revenge-rapes was the notion that women were collectively liable for the rapists' problems. In some cases, victims were substitutes for significant women on whom the men desired to take revenge. In other cases, victims were thought to represent all women, and rape was used to punish, humiliate, and "put them in their place." In both cases women were seen as a class, a category, not as individuals. For some men, rape was almost an afterthought, a bonus added to burglary or robbery. Other men gained access to sexually unavailable or unwilling women through rape. For this group of men, rape was a fantasy come true, a particularly exciting form of impersonal sex which enabled them to dominate and control women, by exercising a singularly male form of power. These rapists talked of the pleasures of raping—how for them it was a challenge, an adventure, a dangerous and "ultimate" experience. Rape made them feel good and, in some cases, even elevated their self-image.

The pleasure these men derived from raping reveals the extreme to which they objectified women. Women were seen as sexual commodities to be used or conquered rather than as human beings with rights and feelings. One young man expressed the extreme of the contemptful view of women when he confided to the female researcher.

> Rape is a man's right. If a woman doesn't want to give it, the man should take it. Women have no right to say no. Women are made to have sex. It's all they are good for. Some women would rather take a beating, but they always give in; it's what they are for.

This man murdered his victim because she wouldn't "give in."

Undoubtedly, some rapes, like some of all crimes, are idiopathic. However, it is not necessary to resort to pathological motives to account for all rape or other acts of sexual violence. Indeed, we find that men who rape have something to teach us about the cultural roots of sexual aggression. They force us to acknowledge that rape is more than an idiosyncratic act committed by a few "sick" men. Rather, rape can be viewed as the end point in a continuum of sexually aggressive behaviors that reward men and victimize women. In the way that motives for committing any criminal act can be rationally determined, reasons for rape can also be determined. Our data demonstrate that some men rape because they have learned that in this culture, sexual violence is rewarding. Significantly, the overwhelming majority of these rapists indicated they never thought they would go to prison for what they did. Some did not fear imprisonment because they did not define their behavior as rape. Others knew that women frequently do not report rape and of those cases that are reported, conviction rates are low, and therefore they felt secure. These men perceived rape as a rewarding, low-risk act. Understanding that otherwise normal men can and do rape is critical to the development of strategies for prevention.

We are left with the fact that all men do not rape. In view of the apparent rewards and cultural supports for rape, it is important to ask why some men do not rape. Hirschi (1969) makes a similar observation about delinquency. He argues that the key question is not "Why do they do it?" but rather "Why don't we do it?" (p. 34). Likewise, we may be seeking an answer to the wrong question about sexual assault of women. Instead of asking men who rape "Why?" perhaps we should be asking men who don't "Why not?"

References

Abel, G., J. Becker, and L. Skinner (1980). "Aggressive behavior and sex." *Psychiatric Clinics of North America* 3:133–51.

Bart, P. (1979). "Rape as a paradigm of sexism in society—victimization and its discontents." *Women's Studies International Quarterly* 2: 347–57.

Black, D. (1983). "Crime as social control." *American Sociological Review* 48: 34–45.

Blumberg, R. L. (1979). "A paradigm for predicting the position of women: policy implications and problems." Pp. 113–42 in J. Lipman-Blumen and J. Bernard (eds.), *Sex Roles and Social Policy*. London: Sage Studies in International Sociology.

Broude, G., and S. Green (1976). "Cross-cultural codes on twenty sexual attitudes and practices." *Ethnology* 15: 409–28.

Brownmiller, S. (1975). *Against Our Will*. New York: Simon & Schuster.

Fisher, G., and E. Rivlin (1971). "Psychological needs of rapists." *British Journal of Criminology* 11: 182–85.

Griffin, S. (1971, September 10). "Rape: The all American crime." *Ramparts*, pp. 26–35.

Groth, N. (1979). *Men Who Rape*. New York: Plenum Press.

Hammer, E., and I. Jacks (1955). "A study of Rorschach flexnor and extensor human movements." *Journal of Clinical Psychology* 11: 63–67.

Herman, D. (1984). "The rape culture." Pp. 20–39 in J. Freeman (ed.), *Women: A Feminist Perspective*. Palo Alto, CA: Mayfield.

Hirschi, T. (1969). *Causes of Delinquency*. Berkeley: University of California Press.

Hoebel, E. A. (1954). *The Law of Primitive Man*. Boston: Harvard University Press.

Johnson, A. G. (1980). "On the prevalence of rape in the United States." *Signs* 6: 136–46.

Kanin, E. (1957). "Male aggression in dating-courtship relations." *American Journal of Sociology* 63: 197–204.

———— (1965). "Male sex aggression and three psychiatric hypotheses." *Journal of Sex Research* 1: 227–29.

———— (1967). "Reference groups and sex conduct norm violation." *Sociological Quarterly* 8: 495–504.

———— (1969). "Selected dyadic aspects of male sex aggression." *Journal of Sex Research* 5: 12–28.

Kasinsky, R. (1975, September). Rape: a normal act? *Canadian Forum*, pp. 18–22.

Kirkpatrick, C., and E. Kanin (1957). "Male sex aggression on a university campus." *American Sociological Review* 22: 52–58.

Koss, M. P., and K. E. Leonard (1984). "Sexually aggressive men: empirical findings and theoretical implications." Pp. 213–32 in N. M. Malamuth and E. Donnerstein (eds.), *Pornography and Sexual Aggression*. New York: Academic Press.

LaFree, G. (1980). "The effect of sexual stratification by race on official reactions to rape." *American Sociological Review 45:* 824–54.

———— (1982). "Male power and female victimization: towards a theory of interracial rape." *American Journal of Sociology 88:* 311–28.

Llewellyn, K. N., and E. A. Hoebel (1941). *The Cheyenne Way: Conflict and Case Law in Primitive Jurisprudence*. Norman: University of Oklahoma Press.

Malamuth, N., S. Haber, and S. Feshback (1980). "Testing hypotheses regarding rape: exposure to sexual violence, sex difference, and the 'normality' of rapists." *Journal of Research in Personality 14:* 121–37.

Malamuth, N., M. Heim, and S. Feshback (1980). "Sexual responsiveness of college students to rape depictions: inhibitory and disinhibitory effects." *Social Psychology 38:* 399–408.

Meyer, T. J. (1984, December 5). "'Date rape': a serious problem that few talk about." *Chronicle of Higher Education*.

Morgan, R. (1980). "Theory and practice: pornography and rape." Pp. 134–40 in L. Lederer (ed.), *Take Back the Night: Women on Pornography*. New York: William Morrow.

Rada, R. (1978). *Clinical Aspects of Rape*. New York: Grune & Stratton.

Russell, D. (1975). *The Politics of Rape*. New York: Stein & Day.

Sanday, P. R. (1979). *The Socio-Cultural Context of Rape*. Washington, D.C.: U.S. Dept. of Commerce, National Technical Information Service.

Scully, D., and J. Marolla (1984). "Convicted rapists' vocabulary of motive: excuses and justifications." *Social Problems 31:* 530–44.

———— (1985). "Rape and psychiatric vocabulary of motive: alternative perspectives." Pp. 294–312 in A. W. Burgess (ed.), *Rape and Sexual Assault: A Research Handbook*. New York: Garland Publishing.

Smith, D. (1976). "The social context of pornography." *Journal of Communications 26:* 16–24.

Smithyman, S. (1978). *The Undetected Rapist*. Unpublished dissertation, Claremont Graduate School.

West, D. J. (1983). "Sex offenses and offending." Pp. 1–30 in M. Tonry and N. Morris (eds.), *Crime and Justice: An Annual Review of Research*. Chicago: University of Chicago Press.

Weis, K., and S. Borges (1973). "Victimology and rape: The case of the legitimate victim." *Issues in Criminology 8:* 71–115.

Wheeler, H. (1985). "Pornography and rape: a feminist perspective." Pp. 374–91 in A. W. Burgess (ed.), *Rape and Sexual Assault: A Research Handbook*. New York: Garland Publishing.

6 Doing Fieldwork Among the Yąnomamö

NAPOLEON A. CHAGNON

As stated in the second reading, the primary difference between sociology and anthropology is the choice of research setting. That is, sociologists usually study people living in industrialized societies, while anthropologists focus on preliterate and peasant groups. This distinction does not always hold, however, as some anthropologists do research in urban settings, and occasionally a sociologist wanders into peasant society or even preliterate territory. Consequently, it makes little difference that the fieldwork reported here was done by an anthropologist, for if a sociologist had done participant observation among the Yąnomamö, he or she would have written a similar account of those experiences. (Sociologists, however, are considerably less interested in kinship relations.)

To anticipate Part III, wherein we focus on culture, note how the culture of the Yąnomamö sets the stage for their behaviors. Although from our perspective their behaviors are strange, this is the way of life that the Yąnomamö have learned. What they experience is as natural for them as our way of life is for us. But for someone from our culture to experience Yąnomamö life is to encounter an alien world, as Chagnon discovered firsthand. Chagnon experienced *culture shock*—that is, the fundamentals of life that he had learned no longer applied, and he was most uncomfortable with what he confronted. How would you have felt in his place?

THE YĄNOMAMÖ INDIANS live in southern Venezuela and the adjacent portions of northern Brazil. Some 125 widely scattered villages have populations ranging from 40 to 250 inhabitants, with 75 to 80 people the most usual number. In total numbers their population probably approaches 10,000 people, but this is merely a guess. Many of the villages have not yet been contacted by outsiders, and nobody knows for sure exactly how many uncontacted villages there are, or how many people live in them. By comparison to African or Melanesian tribes, the Yąnomamö population is small. Still, they are one of the largest unacculturated tribes left in all of South America.

But they have a significance apart from tribal size and cultural purity: the Yąnomamö are still actively conducting warfare. It is in the nature of man to fight, according to one of their myths, because the blood of "Moon" spilled on this layer of the cosmos, causing men to become fierce. I describe the Yąnomamö as "the fierce people" because that is the most accurate single phrase that describes them. That is how they conceive themselves to be, and that is how they would like others to think of them.

I spent nineteen months with the Yąnomamö, during which time I acquired some proficiency in their language and, up to a point, submerged myself in their culture and way of life. The thing that impressed me most was the importance of aggression in their culture. I had the opportunity to witness a good many incidents that expressed individual vindictiveness on the one hand and collective bellicosity on the other. These ranged in seriousness from the ordinary incidents of wife beating and chest pounding to dueling and organized raiding by parties that set out with the intention of ambushing and killing men from enemy villages. One of the villages was raided approximately twenty-five times while I conducted the fieldwork, six times by the group I lived among. . . .

This is not to state that primitive man everywhere is unpleasant. By way of contrast, I have also done limited fieldwork among the Yąnomamö's northern neighbors, the Carib-speaking Makiritare Indians. This group was very pleasant and charming, all of them anxious to help me and honor bound to show any visitor the numerous courtesies of their system of etiquette. In short, they approached the image of primitive man that I had conjured up, and it was sheer pleasure to work with them. . . .

My first day in the field illustrated to me what my teachers meant when they spoke of "culture shock." I had traveled in a small, aluminum rowboat propelled by a large outboard motor for two and a half days. This took me from the Territorial capital, a small town on the Orinoco River, deep into Yąnomamö country. On the morning of the third day we reached a small mission settlement, the field "headquarters" of a group of Americans who were working in two Yąnomamö villages. The missionaries had come out of these villages to hold their annual conference on the progress of their mission work, and were conducting their meetings when I arrived. We picked up a passenger at the mission station, James P. Barker, the first non-Yąnomamö to make a sustained, permanent contact with the tribe (in 1950). He had just returned from a year's furlough in the United States, where I had earlier visited him before leaving for Venezuela. He agreed to accompany me to the village I had selected for my base of operations to introduce me to the Indians. This village was also his own home base, but he had not been there for over a year and did not plan to join me for another three months. Mr. Barker had been living with this particular group about five years.

We arrived at the village, Bisaasi–teri, about 2:00 P.M. and docked the boat along the muddy bank at the terminus of the path used by the Indians to fetch their drinking water. It was hot and muggy, and my clothing was soaked with perspiration. It clung uncomfortably to my body, as it did thereafter for the remainder of the work. The small, biting gnats were out in astronomical numbers, for it was the beginning of the dry season. My face and hands were swollen from the venom of their numerous stings. In just a few moments I was to meet my first Yąnomamö, my first primitive man. What would it be like? I had visions of entering the village and seeing 125 social facts running about calling each other kinship terms and sharing food, each waiting and anxious to have me collect his genealogy. I would wear them out in turn. Would they like me? This was important to me; I wanted them to be so fond of me that they would adopt me into their kinship system and way of life, because I had heard that successful anthropologists always get adopted by their people. I had learned during my seven years of anthropological training at the University of Michigan that kinship was equivalent to society in primitive tribes and that it was a moral way of life, "moral" being something "good" and "desirable." I was determined to work my way into their moral system of kinship and become a member of their society.

My heart began to pound as we approached the village and heard the buzz of activity within the circular compound. Mr. Barker commented that he was anxious to see if any changes had taken place while he was away and wondered how many of them had died during his absence. I felt into my back pocket to make sure that my notebook was there and felt personally more secure when I touched it. Otherwise, I would not have known what to do with my hands.

I looked up and gasped when I saw a dozen burly, naked, filthy, hideous men staring at us down the shafts of their drawn arrows! Immense wads of green tobacco were stuck between their lower teeth and lips making them look even more hideous, and strands of dark-green slime dripped or hung from their noses. We arrived at the village while the men were blowing a hallucinogenic drug up their noses. One of the side effects of the drug is a runny nose. The mucus is always saturated with the green powder and the Indians usually let it run freely from their nostrils. My next discovery was that there were a dozen or so vicious, underfed dogs snapping at my legs, circling me as if I were going to be their next meal. I just stood there holding my notebook, helpless and pathetic. Then the stench of the decaying vegetation and filth struck me and I almost got sick. I was horrified. What sort of a welcome was this for the person who came here to live with you and learn your way of life, to become friends with you? They put their weapons down when they recognized Barker and returned to their chanting, keeping a nervous eye on the village entrances.

We had arrived just after a serious fight. Seven women had been abducted the day before by a neighboring group, and the local men and their guests had just that morning recovered five of them in a brutal club fight that nearly ended in a shooting war. The abductors, angry because they lost five of the seven captives, vowed to raid the Bisaasi–teri. When we arrived and entered the village unexpectedly, the Indians feared that we were the raiders. On several occasions during the next two hours the men in the village jumped to their feet, armed themselves, and waited nervously for the noise outside the village to be identified. My enthusiasm for collecting ethnographic curiosities diminished in proportion to the number of times such an alarm was raised. In fact, I was relieved when Mr. Barker suggested that we sleep across the river for the evening. It would be safer over there.

As we walked down the path to the boat, I pondered the wisdom of having decided to spend a year and a half with this tribe before I had even seen what they were like. I am not ashamed to admit, either, that had there been a diplomatic way out, I would have ended my fieldwork then and there. I did not look forward to the next day when I would be left alone with the Indians; I did not speak a word of their language, and they were decidedly different from what I had imagined them to be. The whole situation was depressing, and I wondered why I ever decided to switch from civil engineering to anthropology in the first place. I had not eaten all day, I was soaking wet from perspiration, the gnats were biting me, and I was covered with red pigment, the result of a dozen or so complete examinations I had been given by as many burly Indians. These examinations capped an otherwise grim day. The Indians would blow their noses into their hands, flick as much of the mucus off that would separate in a snap of the wrist, wipe the residue into their hair, and then carefully examine my face, arms, legs, hair, and the contents of my pockets. I asked Mr. Barker how to say "Your hands are dirty"; my comments were met by the Indians in the following way: They would "clean" their hands by spitting a quantity of slimy tobacco juice into them, rub them together, and then proceed with the examination.

Mr. Barker and I crossed the river and slung our hammocks. When he pulled his hammock out of a rubber bag, a heavy, disagreeable odor of mildewed cotton came with it. "Even the missionaries are filthy," I thought to myself. Within two weeks everything I owned smelled the same way, and I lived with the odor for the remainder of the fieldwork. My own habits of personal cleanliness reached such levels that I didn't even mind being examined by the Indians, as I was not much cleaner than they were after I had adjusted to the circumstances.

So much for my discovery that primitive man is not the picture of nobility and sanitation I had conceived him to be. I soon discovered that it was an enormously time-consuming task to maintain my own body in the manner to which it had grown accustomed in the relatively antiseptic environment of the northern United States. Either I could be relatively well fed and relatively comfortable in a fresh change of clothes and do very little fieldwork, or, I could do considerably more fieldwork and be less well fed and less comfortable.

It is appalling how complicated it can be to make oatmeal in the jungle. First, I had to make two trips to the river to haul the water. Next, I had to prime my kerosene stove with alcohol and get it burning, a tricky procedure when you are trying to mix powdered milk and fill a coffee pot at the same time: the alcohol prime always burned out before I could turn the kerosene on, and I would have to start all over. Or, I would turn the kerosene on, hoping that the element was still hot enough to vaporize the fuel, and start a small fire in my palm-thatched hut as the liquid kerosene squirted all over the table and walls and ignited. It was safer to start over with the alcohol. Then I had to boil the oatmeal and pick the bugs out of it. All my supplies, of course, were carefully stored in Indian-proof, ratproof, moisture-proof, and insect-proof containers, not one of which ever served its purpose adequately. Just taking things out of the multiplicity of containers and repacking them afterward was a minor project in itself. By the time I had hauled the water to cook with, unpacked my food, prepared the oatmeal, milk, and coffee, heated water for dishes, washed and dried the dishes, repacked the food in the containers, stored the containers in locked trunks and cleaned up my mess, the ceremony of preparing breakfast had brought me almost up to lunch time.

Eating three meals a day was out of the question. I solved the problem by eating a single meal that could be prepared in a single container, or, at most, in two containers, washed my dishes only when there were no clean ones left, using cold river water, and wore each change of clothing at least a week to cut down on my laundry problem, a courageous undertaking in the tropics. I was also less concerned about sharing my provisions with the rats, insects, Indians, and the elements, thereby eliminating the need for my complicated storage process. I was able to last most of the day on *cafe con leche*, heavily sugared espresso coffee diluted about five to one with hot milk. I would prepare this in the evening and store it in a thermos. Frequently, my single meal was no more complicated than a can of sardines and a package of crackers. But at least two or three times a week I would do something sophisticated, like make oatmeal or boil rice and add a can of tuna fish or tomato paste to it. I even saved time by devising a water system that obviated the trips to the river. I had a few sheets of zinc roofing brought in and made a rain-water trap. I caught the water on the zinc surface, funneled it into an empty gasoline drum, and then ran a plastic hose from the drum to my hut. When the drum was exhausted in the dry season, I hired the Indians to fill it with water from the river.

I ate much less when I traveled with the Indians to visit other villages. Most of the time my travel diet consisted of roasted or boiled green plantains that I obtained from the Indians, but I always carried a few cans of sardines with me in case I got lost or stayed away longer than I had planned. I found peanut butter and crackers a very nourishing food, and a simple one to prepare on trips. It was nutritious and portable, and only one tool was required to prepare the meal, a hunting knife that could be cleaned by wiping the blade on a leaf. More importantly, it was one of the few foods the Indians would let me eat in relative peace. It looked too much like animal feces to them to excite their appetites.

I once referred to the peanut butter as the dung of cattle. They found this quite repugnant. They did not know what "cattle" were, but were generally aware that I ate several canned products of such an animal. I perpetrated this myth, if for no other reason than to have some peace of mind while I ate. Fieldworkers develop strange defense mechanisms, and this was one of my own forms of adaptation. On another occasion I was eating a can of frankfurters and growing very weary of the demands of one of my guests for a share in my meal. When he asked me what I was eating, I replied: "Beef." He then asked, "What part of the animal are you eating?" to which I replied, "Guess!" He stopped asking for a share.

Meals were a problem in another way. Food sharing is important to the Yąnomamö in the context of displaying friendship. "I am hungry," is almost a form of greeting with them. I could not possibly have brought enough food with me to feed the entire village, yet they seemed not to understand this. All they could see was that I did not share my food with them at each and every meal. Nor could I enter into their system of reciprocities with respect to food; every time one of them gave me something "freely," he would dog me for months to pay him back, not with food, but with steel tools. Thus, if I accepted a plantain from someone in a different village while I was on a visit, he would most likely visit me in the future and demand a machete as payment for the time that he "fed" me. I usually reacted to these kinds of demands by giving a banana, the customary reciprocity in their culture—food for food—but this would be a disappointment for the individual who had visions of that single plantain growing into a machete over time.

Despite the fact that most of them knew I would not share my food with them at their request, some of them always showed up at my hut during mealtime. I gradually became accustomed to this and learned to ignore their persistent demands while I ate. Some of them would get angry because I failed to give in, but most of them accepted it as just a peculiarity of the subhuman foreigner. When I did give in, my hut quickly filled with Indians, each demanding a sample of the food that I had given one of them. If I did not give all a share, I was that much more despicable in their eyes.

A few of them went out of their way to make my meals unpleasant, to spite me for not sharing; for example, one man arrived and watched me eat a cracker with honey on it. He immediately recognized the honey, a particularly esteemed Yąnomamö food. He knew that I would not share my tiny bottle and that it would be futile to ask. Instead, he glared at me and queried icily, "Shaki![1] What kind of animal semen are you eating on that cracker?" His question had the desired effect, and my meal ended.

Finally, there was the problem of being lonely and separated from your own kind, especially your family. I tried to overcome this by seeking personal friendships among the Indians. This only complicated the matter because all my friends simply used my confidence to gain privileged access to my cache of steel tools and trade goods, and looted me. I would be bitterly disappointed that my "friend" thought no more of me than to finesse our relationship exclusively with the intention of getting at any locked up possessions, and my depression would hit new lows every time I discovered this. The loss of the possession bothered me much less than the shock that I was, as far as most of them were concerned, nothing more than a source of desirable items; no holds were barred in relieving me of these, since I was considered something subhuman, a non-Yąnomamö .

The thing that bothered me most was the incessant, passioned, and aggressive demands the Indians made. It would become so unbearable that I would have to lock myself in my mud hut every once in a while just to escape from it: Privacy is one of Western culture's greatest achievements. But I did not want privacy for its own sake; rather, I simply had to get away from the begging. Day and night for the entire time I lived with the Yąnomamö I was plagued by such demands as: "Give me a knife, I am poor!"; "If you don't take me with you on your next trip to Widokaiya–teri I'll chop a hole in your canoe!"; "Don't point your camera at me or I'll hit you!"; "Share your food with me!"; "Take me across the river in your canoe and be quick about it!"; "Give me a cooking pot!"; "Loan me your flashlight so I can go hunting tonight!"; "Give me medicine . . . I itch all over!"; "Take us on a week-long hunting trip with your shotgun!"; and "Give me an axe or I'll break into your hut when you are away visiting and steal one!" And so I was bombarded by such demands day after day, months on end, until I could not bear to see an Indian.

It was not as difficult to become calloused to the incessant begging as it was to ignore the sense of urgency, the impassioned tone of voice, or the intimidation and aggression with which the demands were made. It was likewise difficult to adjust to the fact that the Yąnomamö refused to accept "no" for an answer until or unless it seethed with passion and intimidation—which it did after six months. Giving in to a demand always established a new threshold; the next demand would be for a bigger item or favor, and the anger of the Indians even greater if the demand was not met. I soon learned that I had to become very much like the Yąnomamö to be able to get along with them on their terms: sly, aggressive, and intimidating.

Had I failed to adjust in this fashion I would have lost six months of supplies to them in a single day or would have spent most of my time ferrying them around in my canoe or hunting for them. As it was, I did spend a considerable amount of time doing these things and did succumb to their outrageous demands for axes and machetes, at least at first. More importantly, had I failed to demonstrate that I could not be pushed around beyond a certain point, I would have been the subject of far more ridicule, theft, and practical jokes than was the actual case. In short, I had to acquire a certain proficiency in their kind of interpersonal politics and to learn how to imply subtly that certain potentially undesirable consequences might follow if they did such and such to me. They do this to each other in order to establish precisely the point at which they cannot goad an individual any further without precipitating retaliation. As soon as I caught on to this and realized that much of their aggression was stimulated by their desire to discover my flash point, I got along much better with them and regained some lost ground. It was sort of like a political game that everyone played, but one in which each individual sooner or later had to display some sign that his bluffs and implied threats could be backed up. I suspect that the frequency of wife beating is a component of this syndrome, since men can display their ferocity and show others that they are capable of violence. Beating a wife with a club is considered to be an acceptable way of displaying ferocity and one that does not expose the male to much danger. The important thing is that the man has displayed his potential for violence and the implication is that other men better treat him with respect and caution.

After six months, the level of demand was tolerable in the village I used for my headquarters. The Indians and I adjusted to each other and knew what to expect with regard to demands on their part for goods, favors, and services. Had I confined my fieldwork to just that village alone, the field experience would have been far more enjoyable. But, as I was interested in the demographic pattern and social organization of a much larger area, I made regular trips to some dozen different villages in order to collect genealogies or to recheck those I already had. Hence, the intensity of begging and intimidation was fairly constant for the duration of the fieldwork. I had to establish my position in some sort of pecking order of ferocity at each and every village.

For the most part, my own "fierceness" took the form of shouting back at the Yąnomamö as loudly and as passionately as they shouted at me, especially at first, when I did not know much of their language. As I became more proficient in their language and learned more about their political tactics, I became more sophisticated in the art of bluffing. For example, I paid one young man a machete to cut palm trees and make boards from the wood. I used these to fashion a platform in the bottom of my dugout canoe to keep my possessions dry when I traveled by river. That afternoon I was doing informant work in the village; the long-awaited mission supply boat arrived, and most of the Indians ran out of the village to beg goods from the crew. I continued to work in the village for another hour or so and went down to the river to say "hello" to the men on the supply boat. I was angry when I discovered that the Indians had chopped up all my palm boards and used them to paddle their own canoes across the river. I knew that if I overlooked this incident I would have invited them to take even greater liberties with my goods in the future. I crossed the river, docked amidst their dugouts, and shouted for the Indians to come out and see me. A few of the culprits appeared, mischievous grins on their faces. I gave a spirited lecture about how hard I had worked to put those boards in my canoe, how I had paid a machete for the wood, and how angry I was that they destroyed my work in their haste to cross the river. I then pulled out my hunting knife and, while their grins disappeared, cut each of their canoes loose, set them into the current, and let them float away. I left without further ado and without looking back.

They managed to borrow another canoe and, after some effort, recovered their dugouts. The headman of the village later told me with an approving chuckle that I had done the correct thing. Everyone in the village, except, of course, the culprits, supported and defended my action. This raised my status.

Whenever I took such action and defended my rights, I got along much better with the Yąnomamö. A good deal of their behavior toward me was directed with the forethought of establishing the point at which I would react defensively. Many of them later reminisced about the early days of my work when I was "timid" and a little afraid of them, and they could bully me into giving goods away.

Theft was the most persistent situation that required me to take some sort of defensive action. I simply could not keep everything I owned locked in trunks, and the Indians came into my hut and left at will. I developed a very effective means for recovering almost all the stolen items. I would simply ask a child who took the item and then take that person's hammock when he was not around, giving a spirited lecture to the others as I marched away in a faked rage with the thief's hammock. Nobody ever attempted to stop me from doing this, and almost all of them told me that my technique for recovering my possessions was admirable. By nightfall the thief would either appear with the stolen object or send it along with someone else to make an exchange. The others would heckle him for getting caught and being forced to return the item.

With respect to collecting the data I sought, there was a very frustrating problem. Primitive social organization is kinship organization, and to understand the Yąnomamö way of life I had to collect extensive genealogies. I could not have deliberately picked a more difficult group to work with in this regard: They have very stringent name taboos. They attempt to name people in such a way that when the person dies and they can no longer use his name, the loss of the word in the language is not inconvenient. Hence, they name people for specific and minute parts of things, such as "toenail of some rodent," thereby being able to retain the words "toenail" and "(specific) rodent," but not being able to refer directly to the toenail of that rodent. The taboo is maintained even for the living: One mark of prestige is the courtesy others show you by not using your name. The sanctions behind the taboo seem to be an unusual combination of fear and respect.

I tried to use kinship terms to collect genealogies at first, but the kinship terms were so ambiguous that I ultimately had to resort to names. They were quick to grasp that I was bound to learn everybody's name and reacted, without my knowing it, by inventing false names for everybody in the village. After having spent several months collecting names and learning them, this came as a disappointment to me: I could not cross-check the genealogies with other informants from distant villages.

They enjoyed watching me learn these names. I assumed, wrongly, that I would get the truth to each question and that I would get the best information by working in public. This set the stage for converting a serious project into a farce. Each informant tried to outdo his peers by inventing a name even more ridiculous than what I had been given earlier, or by asserting that the individual about whom I inquired was married to his mother or daughter, and the like. I would have the informant whisper the name of the individual in my ear, noting that he was the father of such and such a child. Everybody would then insist that I repeat the name aloud, roaring in hysterics as I clumsily pronounced the name. I assumed that the laughter was in response to the violation of the name taboo or to my pronunciation. This was a reasonable interpretation, since the individual whose name I said aloud invariably became angry. After I learned what some of the names meant, I began to understand what the laughter was all about. A few of the more colorful examples are: "hairy vagina," "long penis," "feces of the harpy eagle," and "dirty rectum." No wonder the victims were angry.

I was forced to do my genealogy work in private because of the horseplay and nonsense. Once I did so, my informants began to agree with each other and I managed to learn a few new names, real names. I could then test any new informant by collecting a genealogy from him that I knew to be accurate. I was able to weed out the more mischievous informants this way. Little by little I extended the genealogies and learned the real names. Still, I was unable to get the names of the dead and extend the genealogies back in time, and even my best informants continued to deceive me about their own close relatives. Most of them gave me the name of a living man as the father of some individual in order to avoid mentioning that the actual father was dead.

The quality of a genealogy depends in part on the number of generations it embraces, and the name taboo prevented me from getting any substantial information about deceased ancestors. Without this information, I could not detect marriage patterns through time. I had to rely on older informants for this information, but these were the most reluctant of all. As I became more proficient in the language and more skilled at detecting lies, my informants became better at lying. One of them in particular was so cunning and persuasive that I was shocked to discover that he had been inventing his information. He specialized in making a ceremony out of telling me false names. He would look around to make sure nobody was listening outside my hut, enjoin me to never mention the name again, act very nervous and spooky, and then grab me by the head to whisper the name very softly into my ear. I was always elated after an informant session with him, because I had several generations of dead ancestors for the living people. The others refused to give me this information. To show my gratitude, I paid him quadruple the rate I had given the others. When word got around that I had increased the pay, volunteers began pouring in to give me genealogies.

I discovered that the old man was lying quite by accident. A club fight broke out in the village one day, the result of a dispute over the possession of a woman. She had been promised to Rerebawa, a particularly aggressive young man who had married into the village. Rerebawa had already been given her older sister and was enraged when the younger girl began having an affair with another man in the village, making no attempt to conceal it from him. He challenged the young man to a club fight, but was so abusive in his challenge that the opponent's father took offense and entered the village circle with his son, wielding a long club. Rerebawa swaggered out to the duel and hurled insults at both of them, trying to goad them into striking him on the head with their clubs. This would have given him the opportunity to strike them on the head. His opponents refused to hit him, and the fight ended. Rerebawa had won a moral victory because his opponents were afraid to hit him. Thereafter, he swaggered around and insulted the two men behind their backs. He was genuinely angry with them, to the point of calling the older man by the name of his dead father. I quickly seized on this as an opportunity to collect an accurate genealogy and pumped him about his adversary's ancestors. Rerebawa had been particularly nasty to me up to this point, but we became staunch allies: We were both outsiders in the local village. I then asked about other dead ancestors and got immediate replies. He was angry with the whole group and not afraid to tell me the names of the dead. When I compared his version of the genealogies to that of the old man, it was obvious that one of them was lying. I challenged his information, and he explained that everybody knew that the old man was deceiving me and bragging about it in the village. The names the old man had given me were the dead ancestors of the members of a village so far away that he thought I would never have occasion to inquire about them. As it turned out, Rerebawa knew most of the people in that village and recognized the names.

I then went over the complete genealogical records with Rerebawa, genealogies I had presumed to be in final form. I had to revise them all because of the numerous lies and falsifications they contained. Thus, after five months of almost constant work on the genealogies of just one group, I had to begin almost from scratch!

Discouraging as it was to start over, it was still the first real turning point in my fieldwork. Thereafter, I began taking advantage of local arguments and animosities in selecting my informants, and used more extensively individuals who had married into the group. I began traveling to other villages to check the genealogies, picking villages that were on strained terms with the people about whom I wanted information. I would then return to my base camp and check with local informants the accuracy of the new information. If the informants became angry when I mentioned the new names I acquired from the unfriendly group, I was almost certain that the information was accurate. For this kind of checking I had to use informants whose genealogies I knew rather well: they had to be distantly enough related to the dead person that they would not go into a rage when I mentioned the name, but not so remotely related that they would be uncertain of the accuracy of the information. Thus, I had to make a list of names that I dared not use in the presence of each and every informant. Despite the precautions, I occasionally hit a name that put the informant into a rage, such as that of a dead brother or sister that other informants had not reported. This always terminated the day's work with that informant, for he would be too touchy to continue any further, and I would be reluctant to take a chance on accidentally discovering another dead kinsman so soon after the first.

These were always unpleasant experiences, and occasionally dangerous ones, depending on the temperament of the informant. On one occasion I was planning to visit a village that had been raided about a week earlier. A woman whose name I had on my list had been killed by the raiders. I planned to check each individual on the list one by one to estimate ages, and I wanted to remove her name so that I would not say it aloud in the village. I knew that I would be in considerable difficulty if I said this name aloud so soon after her death. I called on my original informant and asked him to tell me the name of the woman who had been killed. He refused, explaining that she was a close relative of his. I then asked him if he would become angry if I read off all the names on the list. This way he did not have to say her name and could merely nod when I mentioned the right one. He was a fairly good friend of mine, and I thought I could predict his reaction. He assured me that this would be a good way of doing it. We were alone in my hut so that nobody could overhear us. I read the names softly, continuing to the next when he gave a negative reply. When I finally spoke the name of the dead woman he flew out of his chair, raised his arm to strike me, and shouted: "You son-of-a-bitch!² If you ever say that name again, I'll kill you!" He was shaking with rage, but left my hut quietly. I shudder to think what might have happened if I had said the name unknowingly in the woman's village. I had other, similar experiences in different villages, but luckily the dead person had been dead for some time and was not closely related to the individual into whose ear I whispered the name. I was merely cautioned to desist from saying any more names, lest I get people angry with me.

I had been working on the genealogies for nearly a year when another individual came to my aid. It was Kaobawa, the headman of Upper Bisaasi–teri, the group in which I spent most of my time. He visited me one day after the others had left the hut and volunteered to help me on the genealogies. He was poor, he explained, and needed a machete. He would work only on the condition that I did not ask him about his own parents and other very close kinsmen who were dead. He also added that he would not lie to me as the others had done in the past. This was perhaps the most important single event in my fieldwork, for out of this meeting evolved a very warm friendship and a very profitable informant–fieldworker relationship.

Kaobawa's familiarity with his group's history and his candidness were remarkable. His knowledge of details was almost encyclopedic. More than that, he was enthusiastic and encouraged me to learn details that I might otherwise have ignored. If there were things he did not know intimately, he would advise me to wait until he could check things out with someone in the village. This he would do clandestinely, giving me a report the next day. As I was constrained by my part of the bargain to avoid discussing his close dead kinsmen, I had to rely on Rerebawa for this information. I got Rerebawa's genealogy from Kaobawa.

Once again I went over the genealogies with Kaobawa to recheck them, a considerable task by this time: they included about two thousand names, representing several generations of individuals from four different villages. Rerebawa's information was very accurate, and Kaobawa's contribution enabled me to trace the genealogies further back in time. Thus, after nearly a year of constant work on genealogies, Yąnomamö demography and social organization began to fall into a pattern. Only then could I see how kin groups formed and exchanged women with each other over time, and only then did the fissioning of larger villages into smaller ones show a distinct pattern. At this point I was able to begin formulating more intelligent questions because there was now some sort of pattern to work with. Without the help of Rerebawa and Kaobawa I could not have made very much sense of the plethora of details I had collected from dozens of other informants.

Kaobawa is about 40 years old. I say "about" because the Yąnomamö numeration system has only three numbers: one, two, and more-than-two. He is the headman of Upper Bisaasi–teri. He has had five or six wives so far and temporary affairs with as many more women, one of which resulted in a child. At the present time he has just two wives, Bahimi and Koamashima.

He has had a daughter and a son by Bahimi, his eldest and favorite wife. Koamashima, about 20 years old, recently had her first child, a boy. Kaobawa may give Koamashima to his youngest brother. Even now the brother shares in her sexual services. Kaobawa recently gave his third wife to another of his brothers because she was beshi: "horny." In fact, this girl had been married to two other men, both of whom discarded her because of her infidelity. Kaobawa had one daughter by her; she is being raised by his brother.

Kaobawa's eldest wife, Bahimi, is about thirty-five years old. She is his first cross-cousin. Bahimi was pregnant when I began my fieldwork, but she killed the new baby, a boy, at birth, explaining tearfully that it would have competed with Ariwari, her nursing son, for milk. Rather than expose Ariwari to the dangers and uncertainty of an early weaning, she killed the new child instead. By Yąnomamö standards, she and Kaobawa have a very tranquil household. He only beats her once in a while, and never very hard. She never has affairs with other men.

Kaobawa is quiet, intense, wise, and unobtrusive. He leads more by example than by threats and coercion. He can afford to be this way as he established his reputation for being fierce long ago, and other men respect him. He also has five mature brothers who support him, and he has given a number of his sisters to other men in the village, thereby putting them under some obligation to him. In short, his "natural" following (kinsmen) is large, and he does not have to constantly display his ferocity. People already respect him and take his suggestions seriously.

Rerebawa is much younger, only about twenty-two years old. He has just one wife by whom he has had three children. He is from Karohi–teri, one of the villages to which Kaobawa's is allied. Rerebawa left his village to seek a wife in Kaobawa's group because there were no eligible women there for him to marry.

Rerebawa is perhaps more typical than Kaobawa in the sense that he is concerned about his reputation for ferocity and goes out of his way to act tough. He is, however, much braver than the other men his age and backs up his threats with action. Moreover, he is concerned about politics and knows the details of intervillage relationships over a large area. In this respect he shows all the attributes of a headman, although he is still too young and has too many competent older brothers in his own village to expect to move easily into the position of leadership there.

He does not intend to stay in Kaobawa's group and has not made a garden. He feels that he has adequately discharged his obligations to his wife's parents by providing them with fresh game for three years. They should let him take the wife and return to his own village with her, but they refuse and try to entice him to remain permanently in Bisaasi–teri to provide them with game when they are old. They have even promised to give him their second daughter if he will stay permanently.

Although he has displayed his ferocity in many ways, one incident in particular shows what his character is like. Before he left his own village to seek a wife, he had an affair with the wife of an older brother. When he was discovered, his brother attacked him with a club. Rerebawa was infuriated so he grabbed an axe and drove his brother out of the village after soundly beating him with flat of the blade. The brother was so afraid that he did not return to the village for several days. I recently visited his village with him. He made a point to introduce me to this brother. Rerebawa dragged him out of his hammock by the arm and told me, "This is the brother whose wife I had an affair with," a deadly insult. His brother did nothing and slunk back into his hammock, shamed, but relieved to have Rerebawa release the vise-grip on his arm.

Despite the fact that he admires Kaobawa, he has a low opinion of the others in Bisaasi–teri. He admitted confidentially that he thought Bisaasi–teri was an abdominable group: "This is a terrible neighborhood! All the young men are lazy and cowards and everybody is committing incest! I'll be glad to get back home." He also admired Kaobawa's brother, the headman of Monou–teri. This man was killed by raiders while I was doing my fieldwork. Rerebawa was disgusted that the others did not chase the raiders when they discovered the shooting: "He was the only fierce one in the whole group; he was my close friend. The cowardly Monou–teri hid like women in the jungle and didn't even chase the raiders!"

Even though Rerebawa is fierce and capable of being quite nasty, he has a good side as well. He has a very biting sense of humor and can entertain the group for hours on end with jokes and witty comments. And, he is one of few Yąnomamö that I feel I can trust. When I returned to Bisaasi–teri after having been away for a year, Rerebawa was in his own village visiting his kinsmen. Word reached him that I had returned, and he immediately came to see me. He greeted me with an immense bear hug and exclaimed, "Shaki! Why did you stay away so long? Did you know that my will was so cold while you were gone that at times I could not eat for want of seeing you?" I had to admit that I missed him, too.

Of all the Yąnomamö I know, he is the most genuine and the most devoted to his culture's ways and values. I admire him for that, although I can't say that I subscribe to or endorse these same values. By contrast, Kaobawa is older and wiser. He sees his own culture in a different light and criticizes aspects of it he does not like. While many of his peers accept some of the superstitions and explanatory myths as truth and as the way things ought to be, Kaobawa questions them and privately pokes fun at some of them. Probably, more of the Yąnomamö are like Rerebawa, or at least try to be.

Notes

1. "Shaki," or, rather, "Shakiwa," is the name they gave me because they could not pronounce "Chagnon." They like to name people for some distinctive

feature when possible. *Shaki* is the name of a species of noisome bee; they accumulate in large numbers around ripening bananas and make pests of themselves by eating into the fruit, showering the people below with the debris. They probably adopted this name for me because I was also a nuisance, continuously prying into their business, taking pictures of them, and, in general, being where they did not want me.

2. This is the closest English translation of his actual statement, the literal translation of which would be nonsensical in our language.

PART III

The Cultural Context of Social Life

What is culture? Sometimes the concept is easier to grasp by description than by definition. For example, when we meet someone from a different culture, that person's culture is immediately evident to us. We see it in his or her clothing, jewelry, and body language. We hear it as that person speaks a different language, and when he or she expresses beliefs about life, or opinions of what is valuable or worthwhile. These characteristics, especially when they contrast sharply with our own, alert us to broad differences in the way the person was raised—to that person's culture. Changnon's first glimpse of the Yąnomamö certainly left no doubt that he was face-to-face with a different culture.

Culture consists of *material* things, such as art, weapons, utensils, machines, or (from the above example) clothing and jewelry. Culture is also *nonmaterial*, consisting of the general beliefs and patterns of behavior common to a group of people. Nonmaterial culture is of primary interest to sociologists, for it provides the broad framework that people use to interpret life. Culture is the lens through which we see the world, the basis on which we construct reality and make our decisions.

Understanding how culture affects people's lives is essential to attaining a sociological imagination. But while we may become aware of culture's pervasive influence when we meet someone from a different culture, our perception of our *own* culture is quite another matter. We usually take *our* speech, *our* body language, *our* beliefs, and *our* ways of doing things for granted. We assume that they are normal or natural, and almost without exception we perform them without question. As Ralph Linton has said, "The last thing a fish would ever notice would be water." So it is with us:

79

Except for unusual circumstances, the effects of our own culture generally remain imperceptible to us.

Yet culture's significance for our behavior, our orientations to life, and ultimately our very being is profound. Hardly an aspect of who and what we are is untouched by culture. We came into this life without a language, without values, with no ideas about religion, education, war, money, friendship, love, economic necessity, family relationships, duties and privileges, rights and obligations, and so on. We possessed none of these fundamental orientations that we now take for granted and that are so essential in determining the type of people we are. Yet at this point in our lives we all have them. That, we might say, is culture *within* us.

These learned and shared ways of believing and of doing things (another way to define culture) penetrate our beings at an early age and become part of our basic orientations to life. They become part of our assumptions of what normal is. They are the screen through which we perceive and evaluate what is going on around us. Seldom do we question these assumptions, for as part of our framework for viewing life they themselves remain beyond our ordinary perception.

The rare instances that cause us to become aware of these assumptions, however, can be upsetting. For example, if several Americans arrive at a ticket booth at the same time they will usually line up on the basis of time of arrival. The ticket seller, a member of this culture, also assumes the normalcy of this behavior and sells tickets on a "first come, first served" basis. To us, this seems the natural way of doing things, and we engage in this behavior routinely.

But in northern Africa, where people's ideas of space sharply contrast with ours, when several people want a ticket each pushes his or her way toward the ticket booth. With no conception similar to our "first come, first served" notion, the ticket seller first dispenses tickets to the noisiest, the pushiest, and (not incidentally) those with the longest arms.

When I traveled in northern Africa, I found this part of their culture most upsetting. It violated my basic expectations of the way people *ought* to be—expectations that I did not even know I held until they were so abruptly challenged. At that point I experienced *culture shock*, suddenly unable to depend on the basics of social interaction that I had learned in childhood. However, the fact that I was several inches taller than most Africans, and was able to outreach almost everyone else, helped me to adjust (partially) to this different way of doing things. I never did get used to the idea that pushing ahead of others was "right," though, and always felt guilty about using the accident of my size to receive preferential treatment.

It is to sensitize us to this aspect of life in society—to how cultural factors exert fundamental influences on our lives—that the selections in this third Part are directed. Each reading introduces us to parts of our social lives that ordinarily go unquestioned and unnoticed. Horace Miner helps make visible our basic assumptions about taking care of the body; Edward and Mildred Hall illustrate how culture influences our posture, gestures, facial expressions, and use of space in face-to-face communication; and Erving Goffman helps us to see more clearly how our nonverbal communications are intricate ways by which we attempt to manipulate the opinions that others have of us. These analyses of culture can serve as starting points from which we can begin to analyze other assumptions of reality that we unquestioningly hold, and thus gain a startingly different perceptive of social life—and our own role in it.

7 Body Ritual Among the Nacirema

HORACE MINER

As part of their culture, all peoples develop ideas about proper ways to care for their bodies. The Nacirema, however, have advanced these ideas to a phenomenal degree, and they spend a good deal of their time, energy, and income following the rituals prescribed by their culture. Taking care of the body in the prescribed manner is so important to these people that even a good part of their childrearing revolves around instructing their children in the precise manner of fulfilling their cultural rituals. With intense and prolonged training, accompanied by punishing children who fail to conform while shunning nonconforming adults, it is no wonder that almost all members of the Nacirema culture unquestioningly conform to their prescribed body rituals and dutifully pass them on to their own children.

A better understanding of the Nacirema culture might possibly shed some light on our own way of life.

THE ANTHROPOLOGIST HAS BECOME so familiar with the diversity of ways in which different peoples behave in similar situations that he is not apt to be surprised by even the most exotic customs. In fact, if all of the logically possible combinations of behavior have not been found somewhere in the world, he is apt to suspect that they must be present in some yet undescribed tribe. This point has, in fact, been expressed with respect to clan organization by Murdock. In this light, the magical beliefs and practices of the Nacirema present such unusual aspects that it seems desirable to describe them as an example of the extremes to which human behavior can go.

Professor Linton first brought the ritual of the Nacirema to the attention of anthropologists twenty years ago, but the culture of this people is still very poorly understood. They are a North American group living in the territory between the Canadian Cree, the Yaqui and Tarahumare of Mexico, and the Carib and Arawak of the Antilles. Little is known of their origin, although tradition states that they came from the east.

Nacirema culture is characterized by a highly developed market economy which has evolved in a rich natural habitat. While much of the people's time is devoted to economic pursuits, a large part of the fruits of these labors and a considerable portion of the day are spent in ritual activity. The focus of this activity is the human body, the appearance and health of which loom as a dominant concern in the ethos of the people. While such a concern is certainly not unusual, its ceremonial aspects and associated philosophy are unique.

The fundamental belief underlying the whole system appears to be that the human body is ugly and that its natural tendency is to debility and disease. Incarcerated in such a body, man's only hope is to avert these characteristics through the use of the powerful influences of ritual and ceremony. Every household has one or more shrines devoted to this purpose. The more powerful individuals in the society have several shrines in their houses and, in fact, the opulence of a house is often referred to in terms of the number of such ritual centers it possesses. Most houses are of wattle and daub construction, but the shrine rooms of the more wealthy are walled with stone. Poorer families imitate the rich by applying pottery plaques to their shrine walls.

While each family has at least one such shrine, the rituals associated with it are not family ceremonies but are private and secret. The rites are normally only discussed with children, and then only during the period when they are being initiated into these mysteries. I was able, however, to establish sufficient rapport with the natives to examine these shrines and to have the rituals described to me.

The focal point of the shrine is a box or chest which is built into the wall. In this chest are kept the many charms and magical potions without which no native believes he could live. These preparations are secured from a variety of specialized practitioners. The most powerful of these are the medicine men, whose assistance must be rewarded with substantial gifts. However, the medicine men do not provide the curative potions for their clients, but decide what the ingredients should be and then write them down in an ancient and secret language. This writing is understood only by the medicine men and by the herbalists who, for another gift, provide the required charm.

The charm is not disposed of after it has served its purpose, but is placed in the charm-box of the household shrine. As these magical materials are specific for certain ills, and the real or imagined maladies of the people are many, the charm-box is usually full to overflowing. The magical packets are so numerous that people forget what their purposes were and fear to use them again. While the natives are very vague on this point, we can only assume that the idea in retaining all the old magical materials is that their presence in the charm-box, before which the body rituals are conducted, will in some way protect the worshipper.

Beneath the charm-box is a small font. Each day every member of the family, in succession, enters the shrine room, bows his head before the charm-box, mingles different sorts of holy water in the font, and proceeds with a brief rite of ablution. The holy waters are secured from the Water Temple of the community, where the priests conduct elaborate ceremonies to make the liquid ritually pure.

In the hierarchy of magical practitioners, and below the medicine men in prestige, are specialists whose designation is best translated "holy-mouth-men." The Nacirema have an almost pathological horror of and fascination with the mouth, the condition of which is believed to have a supernatural influence on all social relationships. Were it not for the rituals of the mouth, they believe that their teeth would fall out, their gums bleed, their jaws shrink, their friends desert them, and their lovers reject them. They also believe that a strong relationship exists between oral and moral characteristics. For example, there is a ritual ablution of the mouth for children which is supposed to improve their moral fiber.

The daily body ritual performed by everyone includes a mouth-rite. Despite the fact that these people are so punctilious about care of the mouth, this rite involves a practice which strikes the uninitiated stranger as revolting. It was reported to me that the ritual consists of inserting a small bundle of hog hairs into the mouth, along with certain magical powders, and then moving the bundle in a highly formalized series of gestures.

In addition to the private mouth-rite, the people seek out a holy-mouth-man once or twice a year. These practitioners have an impressive set of paraphernalia, consisting of a variety of augers, awls, probes, and prods. The use of these objects in the exorcism of the evils of the mouth involves almost unbelievable ritual torture of the client. The holy-mouth-man opens the client's mouth and, using the above mentioned tools, enlarges any holes which decay may have created in the teeth. Magical materials are put into these holes. If there are no naturally occurring holes in the teeth, large sections of one or more teeth are gouged out so that the supernatural substance can be applied. In the client's view, the purpose of these ministrations is to arrest decay and draw friends. The extremely sacred and traditional character of the rite is evident in the fact that the natives return to the holy-mouth-men year after year, despite the fact that their teeth continue to decay.

It is to be hoped that, when a thorough study of the Nacirema is made, there will be careful inquiry into the personality structure of these people. One has but to watch the gleam in the eye of a holy-mouth-man, as he jabs an awl into an exposed nerve, to suspect that a certain amount of sadism is involved. If this can be established, a very interesting pattern emerges, for most of the population shows definite masochistic tendencies. It was to these that Professor Linton referred in discussing a distinctive part of the daily body ritual which is performed only by men. This part of the rite involves scraping and lacerating the surface of the face with a sharp instrument. Special women's rites are performed only four times during each lunar month, but what they lack in frequency is made up in barbarity. As part of this ceremony, women bake their heads in small ovens for about an hour. The theoretically interesting point is that what seems to be a preponderantly masochistic people have developed sadistic specialists.

The medicine men have an imposing temple, or *latipso*, in every community of any size. The more elaborate ceremonies required to treat very sick patients can only be performed at this temple. These ceremonies involve not only the thaumaturge but a permanent group of vestal maidens who move sedately about the temple chambers in distinctive costume and head-dress.

The *latipso* ceremonies are so harsh that it is phenomenal that a fair proportion of the really sick natives who enter the temple ever recover. Small children whose indoctrination is still incomplete have been known to resist attempts to take them to the temple because "that is where you go to die." Despite this fact, sick adults are not only willing but eager to undergo the protracted ritual purification, if they can afford to do so. No matter how ill the supplicant or how grave the emergency, the guardians of many temples will not admit a client if he cannot give a rich gift to the custodian. Even after one has gained admission and survived the ceremonies, the guardians will not permit the neophyte to leave until he makes still another gift.

The supplicant entering the temple is first stripped of all his or her clothes. In everyday life the Nacirema avoids exposure of his body and its natural functions. Bathing and excretory acts are performed only in the secrecy of the household shrine, where they are ritualized as part of the body-rites. Psychological shock results from the fact that body secrecy is suddenly lost upon entry into the *latipso*. A man whose own wife has never seen him in an excretory act, suddenly finds himself naked and assisted by a vestal maiden while he performs his natural functions into a sacred vessel. This sort of ceremonial treatment is necessitated by the fact that the excreta are used by a diviner to ascertain the course and nature of the client's sickness. Female clients, on the other hand, find their naked bodies are subjected to the scrutiny, manipulation and prodding of the medicine men.

Few supplicants in the temple are well enough to do anything but lie on their hard beds. The daily ceremonies, like the rites of the holy-mouth-men, involve discomfort and torture. With ritual precision, the vestals awaken their miserable charges each dawn and roll them about on their beds of pain while performing ablutions, in the formal movements of which the maidens are highly trained. At other times they insert magic wands in the supplicant's mouth or force him to eat substances which are supposed to be healing. From time to time the medicine men come to their clients and jab magically treated needles into their flesh. The fact that these temple ceremonies may not cure, and may even kill the neophyte, in no way decreases the people's faith in the medicine men.

There remains one other kind of practitioner, known as a "listener." This witchdoctor has the power to exorcise the devils that lodge in the heads of people who have been bewitched. The Nacirema believe that parents bewitch their own children. Mothers are particularly suspected of putting a curse on children while teaching them the secret body rituals. The counter-magic of the witchdoctor is unusual in its lack of ritual. The patient simply tells the "listener" all his troubles and fears, beginning with the earliest difficulties he can remember. The memory displayed by the Nacirema in these exorcism sessions is truly remarkable. It is not uncommon for the patient to bemoan the rejection he felt upon being weaned as a babe, and a few individuals even see their troubles going back to the traumatic effects of their own birth.

In conclusion, mention must be made of certain practices which have their base in native esthetics but which depend upon the pervasive aversion to the natural body and its functions. There are ritual fasts to make fat people thin and ceremonial feasts to make thin people fat. Still other rites are used to make women's breasts larger if they are small, and smaller if they are large. General dissatisfaction with breast shape is symbolized in the fact that the ideal form is virtually outside the range of human variation. A few women afflicted with almost inhuman hyper-mammary development are so idolized that they make a handsome living by simply going from village to village and permitting the natives to stare at them for a fee.

Reference has already been made to the fact that excretory functions are ritualized, routinized, and relegated to secrecy. Natural reproductive functions are similarly distorted. Intercourse is taboo as a topic and scheduled as an act. Efforts are made to avoid pregnancy by the use of magical materials or by limiting intercourse to certain phases of the moon. Conception is actually very infrequent. When pregnant, women dress so as to hide their condition. Parturition takes place in secret, without friends or relatives to assist, and the majority of women do not nurse their infants.

Our review of the ritual life of the Nacirema has certainly shown them to be a magic-ridden people. It is hard to understand how they have managed to exist so long under the burdens which they have imposed upon themselves. But even such exotic customs as these take on real meaning when they are viewed with the insight provided by Malinowski when he wrote:

"Looking from far and above, from our high places of safety in the developed civilization, it is easy to see all the crudity and irrelevance of magic. But without its power and guidance early man could not have mastered his practical difficulties as he has done, nor could man have advanced to the higher stages of civilization."

8 The Sounds of Silence

EDWARD T. HALL
MILDRED R. HALL

When we refer to communication, we generally think about words. People who are talking, however, use much more than words to communicate with one another. *How* they say things is just as important—sometimes more so—than *what* they say. Their inflections, tones, pauses, cadence, and loudness also convey meanings. If people are speaking face-to-face, their gestures, expressions, mannerisms, and use of space also contain significant messages.

Nonverbal communication is especially significant in conveying feelings and attitudes. Through ways so subtle that they lie beyond even our own perception—and ways so obvious that no one can miss the message—we communicate feelings of comfort and discomfort, trust and distrust, pleasure or tension, suspicions, uncertainties, desires, and a host of other feelings and concerns.

Yet we seldom think about our nonverbal communications. Our body language, for example, usually seems to be "just doing what is natural." Researchers, however, have found little that is "natural" about it. Like our speech, our body language and other forms of nonverbal communication are acquired. Thus, the specific ways by which people communicate these messages vary from one group to another as the Halls make evident in this selection.

BOB LEAVES HIS APARTMENT at 8:15 A.M. and stops at the corner drugstore for breakfast. Before he can speak, the counterman says, "The usual?" Bob nods yes. While he savors his Danish, a fat man pushes onto the adjoining stool and overflows into his space. Bob scowls, and the man pulls himself in as much as he can. Bob has sent two messages without speaking a syllable.

Henry has an appointment to meet Arthur at 11:00 A.M.; he arrives at 11:30. Their conversation is friendly, but Arthur retains a lingering hostility. Henry has unconsciously communicated that he doesn't think the appointment is very important or that Arthur is a person who needs to be treated with respect.

George is talking to Charley's wife at a party. Their conversation is entirely trivial, yet Charley glares at them suspiciously. Their physical proximity and the movements of their eyes reveal that they are powerfully attracted to each other.

José Ybarra and Sir Edmund Jones are at the same party, and it is important for them to establish a cordial relationship for business reasons. Each is trying to be warm and friendly, yet they will part with mutual distrust, and their business transaction will probably fall through. José, in Latin fashion, moves closer and closer to Sir Edmund as they speak, and this movement is being miscommunicated as pushiness to Sir Edmund, who keeps backing away from this intimacy, which in turn is being miscommunicated to José as coldness. The silent languages of Latin and English cultures are more difficult to learn than their spoken languages.

In each of these cases, we see the subtle power of nonverbal communication. The only language used throughout most of the history of humanity (in evolutionary terms, vocal communication is relatively recent), it is the first form of communication you learn. You use this preverbal language, consciously and unconsciously, every day to tell other people how you feel about yourself and them. This language includes your posture, gestures, facial expressions, costume, the way you walk, even your treatment of time and space and material things. All people communicate on several different levels at the same time but are usually aware of only the verbal dialogue and don't realize that they respond to nonverbal messages. But when a person says one thing and really believes something else, the discrepancy between the two can usually be sensed. Nonverbal communication systems are much less subject to the conscious deception that often occurs in verbal systems. When we find ourselves thinking, "I don't know what it is about him, but he doesn't seem sincere" it's usually this lack of congruity between a person's words and his behavior that makes us anxious and uncomfortable.

Few of us realize how much we all depend on body movement in our conversation or are aware of the hidden rules that govern listening behavior. But we know instantly whether or not the person we're talking to is "tuned in," and we're very sensitive to any breach in listening etiquette. In white middle-class American culture, when someone wants to show he is listening to someone else, he looks either at the other person's face or, specifically, at his eyes, shifting his gaze from one eye to the other.

If you observe a person conversing, you'll notice that he indicates he's listening by nodding his head. He also makes little "Hmm" noises. If he agrees with what's being said, he may give a vigorous nod. To show pleasure or affirmation, he smiles; if he has some reservations, he looks skeptical by raising an eyebrow or pulling down the corners of his mouth. If a participant wants to terminate the conversation, he may start shifting his body position, stretching his legs, crossing or uncrossing them, bobbing his foot, or diverting his gaze from the speaker. The more he fidgets, the more the speaker becomes aware that he has lost his audience. As a last measure, the listener may look at his watch to indicate the imminent end of the conversation.

Talking and listening are so intricately intertwined that a person cannot do one without the other. Even when one is alone and talking to onself, there is part of the brain that speaks while another part listens. In all conversations, the listener is positively or negatively reinforcing the speaker all the time. He may even guide the conversation without knowing it, by laughing or frowning or dismissing the argument with a wave of his hand.

The language of the eyes—another age-old way of exchanging feelings— is both subtle and complex. Not only do men and women use their eyes differently, but there are class, generation, regional, ethnic, and national cultural differences. Americans often complain about the way foreigners stare at people or hold a glance too long. Most Americans look away from someone who is using his eyes in an unfamiliar way because it makes them self-conscious. If a man looks at another man's wife in a certain way, he's asking for trouble, as indicated earlier. But he might not be ill-mannered or seeking to challenge the husband. He might be a European in this country who hasn't learned our visual mores. Many American women visiting France or Italy are acutely embarrassed because, for the first time in their lives, men really look at them—their eyes, hair, nose, lips, breasts, hips, legs, thighs, knees, ankles, feet, clothes, hairdo, even their walk. These same women, once they have become used to being looked at often return to the United States and are overcome with the feeling that "No one ever really looks at me anymore."

Analyzing the mass of data on the eyes, it is possible to sort out at least three ways in which the eyes are used to communicate: dominance vs. submission, involvement vs. detachment, and positive vs. negative attitude. In addition, there are three levels of consciousness and control, which can be categorized as follows: (1) conscious use of the eyes to communicate, such as the flirting blink and the intimate nosewrinkling squint; (2) the very extensive category of unconscious but learned behavior governing where the eyes are directed and when (this unwritten set of rules dictates how and under what circumstances the sexes, as well as people of all status categories, look at each other); and (3) the response of the eye itself, which is completely outside both awareness and control—changes in the cast (sparkle) of the eye and the pupillary reflex.

The eye is unlike any other organ of the body, for it is an extension of the brain. The unconscious pupillary reflex and the cast of the eye have been known by people of Middle Eastern origin for years—although most are unaware of their knowledge. Depending on the context, Arabs and others look directly at the eyes or deeply *into* the eyes of their interlocutor. We became aware of this in the Middle East several years ago while looking at jewelry. The merchant suddenly started to push a particular bracelet at a customer and said, "You buy this one." What interested us was that the bracelet was not the one that had been consciously selected by the purchaser.

But the merchant, watching the pupils of the eyes, knew what the purchaser really wanted to buy. Whether he specifically knew *how* he knew is debatable.

A psychologist at the University of Chicago, Eckhard Hess, was the first to conduct systematic studies of the pupillary reflex. His wife remarked one evening, while watching him reading in bed, that he must be very interested in the text because his pupils were dilated. Following up on this, Hess slipped some pictures of nudes into a stack of photographs that he gave to his male assistant. Not looking at the photographs but watching his assistant's pupils, Hess was able to tell precisely when the assistant came to the nudes. In further experiments, Hess retouched the eyes in a photograph of a woman. In one print, he made the pupils small, in another, large; nothing else was changed. Subjects who were given the photographs found the woman with the dilated pupils much more attractive. Any man who has had the experience of seeing a woman look at him as her pupils widen with reflex speed knows that she's flashing him a message.

The eye-sparkle phenomenon frequently turns up in our interviews of couples in love. It's apparently one of the first reliable clues in the other person that love is genuine. To date, there is no scientific data to explain eye sparkle; no investigation of the pupil, the cornea, or even the white sclera of the eye shows how the sparkle originates. Yet we all know it when we see it.

One common situation for most people invovles the use of the eyes in the street and in public. Although eye behavior follows a definite set of rules, the rules vary according to the place, the needs and feelings of the people, and their ethnic background. For urban whites, once they're within definite recognition distance (sixteen to thirty-two feet for people with average eyesight), there is mutual avoidance of eye contact—unless they want something specific: a pickup, a handout, or information of some kind. In the West and in small towns generally, however, people are much more likely to look and greet one another, even if they're strangers.

It's permissible to look at people if they're beyond recognition distance, but once inside this sacred zone, you can only steal a glance at strangers. You *must* greet friends, however; to fail to do so is insulting. Yet, to stare too fixedly even at them is considered rude and hostile. Of course, all of these rules are variable.

A great many blacks, for example, greet each other in public even if they don't know each other. To blacks, most eye behavior of whites has the effect of giving the impression that they aren't there, but this is due to white avoidance of eye contact with *anyone* in the street.

Another very basic difference between people of different ethnic backgrounds is their sense of territoriality and how they handle space. This is the silent communication, or miscommunication, that caused friction between Mr. Ybarra and Sir Edmund Jones in our earlier example. We know from the research that everyone has around himself an invisible bubble of space that contracts and expands depending on several factors: his emotional state, the activity he's performing at the time, and his cultural background. This bubble is a kind of mobile territory that he will defend against intrusion. If he is accustomed to close personal distance between himself and others, his bubble will be smaller than that of someone who's accustomed to greater personal distance. People of northern European heritage—English, Scandinavian, Swiss, and German—tend to avoid contact. Those whose heritage is Italian, French, Spanish, Russian, Latin American, or Middle Eastern like close personal contact.

People are very sensitive to any intrusion into their spatial bubble. If someone stands too close to you, your first instinct is to back up. If that's not possible, you lean away and pull yourself in, tensing your muscles. If the intruder doesn't respond to these body signals, you may then try to protect yourself, using a briefcase, umbrella, or raincoat. Women—especially when traveling alone—often plant their pocketbooks in such a way that no one can get very close to them. As a last resort, you may move to another spot and position yourself behind a desk or a chair that provides screening. Everyone tries to adjust the space around himself in a way that's comfortable for him; most often, he does this unconsciously.

Emotions also have a direct effect on the size of a person's territory. When you're angry or under stress, your bubble expands and you require more space. New York psychiatrist Augustus Kinzel found a difference in what he calls body-buffer zones between violent and nonviolent prison inmates. Dr. Kinzel conducted experiments in which each prisoner was placed in the center of a small room, and then Dr. Kinzel slowly walked toward him. Nonviolent prisoners allowed him to come quite close, while prisoners with a history of violent behavior couldn't tolerate his proximity and reacted with some vehemence.

Apparently, people under stress experience other people as looming larger and closer than they actually are. Studies of schizophrenic patients have indicated that they sometimes have a distorted perception of space, and several psychiatrists have reported patients who experience their body boundaries as filling up an entire room. For these patients, anyone who comes into the room is actually inside their body, and such an intrusion may trigger a violent outburst.

Unfortunately, there is little detailed information about normal people who live in highly congested urban areas. We do know, of course, that the noise, pollution, dirt, crowding, and confusion of our cities induce feelings of stress in most of us, and stress leads to a need for greater space. The man who's packed into a subway, jostled in the street, crowded into an elevator, and forced to work all day in a bull pen or in a small office without auditory or visual privacy is going to be very stressed at the end of his day. He needs places that provide relief from constant overstimulation of his nervous system. Stress from overcrowding is cumulative, and people can tolerate more crowding early in the day than later; note the increased bad temper during the evening rush hour as compared with the morning melee. Certainly one factor in people's desire to commute by car is the need for privacy and relief from crowding (except, often, from other cars); it may be the only time of the day when nobody can intrude.

In crowded public places, we tense our muscles and hold ourselves stiff, and thereby communicate to others our desire not to intrude on their space and, above all, not to touch them. We also avoid eye contact, and the total effect is that of someone who has "tuned out." Walking along the street, our bubble expands slightly as we move in a stream of strangers, taking care not to bump into them. In the office, at meetings, in restaurants, our bubble keeps changing as it adjusts to the activity at hand.

Most white middle-class Americans use four main distances in their business and social relations: intimate, personal, social, and public. Each of these distances has a near and a far phase and is accompanied by changes in the volume of the voice. Intimate distance varies from direct physical contact with another person to a distance of six to eighteen inches and is used for our most private activities—caressing another person or making love. At this distance, you are overwhelmed by sensory inputs from the skin, the fragrance of perfume, even the sound of breathing—all of which literally envelop you. Even at the far phase, you're still within easy touching distance. In general, the use of intimate distance in public between adults is frowned on. It's also much too close for strangers, except under conditions of extreme crowding.

In the second zone—personal distance—the close phase is one and a half to two and a half feet; it's at this distance that wives usually stand from their husbands in public. If another woman moves into this zone, the wife will most likely be disturbed. The far phase—two and a half to four feet— is the distance used to "keep someone at arm's length" and is the most common spacing used by people in conversation.

The third zone—social distance—is employed during business trans- actions or exchanges with a clerk or repairman. People who work together tend to use close social distance—four to seven feet. This is also the distance for conversation at social gatherings. To stand at this distance from someone who is seated has a dominating effect (e.g., teacher to pupil, boss to sec- retary). The far phase of the third zone—seven to twelve feet—is where people stand when someone says, "Stand back so I can look at you." This distance lends a formal tone to business or social discourse. In an executive office, the desk serves to keep people at this distance.

The fourth zone—public distance—is used by teachers in classrooms or speakers at public gatherings. At its farthest phase—twenty-five feet and beyond—it is used for important public figures. Violations of this distance can lead to serious complications. During his 1970 U.S. visit, the president of France, Georges Pompidou, was harassed by pickets in Chicago, who were permitted to get within touching distance. Since pickets in France are kept behind barricades a block or more away, the president was outraged by this insult to his person, and President Nixon was obliged to communicate his concern as well as offer his personal apologies.

It is interesting to note how American pitchmen and panhandlers exploit the unwritten, unspoken conventions of eye and distance. Both take advantage of the fact that once explicit eye contact is established, it is rude to look away, because to do so means to brusquely dismiss the other person and his needs. Once having caught the eye of his mark, the panhandler then locks on, not letting go until he moves through the public zone, the social zone, the personal zone and, finally, into the intimate sphere, where people are most vulnerable.

Touch also is an important part of the constant stream of communication that takes place between people. A light touch, a firm touch, a blow, a caress are all communications. In an effort to break down barriers among people, there's been a recent upsurge in group-encounter activities, in which strangers are encouraged to touch one another. In special situations such as these, the rules for not touching are broken with group approval, and people gradually lose some of their inhibitions.

Although most people don't realize it, space is perceived and distances are set not by vision alone but with all the senses. Auditory space is perceived with the ears, thermal space with the skin, kinesthetic space with the muscles of the body, and olfactory space with the nose. And, once again, it's one's culture that determines how his senses are programmed—which sensory information ranks highest and lowest. The important thing to remember is that culture is very persistent. In this country, we've noted the existence of culture patterns that determine distance between people in the third and fourth generations of some families, despite their prolonged contact with people of very different cultural heritages.

Whenever there is great cultural distance between two people, there are bound to be problems arising from differences in behavior and expectations. An example is the American couple who consulted a psychiatrist about their marital problems. The husband was from New England and had been brought up by reserved parents who taught him to control his emotions and to respect the need for privacy. His wife was from an Italian family and had been brought up in close contact with all the members of her large family, who were extremely warm, volatile, and demonstrative.

When the husband came home after a hard day at the office, dragging his feet and longing for peace and quiet, his wife would rush to him and smother him. Clasping his hands, rubbing his brow, crooning over his weary head, she never left him alone. But when the wife was upset or anxious about her day, the husband's response was to withdraw completely and leave her alone. No comforting, no affectionate embrace, no attention—just solitude. The woman became convinced her husband didn't love her, and in desperation she consulted a psychiatrist. Their problem wasn't basically psychological but cultural.

Why has man developed all these different ways of communicating messages without words? One reason is that people don't like to spell out certain kinds of messages. We prefer to find other ways of showing our feelings. This is especially true in relationships as sensitive as courtship. Men don't like to be rejected, and most women don't want to turn a man down bluntly. Instead, we work out subtle ways of encouraging or discouraging each other that save face and avoid confrontations.

How a person handles space in dating others is an obvious and very sensitive indicator of how he or she feels about the other person. On a first date, if a woman sits or stands so close to a man that he is acutely conscious of her physical presence—inside the intimate-distance zone—the man usually construes it to mean that she is encouraging him. However, before the man starts moving in on the woman, he should be sure what message she's really sending; otherwise, he risks bruising his ego. What is close to someone of northern European background may be neutral or distant to someone of Italian heritage. Also, women sometimes use space as a way of misleading a man, and there are few things that put men off more than women who communicate contradictory messages, such as women who cuddle up and then act insulted when a man takes the next step.

How does a woman communicate interest in a man? In addition to such familiar gambits as smiling at him, she may glance shyly at him, blush, and then look away. Or she may give him a real come-on look and move in very close when he approaches. She may touch his arm and ask for a light. As she leans forward to light her cigarette, she may brush him lightly, enveloping him in her perfume. She'll probably continue to smile at him, and she may use what ethologists call preening gestures—touching the back of her hair, thrusting her breasts forward, tilting her hips as she stands, or crossing her legs if she's seated, perhaps even exposing one thigh or putting a hand on her thigh and stroking it. She may also stroke her wrists as she converses or show the palm of her hand as a way of gaining his attention. Her skin may be unusually flushed or quite pale, her eyes brighter, the pupils larger.

If a man sees a woman whom he wants to attract, he tries to present himself by his posture and stance as someone who is self-assured. He moves briskly and confidently. When he catches the eye of the woman, he may hold her glance a little longer than normal. If he gets an encouraging smile, he'll move in close and engage her in small talk. As they converse, his glance shifts over her face and body. He, too, may make preening gestures—straightening his tie, smoothing his hair, or shooting his cuffs.

How do people learn body language? The same way they learn spoken language—by observing and imitating people around them as they're growing up. Little girls imitate their mothers or an older female. Little boys imitate their fathers or a respected uncle or a character on television. In this way, they learn the gender signals appropriate for their sex. Regional, class, and ethnic patterns of body behavior are also learned in childhood and persist throughout life. . . .

Nonverbal communications signal to members of your own group what kind of person you are, how you feel about others, how you'll fit into and work in a group, whether you're assured or anxious, the degree to which you feel comfortable with the standards of your own culture, as well as deeply significant feelings about the self, including the state of your own psyche. For most of us, it's difficult to accept the reality of another's behavioral system. And, of course, none of us will ever become fully knowledgeable of the importance of every nonverbal signal. But as long as each of us realizes the power of these signals, this society's diversity can be a source of great strength rather than a further—and subtly powerful—source of division.

9 The Presentation of Self in Everyday Life

ERVING GOFFMAN

All the world's a stage
And all the men and women merely players.
They have their exits and their entrances;
And one man in his time plays many parts. . . .
>William Shakespeare
>*As You Like It*, Act 2, Scene 7

This quotation from Shakespeare could well serve as the keynote for the following selection. Taking Shakespeare's statement seriously, Goffman presents a dramaturgical model of human life and uses it as the conceptual framework for understanding life-in-society. In this view, people in everyday life are actors on stage, the audience consists of those persons who observe what others are doing, the parts are the roles that people play (whether occupational, familial, friendship roles, or whatever), the dialogue consists of ritualized conversational exchanges ("Hi. How ya doin'?"; "Hey, bro', wha's hapnin'?"; "How's it goin'?"; the hellos, the goodbyes, and the in-betweens), while the costuming consists of whatever clothing happens to be in style.

Goffman's insightful analysis provides a framework from which we can gain a remarkably different perspective of what we do in life—at home, at school, with friends, while on a date, or while shopping. When understood properly, however, you may find this approach to understanding human behavior disturbing. For example, if we are all actors playing roles on the stage of life, where is the "real me"? Is all of life merely a "put-on," a masquerade of some sort? Does not this framework for understanding human interaction constitute an essentially cynical and manipulative approach to life, a sort of everday Machiavellianism?

WHEN AN INDIVIDUAL ENTERS the presence of others, they commonly seek to acquire information about him or to bring into play information about him already possessed. They will be interested in his general socio-economic status, his conception of self, his attitude toward them, his competence, his trustworthiness, etc. Although some of this information seems to be sought almost as an end in itself, there are usually quite practical reasons for acquiring it. Information about the individual helps to define the situation, enabling others to know in advance what he will expect of them and what they may expect of him. Informed in these ways, the others will know how best to act in order to call forth a desired response from him.

For those present, many sources of information become accessible and many carriers (or "sign-vehicles") become available for conveying this information. If unacquainted with the individual, observers can glean clues from his conduct and appearance which allow them to apply their previous experience with individuals roughly similar to the one before them or, more important, to apply untested stereotypes to him. They can also assume from past experience that only individuals of a particular kind are likely to be found in a given social setting. They can rely on what the individual says about himself or on documentary evidence he provides as to who and what he is. If they know, or know of, the individual by virtue of experience prior to the interaction, they can rely on assumptions as to the persistence and generality of psychological traits as a means of predicting his present and future behavior.

However, during the period in which the individual is in the immediate presence of the others, few events may occur which directly provide the others with the conclusive information they will need if they are to direct wisely their own activity. Many crucial facts lie beyond the time and place of interaction or lie concealed within it. For example, the "true" or "real" attitudes, beliefs, and emotions of the individual can be ascertained only indirectly, through his avowals or through what appears to be involuntary expressive behavior. Similarly, if the individual offers the others a product or service, they will often find that during the interaction there will be no time and place immediately available for eating the pudding that the proof can be found in. They will be forced to accept some events as conventional or natural signs of something not directly available to the senses. In Ichheiser's terms,[1] the individual will have to act so that he intentionally or unintentionally *expresses* himself, and the others will in turn have to be *impressed* in some way by him.

The expressiveness of the individual (and therefore his capacity to give impressions) appears to involve two radically different kinds of sign activity: the expression that he *gives*, and the expression that he *gives off*. The first involves verbal symbols or their substitutes which he uses admittedly and solely to convey the information that he and the others are known to attach to these symbols. This is communication in the traditional and narrow sense. The second involves a wide range of action that others can treat as symptomatic of the actor, the expectation being that the action was performed for reasons other than the information conveyed in this way. As we shall have to see, this distinction has an only initial validity. The individual does of course intentionally convey misinformation by means of both of these types of communication, the first involving deceit, the second feigning.

Taking communication in both its narrow and broad sense, one finds that when the individual is in the immediate presence of others, his activity will have a promissory character. The others are likely to find that they must accept the individual on faith, offering him a just return while he is present before them in exchange for something whose true value will not be established until after he has left their presence. (Of course, the others also live by inference in their dealings with the physical world, but it is only in the world of social interaction that the objects about which they make inferences will purposely facilitate and hinder this inferential process.) The security that they justifiably feel in making inferences about the individual will vary, of course, depending on such factors as the amount of information they already possess about him, but no amount of such past evidence can entirely obviate the necessity of acting on the basis of inferences. As William I. Thomas suggested:

> It is also highly important for us to realize that we do not as a matter of fact lead our lives, make our decisions, and reach our goals in everyday life either statistically or scientifically. We live by inference. I am, let us say, your guest. You do not know, you cannot determine scientifically, that I will not steal your money or your spoons. But inferentially I will not, and inferentially you have me as a guest.[2]

Let us now turn from the others to the point of view of the individual who presents himself before them. He may wish them to think highly of him, or to think that he thinks highly of them, or to perceive how in fact he feels toward them, or to obtain no clearcut impression; he may wish to ensure sufficient harmony so that the interaction can be sustained, or to defraud, get rid of, confuse, mislead, antagonize, or insult them. Regardless of the particular objective which the individual has in mind and of his motive for having this objective, it will be in his interests to control the conduct of the others, especially their responsive treatment of him.[3] This control is achieved largely by influencing the definition of the situation which the others come to formulate, and he can influence this definition by expressing himself in such a way as to give them the kind of impression that will lead them to act voluntarily in accordance with his own plan. Thus, when an individual appears in the presence of others, there will usually be some reason for him to mobilize his activity so that it will convey an impression to others which it is in his interests to convey. Since a girl's dormitory mates will glean evidence of her popularity from the calls she receives on the phone, we can suspect that some girls will arrange for calls to be made, and Willard Waller's finding can be anticipated.

It has been reported by many observers that a girl who is called to the telephone in the dormitories will often allow herself to be called several times, in order to give all the other girls ample opportunity to hear her paged.[4]

Of the two kinds of communication—expressions given and expressions given off—this report will be primarily concerned with the latter, with the more theatrical and contextual kind, the non-verbal, presumably unintentional kind, whether this communication be purposely engineered or not. As an example of what we must try to examine, I would like to cite at length a novelistic incident in which Preedy, a vacationing Englishman, makes his first appearance on the beach of his summer hotel in Spain:

> But in any case he took care to avoid catching anyone's eye. First of all, he had to make it clear to those potential companions of his holiday that they were of no concern to him whatsoever. He stared through them, round them, over them—eyes lost in space. The beach might have been empty. If by chance a ball was thrown his way, he looked surprised; then let a smile of amusement lighten his face (Kindly Preedy), looked round dazed to see that there *were* people on the beach, tossed it back with a smile to himself and not a smile *at* the people, and then resumed carelessly his nonchalant survey of space.
>
> But it was time to institute a little parade, the parade of the Ideal Preedy. By devious handlings he gave any one who wanted to look a chance to see the title of the book—a Spanish translation of Homer, classic thus, but not daring, cosmopolitan too—and then gathered together his beachwrap and bag into a neat sand-resistant pile (Methodical and Sensible Preedy), rose slowly to stretch at ease his huge frame (Big-Cat Preedy), and tossed aside his sandals (Carefree Preedy, after all).
>
> The marriage of Preedy and the sea! there were alternate rituals. The first involved the stroll that turns into a run and a dive straight into the water, thereafter smoothing into a strong splashless crawl towards the horizon. But of course not really to the horizon. Quite suddenly he would turn on to his back and thrash great white splashes with his legs, somehow thus showing that he could have swum further had he wanted to, and then would stand up a quarter out of water for all to see who it was.
>
> The alternative course was simpler, it avoided the cold-water shock and it avoided the risk of appearing too high-spirited. The point was to appear to be so used to the sea, the Mediterranean, and this particular beach, that one might as well be in the sea as out of it. It involved a slow stroll down and into the edge of the water—not even noticing his toes were wet, land and water all same to *him!*—with his eyes up at the sky gravely surveying portents, invisible to others, of the weather (Local Fisherman Preedy).[5]

The novelist means us to see that Preedy is improperly concerned with the extensive impressions he feels his sheer bodily action is giving off to those around him. We can malign Preedy further by assuming that he has acted merely in order to give a particular impression, that this is a false impression, and that the others present receive either no impression at all, or worse still, the impression that Preedy is affectedly trying to cause them to receive this particular impression. But the important point for us here is that the kind of impression Preedy thinks he is making is in fact the kind of impression that others correctly and incorrectly glean from someone in their midst.

I have said that when an individual appears before others his actions will influence the definition of the situation which they come to have. Sometimes the individual will act in a thoroughly calculating manner, expressing himself in a given way solely in order to give the kind of impression to others that is likely to evoke from them a specific response he is concerned to obtain. Sometimes the individual will be calculating in his activity but be relatively unaware that this is the case. Sometimes he will intentionally and consciously express himself in a particular way, but chiefly because the tradition of his group or social status require this kind of expression and not because of any particular response (other than vague acceptance or approval) that is likely to be evoked from those impressed by the expression. Sometimes the traditions of an individual's role will lead him to give a well-designed impression of a particular kind and yet he may be neither consciously nor unconsciously disposed to create such an impression. The others, in their turn, may be suitably impressed by the individual's efforts to convey something, or may misunderstand the situation and come to conclusions that are warranted neither by the individual's intent nor by the facts. In any case, in so far as the others act *as if* the individual had conveyed a particular impression, we may take a functional or pragmatic view and say that the individual has "effectively" projected a given definition of the situation and "effectively" fostered the understanding that a given state of affairs obtains.

There is one aspect of the others' response that bears special comment here. Knowing that the individual is likely to present himself in a light that is favorable to him, the others may divide what they witness into two parts: a part that is relatively easy for the individual to manipulate at will, being chiefly his verbal assertions, and a part in regard to which he seems to have little concern or control, being chiefly derived from the expressions he gives off. The others may then use what are considered to be the ungovernable aspects of his expressive behavior as a check upon the validity of what is conveyed by the governable aspects. In this a fundamental asymmetry is demonstrated in the communication process, the individual presumably being aware of only one stream of his communication, the witness of this stream and one other. For example, in Shetland Isle one crofter's wife, in serving native dishes to a visitor from the mainland of Britain, would listen with a polite smile to his polite claims of liking what he was eating; at the same time she would take note of the rapidity with which the visitor lifted his fork or spoon to his mouth, the eagerness with which he passed food into his mouth, and the gusto expressed in chewing the food, using these signs as a check on the stated feelings of the eater. The same woman, in order to discover what one acquaintance (A) "actually" thought of another acquaintance (B), would wait until B was in the presence of A but engaged in conversation with still another person (C). She would then covertly examine the facial expressions of A as he regarded B in conversation with C. Not being in conversation with B, and not being directly observed by him, A would sometimes relax usual constraints and tactful deceptions, and freely express what he was "actually" feeling about B. This Shetlander, in short, would observe the unobserved observer.

Now given the fact that others are likely to check up on the more controllable aspects of behavior by means of the less controllable, one can expect that sometimes the individual will try to exploit this very possibility, guiding the impression he makes through behavior felt to be reliably informing.[6] For example, in gaining admission to a tight social circle, the participant observer may not only wear an accepting look while listening to an informant, but may also be careful to wear the same look when observing the informant talking to others; observers of the observer will then not as easily discover where he actually stands. A specific illustration may be cited from Shetland Isle. When a neighbor dropped in to have a cup of tea, he would ordinarily wear at least a hint of an expectant warm smile as he passed through the door into the cottage. Since lack of physical obstructions outside the cottage and lack of light within it usually made it possible to observe the visitor unobserved as he approached the house, islanders sometimes took pleasure in watching the visitor drop whatever expression he was manifesting and replace it with a sociable one just before reaching the door. However, some visitors, in appreciating that this examination was occurring, would blindly adopt a social face a long distance from the house, thus ensuring the projection of a constant image.

This kind of control upon the part of the individual reinstates the symmetry of the communication process, and sets the stage for a kind of information game—a potentially infinite cycle of concealment, discovery, false revelation, and rediscovery. It should be added that since the others are likely to be relatively unsuspicious of the presumably unguided aspect of the individual's conduct, he can gain much by controlling it. The others of course may sense that the individual is manipulating the presumably spontaneous aspects of his behavior, and seek in this very act of manipulation some shading of conduct that the individual has not managed to control. This again provides a check upon the individual's behavior, this time his presumably uncalculated behavior, thus re-establishing the asymmetry of the communication process. Here I would like only to add the suggestion that the arts of piercing an individual's effort at calculated unintentionality seem better developed than our capacity to manipulate our own behavior, so that regardless of how many steps have occurred in the information game, the witness is likely to have the advantage over the actor, and the initial asymmetry of the communication process is likely to be retained.

When we allow that the individual projects a definition of the situation when he appears before others, we must also see that the others, however passive their role may seem to be, will themselves effectively project a definition of the situation by virtue of their response to the individual and by virtue of any lines of action they initiate to him. Ordinarily the definitions of the situation projected by the several different participants are sufficiently attuned to one another so that open contradiction will not occur. I do not mean that there will be the kind of consensus that arises when each individual present candidly expresses what he really feels and honestly agrees with the expressed feelings of the others present. This kind of harmony is an optimistic ideal and in any case not necessary for the smooth working of society. Rather, each participant is expected to suppress his immediate heartfelt feelings, conveying a view of the situation which he feels the others will be able to find at least temporarily acceptable. The maintenance of this surface of agreement, this veneer of consensus, is facilitated by each participant concealing his own wants behind statements which assert values to which everyone present feels obliged to give lip service. Further, there is usually a kind of division of definitional labor. Each participant is allowed to establish the tentative official ruling regarding matters which are vital to him but not immediately important to others, e.g., the rationalizations and justifications by which he accounts for his past activity. In exchange for this courtesy he remains silent or noncommittal on matters important to others but not immediately important to him. We have then a kind of interactional *modus vivendi*. Together, the participants contribute to a single over-all definition of the situation which involves not so much a real argument as to what exists but rather a real agreement as to whose claims concerning what issues will be temporarily honored. Real agreement will also exist concerning the desirability of avoiding an open conflict of definitions of the situation.[7] I will refer to this level of agreement as a "working consensus." It is to be understood that the working consensus established in one interaction setting will be quite different in content from the working consensus established in a different type of setting. Thus, between two friends at lunch, a reciprocal show of affection, respect, and concern for the other is maintained. In service occupations, on the other hand, the specialist often maintains an image of disinterested involvement in the problem of the client, while the client responds with a show of respect for the competence and integrity of the specialist. Regardless of such differences in content, however, the general form of these working arrangements is the same.

In noting the tendency for a participant to accept the definitional claims made by the others present, we can appreciate the crucial importance of the information that the individual *initially* possesses or acquires concerning his fellow participants, for it is on the basis of this initial information that the individual starts to define the situation and starts to build up lines of responsive action. The individual's initial projection commits him to what he is proposing to be and requires him to drop all pretenses of being other things. As the interaction among the participants progresses, additions and modifications in this initial informational state will of course occur, but it is essential that these later developments be related without contradiction to, and even built up from, the initial positions taken by the several participants. It would seem that an individual can more easily make a choice as to what line of treatment of demand from and extend to the others present at the beginning of an encounter than he can alter the line of treatment that is being pursued once the interaction is under way.

In everyday life, of course, there is a clear understanding that first impressions are important. Thus, the work adjustment of those in service occupations will often hinge upon a capacity to seize and hold the initiative in the service relation, a capacity that will require subtle aggressiveness on the part of the server when he is of lower socio-economic status than his client. W. F. Whyte suggests the waitress as an example:

> The first point that stands out is that the waitress who bears up under pressure does not simply respond to her customers. She acts with some skill to control their behavior. The first question to ask when we look at the customer relationship is, "Does the waitress get the jump on the customer, or does the customer get the jump on the waitress?" The skilled waitress realizes the crucial nature of this question. . . .
>
> The skilled waitress tackles the customer with confidence and without hesitation. For example, she may find that a new customer has seated himself before she could clear off the dirty dishes and change the cloth. He is now leaning on the table studying the menu. She greets him, says, "May I change the cover, please?" and, without waiting for an answer, takes his menu away from him so that he moves back from the table, and she goes about her work. The relationship is handled politely but firmly, and there is never any question as to who is in charge.[8]

When the interaction that is initiated by "first impressions" is itself merely the initial interaction in an extended series of interactions involving the same participants, we speak of "getting off on the right foot" and feel that it is crucial that we do so. Thus, one learns that some teachers take the following view:

> You can't ever let them get the upper hand on you or you're through. So I start out tough. The first day I get a new class in, I let them know who's boss. . . . You've got to start off tough, then you can ease up as you go along. If you start out easy-going, when you try to be tough, they'll just look at you and laugh.[9]

Similarly, attendants in mental institutions may feel that if the new patient is sharply put in his place the first day on the ward and made to see who is boss, much future difficulty will be prevented.[10]

Given the fact that the individual effectively projects a definition of the situation when he enters the presence of others, we can assume that events may occur within the interaction which contradict, discredit, or otherwise throw doubt upon this projection. When these disruptive events occur, the interaction itself may come to a confused and embarrassed halt. Some of the assumptions upon which the responses of the participants had been predicted become untenable, and the participants find themselves lodged in an interaction for which the situation has been wrongly defined and is now no longer defined. At such moments the individual whose presentation has been discredited may feel ashamed while the others present may feel hostile, and all the participants may come to feel ill at ease, nonplussed, out of countenance, embarrassed, experiencing the kind of anomy that is generated when the minute social system of face-to-face interaction breaks down.

In stressing the fact that the initial definition of the situation projected by an individual tends to provide a plan for the cooperative activity that follows—in stressing this action point of view—we must not overlook the crucial fact that any projected definition of the situation also has a distinctive moral character. It is this moral character of projections that will chiefly concern us in this report. Society is organized on the principle that any individual who possesses certain social characteristics has a moral right to expect that others will value and treat him in an appropriate way. Connected with this principle is a second, namely that an individual who implicitly or explicitly signifies that he has certain social characteristics ought in fact to be what he claims he is. In consequence, when an individual projects a definition of the situation and thereby makes an implicit or explicit claim to be a person of a particular kind, he automatically exerts a moral demand upon the others, obliging them to value and treat him in the manner that persons of his kind have a right to expect. He also implicitly forgoes all claims to be things he does not appear to be[11] and hence forgoes the treatment that would be appropriate for such individuals. The others find, then, that the individual has informed them as to what is and as to what they *ought* to see as the "is."

One cannot judge the importance of definitional disruptions by the frequency with which they occur, for apparently they would occur more frequently were not constant precautions taken. We find that preventive practices are constantly employed to avoid these embarrassments and that corrective practices are constantly employed to compensate for discrediting occurrences that have not been successfully avoided. When the individual employs these strategies and tactics to protect his own projections, we may refer to them as "defensive practices"; when a participant employs them to save the definition of the situation projected by another, we speak of "protective practices" or "tact." Together, defensive and protective practices comprise the techniques employed to safeguard the impression fostered by an individual during his presence before others. It should be added that while we may be ready to see that no fostered impression would survive if defensive practices were not employed, we are less ready perhaps to see that few impressions could survive if those who received the impression did not exert tact in their reception of it.

In addition to the fact that precautions are taken to prevent disruption of projected definitions, we may also note that an intense interest in these disruptions comes to play a significant role in the social life of the group. Practical jokes and social games are played in which embarrassments which are to be taken unseriously are purposely engineered.[12] Fantasies are created in which devastating exposures occur. Ancedotes from the past—real, embroidered, or fictitious—are told and retold, detailing disruptions which occurred, almost occurred, or occurred and were admirably resolved. There seems to be no grouping which does not have a ready supply of these games, reveries, and cautionary tales, to be used as a source of humor, a catharsis for anxieties, and a sanction for inducing individuals to be modest in their claims and reasonable in their projected expectations. The individual may tell himself through dreams of getting into impossible positions. Families tell of the time a guest got his dates mixed and arrived when neither the house nor anyone in it was ready for him. Journalists tell of times when an all-too-meaningful misprint occurred, and the paper's assumption of objectivity or decorum was humorously discredited. Public servants tell of times a client ridiculously misunderstood form instructions, giving answers which implied an unanticipated and bizarre definition of the situation.[13] Seamen, whose home away from home is rigorously he-man, tell stories of coming back home and inadvertently asking mother to "pass the fucking butter."[14] Diplomats tell of the time a near-sighted queen asked a republican ambassador about the health of his king.[15]

To summarize, then, I assume that when an individual appears before others he will have many motives for trying to control the impression they receive of the situation.

Notes

1. Gustav Ichheiser, "Misunderstandings in Human Relations," Supplement to *The American Journal of Sociology*, 55 (September, 1949):6–7.

2. Quoted in E. H. Volkart, editor, *Social Behavior and Personality*, Contributions of W. I. Thomas to Theory and Social Research (New York: Social Science Research Council, 1951), p. 5.

3. Here I owe much to an unpublished paper by Tom Burns of the University of Edinburgh. He presents the argument that in all interaction a basic underlying theme is the desire of each participant to guide and control the responses made by the others present. A similar argument has been advanced by Jay Haley in a recent unpublished paper, but in regard to a special kind of control, that having to do with defining the nature of the relationship of those involved in the interaction.

4. Willard Waller, "The Rating and Dating Complex," *American Sociological Review*, 2:730.

5. William Sansom, *A Contest of Ladies* (London: Hogarth, 1956), pp. 230–32.

6. The widely read and rather sound writings of Stephen Potter are concerned in part with signs that can be engineered to give a shrewd observer the apparently incidental cues he needs to discover concealed virtues the gamesman does not in fact possess.

7. An interaction can be purposely set up as a time and place for voicing differences in opinion, but in such cases participants must be careful to agree not to disagree on the proper tone of voice, vocabulary, and degree of seriousness in which all arguments are to be phrased, and upon the mutual respect which disagreeing participants must carefully continue to express toward one another. This debaters' or academic definition of the situation may also be invoked suddenly and judiciously as a way of translating a serious conflict of views into one that can be handled within a framework acceptable to all present.

8. W. F. Whyte, "When Workers and Customers Meet," Chap. VII, *Industry and Society*, ed. W. F. Whyte (New York: McGraw-Hill, 1946), pp. 132–33.

9. Teacher interview quoted by Howard S. Becker, "Social Class Variations in the Teacher–Pupil Relationship," *Journal of Educational Sociology*, 25:459.

10. Harold Taxel, "Authority Structure in a Mental Hospital Ward" (unpublished Master's thesis, Department of Sociology, University of Chicago, 1953).

11. This role of the witness in limiting what it is the individual can be has been stressed by Existentialists, who see it as a basic threat to individual freedom. See Jean-Paul Sartre, *Being and Nothingness*, trans. by Hazel E. Barnes (New York: Philosophical Library, 1956), pp. 365 ff.

12. Erving Goffman, "Communication Conduct in an Island Community" (unpublished Ph. D. dissertation, Department of Sociology, University of Chicago, 1953), pp. 319–27.

13. Peter Blau, *Dynamics of Bureaucracy; A Study of Interpersonal Relationships in Two Government Agencies*, 2nd ed. (Chicago: University of Chicago Press, 1963).

14. Walter M. Beattie, Jr., "The Merchant Seaman" (unpublished M. A. Report, Department of Sociology, University of Chicago, 1950), p. 35.

15. Sir Frederick Ponsonby, *Recollections of Three Reigns* (New York: Dutton, 1952), p. 46.

PART IV   Socialization and Gender

ESSENTIAL TO OUR SURVIVAL following birth is *socialization*—learning to become full-fledged members of a human group. As we saw in Part III, this learning involves such fundamental, taken–for–granted aspects of group life as ideas of health and morality, and the many nuances of nonverbal communication. We saw that socialization involves learning rules (what we should and should not do under different circumstances) and values (what is considered good or bad), as well as expectations about how we should present the self in different social settings.

The agents of socialization include our parents, brothers and sisters and other relatives, friends, and neighbors, as well as clergy and school teachers. They also include people we do not know and never will know, such as clerks and shoppers who, by their very presence—and the expectations we know they have of us—help to bring our behavior under control at one or another particular moment and thereby shape it for similar situations in the future. Through this process of socialization each of us develops a particular *personality*, the tendency to behave in a certain manner that carries over from one situation to another.

Essential to our identity formation is socialization into gender—that is, our learning masculinity and femininity. (The term *sex* refers to biological characteristics, while the term *gender* refers to social expectations based on those characteristics. We inherit our sex, but we learn our gender. Sex is male or female, while gender is masculinity or femininity.)

Although we come into this world with the biological equipment of a male or female, these physical organs do not determine what we shall be like as a male or a female. Whether or not we defer to members of the

109

opposite sex, for example, is not an automatic result of our particular sexual equipment but is due to what we learn is proper for us because of the particular biological equipment we possess. This learning process is called *gender or sex role socialization.*

Our gender extends into almost every area of our lives, even into situations for which it may be quite irrelevant. For example, if we are grocery clerks, by means of our clothing, language, and gestures we communicate to others that we are *male* or *female* clerks. Because gender cuts across most other aspects of social life, it is sometimes referred to as a *master trait.*

Challenged for generations (the Women's Movement was active before our grandparents were born), the traditional expectations attached to the sexes have undergone substantial modification in recent years. One can no longer safely assume particular behavior on the part of another simply because of that person's sex. In spite of such changes, however, most Americans appear to follow rather traditional lines as they socialize their children. The changes take place slowly, and male dominance remains a fact of social life.

What would we humans be like if we were untouched by culture? Although there is much speculation, no one knows the answer to that question, for any behavior or attitude that we examine is embedded within cultural learning. The closest we can come is to look at children who have received the least introduction to a culture—as Kingsley Davis does in his analysis of Anna and Isabelle. Even isolated children, however, have still been exposed to a culture, although minimally. One really cannot think of humanity apart from culture, then, for culture shapes humanity.

In the past, an occasional naked child was discovered living alone in the wilderness, walking and crawling on all fours, pouncing on small animals and eating them raw. Such *feral* ("wild") *children* were thought to have been raised by animals and to be untouched by human culture. Although documented cases of feral children exist—one boy discovered in 1798 was even studied intensely by scientists—the presumption today is that feral children had been abandoned by their parents because they were retarded. Consequently, the study of feral children does not answer the question of what humans would be like if they were untouched by culture. If it did, the answer would not be encouraging—granted the lack of language, the devouring of small animals, and so on.

It is through our association with other humans, then, that we learn what it means to be human. Essential to this process is gender socialization, the primary focus in Part IV. We want to explore the question of how males and females learn gender, the sex roles they are socially destined to play. Memories of childhood may surface while reading James M. Henslin's analysis of some of the processes by which males are socialized into social dominance. By focusing on childhood, he examines experiences that direct males into a world drastically distinct from the female world, that often lead boys and men to think of themselves as superior, and that later cause them difficulty communicating in depth with women and in maintaining "significant relationships" with the opposite sex. Barrie Thorne and Zella Luria then place the sociological spotlight on the world of children, examining how school children separate their activities and friendships on the basis of sex, and engage in forms of play that help maintain male dominance in society. Then Nancy Henley, Mykol Hamilton, and Barrie Thorne look at how communication, both verbal and nonverbal, helps maintain traditional boundaries between the sexes. The final article, by Mark Synder, examines how stereotypes in everyday life create expectations that people unwittingly fulfill.

Taken together, these articles help us to better understand how gender pervades our lives. They ought to provide considerable insight into your own socialization into gender—how you became masculine or feminine, and how once propeled into that role, social constraints continue to influence your attitudes and behavior.

10 Extreme Isolation

KINGSLEY DAVIS

What could the editor possibly mean by the subtitle in the table of contents: "Learning to be human"? Isn't it obvious that we humans are born human? Certainly that is true concerning our *biological* characteristics, that is, our possession of arms, legs, head, and torso, as well as our internal organs.

But to act like other people, to think the way others think— and perhaps even the ability itself to think—are *learned* characteristics. These are the result of years of exposure to people living in groups.

Just how much does biology contribute to what we are, and how much is due to social life? (Or, in Davis's terms, what are the relative contributions of the biogenic and the sociogenic factors?) Although this question has intrigued many, no one has yet been able to unravel its mystery. According to Davis's observations, however, the contributions of the social group are much farther reaching and of greater fundamental consequence than most of us imagine. Certainly these include our speech, which helps shape our basic attitudes and orientations to life, but, as indicated in this article, the social group may even contribute such ordinarily presumed biological characteristics as our ability to walk. Although this selection will not present any "final answers" to this age-old question, it should stir up your sociological imagination.

EARLY IN 1940 THERE APPEARED . . . an account of a girl called Anna.[1] She had been deprived of normal contact and had received a minimum of human care for almost the whole of her first six years of life. At this time observations were not complete and the report had a tentative character. Now, however, the girl is dead, and with more information available,[2] it is possible to give a fuller and more definitive description of the case from a sociological point of view.

Anna's death, caused by hemorrhagic jaundice, occurred on August 6, 1942. Having been born on March 1 or 6,[3] 1932, she was approximately ten and a half years of age when she died. The previous report covered her development up to the age of almost eight years; the present one recapitulates the earlier period on the basis of new evidence and then covers the last two and a half years of her life.

Early History

The first few days and weeks of Anna's life were complicated by frequent changes of domicile. It will be recalled that she was an illegitimate child, the second such child born to her mother, and that her grandfather, a widowed farmer in whose house her mother lived, strongly disapproved of this new evidence of the mother's indiscretion. This fact led to the baby's being shifted about.

Two weeks after being born in a nurse's private home, Anna was brought to the family farm, but the grandfather's antagonism was so great that she was shortly taken to the house of one of her mother's friends. At this time a local minister became interested in her and took her to his house with an idea of possible adoption. He decided against adoption, however, when he discovered that she had vaginitis. The infant was then taken to a children's home in the nearest large city. This agency found that at the age of only three weeks she was already in a miserable condition, being "terribly galled and otherwise in very bad shape." It did not regard her as a likely subject for adoption but took her in for a while anyway, hoping to benefit her. After Anna had spent nearly eight weeks in this place, the agency notified her mother to come and get her. The mother responded by sending a man and his wife to the children's home with a view to their adopting Anna, but they made such a poor impression on the agency that permission was refused. Later the mother came herself and took the child out of the home and then gave her to this couple. It was in the home of this pair that a social worker found the girl a short time thereafter. The social worker went to the mother's home and pleaded with Anna's grandfather to allow the mother to bring the child home. In spite of threats, he refused. The child, by then more than four months old, was next taken to another children's home in a near-by town. A medical examination at this time revealed that she had impetigo, vaginitis, umbilical hernia, and a skin rash.

Anna remained in this second children's home for nearly three weeks, at the end of which time she was transferred to a private foster-home. Since, however, the grandfather would not, and the mother could not, pay for the child's care, she was finally taken back as a last resort to the grandfather's house (at the age of five and a half months). There she remained, kept on the second floor in an attic-like room because her mother hesitated to incur the grandfather's wrath by bringing her downstairs.

The mother, a sturdy woman weighing about 180 pounds, did a man's work on the farm. She engaged in heavy work such as milking cows and tending hogs and had little time for her children. Sometimes she went out at night, in which case Anna was left entirely without attention. Ordinarily, it seems, Anna received only enough care to keep her barely alive. She appears to have been seldom moved from one position to another. Her clothing and bedding were filthy. She apparently had no instruction, no friendly attention.

It is little wonder that, when finally found and removed from the room in the grandfather's house at the age of nearly six years, the child could not talk, walk, or do anything that showed intelligence. She was in an extremely emaciated and undernourished condition, with skeletonlike legs and a bloated abdomen. She had been fed on virtually nothing except cow's milk during the years under her mother's care.

Anna's condition when found, and her subsequent improvement, have been described in the previous report. It now remains to say what happened to her after that.

Later History

In 1939, nearly two years after being discovered, Anna had progressed, as previously reported, to the point where she could walk, understand simple commands, feed herself, achieve some neatness, remember people, etc. But she still did not speak, and, though she was much more like a normal infant of something over one year of age in mentality, she was far from normal for her age.

On August 30, 1939, she was taken to a private home for retarded children, leaving the county home where she had been for more than a year and a half. In her new setting she made some further progress, but not a great deal. In a report of an examination made November 6 of the same year, the head of the institution pictured the child as follows:

> Anna walks about aimlessly, makes periodic rhythmic motions of her hands, and, at intervals, makes guttural and sucking noises. She regards her hands as if she had seen them for the first time. It was impossible to hold her attention for more than a few seconds at a time—not because of distraction due to external stimuli but because of her inability to concentrate. She ignored the task in hand to gaze vacantly about the room. Speech is entirely lacking. Numerous unsuccessful attempts have been made with her in the hope of developing initial sounds. I do not believe that this failure is due to negativism or deafness but that she is not sufficiently developed to accept speech at this time. . . . The prognosis is not favorable. . . .

More than five months later, on April 25, 1940, a clinical psychologist, the late Professor Francis N. Maxfield, examined Anna and reported the following: large for her age; hearing "entirely normal"; vision apparently normal; able to climb stairs; speech in the "babbling stage" and "promise for developing intelligible speech later seems to be good." He said further that "on the Merrill–Palmer scale she made a mental score of 19 months. On the Vineland social maturity scale she made a score of 23 months.[4]

Professor Maxfield very sensibly pointed out that prognosis is difficult in such cases of isolation. "It is very difficult to take scores on tests standardized under average conditions of environment and experience," he wrote, "and interpret them in a case where environment and experience have been so unusual." With this warning he gave it as his opinion at that time that Anna would eventually "attain an adult mental level of six or seven years."[5]

The school for retarded children, on July 1, 1941, reported that Anna had reached 46 inches in height and weighed 60 pounds. She could bounce and catch a ball and was said to conform to group socialization, though as a follower rather than a leader. Toilet habits were firmly established. Food habits were normal, except that she still used a spoon as her sole implement. She could dress herself except for fastening her clothes. Most remarkable of all, she had finally begun to develop speech. She was characterized as being at about the two-year level in this regard. She could call attendants by name and bring in one when she was asked to. She had a few complete sentences to express her wants. The report concluded that there was nothing peculiar about her, except that she was feebleminded—"probably congenital in type."[6]

A final report from the school made on June 22, 1942, and evidently the last report before the girl's death, pictured only a slight advance over that given above. It said that Anna could follow directions, string beads, identify a few colors, build with blocks, and differentiate between attractive and unattractive pictures. She had a good sense of rhythm and loved a doll. She talked mainly in phrases but would repeat words and try to carry on a conversation. She was clean about clothing. She habitually washed her hands and brushed her teeth. She would try to help other children. She walked well and could run fairly well, though clumsily. Although easily excited, she had a pleasant disposition.

Interpretation

Such was Anna's condition just before her death. It may seem as if she had not made much progress, but one must remember the condition in which she had been found. One must recall that she had no glimmering of speech, absolutely no ability to walk, no sense of gesture, not the least capacity to feed herself even when the food was put in front of her, and no comprehension of cleanliness. She was so apathetic that it was hard to tell whether or not she could hear. And all this at the age of nearly six years. Compared with this condition, her capacities at the time of her death seem striking indeed, though they do not amount to much more than a two-and-a-half-year mental level. One conclusion therefore seems safe, namely, that her isolation prevented a considerable amount of mental development that was undoubtedly part of her capacity. Just what her original capacity was, of course, is hard to say; but her development after her period of confinement (including the ability to walk and run, to play, dress, fit into a social situation, and, above all, to speak) shows that she had at least this capacity—capacity that never could have been realized in her original condition of isolation.

A further question is this: What would she have been like if she had received a normal upbringing from the moment of birth? A definitive answer would have been impossible in any case, but even an approximate answer is made difficult by her early death. If one assumes, as was tentatively surmised in the previous report, that it is "almost impossible for any child to learn to speak, think, and act like a normal person after a long period of early isolation," it seems likely that Anna might have had a normal or near-normal capacity, genetically speaking. On the other hand, it was pointed out that Anna represented "a marginal case, [because] she was discovered before she had reached six years of age," an age "young enough to allow for some plasticity."[7] While admitting, then, that Anna's isolation *may* have been the major cause (and was certainly a minor cause) of her lack of rapid mental progress during the four and a half years following her rescue from neglect, it is necessary to entertain the hypothesis that she was congenitally deficient.

In connection with this hypothesis, one suggestive though by no means conclusive circumstance needs consideration, namely, the mentality of Anna's forebears. Information on this subject is easier to obtain, as one might guess, on the mother's than on the father's side. Anna's maternal grandmother, for example, is said to have been college educated and wished to have her children receive a good education, but her husband, Anna's stern grandfather, apparently a shrewd, hard-driving, calculating farmowner, was so penurious that her ambitions in this direction were thwarted. Under the circumstances her daughter (Anna's mother) managed, despite having to do hard work on the farm, to complete the eighth grade in a country school. Even so, however, the daughter was evidently not very smart. "A schoolmate of [Anna's mother] stated that she was retarded in school work; was very gullible at this age; and that her morals even at this time were discussed by other students." Two tests administered to her on March 4, 1938, when she was thirty-two years of age, showed that she was mentally deficient. On the Standard Revision of the Binet–Simon Scale her performance was equivalent to that of a child of eight years, giving her an I.Q. of 50 and indicating mental deficiency of "middle-grade moron type."[8]

As to the identity of Anna's father, the most persistent theory holds that he was an old man about seventy-four years of age at the time of the girl's birth. If he was the one, there is no indication of mental or other biological deficiency, whatever one may think of his morals. However, some-one else may actually have been the father.

To sum up: Anna's heredity is the kind that *might* have given rise to innate mental deficiency, though not necessarily.

Comparison with Another Case

Perhaps more to the point than speculations about Anna's ancestry would be a case for comparison. If a child could be discovered who had been isolated about the same length of time as Anna but had achieved a much quicker recovery and a greater mental development, it would be a stronger indication that Anna was deficient to start with.

Such a case does exist. It is the case of a girl found at about the same time as Anna and under strikingly similar circumstances. A full description of the details of this case has not been published, but in addition to newspaper reports, an excellent preliminary account by a speech specialist, Dr. Marie K. Mason, who played an important role in the handling of the child, has appeared.[9] Also the late Dr. Francis N. Maxfield, clinical psychologist at Ohio State University, as was Dr. Mason, has written an as yet unpublished but penetrating analysis of the case.[10] Some of his observations have been included in Professor Zingg's book on feral man.[11] The following discussion is drawn mainly from these enlightening materials. The writer, through the kindness of Professors Mason and Maxfield, did have a chance to observe the girl in April, 1940, and to discuss the features of her case with them.

Born apparently one month later than Anna, the girl in question, who has been given the pseudonym Isabelle, was discovered in November, 1938, nine months after the discovery of Anna. At the time she was found she was approximately six and a half years of age. Like Anna, she was an illegiti-mate child and had been kept in seclusion for that reason. Her mother was a deaf-mute, having become so at the age of two, and it appears that she and Isabelle had spent most of their time together in a dark room shut off from the rest of the mother's family. As a result Isabelle had no chance to develop speech; when she communicated with her mother, it was by means of gestures. Lack of sunshine and inadequacy of diet had caused Isabelle to become rachitic. Her legs in particular were affected; they "were so bowed that as she stood erect the soles of her shoes came nearly flat together, and she got about with a skittering gait."[12] Her behavior toward strangers, especially men, was almost that of a wild animal, manifest-ing much fear and hostility. In lieu of speech she made only a strong croaking sound. In many ways she acted like an infant. "She was apparently utterly unaware of relationships of any kind. When presented with a ball for the first time, she held it in the palm of her hand, then reached out and stroked my face with it. Such behavior is comparable to that of a child of six months."[13]

At first it was even hard to tell whether or not she could hear, so unused were her senses. Many of her actions resembled those of deaf children.

It is small wonder that, once it was established that she could hear, specialists working with her believed her to be feeble-minded. Even on nonverbal tests her performance was so low as to promise little for the future. Her first score on the Stanford–Binet was 19 months, practically at the zero point of the scale. On the Vineland social maturity scale her first score was 39, representing an age level of two and a half years.[14] "The general impression was that she was wholly uneducable and that any attempt to teach her to speak, after so long a period of silence, would meet with failure."[15]

In spite of this interpretation, the individuals in charge of Isabelle launched a systematic and skillful program of training. It seemed hopeless at first. The approach had to be through pantomime and dramatization, suitable to an infant. It required one week of intensive effort before she even made her first attempt at vocalization. Gradually she began to respond, however, and, after the first hurdles had at last been overcome, a curious thing happened. She went through the usual stages of learning characteristic of the years from one to six not only in proper succession but far more rapidly than normal. In a little over two months after her first vocalization she was putting sentences together. Nine months after that she could identify words and sentences on the printed page, could write well, could add to ten, and could retell a story after hearing it. Seven months beyond this point she had a vocabulary of 1,500–2,000 words and was asking complicated questions. Starting from an educational level of between one and three years (depending on what aspect one considers), she had reached a normal level by the time she was eight and a half years old. In short, she covered in two years the stages of learning that ordinarily require six.[16] Or, to put it another way, her I.Q. trebled in a year and a half.[17] The speed with which she reached the normal level of mental development seems analogous to the recovery of body weight in a growing child after an illness, the recovery being achieved by an extra fast rate of growth for a period after the illness until normal weight for the given age is again attained.

When the writer saw Isabelle a year and a half after her discovery, she gave him the impression of being a very bright, cheerful, energetic little girl. She spoke well, walked and ran without trouble, and sang with gusto and accuracy. Today she is over fourteen years old and has passed the sixth grade in a public school. Her teachers say that she participates in all school activities as normally as other children. Though older than her classmates, she has fortunately not physically matured too far beyond their level.[18]

Clearly the history of Isabelle's development is different from that of Anna's. In both cases there was exceedingly low, or rather blank, intellectual level to begin with. In both cases it seemed that the girl might be congenitally feeble-minded. In both a considerably higher level was reached later on. But the Ohio girl achieved a normal mentality within two years, whereas Anna was still marked inadequate at the end of four and a half years. This difference in achievement may suggest that Anna had less initial capacity. But an alternative hypothesis is possible.

One should remember that Anna never received the prolonged and expert attention that Isabelle received. The result of such attention, in the case of the Ohio girl, was to give her speech at an early stage, and her subsequent rapid development seems to have been a consequence of that. "Until Isabelle's speech and language development, she had all the characteristics of a feeble-minded child." Had Anna, who, from the standpoint of psychometric tests and early history, closely resembled this girl at the start, been given a mastery of speech at an earlier point by intensive training, her subsequent development might have been much more rapid. [19]

The hypothesis that Anna began with a sharply inferior mental capacity is therefore not established. Even if she were deficient to start with, we have no way of knowing how much so. Under ordinary conditions she might have been a dull normal or, like her mother, a moron. Even after the blight of her isolation, if she had lived to maturity, she might have finally reached virtually the full level of her capacity, whatever it may have been. That her isolation did have a profound effect upon her mentality, there can be no doubt. This is proved by the substantial degree of change during the four and a half years following her rescue.

Consideration of Isabelle's case serves to show, as Anna's case does not clearly show, that isolation up to the age of six, with failure to acquire any form of speech and hence failure to grasp nearly the whole world of cultural meaning, does not preclude the subsequent acquisition of these. Indeed, there seems to be a process of accelerated recovery in which the child goes through the mental stages at a more rapid rate than would be the case in normal development. Just what would be the maximum age at which a person could remain isolated and still retain the capacity for full cultural acquisition is hard to say. Almost certainly it would not be as high as age fifteen; it might possibly be as low as age ten. Undoubtedly various individuals would differ considerably as to the exact age.

Anna's is not an ideal case for showing the effects of extreme isolation, partly because she was possibly deficient to begin with, partly because she did not receive the best training available, and partly because she did not live long enough. Nevertheless, her case is instructive when placed in the record with numerous other cases of extreme isolation. This and the previous article about her are meant to place her in the record. It is to be hoped that other cases will be described in the scientific literature as they are discovered (as unfortunately they will be), for only in these rare cases of extreme isolation is it possible "to observe *concretely separated* two factors in the development of human personality which are always otherwise only analytically separated, the biogenic and the sociogenic factors." [20]

Notes

1. Kingsley Davis, "Extreme Social Isolation of a Child," *American Journal of Sociology*, XLV (January, 1940), 554–65.

2. Sincere appreciation is due to the officials in the Department of Welfare, Commonwealth of Pennsylvania, for their kind cooperation in making available the records concerning Anna and discussing the case frankly with the writer. Helen C. Hubbell, Florentine Hackbusch, and Eleanor Mecklenburg were particularly helpful, as was Fanny L. Matchette. Without their aid neither of the reports on Anna could have been written.

3. The records are not clear as to which day.

4. Letter to one of the state officials in charge of the case.

5. *Ibid.*

6. Progress report of the school.

7. Davis, *op. cit.*, p. 564.

8. The facts set forth here as to Anna's ancestry are taken chiefly from a report of mental tests administered to Anna's mother by psychologists at a state hospital where she was taken for this purpose after the discovery of Anna's seclusion. This excellent report was not available to the writer when the previous paper on Anna was published.

9. Marie K. Mason, "Learning to Speak after Six and One-Half Years of Silence," *Journal of Speech Disorders*, VII (1942), 295–304.

10. Francis N. Maxfield, "What Happens When the Social Environment of a Child Approaches Zero." The writer is greatly indebted to Mrs. Maxfield and to Professor Horace B. English, a colleague of Professor Maxfield, for the privilege of seeing this manuscript and other materials collected on isolated and feral individuals.

11. J. A. L. Singh and Robert M. Zingg, *Wolf-Children and Feral Man* (New York: Harper & Bros., 1941), pp. 248–51.

12. Maxfield, unpublished manuscript cited above.

13. Mason, *op. cit.*, p. 299.

14. Maxfield, unpublished manuscript.

15. Mason, *op. cit.*, p. 299.

16. *Ibid.*, pp. 300–304.

17. Maxfield, unpublished manuscript.

18. Based on a personal letter from Dr. Mason to the writer, May 13, 1946.

19. This point is suggested in a personal letter from Dr. Mason to the writer, October 22, 1946.

20. Singh and Zingg, *op. cit.*, pp. xxi–xxii, in a foreword by the writer.

11 On Becoming Male: Reflections of a Sociologist on Childhood and Early Socialization

JAMES M. HENSLIN

Although this area of social life is enveloped in social change, men still dominate the social institutions of the Western world: law, politics, business, religion, education, the military, medicine, science, sports, and in many ways, even the family. In spite of far-reaching social change, women often find themselves in the more backstage, nurturing, and supportive roles—and those roles are generally supportive of the more dominant roles men play.

Why? Is this a consequence of genetic heritage—males and females being born with different predispositions? Or is it due to culture, because males are socialized into dominance? While there is considerable debate on this matter, sociologists side almost unanimously with the proponents of socialization. In this article, Henslin analyzes some of the socialization experiences that place males in a distinctive social world and prepare them for dominance. This selection is an attempt to penetrate the taken-for-granted, behind-the-scenes aspects of socialization into masculine sexuality. You might find it useful to contrast your experiences in growing up with those the author describes.

ACCORDING TO THE PREVAILING sociological perspective, our masculinity or femininity is not biologically determined. Although our biological or genetic inheritance gives each of us the sex organs of a male or female, how our "maleness" or "femaleness" is expressed depends on what we learn. Our masculinity or femininity, that is, what we are like as sexual beings—our orientations and how we behave as a male or a female—does not depend on biology but on social learning. It can be said that while our gender is part of our biological inheritance, our sexuality (or masculinity or femininity) is part of our social inheritance.

If this sociological position is correct—that culture, not anatomy, is our destiny—how do we become the "way we are"?[1] What factors shape or influence us into becoming masculine or feminine? If our characteristic behaviors do not come from our biology, how do we end up having those that we do have? What is the *process* by which we come to possess behaviors typically associated with our gender? If they *are* learned, how do our behaviors, attitudes, and other basic orientations come to be felt by us as natural and essential to our identity? (And they are indeed essential to our identity.) In what ways is the process of "becoming" related to the social structure of society?

Not only would it take volumes to answer these questions fully, but it would also be impossible, since the answers are only now slowly being unraveled by the researchers. In this short and rather informal article, I will be able only to indicate some of the basics underlying this foundational learning. I will focus exclusively on being socialized into masculinity, and will do this by reflecting on (1) my own experience in "becoming"; (2) my observations as a sociologist of the experiences of others; and (3) what others have shared with me concerning their own experiences. The reader should keep in mind that this article is meant to be neither definitive nor exhaustive, but is designed to depict general areas of male socialization and thereby to provide insight into the acquisition of masculinity in our culture.

In the Beginning . . .

Except for a few rare instances,[2] each of us arrives in this world with a clearly definable physical characteristic that sets us apart from about half the rest of the world. This characteristic makes a literal world of difference. Our parents become excited about whether we have been born with a penis or a vagina. They are usually either happy or disappointed about which organ we possess, seldom feeling neutral about the matter. They announce it to friends, relatives, and often to complete strangers ("It's a boy!" "It's a girl!"). Regardless of how they feel about it, on the basis of our possessing a particular physical organ they purposely, but both consciously and subconsciously, separate us into two worlds. Wittingly and unwittingly, they thereby launch us onto a career that will encompass almost every aspect of our lives—and will remain with us until death.

Colors, Clothing, and Toys

While it is not more masculine or feminine than red, yellow, purple, orange, white, or black, the color blue has become arbitrarily associated with *infantile masculinity.* After what is usually a proud realization that the neonate possesses a penis (which marks him as a member of the overlords of the universe), the inheritor of dominance is wrapped in blue. This color is merely an arbitrary choice, as originally any other would have done as well. But now that the association is made, no other will do. The announcing colors maintain their meaning for only a fairly short period, gradually becoming sexually neutralized.[3] Pink, however, retains at least part of its meaning of sexuality, for even as adults males tend to shy away from it.

Our parents gently and sometimes not so gently push us onto a predetermined course. First they provide clothing designated appropriate to our masculine status. Even as infants our clothing displays sexual significance, and our parents are extremely careful that we never are clothed in either dresses or ruffles. For example, while our plastic panties are designed to keep mothers, fathers, and their furniture and friends dry, our parents make absolutely certain that ours are never pink with white ruffles. Even if our Mom had run out of all other plastic panties, she would rather stay home than take us out in public wearing ruffled pinkies. Mom would probably feel a twinge of guilt over such cross-dressing even in private.[4]

So both Mom and Dad are extremely cautious about our clothing. Generally plain, often simple, and usually sturdy, our clothing is designed to take the greater "rough and tumble" that they know boys are going to give it. They also choose clothing that will help groom us into future adult roles; depending on the style of the period, they dress us in little sailor suits, miniature jogging togs, or two-piece suits with matching ties. Although at this early age we could care less about such things, and their significance appears irrelevant to us, our parents' concern is always present. If during a supermarket expedition even a stranger mistakes our sexual identity, this agitates our parents, challenging their sacred responsibility to maintain the reality-ordering structure of the sex worlds. Such mistaken identification forces them to rethink their activities in proper sex typing, their deep obligation to make certain that their offspring is receiving the right start in life. They will either ascribe the mistake to the stupidity of the stranger or immediately forswear some particular piece of clothing.

Our parents' "gentle nudging" into masculinity does not overlook our toys. These represent both current activities thought sexually appropriate and those symbolic of our future masculinity of courage, competition, and daring. We are given trucks, tanks, and guns. Although our mother might caution us about breaking them, it is readily apparent by her tone and facial expressions that she does not mean what she says. We can continue to bang them together roughly, and she merely looks at us—sometimes quite uncomprehendingly, and occasionally muttering something to the effect that boys will be boys. We somehow perceive her sense of confirmation and we bang them all the more, laughing gleefully at the approval we know it is bringing.

Play and the Sexual Boundaries of Tolerance

We can make all sorts of expressive sounds as we play. We can shout, grunt, and groan on the kitchen floor or roll around in the sandbox. As she shoves us out the door, Mom always cautions us not to get dirty, but when we come in filthy her verbal and gestural disapproval is only mild. From holistic perception, of which by now we have become young masters, we have learned that no matter what Mom's words say, they do not represent the entirety of her feelings.

When we are "all dressed up" before going somewhere, or before company comes, Mom acts differently. We learn that at those times she means what she says about not getting dirty. If we do not want "fire in our pants," we'd better remain clean—at least for a while, for we also learn that after company has come and has had a glimpse of the neat and clean little boy (or, as they say, "the nice little gentleman" or the "fine young man"), we can go about our rough and tumble ways. Pushing, shouting, running, climbing, and other expressions of competition, glee, and freedom then become permissible. We learn that the appearance required at the beginning of a visit is quite unlike that which is passable at the end of the visit.

Our more boisterous and rougher play continues to help us learn the bounds of our parents' tolerance limits. As we continuously test those limits, somewhat to our dismay we occasionally find ourselves having crossed beyond them. Through what is at times painful trial and error, we learn both the limits and how they vary with changed cirucmstance. We eventually learn those edges extremely well and know, for example, precisely how much more we can "get away with" when company comes than when only the immediate family is present, when Mom and Dad are tired or when they are arguing.

As highly rational beings, who are seldom adequately credited by adults for our keen cunning, we learn to calculate those boundaries exceedingly carefully. We eventually come to the point where we know precisely where the brink is—that one more word of back talk, one more quarrel with our brother, sister, or friend, even a small one, or even one more whine will move our parents from words to deeds, and their wrath will fall abruptly upon us with full force. Depending on our parents' orientation to childrearing (or often simply upon their predilection of the moment, for at these times theory tends to fly out the window), this will result in either excruciating humiliation in front of our friends accompanied by horrible (though momentary) physical pain, or excruciating humiliation in front of our friends accompanied by the horrifying (and longer) deprivation of a privilege (which of course we know is really a "right" and is being unjustifiably withheld from us).

On Freedom and Being

As we calculate those boundaries of tolerance (or in the vernacular used by our parents and well understood by us, find out how much they can "stand"), we also learn something about our world vis-à-vis that of those strange female creatures who coinhabit our space. We learn that we can get dirtier, play rougher, speak louder, act more crudely, wander farther from home, stay away longer, and talk back more.

We see that girls live in a world foreign to ours. Theirs is quieter, neater, daintier, and in general more subdued. Sometimes our worlds touch, but then only momentarily. We learn, for example, that while little sisters might be all right to spend an occasional hour with on a rainy afternoon, they are, after all, "only girls." They cannot really enter our world, and we certainly do not want to become part of theirs, with its greater restrictions and fewer challenges. Occasionally, we even find ourselves delighting in this distinction as we taunt them about not being able to do something because it is "not for girls."

If we sometimes wonder about the reason for the differences between our worlds, our curiosity quickly runs its course, for we know deep down that these distinctions are proper. They are *girls*, and, as our parents have told us repeatedly, we are NOT girls. We have internalized the appropriateness of our worlds; some things are right for us, others for them. Seldom are we sorry for the tighter reins placed on girls. We are just glad that we are not one of "them." We stick with "our own kind" and immensely enjoy our greater freedom. Rather than lose ourselves in philosophical reflections about the inequalities of this world (greatly beyond our mental capacities at this point anyway), we lose ourselves in exultation over our greater freedom and the good fortune that made us boys instead of girls.

That greater freedom becomes the most prized aspect of our existence. Before we are old enough to go to school (and later, during summer or weekends and any other nonschool days), when we awaken in the morning we can hardly wait to get our clothes on. Awaiting us is a world of adventure. If we are up before Mom, we can go outside and play in the yard. Before venturing beyond voice distance, however, we have to eat our "wholesome" breakfast, one that somehow is always in the process of "making a man" out of us. After this man-producing breakfast, which might well consist of little more than cereal, we are free to roam, to discover, to experience. There are no dishes to do, no dusting, sweeping, or cleaning. Those things are for sisters, mothers, and other females.

Certainly we have spatial and associational restrictions placed on us, but they are much more generous than those imposed on girls of our age. We know how many blocks we can wander and whom we are allowed to see. But just as significant, we know how to go beyond that distance without getting caught and how to play with the "bad boys" and the "too big boys" without Mom's ever being the wiser. So long as we are home within a certain time limit, in spite of verbal restrictions we really are free to come and go.

We do learn to accept limited responsibility in order to guard our freedom, and we are always pestering other mothers for the time or, when we are able, arranging for them to tell us when it is "just about noon" so we can make our brief appearance for lunch—and then quickly move back into the exciting world of boy activities. But we also learn to lie a lot, finding out that it is better to say anything plausible rather than to admit that we violated the boundaries and be "grounded," practically the worst form of punishment a boy can receive. Consequently, we learn to deny, to avoid, to deceive, to tell half-truths, and to involve ourselves in other sorts of subterfuge rather than to admit violations that might restrict our freedom of movement.

Our freedom is infinitely precious to us, for whether it is cops and robbers or space bandits, the Lone Ranger or Darth Vader, ours is an imaginary world filled with daring and danger. Whether it is six-shooters with bullets or space missiles with laser disintegrators, we are always shooting or getting shot. There are always the good guys and the bad guys. Always there is a moral victory to be won. We are continuously running, shouting, hiding, and discovering. The world is filled with danger, with the inopportune and unexpected lurking just around the corner. As the enemy stalks us, the potential of sudden discovery and the sweet joys of being undetected are unsurpassable. Nothing in adulthood, in spite of its great allure, its challenges and victories yet to be experienced, will ever be greater than this intense bliss of innocence—and part of the joy of this period lies in being entirely unaware of that savage fact of life.

. . . And the Twain Shall Never Meet

Seldom do we think about being masculine. Usually we are just being. The radical social differences that separate us from girls have not gone unnoticed, of course. Rather, these essential differences in life-orientations not only have penetrated our consciousness but have saturated our very beings. Our initial indifference to things male and female has turned to violent taste and distaste. We have learned our lessons so well that we sometimes end up teaching our own mothers lessons in sexuality. For example, we would rather be caught dead than to wear sissy clothing, and our tantrums will not cease until our mothers come to their senses and relent concerning putting something on us that we consider sissified.

We know there are two worlds, and we are grateful for the one we are in. Ours is superior. The evidence continually surrounds us, and we exult in masculine privilege. We also protect our sexual boundaries from encroachment and erosion. The encroachment comes from tomboys who strive to become part of our world. We tolerate them—up to a point. But by excluding them from some activities, we let them know that there are irrevocable differences that forever separate us.

The erosion comes from sissies. Although we are not yet aware that we are reacting to a threat to our developing masculine identity, we do know that sissies make us uncomfortable. We come to dislike them intensely. To be a sissy is to be a traitor to one's very being. It is to be "like a girl," that which we are not—and that which we definitely never will be.

Sissies are to be either pitied or hated. While they are not girls, neither are they real boys. They look like us, but they bring shame on us because they do not represent anything we are. We are everything they are not. Consequently, we separate ourselves from them in the most direct manner possible. While we may be brutal, this breach is necessary, for we must define clearly the boundaries of our own existence—and one way that we know who we are is by knowing what we are not.

So we shame sissies. We make fun of anyone who is not the way he "ought" to be. If he hangs around the teacher or girls during recess instead of playing our rough and tumble games, if he will not play sports because he is afraid of getting dirty or being hurt, if he backs off from a fight, if he cries or whines, or even if he gets too many A's, we humiliate and ridicule him. We gather around him in a circle. We call him a sissy. We say, "Shame! Shame!" We call him gay and queer. We tell him he is a girl and not fit for us.

And as far as we are concerned, he never will be fit for us. He belongs to some strange status, not quite a girl and not quite a boy. Whatever he is, he certainly is not one of us. WE don't cry when we are punished or hurt. WE don't hang around girls. WE are proud of our average grades. WE play rough games. WE are not afraid of getting hurt. (Or if we are, we would never let it show.) WE are not afraid of sassing the teacher—or at least of calling the teacher names when his or her back is turned. We know who we are. We are boys.

The Puberty Shock

We never know, of course, how precarious our sexual identity is. From birth we have been set apart from females, and during childhood we have severely separated ourselves both from females and from those who do not match our standards of masculinity. Our existence is well defined, our world solid. By the end of grade school the pecking order is clear. For good or ill, each of us has been locked into a system of well-honed, peer-determined distinctions, our destiny determined by a heavily defended social order. Our masculine world seems secure, with distinct boundaries that clearly define "us" from "them." We know who we are, and we are cocky about it.

But then comes puberty, and overnight the world undergoes radical metamorphosis. Girls suddenly change. Right before our eyes the flat chests we have always taken for granted begin to protrude. Two little bumps magically appear, and while we are off playing our games, once in a while we cast quizzical glances in the direction of the girls. Witnessing a confusing, haunting change, we shrug off the dilemma and go back to our games.

Then the change hits us. We feel something happening within our own bodies. At first the feeling is vague, undefined. There is no form to it. We just know that something is different. Then we begin to feel strange stirrings within us. These stirrings come on abruptly, and that abruptness begins to shake everything loose in our secure world. Until this time our penis has never given us any particular trouble. It has just "been there," appended like a finger or toenail. It has been a fact of life, something that "we" had and "they" didn't. But now it literally springs to life, taking on an existence of its own and doing things that we once could not even imagine would ever take place. This sometimes creates embarrassment, and there are even times when, called to the blackboard to work out some problem, we must play dumb because of the bulge that we never willed.

It is a new game. The girls in our class are different. We are different. And we never will be the same.

We are forced into new concepts of masculinity. We find this upsetting, but fortunately we do not have to begin from scratch. We can build on our experiences, for mostly the change involves just one area of our lives, girls, and we are able to keep the rest intact. We can still swagger, curse, sweat, get dirty, and bloody ourselves in our games. While the girls still watch us admiringly from the sidelines as we "do our manly thing," we also now watch them more closely as they "do their womanly thing" and strut before us in tight sweaters.

While the girls still admire our toughness, a change is now demanded. At times we must show gentleness. We must be cleaner and watch our language more than before. We must even show consideration. Those shifting requirements are not easy to master, but we have the older, more experienced boys to count on—and they are more than willing to initiate us into this new world and, while doing so, to demonstrate their (always) greater knowledge and skills in traversing the social world.

The Transition into Artificiality

It is with difficulty that we make the transition. A new sexuality is really required, and such radical change could be easy for no one. We already have been fundamentally formed, and what we really learn at this point is to be more adept role-players. We behave one way when we are with the guys. This is the "natural" way, the way we feel. It is relaxed and easy. And we learn to act a different way while we are around girls. This form of presentation we find more contrived and artificial, for it requires greater politeness, consideration, and gentleness. In other words, it is contrary to all that we have previously learned, to all that we have become.

Consequently we hone our acting skills, the ability to put on expected performances. We always have been actors; it is just that we learned our earlier role at a more formative period, and, *having formed us*, this role now provides greater fit. And acting differently while we are around females is nothing new. We have been practicing that since we were at our mother's knee. But now the female expectations are more pressing as our worlds more frequently cross. Although we become fairly skilled at meeting these expectations, they never become part of our being. Always they consist of superficial behaviors added onto what is truly and, by this time, "naturally" us.

This lesson in artificiality reinforces our many exercises in manipulation. We learn that to get what we want, whether that be an approving smile, a caress, a kiss, or more, we must meet the expectations of the one from whom we desire something. We are no strangers to this foundational fact of life, of course, but the masks we must wear in these more novel situations, our uncomfortable gestures and the requisite phrasing, make us awkward strangers to ourselves. We wonder why we are forced into situations that require such constant posing and posturing.

But awkward or not (and as we become more proficient in the game, much of the initial discomfort leaves), we always come back for more. By now sports and games with the fellows are no longer enough. Females seemingly hold the key to our happiness. They can withhold or grant as they see fit. And for favors to be granted, this demanding intersexual game must be played.

The Continuing Masculine World—and Marriage

Eventually we become highly adept players in this intersexual game. We even come to savor our maturing manipulative abilities as the game offers highly stimulating physical payoffs. Our growing skills let us determine if a particular encounter will result in conquest, and thus calculate if it is worth the pursuit. To meet the challenge successfully provides yet another boost to our masculinity.

The hypocrisies and deceits the game requires sometime disturb us. We really want to be more honest than the game allows. But we do not know how to bring that about—and still succeed at the game *and* our masculinity.

Discomforts arising from the game, especially the intimate presence of the female world, must be relieved. Manly activities provide us refuge from this irritant, endeavors in which we men can truly understand one another, where we share a world of aspiration, conflict and competition. Here we can laugh at the same things and talk the way we really feel with much less concern about the words we choose. We know that among men our interests, activities, and desires form an essential part of a shared, self-encapsulating world.

To continue to receive the rewards offered by females, on occasion we must leave our secure world of manliness momentarily to penetrate the conjoint world occupied by our feminine counterparts. But such leave-takings remain temporary, never a "real" part of us. Always waiting for us are the "real" conversations that reflect the "real" world, that exciting realm whose challenging creativity, competition, and conflict help make life worth living.

And we are fortunate in having at our fingertips a socially constructed semi-imaginary masculine world, one we can summon at will to retreat into its beckoning confines. This world of televised football, basketball, wrestling, boxing, hockey, soccer, and car racing is part of the domain of men. At least here is a world, manly and comfortable, that offers us refuge from that threatening feminine world, allowing us to withdraw from its suffocating demands of sharing and intimacy. This semi-imaginary world offers continual appeal because it summons up subconscious feelings from our childhood, adolescence, and, eventually as we grow older, early manhood.

Many of us would not deny that the characteristics we males learn or, if you prefer, the persons we tend to become, fail to provide an adequate basis for developing fulfilling intersexual relationships. But those characteristics, while underlying what is often the shallowness of our relationships with females, are indeed us. They are the logical consequence of our years of learning our culture. We have become what we have been painstakingly shaped to become. Although willing participants in our social destiny, we are heirs of a cultural inheritance that preceded our arrival on the social scene.

Some of us, only with great difficulty, have overcome our masculine socialization into intersexual superficiality and have developed relationships with wives and girlfriends that transcend the confines of those cultural dictates. But such relearning, painfully difficult, comes at a price, leaving in its wake much hurt and brokenness.

Hardly any of this process of becoming a man in our society augurs well for marriage. The separateness of the world that we males join at birth signals our journey into an intricate process whereby we become a specifically differentiated type of being. Our world diverges in almost all respects from the world of females. Not only do we look different, not only do we talk differently and act differently, but our fundamental thinking and orientations to life sharply contrast with theirs. This basic divergence is difficult for females to grasp and, when grasped, is often accompanied by a shudder of disbelief and distaste at the revelatory insight into such dissimilar reality. Yet we are expected to unite permanently with someone from this contradispositional world and, in spite of our essential differences, not only to share a life space but also to join our goals, hopes, dreams, and aspirations.

Is it any wonder, then, that in the typical case men remain strangers to women, women to men, with marriage a crucible of struggle?

Notes

1. The diversity of opinion among sociologists regarding the nature/nurture causes of behavioral differences of males and females is illustrated in *Society* magazine (September/October 1986:4–39). The connection between ideology and theoretical interpretation of data is especially apparent in this heated exchange.

2. Of about one in every 30,000 births, the sex of a baby is unclear. A genetic disorder called congenital adrenal hyperplasis results in the newborn's having parts of both male and female genitals (*St. Louis Globe-Democrat*, March 10–11, 1979, p. 3D).

3. When people (almost exclusively women) are invited to a baby shower and the expectant mother has not yet given birth (or if they wish to take advantage of a sale and buy a gift in advance of the delivery), they find themselves in a quandary. The standard solution to this problem of not knowing the sex of the child (at least in the Midwest) is to purchase either clothing of yellow color or a "sex neutral" item.

4. Duly noted, of course, is the historical arbitrariness and relativity of the gender designation of clothing, with the meaning of ruffles and other stylistic variations depending on the historical period.

12 Sexuality and Gender in Children's Daily Worlds

BARRIE THORNE
ZELLA LURIA

In this selection, two sociologists take children's play seriously and examine its implications for relations between males and females. Their observations are likely to bring back many memories of your childhood. You will also become aware that children's play is not simply play, but has serious sociological meaning—in this instance the fierce maintenance of social boundaries between males and females.

To gather their data, Thorne and Luria studied fourth- and fifth-graders in four schools within three states. They found that the children usually are very careful to separate their friendships and activities on the basis of sex. Girls of this age are more concerned about "being nice," while the interests of boys center on sports and testing the limits of rules. The larger groups into which they band provide each boy a degree of protection and anonymity. The sociological significance of children's play is that both boys and girls are helping to socialize one another into primary adult gender roles, females being more concerned with intimacy, emotionality, and romance, and boys with sexuality. They are writing the "scripts" that they will follow as adults.

THE AMBIGUITIES OF "SEX"—a word used to refer to biological sex, to cultural gender, and also to sexuality—contain a series of complicated questions. Although our cultural understandings often merge these three domains, they can be separated analytically; their interrelationships lie at the core of the social organization of sex and gender. In this paper we focus on the domains of gender and sexuality as they are organized and experienced among elementary school children, especially nine- to eleven-year-olds. This analysis helps illuminate age-based variations and transitions in the organization of sexuality and gender.

We use "gender" to refer to cultural and social phenomena—divisions of labor, activity, and identity which are associated with but not fully determined by biological sex. The core of sexuality, as we use it here, is desire and arousal. Desire and arousal are shaped by and associated with socially learned activities and meanings which Gagnon and Simon (1973) call "sexual scripts." Sexual scripts—defining who does what, with whom, when, how, and what it means—are related to the adult society's view of gender (Miller and Simon, 1981). Nine- to eleven-year-old children are beginning the transition from the gender system of childhood to that of adolescence. They are largely defined (and define themselves) as children, but they are on the verge of sexual maturity, cultural adolescence, and a gender system organized around the institution of heterosexuality. Their experiences help illuminate complex and shifting relationships between sexuality and gender.

First we explore the segregated gender arrangements of middle childhood as contexts for learning adolescent and adult sexual scripts. We then turn from their separate worlds to relations *between* boys and girls, and examine how fourth- and fifth-grade children use sexual idioms to mark gender boundaries. Separate gender groups and ritualized, asymmetric relations between girls and boys lay the groundwork for the more overtly sexual scripts of adolescence.

The Daily Separation of Girls and Boys

Gender segregation—the separation of girls and boys in friendships and casual encounters—is central to daily life in elementary schools. A series of snapshots taken in varied school settings would reveal extensive spatial separation between girls and boys. When they choose seats, select companions for work or play, or arrange themselves in line, elementary school children frequently cluster into same-sex groups. At lunchtime, boys and girls often sit separately and talk matter-of-factly about "girls' tables" and "boys' tables." Playgrounds have gendered spaces: boys control some areas and activities, such as large playing fields and basketball courts; and girls control smaller enclaves like jungle-gym areas and concrete spaces for hopscotch or jump-rope. Extensive gender segregation in everyday encounters and in friendships has been found in many other studies of elementary- and middle-school children. Gender segregation in elementary and middle schools has been found to account for more segregation than race (Schofield, 1982).

Gender segregation is not total. Snapshots of school settings would also reveal some groups with a fairly even mix of boys and girls, especially in games like kickball, dodgeball, and handball, and in classroom and playground activities organized by adults. Some girls frequently play with boys, integrating their groups in a token way, and a few boys, especially in the lower grades, play with groups of girls. In general, there is more gender segregation when children are freer to construct their own activities.

Most of the research on gender and children's social relations emphasizes patterns of separation, contrasting the social organization and cultures of girls' groups with those of boys. In brief summary: Boys tend to interact in larger and more publicly-visible groups; they more often play outdoors, and their activities take up more space than those of girls. Boys engage in more physically aggressive play and fighting; their social relations tend to be overtly hierarchical and competitive. Organized sports are both a central activity and a major metaphor among boys; they use a language of "teams" and "captains" even when not engaged in sports.

Girls more often interact in smaller groups or friendship pairs, organized in shifting alliances. Compared with boys, they more often engage in turn-taking activities like jump-rope and doing tricks on the bars, and they less often play organized sports. While boys use a rhetoric of contests and teams, girls describe their relations using language which stresses cooperation and "being nice." But the rhetorics of either group should not be taken for the full reality. Girls *do* engage in conflict, although it tends to take more indirect forms than the direct insults and challenges more often found in interactions among boys, and between girls and boys.

Interaction Among Boys

In daily patterns of talk and play, boys in all-male groups often build towards heightened and intense moments, moments one can describe in terms of group arousal with excited emotions. This especially happens when boys violate rules.

Dirty words are a focus of rules, and rule breaking, in elementary schools. Both girls and boys know dirty words, but flaunting of the words and risking punishment for their use was more frequent in boys' than in girls' groups in all the schools we studied. In the middle-class Massachusetts public school, both male and female teachers punished ballplayers for [their dirty words]. But teachers were not present after lunch and before school, when most group-directed play took place. A female paraprofessional, who alone managed almost 150 children on the playground, never intervened to stop bad language in play; the male gym teacher who occasionally appeared on the field at after-lunch recess always did. Boys resumed dirty talk immediately after he passed them. Dirty talk is a staple part of the repertoire of the boys' groups (also see Fine, 1980). Such talk defines their groups as, at least in part, outside the reach of the school's discipline.

Some of the dirty talk may be explicitly sexual, as it was in the Massachusetts public school when a group of five fifth-grade boys played a game called "Mad Lib" (also described in Luria, 1983). The game consisted of a paragraph (in this case, a section of a textbook discussing the U.S. Constitution) with key words deleted, to be filled in by the players. Making the paragraph absurd and violating rules to create excitement seemed to be the goal of the game. The boys clearly knew that their intentions were "dirty": they requested the field observer not to watch the game.

Sports, dirty words, and testing the limits are part of what boys teach boys how to do. The assumption seems to be: dirty words, sports interest and knowledge, and transgression of politeness are closely connected.

RULE TRANSGRESSION: COMPARING GIRLS' AND BOYS' GROUPS

Rule transgression in *public* is exciting to boys in their groups. Boys' groups are attentive to potential consequences of transgression, but, compared with girls, groups of boys appear to be greater risk-takers. Adults tending and teaching children do not often undertake discipline of an entire boys' group; the adults might lose out and they cannot risk that. Girls are more likely to affirm the reasonableness of rules, and, when it occurs, rule-breaking by girls is smaller scale. This may be related to the smaller size of girls' groups and to adults' readiness to use rules on girls who seem to believe in them. It is dubious if an isolated pair of boys (a pair is the model size of girls' groups) could get away with the rule-breaking that characterizes the larger male group. A boy may not have power, but a boys' *group* does. Teachers avoid disciplining whole groups of boys, partly for fear of seeming unfair. Boys rarely identify those who proposed direct transgressions and, when confronted, they claim (singly), "I didn't start it; why should I be punished?"

Boys are visibly excited when they break rules together—they are flushed as they play, they wipe their hands on their jeans, some of them look guilty. The Mad Lib game described above not only violates rules, it also evokes sexual meanings within an all-male group. Arousal is not purely individual; in this case, it is shared by the group. . . . The audience for the excitement is the gender-segregated peer group, where each boy increases the excitement by adding still a "worse" word. All of this takes place in a game ("rules") context, and hence with anonymity despite the close-up contact of the game.

While we never observed girls playing a Mad Lib game of this sort, some of our female students recall playing the game in grade school but giving it up after being caught by teachers, or out of fear of being caught. Both boys and girls may acquire knowledge of the game, but boys repeatedly perform it because their gender groups give support for transgression.

These instances all suggest that boys experience a shared, arousing context for transgression, with sustained gender group support for rule-breaking. Girls' groups may engage in rule-breaking, but the gender group's support for repeated public transgression is far less certain. The smaller size of girls' gender groupings in comparison with those of boys, and girls' greater susceptibility to rules and social control by teachers, make girls' groups easier to control. Boys' larger groups give each transgressor a degree of anonymity. Anonymity—which means less probability of detection and punishment—enhances the contagious excitement of rule-breaking.

The higher rates of contagious excitement, transgression, and limit-testing in boys' groups means that when they are excited, boys are often "playing" to male audiences. The public nature of such excitement forges bonds among boys. This kind of bonding is also evident when boys play team sports, and when they act aggressively toward marginal or isolated boys. Such aggression is both physical and verbal (taunts like "sissy," "fag," or "mental"). Sharing a target of aggression may be another source of arousal for groups of boys.

THE TIE TO SEXUALITY IN MALES

When Gagnon and Simon (1973) argued that there are gender-differentiated sexual scripts in adolescence, they implied what our observations suggest: the gender arrangements and subcultures of middle childhood prepare the way for the sexual scripts of adolescence. Fifth and sixth grade boys share pornography, in the form of soft-core magazines like *Playboy* and *Penthouse*, with great care to avoid confiscation. Like the Mad Lib games with their forbidden content, soft-core magazines are also shared in all-male contexts, providing explicit knowledge about what is considered sexually arousing and about attitudes and fantasies. Since pornography is typically forbidden for children in both schools and families, this secret sharing occurs in a context of rule-breaking.

While many theorists since Freud have stressed the importance of boys loosening ties and identification with females (as mother surrogates), few theorists have questioned why "communally-aroused" males do not uniformly bond sexually to other males. If the male groups of fifth and sixth grade are the forerunners of the "frankly" heterosexual gender groups of the junior and high school years, what keeps these early groups from open homosexual expression? Scripting in same-gender peer groups may, in fact, be more about gender than about sexual orientation. Boys, who will later view themselves as having homosexual or heterosexual preferences, are learning patterns of masculinity. The answer may also lie in the teaching of homophobia.

By the fourth grade, children, especially boys, have begun to use homophobic labels—"fag," "faggot," "queer"—as terms of insult, especially for marginal boys. They draw upon sexual allusions (often not fully understood, except for their negative and contaminating import) to reaffirm male hierarchies and patterns of exclusion. As "fag" talk increases, relaxed and cuddling patterns of touch decrease among boys. Kindergarten and first-grade boys touch one another frequently and with ease, with arms around shoulders, hugs, and holding hands. By fifth grade, touch among boys becomes more constrained, gradually shifting to mock violence and the use of poking, shoving, and ritual gestures like "give five" (flat hand slaps) to express bonding. The tough surface of boys' friendships is no longer like the gentle touching of girls in friendship.

Interaction Among Girls

In contrast with the larger, hierarchical organization of groups of boys, fourth- and fifth-grade girls more often organize themselves in pairs of "best friends" linked in shifting coalitions. These pairs are not "marriages"; the pattern is more one of dyads moving into triads, since girls often participate in two or more pairs at one time. This may result in quite complex social networks. Girls often talk about who is friends with or "likes" whom; they continually negotiate the parameters of friendships.

For example, in the California school, Chris, a fifth-grade girl, frequently said that Kathryn was her "best friend." Kathryn didn't proclaim the friendship as often; she also played and talked a lot with Judy. After watching Kathryn talk to Judy during a transition period in the classroom, Chris went over, took Kathryn aside, and said with an accusing tone, "You talk to Judy more than me." Kathryn responded defensively, "I talk to you as much as I talk to Judy."

In talking about their relationships with one another, girls use a language of "friends," "nice," and "mean." They talk about who is most and least "liked," which anticipates the concern about "popularity" found among junior high and high school girls (Eder, 1985). Since relationships sometimes break off, girls hedge bets by structuring networks of potential friends. The activity of constructing and breaking dyads is often carried out through talk with third parties. Some of these processes are evident in a sequence recorded in a Massachusetts school:

> The fifth-grade girls, Flo and Pauline, spoke of themselves as "best friends," while Flo said she was "sort of friends" with Doris. When a lengthy illness kept Pauline out of school, Flo spent more time with Doris. One day Doris abruptly broke off her friendship with Flo and began criticizing her to other girls. Flo, who felt very badly, went around asking others in their network, "What did I do? Why is Doris being so mean? Why is she telling everyone not to play with me?"

On school playgrounds girls are less likely than boys to organize themselves into team sports. They more often engage in small-scale, turn-taking kinds of play. When they jump rope or play on the bars, they take turns performing and watching others perform in stylized movements which may involve considerable skill. Sometimes girls work out group choreographies, counting and jumping rope in unison, or swinging around the bars. In other synchronized body rituals, clusters of fifth- and sixth-grade girls practice cheerleading routines or dance steps. In interactions with one another, girls often use relaxed gestures of physical intimacy, moving bodies in harmony, coming close in space, and reciprocating cuddly touches. We should add that girls also poke and grab, pin one another from behind, and use hand-slap rituals like "giving five," although less frequently than boys.

In other gestures of intimacy, which one rarely sees among boys, girls stroke or comb their friends' hair. They notice and comment on one another's physical appearance such as haircuts or clothes. Best friends monitor one another's emotions. They share secrets and become mutually vulnerable through self-disclosure, with an implicit demand that the expression of one's inadequacy will induce the friend to disclose a related inadequacy. In contrast, disclosure of weakness among boys is far more likely to be exposed to others through joking or horsing around.

IMPLICATIONS FOR SEXUALITY

Compared with boys, girls are more focused on constructing intimacy and talking about one-to-one relationships. Their smaller and more personal groups provide less protective anonymity than the larger groups of boys. Bonding through mutual self-disclosure, especially through disclosure of vulnerability, and breaking off friendships by "acting mean," teach the creation, sustaining, and ending of emotionally intimate relations. Girls' preoccupation with who is friends with whom, and their monitoring of cues of "nice" and "mean," liking and disliking, teach them strategies for forming and leaving personal relationships. In their interactions girls show knowledge of motivational rules for dyads and insight into both outer and inner realities of social relationships. Occasionally, girls indicate that they see boys as lacking such "obvious" knowledge.

Girls' greater interest in verbally sorting out relationships was evident during an incident in the Massachusetts public school. The fifth-grade boys often insulted John, a socially isolated boy who was not good at sports. On one such occasion during gym class, Bill, a high status boy, angrily yelled "creep" and "mental" when John fumbled the ball. The teacher stopped the game and asked the class to discuss the incident. Both boys and girls vigorously talked about "words that kill," with Bill saying he was sorry for what he said, that he had lost control in the excitement of the game. The girls kept asking, "How could anyone do that?" The boys kept returning to, "When you get excited, you do things you don't mean." Both girls and boys understood and verbalized the dilemma, but after the group discussion the boys dropped the topic. The girls continued to converse, with one repeatedly asking, "How could Bill be so stupid? Didn't he know how he'd make John feel?"

When talking with one another, girls use dirty words much less often than boys do. The shared arousal and bonding among boys which we think occurs around public rule-breaking has as its counterpart the far less frequent giggling sessions of girls, usually in groups larger than three. The giggling often centers on carefully guarded topics, sometimes, although not always, about boys.

The sexually related discourse of girls focuses less on dirty words than on themes of romance. In the Michigan school, first- and second-grade girls often jumped rope to rhymes about romance. A favorite was, "Down in the Valley Where the Green Grass Grows," a saga of heterosexual romance which, with the name of the jumper and a boy of her choice filled in, concludes: ". . . along came Jason, and kissed her on the cheek . . . first comes love, then comes marriage, then along comes Cindy with a baby carriage." In the Michigan and California schools, fourth- and fifth-grade girls talked privately about crushes and about which boys were "cute," as shown in the following incident recorded in the lunchroom of the Michigan school:

> The girls and boys from one of the fourth-grade classes sat at separate tables. Three of the girls talked as they peered at a nearby table of fifth-grade boys, "Look behind you," one said. "Ooh," said the other two. "That boy's named Todd." "I know where my favorite guy is . . . there," another gestured with her head while her friends looked.

In the Massachusetts private school, fifth-grade girls plotted about how to get particular boy–girl pairs together.

As Gagnon and Simon (1973) have suggested, two strands of sexuality are differently emphasized among adolescent girls and boys. Girls emphasize and learn about the emotional and romantic before the explicitly sexual. The sequence for boys is the reverse; commitment to sexual acts precedes commitment to emotion-laden, intimate relationships and the rhetoric of romantic love. Dating and courtship, Gagnon suggests, are processes in which each sex teaches the other what each wants and expects. The exchange, as they point out, does not always go smoothly. Indeed, in heterosexual relationships among older adults, tension often persists between the scripts (and felt needs) of women and of men.

Children's Sexual Meanings and the Construction of Gender Arrangements

Girls and boys, who spend considerable time in gender-separate groups, learn different patterns of interaction which, we have argued, lay the groundwork for the sexual scripts of adolescence and adulthood. However, sexuality is not simply delayed until adolescence. Children engage in sexual practices—kissing, erotic forms of touch, masturbation, and sometimes intercourse. As school-based observers, we saw only a few overt sexual activities among children, mostly incidents of public, cross-gender kissing, surrounded by teasing, chasing, and laughter.

HETEROSEXUAL TEASING AND THE IMPORTANCE OF THIRD PARTIES

The special loading of sexual words and gestures makes them useful for accomplishing non-sexual purposes. Sexual idioms provide a major resource which children draw upon as they construct and maintain gender segregation. Through the years of elementary school, children use with increasing frequency heterosexual idioms—claims that a particular girl or boy "likes," "has a crush on," or is "goin' with" someone from the other gender group.

Children's language for heterosexual relationships consists of a very few, often repeated, and sticky words. In a context of teasing, the charge that a particular boy "likes" a particular girl (or vice versa) may be hurled like an insult. The difficulty children have in countering such accusations was evident in a conversation between the observer and a group of third-grade girls in the lunchroom at the Michigan school:

> Susan asked me what I was doing, and I said I was observing the things children do and play. Nicole volunteered, "I like running when boys chase all the girls. See Tim over there? Judy chases him all around the school. She likes him." Judy, sitting across the table, quickly responded, "I hate him. I like him for a friend." "Tim loves Judy," Nicole said in a loud, sing-song voice.

Sexual and romantic teasing marks social hierarchies. The most popular children and the pariahs—the lowest status, excluded children—are most frequently mentioned as targets of "liking." Linking someone with a pariah suggests shared contamination and is an especially vicious tease.

When a girl or boy publicly says that she or he "likes" someone or has a boyfriend or girlfriend, that person defines the romantic situation and is less susceptible to teasing than those targeted by someone else. Crushes may be secretly revealed to friends, a mark of intimacy, especially among girls. The entrusted may then go public with the secret ("Wendy likes John"), which may be experienced as betrayal, but which also may be a way of testing the romantic waters. Such leaks, like those of government officials, can be denied or acted upon by the original source of information.

Third parties—witnesses and kibbitzers—are central to the structure of heterosexual teasing. The teasing constructs dyads (very few of them actively "couples"), but within the control of larger gender groups. Several of the white fifth graders in the Michigan and California schools and some of the black students in the Massachusetts schools occasionally went on dates, which were much discussed around the schools. Same-gender groups provide launching pads, staging grounds, and retreats for heterosexual couples, both real and imagined. Messengers and emissaries go between groups, indicating who likes whom and checking out romantic interest. By the time "couples" actually get together (if they do at all), the groups and their messengers have provided a network of constructed meanings, a kind of agenda for the pair. As we have argued, gender-divided peer groups sustain different meanings of the sexual. They also regulate heterosexual behavior by helping to define the emerging sexual scripts of adolescence (who "likes" whom, who might "go with" whom, what it means to be a couple).

HETEROSEXUALLY CHARGED RITUALS

Boundaries between boys and girls are also emphasized and maintained by heterosexually charged rituals like cross-sex chasing. Formal games of tag and informal episodes of chasing punctuate life on playgrounds. The informal episodes usually open with a provocation—taunts like "You can't get me!" or "Slobber monster!"; bodily pokes; or the grabbing of possessions like a hat or scarf. The person who is provoked may ignore the taunt or poke, handle it verbally ("Leave me alone!"), or respond by chasing. After a chasing sequence, which may end after a short run or a pummeling, the chaser and chased may switch roles.

Chasing has a gendered structure. When boys chase one another, they often end up wrestling or in mock fights. When girls chase girls, they less often wrestle one another to the ground. Unless organized as a formal game like "freeze tag," same-gender chasing goes unnamed and usually undiscussed. But children set apart cross-gender chasing with special names—"girls chase the boys," "boys chase the girls"; "the chase"; "chasers"; "chase and kiss"; "kiss-chase"; "kissers and chasers"; "kiss or kill"—and with animated talk about the activity. The names vary by region and school, but inevitably contain both gender and sexual meanings.

When boys and girls chase one another, they become, by definition, separate teams. Gender terms override individual identities, especially for the other team: "Help, a girl's chasin' me!"; "C'mon Sarah, let's get that boy"; "Tony, help save me from the girls." Individuals may call for help from, or offer help to, others of their gender. In acts of treason they may also grab someone of their gender and turn them over to the opposing team, as when, in the Michigan school, Ryan grabbed Billy from behind, wrestled him to the ground, and then called, "Hey girls, get 'im."

Names like "chase and kiss" mark the sexual meanings of cross-gender chasing. The threat of kissing—most often girls threatening to kiss boys— is a ritualized form of provocation. Teachers and aides are often amused by this form of play among children in the lower grades. They are more perturbed by cross-gender chasing among fifth- and sixth-graders, perhaps because at those ages some girls "have their development" (breasts make sexual meanings seem more consequential), and because of the more elaborate patterns of touch and touch avoidance in chasing rituals among older children. The principal of one Michigan school forbade the sixth-graders from playing "pom-pom," a complicated chasing game, because it entailed "inappropriate touch."

Cross-gender chasing is sometimes structured around rituals of pollution, such as "cooties," where individuals or groups are treated as contaminating or "carrying germs." Children have rituals for transferring cooties (usually touching someone else and shouting "You've got cooties!"), for immunization (e.g., writing "CV" for "cootie vaccination" on their arms), and for eliminating cooties (e.g., saying "no gives" or using "cootie catchers" made of folded paper. Boys may transmit cooties, but cooties usually originate with girls. One version of cooties played in Michigan is called "girl stain." Although cooties is framed as play, the import may be serious. Female pariahs—the ultimate school untouchables by virtue of gender and some added stigma such as being overweight or from a very poor family—are sometimes called "cootie queens" or "cootie girls." Conversely, we have never heard or read about "cootie kings" or "cootie boys."

In these cross-gender rituals girls are defined as sexual. Boys sometimes threaten to kiss girls, but it is girls' kisses and touch which are deemed especially contaminating. Girls more often use the threat of kissing to tease boys and to make them run away, as in this example recorded among fourth-graders on the playground of the California school:

> Smiling and laughing, Lisa and Jill pulled a fourth-grade boy along by his hands, while a group of girls sitting on the jungle-gym called out, "Kiss him, kiss him." Grabbing at his hair, Lisa said to Jill, "Wanna kiss Jonathan?" Jonathan got away, and the girls chased after him. "Jill's gonna kiss your hair," Lisa yelled.

The use of kisses as a threat is double-edged, since the power comes from the threat of pollution. A girl who frequently uses this threat may be stigmatized as a "kisser."

Gender-marked rituals of teasing, chasing, and pollution heighten the boundaries between boys and girls. They also convey assumptions which get worked into later sexual scripts: (1) that girls and boys are members of distinctive, opposing, and sometimes antagonistic groups; (2) that cross-gender contact is potentially sexual and contaminating, fraught with both pleasure and danger; and (3) that girls are more sexually-defined (and polluting) than boys.

Conclusion

Social scientists have often viewed the heterosexual dating rituals of adolescence—when girls and boys "finally" get together—as the concluding stage after the separate, presumably non-sexual, boys' and girls' groups that are so prevalent in childhood. We urge a closer look at the organization of sexuality and of gender in middle and late childhood. The gender-divided social worlds of children are not totally asexual. And same-gender groups have continuing import in the more overtly sexual scripts of adolescence and adulthood.

From an early age "the sexual" is prescriptively heterosexual and male homophobic. Children draw on sexual meanings to maintain gender segregation—to make cross-gender interaction risky and to mark and ritualize boundaries between "the boys" and "the girls." In their separate gender groups, girls and boys learn somewhat different patterns of bonding—boys sharing the arousal of group rule-breaking; girls emphasizing the construction of intimacy, and themes of romance. Coming to adolescent sexual intimacy from different and asymmetric gender subcultures, girls and boys bring somewhat different needs, capacities, and types of knowledge.

References

Eder, Dona (1985). "The cycle of popularity: interpersonal relations among female adolescents." *Sociology of Education 58:* 154–65.

Fine, Gary Alan (1980). "The natural history of preadolescent male friendship groups." Pp. 293–320 in Hugh C. Foot, Antony J. Chapman, and Jean R. Smith (eds.), *Friendship and Social Relations in Children.* New York: Wiley.

Gagnon, John H., and William Simon (1973). *Sexual Conduct.* Chicago: Aldine.

Luria, Zella (1983). "Sexual fantasy and pornography: two cases of girls brought up with pornography." *Archives of Sexual Behavior 11:* 395–404.

Miller, Patricia Y., and William Simon (1981). "The Development of Sexuality in Adolescence." Pp. 383–407 in Joseph Adelson (ed.), *Handbook of Adolescent Psychology.* New York: Wiley.

Schofield, Janet (1982). *Black and White in School.* New York: Praeger.

13 Womanspeak and Manspeak

NANCY HENLEY
MYKOL HAMILTON
BARRIE THORNE

We acquire language early, and with its learning comes a perception of the world. That is, the language we learn does not consist only of words and sounds, and the rules for putting them together. It also contains ways of viewing the self and others, and of expressing those views.

So it also is with our nonverbal language. As noted in the selection by the Halls (article 8), we learn to communicate nonverbally at such an early age that most of it is below our level of awareness. Most of the time we unthinkingly move our bodies, use space, smile, touch, look at others. As we do so, however, our nonverbal language reflects the self and our relationships to others. It also establishes ways of seeing ourselves and others. Only in the last couple of decades have researchers studied such aspects of verbal and nonverbal language.

This selection is an example of how both our research into, and our general sensitivity concerning, this important social area are growing. In it Henley, Hamilton, and Thorne analyze the role of sexism in communication. After a brief review of how our language defines, ignores, and deprecates females, the authors concentrate on nonverbal communication. Note how the communication patterns we learn as children help to maintain male dominance.

A WOMAN STARTS TO SPEAK but stops when a man begins to talk at the same time; two men find that a simple conversation is escalating into full-scale competition; a junior high school girl finds it hard to relate to her schoolbooks, which are phrased in the terminology of a male culture and refer to people as "men"; a woman finds that when she uses the gestures men use for attention and influence, she is responded to sexually; a female college student from an all-girl high school finds a touch or glance from males in class intimidating.

What is happening here? First, there are differences between female and male speech styles, and the sexes are often spoken about in different ways. Male nonverbal communication also has certain elements and effects that distinguish it from its female counterpart. Moreover, females and males move in a context of sexual inequality and strongly differentiated behavioral expectations. Because interaction with others always involves communication of some sort, verbal and nonverbal, it is through communication that much of our pattern of sexist interaction is learned and perpetuated. . . .

Language has been used in the past, and is still used, to dehumanize a people into submission; it both reflects and shapes the culture in which it is embedded.

The Sexist Bias of English

Sexism in the English language takes three main forms: It ignores; it defines; it deprecates.

IGNORING

Most of us are familiar with ways in which our language ignores females. The paramount example of this is the masculine "generic," which has traditionally been used to include women as well as men. We are taught to use *he* to refer to someone whose sex is unspecified, as in the sentence, "Each entrant should do his best." We are told that using *they* in such a case ("Everyone may now take their seat") is ungrammatical; yet Bodine (1975) reports that prior to the eighteenth century, *they* was widely used in this way. Grammarians who insist that we use *he* for numerical agreement with the antecedent overlook the disagreement in gender such usage may entail. Current grammars condemn "he or she" as clumsy, and the singular "they" as inaccurate, but expect pupils to achieve both elegance of expression and accuracy by referring to women as *he*. Despite the best efforts of grammarians, however, singular *they* has long been common in informal conversation and is becoming more frequent even in formal speech and writing.

Many people who claim they are referring to both females and males when they use the word *he* switch to the feminine pronoun when they speak of someone in a traditionally feminine occupation, such as homemaker or schoolteacher or nurse, raising questions about the inclusion of females in the masculine pronoun. Although compared to specific masculine reference the masculine "generic" occurs infrequently, it has a high occurrence in many of our lives; MacKay (1983) estimates that highly educated Americans are exposed to it a million times in their lifetimes. . . .

DEFINING

Language both reflects and helps maintain women's secondary status in our society, by defining her and her "place." Man's power to define through naming is illustrated in the tradition of a woman's losing her own name, and taking her husband's, when she marries; the children of the marriage also have their father's name, showing that they too are his possessions. The view of females as possessions is further evidenced in the common practice of applying female names and pronouns to material possessions such as cars ("Fill 'er up!"), machines, and ships. . . .

The fact that our language generally ignores women also means that when it does take note of them, it often defines their status. Thus "lady doctor," "lady judge," "lady professor," "lady pilot" all indicate exceptions to the rule of finding males in these occupations. Expressions like "male nurse" are much less common, because many more occupations are typed as male and because fewer men choose to enter female-typed occupations than vice versa. Even in cases in which a particular field is female-typed, males who enter it often have a term of their own, with greater prestige, such as *chef* or *couturier*. Of course, patterns of usage subtly reinforce our occupational stereotypes; and deeper undertones further reinforce stereotypes concerning propriety and competency. . . .

DEPRECATING

The deprecation of women in the English language can be seen in the connotations and meanings of words applied to male and female things. The very word *virtue* comes from an old root meaning *man*; to be *virtuous* is, literally, to be "manly." Different adjectives are applied to the actions or productions of the different sexes: Women's work may be referred to as *pretty* or *nice*; men's work will more often elicit adjectives like *masterful*, *brilliant*. While words such as *king, prince, lord, father* have all maintained their elevated meanings, the similar words *queen, madam,* and *dame* have acquired debased meanings.

A woman's sex is treated as if it were the most salient characteristic of her being; this is not the case for males. This discrepancy is the basis for much of the defining of women, and it underlies much of the accompanying deprecation. Sexual insult is applied overwhelmingly to women; Stanley (1977), in researching terms for sexual promiscuity, found 220 terms for a sexually promiscuous woman, but only 22 terms for a sexually promiscuous man. Furthermore, trivialization accompanies many terms applied to females. . . . The feminine endings *-ess* and *-ette*, and the female prefix *lady*, are added to many words which are not really male-specific. Thus we have the trivialized terms *poetess, authoress, aviatrix, majorette, usherette*. Male sports teams are given names of strength and ferocity: "Rams," "Bears," "Jets." Women's sports teams often have cute names like "Rayettes," "Rockettes." As Alleen Nilsen (1972) has put it,

> The chicken metaphor tells the whole story of a girl's life. In her youth she
> is a *chick*, then she marries and begins feeling *cooped up*, so she goes to *hen*

parties where she *cackles* with her friends. Then she has her *brood* and begins to *henpeck* her husband. Finally she turns into an *old biddy*. (p. 109)

. . . Recent research on conversational interaction reflects the attempt to conceptualize language not in terms of isolated variables nor as an abstract code, but within contexts of use, looking at features of conversation within the give-and-take of actual talk. Pamela Fishman (1983) analyzed recurring patterns in many samples of the household conversations of three heterosexual couples. Although the women tried more often than the men to initiate conversations, the women succeeded less often because of minimal responses from their male companions. In contrast, the women pursued topics the men raised, asked more questions, and did more verbal support-work than the men. Fishman concluded that the conversations were under male control, but were mainly produced by female work.

Self-Disclosure

Self-disclosure is another variable that involves language but goes beyond it. Research studies have found that women disclose more personal information to others than men do. Subordinates (in work situations) are also more likely to self-disclose than superiors. People in positions of power are required to reveal little about themselves, yet typically know much about the lives of others—perhaps the ultimate exemplar of this principle is the fictional Big Brother.

According to the research of Jack Sattel (1983), men exercise and maintain power over women by withholding self-disclosure. An institutional example of this use of power is the psychiatrist (usually male), to whom much is disclosed (by a predominantly female clientele), but who classically maintains a reserved and detached attitude, revealing little or nothing of himself. Nonemotionality is the "cool" of the professional, the executive, the poker player, the street-wise operator. Smart men—those in power, those who manipulate others—maintain unruffled exteriors. . . .

Nonverbal Communication

Although we are taught to think of communication in terms of spoken and written language, nonverbal communication has much more impact on our actions and reactions than does verbal. One psychological study concluded, on the basis of a laboratory study, that nonverbal messages carry over four times the weight of verbal messages when both are used in interaction. Yet, there is much ignorance and confusion surrounding the subtler nonverbal form, which renders it a perfect avenue for the unconscious manipulation of others. Nonverbal behavior is of particular importance for women, because their socialization to docility and passivity makes them likely targets for subtle forms of social control, and their close contact with men—for example as wives and secretaries—entails frequent verbal and nonverbal interaction with those in power. Additionally, women have been found to be more sensitive than men to nonverbal cues, perhaps because their survival depends upon it. (Blacks have also been shown to be better than whites at interpreting nonverbal signals.) . . .

DEMEANOR

Persons of higher status have certain privileges of demeanor that their subordinates do not: the boss can put his feet on the desk and loosen his tie, but workers must be more careful in their behavior. Also, the boss had better not put her feet on the desk; women are restricted in their demeanor. Goffman (1967) observed that in hospital staff meetings, the doctors (usually male, and always of high status) had the privilege of swearing, changing the topic of conversation, and sitting in undignified positions. They could lounge on the (mostly female) nurses' counter and initiate joking sessions. Attendants and nurses, of lower status, had to be more circumspect in their demeanor. Women are also denied privileges of swearing and sitting in the undignified positions allowed to men; in fact, women are explicitly required to be more cautious than men by all standards, including the well-known double one. This requirement of propriety is similar to women's use of more proper speech forms, but the requirement for nonverbal behavior is much more compelling.

Body tension is another sex-differentiated aspect of demeanor. In laboratory studies of conversation, communicators are more relaxed with lower-status addressees than with higher-status ones, and they are more relaxed with females than with males. Also, males are generally more relaxed than females; females' somewhat tenser postures are said to convey submissive attitudes (Mehrabian 1972).

USE OF SPACE

Women's general bodily demeanor must be restrained and restricted; their femininity is gauged, in fact, by how little space they take up, while masculinity is judged by males' expansiveness and the strength of their flamboyant gestures. Males control both greater territory and greater personal space, a situation associated with dominance and high status in both human beings and animals. Both field and laboratory studies have found that people tend to approach females more closely than males, to seat themselves closer to females and otherwise intrude on their territory, and to cut across their paths. In the larger aspect of space, women are also less likely to have their own room or other private space in the home.

LOOKING AND STARING—EYE CONTACT

Eye contact is greatly influenced by sex. It has been repeatedly found that in interactions, women look more at the other person than men do and maintain mutual eye contact longer. . . . Other writers have observed that rather than stare, women tend more than men to avert the gaze, especially when stared at by men. Public staring, clothing designed to reveal the contours of the body, and public advertising which lavishly flashes women across billboards and through magazines, all make females a highly visible sex. Visual information about women is readily available, just as their personal information is available through greater self-disclosure.

SMILING

The smile is women's badge of appeasement. . . . Women engage in more smiling than men do, whether they are truly happy or not. Research has confirmed this. Erving Goffman (1979) analyzed the depiction of gender in U.S. print advertising and concluded that women's smiles are ritualistic mollifiers; women smile more, and more expansively, than men. The smile is a requirement of women's social position and is used as a gesture of submission. . . . The smile is generally thought to signal to an aggressor that the subordinate individual intends no harm. In many women, and in other subordinate persons, smiling has reached the status of a nervous habit.

TOUCHING

Touching is another gesture of dominance, and cuddling to the touch is its corresponding gesture of submission. Touching is reportedly used by primates to maintain a dominance order, and it is likely that it is used by human beings in the same way. Just as the boss can put a hand on the worker, the master on the servant, the teacher on the student, the business executive on the secretary, so men more frequently put their hands on women, despite a folk mythology to the contrary. . . . Much of this touching goes unnoticed because it is expected and taken for granted, as when men steer women across the street, through doorways, around corners, into elevators, and so on. The male doctor or lawyer who holds his female client's hand overlong, and the male boss who puts his hand on the female secretary's arm or shoulder when giving her instructions, are easily recognizable examples of such everyday touching of women by men. There is also the more obtrusive touching: the "pawing" by sexually aggressive males: the pinching of waitresses and female office and factory workers; and the totally unexpected and unwelcomed tactual familiarity women are subjected to from complete strangers on the street.

Many interpret this pattern of greater touching by males as a reflection of sexual interest and of a greater level of sexuality among men than women. This explanation, first of all, ignores the fact that touching is a status and dominance signal for human and animal groups. . . . It also ignores the findings of sexual research, which gives us no reason to expect any greater sexual drive in males than in females. Rather, males in our culture have more freedom and encouragement to express their sexuality, and they are also accorded more freedom to touch others. Touching carries the connotation of possession when used with objects, and the wholesale touching of women carries the message that women are community property. . . .

INTIMACY AND STATUS IN NONVERBAL GESTURES

There is another side to touching, one which is much better understood: Touching symbolizes friendship and intimacy. To speak of the power dimension of touching is not to rule out the intimacy dimension. A particular touch may have both components and more, but it is the *pattern* of touching between two individuals that tells us most about their relationship. When touching is symmetrical—that is, when both parties have equal touching privileges—it conveys information about the *intimacy* dimension of the relationship: much touching indicates closeness, and little touching indicates distance. When one party is free to touch the other but not vice versa, we gain information about the *status*, or power, dimension: the person with greater touching privileges is of higher status or has more power. Even when there is mutual touching between two people, it is most likely to be initiated by the higher status person; e.g., in a dating relationship it is usually the male who first puts an arm around the female or begins holding hands.

GESTURES OF DOMINANCE AND SUBMISSION

We have named several gestures of dominance (invasion of personal space, touching, staring) and of submission (allowing oneself to be touched, averting the eyes, and smiling). Pointing may be interpreted as another gesture of dominance, and the corresponding submissive action is to stop talking or acting. In conversation, interruption often functions as a gesture of dominance, and allowing interruption signifies submission. Often mock play between males and females also carries strong physical overtones of dominance: the man squeezing the woman too hard, "pretending" to twist her arm, playfully lifting her and tossing her from man to man, chasing, catching and spanking her. This type of "play" is also frequently used to control children and to maintain a status hierarchy among male teenagers.

Breaking the Mold—a First Step

Women can reverse these nonverbal interaction patterns with probably greater effect than can be achieved through deliberate efforts to alter speech patterns. Women can stop smiling unless they are happy, stop lowering their eyes, stop getting out of men's way on the street, and stop letting themselves be interrupted. They can stare people in the eye, be more relaxed in demeanor (when they realize it is more a reflection of status than of morality), and touch when they feel it is appropriate. Men can likewise become aware of what they are signifying nonverbally. They can restrain their invasions of personal space, touching (if it's not mutual), and interrupting. They may also benefit by losing their cool and feeling free to display their more tender emotions. Males and females who have responsibility for socializing the next generation—that is, parents and teachers particularly—should be especially aware of what they are teaching children about dominance, power, and privilege through nonverbal communication.

References

Bodine, A. (1975). Androcentrism in prescriptive grammar. Singular "they," sex-indefinite "he," and "he or she." *Lang. in Soc., 4:* 129–146.

Fishman, P. (1983). Interaction: The work women do. In B. Thorne, C. Kramarae, & N. Henley, Eds., *Language, gender and society.* Rowley, MA: Newbury House.

Goffman, E. (1967). The nature of deferences and demeanor. In *Interaction ritual* (pp. 47–95). New York: Anchor.

Goffman, E. (1979). *Gender advertisements.* New York: Harper & Row.

MacKay, D. G. (1983). Prescriptive grammar and the pronoun problem. In B. Thorne, C. Kramarae, & N. Henley, Eds., *Language, gender and society.* Rowley, MA: Newberry House.

Mehrabian, A. (1972). *Nonverbal Communication.* Chicago: Aldine Atherton.

Nilsen, A. P. (1972). Sexism in English: A feminist view. In N. Hoffman, C. Secor, and A. Tinsley, Eds., *Female Studies VI* (pp. 102–09). Old Westbury, NY: Feminist Press.

Sattel, J. (1983). Men, inexpressiveness, and power. In B. Thorne, C. Kramarae, & N. Henley, Eds., *Language, gender and society.* Rowley, MA: Newbury House.

Stanley, J. P. (1977). Paradigmatic Woman: The prostitute. In B. Shores and C. P. Hines, Eds., *Papers in Language Variation* (pp. 303–21). University, AL: University of Alabama Press.

14 Self-Fulfilling Stereotypes

MARK SNYDER

When you hear the word *stereotype*, you are likely to think of something negative—perhaps a teacher sternly warning you not to stereotype others. Stereotyping, however—*in its essential meaning of placing people and objects into classifications*—is indispensable for human interaction. It appears that *to be human is to stereotype*, for part of our humanity is the capacity to generalize from one object to others with similar characteristics. To help us negotiate everyday life, all of us depend on stereotypes—including those who warn us against stereotyping!

The problem, then, is not stereotyping, for this we cannot help but do. The problem is that we sometimes classify others into unfair, unflattering categories—what most people mean when they use the term "stereotype." Such negative stereotypes can be very harmful. They set up obstacles that divide group from group and prevent us from entering more fully into relationships with persons who differ from us. In this selection, Snyder even shows that stereotypes can take on a life of their own. Perhaps the most significant statement in his article is: "Stereotypes are not merely beliefs or attitudes that exist in a vacuum; they are reinforced by the behavior of both prejudiced people and the targets of their prejudice."

Perhaps, through awareness of this process (and especially of the finding that *stereotypes socially reproduce their imagery*), we can open our classifications to encompass a broader range of human characteristics. After all, positive stereotypes produce positive traits—and that, for male–female relations, is a gain for us all.

GORDON ALLPORT, THE HARVARD PSYCHOLOGIST who wrote a classic work on the nature of prejudice, told a story about a child who had come to believe that people who lived in Minneapolis were called monopolists. From his father, moreover, he had learned that monopolists were evil folk. It wasn't until many years later, when he discovered his confusion, that his dislike of residents of Minneapolis vanished.

Allport knew, of course, that it was not so easy to wipe out prejudice and erroneous stereotypes. Real prejudice, psychologists like Allport argued, was buried deep in human character, and only a restructuring of education could begin to root it out. Yet many people whom I meet while lecturing seem to believe that stereotypes are simply beliefs or attitudes that change easily with experience. Why do some people express the view that Italians are passionate, blacks are lazy, Jews materialistic, or lesbians mannish in their demeanor? In the popular view, it is because they have not learned enough about the diversity among these groups and have not had enough contact with members of the groups for their stereotypes to be challenged by reality. With more experience, it is presumed, most people of good will are likely to revise their stereotypes.

My research over the past decade convinces me that there is little justification for such optimism—and not only for the reasons given by Allport. While it is true that deep prejudice is often based on the needs of pathological character structure, stereotypes are obviously quite common even among fairly normal individuals. When people first meet others, they cannot help noticing certain highly visible and distinctive characteristics: sex, race, physical appearance, and the like. Despite people's best intentions, their initial impressions of others are shaped by their assumptions about such characteristics.

What is critical, however, is that these assumptions are not merely beliefs or attitudes that exist in a vacuum; they are reinforced by the behavior of both prejudiced people and the targets of their prejudice. In recent years, psychologists have collected considerable laboratory evidence about the processes that strengthen stereotypes and put them beyond the reach of reason and good will.

My own studies initially focused on first encounters between strangers. It did not take long to discover, for example, that people have very different ways of treating those whom they regard as physically attractive and those whom they consider physically unattractive, and that these differences tend to bring out precisely those kinds of behavior that fit with stereotypes about attractiveness.

In an experiment that I conducted with my colleagues Elizabeth Decker Tanke and Ellen Berscheid, pairs of college-age men and women met and became acquainted in telephone conversations. Before the conversations began, each man received a Polaroid snapshot, presumably taken just moments before, of the woman he would soon meet. The photograph, which had actually been prepared before the experiment began, showed either a physically attractive woman or a physically unattractive one. By randomly choosing which picture to use for each conversation, we insured that there was no consistent relationship between the attractiveness of the woman in the picture and the attractiveness of the woman in the conversation.

By questioning the men, we learned that even before the conversations began, stereotypes about physical attractiveness came into play. Men who looked forward to talking with physically attractive women said that they expected to meet decidedly sociable, poised, humorous, and socially adept people, while men who thought that they were about to get acquainted with unattractive women fashioned images of rather unsociable, awkward, serious, and socially inept creatures. Moreover, the men proved to have very different styles of getting acquainted with women whom they thought to be attractive and those whom they believed to be unattractive. Shown a photograph of an attractive woman, they behaved with warmth, friendliness, humor, and animation. However, when the woman in the picture was unattractive, the men were cold, uninteresting, and reserved.

These differences in the men's behavior elicited behavior in the women that was consistent with the men's stereotyped assumptions. Women who were believed (unbeknown to them) to be physically attractive behaved in a friendly, likeable, and sociable manner. In sharp contrast, women who were perceived as physically unattractive adopted a cool, aloof, and distant manner. So striking were the differences in the women's behavior that they could be discerned simply by listening to tape recordings of the women's side of the conversations. Clearly, by acting upon their stereotyped beliefs about the women whom they would be meeting, the men had initiated a chain of events that produced *behavioral confirmation* for their beliefs.

Similarly, Susan Anderson and Sandra Bem have shown in an experiment at Stanford University that when the tables were turned—when it is women who have pictures of men they are to meet on the telephone—many women treat the men according to their presumed physical attractiveness, and by so doing encourage the men to confirm their stereotypes. Little wonder, then, that so many people remain convinced that good looks and appealing personalities go hand in hand.

Sex and Race

It is experiments such as these that point to a frequently unnoticed power of stereotypes: the power to influence social relationships in ways that create the illusion of reality. In one study, Berna Skrypnek and I arranged for pairs of previously unacquainted students to interact in a situation that permitted us to control the information that each one received about the apparent sex of the other. The two people were seated in separate rooms so that they could neither see nor hear each other. Using a system of signal lights that they operated with switches, they negotiated a division of labor, deciding which member of the pair would perform each of several tasks that differed in sex-role connotations. The tasks varied along the dimensions of masculinity and femininity: sharpen a hunting knife (masculine), polish a pair of shoes (neutral), iron a shirt (feminine).

One member of the team was led to believe that the other was, in one condition of the experiment, male; in the other, female. As we had predicted, the first member's belief about the sex of the partner influenced the outcome of the pair's negotiations. Women whose partners believed them to be men generally chose stereotypically masculine tasks; in contrast, women whose partners believed that they were women usually chose stereotypically feminine tasks. The experiment thus suggests that much sex-role behavior may be the product of other people's stereotyped and often erroneous beliefs.

In a related study at the University of Waterloo, Carl von Baeyer, Debbie Sherk, and Mark Zanna have shown how stereotypes about sex roles operate in job interviews. The researchers arranged to have men conduct simulated job interviews with women supposedly seeking positions as research assistants. The investigators informed half of the women that the men who would interview them held traditional views about the ideal woman, believing her to be very emotional, deferential to her husband, home-oriented, and passive. The rest of the women were told that their interviewer saw the ideal woman as independent, competitive, ambitious, and dominant. When the women arrived for their interviews, the researchers noticed that most of them had dressed to meet the stereotyped expectations of their prospective interviewers. Women who expected to see a traditional interviewer had chosen very feminine-looking makeup, clothes, and accessories. During the interviews (videotaped through a one-way mirror) these women behaved in traditionally feminine ways and gave traditionally feminine answers to questions such as "Do you have plans to include children and marriage with your career plans?"

Once more, then, we see the self-fulfilling nature of stereotypes. Many sex differences, it appears, may result from the images that people create in their attempts to act out accepted sex roles. The implication is that if stereotyped expectations about sex roles shift, behavior may change, too. In fact, statements by people who have undergone sex-change operations have highlighted the power of such expectations in easing adjustment to a new life. As the writer Jan Morris said in recounting the story of her transition from James to Jan: "The more I was treated as a woman, the more woman I became."

The power of stereotypes to cause people to confirm stereotyped expectations can also be seen in interracial relationships. In the first of two investigations done at Princeton University by Carl Word, Mark Zanna, and Joel Cooper, white undergraduates interviewed both white and black job applicants. The applicants were actually confederates of the experimenters, trained to behave consistently from interview to interview, no matter how the interviewers acted toward them.

To find out whether or not the white interviewers would behave differently toward white and black job applicants, the researchers secretly videotaped each interview and then studied the tapes. From these, it was apparent that there were substantial differences in the treatment accorded blacks and whites. For one thing, the interviewers' speech deteriorated when they talked to blacks, displaying more errors in grammar and pronunciation. For another, the interviewers spent less time with blacks than with whites and showed less "immediacy," as the researchers called it, in their manner. That is, they were less friendly, less outgoing, and more reserved with blacks.

In the second investigation, white confederates were trained to approximate either the immediate or the non-immediate interview styles that had been observed in the first investigation as they interviewed white job applicants. A panel of judges who evaluated the tapes agreed that applicants subjected to the nonimmediate styles performed less adequately and were more nervous than job applicants treated in the immediate style. Apparently, then, the blacks in the first study did not have a chance to display their qualifications to the best advantage. Considered together, the two investigations suggest that in interracial encounters, racial stereotypes may constrain behavior in ways that cause both blacks and whites to behave in accordance with those stereotypes.

Rewriting Biography

Having adopted stereotyped ways of thinking about another person, people tend to notice and remember the ways in which that person seems to fit the stereotype, while resisting evidence that contradicts the stereotype. In one investigation that I conducted with Seymour Uranowitz, student subjects read a biography of a fictitious woman named Betty K. We constructed the story of her life so that it would fit the stereotyped images of both lesbians and heterosexuals. Betty, we wrote, never had a steady boyfriend in high school, but did go out on dates. And although we gave her a steady boyfriend in college, we specified that he was more of a close friend than anything else. A week after we had distributed this biography, we gave our subjects some new information about Betty. We told some students that she was now living with another woman in a lesbian relationship; we told others that she was living with her husband.

To see what impact stereotypes about sexuality would have on how people remembered the facts of Betty's life, we asked each student to answer a series of questions about her life history. When we examined their answers, we found that the students had reconstructed the events of Betty's past in ways that supported their own stereotyped beliefs about her sexual orientation. Those who believed that Betty was a lesbian remembered that Betty had never had a steady boyfriend in high school, but tended to neglect the fact that she had gone out on many dates in college. Those who believed that Betty was now a heterosexual tended to remember that she had formed a steady relationship with a man in college, but tended to ignore the fact that this relationship was more of a friendship than a romance.

The students showed not only selective memories but also a striking facility for interpreting what they remembered in ways that added fresh support for their stereotypes. One student who accurately remembered that a supposedly lesbian Betty never had a steady boyfriend in high school confidently pointed to that fact as an early sign of her lack of romantic or sexual interest in men. A student who correctly remembered that a purportedly lesbian Betty often went out on dates in college was sure that these dates were signs of Betty's early attempts to mask her lesbian interests.

Clearly, the students had allowed their preconceptions about lesbians and heterosexuals to dictate the way in which they interpreted and reinterpreted the facts of Betty's life. As long as stereotypes make it easy to bring to mind evidence that supports them and difficult to bring to mind evidence that undermines them, people will cling to erroneous beliefs.

Stereotypes in the Classroom and Work Place

The power of one person's beliefs to make other people conform to them has been well demonstrated in real life. Back in the 1960s, as most people well remember, Harvard psychologist Robert Rosenthal and his colleague Lenore Jacobson entered elementary-school classrooms and identified one out of every five pupils in each room as a child who could be expected to show dramatic improvement in intellectual achievement during the school year. What the teachers did not know was that the children had been chosen on a random basis. Nevertheless, something happened in the relationships between teachers and their supposedly gifted pupils that led the children to make clear gains in test performance.

It can also do so on the job. Albert King, now a professor of management at Northern Illinois University, told a welding instructor in a vocational training center that five men in his training program had unusually high aptitude. Although these five had been chosen at random and knew nothing of their designation as high-aptitude workers, they showed substantial changes in performance. They were absent less often than were other workers, learned the basics of the welder's trade in about half the usual time, and scored a full 10 points higher than other trainees on a welding test. Their gains were noticed not only by the researcher and by the welding instructor, but also by other trainees, who singled out the five as their preferred co-workers.

Might not other expectations influence the relationships between supervisors and workers? For example, supervisors who believe that men are better suited to some jobs and women to others may treat their workers (wittingly or unwittingly) in ways that encourage them to perform their jobs in accordance with stereotypes about differences between men and women. These same stereotypes may determine who gets which job in the first place. Perhaps some personnel managers allow stereotypes to influence, subtly or not so subtly, the way in which they interview job candidates, making it likely that candidates who fit the stereotypes show up better than job-seekers who do not fit them.

Unfortunately, problems of this kind are compounded by the fact that members of stigmatized groups often subscribe to stereotypes about themselves. That is what Amerigo Farina and his colleagues at the University of Connecticut found when they measured the impact upon mental patients of believing that others knew their psychiatric history. In Farina's study, each mental patient cooperated with another person in a game requiring teamwork. Half of the patients believed that their partners knew they were patients; the other half believed that their partners thought they were nonpatients. In reality, the nonpatients never knew a thing about anyone's psychiatric history. Nevertheless, simply believing that others were aware of their history led the patients to feel less appreciated, to find the task more difficult, and to perform poorly. In addition, objective observers saw them as more tense, more anxious, and more poorly adjusted than patients who believed that their status was not known. Seemingly, the belief that others perceived them as stigmatized caused them to play the role of stigmatized patients.

Consequences for Society

Apparently, good will and education are not sufficient to subvert the power of stereotypes. If people treat others in such a way as to bring out behavior that supports stereotypes, they may never have an opportunity to discover which of their stereotypes are wrong.

I suspect that even if people were to develop doubts about the accuracy of their stereotypes, chances are they would proceed to test them by gathering precisely the evidence that would appear to confirm them.

The experiments I have described help to explain the persistence of stereotypes. But, as is so often the case, solving one puzzle only creates another. If by acting as if false stereotypes were true, people lead others, too, to act as if they were true, why do the stereotypes not come to *be* true? Why, for example, have researchers found so little evidence that attractive people are generally friendly, sociable, and outgoing and that unattractive people are generally shy and aloof?

I think that the explanation goes something like this: Very few among us have the kind of looks that virtually everyone considers either very attractive or very unattractive. Our looks make us rather attractive to some people but somewhat less attractive to other people. When we spend time with those who find us attractive, they will tend to bring out our more sociable sides, but when we are with those who find us less attractive, they will bring out our less sociable sides. Although our actual physical appearance does not change, we present ourselves quite differently to our admirers and to our detractors. For our admirers we become attractive people, and for our detractors we become unattractive. This mixed pattern of behavior will prevent the development of any consistent relationship between physical attractiveness and personality.

Now that I understand some of the powerful forces that work to perpetuate social stereotypes, I can see a new mission for my research. I hope, on the one hand, to find out how to help people see the flaws in their stereotypes. On the other hand, I would like to help the victims of false stereotypes find ways of liberating themselves from the constraints imposed on them by other members of society.

PART V Social Groups and Social Structure

N̲O ONE IS ONLY A MEMBER OF HUMANITY in general; each of us is also a member of particular social groups. We live in a certain country and in a particular neighborhood. We belong to a family and are members of an ethnic group. Most of us work at a job and have friends, and many of us belong to churches, clubs, and other social organizations. The articles in this Part are meant to sensitize us to how social groups and social structure have far-reaching effects on our own lives. Let us see what some of those effects are.

No fact of social life is more important than group membership. *To belong to a group is to yield to others the right to make certain decisions about our behavior, while assuming obligations to act according to the expectations of those others.* This is illustrated by a parent saying to a teenage daughter or son: "As long as you are living under my roof, you had better be home by midnight." As a member of the family, the daughter or son is expected to conform to the parents' expectations, and in this instance the parents are saying that as long as she or he wants to remain a member of the social group known as the household, her or his behavior must conform to their expectations. So it is with *all* the social groups to which we belong: By our membership and participation in them we relinquish to others at least some control over our own lives.

Those social groups that provide little option to belong or not are called *involuntary memberships* or *associations*. These include our family and the sexual, ethnic, and racial groups into which we are born. In contrast, those social groups to which we choose whether or not to belong are called *voluntary memberships* or *associations*. The Boy and Girl Scouts, professional associations, church groups, clubs, friendship cliques, and work groups

161

are examples. In certain instances we willingly, sometimes even gladly, conform to their rules and expectations in order to become members. In all, we must alter some of our behaviors in order to belong to them and to remain members in good standing.

Of course, not all memberships in voluntary associations involve the same degree of willingness to yield to others a measure of control over our lives; and there even are occasions, as in some occupational situations, when we can hardly bear to be a member of the group but feel that, under the circumstances, we have no choice. *Both* types of membership vitally affect our lives, for our participation in specific social groups shapes our ideas as well as our orientations to life.

It is easy to see that social groups have far-reaching effects on our lives—for, as we saw in Part IV, we would not even be "human" without group membership—but what about the second term that heads the title of this present Part? What does *social structure* mean? By this term, sociologists mean that the various social groups making up our lives are not simply a random collection of components; rather, they are interrelated.

I know that if any term in sociology sounds vague and irrelevant, it is "social structure." This term, however, also refers to highly significant matters—for *the social organization that underlies your life determines your relationships with others.* To better see what this term means, we can note that "social structure" encompasses five "levels." As I summarize them, I shall go from the broadest to the smallest levels. The first two levels are *inter*societal; that is, they refer to international relationships, while the next three levels are *intra*societal; that is, they refer to relationships within a society.

First, on the broadest level, social structure refers to relationships among blocs (or groups) of nations, such as the West's dependence on the Mideast for much of its oil, and the domination of the Third World (the poor, nonindustrialized nations) by the First World (the rich, industrialized nations). The *second* level, the next broadest, refers to relationships between particular nations, such as the extensive role that the United States plays in the Canadian economy. These first two levels—the international dimensions of social structure—sensitize us to relationships based on historical events as well as current balances of power and resources.

The *third* level, also quite broad, refers to how the social institutions *within* a society are related to one another. This level sensitizes us to how political decisions affect the military, how economic change affects families, and the like. The *fourth,* a more medium level, refers to relationships between smaller social groups, such as the relationship between McDonald's and other firms in the fast-food business. The *fifth,* the smallest level, deals with such matters as how people are organized within some particular group—such as an individual's role as leader or follower; or the parents' authority over their young children that empowers them to determine what the children will eat, where they will live, what schools they will attend, and how they are to be disciplined.

Part V, which focuses on the influences of social groups and social structure on our lives, opens with a provocative question. Just how much control do groups have? Because of them, will people even willingly participate in acts that go against their conscience? As Philip Meyer's recounting of the classic experiments of Stanley Milgram illustrates, groups do have such coercive power.

The next three selections focus on city life. Elijah Anderson examines the uneasy coexistence of ghetto dwellers and middle-class gentrifiers (those who are reclaiming an area of the city from the poor). Their interactions, often tense, are marked by social class distinctions—those between the middle class and the poor—as well as by race. James M. Henslin's analysis of fleeting urban interactions, those between cab drivers and passengers, reveals some of the social bases of trust, that component of social life so essential to almost all human life. John R. Coleman's focus on the urban homeless pinpoints the debilitating isolation that sometimes exists in the city.

The final three articles examine interaction in smaller settings. Clifton D. Bryant details cockfights, a surprisingly popular but largely invisible subterranean activity. William E. Thompson turns our attention to the work setting, as he analyzes how workers struggle with the assembly line in the meat-packing industry. Finally, James M. Henslin and Mae A. Biggs use Goffman's dramaturgical model to uncover the means by which nonsexuality is sustained during the vaginal examination.

Except for the opening article, which reports the results of a laboratory experiment, these authors used *participant observation* to gain their information. For many years, Anderson lived in the neighborhood he describes. Henslin drove cabs. Coleman wandered the city streets and slept in shelters for the homeless. Bryant attended cockfights. Thompson worked in a meat-packing plant, and Biggs as a gynecological nurse.

As these researchers *participated* in the lives of the people they were studying, they systematically *observed* what was happening (hence the label participant observation). To gather their data, participant observers sometimes place greater emphasis on observing people, at other times on participating in their lives. Biggs, for example, was a more detached observer of events as she worked as a nurse, while Anderson participated for years in the neighborhood on which he reports. Regardless of whether participation or observation receives the greater emphasis, however, when a researcher reports on observations of a social setting, the term "participant observation" is used to describe this method of studying social life. (Other terms that refer to this technique of studying people are "field research," "ethnographic research," and "qualitiative research.") Largely because of this research method, these authors provide rich, detailed descriptions that, by retaining some of the flavor of the settings, bring the reader close to the events that occurred.

As I stressed in my article on research methods in Part II, a chief concern of sociologists is that they gather accurate information about the people they study. To do this, sociologists try to be objective, to leave their biases behind both when they gather data and as they interpret those data for the book and articles and other reports they write. A primary distinction between the research methods of sociology is whether they are *quantitative* or *qualitative*. Participant observation is an example of a qualitative method, and is more exploratory or descriptive. Quantitative methods place the emphasis on measuring precise differences between individuals and groups.

Through their training and experience, sociologists come to prefer some particular method of gathering data. They also associate with one another on the basis of the subject matter they are interested in *and* on the basis of the methods of research they employ. Consequently, the qualitative and quantitative approaches to social research have become critical identifiers among sociologists. Although sociologists have their preferences, and sometimes feel strongly about the matter, both qualitative and quantitative methods are valid means with which to gather data about social life.

In this book the emphasis is on studies that use the qualitative approach. I believe that the selections impart the flavor, meanings, and experiences of the groups being studied. As I see it (and as probably does your instructor), this approach best imparts the excitement of sociological discovery.

15 If Hitler Asked You to Electrocute a Stranger, Would You? Probably

PHILIP MEYER

Let's take the title of this selection seriously for a moment. Suppose that Hitler did ask you to electrocute a stranger, would you? "Of course, I wouldn't" is our immediate response. "*I* wouldn't even *hurt* a stranger just because someone asked me, much less electrocute the person."

Such an answer certainly seems reasonable, but unfortunately it may not be true. Consider two aspects of the power of groups over our lives. First, we all do things that we prefer not to—from going to work and taking tests when we really want to stay in bed to mowing the grass or doing the dishes when we want to watch television. Our roles and relationships require that we do them, and our own preferences become less important than fulfilling the expectations of others. Second, at least on occasion, most of us feel social pressures so strongly that we do things that conflict with our morals. Both these types of behavior are fascinating to sociologists, for they indicate how social structure—the way society is organized—shapes our lives.

But electrocute someone? Isn't that carrying the point a little too far? One would certainly think so. The experiments described in this selection, however, indicates that people's positions in groups are so significant that even "nice, ordinary" people will harm strangers upon request. You may find the implications of authority and roles arising from these experiments disturbing. Many of us do.

IN THE BEGINNING, Stanley Milgram was worried about the Nazi problem. He doesn't worry much about the Nazis anymore. He worries about you and me, and, perhaps, himself a little bit too.

Stanley Milgram is a social psychologist, and when he began his career at Yale University in 1960 he had a plan to prove, scientifically, that Germans are different. The Germans-are-different hypothesis had been used by historians, such as William L. Shirer, to explain the systematic destruction of the Jews by the Third Reich. One madman could decide to destroy the Jews and even create a master plan for getting it done. But to implement it on the scale that Hitler did meant that thousands of other people had to go along with the scheme and help to do the work. The Shirer thesis, which Milgram set out to test, is that Germans have a basic character flaw which explains the whole thing, and this flaw is a readiness to obey authority without question, no matter what outrageous acts the authority commands.

The appealing thing about this theory is that it makes those of us who are not Germans feel better about the whole business. Obviously, you and I are not Hitler, and it seems equally obvious that we would never do Hitler's dirty work for him. But now, because of Stanley Milgram, we are compelled to wonder. Milgram developed a laboratory experiment which provided a systematic way to measure obedience. His plan was to try it out in New Haven on Americans and then go to Germany and try it out on Germans. He was strongly motivated by scientific curiosity, but there was also some moral content in his decision to pursue this line of research, which was in turn colored by his own Jewish background. If he could show that Germans are more obedient than Americans, he could then vary the conditions of the experiment and try to find out just what it is that makes some people more obedient than others. With this understanding, the world might, conceivably, be just a little bit better.

But he never took his experiment to Germany. He never took it any farther than Bridgeport. The first finding, also the most unexpected and disturbing finding, was that we Americans are an obedient people: not blindly obedient, and not blissfully obedient, just obedient. "I found so much obedience," says Milgram softly, a little sadly, "I hardly saw the need for taking the experiment to Germany."

There is something of the theater director in Milgram, and his technique, which he learned from one of the old masters in experimental psychology, Solomon Asch, is to stage a play with every line rehearsed, every prop carefully selected, and everybody an actor except one person. That one person is the subject of the experiment. The subject, of course, does not know he is in a play. He thinks he is in real life. The value of this technique is that the experimenter, as though he were God, can change a prop here, vary a line there, and see how the subject responds. Milgram eventually had to change a lot of the script just to get people to stop obeying. They were obeying so much, the experiment wasn't working—it was like trying to measure oven temperature with a freezer thermometer.

The experiment worked like this: If you were an innocent subject in Milgram's melodrama, you read an ad in the newspaper or received one in the mail asking for volunteers for an educational experiment. The job would take about an hour and pay $4.50. So you make an appointment and go to an old Romanesque stone structure on High Street with the imposing name of The Yale Interaction Laboratory. It looks something like a broadcasting studio. Inside, you meet a young, crew-cut man in a laboratory coat who says he is Jack Williams, the experimenter. There is another citizen, fiftyish, Irish face, an accountant, a little overweight, and very mild and harmless looking. This other citizen seems nervous and plays with his hat while the two of you sit in chairs side by side and are told that the $4.50 checks are yours no matter what happens. Then you listen to Jack Williams explain the experiment.

It is about learning, says Jack Williams in a quiet, knowledgeable way. Science does not know much about the conditions under which people learn and this experiment is to find out about negative reinforcement. Negative reinforcement is getting punished when you do something wrong, as opposed to positive reinforcement which is getting rewarded when you do something right. The negative reinforcement in this case is electric shock. You notice a book on the table, titled, *The Teaching-Learning Process*, and you assume that this has something to do with the experiment.

Then Jack Williams takes two pieces of paper, puts them in a hat, and shakes them up. One piece of paper is supposed to say, "Teacher" and the other, "Learner." Draw one and you will see which you will be. The mild-looking accountant draws one, holds it close to his vest like a poker player, looks at it, and says, "Learner." You look at yours. It says, "Teacher." You do not know that the drawing is rigged, and both slips say "Teacher." The experimenter beckons to the mild-mannered "learner."

"Want to step right in here and have a seat, please?" he says. "You can leave your coat on the back of that chair . . . roll up your right sleeve, please. Now what I want to do is strap down your arms to avoid excessive movement on your part during the experiment. This electrode is connected to the shock generator in the next room.

"And this electrode paste," he says, squeezing some stuff out of a plastic bottle and putting it on the man's arm, "is to provide a good contact and to avoid a blister or burn. Are there any questions now before we go into the next room?"

You don't have any, but the strapped-in "learner" does.

"I do think I should say this," says the learner. "About two years ago, I was in the veterans' hospital . . . they detected a heart condition. Nothing serious, but as long as I'm having these shocks, how strong are they—how dangerous are they?"

Williams, the experimenter, shakes his head casually. "Oh, no," he says. "Although they may be painful, they're not dangerous. Anything else?"

Nothing else. And so you play the game. The game is for you to read a series of word pairs: for example, blue-girl, nice-day, fat-neck. When you finish the list, you read just the first word in each pair and then a multiple-choice list of four other words, including the second word of the pair. The learner, from his remote, strapped-in position, pushes one of four switches to indicate which of the four answers he thinks is the right one. If he gets it right, nothing happens and you go on to the next one. If he gets it wrong, you push a switch that buzzes and gives him an electric shock. And then you go on to the next word. You start with 15 volts and increase the number of volts by 15 for each wrong answer. The control board goes from 15 volts on one end to 450 volts on the other. So that you know what you are doing, you get a test-shock yourself, at 45 volts. It hurts. To further keep you aware of what you are doing to that man in there, the board has verbal descriptions of the shock levels, ranging from "Slight Shock" at the left-hand side, through "Intense Shock" in the middle, to "Danger: Severe Shock" toward the far right. Finally, at the very end, under 435- and 450-volt switches, there are three ambiguous X's. If, at any point, you hesitate, Mr. Williams calmly tells you to go on. If you still hesitate, he tells you again.

Except for some terrifying details, which will be explained in a moment, this is the experiment. The object is to find the shock level at which you disobey the experimenter and refuse to pull the switch.

When Stanley Milgram first wrote this script, he took it to 14 Yale psychology majors and asked them what they thought would happen. He put it this way: Out of one hundred persons in the teacher's predicament, how would their break-off points be distributed along the 15- to 450-volt scale? They thought a few would break off very early, most would quit someplace in the middle, and a few would go all the way to the end. The highest estimate of the number out of 100 who would go all the way to the end was three. Milgram then informally polled some of his fellow scholars in the psychology department. They agreed that very few would go to the end. Milgram thought so too.

"I'll tell you quite frankly," he says, "before I began this experiment, before any shock generator was built, I thought that most people would break off at "Strong Shock' or "Very Strong Shock.' You would get only a very, very small proportion of people going out to the end of the shock generator, and they would constitute a pathological fringe."

In his pilot experiments, Milgram used Yale students as subjects. Each of them pushed the shock switches, one by one, all the way to the end of the board.

So he rewrote the script to include some protests from the learner. At first, they were mild, gentlemanly, Yalie protests, but "it didn't seem to have as much effect as I thought it would or should," Milgram recalls. "So we had more violent protestation on the part of the person getting the shock. All of the time, of course, what we were trying to do was not to create a macabre situation, but simply to generate disobedience. And that was one of the first findings. This was not only a technical deficiency of the experiment, that we didn't get disobedience. It really was the first finding: that obedience would be much greater than we had assumed it would be and disobedience would be much more difficult than we had assumed."

As it turned out, the situation did become rather macabre. The only meaningful way to generate disobedience was to have the victim protest with great anguish, noise, and vehemence. The protests were tape-recorded so that all the teachers ordinarily would hear the same sounds and nuances, and they started with a grunt at 75 volts, proceeded through a "Hey, that really hurts," at 125 volts, got desperate with, "I can't stand the pain, don't do that," at 180 volts, reached complaints of heart trouble at 195, an agonized scream at 285, a refusal to answer at 315, and only heartrending, ominous silence after that.

Still, 65 percent of the subjects, 20- to 50-year-old American males, everyday, ordinary people, like you and me, obediently kept pushing those levers in the belief that they were shocking the mild-mannered learner, whose name was Mr. Wallace, and who was chosen for the role because of his innocent appearance, all the way up to 450 volts.

Milgram was now getting enough disobedience so that he had something he could measure. The next step was to vary the circumstances to see what would encourage or discourage obedience. There seemed very little left in the way of discouragement. The victim was already screaming at the top of his lungs and feigning a heart attack. So whatever new impediment to obedience reached the brain of the subject had to travel by some route other than the ear. Milgram thought of one.

He put the learner in the same room with the teacher. He stopped strapping the learner's hand down. He rewrote the script so that at 150 volts the learner took his hand off the shock plate and declared that he wanted out of experiment. He rewrote the script some more so that the experimenter then told the teacher to grasp the learner's hand and physically force it down on the plate to give Mr. Wallace his unwanted electric shock.

"I had the feeling that very few people would go on at that point, if any," Milgram says. "I thought that would be the limit of obedience that you would find in the laboratory."

It wasn't.

Although [years have] gone by, Milgram still remembers the first person to walk into the laboratory in the newly rewritten script. He was a construction worker, a very short man. "He was so small," says Milgram, "that when he sat on the chair in front of the shock generator, his feet didn't reach the floor. When the experimenter told him to push the victim's hand down and give the shock, he turned to the experimenter, and he turned to the victim, his elbow went up, he fell down on the hand of the victim, his feet kind of tugged to one side, and he said, 'Like this, boss?' Zzumph!"

The experiment was played out to its bitter end. Milgram tried it with 40 different subjects. And 30 percent of them obeyed the experimenter and kept on obeying.

"The protests of the victim were strong and vehement, he was screaming his guts out, he refused to participate, and you had to physically struggle with him in order to get his hand down on the shock generator," Milgram remembers. But 12 out of 40 did it.

Milgram took his experiment out of New Haven. Not to Germany, just 20 miles down the road to Bridgeport. Maybe, he reasoned, the people obeyed because of the prestigious setting of Yale University. If they couldn't trust a learning center that had been there for two centuries, whom could they trust? So he moved the experiment to an untrustworthy setting.

The new setting was a suite of three rooms in a run-down office building in Bridgeport. The only identification was a sign with a fictitious name: "Research Associates of Bridgeport." Questions about professional connections got only vague answers about "research for industry."

Obedience was less in Bridgeport. Forty-eight percent of the subjects stayed for the maximum shock, compared to 65 percent at Yale. But this was enough to prove that far more than Yale's prestige was behind the obedient behavior.

[Since the experiments] Stanley Milgram has been trying to figure out what makes ordinary American citizens so obedient. The most obvious answer—that people are mean, nasty, brutish, and sadistic—won't do. The subjects who gave the shocks to Mr. Wallace to the end of the board did not enjoy it. They groaned, protested, fidgeted, argued, and in some cases, were seized by fits of nervous, agitated giggling.

"They even try to get out of it," says Milgram, "but they are somehow engaged in something from which they cannot liberate themselves. They are locked into a structure, and they do not have the skills or inner resources to disengage themselves. . . ."

"The results, as seen and felt in the laboratory," he has written, "are disturbing. They raise the possibility that human nature, or more specifically the kind of character produced in American democratic society, cannot be counted on to insulate its citizens from brutality and inhumane treatment at the direction of malevolent authority. A substantial proportion of people do what they are told to do, irrespective of the content of the act and without limitation of conscience, so long as they perceive that the command comes from a legitimate authority. If, in this study, an anonymous experimenter can successfully command adults to subdue a 50-year-old man and force on him painful electric shocks against his protest, one can only wonder what government, with its vastly greater authority and prestige, can command of its subjects. . . ."

Stanley Milgram has his problems, too. He believes that in the laboratory situation, he would not have shocked Mr. Wallace. His professional critics reply that in his real-life situation he has done the equivalent. He has placed innocent and naive subjects under great emotional strain and pressure in selfish obedience to his quest for knowledge. When you raise this issue with Milgram, he has an answer ready. There is, he explains patiently, a critical difference between his naive subjects and the man in the electric chair. The man in the electric chair (in the mind of the naive subject) is helpless, strapped in. But the naive subject is free to go at any time.

Immediately after he offers this distinction, Milgram anticipates the objection.

"It's quite true," he says, "that this is almost a philosophic position, because we have learned that some people are psychologically incapable of disengaging themselves. But that doesn't relieve them of the moral responsibility."

The parallel is exquisite. "The tension problem was unexpected," says Milgram in his defense. But he went on anyway. The naive subjects didn't expect the screaming protests from the strapped-in learner. But they went on.

"I had to make a judgment," says Milgram. "I had to ask myself, was this harming the person or not? My judgment is that it was not. Even in the extreme cases, I wouldn't say that permanent damage results."

Sound familiar? "The shocks may be painful," the experimenter kept saying, "but they're not dangerous."

After the series of experiments was completed, Milgram sent a report of the results to his subjects and a questionnaire, asking whether they were glad or sorry to have been in the experiment. Eighty-three and seven-tenths percent said they were glad and only 1.3 percent were sorry; 15 percent were neither sorry nor glad. However, Milgram could not be sure at the time of the experiment that only 1.3 percent would be sorry.

Kurt Vonnegut, Jr., put one paragraph in the preface to *Mother Night*, in 1966, which pretty much says it for the people with their fingers on the shock-generator switches, for you and me, and maybe even for Milgram. "If I'd been born in Germany," Vonnegut said, "I suppose I would have *been* a Nazi, bopping Jews and gypsies and Poles around, leaving boots sticking out of snowbanks, warming myself with my sweetly virtuous insides. So it goes."

Just so. One thing that happened to Milgram back in New Haven during the days of the experiment was that he kept running into people he'd watched from behind the one-way glass. It gave him a funny feeling, seeing those people going about their everyday business in New Haven and knowing what they would do to Mr. Wallace if ordered to. Now that his research results are in and you've thought about it, you can get this funny feeling too. You don't need one-way glass. A glance in your own mirror may serve just as well.

16 Streetwise

ELIJAH ANDERSON

Master statuses are those characteristics that cut across an individual's statuses. As noted in the introduction to Part IV, gender is an example of a master status. A woman may be a professor, physician, or laborer, but she is perceived as a *female* professor, a *female* physician, or a *female* laborer. Similarly, ex-con, convicted rapist, multimillionaire, paraplegic, and elderly are master statuses. No matter what else the individual may do in life, their activities are perceived through the screen of these statuses. In this article Elijah Anderson, who did participant observation in a changing neighborhood for 14 years, analyzes how the master status of "young black male" affects interaction.

Anderson lives in the Philadelphia neighborhood he refers to as the Village-Northton. The Village has undergone *gentrification*, a process by which the relatively affluent move into an urban area inhabited by the poor and renovate the buildings. Gentrification increases property values, and the neighborhood becomes too expensive for the poor to remain. Next to the Village is a ghetto, whose high crime rate spills over into the Village. Consequently, for the relatively affluent blacks and whites who are living in the Village, the presence of strangers makes even walking down the street a problem, and the middle class interacts uneasily with the poor. This selection examines public interaction when distrust and the threat of violence enshroud people's relationships.

AN OVERWHELMING NUMBER OF young black males in the Village are committed to civility and law-abiding behavior. They often have a hard time convincing others of this, however, because of the stigma attached to their skin color, age, gender, appearance, and general style of self-presentation. Moreover, most residents ascribe criminality, incivility, toughness, and street smartness to the anonymous black male, who must work hard to make others trust his common decency.

This state of affairs is worth exploring [because] . . . the situation of young black men as a group encapsulates the stigmatizing effect of "negative" status-determining characteristics, in this case gender and race. Because public encounters between strangers on the streets of urban American are by nature brief, the participants must draw conclusions about each other quickly, and they generally rely on a small number of cues. This process is universal, and it unavoidably involves some prejudging—prejudice—but its working out is especially prominent in the public spaces of the Village-Northton. . . .

The residents of the area, including black men themselves, are likely to defer to unknown black males, who move convincingly through the area as though they "run it," exuding a sense of ownership. They are easily perceived as symbolically inserting themselves into any available social space, pressing against those who might challenge them. The young black males, the "big winners" of these little competitions, seem to feel very comfortable as they swagger confidently along. Their looks, their easy smiles, and their spontaneous laughter, singing, cursing, and talk about the intimate details of their lives, which can be followed from across the street, all convey the impression of little concern for other pedestrians. The other pedestrians, however, are very concerned about them. . . .

People, black or white, who are more familiar with the black street culture are less troubled by sharing the streets with young black males. Older black men, for instance, frequently adopt a refined set of criteria. In negotiating the streets, they watch out particularly for a certain *kind* of young black male; "jitterbugs" or those who might belong to "wolf packs," small bands of black teenage boys believed to travel about the urban areas accosting and robbing people.

Many members of the Village community, however, both black and white, lack these more sophisticated insights. Incapable of making distinctions between law-abiding black males and others, they rely for protection on broad stereotypes based on color and gender, if not outright racism. They are likely to misread many of the signs displayed by law-abiding black men, thus becoming apprehensive of almost any black male they spot in public. . . . The "master status-determining characteristic" of race (Hughes 1945) is at work in the most casual street encounter. Becker's application of Hughes's conception of the contradictions and dilemmas of status has special relevance:

> Some statuses, in our society as in others, override all other statuses and have a certain priority. Race is one of these. Membership in the Negro race, as socially defined, will override most other status considerations in most situations; the fact that one is a physician or middle class or female will not protect one from being treated as a Negro first and any of these other things second. The status of deviant (depending on the kind of deviance) is this kind of master status. One receives the status as a result of breaking a rule, and the identification proves to be more important than most others. One will be identified as a deviant first, before other identifications are made. The question raised: "What kind of person would break such an important rule?" And the answer

given: "One who is different from the rest of us, who cannot or will not act as a moral human being and therefore might break other important rules." The deviant identification becomes the controlling one.

Treating a person as though he were generally rather than specifically deviant produces a self-fulfilling prophecy. It sets in motion several mechanisms which conspire to shape the person in the image people have of him. (Becker 1963, 33, 34)

In the minds of many Village residents, black and white, the master status of the young black male is determined by his youth, his blackness, his maleness, and what these attributes have come to stand for in the shadow of the ghetto. . . .

Because public interactions generally matter for only a few crucial seconds, people are conditioned to rapid scrutiny of the looks, speech, public behavior, gender, and color of those sharing the environment. . . . The central strategy in maintaining safety on the streets is to avoid strange black males. The public awareness is color-coded: white skin denotes civility, law-abidingness, and trustworthiness, while black skin is strongly associated with poverty, crime, incivility, and distrust. Thus an unknown young black male is readily deferred to. If he asks for anything, he must be handled quickly and summarily. If he is persistent, help must be summoned.

This simplistic racial interpretation of crime creates a "we/they" dichotomy between whites and blacks. Yet here again the underlying issue is class. . . . Middle-income blacks in the Village, who also are among the "haves," often share a victim mentality with middle-income whites and appear just as distrustful of black strangers. Believing they are immune to the charge of racism, Village blacks make some of the same remarks as whites do, sometimes voicing even more incisive observations concerning "street blacks" and black criminality. . . .

Street Etiquette

A set of informal rules has emerged among residents and other users of the public spaces of the Village. These rules allow members of diverse groups orderly passage with the promise of security, or at least a minimum of trouble and conflict. . . . The process begins something like this. One person sees another walking down the street alone, with another person, or perhaps with a few others. Those seen might be getting out of an unusual car, riding a ten-speed bicycle, walking a dog, strolling on the grounds of a dwelling in the neighborhood, or simply crossing the street at the light or leaving a store carrying groceries. The sight of people engaging in such everyday activities helps to convey what may be interpreted as the usual picture of public life—what residents take for granted.

Skin, color, gender, age, dress, and comportment are important markers that characterize and define the area. Depending on the observer's biases, such specific markers can become the most important characteristics determining the status of those being watched, superseding other meaningful attributes. However, the most important aspect of the situation is simply that the observer takes mental note of the other person: a significant social contact, though usually not a reciprocal one, is made. The person seen, and the category he or she is believed to represent, comes to be considered an ordinary part of the environment.

Although the initial observation is important, it is not the crucial element in "knowing about" others and feeling comfortable. Rather, it helps determine the social context for any other meaningful interactions, whether unilateral or bilateral. It gives users of the streets a sense of whom to expect where and when, and it allows them to adjust their plans accordingly.

The significance of the initial encounter is contingent upon subsequent meetings and interactions. If the person is never seen again, the encounter gradually loses significance. But if the observer sees the person again or meets others who are similar, the initial impression may become stronger and might develop into a theory about the category of people, a working conception of a social type. The strength of such impressions—nurtured and supported through repeated encounters, observations, and talk with other residents—gradually builds.

Background information and knowledge may provide a basis for social connection. A stranger may be seen in one context, then in another, then in a third. In time the observer might say to himself, "I know that person." Certainly he does know the person, if only by sight. He has noticed him many times in various neighborhood contexts, and with each successive encounter he has become increasingly familiar with him and the class he has come to represent. Probably the two are not yet speaking, though they may have exchanged looks that establish the minimal basis for trust. If asked directly, the observer might say, "Yeah, I've seen him around." In this way strangers may know each other and obtain a degree of territorial communion without ever speaking a word. It is quite possible that they will never reach speaking terms.

But there are circumstances where the social gap between visual and verbal interaction in public is pressed and the relationship between incomplete strangers is required to go further. People sometimes feel silly continually passing others they know well by sight without speaking to them. They may resolve their discomfort by greeting to them or by contrived avoidance. If they choose to speak, they may commit themselves to a series of obligatory greetings.

Introductions may also occur when two people who have seen each other in the neighborhood for some time happen to meet in a different part of town; there, despite some awkwardness, they may feel constrained to greet each other like long-lost friends. Perhaps they had not yet reached the point of speaking but had only warily acknowledged one another with knowing looks, or even with the customary offensive/defensive scowl used on the street for keeping strangers at a distance. After this meeting, previously distant Villagers may begin to speak regularly on the neighborood streets. In this way trust can be established between strangers, who may then come to know each other in limited ways or very well.

Just the fact of their regular presence offers a sense of security, or at least continuity, to their neighbors. Thus, many people walk the streets with a confidence that belies their serious concerns. They use those they "know" as buffers against danger. Although they may still be strangers, they feel they can call on each other as allies when neighborhood crises emerge, when they would otherwise be seriously short of help, or when they must protect themselves or their loved ones. For example, during emergencies such as house fires, street crimes in which someone clearly needs help, or some other event where partial strangers have an opportunity to gather and compare notes with neighbors who seemed out of reach before, they may first provide help and only then reach out a hand and introduce themselves, saying, "Hello, my name is . . ."

EYE WORK

Many blacks perceive whites as tense or hostile to them in public. They pay attention to the amount of eye contact given. In general, black males get far less time in this regard than do white males. Whites tend not to "hold" the eyes of a black person. It is more common for black and white strangers to meet each other's eyes for only a few seconds, and then to avert their gaze abruptly. Such behavior seems to say, "I am aware of your presence," and no more. Women especially feel that eye contact invites unwanted advances, but some white men feel the same and want to be clear about what they intend. This eye work is a way to maintain distance, mainly for safety and social purposes. . . .

Many people, particularly those who see themselves as more economically privileged than others in the community, are careful not to let their eyes stray, in order to avoid an uncomfortable situation. As they walk down the street they pretend not to see other pedestrians, or they look right at them without speaking, a behavior many blacks find offensive.

Moreover, whites of the Village often scowl to keep young blacks at a social and physical distance. As they venture out on the streets of the Village and, to a lesser extent, of Northton, they may plant this look on their faces to ward off others who might mean them harm. Scowling by whites may be compared to gritting by blacks as a coping strategy. At times members of either group make such faces with little regard for circumstances, as if they were dressing for inclement weather. But on the Village streets it does not always storm, and such overcoats repel the sunshine as well as the rain, frustrating many attempts at spontaneous human communication.

MONEY

Naturally, given two adjacent neighborhoods representing "haves" and "have-nots," there is tremendous anxiety about money: how much to carry, how to hold it, how to use it safely in public. As in other aspects of Village life, shared anecdotes and group discussions help newcomers recognize the underlying rules of comportment.

Perhaps the most important point of etiquette with regard to money in public places is to be discreet. For example, at the checkout counter one looks into one's wallet or purse and takes out only enough to cover the charge, being careful that the remaining contents are not on display. Further, one attempts to use only small bills so as not to suggest that one has large ones.

When walking on the streets at night, it is wise to keep some money in a wallet or purse and hide the rest in other parts of one's clothing—some in a jacket pocket, some in the back pocket of one's jeans, maybe even some in a sock. In this way one would not lose everything in a mugging, yet the mugger would get something to appease him.

A final rule, perhaps the most critical, is that in a potentially violent situation it is better to lose one's money than one's life. Thus the person who plans to travel at dangerous times or in dangerous areas should have some money on hand in case of an assault:

> It was 9:00 P.M., and the Christmas party had ended. I was among the last to leave. John [a forty-five-year-old professional], the host, had to run an errand and asked if I wanted to go with him. I agreed. While I was waiting, Marsha, John's wife, said in a perfectly serious voice, "Now, John, before you go, do you have $10 just in case you get mugged?" "No, I don't have it, do you?"
>
> Marsha fetched $10 and gave it to John as what was in effect protection money, a kind of consolation prize designed to cool out a prospective mugger. As we walked the three blocks or so on the errand, John said, "We've come two blocks, and it's not so bad." His tone was that of a nervous joke, as though he really half expected to encounter muggers.

The reality of the Village is that residents can make their lives safer by "expecting" certain problems and making plans to cope with them. The mental preparation involved—imagining a bad situation and coming up with the best possible solution, acting it out in one's mind—may well be a valuable tool in learning to behave safely on the streets. . . .

OTHER SAFETY RULES AND STRATEGIES

Dress is an important consideration when walking the Village streets, day or night. Women wear clothing that negates stereotypical "female frailty" and symbolizes aggressiveness. Unisex jackets, blue jeans, and sneakers are all part of the urban female costume. "Sexy" dresses are worn only when women are in a group, accompanied by a man, or traveling by car.

Village men also stick to practical, nonshowy clothing. Most times this means blue jeans or a sweat suit. More expensive clothing is relegated to daytime work hours or, as for females, travel by car.

The safety of cars and things in them is a major worry. Newcomers learn to park on the east-west streets to avoid nighttime vandalism and theft. They buy "crime locks" and hood locks for their cars. They learn, sometimes through painful error, to remove attractive items like tape decks and expensive briefcases, or anything that looks valuable, before they lock up and leave.

Their homes may be similarly barricaded. They sometimes have chains for their bicycles, bars for their first-floor windows, and dead bolts for their back doors. Some install elaborate and expensive burglar alarms or keep dogs for the same purpose. They may build high fences to supplement the quaint waist-high wrought-iron fences from the early 1900s when the wealthy still claimed hegemony in the area.

Watching from the car as companions go into their houses is a standard precaution for city dwellers. The driver idles the motor out front and keeps an eye on the street until the resident has unlocked the door and is safely inside. This common practice has become ritualized in many instances, perhaps more important as a sign of a caring bond between people than as a deterrent of assault. It helps to make people feel secure, and residents understand it as a polite and intelligent action.

But some people are given to overreaction and to overelaboration of "mug-proofing" behaviors and are likely to see a potential mugger in almost anyone with certain attributes, most noticeably black skin, maleness, and youth. A middle-aged white woman told me this story:

> I had a white taxi driver drive me home once, and he was horrified at the neighborhood I lived in. It was night, and he told me what a horrible neighborhood I lived in, speaking of how dangerous it was here. He said, "This neighborhood is full of blacks. You'll get raped, you'll get murdered, or robbed." I replied, "I've lived here for a long time. I really like this neighborhood." He let me out on the opposite side of Thirty-fourth Street. He said, "OK, you go straight in your door, and I'll cover you." And he pulled out a gun. I said, "Please put it away." But he wouldn't. I was scared to death he was going to shoot me or something as I walked toward the house. It was so offensive to me that this man [did this], whom I trusted less than I trusted any of my neighbors, even those I knew only by sight. I felt sick for days.

The woman surmised that the taxi driver "must have been from a white ethnic and working-class background." It is commonly assumed among local blacks that such men feel especially threatened by blacks. But some middle- and upper-middle class whites within the Village are susceptible to similar situational behavior.

Street Wisdom

. . . Street wisdom and street etiquette are comparable to a scalpel and a hatchet. One is capable of cutting extremely fine lines between vitally different organs; the other can only make broader, more brutal strokes. . . .

The streetwise individual thus becomes interested in a host of signs, emblems, and symbols that others exhibit in everyday life. Besides learning the "safety signals" a person might display—conservative clothing, a tie, books, a newspaper—he also absorbs the vocabulary and expressions of the street. If he is white, he may learn for the first time to make distinctions among different kinds of black people. He may learn the meaning of certain styles of hats, sweaters, jackets, shoes, and other emblems of the subculture, thus rendering the local environment "safer" and more manageable. . . .

A primary motivation for acquiring street wisdom is the desire to have the upper hand. It is generally believed that this will ensure safe passage, allowing one to outwit a potential assailant. In this regard a social game may be discerned. Yet is is a serious game, for failing could mean loss of property, injury, or even death. To prevail means simply to get safely to one's destination, and the ones who are most successful are those who are "streetwise." Street wisdom is really street etiquette wisely enacted. . . .

Typically, those generally regarded as streetwise are veterans of the public spaces. They know how to get along with strangers, and they understand how to negotiate the streets. They know whom to trust, whom not to trust, what to say through body language or words. They have learned how to behave effectively in public. Probably the most important consideration is the experience they have gained through encounters with "every kind of stranger." Although one may know about situations through the reports of friends or relatives, this pales in comparison with actual experience. It is often sheer proximity to the dangerous streets that allows a person to gain street wisdom and formulate some effective theory of the public spaces. As one navigates there is a certain edge to one's demeanor, for the streetwise person is both wary of others and sensitive to the subtleties that could salvage safety out of danger.

The longer people live in this locale, having to confront problems on the streets and public spaces every day, the greater chance they have to develop a sense of what to do without seriously compromising themselves.

Further, the longer they are in the area, the more likely they are to develop contacts who might come to their aid, allowing them to move boldly.

This self-consciousness makes people likely to be alert and sensitive to the nuances of the environment. More important, they will project their ease and self-assurance to those they meet, giving them the chance to affect the interaction positively. For example, the person who is "streetdumb," relying for guidance on the most superficial signs, may pay too much attention to skin color and become needlessly tense just because the person approaching is black. A streetwise white who meets a black person will probably just go about his or her business. In both cases the black person will pick up the "vibe" being projected—in the first instance fear and hostility, in the second case comfort and a sense of commonality. There are obviously times when the "vibe" itself could tip the balance in creating the subsequent interaction.

CRISIS AND ADAPTATION

Sometimes the balance tips severely, and the whole neighborhood reacts with shock and alarm. A wave of fear surges through the community when violent crimes are reported by the media or are spread by word of mouth through the usually peaceful Village. One February a young woman, a new mother, was stabbed and left for dead in her home on one of the well-traveled north-south streets. Her month-old baby was unharmed, but it was weeks before the mother, recuperating in the hospital, remembered she had recently given birth. Word of how the stabbing occurred spread up and down the blocks of the Village. Neighbors said the woman often went out her back door to take out the garbage or call in the dog. But to uninitiated newcomers, the brick streets and large yards seem deceptively peaceful. Crises like these leave in their wake a deeper understanding of the "openness" that characterizes this quaint area of the city.

They also separate those who survive by brittle etiquette from those who—despite increased temporary precautions—can continue to see strangers as individuals. Less than half a block away from the scene of the attack, in a building facing an east-west street, a friend of the young mother was overcome with fear. Her husband was scheduled to go out of town the week after the vicious attack on her friend. She was so frightened that he had to arrange for a neighbor to "baby-sit" with his wife and children at night while he was away.

Security all over the Village was tightened for a time. People who used to go in and out, feeding the birds, shoveling walks, visiting their neighbors and friends, no longer came and went so carelessly. As the news traveled, fear rippled out from the young victim's immediate neighbors to affect behavior in other parts of the Village. One young black man reported that after the attack he was greeted with suspicious stares on his way to Mr. Chow's.

"Everyone's looking over their shoulder suddenly," he said. "All black people are suspects."

"It makes you stop and wonder about living here," said one young mother shortly after the stabbing became the main item of conversation. "I've never lived in such a dangerous neighborhood. I run upstairs and leave my back door open sometimes. Like today, I got both kids and took them upstairs, and all of a sudden I said, "Oh, no! I left the door unlocked!' and I just stopped what I was doing and ran downstairs to lock it." This kind of fear-induced behavior occurs as neighbors work out their group perspective on what is possible, if not probable, in the aftermath of such a crime.

Violence causes residents to tense up and begin taking defensive action again. They may feel uncomfortable around strangers on the streets, particularly after dark. They become especially suspicious of black males. An interview with a young black man from the area sheds some light on how residents react to neighborhood blacks shortly after a violent incident:

> People come out of the door and they're scared. So when they see blacks on the streets they try to get away. Even ones who live right next door. All of a sudden they change attitudes toward each other. They're very suspicious. The guy that killed that lady and her husband down on Thirty-fourth in the Villlage, he from the Empire [gang]. He tried to rape the lady right in front of the husband—he stabbed the husband and killed him. He'll get the electric chair now; they gave him the death penalty. They caught him comin' out. Wouldn't been so bad, the cops got another call to next door to where he did it at. She was screamin' and the cops heard and came around to the door.
>
> After that happened, you could feel the vibes from whites. When things like that happen, things get very tense between blacks and whites. And you can feel it in the way they look at you, 'cause they think you might be the one who might do the crime. Everytime they see a black they don't trust 'em. Should stay in their own neighborhood.
>
> That's the Village. They paranoid.

In time the fear recedes. Through successive documentations and neighborhood gossip, Villagers slowly return to some level of complacency, an acceptance of the risks of living in the city. Familiar people on the streets are "mapped" and associated with their old places, much as veteran Villagers have mapped them before. Streets, parks, and playgrounds are again made theirs. When these mental notations remain reliable and undisturbed for a time, a kind of "peace" returns. More and more can be taken for granted. Night excursions become more common. Children may be given a longer tether. Villagers gather and talk about the more pleasant aspects of neighborhood life. But they know, and are often reminded, that the peace is precarious. . . .

References

Becker, Howard S. 1963. *Outsiders: Studies in the sociology of deviance.* New York: Macmillan.

Hughes, Everett C. 1945. Dilemmas and contradictions of status. *American Journal of Sociology* 50:353-59.

17 Trust and Cabbies

JAMES M. HENSLIN

There are two types of participant observation: *overt*, in which the group is aware that a researcher is in their midst, and *covert*, in which the group does not know so. This study was done by covert participation observation. The researcher was known by the other drivers as simply another cabbie. Because they did not know they were being studied, the cabbies did not change their behavior (or expressions of attitudes) in order to match their ideas of what they thought a researcher might expect. Thus covert participant observation allowed full access to both the subtlety and the richness of interaction as it occurred in this natural setting.

When Henslin became a cab driver, he entered an unfamiliar world, a world where many assumptions of what is normal differed from those he had previously experienced. Directly encountering constrasting assumptions of life prodded him to question fundamental aspects of cabbie interaction. As he laid these bare, he was able to examine components of trust, a foundational aspect of our own everyday lives. This analysis is an attempt to share with you what goes into the cab driver's perception of trust or distrust of passengers. Perhaps this analysis will help make more visible some of the background assumptions with which you approach life.

TRUST IS A FUNDAMENTAL ASPECT of anyday/everyday-life-in-society.[1] We all deal with trust all the time. It is with us each day as we go about our regular routines, but it is one of those taken-for-granted aspects of life-in-society that we seldom analyze. At times we may be sharply aware of our distrust of others and be quite verbal in specifying why. At other times we may be only vaguely aware that we are uneasy and distrustful in the presence of a certain person, being unable even to specify the factors that have led to our distrust. There are also occasions when we are very trusting and comfortable in the presence of others, but when we would be "hard put" to explain just why this was so.

We usually miss the subtlety of our own perceptions when it comes to trust. The probable reason is that most of the behavioral cues by which we are judging the "trustability" of others are finely honed characteristics about which we have been socialized since we were children. Although these variables are continually affecting our lives, and we routinely make both important and trivial decisions on the basis of them, they ordinarily lie below the threshold of our awareness.

As such, if we are asked why we didn't trust a particular person, rather than being able to specify the relevant variables, we might more likely say something like, "I just didn't like the looks of him." And it is true that we *didn't* like the looks of him. But what are the variables that go into determining whether we like or do not like the looks of someone? To move in the direction of an answer to this question, we shall examine what trust means for the cab driver, looking specifically at what determines whether cab drivers will accept someone as their passenger.

Definition

Erving Goffman[2] has developed useful concepts concerning the *front* of performers (the expressive equipment that serves to define the situation for the observer) that can be utilized as a conceptual framework in analyzing how cab drivers determine whether an individual can be trusted to become their passenger or not. Goffman states that there are three standard parts to front. The first is a general aspect: the *setting*, which consists of the background items that supply scenery and props for the performance, e.g., furniture, decor, and physical layout. The other two are personal aspects: the individual's *appearance* (the stimuli that tell the observer the individual's social statuses, e.g., clothing), and *manner* (the stimuli that tell the observer the role that someone will play on a particular occasion or the way in which people will play their roles, e.g., being meek or haughty). Goffman adds that the audience ordinarily expects a "fit" or coherence among these standard parts of the front.

Actors are continually offering definitions of themselves to audiences. The audience, by checking the fit of the parts that compose the front of the actor, determines whether it will accept or reject the offered definition. *Trust consists of an actor offering a definition of himself or herself and an audience being willing to interact with the actor on the basis of that definition.* If the audience does not accept the definition of the actor and is not willing to interact with the actor on the basis of the definition that he or she offers, the situation is characterized by *distrust*.

Thus trust, more fully, is conceptualized for our purposes as consisting of:

1. The offering of a definition of self by an actor;
2. Such that when the audience perceives fit between the parts of the front of the actor;

3. And accepts this definition as valid;
4. The audience is willing, without coercion, to engage in interaction with the actor;
5. The interaction being based on the accepted definition of the actor, and;
6. The continuance of this interaction being dependent on the continued acceptance of this definition, or the substitution of a different definition that is also satisfactory to the audience.

Trust and Accepting Someone as a Passenger

The major definition people offer of themselves that cab drivers are concerned with is that of "passenger." In trying to hire a cab, an individual is in effect saying to the cab driver, "I am (or more accurately, I want to be) a passenger"; that is, I will fulfill the role obligations of a passenger. In the driver's view the role obligations of "passenger" include having a destination, being willing to go to a destination for an agreed upon rate, being able and willing to pay the fare, and not robbing or harming the cab driver. If a cab driver accepts someone as a passenger—is interacting with the individual on the basis of this definition—it means, according to our conceptualization, that trust is present.

How does the cab driver know whether it is safe to accept someone's definition of himself or herself as a passenger and interact with that person on the basis of that definition; that is, how does the driver know whether to trust the person? This is our major concern here. We shall now try to explicate what enters into such a decision by the cab driver. The table on pages 186–187 diagrams the variables we shall examine.

Cab drivers typically accept as passengers those to whom they have been dispatched, especially when they are sent to a middle- or upper-class residential area during daylight hours. They are progressively less likely to do so as the time becomes later or as the neighborhood becomes more lower-class or more black. When these three conditions of time, social class, and race are combined, they are least likely to accept someone as a passenger.

From past experiences drivers assume that they are safer as the *neighborhood* becomes "better." This is even more the case when the passenger emerges from the residence to which the driver has been dispatched. Hence the driver assumes that there is a connection between such callers and their point of departure. Responsible people whom one can trust to be "good passengers" live in neighborhoods like these. If callers live in such an area, they are good passengers; if the callers don't actually live there, then they must be known by those who do live in the location from which they are now emerging, so it is unlikely that such individuals would be anything other than good passengers. This latter case illustrates "trackability"; that is,

Variables That, in the Cab Driver's View, Lead to Greater or Lesser Trust of One Who Wants To Be (or Has Become) a Passenger

TRUST	TYPE OF ORDER		TIME
HI	Dispatched order	Regular rider or charge customer	Day
LO	Flag load	Stranger	Night

CHARACTERISTICS OF LOCATION

TRUST	Match with Physical Reality	Social Class	Racial Make-up	Driver's Knowledge of	Illumination and Habitation
HI	Matches (is a location)	(a) Upper class (b) Middle class	White	Known to driver	Light, inhabited area
LO	Doesn't match (is a non-location)	Lower class (poverty area)	Black (ghetto area)	Strange to driver	Dark, deserted area

CHARACTERISTICS OF PASSENGER

TRUST	Social Class	Race	Sex	Age	Sobriety
HI	(a) Upper class (b) Middle class	White	Female	(a) Very old (b) Very young	(a) Sober (b) "High" (c) Drunk (d) Very drunk
LO	Lower class (poverty)	Black	Male	Ages between above	(a) Sober (b) "High" (c) Drunk

TRUST BEHAVIOR OF PASSENGER

	Emergent Behavior	Sitting Behavior Where	Sitting Behavior How	Rationality of Behavior
HI	Seen to emerge from primary location	(a) In rear, diagonal from driver (b) in front	"Open sitting"	Acts rationally
LO	Not seen to emerge from primary location	In rear, behind driver	Sitting that seems to conceal passenger	Acts irrationally

TRUST DISPATCHER

	DISPATCHER	PREVIOUS EXPERIENCE WITH A GIVEN VARIABLE	SUMMARY OF THE VARIABLES OF THIS TABLE
HI	(a) Dispatches order without comment (b) Offers assurance	Positive experience: "Known that can be trusted"	Matches any stereotype the driver has of a trusted category
LO	Dispatches order with a warning	(a) Negative experience: "Known that cannot be trusted" (b) No experience: "Not known whether can be trusted"	Matches any stereotype the driver has of a distrusted category

the riders can be traced back to their point of origin and their association with the residence or with the people who live in that residence. Those who possess the greatest amount of trackability, and in whom the drivers place the greatest trust, are *regular riders* who routinely use cabs in their activities and who consequently become known to the drivers. (In many of these cases, the interaction between cab drivers and regular riders moves into the personal sphere.[3])

However, this is not the case when a driver is dispatched to a potential passenger in a neighborhood where, in the driver's view, less responsible types of people live, people who are not as financially established, who do not own their own homes, and whose trackability is low. The drivers view poor or black neighborhoods as an indication of correspondingly less responsibility and trackability on the part of potential passengers. Accordingly, they trust persons from these origins less, and the likelihood increases that they will be rejected as passengers.

The same is true of *time of day*. A driver feels that daylight provides greater trackability, because it is possible to get a better look at the passenger and to observe much more about him than he is able to at night. This means that he can notice any discrepancies or lack of fit among the parts of the front of the passenger, especially in terms of his appearance and manner. Thus, in a lower-class or black neighborhood the cab driver can "look over good" any potential passenger, whether the passenger has phoned for a cab or is trying to flag down the driver. The driver can observe quickly and well any discrepancies about the potential passenger's manner, and in the case of a flag load, determine whether to stop or not. At night the drivers simply cannot see as well, so that with the lateness of the hour they are progressively less likely to stop for passengers in such areas.

Night and trust work out in practice the following way. A driver will always enter certain neighborhoods at any time of the night or day, for a dispatched order to a residence. These are the upper- and middle-class neighborhoods of the city. They are, however, less likely to accept as a passenger someone who is calling from a phone booth in this area because the trackability is lower, and because the connection between the caller and the residents of that neighborhood becomes more tenuous; that is, it could be anyone calling from a public phone booth, including, and more likely, someone who doesn't belong there.

Drivers will enter some neighborhoods during the day for a dispatched order and also stop for a flag load, yet at night they will enter only for dispatched orders. That is, the drivers assume that one can trust people at night in this neighborhood if there is a call from an apartment for a cab, but not if a person is flagging from the street. In this type of neighborhood, veteran drivers frequently exhort novice drivers to be very careful to observe that their passenger is actually coming from the house to which they were dispatched, and not from an area nearby the house. If the house has a light on inside, then so much the better. (If there is no light on inside, it becomes difficult to tell whether or not the person is actually coming from within the house.)

Finally, there are neighborhoods that drivers will enter for a dispatched order during the day, and perhaps reluctantly stop for flag loads during the day, but that they will not enter at night to pick up any passengers, dispatched or otherwise. This is true of the hard core ghetto of the city studied, St. Louis. The demand for cabs from this area is serviced by a black cab firm.

Sex is another variable used by drivers to size up a passenger. Under almost all circumstances a driver will exhibit greater trust for a female passenger than for a male passenger.[4] The following comment by a driver illustrates this trust of the female:

> I was driving down Union and Delmar about two o'clock this morning, and this woman hollered "Taxi." I wouldn't have stopped at that time in the morning, but I saw it was a woman, so I stopped for her. At least I thought it was a woman. And she gets into the cab, and she turns out to be a guy all dressed up like a woman.

Aside from the humor present in this case, the driver furnishes us with an excellent illustration of the differential trust cab drivers have of females. Union and Delmar is on the fringe of the ghetto, and drivers would ordinarily stop for flag loads during the day there, but not at this time of night. The driver, however, typically stops for a woman in this area at a time when, according to his own statement, he would not think of stopping for a male who was trying to flag him down.

Another determinant of trust is that of *age*. If passengers are quite aged, the driver will trust them. I was unaware of the influence of this variable until the following took place:

> About midnight I was dispatched to an apartment building where I picked up two men who appeared to be in their seventies or eighties. As we drove along I started to count the money that was in my pocket. Ordinarily every time I accumulated five dollars over enough to make change for a ten I would put the excess away to make certain that it would be safe in case of robbery. I thought to myself, "I should put this away," but then I thought, "No, these guys aren't going to rob me." It was at this point that I realized that I felt safe from robbery because of their ages. These men were not too spry; they walked with the aid of canes; and they didn't look as though they were physically able to rob me.[5]

The same applies at the other end of the age continuum; children are more trusted than adults. Very young children, at least, are physically incapable of carrying out a robbery or of harming the driver, and as they become older, until they reach a certain age or size, can do so only with difficulty.

Another relevant personal characteristic is the *degree of sobriety* of the passenger. This variable does not operate by itself, however; it operates rather as a "potentiator."[6] The passenger's degree of sobriety takes on meaning for the driver only in conjunction with other variables. Thus sobriety allows the other variables to retain their meaning, but different levels of intoxication intensify the meaning of the other variables. Passengers who reach a level of intoxication that is described by drivers as "They are high," are more trusted. Such passengers are more likely to increase their tips or be amenable to the driver's suggestions. At the same time, this level of intoxication makes those who do not normally meet the criteria of a passenger even less trusted. The driver views such individuals, when they are "high," as being even more likely than when sober to "try something funny."

When intoxication is greater than "high," and the passengers could be called "drunk," drivers have less trust, regardless of whether they meet the criteria of good passengers or not. This is because of the basic unpredictability of a drunk, or as the drivers say, "Ya don't know what a drunk is gonna do." Yet when intoxication is to the point where the passenger has little control over his or her actions (close to being "dead drunk" or "passed out"), trust again increases. Such persons become defined by drivers as being unable to carry out evil intentions even if they wanted to. The person inebriated to this degree, of course, easily becomes prey for the cab driver.[7]

The *secondary location*, the destination to which the passenger is going, is another variable that determines trust for the cab driver. In the driver's view, the passenger's destination is frequently considered to be part of the passsenger. Thus, if a passenger is going to an area that the driver distrusts, the driver's distrust of the area may be transferred to the passenger who, until giving the destination, had been trusted. That is, if this same passenger were going to a location that the driver trusted, the driver would not give a second thought about this passenger. If everything else is the same— except that the passenger wants to go to an area that the driver doesn't trust—the driver will begin to wonder about the trustworthiness of the passenger, and will begin to question the correctness of the original decision to trust this individual as a passenger. The driver will wonder why the passenger is going into that area, an area that drivers themselves don't like to enter.[8] Usually the reason becomes apparent: sometimes the driver elicits the information, either directly or indirectly, and sometimes the passenger, aware of the driver's concerns, volunteers the information. Usual reasons for this discrepancy involve such things as the passenger's place of residence versus place of work (e.g., a black domestic returning by cab to the ghetto), or continuing relationships with friends and relatives who have not moved out of the ghetto, or "slumming" by persons who are out for kicks that they can't receive in their usual haunts.

Another way that the passenger's destination can communicate distrust to the driver is the driver's perception of the destination as a *non-location;*

that is, there is no "match" between the location given and a corresponding location in physical reality. For example, a street address is given, but the street does not run as far as the number indicates. In this case, too, the driver will seek an explanation for the discrepancy, and many times a plausible explanation exists; for example, the person has read the number incorrectly. If a plausible explanation is not readily available, or if the individual is one for whom low trust exists, this fiction will lead to distrust.

If no specific destination is given, this too can lead to distrust. A passenger telling a driver to "just drive around" is suspect unless there is a satisfactory explanation for this lack of a specific destination: for example, a tourist who wants to see various parts of the city or a woman who wants to be driven around the park because it is a beautiful day. Where the explanation is not readily available, drivers are likely to suspect that the passenger might be setting them up for robbery.

The secondary location also communicates trust. A passenger who gives a destination in a "good" part of town, or an area that the driver already trusts, is less likely to be under the driver's suspicion than in the above case. In some instances, the secondary location can even mitigate distrust that has developed for other reasons. For example:

> It was about 1:00 A.M. I had taken a practical nurse home after her work shift and ended up in part of the ghetto. Since I was next to a stand, I decided to park there. As I was pulling into the space, I saw a man standing at the bus stop which was next to the stand, with his arm held out horizontally and wagging his finger a bit. He was a large black male wearing a dark blue overcoat. He opened the back door of the cab, and my first thought was, "Well, here goes! I'm going to be robbed. I'd better turn on the tape recorder and get this on tape!" After he got into the cab, he said, "I want to go to Richmond Heights. You know where Richmond Heights is?"

Although there was originally a high level of distrust of this passenger, when he gave his destination I was much reassured. My perception at that time of the black community in Richmond Heights was that of a small community of blacks in the midst of middle-class whites, a black community that was "solid," composed of black professional and working people. His destination was "paired" with him, and I figured if he were going to where this class of blacks live, that I did not have to worry about being robbed.

Many variables affect trust that are not as easily analyzable as the above variables. Many of these are subtle interactional cues that communicate much to the driver but that are difficult to explicate. Such a variable is the *sitting behavior* of the passenger. It is possible for passengers to sit in such a way that they communicate "evil intention" to the driver, failing to make their manner fit the rest of their front or their definition of themselves as trustworthy passengers. In the above case, for example:

After I was reassured about this passenger because of his destination, I noticed by means of the mirror that he was sitting in a slumped-over position in the extreme right-hand side of the back seat. It seemed that he could be sitting this way to hide his face from me. I decided to turn around and get a good look at him. I turned around and made some innocuous comment about directions, and as I did I noticed that he was sleeping. When he heard my question his eyes popped open, and he began to respond. It was then obvious that his manner of sitting was due to his sleepiness, and I was again reassured.

Another type of sitting behavior that lessens a driver's trust of passengers concerns single passengers. A single passenger will almost invariably sit on the right-hand side of the back seat (the side diagonal from the driver), or, at times, in the front seat next to the driver. The driver views either of these positions as appropriate for a single passenger. Occasionally, however, a passenger will sit directly behind the driver in the back seat. This ordinarily makes drivers uncomfortable and wary of the passenger; they begin to wonder why the passenger is sitting there. Interaction between the driver and passenger is more difficult in this position, and the cab driver cannot easily keep tabs on what the passenger is doing.

There are additional subtle interaction cues that affect a driver's trust of passengers. They range from somebody's looks (e.g., "sneaky, slitty eyes") to body posture and beyond. Cab drivers interpret and react to others in stereotypical ways on the basis of the symbols to which they have been socialized. It is obvious that there are any number of such cues, gestures, or symbols that lead to trust or distrust. Most of these are beyond the scope of this analysis except to state the obvious: When drivers deal with symbols to which they have feelings of distrust attached, they will distrust the bearer of the symbol, the passenger.

> DISPATCHER: Twenty-third and Choteau. . . .
> DRIVER: ((   ))*
> DISPATCHER: It's fine if you can't. Don't take any chances. . . .
> DRIVER: ((   ))
> DISPATCHER: I don't like the order myself. *I don't like the sound of the man's voice.* . . .

This order was given at 1:10 A.M., and the dispatcher himself was answering incoming calls. According to his statement, there was something about the caller's voice that made him reluctant to dispatch a cab. But what was it about the caller's voice that led him to this reaction? It is this type of variable, though both interesting and important in determining trust, to which our data unfortunately does not lend itself for analysis.

Because dispatchers play a vital role in the communication process

---

* Double parentheses represent statements by the dispatcher to the driver that cannot be heard by other drivers.

of dispatching drivers to passengers, they are important in determining whether a driver will trust a potential passenger to become an actual passenger or not. The above taped conversation concluded with:

> DISPATCHER: No. It is *not* a Missouri Boiler order! It is *not* a Missouri Boiler order! It's a terminal railroad man on Twenty-third and Choteau, on Twenty-third street north of Choteau. . . .
> DRIVER: ((   ))
> DISPATCHER: Let me know if you get the man or if you do not get him. . . . .

The driver, who wants and needs the order at this slack period, tries to tie the order in with the known and trusted. That is, workers getting off the swing shift at Missouri Boiler sometimes take cabs, and they can be trusted. Perhaps this is such an order. But the dispatcher, showing his impatience with the driver's lack of knowledge that the address he gave is not that of Missouri Boiler, tells the driver that it is not that kind of order and the caller should be carefully approached. The dispatcher then does an unusual thing—he makes the dispatcher order optional at the discretion of the driver. Ordinarily a dispatched order becomes a sacred thing to the driver, not an option. It is a responsibility for which drivers assume completion and for which they can be fired if they fail to complete. Yet here in the view of both the cab driver and of the dispatcher, the driver need not accept the responsibility for completing an order when the passenger cannot be trusted.[9]

Dispatchers, when they are able, offer assurance to drivers who do not have enough cues to know whether they can trust a passenger or not. The following example illustrates this:

> DISPATCHER: You have to go in the rear of the court to get in there, Driver. We had that last night, so it's all right. . . .

The dispatcher is assuring the driver that the people waiting are acceptable as passengers; that is, although the driver is reluctant to go in the back, where it is perhaps dark, the dispatcher says that it is all right to do so: this is not a set-up for a robbery. How can the dispatcher give such an assurance? As he states, there had been an order from that location the night before and it turned out to be an acceptable passenger. In this case, the setting, "in the rear of the court at night," did not fit the driver's estimation of acceptability for trusting someone to become a passenger, but, because the dispatcher has had a previous rewarding experience with this lack of fit, he knows that it is all right, and he is able to assure the driver.

The passenger of mine who best incorporated most of the above variables of distrust within a single case and who illustrates other variables that have not been explicated was the following:

About 2:00 A.M. I was dispatched to just within the ghetto, to a hotel which also serves as a house of prostitution. My passenger turned out to be a drunk, elderly, black male, who chose to sit next to me in the front seat. He ordered me to take him to East St. Louis and said, "We're going to a rough neighborhood. Lock your doors. Roll up your windows."

The passenger then began talking to himself. As he did so, I thought he was talking to me, and I said, "What did you say?" He looked up and said, "None of your business!" He then continued talking to himself. As we passed the Atlas Hotel in the 4200 block of Delmar, he made the comment that he should have stopped there and seen someone, but that since we had already passed it I should go on. I said, "No, that's all right. I'll take you there," and I drove around the block to the hotel. He got out and was about to leave when I said, "I'll wait for you, but you'll have to pay what's on the meter." He became rather angry, gave me some money, and then urinated against the side of the cab. I drove on without him.

This man was distrusted because he was a stranger, a male, a black, at night, had been drinking, was coming from the edge of the ghetto, going to a ghetto area, which area was "unknown" to the driver, and acted irrationally by speaking aloud to himself.

The driver has less trust for someone who acts irrationally, just as most members of society would have less trust for someone who exhibited this type of behavior. Because the individual was irrational, predictability of his behavior decreased. TO TRUST SOMEONE MEANS THAT ONE IS PREDICTING THAT PERSON'S BEHAVIOR ON THE BASIS OF ACCEPTANCE OF THAT PERSON'S IDENTITY. This is what cannot be done with someone who does not act as we have learned that "ordinary" persons act.

Cab drivers have less trust for areas that they do not know—that is, areas whose layout they are unfamiliar with—because they cannot easily maneuver their cabs or plan and carry out routes in such areas. Control in such situations passes from the driver to the passenger who possesses such knowledge. *To enter an interaction with someone who possesses the greater control requires trust that the other individual will not use this control to his or her advantage and to one's own disadvantage,* in this case such things as robbery or not paying the fare.

Conclusion

Cabbies will usually accept people's definition of themselves as belonging to the category "passenger," and they almost without exception will do so when they are dispatched to an order. However, under some circumstances, especially flag loads, the cab driver will refuse to allow potential passengers to become passengers and will not let them ride in the cab. In examining how cab drivers differentiate between those whom they allow to become their passengers and those they do not, I have attempted to delineate the variables that go into this foundational aspect of our life-in-society—trust.

Although the specific interaction situation in which trust has been analyzed is that of cab drivers as they go about their daily routines, the import of this analysis extends beyond the cab driver–passenger interaction situation to all life-in-society. The specific variables that lead to trust and distrust change with each situation, but the fundamental principles of evaluating others are the same. Your world is also composed of situations in which people are continually offering you a definition of themselves, and you must, and do, evaluate that definition on the basis of your perception of the fit or misfit among the parts presented that you have learned to associate with that particular front. Your evaluation, like the cabbie's, although perhaps based on differing expectations of parts to be associated with particular fronts, leads to a reaction of trust or distrust. Hopefully, through an analysis of the way trust operates in the cabbie's life, you have gained both a clearer perception of the principles underlying trust in your own social world and a more complete understanding of your reactions to others within that world.

Notes

1. This article is a version of Chapter VI of *The Cab Driver: An Interactional Analysis of An Occupational Culture*, unpublished dissertation, Washington University, 1967: 214–250. A different version has appeared in *Sociology and Everyday Life*, Marcello Truzzi, ed. Englewood Cliffs, NJ: Prentice-Hall, 1968: 138–58.

2. Erving Goffman, *The Presentation of Self in Everyday Life*, Garden City, NY: Doubleday Anchor Books, 1959: 22–30.

3. This is true for Metro Cab even though it does not allow "personals," i.e., passengers who are allowed to phone the company and ask for "my" driver, regardless of spatial rules. Where this is allowed, we would be a step closer to "maximum trust." Personals would be more common in smaller towns, but they also exist in St. Louis with some of the smaller cab companies. A specific type of regular rider is the "charge customer," the passenger who has a charge account with Metro, who, instead of paying cash, fills out and signs a charge slip. Like most charge accounts, such customers are billed monthly by the company.

4. This was evidenced by the incredulity and shock Metro drivers expressed when during the Christmas season of 1964 it was learned that a female passenger had robbed a cab driver.

5. I assume that health would be another such variable; that is, if someone were sick or weak, the driver would have fewer reservations about accepting that person as a passenger. One's perception of health could, of course, be erroneous. The individual could be faking an illness—or even rob due to the needs caused by the illness. Potential passengers can, of course, also be faking their sex (see quotation above), their residence, their social class, and their agedness. But we are here

speaking of the drivers' perceptions as they relate to trust and the acceptance of passengers, not the accuracy of those perceptions.

6. "Potentiate" or "potentiator" is a term used by chemists to refer to a substance that makes the action of other chemicals more powerful or effective or active. It is different from a catalyst because it is consumed in the reaction. I am indebted to Elliott G. Mishler for this analogy.

7. For an analysis of extortive practices of cabbies, see James M. Henslin, "Sex and Cabbies," in *Studies in The Sociology of Sex,* James M. Henslin, ed. New York: Appleton-Century-Crofts, 1971: 192–223.

8. In addition to the ghetto and other lower-class "tough neighborhoods," other areas of the city that will elicit distrust, unless there is an adequate "account" given, are areas of the city that are relatively deserted, especially at night, such as a small back street or a dead-end street with few or no lights, or a warehouse or riverfront section of town.

9. It is again, of course, irrelevant whether the passenger can, in fact, be trusted. It is the driver's perception of trust that matters.

18 Diary of a Homeless Man

JOHN R. COLEMAN

Can you imagine yourself being without a home? Think of what it must be like not to have a house or apartment, not to have your own room or even one you must share with a sibling. No living room with television, no kitchen with a refrigerator you can "raid" whenever you want. Night falls, and you don't know where you'll sleep. Day breaks, and you still have no place to go, nothing to do—and no one who cares.

Such is life for some people in our society—the discards of the advanced technological society, those who have been left behind in our culturally mandated frantic pursuit after material wealth. Like others, Coleman, a college president, had seen these strange people on the streets of the city. Like others, he wondered what their life was like. But unlike most others, he decided to find out first hand—by directly experiencing their world. He left his comfortable, middle-class home and joined the street people. This is his engrossing account of that experience.

Wednesday, 1/19

Somehow, 12 degrees at 6 A.M. was colder than I had counted on. I think of myself as relatively immune to cold, but standing on a deserted sidewalk outside Penn Station with the thought of ten days ahead of me as a homeless man, the immunity vanished. When I pulled my collar closer and my watch cap lower, it wasn't to look the part of a street person; it was to keep the wind out.

My wardrobe wasn't much help. I had bought my "new" clothes—flannel shirt, baggy sweater, torn trousers, the cap and the coat—the day before on Houston Street for $19. "You don't need to buy shoes," the shop-keeper had said. "The ones you have on will pass for a bum's." I was hurt; they were shoes I often wore to the office.

Having changed out of my normal clothes in the Penn Station men's room and stowed them in a locker, I was ready for the street. Or thought so.

Was I imagining it, or were people looking at me in a completely different way? I felt that men, especially the successful-looking ones in their forties and over, saw me and wondered. For the rest, I wasn't there.

At Seventh Avenue and 35th Street, I went into a coffee shop. The counterman looked me over carefully. When I ordered the breakfast special— 99 cents plus tax—he told me I'd have to pay in advance. I did (I'd brought $40 to see me through the ten days), but I noticed that the other customers were given checks, and paid only when they left.

By 9:30, I had read a copy of the *Times* retrieved from a trash basket; I had walked most of the streets around the station; I had watched the construction at the new convention center. There was little else to do.

Later, I sat and watched the drug sales going on in Union Square. Then I went into the Income Maintenance Center on 14th Street and watched the people moving through the welfare lines. I counted the trucks on Houston Street.

I vaguely remembered a quote to the effect that "idleness is only enjoyable when you have a lot to do." It would help to be warm, too.

There was ample time and incentive to stare at the other homeless folk on the street. For the most part, they weren't more interesting than the typical faces on Wall Street or upper Madison Avenue. But the extreme cases caught and held the eye. On Ninth Avenue, there was a man on the sidewalk directing an imaginary (to me) flow of traffic. And another, two blocks away, tracing the flight of planes or birds—or spirits—in the winter sky. And there was a woman with gloves tied to her otherwise bare feet.

Standing outside the Port Authority Bus Terminal was a man named Howard. He was perhaps my age, but the seasons had left deeper marks on his face. "Come summertime, it's all going to be different," he told me. "I'm going to have a car to go to the beach. And I'm going to get six lemons and make me a jug of ice-cold lemonade to go with the car.

"This whole country's gone too far with the idea of one person being at the top. It starts with birthday parties. Who gets to blow out the candle? One person. And it takes off from there. If we're ever going to make things better, we gotta start with those candles."

Was there any chance of people like us finding work?

"Jobs are still out there for the young guys who want them," Howard said. "But there's nothing for us. Never again. No, I stopped dreaming about jobs a long time ago. Now I dream about cars. And lemonade."

Drugs and alcohol are common among the homeless. The damage done by them was evident in almost every street person I saw. But which was cause and which was effect? Does it matter, once this much harm has been done?

My wanderings were all aimless. There was no plan, no goal, no reason to be anywhere at any time. Only hours into this role, I felt a useless part of the city streets. I wasn't even sure why I was doing this. . . .

A weathered drifter told me about a hideaway down in the bowels of the station, where it was warm and quiet. I found my way there and lay down on some old newspapers to sleep.

How long did I sleep? It didn't seem long at all. I was awakened by a flashlight shining in my eyes, and a voice, not an unkind one, saying, "You can't sleep here. Sorry, but you have to go outside."

I hadn't expected to hear that word "sorry." It was touching.

I left and walked up to 47th Street, between Fifth and Madison Avenues, where I knew there was a warm grate in the sidewalk. (I've been passing it every morning for over five years on my way to work.) One man was asleep there already. But there was room for two, and he moved over.

Thursday, 1/20

When you're spending the night on the street, you learn to know morning is coming by the kinds of trucks that roll by. As soon as there are other than garbage trucks—say, milk or bread trucks—you know the night will soon be over.

I went back to Penn Station to clean up in the washroom. The care with which some of the other men with me bathed themselves at the basins would have impressed any public-health officer. And I couldn't guess from the appearance of their clothes who would be the most fastidious.

I bought coffee and settled back to enjoy it out of the main traffic paths in the station. No luck. A cop found me and told me to take it to the street.

After breakfast ($1.31 at Blimpie), I walked around to keep warm until the public library opened. I saw in a salvaged copy of the *Times* that we had just had our coldest night of the year, well below zero with the windchill factor, and that a record 4,635 people had sought shelter in the city's hostels.

The library was a joy. The people there treated me the same as they might have had I been wearing my business suit. To pass the time, I got out the city's welfare reports for 50 years ago. In the winter of 1933, the city had 4,524 beds available for the homeless, and all were said to be filled every night. The parallel to 1983 was uncanny. But, according to the reports, the man in charge of the homeless program in 1933, one Joseph A. Manning, wasn't worried about the future. True, the country was in the midst of a depression. But there had been a slight downturn in the numbers served in the shelters in the two months immediately preceding his report. This meant, wrote Manning, that "the depression, in the parlance of the ring, is K.O.'d."

Already, I notice changes in me. I walk much more slowly. I no longer see a need to beat a traffic light or to be the first through a revolving door. Force of habit still makes me look at my wrist every once in a while.

But there's no watch there, and it wouldn't make any difference if there were. The thermometer has become much more important to me now than any timepiece could be. . . .

The temperature rose during the day. Just as the newspaper headlines seem to change more slowly when you're on the streets all day long, so the temperature seems to change more rapidly and tellingly.

At about 9 P.M., I went back to the heated grate on 47th Street. The man who had been there last night was already in place. He made it clear that there was again room for me.

I asked him how long he had been on the streets.

"Eleven years, going on twelve," he said.

"This is only my second night."

"You may not stick it out. This isn't for every man."

"Do you ever go into the shelters?"

"I couldn't take that. I prefer this anytime."

Friday, 1/21

When I left my grate mate—long before dawn—he wished me a good day. I returned the gesture. He meant his, and I meant mine.

In Manhattan's earliest hours, you get the feeling that the manufacture and removal of garbage is the city's main industry. So far, I haven't been lucky or observant enough to rescue much of use from the mounds of trash waiting for the trucks and crews. The best find was a canvas bag that will fit nicely over my feet at night.

I'm slipping into a routine: Washing up at the station. Coffee on the street. Breakfast at Blimpie. A search for the *Times* in the trash baskets. And then a leisurely stretch of reading in the park.

Some days bring more luck than others. Today I found 20 cents in a pay-phone slot and heard a young flutist playing the music of C.P.E. Bach on Sixth Avenue between 9th and 10th streets. A lot of people ignored her, even stepped over her flute case as if it were litter on the sidewalk. More often than not, those who put money in the case looked embarrassed. They seemed to be saying, "Don't let anyone see me being appreciative."

By nightfall, the streets were cruelly cold once again. . . .

I headed for the 47th Street grate again but found my mate gone. There was no heat coming up through it. Do they turn it off on Friday nights? Don't we homeless have any rights?

On the northwest corner of Eighth Avenue and 33rd Street, there was a blocked-off subway entrance undergoing repair. I curled up against the wall there under some cardboard sheets. Rain began to fall, but I stayed reasonably dry and was able to get to sleep.

At some point, I was awakened by a man who had pulled back the upper piece of cardboard.

"You see my partner here. You need to give us some money."

I was still half-asleep. "I don't have any."

"You must have something, man."

"Would I be sleeping here in the rain if I did?"

His partner intervened. "C'mon. Leave the old bastard alone. He's not worth it."

"He's got something. Get up and give it to us."

I climbed to my feet and began fumbling in my pocket. Both men were on my left side. That was my chance. Suddenly I took off and ran along 33rd Street toward Ninth Avenue. They gave no chase. And a good thing, too, because I was too stiff with cold to run a good race.

Saturday, 1/22

A man I squatted next to in a doorway on 29th Street said it all: "The onliest thing is to have a warm place to sleep. That and having somebody care about you. That'd be even onlier."

He had what appeared to be rolls of paper toweling wrapped around one leg and tied with red ribbon. But the paper, wet with rain by now, didn't seem to serve any purpose.

I slept little. The forecast was for more rain tomorrow, so why wish the night away?

The morning paper carried news of Mayor Koch's increased concern about the homeless.

But what can he do? He must worry that the more New York does to help, the greater the numbers will grow. At the moment he's berating the synagogues for not doing anything to take street people in.

Watching people come and go at the Volvo tennis tournament at Madison Square Garden, I sensed how uncomfortable they were at the presence of the homeless. Easy to love in the abstract, not so easy face to face.

It's no wonder that the railway police are under orders to chase us out of sight.

Perhaps a saving factor is that we're not individuals. We're not people anybody knows. So far I've had eye contact with only three people who know me in my other life. None showed a hint of recognition. One was the senior auditor at Arthur Andersen & Company, the accounting firm that handles the Clark Foundation, my employer. One was a fellow lieutenant in the Auxiliary Police Force, a man with whom I had trained for many weeks. And one was an owner in the cooperative apartment where I live. . . .

Early in the evening I fell asleep on the Seventh Avenue steps outside the Garden. Three Amtrak cops shook me awake to ask if two rather good-looking suitcases on the steps were mine. I said that I had never seen them.

One cop insisted that I was lying, but then a black man appeared and said they belonged to a friend of his. The rapid-fire questioning from two of the cops soon made that alibi rather unlikely. The third cop was going through the cases and spreading a few of the joints he found inside on the ground.

As suddenly as it had begun, the incident was over. The cops walked away, and the man retrieved the bags. I fell back to sleep. Some hours later when I woke up again, the black man was still there, selling.

Sunday, 1/23

A new discovery of a warm and dry, even scenic, place to sit on a rainy day: the Staten Island Ferry.

For one 25-cent fare, I had four crossings of the harbor, read all I wanted of the copy of the Sunday *Times* I'd found, and finished the crossword puzzle.

When I got back to the Garden, where the tennis tournament was in its last hours, I found the police were being extra diligent in clearing us away from the departing crowds. One older woman was particularly incensed at being moved. "You're ruining my sex life," she shouted. "That's what you're doing. My sex life. Do you hear?"

A younger woman approached me to ask if I was looking for love. "No, ma'am. I'm just trying to stay out of the rain." . . .

So, back to the unused subway entrance, because there was still no heat across town on the 47th Street grate.

The night was very cold. Parts of me ached as I tried to sleep. Turning over was a chore, not only because the partially wet cardboard had to be rearranged with such care, but also because the stiffer parts of my body seemed to belong to someone else. Whatever magic there was in those lights cutting down through the fog was gone by now. All I wanted was to be warm and dry once more. Magic could wait.

Monday, 1/24

Early this morning I went to the warren of employment agencies on 14th Street to see if I could get a day's work. There was very little action at most of these last-ditch offices, where minimum wages and sub-minimum conditions are the rule.

But I did get one interview and thought I had a dishwashing job lined up. I'd forgotten one thing. I had no identification with me. No identification, no job.

There was an ageless, shaggy woman in Bryant Park this morning who delivered one of the more interesting monologues I've heard. For a full ten minutes, with no interruption from me beyond an occasional "Uh-huh," she analyzed society's ills without missing a beat.

Beginning with a complaint about the women's and men's toilets in the park being locked ("What's a poor body to do?"), she launched into the strengths of the Irish, who, though strong, still need toilets more than others, and the weaknesses of the English and the Jews, the advantages of raising turkeys over other fowl, and the wickedness of Eleanor Roosevelt in letting the now Queen Mother and that stuttering king of hers rave so much about the hot dogs served at Hyde Park that we had no alternative but to enter World War II on their side. The faulty Russian satellite that fell into the Indian Ocean this morning was another example of shenanigans, she said. It turns out the Russians and Lady Diana, "that so-called Princess of Wales," are in cahoots to keep us so alarmed about such things far away from home that we don't get anything done about prayer in schools or the rest of it. But after all, what would those poor Protestant ministers do for a living if the children got some real religion in school, like the kind we got from the nuns, God bless them?

That at least was the gist of what she said. I know I've missed some of the finer points.

At 3:30 P.M., with more cold ahead, I sought out the Men's Shelter at 8 East 3rd Street. This is the principal entry point for men seeking the city's help. It provides meals for 1,300 or so people every day and beds for some few of those. I had been told that while there was no likelihood of getting a bed in this building I'd be given a meal here and a bed in some other shelter.

I've seen plenty of drawings of London's workhouses and asylums in the times of Charles Dickens. Now I've seen the real thing, in the last years of the twentieth century in the world's greatest city.

The lobby and the adjacent "sitting room" were jammed with men standing, sitting, or stretched out in various positions on the floor. It was as lost a collection of souls as I could have imagined. Old and young, scarred and smooth, stinking and clean, crippled and hale, drunk and sober, ranting and still, parts of another world and parts of this one. The city promises to take in anyone who asks. Those rejected everywhere else find their way to East 3rd Street.

The air was heavy with the odors of Thunderbird wine, urine, sweat, and, above all, nicotine and marijuana. Three or four Human Resources Administration police officers seemed to be keeping the violence down to tolerable levels, but barely so.

After a long delay, I got a meal ticket for dinner and was told to come back later for a lodging ticket.

It was time to get in line to eat. This meant crowding into what I can only compare to a cattle chute in a stockyard. It ran along two walls of the sitting room and was already jammed. A man with a bullhorn kept yelling at us to stand up and stay in line. One very old and decrepit (or drunk?) man couldn't stay on his feet. He was helped to a chair, from which he promptly fell onto the floor. The bullhorn man had some choice obscenities for him, but they didn't seem to have any effect. The old man just lay there; and we turned our thoughts back to the evening meal.

I made a quick, and probably gross unfair, assessment of the hundreds of men I could see in the room. Judging them solely by appearance, alertness, and body movements, I decided that one-quarter of them were perfectly able to work; they, more likely than not, were among the warriors who helped us win the battle against inflation by the selfless act of joining the jobless ranks. Another quarter might be brought back in time into job-readiness by some counseling and some caring for them as individuals. But the other half seemed so ravaged by illness, addiction, and sheer neglect that I couldn't imagine them being anything but society's wards from here on out to—one hopes—a peaceful end.

At the appointed hour, we were released in groups of twenty or thirty to descend the dark, filthy steps to the basement eating area. The man with the bullhorn was there again, clearly in charge and clearly relishing the extra power given to his voice by electric amplification. He insulted us collectively and separately without pause, but because his vocabulary was limited it tended to be the same four-letter words over and over.

His loudest attack on me came when I didn't move fast enough to pick up my meal from the counter. His analysis of certain flaws in my white ancestry wasn't hard to follow, even for a man in as much of a daze as I was.

The shouting and the obscenities didn't stop once we had our food. Again and again we were told to finish and get out. Eating took perhaps six minutes, but those minutes removed any shred of dignity a man might have brought in with him from the street.

Back upstairs, the people in charge were organizing the people who were to go to a shelter in Brooklyn. Few had volunteered, so there was more haranguing.

In the line next to the one where I was waiting for my lodging ticket a fight suddenly broke out. One man pulled a long knife from his overcoat pocket. The other man ran for cover, and a police officer soon appeared to remove the man with the knife from the scene. The issue, it seems, was one of proper places in the line.

There still weren't enough Brooklyn volunteers to suit the management, so they brought in their big gun: Mr. Bullhorn. "Now, listen up," he barked. "There aren't any buses going to Ft. Washington [another shelter] until 11:30, so if you want to get some sleep, go to Brooklyn. Don't ask me any questions. Just shut up and listen. It's because you don't listen up that you end up in a place like this."

I decided to ask a question anyway, about whether there would still be a chance for me to go to Brooklyn once I got my lodging ticket. He turned on me and let me have the full force of the horn: "Don't ask questions, I said. You're not nobody."

The delays at the ticket-issuing window went on and on. Three staff members there seemed reasonably polite and even efficient. The fourth and heaviest one—I have no idea whether it was a man or woman—could not have moved more slowly without coming to a dead halt. The voice of someone who was apparently a supervisor came over the public-address system from time to time to apologize for the delay in going to the Ft. Washington shelter, which was in an armory, but any good he did from behind the scenes was undone by the staff out front and a "see-no-work, hear-no-work, do-no-work" attendant in the office.

As 11:30 approached, we crowded back into the sitting room to get ready to board the buses. A new martinet had appeared on the scene. He got as much attention through his voice, cane, and heavy body as Mr. Bullhorn had with his amplifying equipment. But his new man was more openly vile and excitable; he loved the power that went with bunching us all up close together and then ordering us to stretch out again in a thinner line. We practiced that routine several times. . . .

Long after the scheduled departure, the lines moved. We sped by school buses to the armory at Ft. Washington Avenue and 168th Street. There we were met, just before 2:30 A.M., by military police, social workers, and private guards. They marched us into showers (very welcome), gave us clean underwear, and sent us upstairs to comfortable cots arranged in long rows in a room as big as a football field.

There were 530 of us there for the night, and we were soon quiet.

Tuesday, 1/25

We were awakened at 6 A.M. by whistles and shouting, and ordered to get back onto the buses for the return trip to lower Manhattan as soon as possible.

Back at 8 East 3rd Street, the worst of the martinets were off duty. So I thought breakfast might be a bit quieter than dinner had been. Still, by eight, I had seen three incidents a bit out of the ordinary for me.

A man waiting for breakfast immediately ahead of me in the cattle chute suddenly grabbed a chair from the adjoining area and prepared to break it over his neighbor's head. In my haste to get out of the way, I fell over an older man sleeping against the wall. After some shouts about turf, things cooled off between the fighters, and the old man forgave me.

In the stairwell leading down to the eating area, a young man made a sexual advance to me. When I withdrew from him and stupidly reached for my coat pocket, he thought I was going for a weapon. He at once pinned me against the wall and searched my pockets; there was nothing there.

As I came out of the building onto East 3rd Street, two black Human Resources Administration policemen were bringing two young blacks into the building. One officer had his man by the neck. The other officer had his man's hands cuffed behind his back and repeatedly kicked him hard in the buttocks.

My wanderings were still more aimless today. I couldn't get East 3rd Street out of my mind. What could possibly justify some of that conduct? If I were a staff member there, would I become part of the worst in that pattern? Or would I simply do as little, and think as little, as possible?

At day's end I can't recall much of where I went or why I went there. Only isolated moments remain with me. Like . . . staring at the elegant crystal and silver in the shops just north of Madison Square Park and wondering what these windows say to the people I'd spent the night with.

Much too soon it was time to go back to the shelter for dinner and another night. At first I thought I didn't have the guts to do it again. Does one have to do *this* to learn who the needy are? I wanted to say, "Enough! There's only so much I need to see."

But I went back to the shelter anyway, probably because it took more guts to quit than it did to go ahead.

A man beside me in the tense dinner line drove one truth of this place home to me. "I never knew hell came in this color," he said.

I was luckier in my assignment for the night. I drew the Keener Building, on Wards Island, a facility with a capacity of 416 men. The building was old and neglected, and the atmosphere of a mental hospital, which it once was, still hung over it. But the staff was polite, the rooms weren't too crowded (there were only twelve beds in Room 326), the single sheet on each bed was clean, and there was toilet paper in the bathroom.

There were limits and guards and deprivations, but there was also an orderliness about the place. Here, at least, I didn't feel I had surrendered all of my dignity at the door.

Wednesday, 1/26

. . . Back to the shelter on East 3rd Street for dinner.

There is simply no other situation I've seen that is so devoid of any graces at all, so tense at every moment, or so empty of hope. The food isn't bad, and the building is heated; that's all it has going for it.

The only cutlery provided is a frail plastic spoon. With practice you can spread hard oleo onto your bread with the back of one. If there's liver or ham, you don't have to cut it; just put it between the two pieces of bread that go with each meal. Everything else—peas, collard greens, apple pudding, plums—can be managed with the spoon. And talk over dinner or sipping, rather than gulping, coffee isn't all that important.

What is hardest to accept is the inevitable jungle scene during the hour you stand in line waiting to eat. Every minute seems to be one that invites an explosion. You know instinctively that men can't come this often to the brink without someone going over. One person too many is going to try to jump ahead in line. One particular set of toes is going to be stepped on by mistake. And the lid is going to blow.

The most frightening people here are the many young, intensely angry blacks. Hatred pours out in all of their speech and some of their actions. I could spend a lot of time imagining how and why they became so completely angry—but if I were the major, the counselor, or the man with the bullhorn, I wouldn't know how to divert them from that anger any more. Hundreds and hundreds of men here have been destroyed by alcohol or drugs. A smaller, but for me more poignant, number are being destroyed by hate.

Their loudest message—and because their voices are so strong it is very loud indeed—is "Respect me, man." The constant theme is that someone or some group is putting them down, stepping on them, asking them to conform to a code they don't accept, getting in their way, writing them off.

So most of the fights begin over turf. A place in line. A corner to control. The have-nots scrapping with the have-nots. . . .

Tonight, I chose the Brooklyn shelter because I thought the buses going there would leave soonest. The shelter, a converted school, is on Williams Avenue and has about 400 beds.

We left in fairly good time but learned when we got to the shelter that no new beds would be assigned until after 11 P.M. We were to sit in the auditorium until then.

At about ten, a man herded as many of us newcomers as would listen to him into a corner of the auditorium. There he delivered an abusive diatribe outlining the horror that lay ahead for our possessions and our bodies during the night to come. It made the ranting at East 3rd Street seem tame.

It's illustrative of what the experience of homelessness and helplessness does to people that all of us—regardless of age, race, background, or health—listened so passively.

Only at midnight, when some other officials arrived, did we learn that this man had no standing whatsoever. He was just an underling who strutted for his time on the stage before any audience cowed enough to take what he dished out. . . .

Thursday, 1/27

Back on the street this morning, I became conscious of how little time I had left to live this way. There seemed so much still to do, and so little time in which to do it.

One part of me tells me I have been fully a part of this. I know I walk with slower steps and bent shoulders. . . . I know I worry a lot more about keeping clean.

But then I recall how foolish that is, I'm acting. This will end tomorrow night. I can quit any time I want to. And unlike my mate from 47th Street, I haven't the slightest idea of what eleven years of sleeping on a grate amount to.

Early this afternoon, I went again to the Pavilion restaurant, where I had eaten five times before. I didn't recognize the man at the cash register.

"Get out," he said.

"But I have money."

"You heard me. Get out." His voice was stronger.

"That man knows me," I said, looking toward the owner in the back of the restaurant.

The owner nodded, and the man at the register said, "Okay, but sit in the back."

If this life in the streets had been real, I'd have gone out the door at the first "Get out." And the assessment of me as not worthy would have been self-fulfilling; I'd have lost so much respect for myself that I wouldn't have been worthy of being served the next time. The downward spiral would have begun.

Until now I haven't understood the extent of nicotine addiction. Dependencies on drugs and alcohol have been around me for a long time, but I thought before that smoking was a bad habit rather easy to overcome.

How many times have I, a nonsmoker, been begged for a cigarette in these days? Surely hundreds. Cigarettes are central. A few folks give them away, a small number sell them for up to 8 cents apiece, and almost all give that last pathetic end of a butt to the first man who asks for what little bit is left. I know addiction now as I didn't before.

Tonight, after a repeat of the totally degrading dinner-line scene at East 3rd Street, I signed up for Keener once again. No more Brooklyn for me.

Sitting upstairs with the other Keener-bound men, I carelessly put my left foot on the rung of the chair in front of me, occupied by a young black.

"Get your foot off, yo."

("Yo" means "Hey, there," "Watch yourself," "Move along," and much more.)

I took it off. "Sorry," I said.

But it was too late. I had broken a cardinal rule. I had violated the man's turf. As we stood in the stairwell waiting for the buses, he told a much bigger, much louder, much angrier friend what I had done.

That man turned on me.

"Wait till we get you tonight, whitey. You stink. Bad. The worst I've ever smelled. And when you put your foot on that chair, you spread your stink around. You better get yourself a shower as soon as we get there, but it won't save you later on. . . . And don't sit near me or him on the bus. You hear, whitey?"

I didn't reply.

The bombardment went on as we mounted the bus. No one spoke up in my defense. Three people waved me away when I tried to sit next to them. The next person, black and close to my age, made no objection when I sat beside him.

The big man continued the tirade for a while, but he soon got interested in finding out from the driver how to go about getting a bus-driver's license. Perhaps he had come down from a high.

I admit I was scared. I wrote my name, address, and office telephone number on a piece of paper and slipped it into my pocket. At least someone would know where to call if the threats were real. I knew I couldn't and wouldn't defend myself in this setting.

While we stood in line on Wards Island waiting for our bed assignments, there were plenty of gripes about the man who was after me. But no one said anything directly to him. Somehow it didn't seem that this was the night when the meek would inherit the earth.

I slept fitfully. I don't like lying with the sheet hiding my face.

Friday, 1/28

I was up and out of Keener as early as possible. That meant using some of my little remaining money for a city-bus ride back to Manhattan, but it was worth it to get out of there.

After breakfast on East 3rd Street, I was finished with the public shelters. That was an easy break for me to make, because I had choices and could run.

The day was cold and, for the early hours, clear. I washed the memory of the big man at 3rd Street out of my mind by wandering through the Fulton Fish Market. I walked across the Brooklyn Bridge and even sang as I realized how free I was to relax and enjoy its beauty.

With a cup of coffee and the *Times*, I sat on a cinder block by the river and read. In time, I wandered through the Wall Street district and almost learned the lay of some of the streets.

I walked up to the Quaker Meeting House at Rutherford Place and 15th Street. Standing on the porch outside, I tried hard to think how the doctrine that "there is that of God in every person" applied to that man last night and to some of the others I had encountered in these ten days. I still think it applies, but it isn't always easy to see how. . . .

Darkness came. I got kicked out of both the bus terminal and Grand

Central. I got my normal clothes out of the locker at Penn Station, changed in the men's room, and rode the AA train home.

My apartment was warm, and the bed was clean.

That's the onliest thing.

19 Cockfighting: America's Invisible Sport

CLIFTON D. BRYANT

Unlike preliterate groups such as the Yąnomamö, the subject of article 6, a large, industrialized society is made up of millions of groups. Some groups, such as families or good friends, are *primary*; that is, they are small and their relationships are informal, face-to-face, long-term, and intimate. Other groups are *secondary*; that is, they are larger, and their relationships are more formal and less emotionally expressive. Although primary groups generally meet deep emotional needs, secondary groups, such as volunteer organizations, are also vital for our well-being. They are a form of social organization that helps to get society's work done.

The differences between primary and secondary groups are not always clear-cut. Work groups, for example, may blend characteristics of each type, while a church or synagogue may be primary for some, but will remain secondary for others. The relationships among a society's groups, both primary and secondary, constitute the *social structure* of a society.

Some groups come together only for specific purposes; the individuals interact briefly, then disband. Although brief, the interaction may be intense, stimulating, and highly rewarding. A group's activities may also be illegal and their meetings clandestine. Bryant describes a group whose subterranean activities are so extensive that he calls it America's invisible sport.

The room is dim but the "pit" with an earthen floor in the center is brightly illuminated by overhead lights. Rows of banked seats or bleachers surround the pit. The glowing signs over the exit door stand out in the dim atmosphere and light from the surrounding rooms filters into the arena.

A referee and two men known as "handlers," carrying gamefowl roosters, file into the approximately 20 foot wide pit. A center line is drawn on the clay floor of the pit. Other lines are etched in the floor parallel to and 22 inches on either side of the center line. These are the "short" lines. A second set of lines is drawn on the floor parallel to and four feet on either side of the center line. These are the "score" lines. All of these floor markings play a role in the mechanics of the fight. The birds have been matched for weight. They have also had sharpened metal spurs or "gaffs" tied to their legs.

Inside the pit, the handlers move to opposite sides of the pit to get their birds "loosened" up or warmed up. This may include letting the bird walk about, tossing it into the air, massaging its legs or wings, or even teasing it to agitate it. The referee checks the leg bands on the birds to ensure that there are no substitutions, and the handlers, standing on the short lines, extend their arms so the birds can peck at each other, a process known as "billing." The referee calls "Handle!" and the handlers return to the "score" lines, eight feet apart, with their cocks.

During these preliminaries, the spectators have been betting. Members of the audience may stand up and call out their best offers, not unlike stock brokers. Someone far across the room may catch the eye of a person calling out a bet offer and by simply raising his hand, indicates acceptance of the bet. The offerer points to the bird of his choice and then to himself. The acceptor nods his agreement and the deal is sealed. After the fight the loser usually delivers the money he lost on the bet, but sometimes he simply crumples up a bill and tosses it to the winner. The sound of betting subsides as the match is about to begin.

Back in the pit, the referee yells "Pit!" and the handlers release the cocks, their hackle feathers erect and their tail feathers flared out. The birds rush toward each other, sometimes stopping about a foot apart, cautiously circling, looking for an opening to attack. In the initial assault one bird often flutters up a foot or so off the ground like a startled pheasant on the rise, to gain advantage for a kick with its spurs. The other cock usually parries by also flying off the ground for a kick. The resulting collision sounds like a paddle striking a cardboard box. There is a flurry of feathers in the air.

The cocks circle and again wing to attack. If the spur of one bird becomes lodged in the other bird, the referee calls "Handle!" and the two men rush to separate the birds. They have a period of time to refresh their birds, much as with a prizefighter between rounds. They may massage the bird's legs, stretch its wings, blow down the rooster's throat—in the fashion of artificial respiration—or even lick the front of the cock's head. The referee calls "Pit!" and the fight resumes. In time, one bird will strike the telling blow and his opponent goes down. A downed bird may try to fight back from his disabled position, and the surviving bird may rush over to peck at the wounded or dead bird and frequently crows to signal his victory. The men with their cocks, alive and dead, depart the pit.

Bets are paid off. Conversation concerning the past fight continues for a few minutes, and then subsides as betting on the new match becomes more vocal and energetic. Some members of the audience may follow the fight, unconsciously moving their bodies as if physically involved in the match, in a manner similar to spectators at a boxing match or hockey game. Also, some spectators may shout exclamations of encouragement, warning, or advice to their champion, using phrases such as "shoot him," "hit him again," or "take him now," particularly in an energetic match. However, this cheering never reaches the volume or intensity of fans yelling at a football game. The sport of cockfighting, which involves humans and animals, is by intent violent, and is conducted in a clandestine, "underground" fashion. It is, in effect, America's invisible sport.

Cockfighting: The Image and the Reality

Many Americans have never heard of cockfighting. Some of those who have believe that it, like other so-called "blood sports," passed from the American scene in the nineteenth century. Of those who know it exists today, many believe that the sport is an anachronistic practice that has declined almost to non-existence and that it is largely confined to isolated rural areas in a few states. Its followers, according to stereotypical public image, are mostly lower-class, uneducated, unemployed "riff-raff" with criminal and/or deviant propensities (Bryant and Li, 1991b).

Most Americans would be startled to learn that all of these assumptions are invalid. Cockfighting is alive and well, and flourishing in large cities and smaller communities, as well as in rural areas. The sport cuts across all walks of life, various income levels, and its devotees include Euro-Americans, African Americans, Asian Americans, and Hispanic Americans. Cockers, or gamefowl enthusiasts, as they are known, include white-collar and blue-collar workers, professionals of all types, farmers and ranchers, truck drivers and school teachers. Cockers are rich and poor, Democrat and Republican, Catholics, Protestants, and Jews, and conservatives and liberals. They resemble mainstream Americans in almost every way, with one exception—they like to "fight chickens."

The "Mechanics" of Cockfighting

Cockfighting is a sport that is simple in its basics and complex in its nuances (for a detailed account of cockfighting, see Herzog, 1985). Two roosters of a particular variety of poultry known as gamefowl are placed within a small enclosure known as a "pit" or "cockpit" (yes, this term referring to the operating area of an airplane derives from cockfighting). The birds are territorial and are genetically programmed to fight any male bird of their species to the death. This tendency is facilitated by attaching "heels" or "gaffs" (needle-like spurs) to the legs of the birds. Armed with their spurs, the birds attack each other and ultimately one succeeds in killing the other. This is the simple aspect of the sport.

The complex nuances revolve around the propagation and conditioning of the birds. Every cocker has his own highly individualized notions concerning which genetic mixtures of gamefowl strains produce the most aggressive and effective birds—the best bloodlines, as it were. The birds require no training, inasmuch as they are instinctive fighters, but there are different approaches to conditioning (i.e., feeding, exercising, etc.) and each school has its adherents. The combinations and permutations of breeding and conditioning options are almost infinite.

The Social History of Cockfighting

Cockfighting may well be the oldest spectator sport on earth (for a detailed historical overview of cockfighting, see Bryant, 1982). It likely originated as long as 6,000 or 7,000 years ago in Southeast Asia. By 2000 B.C. cockfighting had migrated westward along with the domestication of poultry, first to India and then to the Middle East. Over the centuries many groups, including Persians, Macedonians, Greeks, Phoenicians, and ultimately Romans, took up the sport. As the Roman Legionnaires marched over Europe, they took fighting cocks along with them for entertainment, spreading the sport even further. In England, cockfighting was extremely popular, and Henry VIII elevated cockfighting to a "royal diversion" when he had a cockpit constructed at his palace, Whitehall. Subsequent monarchs including James I and Charles II were said to be equally enthusiastic about cockfighting.

The colonists brought cockfighting to America, perhaps as early as 1650. Various U.S. presidents, such as George Washington, Thomas Jefferson, and Andrew Jackson, were avid cockfighters. Abraham Lincoln was said to have been a referee at cockfights, as well as a fan. More recently, Lyndon Johnson is reported to have occasionally attended a cockfight. Cockfighting is perhaps the most "traditional" of American sports.

The strong imprint of cockfighting on our language indicates how it has embedded itself in the fabric of American culture. Examples are "cockstrong," "cocksure," being "pitted" against each other in competition, "crestfallen" and performances "in the round." As stated earlier, the cabin of an airplane is a "cockpit." Even the American institution of the mixed drink—the "cocktail"—owes its etymology to cockfighting. "Cock-ale" was a spiritous drink fed to fighting cocks in training. And legend has it that spectators at a cockfight used to toast the cock that had the most tail feathers left after the fight. The drink was supposed to contain the same number of ingredients as the number of tail feathers remaining, thus the appellation "cocktail."

Cockfighting as Stigmatized Sport

Cockfighting has always had its critics and detractors (see McCaghy and Neal, 1974). While the Greeks were nearly fanatical in their enthusiasm for cockfighting, the Romans originally disdained it derisively referring to the sport as the "Greek Diversion." In time, the Romans became equally enthusiastic about the sport and reckless in their gambling on the birds. Columbella, a Roman writer of the first century A.D., commented that "devotees (of cockfighting) often spent their entire patrimony in betting at the pitside." In Europe and England, cockfighting also received its share of social condemnation. Oliver Cromwell managed to outlaw it for a time during his rule. Numerous writers attacked the practice because they believed that deriving pleasure from observing animal violence was debasing and had a demoralizing, if not brutalizing, effect on the spectators. They were particularly concerned that it might make them "unfitted" for work.

In the United States, where agrarian society gave way to industrialization later than in England, the social opposition to cockfighting and other "blood sports" was based more on the immorality of gambling on the fights. Another factor was that devotees tended to be enthusiastic to the point of fanaticism, which intruded on more socially productive activities such as work, church, and community affairs. In time, the issue of animal cruelty became as heated as in England. Today, cockfighting is still legal in a few states such as Louisiana, Oklahoma, and Arizona. It is "tolerated" to a modest degree in some states where it is illegal, with laws outlawing the sport enforced only irregularly depending on local sentiments. In a number of states, laws banning the sport are vigorously enforced, and violaters face felony convictions. Faced with social condemnation and legal opposition, cockfighting has moved underground and become a socially "invisible" sport (see Bryant, 1991).

The Invisible Sport

With the exception of an occasional newspaper item about a law enforcement raid on a cockpit, most Americans are unaware of the sport. Cockfighting flourishes, however, in a clandestine mode. There is no accurate census of the number of cockpits in the United States, but certainly there are in excess of several thousand. Some sources claim that there are between 250 and 1,000 pits in New York City alone, often in basements of old buildings (Cox, 1977:8; McCaghy and Neal, 1974:558). Similarly, there is no complete count of cockers. Probably 20,000 to 40,000 regular and committed gamefowl enthusiasts make up the "core" of the sport (Bryant, 1991:19), and perhaps another 40,000 to 100,000 "supporters" who attend fights less frequently have some type of ancillary involvement in the sport, such as manufacturing or selling products like feed, medications, cages, and the like. In addition, there may be as many as 70,000 breeders of fighting cocks in the country (*Grit and Steel* 1970:20, 31) who annually produce several hundred thousand birds for American cockpits and export more than 12,000 fighting cocks to the Philippines, the West Indies, and Latin America. Finally, the "fans" of cockfighting number another 100,000 to 200,000. They attend fights, are well conversant with the details of the sport, may gamble on the fights, and may have once owned or fought birds. Thus, the total number of gamefowl fanciers probably is about 250,000 to 350,000.

Three monthly periodicals devoted to the sport, *Grit and Steel, The Feathered Warrior,* and *The Gamecock,* keep devotees informed of upcoming "mains" and "derbies" (fights) and the results of recent matches. Each has a circulation of approximately 10,000. Cockfighting represents an "industry" of significant size in terms of the monies generated by the sale of birds, feeds, supplements, medications, supplies, books, pamphlets, periodicals, and the admission to pits and the subsequent sale of food and refreshments. Some estimate a total of between $20,000,000 and $40,000,000 (possibly as high as $75,000,000). Cockfighting is big business.

Cockfighting has a strong subcultural dimension, and some call its participants a "fraternity" (McCaghy and Neal, 1974). Many members in the "core" know hundreds or even thousands of other members in various parts of the country. They travel about the nation, attending fights in many states, as well as conventions of state and national gamefowl organizations, where they socialize with other cockers. The sport of cockfighting provides the basis for camaraderie, a commonality of interests and activities, and a strong sense of social identity and even community. Cockfights can be classified along a social continuum based on context, and on size and type of audience in attendance at the pit. The actual dynamics of the cockfight itself (as described above) tend to be much the same, regardless of the type of pit.

Types of Cockfights

THE COCKFIGHT AT A "BRUSH PIT"

At one end of the continuum is the cockfight conducted in a "brush pit," often a rudimentary arrangement constructed in a deserted barn, shed, or outbuilding in some isolated rural area. One researcher (Hawley, 1982:67) comments that "the prototypical brush pit is in a remote rural location, usually not readily identifiable as such from an observer passing by in an automobile." He goes on to say that there may even be lookouts with "CB radio walkie-talkies" at the gates to the property. In areas where there is strong opposition to cockfighting, and/or where law enforcement is not sympathetic to the sport, security may be tight and attendance furtive. In locales with greater tolerance of cockfighting, the "brush pit" may not have to be "hidden" but may only be situated in such a way as to have a low profile and thus not antagonize the local citizenry. Such pits are often constructed of simple materials (plywood, sheet metal, etc.) and display a "make-do," or fabricated rather than purchased quality (Donlon, 1990:281). Their general layout, however, is usually quite traditional. They are, in effect, smaller "do-it-yourself" versions of the larger commercial pits found in some states. These pits may contain a curious mixture of the old and the new; a pot-bellied stove for heating and fluorescent lights for illumination, for example (Cobb, 1978:88).

The spectators at "brush pits" may be a small group of locals, perhaps farmers, blue-collar employees, or self-employed craftsmen—"good ole boys," as some writers might characterize them, who gather on a Sunday to conduct a "hack fight" (a relatively impromptu contest that may not necessarily involve carefully matched weights of the birds). The participants and spectators, contrary to stereotype, are generally not unkempt or wearing dirty or shabby attire. Hawley (1982:69) describes them:

> At most pits the mode of dress is decidedly casual but usually not abjectly sloppy. Denims predominate and new overalls and western wear are *de riguer*. Some of the participants and spectators may wear items of clothing, hats, or jewelry embazoned with chickens in combative posture. These items are widely advertised in the cockfighting press. Baseball, or billed-style, hats are the dominant form of headgear; no urban cowboys these! Since cockfights are often held on Sunday, the more "respectable" elements show up after church is over at noon and are often dressed in polyester jumpsuits and vinyl shoes. For all spectators and participants, comfort and utility seem to be the deciding factor in one's choice of attire.

Some "brush pits," however, may be relatively large, accommodating 100–200 persons or more, and may even provide toilet facilities and some spartan concession stands where coffee and sandwiches or simple hot food can be purchased. Alcoholic beverages are customarily *not* sold (Hawley, 1982:70). Cockfights at "brush pits" often tend to be relatively private inasmuch as most of the participants are likely to know each other, or at least know of each other. Strangers, unless accompanied by a sponsor, may be viewed with suspicion, or in some instances not even admitted. Women are less likely to attend such gatherings, wives and daughters are sometimes present. Because fights at "brush pits" lack the "pageantry" or social characteristics of cockfights at larger commercial pits, they are usually not as appealing to females. Activity at the "brush pits" resembles the stereotypical images of cockfighting often found in the popular literature.

THE "SOCIETY" COCKFIGHT

Many would label the term "Society Cockfight" an oxymoron, finding the idea of high-status spectators and participants at a cockfight to be an incongruous notion. There are such events, however. As mentioned earlier, for centuries cockfighting was a "royal" sport in England, and in America cockfighting was avidly pursued by the landed gentry. Many persons of high status, including several presidents, have been enthusiastic gamefowl fanciers.

In many elite country clubs in Latin American nations, a cockpit is as prominent on the club grounds as a swimming pool or tennis court. In the Philippines, cockfighting is almost the national sport for rich and poor alike. Most Philippine communities of any size have cockpits. Some, resembling small colleseums, border on the lavish, with air conditioning, padded seats, and other amenities. Such cockpits are designed to accommodate the more affluent class of spectators. Imelda Marcos, when still first lady of the Philippines, sponsored a "charity" cockfight in Manila to raise money for some of her favorite causes. The social position of those who attended can be inferred from the door prize—a Mercedez Benz automobile.

In the United States, "society" cockfights, like other types of matches, must be conducted in a clandestine fashion. One such event I attended was particularly memorable. While being interviewed about my cockfighting research on a local television station in a small Middle Atlantic city several years ago, I mentioned my interest in learning more about "society cockfights." Not too long thereafter, I received a printed invitation to attend a combined cockfight and cocktail party at a large horse farm not far from the city. At the appointed time, my spouse and I journeyed to the farm where the social gathering was to be held. On the large and well maintained premises, one building housed a permanent cockpit. The party was held outside around the cockfight building. For the most part, the automobiles parked about the area were expensive vehicles, often of a sporting or casual variety— luxury four-wheel drive vehicles such as Jeep Wagoneers, Buick Station Wagons, large vans, as well as a variety of imported sports cars.

The social affair, hosted by the elderly widow who owned the farm, was an annual event sponsored by a small "club" of gentlemen who had been fighting cocks for two or more generations. Membership was exclusive and limited to the original membership or their heirs. No new outside members were accepted and only when one member died was his son or some other close male heir eligible to join. The grandfathers of some of the present members had been founders of the club. There was a trophy for the winner, and the annual event was steeped in tradition. The members of the club were widely known as top breeders of gamecocks, and the annual fights were renowned for the quality of the birds and their performance. Over the years, the occasion had evolved from merely a cockfight with refreshments for the members and their families to an elaborate spring soiree for a select segment of the community. Each club member was permitted to invite a certain number of guests and such invitations were eagerly sought. The annual cockfight and cocktail party had become *the* social and sporting event of the spring.

The guests, many of whom were already in attendance when we arrived, were attired in tasteful dress that would have been eminently appropriate for an outside cocktail party at an upscale country club. Some of the gentlemen wore coats and ties, while others wore tailored slacks and short sleeved shirts. A few, who were to be directly involved in the cockfighting activities, wore more casual clothing, such as chinos or crisp neutral colored coveralls. Some of the ladies wore cocktail dresses, while others wore slacks and blouses. Many wore high-heeled shoes. Those who were part of the "core," or involved group, tended to be more casually dressed, while those who had been invited as guests and spectators were more formally attired. Whatever the clothing, it was invariably fashionable and "pricey."

The invited guests were local professionals, merchants, entrepreneurs, and ranchers from the surrounding area. There were physicians, politicians, a judge, attorneys, real estate agents, owners of businesses, and members of the local "sporting set." The ladies and gentlemen were well tanned, reflecting their outdoors proclivities. They were golfers, tennis players, horseback riders, and boaters. Some were cockfighters, but many were not. The latter came for the social interaction as much as for the cockfighting.

Behind the bar set up in the cockpit building was a white-coated, black, elderly servant, a long-time family retainer of the hostess. The choice of drinks seemed to be gin and tonic or bourbon and "branch." The "branch" was naturally cold water drawn from a deep well on the premises and kept on the bar in a cedar bucket and ladled out with a dipper. Tap water and bourbon would simply not do! Another servant was cutting up wheels of cheese for hors d'oeuvres at a near-by table, while the other two servants prepared hamburgers over a charcoal fire.

The building itself was quite spartan, with the typical clay pit surrounded by old seats and benches, suggesting that it was used only irregularly, and then only for relatively small groups of spectators. Hung conspicuously on a side wall of the building was a large American flag. What was most engaging, however, was the lighting fixture hanging above the pit. It was an enormous antique, stained-glass, Tiffany chandelier. This had been purchased in a Paris antique gallery many years before by the owner of the horse farm. Its real charm, however, lay in the fact that supposedly it had originally hung in a French bordello at the turn of the century.

Partygoers milled about outside the building exchanging casual conversation, which often revolved around other sporting activities—upcoming golf games, fox hunts, horse races—or land, livestock, and show dogs. This was a group for whom leisure and recreation were as vigorous pursuits as career and vocation. One gentleman stuck his head out of the door of the building and yelled "chicken in the pit!" The matches had begun. The crowd moved inside, drinks in hand, and took seats in the small bleachers or stood at the rear. The spectacle in the pit followed the usual format—two game-cocks, two handlers, and one referee. The birds were of good quality and the fights were spirited. After a decent interval, the guests who were not dedicated cockers moved away from the pit and resumed their conversations. The hamburgers were ready, and people could go through the food line at their leisure. Some took their food and drink back to the seating area and watched more fights. After a number of matches, the guests developed a curious mannerism. Those holding cocktails placed one hand slightly above the top of the glass they were holding. The reason soon became evident. In a cockfight, the feathers literally do fly. Large feathers fall to the floor of the pit and after several fights, an attendant rakes up the feathers between matches so they will not impede the movement of birds in the next fight. The smaller feathers, some pin feathers as tiny as threads, drift into the air and are blown about the room. The protective hand over the cocktail glass kept these small pin feathers from falling into the glass.

The fights were the center of attention throughout the afternoon and into the evening, with one exception. This was the afternoon of the Kentucky Derby. Someone keeping track of the time suddenly turned on the TV set on a wall shelf and yelled, "Derby's on!" Conversation ceased, and all heads turned toward the TV screen. The Derby was watched with appropriate emotional comments and cheers as various favorite horses pulled toward the lead. After the Derby, the cockfight resumed.

Throughout the party, the spectators had become only mildly animated, and the voice level around the pit was little more than conversational, punctuated occasionally by muted exclamations when something unusual happened in the pit—a quick kill in the early moments of the fight or a cock that seemed to be down and dying suddenly leaping to its feet and aggressively attacking the other bird. As the evening wore on, some guests moved away from the pit to talk with others and, in time, began to depart. Ultimately, only the true gamefowl enthusiasts remained. The scheduled fights were concluded, the scores tallied, the trophy awarded, and champagne toasts exchanged. Almost on a whim, one of the participants proposed a "Battle Royal" as a finale. After some brief discussion, the participants agreed and all of the birds still alive and in fighting form—approximately a dozen or so—were released in the pit. Accompanied by a good bit of crowing, the birds began attacking each other, sometimes concentrating on one opponent and sometimes attacking other birds sequentially. From time to time a wounded bird would lie still on the pit floor as if dead. When its opponent crowed to signal its victory, the sound would stimulate the adrenaline in the "dead" bird, who would leap to its feet and again attack the enemy cock. Ultimately the number dwindled to a few and then to two. Like all fights, the final one was to the death. The bird that prevailed, by virtue of being the only survivor, was saluted as the champion of the "Battle Royal." The spectators departed, sated from the full feast of food, drink, sociability, and primal entertainment.

THE COCKFIGHT AT THE COMMERCIAL PIT

Most serious cockfighting takes place at large commercial pits—arenas constructed in a more permanent fashion, often housed in metal buildings or concrete block structures. In states such as Arizona, Oklahoma, or Louisiana, where cockfighting is legal, the pit building may be quite conspicuous, sometimes located along a well-traveled road. Where cockfighting is illegal, pits are usually well hidden on private land in remote areas away from towns or are relatively unobtrusive if located in more accessible places. Obviously, they cannot be so well hidden that they are completely unknown to local law enforcement authorities. Because of prevailing local values and sentiments, however, the authorities may tolerate cockfighting as long as it maintains a low public visibility.

Commercial pits are often large, accommodating up to 500 or more spectators. They usually have holding cages for cocks awaiting fights, areas for "heeling" the birds, toilet facilities (sometimes with door signs reading "hens" and "roosters," or "chicks" and "cocks"), concession areas (often including short order restaurant areas), and space for score keepers. The general atmosphere is not unlike that at any other type of sporting activity. One characteristic of pits that seems to be widespread, if not universal, is that no beer or other alcoholic beverages are sold and usually there are signs saying "No Drinking Permitted" (Cobb, 1978:78; Hawley, 1982:70). As with other sports or even card playing, it is felt that drinking interferes with concentration. At some derbies there may be some drinking by spectators in cars parked about the grounds (Hawley, 1982:68), but generally it is not in evidence inside the pit building. Drunks are usually not tolerated. Other characteristics include a relatively moderate noise level throughout the pit building (although admittedly louder than at "society" cockfights) and even during the matches—in contrast to a much higher decibel level at some other sporting events such as basketball games.

Many commercial pits are known as "family pits," and, indeed, it is not unusual to see wives, mothers, and children of all ages in attendance (Cobb, 1978:93: Hawley, 1982:74). Cockfighting is often a family affair, with spouses and children assisting in the raising and conditioning of birds (Bryant and Li, 1991b:46–49). Accordingly, the wives and children enjoy seeing the fruits of their labors in the form of victorious cocks. Sometimes, a youngster may even enter a cock he has personally raised and conditioned in a match, although it would be unusual to see a handler who is not an adult. Handlers are usually men, but occasionally a female handler will be seen (Cobb,

1978:93), and from time to time some pits even sponsor "powder-puff" derbies where all the handlers are female (Hawley, 1982:74). Perhaps because of the presence of family members, there seems to be a minimal use of profanity or crude language in the pit house.

The spectators appear to be of all ages, from preteen children to persons of advanced years, although most tend to be between 25 and 50 years old. Teenagers of both sexes are frequently in the audience, and the girls (often the daughters of participating cockers) sometimes place bets. In many instances, the girls are excellent judges of fighting cocks, having grown up with game fowl in their yards. Many teenaged males are active bettors, walking about with small note pads to keep up with their wagers. Middle-aged women may sometimes also be active and enthusiastic bettors (Cobb, 1978:93).

The racial ethnic mix depends on the region of the country. In the Southwest, for example, a high proportion of Hispanics may attend these events while blacks may be seen at southern pits. On the West Coast and in Hawaii, there are frequently significant numbers of Asian Americans in attendance. The dress of the spectators at commercial pits is mixed, but usually casual—sometimes Western with the requisite boots, sometimes slacks and sport shirts with wind breakers, frequently denims, khakis, or chinos, increasingly camo fatigues, and occasionally a sports coat.

Commercial pits leave the impression of the rural small town—orderly, relaxed, and casual, with family, friends, and neighbors enjoying a relaxing and engaging weekend respite from routine. Most of all, there is a total and complete acceptance of the cockfight as a normal, comfortable cultural pattern, as American as apple pie, motherhood, and the Chevrolet.

Conclusion

Cockfighting, as old as civilization, is a traditional part of American culture. Changing times, however, have placed cockfighting at the center of heated controversy. Adherents assert that their avocation is their traditional heritage, their right, and an enormously challenging, engaging, and rewarding recreational pursuit, with significant real and symbolic benefits. Moderate opponents view the sport as anachronistic and inappropriate in today's times. More strident opponents claim that it is barbaric and degenerate, unfit for a civilized society. Cockfighting and its opposition are in an ideological stalemate.

From a sociological perspective, the controversy surrounding cockfighting is a symbolic conflict and a metaphor for the clash of two overriding value systems in U.S. society—between the instrumental orientation of times past and today's affective/expressive orientation. In earlier centuries, and especially in rural or frontier society, life was harsh and survival problematic. Sensitivity and sentimentality were luxuries, if not vices, that few could afford, and "toughness" was a common virtue. The expedient and instrumental approach to life gave everything a purpose. Animals—whether horse, cow, dog, or gamecock—were "tools" to be used for human benefit without regard for their sensibilities. Such was the nature of existence.

In contrast, in today's "kinder and gentler" culture, with its animal rights movement and pervasive animal anthropormorphisms, the affective/expressive orientation holds that animals are the social and moral equivalents of humans and should, accordingly, be treated as humans. Thus, animal-related, human behavior is viewed through two widely disparate perspectives.

In Western, industrialized societies, the modal motivation for social behavior has developed in two separate directions. In a best-selling book titled *The Lonely Crowd*, David Riesman and his colleagues said the American national character or value emphasis was moving from a traditional "inner directed" orientation to one that is "other directed." The "inner directed" person is guided by resolute conviction, a personal sense of mission, and a well defined feeling of what is right and wrong, all acquired through early family and community socialization. The "inner directed" person is a rugged individualist who follows his or her own dictates and beliefs, regardless of what others think. This person values individual rights—including privacy, private property, and minding "one's own buisness."

Perception of social approval in contrast, guides the "other directed" individual. He or she gives priority to the group rather than to the individual, and places high value on change and moderation—the "happy medium," as it were. Such an individual strongly believes in "improvement" of social life, including a movement toward collectivism, and stresses cooperation, consensus, and concern for the common cause. "Other directed" people are convinced that the public concern supersedes private belief and privilege, and that the suppression of individual rights is well justified if it contributes to the collective good.

In the very simplest terms, the cockfighter feels that he should be allowed to pursue his avocation because his forebearers did, because it represents the "natural order" of things, because he sees socially redeeming value in it, and because he believes it to be his personal and inalienable right in a free society. Opponents of cockfighting, on the other hand, think the sport should be outlawed because they find it socially and morally reprehensible, an affront to common decency and community propriety, antithetical to the common good and, thus, indefensible on the basis of any grounds.

Oil and water do not mix!

References

Bryant, Clifton D. (1982). "Cockfighting in Sociohistorical Context: Some Sociological Observations on a Socially Disvalued Sport. Part I: *The Gamecock, 45* (1): 80–85; Part II: *45* (2): 65–70.

Bryant, Clifton D. (1991). "Deviant Leisure and Clandestine Lifestyle: Cockfighting as a Socially Disvalued Sport," *World Leisure and Recreation* (Official Publication of the World Leisure and Recreation Association) *33* (2): 17–21.

Bryant, Clifton D., and Li Li. (1991a) *The National Gamefowl Fanciers Survey: A Research Report (Volume One).* Blacksburg (VA): Department of Sociology, Virginia Polytechnic Institute and State University.

Bryant, Clifton D., and Li Li. (1991b). "A Statistical Value Profile of Cockfighters," *Sociology and Social Research 75* (4): 199–209.

Cobb, James E., "Cockfighting in East Tennessee," pp. 75–96 in Charles A. Faulkner and Carol Buckles (eds.), *Glimpses of Southern Appalachian Folk Culture: Papers in Memory of Norbert T. Riedl.* Tennessee Anthropological Association, Miscellaneous Paper No. 3, 1978.

Cox, C. (1977). "Cockfighting: An Unfashionable View," *Esquire*, pp. 8–15.

Donlon, Jon. (1990). "Fighting Cocks, Feathered Warriors, and Little Heroes," *Play and Culture 3*: 273–285.

Hawley, F. Frederick. *Organized Cockfighting: A Deviant Recreational Subculture.* Unpublished Ph.D. dissertation, Louisiana State University, Baton Rouge (1982).

Grit and Steel (October 1970). pp. 20 & 31.

Herzog, Harold A., Jr. (1985). "Hackfights and Derbies," *Appalachian Journal 12* (2): 114–123.

McCaghy, Charles H., and Arthur G. Neal. (1974). "The Fraternity of Cockfighters: Ethical Embellishments of an Illegal Sport," *Journal of Popular Culture 8*: 557–569.

Parker, Gary L. (1986). "An Outlet for Male Aggression: The Secret Fraternity of the Southern Cockfighter," *Tennessee Anthropologist 11* (1): 21–26.

Riesman, David, Nathan Glazer, and Ruell Denny. (1950). *The Lonely Crowd.* New Haven: Yale University Press.

20 Hanging Tongues: A Sociological Encounter with the Assembly Line

WILLIAM E. THOMPSON

Few of us are born so wealthy—or so deprived—that we do not have to work for a living. Some jobs seem to be of little importance, as with those we take during high school and college. We simply accept what is available and look at it as a temporary activity to help us get by for the time being. When its time is up, we discard it as we would worn-out clothing. In contrast, the jobs we take after we have completed our education—those full-time, more or less permanent endeavors at which we labor so long and hard—in these we invest much of ourselves. In turn, as our schedules come to revolve around their demands, we become aware of how central these jobs are to our lives.

All jobs, however, whether full-time and permanent or temporary, expedient, and discarded, are significant for our lives. Each contributes in its own way to our thinking and attitudes, becoming a part of the general stockpile of experiences that culminates in our basic orientation to life. Because of the significance of work for our lives, then, sociologists pay a great deal of attention to the work setting. They focus on interaction in that setting, as well as the social organization of work and its constraints, benefits, and other outcomes.

Of all jobs, one of the most demanding, demeaning, and demoralizing is that of the assembly line. Those of us who have worked on an assembly line have shared a work experience unlike any other, and for many of us education was the way by which we escaped from this form of modern slavery. As Thompson examines the assembly line in the meat-packing industry, he makes evident how this job affects all aspects of the workers' lives. His analysis provides a good framework for you to use in reflecting on your own work experiences.

THIS QUALITATIVE SOCIOLOGICAL STUDY analyzes the experience of working on a modern assembly line in a large beef plant. It explores and examines a special type of assembly line work which involves the slaughtering and processing of cattle into a variety of products intended for human consumption and other uses.

Working in the beef plant is "dirty work," not only in the literal sense of being drenched with perspiration and beef blood, but also in the figurative sense of performing a low-status, routine, and demeaning job. Although the work is honest and necessary in a society which consumes beef, slaughtering and butchering cattle is generally viewed as an undesirable and repugnant job. In that sense, workers at the beef plant share some of the same experiences as other workers in similarly regarded occupations (for example, ditchdiggers, garbage collectors, and other types of assembly line workers). . . .

The Setting

The setting for the field work was a major beef processing plant in the Midwest. At the time of the study, the plant was the third largest branch of a corporation which operated ten such plants in the United States. . . .

The beef plant was organizationally separated into two divisions: Slaughter and Processing. This study focused on the Slaughter division in the area of the plant known as the *kill floor*. A dominant feature of the kill floor was the machinery of the assembly line itself. The line was composed of an overhead stainless steel rail which began at the slaughter chute and curved its way around every work station in the plant. Every work station contained specialized machinery for the job performed at that place on the line. Dangling from the rail were hundreds of stainless steel hooks pulled by a motorized chain. Virtually every part of the line and all of the implements (tubs, racks, knives, etc.) were made of stainless steel. The walls were covered with a ceramic tile and the floor was made of sealed cement. There were floor drains located at every work station, so that at the end of each work segment (at breaks, lunch, and shift's end) the entire kill floor could be hosed down and cleaned for the next work period.

Another dominant feature of the kill floor was the smell. Extremely difficult to describe, yet impossible to forget, this smell combined the smells of live cattle, manure, fresh beef blood, and internal organs and their contents. This smell not only permeated the interior of the plant, but was combined on the outside with the smell of smoke from various waste products being burned and could be smelled throughout much of the community. This smell contributed greatly to the general negative feelings about work at the beef plant, as it served as the most distinguishable symbol of the beef plant to the rest of the community. The single most often asked question of me during the research by those outside the beef plant was, "How do you stand the smell?" In typical line workers' fashion, I always responded, "What smell? All I smell at the beef plant is money." . . .

Method

The method of this study was nine weeks of full-time participant observation as outlined by Schatzman and Strauss (1973) and Spradley (1979; 1980). To enter the setting, the researcher went through the standard application process for a summer job. No mention of the research intent was made, though it was made clear that I was a university sociology professor. After initial screening, a thorough physical examination, and a helpful reference from a former student and part-time employee of the plant, the author was hired to work on the *Offal* crew in the Slaughter division of the plant. . . .

The Work

. . . The line speed on the kill floor was 187. That means that 187 head of cattle were slaughtered per hour. At any particular work station, each worker was required to work at that speed. Thus, at my work station, in the period of one hour, 187 beef tongues were mechanically pulled from their hooks; dropped into a large tub filled with water; had to be taken from the tub and hung on a large stainless steel rack full of hooks; branded with a "hot brand" indicating they had been inspected by a USDA inspector; and then covered with a small plastic bag. The rack was taken to the cooler, replaced with an empty one, and the process began again.

It would be logical to assume that if a person worked at a steady, continuous pace of handling 187 tongues per hour, everything would go smoothly; not so. In addition to hanging, branding, and bagging tongues, the worker at that particular station also cleaned the racks and cleaned out a variety of empty stainless steel tubs used to hold hearts, kidneys, and other beef organs. Thus, in order to be free to clean the tubs when necessary, the "tongue-hanger" had to work at a slightly faster pace than the line moved. Then, upon returning from cleaning the tubs, the worker would be behind the line (*in a hole*) and had to work much faster to catch up with the line. Further, one fifteen-minute break and a thirty-minute lunch break were scheduled for an eight-hour shift. Before the "tongue-hanger" could leave his post for one of these, all tongues were required to be properly disposed of, all tubs washed and stored, and the work area cleaned.

My first two nights on the job, I discovered the consequences of working at the line speed (hanging, branding, and bagging each tongue as it fell in the tub). At the end of the work period when everybody else was leaving the work floor for break or lunch, I was furiously trying to wash all the tubs and clean the work area. Consequently, I missed the entire fifteen minute break and had only about ten minutes for lunch. By observing other workers, I soon caught on to the system. Rather than attempting to work at a steady pace consistent with the line speed, the norm was to work sporadically at a very frenzied pace, actually running ahead of the line and plucking tongues from the hooks before they got to the station. With practice, I learned to hang two or three tongues at a time, perform all the required tasks, and then take an unscheduled two or three minute break until the line caught up with me. Near break and lunch everybody worked at a frantic pace, got ahead of the line, cleaned the work areas, and even managed to add a couple of minutes to the scheduled break or lunch.

Working ahead of the line seems to have served as more than merely a way of gaining a few minutes of extra break time. It also seemed to take on a symbolic meaning. The company controlled the speed of the line. Seemingly, that took all element of control over the work process away from the workers. . . . However, when the workers refused to work at line speed and actually worked faster than the line, they not only added a few minutes of relaxation from the work while the line caught up, but they symbolically regained an element of control over the pace of their own work. . . .

Coping

One of the difficulties of work at the beef plant was coping with three aspects of the work: monotony, danger, and dehumanization. While individual workers undoubtedly coped in a variety of ways, some distinguishable patterns emerged.

MONOTONY

The monotony of the line was almost unbearable. At my work station, a worker would hang, brand, and bag between 1,350 and 1,500 beef tongues in an eight-hour shift. With the exception of the scheduled fifteen-minute break and a thirty-minute lunch period (and sporadic brief gaps in the line), the work was mundane, routine, and continuous. As in most assembly line work, one inevitably drifted into daydreams (e.g., Garson, 1975; King, 1978; Linhart, 1981). It was not unusual to look up or down the line and see workers at various stations singing to themselves, tapping their feet to imaginary music, or carrying on conversations with themselves. I found that I could work with virtually no attention paid to the job, with my hands and arms almost automatically performing their tasks. In the meantime, my mind was free to wander over a variety of topics, including taking mental notes. In visiting with other workers, I found that daydreaming was the norm. Some would think about their families, while others fantasized about sexual escapades, fishing, or anything unrelated to the job. One individual who was rebuilding an antique car at home in his spare time would meticulously mentally rehearse the procedures he was going to perform on the car the next day.

Daydreaming was not inconsequential, however. During these periods, items were most likely to be dropped, jobs improperly performed, and accidents incurred. Inattention to detail around moving equipment, stainless steel hooks, and sharp knives invariably leads to dangerous consequences. Although I heard rumors of drug use to help fight the monotony, I never saw any workers take any drugs nor saw any drugs in any workers' possession. It is certainly conceivable that some workers might have taken something to help them escape the reality of the line, but the nature of the work demanded enough attention that such a practice could be ominous.

DANGER

The danger of working in the beef plant was well known. Safety was top priority (at least in theory) and management took pride in the fact that only three employee on-the-job deaths had occurred in twelve years. Although deaths were uncommon, serious injuries were not. The beef plant employed over 1,800 people. Approximately three-fourths of those employed had jobs which demanded the use of a knife honed to razor-sharpness. Despite the use of wire-mesh aprons and gloves, serious cuts were almost a daily occurrence. Since workers constantly handled beef blood, danger of infection was ever present. As one walked along the assembly line, a wide assortment of bandages on fingers, hands, arms, necks, and faces could always be seen.

In addition to the problem of cuts, workers who cut meat continuously sometimes suffered muscle and ligament damage to their fingers and hands. In one severe case, I was told of a woman who worked in processing for several years who had to wear splints on her fingers while away from the job to hold them straight. Otherwise, the muscles in her hand would constrict her fingers into the grip position, as if holding a knife. . . .

When I spoke with fellow workers about the dangers of working in the plant, I noticed interesting defense mechanisms. . . . After a serious accident, or when telling about an accident or death which occurred in years past, the workers would almost immediately dissociate themselves from the event and its victim. Workers tended to view those who suffered major accidents or death on the job in much the same way that nonvictims of crime often view crime victims as either partially responsible for the event, or at least as very different from themselves (Barlow, 1981). "Only a part-timer," "stupid," "careless" or something similar was used, seemingly to reassure the worker describing the accident that it could not happen to him. The reality of the situation was that virtually all the jobs on the kill floor were dangerous, and any worker could have experienced a serious injury at any time. . . .

DEHUMANIZATION

Perhaps the most devastating aspect of working at the beef plant (worse than the monotony and the danger) was the dehumanizing and demeaning elements of the job. In a sense, the assembly line worker became a part of the assembly line. The assembly line is not a tool used by the worker, but a machine which controls him/her. A tool can only be productive in the hands of somebody skilled in its use, and hence becomes an extension of the person using it. A machine, on the other hand, performs specific tasks, thus its operator becomes an extension of it in the production process. . . . When workers are viewed as mere extensions of the machines with which they work, their human needs become secondary in importance to the smooth mechanical functioning of the production process. In a bureaucratic structure, when "human needs collide with systems needs the individual suffers" (Hummel, 1977:65).

Workers on the assembly line are seen as interchangeable as the parts of the product on the line itself. An example of one worker's perception of this phenomenon at the beef plant was demonstrated the day after a fatal accident occurred. I asked the men in our crew what the company did in the case of an employee death (I wondered if there was a fund for flowers, or if the shift was given time off to go to the funeral, etc.). One worker's response was: "They drag off the body, take the hard hat and boots and check 'em out to some other poor sucker, and throw him in the guy's place." While employee death on the job was not viewed quite that coldly by the company, the statement fairly accurately summarized the overall result of a fatal accident, and importance of any individual worker to the overall operation of the production process. It accurately summarized the workers' perceptions about management's attitudes toward them. . . .

Sabotage

It is fairly common knowledge that assemblyline work situations often led to employee sabotage or destruction of the product or equipment used in the production process (Garson, 1975; Balzer, 1976; Shostak, 1980). This is the classic experience of alienation as described by Marx (1964a,b). . . . At the beef plant I quickly learned that there was an art to effective sabotage. Subtlety appeared to be the key. "The art lies in sabotaging in a way that is not immediately discovered," as a Ford worker put it (King, 1978:202). This seemed to hold true at the beef plant as well. . . .

The greatest factor influencing the handling of beef plant products was its status as a food product intended for human consumption. . . . Though not an explicitly altruistic group, the workers realized that the product would be consumed by people (even family, relatives, and friends), so consequently, they rarely did anything to actually contaminate the product.

Despite formal norms against sabotage, some did occur. It was not uncommon for workers to deliberately cut chunks out of pieces of meat for no reason (or for throwing at other employees). While regulations required that anything that touched the floor had to be put in tubs marked "inedible," the informal procedural norms were otherwise. When something was dropped, one usually looked around to see if an inspector or foreman noticed. If not, the item was quickly picked up and put back on the line.

Several explanations might be offered for this type of occurrence. First, since the company utilized a profit-sharing plan, when workers damaged the product, or had to throw edible pieces into inedible tubs (which sold for pet food at much lower prices), profits were decreased. A decrease in profits to the company ultimately led to decreased dividend checks to employees. Consequently, workers were fairly careful not to actually ruin anything. Second, when something was dropped or mishandled and had to be rerouted to "inedible," it was more time-consuming than if the product had been handled properly and kept on the regular line. In other words, if no inspector noticed, it was easier to let it go through on the line. There was a third, and seemingly more meaningful, explanation for this behavior, however. It was against the rules to do it, it was a challenge to do it, and thus it was fun to do it.

The workers practically made a game out of doing forbidden things simply to see if they could get away with it. . . . New workers were routinely socialized into the subtle art of rulebreaking as approved by the line workers. At my particular work station, it was a fairly common practice for other workers who were covered with beef blood to come over to the tub of swirling water designed to clean the tongues, and as soon as the inspector looked away, wash their hands, arms, and knives in the tub. This procedure was strictly forbidden by the rules. If witnessed by a foreman or inspector, the tub had to be emptied, cleaned, and refilled, and all the tongues in the tub at the time had to be put in the "inedible" tub. All of that would be a time-consuming and costly procedure, yet the workers seemed to absolutely delight in successfully pulling off the act. As Balzer (1976:90) indicates:

> Since a worker often feels that much if not all of what he does is done in places designated by the company, under company control, finding ways to express personal freedom from this institutional regimentation is important.

Thus, artful sabotage served as a symbolic way in which the workers could express a sense of individuality, and hence, self-worth.

The Financial Trap

Given the preceding description and analysis for work at the beef plant, why did people work at such jobs? Obviously, there are a multitude of plausible answers to that question. Without doubt, however, the key is money. The current economic situation, the lack of steady employment opportunities (especially for the untrained and poorly educated), combined with the fact that the beef plant's starting wage exceeded the minimum wage by approximately $5.50 per hour emerge as the most important reasons people went to work there.

Despite the high hourly wage and fringe benefits, however, the monotony, danger, and hard physical work drove many workers away in less than a week. During my study, I observed much worker turnover. Those who stayed displayed an interesting pattern which helps explain why they did not leave. Every member of my work crew answered similarly my questions about why they stayed at the beef plant. Each of them took the job directly after high school, because it was the highest-paying job available. Each of them had intended to work through the summer and then look for a better job in the fall. During that first summer on the job they fell victim to what I label the "financial trap."

The "financial trap" was a spending pattern which demanded the constant weekly income provided by the beef plant job. This scenario was first told to me by an employee who had worked at the plant for over nine years. He began the week after his high school graduation, intending only to work that summer in order to earn enough money to attend college in the fall. After about four weeks' work he purchased a new car. He figured he could pay off the car that summer and still save enough money for tuition. Shortly after the car purchase, he added a new stereo sound system to his debt; next came a motorcycle; then the decision to postpone school for one year in order to continue working at the beef plant and pay off his debts. A few months later he married; within a year purchased a house; had a child; and bought another new car. Nine years later, he was still working at the beef plant, hated every minute of it, but in his own words "could not afford to quit." His case was not unique. Over and over again, I heard stories about the same process of falling into the "financial trap." The youngest and newest of our crew had just graduated high school and took the job for the summer in order to earn enough money to attend welding school the following fall. During my brief tenure at the beef plant, he purchased a new motorcycle, a new stereo, and a house trailer. When I left, he told me he had decided to postpone welding school for one year in order "to get everything paid for." I saw the financial trap closing in on him fast; he did too. . . .

Summary and Conclusions

There are at least three interwoven phenomena in this study which deserve further comment and research.

First is the subtle sense of unity which existed among the line workers. . . . The line both symbolically and literally linked every job, and consequently every worker, to each other. . . . A system of "uncooperative teamwork" seemed to combine simultaneously a feeling of "one-for-all, all-for-one, and every man for himself." Once a line worker made it past the first three or four days on the job which "weeded out" many new workers, his status as a *beefer* was assured and the sense of unity was felt as much by the worker of nine weeks as it was by the veteran of nine years. Because the workers maintained largely secondary relationships, this feeling of unification is not the same as the unity typically found on athletic teams, in fraternities, or among various primary groups. Yet it was a significant social force which bound the workers together and provided a sense of meaning and worth. Although their occupation might not be highly respected by outsiders, they derived mutual self-respect from their sense of belonging.

A second important phenomenon was the various coping methods . . . the beef plant line workers developed and practiced . . . for retaining their humanness. Daydreaming, horseplay and occasional sabotage protected their sense of self. Further, the prevailing attitude among workers that it was "us" against "them" served as a reminder that, while the nature of the job might demand subjugation to bosses, machines, and even beef parts, they were still human beings. . . .

A third significant finding was that consumer spending patterns among the beefers seemed to "seal their fate" and make leaving the beef plant almost impossible. A reasonable interpretation of the spending patterns of the beefers is that having a high-income/low-status job encourages a person to consume conspicuously. The prevailing attitude seemed to be "I may not have a nice job, but I have a nice home, a nice car, etc." This conspicuous consumption enabled workers to take indirect pride in their occupations. One of the ways of overcoming drudgery and humiliation on the job was to surround oneself with as many desirable material things as possible off the job. These items (cars, boats, motorcycles, etc.) became tangible rewards for the sacrifices endured at work.

The problem, of course, is that the possession of these expensive items required the continual income of a substantial paycheck which most of these men could only obtain by staying at the beef plant. These spending patterns were further complicated by the fact that they were seemingly "contagious." Workers talked to each other on breaks about recent purchases, thus reinforcing the norm of immediate gratification. A common activity of a group of workers on break or lunch was to run to the parking lot to see a fellow worker's new truck, van, car or motorcycle. Even the seemingly more financially conservative were usually caught up in this activity and often could not wait to display their own latest acquisitions. Ironically, as the workers cursed their jobs, these expensive possessions virtually destroyed any chance of leaving them.

Working at the beef plant was indeed "dirty work." It was monotonous, difficult, dangerous, and demeaning. Despite this, the workers at the beef plant worked hard to fulfill employer expectations in order to obtain financial rewards. Through a variety of symbolic techniques, they managed to overcome the many negative aspects of their work and maintain a sense of self-respect about how they earned their living.

References

Balzer, Richard (1976). *Clockwork: Life In and Outside an American Factory.* Garden City, NY: Doubleday.

Barlow, Hugh (1981). *Introduction to Criminology.* 2d ed. Boston: Little, Brown.

Garson, Barbara (1975). *All the Livelong Day: The Meaning and Demeaning of Routine work.* Garden City, NY: Doubleday.

Hummel, Ralph P. (1977). *The Bureaucratic Experience.* New York: St. Martin's Press.

King, Rick (1978). "In the sanding booth at Ford." Pp. 199–205 in John and Erna Perry (eds.), *Social Problems in Today's World.* Boston: Little, Brown.

Linhart, Robert (translated by Margaret Crosland) (1981). *The Assembly Line.* Amherst: University of Massachusetts Press.

Marx, Karl (1964a). *Economic and Philosophical Manuscripts of 1844.* New York: International Publishing (1844).

_____(1964b). *The Communist Manifesto.* New York: Washington Square Press (1848).

Schatzman, Leonard, and Anselm L. Strauss (1973). *Field Research.* Englewood Cliffs, NJ: Prentice-Hall.

Shostak, Arthur (1980). *Blue Collar Stress.* Reading, MA: Addison-Wesley.

Spradley, James P. (1979). *The Ethnographic Interview.* New York: Holt, Rinehart & Winston.

_____(1980). *Participant Observation.* New York: Holt, Rinehart & Winston.

21 The Sociology of the Vaginal Examination

JAMES M. HENSLIN
MAE A. BIGGS

All of us depend on others for the successful completion of the roles we play. In many ways, this makes cooperation the essence of social life (with due apologies to my conflict-theorist friends). Without teamwork, performances fall apart, people become disillusioned, jobs don't get done—and, ultimately, society is threatened. Accordingly, much of our socialization centers on learning to be good team players.

The work setting lends itself well to examining cooperative interaction and to the socially acceptable handling of differences—of "working arrangements" that defuse threats to fragile social patterns. For example, instructors often accept from students excuses that they know do not match reality. For their part, students often publicly accept what instructors teach, even though they privately disagree with those interpretations. Confrontation not only is unpleasant, and therefore preferable to avoid, but also is a threat to the continuity of interaction. Thus both instructors and students generally allow one another enough leeway to "get on with business" (which some might say is education, while others—more cynical—might say is the one earning a living and the other a degree).

One can gain much insight into the nature of society by trying to identify the implicit understandings that guide our interactions in everyday life. In this selection, Henslin and Biggs draw heavily on Goffman's dramaturgical framework as they focus on the vaginal examination. Note how much teamwork is required to make the definition stick that nothing sexual is occuring.

GENITAL BEHAVIOR IS PROLEMATIC in American society. Americans are socialized at a very early age into society's dictates concerning the situations, circumstances, and purposes of allowable and unallowable genital exposure.

Our thanks to Erving Goffman for commenting on this paper while it was in manuscript form. We have resisted the temptation to use his suggested title, "Behavior in Pubic Places."

After an American female has been socialized into rigorous norms concerning society's expectations in the covering and privacy of specified areas of her body, especially her vagina, exposure of her pubic area becomes something that is extremely problematic for her. Even for a woman who has overcome this particular problem when it comes to sexual relations and is no longer bothered by genital exposure in the presence of her sexual partner, the problem frequently recurs when she is expected to expose her vagina in a nonsexual manner to a male. Such is the case with the vaginal examination. The vaginal examination can become so threatening, in fact, that for many women it not only represents a threat to their feelings of modesty but also threatens their person and their feelings of who they are.

Because emotions are associated with the genital area through the learning of taboos, the vaginal examination becomes an interesting process; it represents a structured interaction situation in which the "privates" no longer remain private. From a sociological point of view, what happens during such interaction? Since a (if not *the*) primary concern of the persons involved is that all the interaction be defined as nonsexual, with even the hint of sexuality being avoided, what structural restraints on behavior operate? How does the patient cooperate in maintaining this definition of nonsexuality? In what ways are the roles of doctor, nurse, and patient performed such that they conjointly contribute to the maintenance of this definition?

This analysis is based on a sample of 12,000 to 14,000 vaginal examinations. The female author served as an obstetrical nurse in hospital settings and as an office nurse for general practitioners for fourteen years, giving us access to this area of human behavior which is ordinarily not sociologically accessible. Based on these observations, we have divided the interaction of the vaginal examination into five major scenes. We shall now examine each of these bounded interactions.

The setting for the vaginal examination may be divided into two areas (see Figure 21.1). Although there are no physical boundaries employed to demarcate the two areas, highly differentiated interaction occurs in each. Area 1, where Scenes I and V are played, includes that portion of the "office-examination" room which is furnished with a desk and three chairs. Area 2, where Scenes II, III, and IV take place, is furnished with an examination table, a swivel stool, a gooseneck lamp, a table for instruments, and a sink with a mirror above it.

Scene I: The Personalized Stage: The Patient as Person

The interaction flow of Scene I is as follows: (a) the doctor enters the "office-examination" room; (b) greets the patient; (c) sits down; (d) asks the patient why she is there; (e) questions her on specifics; (f) decides on a course of action, specifically whether a pelvic examination is needed or not; (g) if he thinks a pelvic is needed, he signals the nurse on the intercom and says, "I want a pelvic in room (X)"; (h) he gets up, and (i) leaves the room.

During this scene the patient is treated as a full person; that is, the courtesies of middle-class verbal exchange are followed, and, in addition to gathering medical information, if the doctor knows the patient well he may intersperse his medical queries with questions about her personal life. The following interaction that occurred during Scene I demonstrates the doctor's treatment of his patient as a full person:

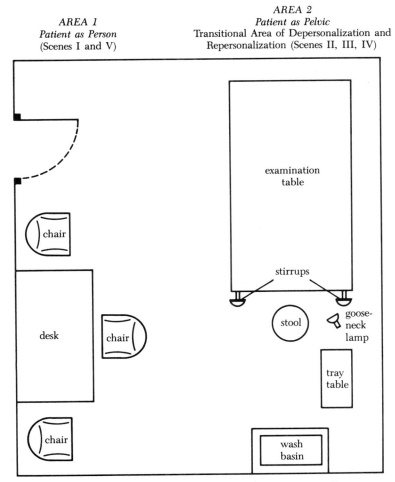

AREA 1
Patient as Person
(Scenes I and V)

AREA 2
Patient as Pelvic
Transitional Area of Depersonalization and
Repersonalization (Scenes II, III, IV)

FIGURE 21.1. The Doctor's Office-Examination Room

DOCTOR (upon entering the room): Hello, Joyce, I hear you're going to Southern
  Illinois University.
PATIENT: Yes, I am. I've been accepted, and I have to have my health record
  completed.

The doctor then seated himself at his desk and began filling out the health
record that the patient gave him. He interspersed his questions concerning
the record form with questions about the patient's teaching, about the area
of study she was pursuing, about her children, their health and their schooling.
He then said, "Well, we have to do this right. We'll do a pelvic on you." He
then announced via the intercom, "I want to do a pelvic on Joyce in room
1." At that point he left the room.

This interaction sequence is typical of the interaction that occurs in
Scene I between a doctor and a patient he knows well. When the doctor
does not know the patient well, he does not include his patient's name,
either her first or last name, in his announcement to the nurse that she
should come into the room. In such a case, he simply says, "I want to do
a pelvic in room 1," or, "Pelvic in room 1." The doctor then leaves the
room, marking the end of the scene.

Scene II: The Depersonalized Stage: Transition from Person to Pelvic

When at the close of Scene I the doctor says, "Pelvic in room (X)," he is
in effect announcing the transition of the person to a pelvic. It is a sort of
advance announcement, however, of a coming event, because the transition
has not yet been effected. The doctor's signal for the nurse to come in is,
in fact, a signal that the nurse should now help with the transition of the
patient from a person to a pelvic. Additionally, it also serves as an announcement to the patient that she is about to undergo this metamorphosis.

The interaction flow which accomplishes the transition from person to
pelvic is as follows: Upon entering the room, the nurse, without preliminaries, tells the patient, "The doctor wants to do a vaginal examination on
you. Will you please remove your panties?" While the patient is undressing,
the nurse prepares the props, positioning the stirrups of the examination
table, arranging the glove, the lubricant, and the speculum (the instrument
which, when inserted into the vagina, allows visual examination of the vaginal tract). She then removes the drape sheet from a drawer and directs
the patient onto the table, covers the patient with the drape sheet, assists
her in placing her feet into the stirrups, and positions her hips, putting
her into the lithotomy position (lying on her back with knees flexed and
out).

MEANING OF THE DOCTOR'S ABSENCE

The doctor's exiting from this scene means that the patient will be undressing in his absence. This is not accidental. In many cases, it is true, the doctor leaves because another patient is waiting, but even when there are no waiting patients, the doctors always exists at the end of Scene I. His leaving means that he will not witness the patient undressing, thereby successfully removing any suggestion whatsoever that a striptease is being performed. From the patient's point of view, the problem of undressing is lessened since a strange male is not present. Thus sexuality is removed from the undressing room, and when the doctor returns, only a particularized portion of her body will be exposed for the ensuing interaction. As we shall see, the doctor is no longer dealing with a person, but he is, rather, confronted by a "pelvic."

THE PROBLEM OF UNDERCLOTHING

Undressing and nudity are problematic for the patient since she has been socialized into not undressing before strangers.[1] Almost without exception, when the woman undresses in Scene II, she turns away from the nurse and the door, even though the door is closed. She removes only her panties in the typical case, but a small number of patients also remove their shoes.

After the patient has removed her panties and/or girdle, the problem for her is what to do with them. Panties and girdles do not have the same meaning as other items of clothing, such as a sweater, that can be casually draped around the body or strewn on furniture. Clothing is considered to be an extension of the self (Gross and Stone 1964), and in some cases the clothing comes to represent the particular part of the body that it covers. In this case, this means that panties represent to women their "private area." Comments made by patients that illustrate the problematics of panty exposure include: "The doctor doesn't want to look at these," "I want to get rid of these before he comes in," and, "I don't want the doctor to see these old things."

Some patients seem to be at a loss in solving this problem and turn to the nurse for guidance, asking her directly what they should do with their underclothing. Most patients, however, do not ask for directions, but hide their panties in some way. The favorite hiding or covering seems to be in or under the purse.[2] Other women put their panties in the pocket of their coat or in the folds of a coat or sweater, some cover them with a magazine, and some cover them with their own body on the examination table. It is rare that a woman leaves her panties exposed somewhere in the room.

THE DRAPE SHEET

Another problematic area in the vaginal examination is what being undressed can signify. Disrobing for others frequently indicates preparation for sexual relations. Since sexuality is the very thing that this scene is oriented toward removing, a mechanism is put into effect to eliminate sexuality—the drape sheet. After the patient is seated on the table, the nurse places a drape sheet from just below her breasts (she still has her blouse on) to over her legs. Although the patient is draped by the sheet, when she is positioned on the table with her legs in the stirrups, her pubic region is exposed. Usually it is not necessary for the doctor even to raise a fold in the sheet in order to examine her genitals.

Since the drape sheet does not cover the genital area, but, rather, leaves it exposed, what is its purpose? The drape sheet depersonalizes the patient. It sets the pubic area apart, letting the doctor view the pubic area in isolation, separating the pubic area from the person. The pubic area or female genitalia becomes an object isolated from the rest of the body. With the drape sheet, the doctor, in his position on the low stool, does not even see the patient's head. He no longer sees or need deal with a person, just the exposed genitalia marked off by the drape sheet. Yet, from the patient's point of view in her supine position, her genitals are covered! When she looks down at her body, she does not see exposed genitalia. The drape sheet effectively hides her pubic area *from herself* while exposing it to the doctor.

THIGH BEHAVIOR

American girls are given early and continued socialization in "limb discipline," being taught at a very early age to keep their legs close together while they are sitting or while they are retrieving articles from the ground. They receive such cautions from their mothers as, "Keep your dress down," "Put your legs together," and "Nice girls don't let their panties show." Evidence of socialization into "acceptable" thigh behavior shows up in the vaginal examination while the women are positioned on the examination table and waiting for the doctor to arrive. They do not let their thighs fall outwards in a relaxed position, but they try to hold their upper or mid-thighs together until the doctor arrives. They do this even in cases where it is very difficult for them to do so, such as when the patient is in her late months of pregnancy.

Although the scene has been played such that desexualization is taking place, and although the patient is being depersonalized such that when the doctor returns he primarily has a pelvic to deal with and not a person at this point in the interaction sequence the patient is still holding onto her sexuality and "personality" as demonstrated by her "proper" thigh behavior. Only later, when the doctor reenters the scene will she fully consent to the desexualized and depersonalized role and let her thighs fall outwards.

After the props are ready and the patient is positioned, the nurse announces to the doctor via intercom that the stage is set for the third scene, saying, "We're ready in room (X)."

Scene III: The Depersonalized Stage: The Person as Pelvic

FACE-TO-PUBIC INTERACTION

The interaction to this point, as well as the use of props, has been structured to project a singular defintion of the situation—that of legitimate doctor–patient interaction and, specifically, the nonsexual examination of a woman's vaginal region by a male. In support of this definition, a team performance is given in this scene (Goffman 1959: 104). Although the previous interaction has been part of an ongoing team performance, it has been sequential, leading to the peak of the performance, the vaginal examination itself. At this time, the team goes into a tandem cooperative act, utilizing its resources to maintain and continue the legitimation of the examination, and by its combined performance reinforcing the act of each team member. The doctor, while standing, places a plastic glove on his right hand, again symbolizing the depersonalized nature of the action—by using the glove he is saying that he will not himself be actually touching the "private area" since the glove will serve as an insulator.[3] It is at this point that he directs related questions to the patient regarding such things as her bowels or bladder. Then, while he is still in this standing position, the nurse in synchronization actively joins the performance by squeezing a lubricant onto his outstretched gloved fingers, and the doctor inserts the index and middle fingers of his right hand into the patient's vagina while externally palpating (feeling) the uterus. He then withdraws his fingers from the vagina, seats himself on the stool, inserts a speculum, and while the nurse positions the gooseneck lamp behind him, he visually examines the cervix.

Prior to this third scene, the interaction has been dyadic only, consisting of nurse and patient in Scene II and doctor and patient in Scene I. In this scene, however, the interaction becomes triadic in the sense that the doctor, nurse, and patient are simultaneously involved in the performance. The term triadic, however, does not even come close to accurately describing the role-playing of this scene. Since the patient has essentially undergone a metamorphosis from a person to an object—having been objectified or depersonalized, the focus of the interaction is now on a specific part of her body. The positioning of her legs and the use of the drape sheet have effectively made her pubic region the interaction focus, not only demarcating the pubic region as the focus of interaction but also blocking out the "talklines" between the doctor and patient, physically obstructing their exchange of glances (Goffman 1963: 161). Interaction between the doctor and the patient is no longer "face-to-face," being perhaps now more accurately described as "face-to-pubic" interaction.

BREASTS AS NONSEXUAL OBJECTS

Projecting and maintaining the definition of nonsexuality in the vaginal examination applies also to other parts of the body that are attributed to have sexual meaning in our culture, specifically the breasts. When the breasts are to be examined in coinjunction with a vaginal examination, a rather interesting ritual is ritually employed in order to maintain the projected definition of nonsexuality. This ritual tries to objectify the breasts by isolating them from the rest of the body, permitting the doctor to see the breasts apart from the person. In this ritual, after the patient has removed her upper clothing, a towel is placed across her breasts, and the drape sheet is then placed on top of the towel. Since the towel in and of itself more than sufficiently covers the breasts, we can only conclude that the purpose of the drape sheet is to further the definition of nonsexual interaction. Additionally, the doctor first removes the sheet from the breasts and exposes the towel. He then lifts the towel from *one* breast, makes his examination, and *replaces* the towel over the breast. He examines the other breast in exactly the same way, again replacing the towel after the examination.

THE NURSE AS CHAPERONE

That interaction in Scene III is triadic is not accidental, nor is it instrumentally necessary. It is, rather, purposely designed, being another means of desexualizing the vaginal examination. Instrumentally, the nurse functions merely to lubricate the doctor's fingers and to hand him the speculum. These acts obviously could be handled without the nurse's presence. It becomes apparent, then, that the nurse plays an entirely different role in this scene, that of chaperone, the person assigned to be present in a male–female role relationship to give assurance to interested persons that no untoward sexual acts take place. Although the patient has been depersonalized, or at least this is the definition that has been offered throughout the performance and is the definition that the team has been attempting to maintain, the possibility exists that the vaginal examination can erupt into a sexual scene. Because of this possibility (or the possible imputation or accusation of sexual behavior having taken place), the nurse is always present.[4] Thus even the possibility of sexual content in the vaginal examination is ordinarily denied by all the role-players. It would appear that such denial serves as a mechanism to avoid apprehension and suspicion concerning the motivations and behaviors of the role-players, allowing the performance to be initiated and to continue smoothly to its logical conclusion.[5]

THE PATIENT AS A NONPERSON TEAM MEMBER

With this definition of objectification and desexualization, the patient represents a vagina disassociated from a person. She has been dramaturgically transformed for the duration of this scene into a nonperson (Goffman 1959:152). This means that while he is seated and performing the vaginal examination, the doctor need not interact with the patient as a person, being, for example, constrained neither to carry on a conversation nor to maintain eye contact with her. Furthermore, this means that he is now permitted to carry on a "side conversation" with the person with whom he does maintain eye contact, his nurse. For example, during one examination the doctor looked up at the nurse and said: "Hank and I really caught some good-sized fish while we were on vacation. He really enjoyed himself." He then looked at his "work" and announced, "Cervix looks good; no inflammation—everything appears fine down here." Such ignoring of the presence of a third person would ordinarily constitute a breach of etiquette for middle-class interactions, but *in this case there really isn't a third person present.* The patient has been "depersonalized," and, correspondingly, the rules of conversation change, and no breach of etiquette has taken place.[6]

The patient, although defined as an object, is actually the third member of the team in the vaginal examination. Her role is to "play the role of being an object"; that is, she contributes her part to the flow of the interaction by acting as an object and not as a person. She contributes to the definition of herself as an object through studied alienation from the interaction, demonstrating what is known as dramaturgical discipline (Goffman 1959:216–18). She studiously gazes at the ceiling or wall, only occasionally allowing herself the luxury (or is it the danger?) of fleeting eye contact with the nurse. Eye contact with the doctor is, of course, prevented by the position of her legs and the drape sheet.

After the doctor tells the patient to get dressed, he leaves the room, and the fourth scene is ready to unfold.

Scene IV: The Repersonalizing Stage: The Transition from Pelvic to Person

During this stage of the interaction the patient undergoes a demetamorphosis, dramaturgically changing from vaginal object to person. Immediately after the doctor leaves, the nurse assists the patient into a sitting position, and she gets off the table. The nurse then asks the patient if she would like to use a towel to cleanse her genital area, and about 80 percent of the patients accepts the offer. In this scene, it is not uncommon for patients to make some statement concerning their relief that the examination is over. Statements such as "I'm glad that's over with" seem to indicate the patient's overt recognition of the changing scene, to acknowledge that she is now entering a different scene in the vaginal drama.

During this repersonalizing stage the patient is concerned with regrooming and recostuming. Patients frequently ask if they look all right, and the common question. "My dress isn't too wrinkled, is it?" appears to indicate the patient's awareness of and desire to be ready for the resumption of roles other than vaginal object. Her dress isn't too wrinkled for what? It must be that she is asking whether it is too wrinkled for (1) her resumption of the role of (patient as) person and (2) her resumption of nonpatient roles.

Modesty continues to operate during this scene, and it is interesting that patients who have just had their genital area thoroughly examined both visually and tactually by the doctor are concerned that this same man will see their underclothing. ("He won't be in before I get my underwear on, will he?") They are now desiring and preparing for the return to the feminine role. They apparently fear that the doctor will reenter the room as they literally have one foot in and one foot out of their panties. They want to have their personal front reestablished to their own satisfaction before the return of this male and the onset of the next scene. For this, they strive for the poise and composure that they deem fitting the person role for which they are now preparing, frequently using either their own pocket-mirror or the mirror above the sink to check their personal front.

During this transitional role patients indicate by their comments to the nurse that they are to again be treated as persons. While they are dressing, they frequently speak about their medical problems, their aches and pains, their fight against gaining weight, or feelings about their pregnancy. In such ways they are reasserting the self and are indicating that they are again entering "personhood."

The patient who best illustrates awareness that she had undergone a process of repersonalization is the woman who, after putting on her panties, said, "There! Just like new again." She had indeed moved out of her necessary but uncomfortable role as object, and her appearance or personal front once again matched her self-concept.

After the patient has recostumed and regroomed, the nurse directs the patient to the chair alongside the doctor's desk, and she then announces via intercom to the doctor, "The patient is dressed," or, "The patient is waiting." It is significant that at this point the woman is referred to as "patient" in the announcement to the doctor and not as "pelvic" as she was at the end of second scene. Sometimes the patient is also referred to by name in this announcement. The patient has completed her demetamorphosis at this point, and the nurse, by the way she refers to her, is officially acknowledging the transition.

The nurse then leaves the room, and her interaction with the patient ceases.

Scene V: The Repersonalized Stage: The Patient as Person Once More

When the doctor makes his third entrance, the patient has again resumed the role of person and is interacted with on this basis. She is both spoken to and receives replies from the doctor, with her whole personal front being visible in the interaction. During this fifth scene the doctor informs the patient of the results of her examination, he prescribes necessary medications, and, wherever indicated, he suggests further care. He also tells the patient whether or not she need see him again.

The significance of the interaction of Scene V for us is that the patient is again allowed to interact *as a person within the role of patient.* The doctor allows room for questions that the patient might have about the results of the examination, and he also gives her the opportunity to ask about other medical problems that she might be experiencing.

Interaction between the doctor and patient terminates as the doctor gets up from his chair and moves toward the door.

Conclusion: Desexualization of the Sacred

In concluding this analysis, we shall briefly indicate that conceptualizing the vagina as a sacred object yields a perspective that appears to be of value in analyzing the vaginal examination. Sacred objects are surrounded by rules protecting the object from being profaned, rules governing who may approach the "sacred," under what circumstances it may be approached, and what may and may not be done during such an approach (Durkheim 1965:51–59). If these rules are followed, the "sacred" will lose none of its "sacredness," but if they are violated, there is danger of the sacred being profaned.

In conceptualizing the vagina in this way, we find, for example, that who may and who may not approach the vagina is highly circumscribed, with the primary person so allowed being one who is ritually related to the possessor of the vagina, the husband. Apart from the husband (with contemporary changes duly noted),[7] except in a medical setting and by the actors about whom we are speaking, no one else may approach the vagina other than the self and still have it retain its sacred character.[8]

Because of this, the medical profession has taken great pains to establish a routine and ritual that will ensure the continued sacredness of the vaginas of its female patients, one that will avoid even the imputation of taboo violation. Accordingly, as we have herein analyzed, this ritual of the vaginal examination allows the doctor to approach the sacred without profaning it or violating taboos by dramaturgically defining the vagina as just another organ of the body, dissociating the vagina from the person, while desexualizing the person into a cooperative object.

Notes

1. With a society that is as clothing conscious and bodily conscious as is ours, undressing and nudity are problematic for many, but perhaps more for females than for males since males are more likely to experience structured situations in which they undress and are nude before others, such as showering after high school physical education classes, while females in the same situation are often afforded a greater degree of privacy with, for example, private shower stalls in place of the mass showers of the males. This is not always the case, however, and Theresa France (private communication) reports that in her classes the females also had communal showers.

2. From a psychiatric orientation this association of the panties with the purse is fascinating, given the Freudian interpretation that the purse signifies the female genitalia.

In some examination rooms, the problem of where to put the undergarments is solved by the provision of a special drawer for them located beneath the examination table.

3. It is true, of course, that the glove also serves instrumental purposes, such as protecting the physician from diseases that might be transmitted by means of digital–vaginal contact—and patients from diseases the physician might transmit from one patient to another.

4. It is interesting to note that even the corpse of a female is defined as being in need of such chaperonage. Erving Goffman, on reading this paper in manuscript form, commented that hospital etiquette dictates that "when a male attendant moves a female stiff from the room to the morgue he be accompanied by a female nurse."

5. Compare what Goffman (1959:104 has to say about secrets shared by team members. Remember that the patient in this interaction is not simply a member of the audience. She is a team member, being also vitally interested in projecting and maintaining the definition of nonsexuality. Another reader of this paper, who wishes to remain anonymous, reports that during one of her pregnancies she had a handsome, young, and unmarried Hungarian doctor and that during vaginal examinations with him she would "concentrate on the instruments being used and the uncomfortableness of the situation" so as not to become sexually aroused.

6. In this situation a patient is "playing the role" of an object, but she is still able to hear verbal exchange, and she could enter the interaction if she so desired. As such, side comments between doctor and nurse must be limited. In certain other doctor-patient situations, however, the patient completely leaves the "person role," such as when the patient is anesthetized, which allows much freer banter among medical personnel. In delivery rooms of hospitals, for example, it is not uncommon

for the obstetrician to comment while stitching the episiotomy, "She's like a new bride now," or, when putting in the final stitch, to say, "This is for the old man." Additionally, while medical students are stitching their first episiotomy, instructing doctors have been known to say, "It's not tight enough. Put one more in for the husband."

7. Consensual approaches by boyfriends certainly run less risk of violating the sacred than at earlier periods in our history, but this depends a good deal on religion, education, age, and social class membership.

8. It is perhaps for this reason that prostitutes ordinarily lack respect: They have profaned the sacred. And in doing so, not only have they failed to limit vaginal access to culturally prescribed individuals, but they have added further violation by allowing vaginal access on a pecuniary basis. They have, in effect, sold the sacred.

References

Durkheim, Emile (1965). *The Elementary Forms of the Religious Life*. New York: The Free Press (1915 copyright by George Allen & Unwin Ltd.).

Goffman, Erving (1959). *The Presentation of Self in Everyday Life*. Garden City, NY: Doubleday, Anchor Books.

Goffman, Erving (1963). *Behavior in Public Places: Notes on the Social Organization of Gatherings*. New York: The Free Press.

Gross, Edward, and Gregory Stone (1964). "Embarrassment and the Analysis of Role Requirements," *American Journal of Sociology 70*: 1–15.

Deviance and Social Control

F OR SOCIETY TO EXIST, people must be able to know what to expect of others. If they couldn't do this, the world would be in chaos. Because the behavior of humans is not controlled by instincts, people develop *norms* (rules and expectations) to provide regularity, or patterns, to social life. Norms provide a high degree of certainty in what would be a hopelessly disoriented world if everyone followed his or her own inclinations and no one knew what to expect of others.

The confidence we can place in others is only relative, however, because not everyone follows all the rules all the time. In fact *deviance*, the violation of rules and expectations, is universal. All members of society violate some of the expectations that others have of them.

The norms that people develop to control one another cover a fascinating variety of human behavior. They include rules and expectations concerning our appearance, manner, and conduct.

1. *Appearance* (what we look like): the norms concerning clothing, make-up, hairstyle, and other such presentational aspects of our body including its cleanliness and odors. These rules also cover the *social extensions of the person*, those objects thought to represent the individual in some way, such as one's home, car, or pet.

2. *Manner* (our style of doing things): the usually informal expectations concerning the way we express ourselves, such as our mannerisms, gestures, and other body language. Manner includes *personal style*, the expectations others have of an individual because of the way he or she has acted in the past (personality, "the way he or she is"), as well as *group style*, the expectations attached to a social group (racial, sexual, occupational, age, and so on—"the way they are"). Rules or expectations of manner are held by the

individual who is a member of a particular group, by other members of the group, and by persons who are not members of the group. These three sources of expectations often conflict.

3. *Conduct* (what we say, what we do): rules covering the rest of human behavior, specifying what one can and cannot do and say under various circumstances. These include rules of *authority* (who has the right to give which orders to whom), rules of *obligation* (who has the responsibility to do what for whom), and rules of *account giving* (what one is expected to say when asked for an explanation, including the degree to which one is expected to be honest, to go into detail, or to avoid implicating others).

These everyday rules of appearance, manner, and conduct cover what we can and cannot say or do to whom, the circumstances under which we can or cannot do or say it, how we should look when we do or say something, and how we must phrase what we say, such as with varying degrees of respect or informality. In other words, hardly a single aspect of our lives goes untouched by rules made by others. We all are immersed in these pervasive expectations. None of us is a free agent, able to do as he or she pleases. Rather, *social control* is a basic fact of social life.

Norms are extremely complex. They vary for the same person under different circumstances, dictating variations in proper attire in a university classroom, at a formal dance, or at the beach. They also differ according to people's social identities—that is, according to the groups to which people are thought to belong. For example, the rules of conduct, appearance, and manner differ for convicts, CEOS, students, children, old people, and men and women—that is, these expectations depend on reputation, prestige, wealth, occupation, age, and gender. In some instances, they also vary according to race.

The rules also change depending on the audience for whom one is performing. For example, as teenagers know so well, their parents' expectations markedly differ from their friends' expectations. Similarly, people often are expected to act one way when they are with members of their own age or racial/ethnic group, but differently when they are with others.

These complex expectations define in and define out: Those who conform to the norms are accorded the status of members in good standing, while those who deviate usually are defined as outsiders of some sort. Viewed with suspicion, deviants are reacted to in a number of ways. They may be given more attention in order to bring them back into line, or they may be ostracized or kicked out of the group. In extreme cases they are tried and imprisoned—or even put to death. In less extreme cases they may be shunned or physically attacked. For mild deviations, they may simply be stared at. People also may gossip about them, divorce them, strike their names from guest lists, or demote or fire them.

This list of some of the social reactions to deviance indicates that people are extremely concerned with rule-following and rule-breaking behaviors.

Deviance challenges fundamental expectations about the way in which social life is run, and affects people's welfare. With such a stake in the conformity of others, people react to deviants—sharply and negatively if they consider the deviance threatening, but tolerantly and perhaps even with amusement if they believe it to be mild.

As the word is used in sociology, "deviance" is not a term of negative judgment, as it usually is when used by nonsociologists. To sociologists the term is meant simply to be descriptive, referring to activities that violate the expectations of others, passing judgment neither on the merit of the rules nor on those who violate them.

In this Part, in which we focus on responses to deviants, we look especially at processes of social control. In the opening selection, James M. Henslin tells the story of an airplane crash in the Andes—looking at how social control operated among the survivors who ate their deceased friends and relatives. William J. Chambliss then examines how different community reactions to lower-class and middle-class delinquents have far-reaching effects on their later lives. Gary T. Marx follows this by analyzing some of the fascinating—but unintended—effects on police who go under-cover. Philip G. Zimbardo then describes his intriguing experiment in which he uncovered organizational bases for the hostile relationships between prisoners and prison guards. Finally, David L. Rosenhan closes this Part by asking the intriguing question of whether or not we can tell the sane from the insane.

22 The Survivors of the F-227

JAMES M. HENSLIN

As has been stressed in previous readings, each culture provides guidelines for how to view the world, and for determining right and wrong. The perspective we learn envelops us much as a fish is immersed in water. Almost all the world's cultures uphold the idea that it is wrong to eat human flesh. (Some exceptions do apply, such as warriors who used to eat the heart or kidneys of slain enemies in an attempt to acquire the source of their strength or courage.) Thus it is safe to say that nowhere in the world is there a culture whose members regularly consume people as food. Yet, in the unusual situation recounted here, that is precisely what happened.

Note how, even in the midst of reluctantly committing acts they themselves found extremely repugnant—and ones they fully knew that the world condemns—this group developed norms to govern their behavior. This was crucial for these survivors, because group support, along with its attendant norms, is critical in maintaining a sense of a "good" self. At the conclusion of the article, Henslin shows how this event is more than simply an interesting story—that it represents the essence of social life.

LOCATED BETWEEN BRAZIL AND ARGENTINA, near Buenos Aires, is tiny Uruguay. On October 12, 1972, a propeller-driven Fairchild F-227 left Uruguay's capital, Montevideo, bound for Santiago, Chile—a distance of about 900 miles. On board were 15 members of an amateur rugby team from Uruguay, along with 25 of their relatives and friends. The pilots, from the Uruguayan Air Force, soon became concerned about turbulence

The events related in this selection are based primarily on Piers Paul Read, *Alive: The Story of the Andes Survivors* (Philadelphia: J. B. Lippincott, 1974), pages 26–39, 70, 81–91, 98, 101, 128, 136–139, 165, 168, 171, 199, and 218. Supplementary sources are "Cannibalism on the Cordillera," *Time,* January 8, 1973:27–28, and Carlos Benales, "70 Days Battling Starvation and Freezing in the Andes: A Chronicle of Man's Unwillingness to Die," *New York Times,* January 1, 1973:3.

over the Andes Mountains. Winds blowing in from the Pacific were colliding with air currents coming from the opposite direction, creating a turbulence that could toss a plane around like a scrap of paper in a wind storm.

Since the threat was so great, the pilots landed in Mendoza, Argentina, where everyone spent the night. The next day, with the weather only slightly improved, the crew debated about turning back. Several of the rugby players taunted them, saying they were cowards. When the captain of a plane which had just flown over the Andes reported that the F-227 should be able to fly over the turbulence, the Fairchild's pilots decided to continue the trip. Once again airborne, the young passengers laughed about its being Friday the 13th as some threw a rugby ball around and others played cards. Many of them still in their teens, and all of them from Uruguay's upper class (two were nephews of the president of Uruguay), they were in high spirits.

Over the Andes the plane flew into a thick cloud, and the pilots had to fly by instrument. Amid the turbulence they hit an "air pocket," and the plane suddenly plunged 3,000 feet. When the passengers abruptly found themselves below the cloud, one young man turned to another and said, "Is it normal to fly so close?" He was referring to the mountainside just 10 feet off the right wing.

With a deafening roar, the right wing sheared off as it hit the side of the mountain. The wing whipped over the plane and knocked off the tail. The steward, the navigator, and three of the rugby players still strapped in their seats were blown out of the gaping hole. Then the left wing broke off and, like a toboggan going 200 miles an hour, the fuselage slid on its belly into a steep, snow-covered valley.

As night fell, the survivors huddled in the wreckage. At 12,000 feet the cold, especially at night, was brutal. There was little fuel, because not much wood is used in the construction of airplanes. They had almost no food—basically some chocolate that the passengers had bought on their overnight stay in Mendoza. There were a few bottles of wine, and the many cartons of cigarettes they had purchased at a duty-free shop.

The twenty-seven who survived the crash expected to be rescued quickly. At most, they thought, they would have to spend the night on the mountain top. Seventy days later, only sixteen remained alive.

The chocolate and wine didn't go very far, and provided little nourishment. The plane, off course by a hundred miles or so and painted white, was not only difficult to track, but virtually invisible against the valley's deep layer of snow: Search planes were unable to locate the wreckage.

As the days went by, the survivors' spirits seemed to be sucked into a hopeless pit. Hunger and starvation began to bear down on them. They felt cold all the time. They became weaker and had difficulty keeping their balance. Their skin became wrinkled, like that of old people. Although no one mentioned it, several of the young men began to realize that their only chance to survive was to eat the bodies of those who died in the crash. The corpses lay strewn in the snow around the plane, perfectly preserved by the bitter cold.

The thought of cutting into the flesh of their friends was too ghastly a prospect to put into words. Finally, however, Canessa, a medical student, brought up the matter with his friends. He asserted that the bodies were no longer people. The soul was gone, he said, and the body was simply meat—and essential to their survival. They were growing weaker, and they could not survive without food. And what food was there besides the corpses? "They are no more human beings than the dead flesh of the cattle we eat at home," he said.

Days later, the topic moved from furtive discussion in a small group to open deliberation among all the survivors. Inside the plane, arguing the matter, Canessa reiterated his position. His three closest friends supported him, adding, "We have a duty to survive. If we don't eat the bodies, it is a sin. We must do this not just for our own sakes but also for our families. In fact," they continued, "God wants us to survive, and He has provided these bodies so we can live." Some, however, just shook their heads, the thought too disturbing to even contemplate.

Serbino pushed the point. He said, "If I die, I want you to eat my body. I want you to use it." Some nodded in agreement. In an attempt to bring a little humor to the black discussion, he added, "If you don't, I'll come back and give you a swift kick in the butt." Some said that while they did not think it would be wrong to eat the bodies, they themselves could never do it. The arguments continued for hours.

Four of the young men went outside. Near the plane, the buttocks of a body protruded from the snow. No one spoke as they stared at it. Wordlessly, Canessa knelt and began to cut with the only instrument he had found, a piece of broken glass. The flesh was frozen solid, and he could cut only slivers the size of matchsticks. Canessa laid the pieces on the roof of the plane, and the young men went back inside. They said that the meat was drying in the sun. The others looked mutely at one another. No one made a move to leave the plane.

Canessa decided that he would have to be the first to act. Going outside, he picked up a sliver of meat. Staring at it, almost transfixed, he became as though paralyzed. He simply couldn't make his hand move to his mouth. Summoning every ounce of courage, he forced his hand upwards. While his stomach recoiled, he pushed the meat inside his mouth and forced himself to swallow. Later, Serbino took a piece. He tried to swallow, but the sliver hung halfway down his throat. Quickly grabbing some snow, he managed to wash it down. Canessa and Serbino were joined by others, who also ate.

The next morning, on the transistor radio they had struggled so hard to get working, their hearts plunged when they heard that the air force had called off the search. The survivors knew that this announcement almost sealed their fate. The only way out, if there was one, was on their own. They held a meeting and decided that the fittest should try to seek help— even though no one knew where to seek it. But none was strong enough to try. With the snow's crust breaking under every step, even to walk was exhausting. There was only one way to regain strength, and, without giving the thought words, everyone knew what it was.

Canessa and Strauch went outside. The corpse was in the same position as before. They took a deep breath and began to hack meat off the bone. They laid the strips on the plane to thaw in the sun. The knowledge that no rescuers were looking for them encouraged others to join in eating the human flesh. They forced themselves to swallow—their consciences, seconded by their stomachs, accusing them of extreme wrongdoing. Still, they forced the flesh down, telling themselves over and over that there was no other way to survive.

Some, however, could not. Javier and Liliana Methol, husband and wife, though they longed to return to their children, could not eat human flesh. They said that the others could do as they liked, but perhaps God wanted them to choose to die.

The survivors began to organize. Canessa took charge of cutting up the bodies, while a group of the younger had the job of preventing the corpses from rotting by keeping them covered with snow. Another group had the task of seeing that the plane was kept in order. Even the weakest had a job to do: They were able to hold pieces of aluminum in the sun to melt snow for drinking water.

The first corpses they ate were those of the crew, strangers to them.

One day, when it was too cold to melt snow, they burned wooden Coca-Cola crates that they had found in the luggage compartment. After they had water, they roasted some meat over the embers. There was only enough heat to brown the pieces, but they found the flavor better—tasting, as they said, like beef, but softer. Canessa said they should never do this again, for heat destroys proteins. "You have to eat it raw to get its full value," he argued. Rejecting his advice, the survivors cooked the meat when they had the chance, about once or twice a week. Daily, the recurring question was, "Are we cooking today?"

Liliana told Javier that after they got back home she wanted to have another baby. He agreed. As they looked at one another, though, they saw eyes sunken into their sockets and bones protruding from their cheeks. They knew there was no hope, unless. . . . Liliana and Javier shuddered as they picked up a piece of meat.

Some never could eat. Although the others argued with them, even trying to force them to eat, they never could overcome their feelings of revulsion. They continued to refuse, and so day by day grew weaker. Others, however, grew accustomed to what they were doing. They became able to cut meat from a body before everyone's eyes. They could even eat larger pieces, which they had to chew and taste.

As time went on, they developed a set of rules. They would not eat the women's bodies. No one *had* to eat. The meat would be rationed, and no one could eat more than his or her share. The three who were going to leave in search of help could eat more than the others. One corpse would always be finished before another would be started. (It was overlooked when those who had the disagreeable job of cutting the corpses ate a little as they cut.)

They refused to eat certain parts of the body—the lungs, the skin, the head, and the genitals.

There were some things they never could get used to, such as cutting up a close friend. When they dug a corpse out of the snow, it was preserved just as it had been at the moment of death. If the eyes had been open when the friend died, they were still open, now staring back at them. Everyone understood that no one had to eat a friend or relative.

Survival work became more organized. Those who could stomach it would cut large chunks from a body and pass them to another team, who would slice them with razor blades into smaller pieces. This was not as disagreeable a task, for, separated from the body, the meat was easier to deal with.

The sheets of fat from a body lay outside the rules. They were dried in the sun until a crust formed. Anyone could eat as much as they wished. But the fat wasn't as popular as the meat.

Also outside the rationing system were the pieces of the first carcasses they had cut up, before they developed the rules. Those pieces lay about the snow, and anyone who wanted could scavenge them. Some could never stomach the liver, others the heart or kidneys, and many could not eat the intestines of the dead. Three young men refused the red meat of the muscles.

The dead became part of their lives. One night, Inciarte reached up to get something from the hat rack and was startled when an icy hand brushed against his cheek. Apparently someone had sneaked it in as a late snack.

Constipation was an unexpected complication of their diet. As day after day went by without defecation, they began to worry that their insides would burst. Eventually they developed a sort of contest, wondering who would be the last hold-out. After 28 days, only two had not defecated. At 32, only one. Finally, on the 34th day, Bobby François joined the others.

The three who had been selected to go in search of rescuers had to solve the problem of preventing their feet from freezing. The skin of the dead provided the solution. By cutting an arm just above and below the elbow, and slowly pulling, the skin came away with its subcutaneous layers of fat. Sewing up the lower end made an insulated pair of socks.

Their bland diet became boring. As their bodies and minds cried out for variety, they began to seek new tastes. After eating the meat from a bone, they would crack it open and scoop out the marrow. Everyone liked the marrow. Some sought out the blood clots from around the heart. Others even ate parts of bodies that had started to rot. (Many were revolted by this, but, as time went on, more of the survivors did the same.)

Canessa, Parrado, and Vizintin were selected to go in search of help. Before they left, Parrado took aside a couple of friends and said that they might run short of food before help could arrive. "I prefer you don't," he whispered, "but I'll understand if you eat my mother and sister."

Ten days after the expeditionaries set out, they stumbled into a shepherd's hut. The news of their survival, long after they had been given up for dead, came as a shock to their friends and relatives. Those still waiting on the mountain were rescued by helicopter—just four days before Christmas.

Although the survivors felt a compulsive need to talk about what they had done, at first physicians and government officials kept the cannibalism a secret. When the news leaked out, however, it made headlines around the world. One survivor explained, "It was like a heart transplant. The dead sustained the living." Another said, "It was like holy communion. God gives us the body and blood of Christ in holy communion. God gave us these bodies and blood to eat."

All were Roman Catholics, and they asked forgiveness. The priests replied that they did not need forgiveness, for they had done nothing wrong. There was no soul in the bodies, the priests explained, and in extreme conditions, if there is no other way to survive, it is permissible to eat the dead. After consultation with relatives, it was decided to bury what was left of the dead at the crash site.

The young men, rejoining their families, became celebrities. They shunned the spotlight, however, banded together, and thought of themselves as special people. As persons who had survived the impossible, they felt that they had a unique purpose in life.

The world's reaction to the events in the Andes was shock and horror—mixed with fascination. As one Chilean paper asked in its headlines, "What would *you* have done?"

The Social Construction of Reality

I was going to let the story stop here, but I was told by a person very influential in my life that I really ought to make the sociology explicit. So let's see what sociological lessons we can derive from this tragedy in the Andes.

First, the main lesson, one from which the other points follow, comes from the symbolic interactionists, who stress that *our world is socially constructed.* By this, they mean that nothing contains built-in meanings. In other words, whatever meaning something has is arbitrary: We humans have given it a particular meaning, but we could just as well have given it a different meaning. *Second,* it is through a social process that we determine meanings; that is, people jointly decide on the meanings to assign events and objects. *Third,* because meanings (or what things symbolize to people) are arbitrary, people can change them. I am aware that these statements may sound extremely vague, but they should become clear as we look at how these survivors constructed their reality.

We might begin by asking what the meaning of a human body is. As with other aspects of life, a group can assign to a body any meaning that it wishes, for, by itself, a body has no meaning. These survivors did not begin to develop their definitions from scratch, however, for they brought to the Andes meanings that they had learned in their culture—basically that a body, while not a person, is still human, and must be treated with respect. A related meaning they had learned is that a human body is "not food." Such an understanding may seem natural to us because it matches our own cultural definitions—which obscures the arbitrary nature of the definition.

Fourth, when circumstances change, definitions can become outmoded—even definitions about fundamental aspects of life. *Fifth,* even though definitions no longer "work," changes in basic orientations do not come easily. *Sixth,* anyone who suggests such changes is likely to be seen as a threatening deviant. Shock, horror, or ridicule may be the reactions, and—for persons who persist on a disorienting course—shunning, ostracism, and violence may result. *Seventh,* the source of radical new ideas is extremely significant in determining whether or not they gain acceptance. *Eighth,* if an individual can drum up group support, then there exists a *social* basis for the new, competing definition. *Ninth,* if the group that offers the new definition can get enough others to accept it, then the common definition of reality will change. *Tenth,* changed circumstances make people more open to accepting new definitions of reality.

In this case, Canessa did not want to appear as a deviant, so he furtively proposed a new definition—entrusting it at first to only a few close friends. Even there, however, since it violated basic definitions acquired in early socialization, it was initially met with resistance. But the friends had high respect for Canessa, who had completed a year of medical school, and they were won over. This small group then proposed their new definition of human bodies to the larger group. Eventually, in the growing realization that death was imminent, this definition won out.

Eleventh, behavior follows definitions. That is, definitions of reality are not just abstract ideas; they also indicate what is allowable. We tend to do what our definitions allow. In this case, when the definition of human bodies changed, so did the survivors' behavior: The changed definition allowed them to eat human corpses.

Twelfth, definitions also follow behavior. That is, as people engage in an activity, they tend to develop ideas that lend support to what they are doing. In this instance, the eating of human flesh—especially since it was a group activity—reinforced the initial definition that had been only tentatively held, that the flesh was no longer human. Eventually, at least for many, the flesh indeed became meat—so much so that some people were even able to take a human hand to bed for a late-night snack.

Thirteenth, for their very survival, all groups must have norms. By allowing people to know what to expect in a given situation, norms provide a basic structure for people's relationships with one another. Without norms, anarchy and chaos would reign.

This principle also applies to groups that make deviance part of their activities. Although a superficial view from the outside may make such groups appear disorganized and without rules, they are in fact very normative. Groups of outlaw motorcyclists, for example, share an elaborate set of rules about what they expect from one another, most of which, like those of other groups, are not in written form. In short, norms cover even deviant activities, for, without them, how can group members know what to expect of one another?

The Andes survivors developed a basic set of norms to provide order to their deviant activity. Some of those norms were:

1. No one had to violate his or her conscience. If someone did not wish to eat human flesh, no one would force them.
2. Some bodies were "off limits."
3. Meat was rationed, with a specified amount for each person:
   a. Fat was outside the rationing system, and
   b. Leftover parts from the first bodies were outside the rationing system.
4. Meat was distributed according to an orderly system, namely:
   a. Everyone who wished to could eat, and
   b. Designated parts of the body could be "wasted."

Fourteenth, human groups tend to stratify, that is, to sort themselves out on a basis of inequality, with some getting more of a group's resources, some less. A norm concerning eating human flesh that I did not mention above illustrates this principle: Those persons deemed most valuable to the group were allowed to eat more. These were persons who were going in search of rescue and those who performed the disagreeable task of cutting up the bodies. This unequal division of resources represents the formation of a basic system of social stratification.

Fifteenth, human groups tend to organize themselves. In this instance, the survivors did not just randomly cut away at the bodies, but specific tasks were assigned. Teamwork developed to coordinate tasks, with some individuals performing specialized jobs in making the meat edible. Even the weakest had a part to play. The incipient social stratification just mentioned is another example of organization. *Sixteenth,* an essential part of the human tendency to organize is the emergence of leadership—to direct and coordinate the activities of others. In this case, Canessa stands out.

Seventeenth, people attempt to maintain a respectable sense of self. These survivors were highly conforming individuals in that they had accepted the norms of their society and were striving for a respectable place within it. They wanted to continue to think of themselves as good people. Yet, they had to make a decision about an activity that went beyond the bounds of what they looked at as normal—one they even knew was defined as highly deviant by "everyone."

Eighteenth, it is possible to maintain a "good" self-image and still engage in deviant activities. Because the essence of human society is the social construction of reality, so the key to the self also lies in how reality is defined. If you can redefine an activity to make it "not deviant," then it does not threaten your sense of a "good" self. In this present instance, the Andes survivors looked on eating human flesh as part of their "duty to survive." To do a duty is a good thing, and, accordingly, the acts required by it cannot be "bad." In fact, they must be "good." (The most infamous example of the use of this basic principle was Hitler's SS, who looked on killing Jews as necessary for the survival of the "Aryan" race and culture. They even termed the slaughter a "good" act and their participation in it as patriotic and self–sacrificing.)

This principle helps many people get through what otherwise would be excruciatingly painful nights—for they would toss sleeplessly owing to a gnawing conscience. Redefinition, by keeping one's sense of self intact, allows people to participate in a variety of acts condemned by society—and even those disapproved by the self. For most people redefinition involves much less dramatic acts than eating human flesh, such as a college student cheating on a test or a boss firing a worker.

Nineteenth, some people participate in deviant acts even though they remain unconvinced about such redefinitions. (Some do not even attempt to redefine them.) They may do so from a variety of motives—from what they consider "sheer necessity" to the desire to reach a future goal. Liliana and Javier, who decided that they wanted a baby, are an example. Such persons have greater difficulty adjusting to their acts than those who redefine them as "good." (Even the latter may have difficulty, for redefinitions may be only partial, especially in the face of competing definitions.)

Twentieth, people feel they must justify their actions to others. This process of justifying the self involves clothing definitions of reality in forms thought to be acceptable to others. In order for definitions to be accepted, they must be made to fit into the others' already-existing definitional frame-work. In this case, the survivors—speaking to a Roman Catholic audience—used the analogy of holy communion to try to justify their act.

Twenty-first, to gain institutional support is to secure a broad, solid base for one's definitions of reality. Then one no longer stands alone, which is to invite insanity, nor is one a member of a small group, which is to invite ridicule and may require cutting off oneself from the larger group. In this case, institutional support was provided by the Roman Catholic Church, which, while not accepting the survivors' analogy of cannibalism as com-munion, allowed them to avoid the label of sin by defining their actions as allowable under the circumstances.

Finally, note that these principles are fundamental to human life. They do not simply apply to the Andes survivors—or to deviants in general—but they underlie human society. For all of us, reality is socially constructed, and the story of the Andes survivors contains the essence of human society.

23 The Saints and the Roughnecks

WILLIAM J. CHAMBLISS

When people deviate from what is expected of them, other people react. But on what do their reactions depend? Do they depend simply on the nature of the deviance itself, or is more involved? If so, what sorts of things?

It is these fascinating questions that William J. Chambliss examines in this study of two groups of delinquents in the same high school. He found that although both groups were involved in serious and repetitive delinquent acts, while one was perceived as a group of saints, the other was viewed as a bunch of roughnecks. After analyzing what influenced people's perceptions, and hence their reactions to the boys, Chambliss examines the far-reaching effects of those reactions. He indicates that in the case of the roughnecks, people's reactions helped lock the boys into behaviors that continued after high school, eventually leading to prison or to low-paying jobs, while social reactions to the saints set them on a life-course that not only meant staying out of prison but also entering well-paying positions of prestige.

EIGHT PROMISING YOUNG MEN—children of good, stable, white upper-middle-class families, active in school affairs, good pre-college students—were some of the most delinquent boys at Hanibal High School. While community residents knew that these boys occasionally sowed a few wild oats, they were totally unaware that sowing wild oats completely occupied the daily routine of these young men. The Saints were constantly occupied with truancy, drinking, wild driving, petty theft, and vandalism. Yet no one was officially arrested for any misdeed during the two years I observed them.

This record was particularly surprising in light of my observations during the same two years of another gang of Hanibal High School students, six lower-class white boys known as the Roughnecks. The Roughnecks were constantly in trouble with police and community even though their rate of delinquency was about equal with that of the Saints. What was the cause of this disparity? the result? The following consideration of the activities, social class, and community perceptions of both gangs may provide some answers.

The Saints from Monday to Friday

The Saints' principal daily concern was with getting out of school as early as possible. The boys managed to get out of school with minimum danger that they would be accused of playing hookey through an elaborate procedure for obtaining "legitimate" release from class. The most common procedure was for one boy to obtain the release of another by fabricating a meeting of some committee, program, or recognized club. Charles might raise his hand in his 9:00 chemistry class and ask to be excused—a euphemism for going to the bathroom. Charles would go to Ed's math class and inform the teacher that Ed was needed for a 9:30 rehearsal of the drama club play. The math teacher would recognize Ed and Charles as "good students" involved in numerous school activities and would permit Ed to leave at 9:30. Charles would return to his class, and Ed would go to Tom's English class to obtain his release. Tom would engineer Charles's escape. The strategy would continue until as many of the Saints as possible were freed. After a stealthy trip to the car (which had been parked in a strategic spot), the boys were off for a day of fun.

Over the two years I observed the Saints, this pattern was repeated nearly every day. There were variations on the theme, but in one form or another, the boys used this procedure for getting out of class and then off the school grounds. Rarely did all eight of the Saints manage to leave school at the same time. The average number avoiding school on the days I observed them was five.

Having escaped from the concrete corridors the boys usually went either to a pool hall on the other (lower-class) side of town or to a café in the suburbs. Both places were out of the way of people the boys were likely to know (family or school officials), and both provided a source of entertainment. The pool hall entertainment was the generally rough atmosphere, the occasional hustler, the sometimes drunk proprietor and, of course, the game of pool. The café's entertainment was provided by the owner. The boys would "accidentally" knock a glass on the floor or spill cola on the counter—not all the time, but enough to be sporting. They would also bend spoons, put salt in sugar bowls and generally tease whoever was working in the café. The owner had opened the café recently and was dependent on the boys' business which was, in fact, substantial since between the horsing around and the teasing they bought food and drinks.

The Saints on Weekends

On weekends the automobile was even more critical than during the week, for on weekends the Saints went to Big Town—a large city with a population of over a million 25 miles from Hanibal. Every Friday and Saturday night most of the Saints would meet between 8:00 and 8:30 and would go into Big Town. Big Town activities included drinking heavily in taverns or nightclubs, driving drunkenly through the streets, and committing acts of vandalism and playing pranks.

By midnight on Fridays and Saturdays the Saints were usually thoroughly high, and one or two of them were often so drunk they had to be carried to the cars. Then the boys drove around town, calling obscenities to women and girls; occasionally trying (unsuccessfully so far as I could tell) to pick girls up; and driving recklessly through red lights and at high speeds with their lights out. Occasionally they played "chicken." One boy would climb out the back window of the car and across the roof to the driver's side of the car while the car was moving at high speed (between 40 and 50 miles an hour); then the driver would move over and the boy who had just crawled across the car roof would take the driver's seat.

Searching for "fair game" for a prank was the boys' principal activity after they left the tavern. The boys would drive alongside a foot patrolman and ask directions to some street. If the policeman leaned on the car in the course of answering the question, the driver would speed away, causing him to lose his balance. The Saints were careful to play this prank only in an area where they were not going to spend much time and where they could quickly disappear around a corner to avoid having their license plate number taken.

Construction sites and road repair areas were the special province of the Saints' mischief. A soon-to-be-repaired hole in the road inevitably invited the Saints to remove lanterns and wooden barricades and put them in the car, leaving the hole unprotected. The boys would find a safe vantage point and wait for an unsuspecting motorist to drive into the hole. Often, though not always, the boys would go up to the motorist and commiserate with him about the dreadful way the city protected its citizenry.

Leaving the scene of the open hole and the motorist, the boys would then go searching for an appropriate place to erect the stolen barricade. An "appropriate place" was often a spot on a highway near a curve in the road where the barricade would not be seen by an oncoming motorist. The boys would wait to watch an unsuspecting motorist attempt to stop and (usually) crash into the wooden barricade. With saintly bearing the boys might offer help and understanding.

A stolen lantern might well find its way onto the back of a police car or hang from a street lamp. Once a lantern served as a prop for a reenactment of the "midnight ride of Paul Revere" until the "play," which was taking place at 2:00 A.M. in the center of a main street of Big Town, was interrupted by a police car several blocks away. The boys ran, leaving the lanterns on the street, and managed to avoid being apprehended.

Abandoned houses, especially if they were located in out-of-the-way places, were fair game for destruction and spontaneous vandalism. The boys would break windows, remove furniture to the yard and tear it apart, urinate on the walls, and scrawl obscenities inside.

Through all the pranks, drinking, and reckless driving the boys managed miraculously to avoid being stopped by police. Only twice in two years was I aware that they had been stopped by a Big Town policeman. Once was for speeding (which they did every time they drove whether they were drunk or sober), and the driver managed to convince the policeman that it was simply an error. The second time they were stopped they had just left a nightclub and were walking through an alley. Aaron stopped to urinate and the boys began making obscene remarks. A foot patrolman came into the alley, lectured the boys and sent them home. Before the boys got to the car one began talking in a loud voice again. The policeman, who had followed them down the alley, arrested this boy for disturbing the peace and took him to the police station where the other Saints gathered. After paying a $5.00 fine, and with the assurance that there would be no permanent record of the arrest, the boy was released.

The boys had a spirit of frivolity and fun about their escapades. They did not view what they were engaged in as "delinquency," though it surely was by any reasonable definition of that word. They simply viewed themselves as having a little fun and who, they would ask, was really hurt by it? The answer had to be no one, although this fact remains one of the most difficult things to explain about the gang's behavior. Unlikely though it seems, in two years of drinking, driving, carousing, and vandalism no one was seriously injured as a result of the Saints' activities.

The Saints in School

The Saints were highly successful in school. The average grade for the group was "B," with two of the boys having close to a straight "A" average. Almost all of the boys were popular and many of them held offices in the school. One of the boys was vice president of the student body one year. Six of the boys played on athletic teams.

At the end of their senior year, the student body selected ten seniors for special recognition as the "school wheels"; four of the ten were Saints. Teachers and school officials saw no problem with any of these boys and anticipated that they would all "make something of themselves."

How the boys managed to maintain this impression is surprising in view of their actual behavior in school. Their technique for covering truancy was so successful that teachers did not even realize that the boys were absent from school much of the time. Occasionally, of course, the system would backfire and then the boy was on his own. A boy who was caught would be most contrite, would plead guilty and ask for mercy. He inevitably got the mercy he sought.

Cheating on examinations was rampant, even to the point of orally communicating answers to exams as well as looking at one another's papers. Since none of the group studied, and since they were primarily dependent on one another for help, it is surprising that grades were so high. Teachers contributed to the deception in their admitted inclination to give these boys (and presumably others like them) the benefit of the doubt. When asked how the boys did in school, and when pressed on specific examinations, teachers might admit that they were disappointed in John's performance, but would quickly add that they "knew that he was capable of doing better," so John was given a higher grade than he had actually earned. How often this happened is impossible to know. During the time that I observed the group, I never saw any of the boys take homework home. Teachers may have been "understanding" very regularly.

One exception to the gang's generally good performance was Jerry, who had a "C" average in his junior year, experienced disaster the next year, and failed to graduate. Jerry had always been a little more nonchalant than the others about the liberties he took in school. Rather than wait for someone to come get him from class, he would offer his own excuse and leave. Although he probably did not miss any more class than most of the others in the group, he did not take the requisite pains to cover his absences. Jerry was the only Saint whom I ever heard talk back to a teacher. Although teachers often called him a "cut up" or a "smart kid," they never referred to him as a troublemaker or as a kid headed for trouble. It seems likely, then, that Jerry's failure his senior year and his mediocre performance his junior year were consequences of his not playing the game the proper way (possibly because he was disturbed by his parents' divorce). His teachers regarded him as "immature" and not quite ready to get out of high school.

The Police and the Saints

The local police saw the Saints as good boys who were among the leaders of the youth in the community. Rarely, the boys might be stopped in town for speeding or for running a stop sign. When this happened the boys were always polite, contrite and pled for mercy. As in school, they received the mercy they asked for. None ever received a ticket or was taken into the precinct by the local police.

The situation in Big Town, where the boys engaged in most of their delinquency, was only slightly different. The police there did not know the boys at all, although occasionally the boys were stopped by a patrolman. Once they were caught taking a lantern from a construction site. Another time they were stopped for running a stop sign, and on several occasions they were stopped for speeding. Their behavior was as before: contrite, polite and penitent. The urban police, like the local police, accepted their demeanor as sincere. More important, the urban police were convinced that these were good boys just out for a lark.

The Roughnecks

Hanibal townspeople never perceived the Saints' high level of delinquency. The Saints were good boys who just went in for an occasional prank. After all, they were well dressed, well mannered and had nice cars. The Roughnecks were a different story. Although the two gangs of boys were the same age, and both groups engaged in an equal amount of wild-oat sowing, everyone agreed that the not-so-well-dressed, not-so-well-mannered, not-so-rich boys were heading for trouble. Townspeople would say, "You can see the gang members at the drugstore, night after night, leaning against the storefront (sometimes drunk) or slouching around inside buying cokes, reading magazines, and probably stealing old Mr. Wall blind. When they are outside and girls walk by, even respectable girls, these boys make suggestive remarks. Sometimes their remarks are downright lewd."

From the community's viewpoint, the real indication that these kids were in trouble was that they were constantly involved with the police. Some of them had been picked up for stealing, mostly small stuff, of course, "but still it's stealing small stuff that leads to big time crimes." "Too bad," people said. "Too bad that these boys couldn't behave like the other kids in town; stay out of trouble, be polite to adults, and look to their future."

The community's impression of the degrees to which this group of six boys (ranging in age from 16 to 19) engaged in delinquency was somewhat distorted. In some ways the gang was more delinquent than the community thought; in other ways they were less.

The fighting activities of the group were fairly readily and accurately perceived by almost everyone. At least once a month, the boys would get into some sort of fight, although most fights were scraps between members of the group or involved only one member of the group and some peripheral hanger-on. Only three times in the period of observation did the group fight together: once against a gang from across town, once against two blacks, and once against a group of boys from another school. For the first two fights the group went out "looking for trouble"—and they found it both times. The third fight followed a football game and began spontaneously with an argument on the football field between one of the Roughnecks and a member of the opposition's football team.

Jack has a particular propensity for fighting and was involved in most of the brawls. He was a prime mover of the escalation of arguments into fights.

More serious than fighting, had the community been aware of it, was theft. Although almost everyone was aware that the boys occasionally stole things, they did not realize the extent of the activity. Petty stealing was a frequent event for the Roughnecks. Sometimes they stole as a group and coordinated their efforts; other things they stole in pairs. Rarely did they steal alone.

The thefts ranged from very small things like paperback books, comics, and ballpoint pens to expensive items like watches. The nature of the thefts varied from time to time. The gang would go through a period of systematically lifting items from automobiles or school lockers. Types of thievery varied with the whim of the gang. Some forms of thievery were more profitable than others, but all thefts were for profit, not just thrills.

Roughnecks siphoned gasoline from cars as often as they had access to an automobile, which was not very often. Unlike the Saints, who owned their own cars, the Roughnecks would have to borrow their parents' cars, an event which occurred only eight or nine times a year. The boys claimed to have stolen cars for joy rides from time to time.

Ron committed the most serious of the group's offenses. With an unidentified associate the boy attempted to burglarize a gasoline station. Although this station had been robbed twice previously in the same month, Ron denied any involvement in either of the other thefts. When Ron and his accomplice approached the station, the owner was hiding in the bushes beside the station. He fired both barrels of a double-barreled shotgun at the boys. Ron was severely injured; the other boy ran away and was never caught. Though he remained in critical condition for several months, Ron finally recovered and served six months of the following year in reform school. Upon release from reform school, Ron was put back a grade in school, and began running around with a different gang of boys. The Roughnecks considered the new gang less delinquent than themselves, and during the following year Ron had no more trouble with the police.

The Roughnecks, then, engaged mainly in three types of delinquency: theft, drinking, and fighting. Although community members perceived that this gang of kids was delinquent, they mistakenly believed that their illegal activities were primarily drinking, fighting, and being a nuisance to passersby. Drinking was limited among the gang members, although it did occur, and theft was much more prevalent than anyone realized.

Drinking would doubtless have been more prevalent had the boys had ready access to liquor. Since they rarely had automobiles at their disposal, they could not travel very far, and the bars in town would not serve them.

Most of the boys had little money, and this, too, inhibited their purchase of alcohol. Their major source of liquor was a local drunk who would buy them a fifth if they would give him enough extra to buy himself a pint of whiskey or a bottle of wine.

The community's perception of drinking as prevalent stemmed from the fact that it was the most obvious delinquency the boys engaged in. When one of the boys had been drinking, even a casual observer seeing him on the corner would suspect that he was high.

There was a high level of mutual distrust and dislike between the Roughnecks and the police. The boys felt very strongly that the police were unfair and corrupt. Some evidence existed that the boys were correct in their perception.

The main source of the boys' dislike for the police undoubtedly stemmed from the fact that the police would sporadically harass the group. From the standpoint of the boys, these acts of occasional enforcement of the law were whimsical and uncalled for. It made no sense to them, for example, that the police would come to the corner occasionally and threaten them with arrest for loitering when the night before the boys had been out siphoning gasoline from cars and the police had been nowhere in sight. To the boys, the police were stupid on the one hand, for not being where they should have been and catching the boys in a serious offense, and unfair on the other hand, for trumping up "loitering" charges against them.

From the viewpoint of the police, the situation was quite different. They knew, with all the confidence necessary to be a policeman, that these boys were engaged in criminal activities. They knew this partly from occasionally catching them, mostly from circumstantial evidence ("the boys were around when those tires were slashed"), and partly because the police shared the view of the community in general that this was a bad bunch of boys. The best the police could hope to do was to be sensitive to the fact that these boys were engaged in illegal acts and arrest them whenever there was some evidence that they had been involved. Whether or not the boys had in fact committed a particular act in a particular way was not especially important. The police had a broader view: their job was to stamp out these kids' crimes; the tactics were not as important as the end result.

Over the period that the group was under observation, each member was arrested at least once. Several of the boys were arrested a number of times and spent at least one night in jail. While most were never taken to court, two of the boys were sentenced to six months' incarceration in boys' schools.

The Roughnecks in School

The Roughnecks' behavior in school was not particularly disruptive. During school hours they did not all hang around together, but tended instead to spend most of their time with one or two other members of the gang who were their special buddies. Although every member of the gang attempted to avoid school as much as possible, they were not particularly successful and most of them attended school with surprising regularity. They considered school a burden—something to be gotten through with a minimum of conflict. If they were "bugged" by a particular teacher, it could lead to trouble. One of the boys, Al, once threatened to beat up a teacher and, according to the other boys, the teacher hid under a desk to escape him.

Teachers saw the boys the way the general community did, as heading for trouble, as being uninterested in making something of themselves. Some were also seen as being incapable of meeting the academic standards of the school. Most of the teachers expressed concern for this group of boys and were willing to pass them despite poor performance, in the belief that failing them would only aggravate the problem.

The group of boys had a grade point average just slightly above "C." No one in the group failed either grade, and no one had better than a "C" average. They were very consistent in their achievement or, at least, the teachers were consistent in their perception of the boys' achievement.

Two of the boys were good football players. Herb was acknowledged to be the best player in the school and Jack was almost as good. Both boys were criticized for their failure to abide by training rules, for refusing to come to practice as often as they should, and for not playing their best during practice. What they lacked in sportsmanship they made up for in skill, apparently, and played every game no matter how poorly they had performed in practice or how many practice sessions they had missed.

Two Questions

Why did the community, the school, and the police react to the Saints as though they were good, upstanding, nondelinquent youths with bright futures but to the Roughnecks as though they were tough, young criminals who were headed for trouble? Why did the Roughnecks and the Saints in fact have quite different careers after high school—careers which, by and large, lived up to the expectations of the community?

The most obvious explanation for the differences in the community's and law enforcement agencies' reactions to the two gangs is that one group of boys was "more delinquent" than the other. Which group was more delinquent? The answer to this question will determine in part how we explain the differential responses to these groups by the members of the community and, particularly, by law enforcement and school officials.

In sheer number of illegal acts, the Saints were the more delinquent. They were truant from school for at least part of the day almost every day of the week. In addition, their drinking and vandalism occurred with surprising regularity. The Roughnecks, in contrast, engaged sporadically in delinquent episodes. While these episodes were frequent, they certainly did not occur on a daily or even a weekly basis.

The difference in frequency of offenses was probably caused by the Roughnecks' inability to obtain liquor and to manipulate legitimate excuses from school. Since the Roughnecks had less money than the Saints, and teachers carefully supervised their school activities, the Roughnecks' hearts may have been as black as the Saints', but their misdeeds were not nearly as frequent.

There are really no clear-cut criteria by which to measure qualitative differences in antisocial behavior. The most important dimension is generally referred to as the "seriousness" of the offenses.

If seriousness encompasses the relative economic costs of delinquent acts, then some assessment can be made. The Roughnecks probably stole an average of about $5.00 worth of goods a week. Some weeks the figure was considerably higher, but these times must be balanced against long periods when almost nothing was stolen.

The Saints were more continuously engaged in delinquency but their acts were not for the most part costly to property. Only their vandalism and occasional theft of gasoline would so qualify. Perhaps once or twice a month they would siphon a tankful of gas. The other costly items were street signs, construction lanterns, and the like. All of these acts combined probably did not quite average $5.00 a week, partly because much of the stolen equipment was abandoned and presumably could be recovered. The difference in cost of stolen property between the two groups was trivial, but the Roughnecks probably had a slightly more expensive set of activities than did the Saints.

Another meaning of seriousness is the potential threat of physical harm to members of the community and to the boys themselves. The Roughnecks were more prone to physical violence; they not only welcomed an opportunity to fight; they went seeking it. In addition, they fought among themselves frequently. Although the fighting never included deadly weapons, it was still a menace, however minor, to the physical safety of those involved.

The Saints never fought. They avoided physical conflict both inside and outside the group. At the same time, though, the Saints frequently endangered their own and other people's lives. They did so almost every time they drove a car, especially if they had been drinking. Sober, their driving was risky; under the influence of alcohol it was horrendous. In addition, the Saints endangered the lives of others with their pranks. Street excavations left unmarked were a very serious hazard.

Evaluating the relative seriousness of the two gangs' activities is difficult. The community reacted as though the behavior of the Roughnecks was a problem, and they reacted as though the behavior of the Saints was not. But the members of the community were ignorant of the array of delinquent acts that characterized the Saints' behavior. Although concerned citizens were unaware of much of the Roughnecks' behavior as well, they were much better informed about the Roughnecks' involvement in delinquency than they were about the Saints'.

Visibility

Differential treatment of the two gangs resulted in part because one gang was infinitely more visible than the other. This differential visibility was a direct function of the economic standing of the families. The Saints had access to automobiles and were able to remove themselves from the sight of the community. In as routine a decision as to where to go to have a milkshake after school, the Saints stayed away from the mainstream of community life. Lacking transportation, the Roughnecks could not make it to the edge of town. The center of town was the only practical place for them to meet since their homes were scattered throughout the town and any noncentral meeting place put an undue hardship on some members. Through necessity the Roughnecks congregated in a crowded area where everyone in the community passed frequently, including teachers and law enforcement officers. They could easily see the Roughnecks hanging around the drugstore.

The Roughnecks, of course, made themselves even more visible by making remarks to passersby and by occasionally getting into fights on the corner. Meanwhile, just as regularly, the Saints were either at the café on one edge of town or in the pool hall at the other edge of town. Without any particular realization that they were making themselves inconspicuous, the Saints were able to hide their time-wasting. Not only were they removed from the mainstream of traffic, but they were almost always inside a building.

On their escapades the Saints were also relatively invisible, since they left Hanibal and traveled to Big Town. Here, too, they were mobile, roaming the city, rarely going to the same area twice.

Demeanor

To the notion of visibility must be added the difference in the responses of group members to outside intervention with their activities. If one of the Saints was confronted with an accusing policeman, even if he felt he was truly innocent of a wrongdoing, his demeanor was apologetic and penitent. A Roughneck's attitude was almost the polar opposite. When confronted with a threatening adult authority, even one who tried to be pleasant, the Roughneck's hostility and disdain were clearly observable. Sometimes he might attempt to put up a veneer of respect, but it was thin and was not accepted as sincere by the authority.

School was no different from the community at large. The Saints could manipulate the system by feigning compliance with the school norms. The availability of cars at school meant that once free from the immediate sight of the teacher, the boys could disappear rapidly. And this escape was well enough planned that no administrator or teacher was nearby when the boys left. A Roughneck who wished to escape for a few hours was in a bind. If it were possible to get free from class, downtown was still a mile away, and even if he arrived there, he was still very visible. Truancy for the Roughnecks meant almost certain detection, while the Saints enjoyed almost complete immunity from sanctions.

Bias

Community members were not aware of the transgressions of the Saints. Even if the Saints had been less discreet, their favorite delinquencies would have been perceived as less serious than those of the Roughnecks.

In the eyes of the police and school officials, a boy who drinks in an alley and stands intoxicated on the street corner is committing a more serious offense than is a boy who drinks to inebriation in a nightclub or a tavern and drives around afterwards in a car. Similarly, a boy who steals a wallet from a store will be viewed as having committed a more serious offense than a boy who steals a lantern from a construction site.

Perceptual bias also operates with respect to the demeanor of the boys in the two groups when they are confronted by adults. It is not simply that adults dislike the posture affected by boys of the Roughneck ilk; more important is the conviction that the posture adopted by the Roughnecks is an indication of their devotion and commitment to deviance as a way of life. The posture becomes a cue, just as the type of the offense is a cue, to the degree to which the known transgressions are indicators of the youths' potential for other problems.

Visibility, demeanor, and bias are surface variables which explain the day-to-day operations of the police. Why do these surface variables operate as they do? Why did the police choose to disregard the Saints' delinquencies while breathing down the backs of the Roughnecks?

The answer lies in the class structure of American society and the control of legal institutions by those at the top of the class structure. Obviously, no representative of the upper class drew up the operational chart for the police which led them to look in the ghettos and on streetcorners— which led them to see the demeanor of lower-class youth as troublesome and that of upper-middle-class youth as tolerable. Rather, the procedures simply developed from experience—experience with irate and influential upper-middle-class parents insisting that their son's vandalism was simply a prank and his drunkenness only a momentary "sowing of wild oats"— experience with cooperative or indifferent, powerless, lower-class parents who acquiesced to the law's definition of their son's behavior.

Adult Careers of the Saints and the Roughnecks

The community's confidence in the potential of the Saints and the Roughnecks apparently was justified. If anything, the community members underestimated the degree to which these youngsters would turn out "good" or "bad."

Seven of the eight members of the Saints went on to college immediately after high school. Five of the boys graduated from college in four years. The sixth one finished college after two years in the army, and the seventh spent four years in the air force before returning to college and receiving a B.A. degree. Of these seven college graduates, three went on for advanced degrees. One finished law school and is now active in state politics, one finished medical school and is practicing near Hanibal, and one boy is now working for a Ph.D. The other four college graduates entered submanagerial, managerial, or executive training positions with larger firms.

The only Saint who did not complete college was Jerry. Jerry had failed to graduate from high school with the other Saints. During his second senior year, after the other Saints had gone on to college, Jerry began to hang around with what several teachers described as a "rough crowd"— the gang that was heir apparent to the Roughnecks. At the end of his second senior year, when he did graduate from high school, Jerry took a job as a used-car salesman, got married, and quickly had a child. Although he made several abortive attempts to go to college by attending night school, when I last saw him (ten years after high school) Jerry was unemployed and had been living on unemployment for almost a year. His wife worked as a waitress.

Some of the Roughnecks have lived up to community expectations. A number of them were headed for trouble. A few were not.

Jack and Herb were the athletes among the Roughnecks and their athletic prowess paid off handsomely. Both boys received unsolicited athletic scholarships to college. After Herb received his scholarship (near the end of his senior year), he apparently did an about-face. His demeanor became very similar to that of the Saints. Although he remained a member in good standing of the Roughnecks, he stopped participating in most activities and did not hang out on the corner as often.

Jack did not change. If anything, he became more prone to fighting. He even made excuses for accepting the scholarship. He told the other gang members that the school had guaranteed him a "C" average if he would come to play football—an idea that seems far-fetched, even in this day of highly competitive recruiting.

During the summer after graduation from high school, Jack attempted suicide by jumping from a tall building. The jump would certainly have killed most people trying it, but Jack survived. He entered college in the fall and played four years of football. He and Herb graduated in four years, and both are teaching and coaching in high schools. They are married and have stable families. If anything, Jack appears to have a more prestigious position in the community than does Herb, though both are well respected and secure in their positions.

Two of the boys never finished high school. Tommy left at the end of his junior year and went to another state. That summer he was arrested and placed on probation on a manslaughter charge. Three years later he was arrested for murder; he pleaded guilty to second degree murder and is serving a 30-year sentence in the state penitentiary.

Al, the other boy who did not finish high school, also left the state in his senior year. He is serving a life sentence in a state penitentiary for first degree murder.

Wes is a small-time gambler. He finished high school and "bummed around." After several years he made contact with a bookmaker who employed him as a runner. Later he acquired his own area and has been working it ever since. His position among the bookmakers is almost identical to the position he had in the gang; he is always around but no one is really aware of him. He makes no trouble and he does not get into any. Steady, reliable, capable of keeping his mouth closed, he plays the game by the rules, even though the game is an illegal one.

That leaves only Ron. Some of his former friends reported that they had heard he was "driving a truck up north," but no one could provide any concrete information.

Reinforcement

The community responded to the Roughnecks as boys in trouble, and the boys agreed with that perception. Their pattern of deviancy was reinforced, and breaking away from it became increasingly unlikely. Once the boys acquired an image of themselves as deviants, they selected new friends who affirmed that self-image. As that self-conception became more firmly entrenched, they also became willing to try new and more extreme deviances. With their growing alienation came freer expression of disrespect and hostility for representatives of the legitimate society. This disrespect increased the community's negativism, perpetuating the entire process of commitment to deviance. Lack of a commitment to deviance works the same way. In either case, the process will perpetuate itself unless some event (like a scholarship to college or a sudden failure) external to the established relationship intervenes. For two of the Roughnecks (Herb and Jack), receiving college athletic scholarships created new relations and culminated in a break with the established pattern of deviance. In the case of one of the Saints (Jerry), his parents' divorce and his failing to graduate from high school changed some of his other relations. Being held back in school for a year and losing his place among the Saints had sufficient impact on Jerry to alter his self-image and virtually to assure that he would not go on to college as his peers did. Although the experiments of life can rarely be reversed, it seems likely in view of the behavior of the other boys who did not enjoy this special treatment by the school that Jerry, too, would have "become something" had he graduated as anticipated. For Herb and Jack outside intervention worked to their advantage; for Jerry it was his undoing.

Selective perception and labeling—finding, processing, and punishing some kinds of criminality and not others—means that visible, poor, nonmobile, outspoken, undiplomatic "tough" kids will be noticed, whether their actions are seriously delinquent or not. Other kids, who have established a reputation for being bright (even though underachieving), disciplined, and involved in respectable activities, who are mobile and monied, will be invisible when they deviate from sanctioned activities. They'll sow their wild oats—perhaps even wider and thicker than their lower-class cohorts—but they won't be noticed. When it's time to leave adolescence most will follow the expected path, settling into the ways of the middle class, remembering fondly the delinquent but unnoticed fling of their youth. The Roughnecks and others like them may turn around, too. It is more likely that their noticeable deviance will have been so reinforced by police and community that their lives will be effectively channeled into careers consistent with their adolescent background.

24 Unintended Consequences of Undercover Work

GARY T. MARX

A seemingly simple sociological principle, but one we could study for years to try to fully comprehend, is that *we tend to become the roles we play*. In other words, as we play a role over time, the attitudes and expectations attached to that role tend to become internalized into the self—that is, they become a part of who we are, of how we perceive right and wrong, of our understandings of the way things ought to be. This intriguing characteristic of role playing is highly significant for society, for it allows its members to convincingly fulfill their assigned roles.

There are two sides to this picture. The more attractive side is that if we play a positive role, we tend to take on its traits. The less attractive side is that if we play a negative role, we tend to take on its qualities—that is, the negative aspects of roles similarly tend to become part of the self. Marx focuses precisely on this aspect of role playing in discussing police who, after going undercover, no longer are able to distinguish between their roles. The "criminal" role lingers even after the role playing is supposed to be over. In some cases, the criminal role even "engulfs" the person, and the individual never is able take up where he or she left off.

This article provides observations that you may be able to apply to your own life. Because roles become an essential part of the self—producing either negative or positive traits—to the extent that you have a choice you can play roles that will produce characteristics you admire and avoid roles that might produce a self that you won't like. Remember, what you play is what you become.

THE FBI's REPUTATION FOR INTEGRITY and its clean-cut, straight arrow image is attributable in part to J. Edgar Hoover's refusal to allow agents to face the temptations and problems confronting undercover police. Similarly, Los Angeles's Chief William Parker felt that the establishment

278

of personal relations between officers and suspects "would invariably fester into a spot of corruption or prove a source of embarrassment even when capably and honestly conducted." As they recognized, the social and psychological consequences for police who play undercover roles can be severe. He who sups with the devil must indeed have a long spoon. What is there about undercover work that is conducive to negative effects on police, and what are these effects?

Undercover situations tend to be more fluid and unpredictable than routine patrol or investigative work. Agents have greater autonomy, and rules and procedures are less clearly defined. The need for secrecy accentuates problems of coordination, increases the potential for error, and lessens the probability that problems will be discovered.

The major organizational problem of any law enforcement agency—how to supervise a dispersed set of employees—is compounded. Undercover agents are removed from the usual controls and supports of a uniform, a badge, a visible supervisor, a fixed time and place for work, radio or beeper calls, and a clearly bounded assignment. These [controls] have both a literal and symbolic significance. Their formal and visible nature enhances accountability by advertising to police and the public who the individual is and what is expected of him.

Social and Psychological Consequences

Unlike conventional police officers, undercover agents tend to be involved primarily with criminals; the deception is continuous, the criminal environment is pervasive. The agent's ability to blend in, to resemble criminals, and to be accepted are necessary conditions for his effectiveness. As an undercover agent with twenty years of experience put in: "A guy who is two degrees off plumb will survive out there, while a choir boy from MIT will be in a lot of trouble."

To the extent that agents develop personal relationships with potential targets, they may experience pressure, ambivalence, and guilt over the betrayal inherent in the deception. Romantic entanglements are an extreme example; more commonly, agents may come to feel sympathy for their targets and develop an understanding of why they behave as they do. A highly productive officer who, before his undercover assignment, saw the world in black-and-white terms reports he became "a different kind of cop." Going undercover, he learned "what it's like to be on the other side of the fence." He started "seeing the criminal element being just regular people, but caught up in their own thing." Another deep-cover agent says: "Boy, it can get gray out there . . . just because a guy's a criminal doesn't mean you can't like him and that he doesn't have the same interest[s] as you do [e.g., baseball or fishing]." Such attitudes can lead to passivity and even the protection of particular targets. Consider, for example, an agent who came to feel close to a target: "He was a 72-year-old guy. The king pin. There was enough evidence. You go to christenings, weddings, Sunday dinner. It's easy to say hey, it's the other guys. He really isn't so bad. I won't testify against him." The agent may falsely report back that the group cannot be penetrated or that no violations are occurring. The fear of being "made" or "burned" (discovered) may also mean the failure to pursue a case vigorously.

Another agent described the feelings of betrayal he had on concluding an operation when his unknowing target "protected" him. In a sell-bust transaction, the agent arranged for contraband to be sold to a suspect he had befriended. The eventual arrest was arranged in such a way as not to cast suspicion upon the agent. When the arrested suspect was interrogated about his source for the contraband, he refused to "give up" the agent.

In contrast, when the agent plays the role of victim and develops a strong identification in this direction, the result may be an overly aggressive crusade. Joseph Wambaugh describes a member of the San Diego decoy squad who played the role of aliens who had been robbed, stabbed, raped, or terrorized: "He began to feel what *they* felt . . . to *feel* the poverty and fear. It made funny pains in the stomach. . . . It made them sigh a lot. Finally it made them mad." In this case, the strong identification meant vigilante actions and personal crusades, as the decoys sought to teach "the crooks that there was a price to pay" for their behavior, regardless of departmental policy and the law.

Covert work is very intense. The agent is always "on." For some agents, the work has an addictive quality as they savor the sense of power, intrigue, excitement, and their protected contact with illegality. They may be both attracted and repelled by the role they play. The strong male bonding and secrecy that are characteristic of police work may take a conspiratorial turn as undercover agents adopt a protective code of silence not unlike that of organized crime.

In his analysis of how patrolmen can avoid becoming corrupted by the use of coercion, William Muir stresses the importance of conversation and interaction with supervisors. The same conditions are likely to reduce the corruption of those licensed to use deception. Yet for the undercover agent these conditions may not be as available. Isolation and secrecy may work against the undercover agent's developing a morality that permits the use of deception in a bounded and principled fashion. Isolation from other contacts and the need to be liked and accepted by members of a criminal subculture can have undesirable consequences. To do well, you must "get your mind inside the bad guy's mind." But "playing the crook" may increase cynicism and ambivalence about the police role and make it easier to rationalize the use of illegal and immoral means, whether for agency or corrupt personal goals. As one agent jokingly put it when asked about his speeding and running stop signs (unrelated to any enforcement effort): "We're here to enforce the law, not to obey it."

When an insensitive supervisor fails to help the agent cope with the moral complexity of the issues or fails to communicate support and questions what the agent does, it may seem to the agent that "everything bad that happens to me comes from the good guys, and everything good comes from the bad guys. You start to wonder." On the other hand, as long as the tactic produces results, some supervisors may not wish to know what agents are doing or what the role is doing to the agent.

The stress the agent experiences can be intense. Some supervisors are more concerned with making cases than with the well-being of their agents. They may not share the priority implicit in the remark of a wise supervisor who said: "Cases will always be there, agents won't." A state police officer who spent two and one-half years undercover reports:

> My nerves are really up. I'm starting to get to where I can't keep a meal down. I would eat with them . . . twenty minutes later, I would be throwing my guts up on the side of the road. I started to feel these chest pains. I really felt like I was having a heart attack. I would have diarrhea on a daily basis.
>
> I go to this doctor . . . I go to my sergeant on the undercover gig the next day and say, "I went to the doc, and he wrote this down for you." I figure this is it. I have a note from the doctor saying I'm under stress, too much stress. They'll have to let me out of this job.
>
> He laughs. I say, "What are you laughing about?"
>
> "We got a million dollars wrapped up in this. You're not physically hurt. You're going through stress. You'll be all right. You can handle it." That's the mentality of cops: You can handle anything. Don't worry about it, kid, you can handle it. I was devastated.

. . . The secrecy required for undercover work offers rich opportunities for shortcuts, financial rewards, and self-aggrandizement. Agents may learn the technical skills needed for complicated offenses. Their knowledge of how police operate lessens the likelihood of discovery, as does the usual absence of a complainant. Moral corrosion or a lowering of standards may occur when agents are granted the power to engage in conspiracies on behalf of law enforcement and are immersed in a seamy, morally relative world.

New York City's elite narcotics force, the SIU (Special Investigating Unit), illustrates many of these issues. Its members gave heroin to informants, set illegal wiretaps, committed perjury, and sometimes took bribes. They also engaged in vigilante tactics, such as seizing drugs and cash and summarily ordering foreign dealers out of the country (referred to as "taking the devil's money to do the Lord's work" or "make them bleed, bust their ass, and steal their weed").

This highly select unit (chosen from the "best guys in all the precincts") roamed the city, had no assigned precinct, and were exempt from many of the bureaucratic restrictions faced by others. Belief in the special elite character of the unit resulted in a lessening of supervision ("they supervise themselves"). The unit made major arrests and seized large quantities of drugs. Its spectacular success did not suggest corruption, but effectiveness and opportunities for corruption often go hand in hand. The unit did not fare well: of 70 SIU detectives, 52 were indicted, 2 committed suicide, and 1 had a mental breakdown.

Undercover agents may come to have an exaggerated sense of their own power. The highly committed members of the elite San Diego decoy unit wanted no part of ordinary police duties and came to feel apart from, and superior to, other police:

> They started to come to work looking like something that fell off a boxcar or was pushed off by a railroad bull. They'd work in their yards or wash their cars or haul fertilizer or whatever, and they'd come to work rank. Unshaven. . . .
>
> They'd tell their wives and friends, and fellow cops who worked patrol and detectives, that they *had* to dress and look and smell like that. That out in the canyons they had to *be* aliens. That their performances might make the difference in whether they lived or died. . . .

A number of the interview, news, and nonfiction and fiction accounts in the literature suggests that some deep-cover agents undergo a striking metamorphosis. As lying becomes a way of life, the agent may become confused about his or her true identify. Familiarity can breed affection as well as contempt. This is particularly likely to the extent that the agent is cut off from friends and becomes immersed in a new life. The phenomenon of "going native" is a danger well known to social science field researchers. A few agents "cross over."

The parallel to the informer who comes to identify with police is the officer who comes to identify with criminals. In his novel *Mother Night*, Kurt Vonnegut observes that "we are what we pretend to be, so we must be careful about what we pretend to be." Or, put more prosaically by a vice-squad detective: "You're working with dope fiends and perverts all day, and a guy on the vice squad usually goes down; he deteriorates; he becomes like the people you work with." Most agents, however, do not turn into "weird guys," even though the potential for adverse effects is there.

A Connecticut officer from a conservative family background spent a year posing as a street person and riding with a motorcycle gang. He was overtaken by the role. He reports: "I knew [it] was a role-playing thing, but I became total, 100 percent involved. I became what I was trying to tell people I was, and it confused me. Believe me, it confused me a lot."

Robert Leuci, who served as the model for the book and film *Prince of the City*, noted a gradual change in himself and the officers he worked with:

> I began to wake up in the morning and look at myself in the mirror and see my reflection—and I didn't like what I saw. . . . I didn't like the way I was dressing. . . . We all started wearing pinkie rings. I *hated* them, but I found myself wearing one . . . spending a lot of money on shoes. . . . It seemed like I was becoming like the people I was *after*. I started looking like Mafia guys. You look at those guys—they talk out of the sides of their mouths— they talk like there's a big criminal conspiracy going on, even if they're only talking to their kids. They're never up front. They live a life of whispers. So then I found myself talking to my father in the same way.

An officer in San Jose describes how he changed after being "buried" in a deep-cover operation:

> This was really strange. . . . For the first nine months I was really nervous and afraid. . . . You meet a lot of bad people and you've got . . . no cover. But I still remember one day . . . something snapped. I just felt it like a jolt going through . . . and I was no longer afraid or nervous. It was like I had a handle on things . . . [and] a short time after that . . . I didn't believe I was a cop.

Most of the same social and psychological factors involving agents and targets are operating in political settings as in criminal ones. But there is an additional paradox here when an ideological issue involves matters of class, age, ethnicity, race, religion, or gender. The agent must share at least some of these attributes in order to be credible, and this common bond increases the likelihood that the agent will understand and sympathize with the group's goals. . . .

An officer's personal habits may change as a result of easily accessible vice opportunities. Police may become consumers or purveyors of the very vice they set out to control. In Chicago, an officer was suspended for operating a prostitution ring. He had initially posed as a pimp and infiltrated the ring as part of a police operation. When the investigation ended, he continued in his role as a pimp. A vice detective referred to involvement with prostitutes as an "occupational habit," then corrected himself, saying, "I mean occupational hazard.". . .

With drugs the problem is more serious. Little is known about police drug use and addiction. Departments have become increasingly concerned as officers raised in a more permissive culture have entered the force. Undercover officers may be even more prone to their use than conventional officers because of greater stress, isolation, and accessibility. Drug use is frequently linked to the covert role and life-style that the agent is affecting. Its use is at least informally justified. Most drug officers certainly do not develop drug problems, but there are tragic cases, and the risk is real. . . .

The strains on a marriage or a relationship are considerable: the odd hours, days, or weeks away from home; unpredictability of work schedules; concern over safety; late-night temptations and partying that the role may bring; and personality and life-style changes that the agent may undergo. The need for secrecy and the inability to share work details and problems, as well as limitations on a spouse's talking to others, can be costly. Knowledge of the agent's skill at acting, deception, and lying can increase paranoia and suspiciousness once initial doubts appear. The wife of one agent observes, "When you live under cover, you live a lie. You can't confide in friends about the pressures on your husband; you can't even tell your children what their father really does. You live under constant strain."

Although extreme, consider the case of an officer who was promoted for his outstanding work in infiltrating an international drug ring. He gained access to the ring by having an affair with one of its female leaders. His wife was proud of his heroic efforts and promotion, but, when the full details of the investigation became clear, she sought a divorce. An officer who got divorced in the middle of a three-year operation observed: "Imagine having a relationship with someone where you can't talk about what you do and where you suddenly say 'I'll see you in a week' and just disappear. There is also stress on her because you may not come back." For some agents, the "job becomes the mistress."

Should the agent be so inclined, the role is supportive of affairs. It also can offer a useful cover, as one supervisor in Los Angeles discovered. He received a call from the wife of an agent who complained that her husband's undercover assignment was keeping him away from home too many nights. The wife did not know that the operation had ended months before. . . .

Leaving the Role

. . . When the investigation ends, the agent may feel relief, but he may be unable simply to return to an ordinary existence. If there is a danger of reprisals, it may be necessary for him to move to a new location and change his appearance and some customary behavior patterns. Apart from this, some agents experience subsequent personality changes and difficulties in readjustment. Ironically, some of the qualities thought to aid in effective undercover work (being outgoing, extroverted, a risk taker, adept at role playing) also may be associated with problems once the role ends.

An experienced officer observed that training a policeman to act like a criminal can be "like training a vicious dog. When you're through with him, you don't know what to do with him." Although this is certainly over-stated, problems may appear in the transition from a covert deep-cover agent to a conventional police role. Like an actor caught up in a stage part, the agent may have trouble leaving the role. There are parallels to the re-entry problems sometimes faced by combat soldiers. The agent may initially find it difficult to shed fully the trappings of the caper, whether it be in language, dress, hairstyle, or conspicuous consumption. He may be hesitant to return false identification or jewelry used in the operation. The agent may miss the more free-wheeling expressive life and work style and the excitement and attention associated with the role. After the high of a successful case, some agents have trouble fitting back into normal office routines. They may have discipline problems and show various neurotic responses and in a few cases appear to have a split personality.

Consider, for example, a northern California police officer who rode with the Hell's Angels for a year and a half. He was responsible for a large number of arrests, including previously almost untouchable higher-level drug dealers. He was praised for doing a "magnificient job." But this came at a cost of heavy drug use, alcoholism, brawling, the breakup of his family, and his inability to fit back into routine police work after the investigation was over. The result was resignation from the force, several bank robberies, and a prison term.

FBI agent John Livingston spent two and a half years posing as a distributor of sexually explicit materials in Operation MiPorn (Miami pornography). The operation—the largest federal pornography investigation ever undertaken—was hailed as a great success and received extensive media coverage. Livingston was praised for his excellent work, but he had trouble separating from his role. He continued to use his undercover name in situations unrelated to his FBI work and to frequent bars and places he had been during the investigation. After two brushes with the law, he was eventually arrested for shoplifting and gave his undercover alias. He split up with his wife and lost many friends. Psychiatric evaluation found that he had difficulty distinguishing his undercover from his real identify. Fourteen indictments that had resulted from his prior covert work were dropped because they were believed to be tainted by the investigator's confusion. Livingston initially demonstrated a "lack of candor" in describing his actions to his superiors. In what another former FBI agent characterized as "shooting our wounded," he was fired from the FBI after 17 years of service. He eventually obtained a disability pension.

Although not experiencing that degree of trouble, a northern California officer reports difficulty in returning to regular police work:

> At first it was really kind of strange and weird and scary and funny. I'd be riding in a patrol car, and I wouldn't be in the frame of mind of a uniformed police officer. I'd see another patrol car, and I'd tense up in knots. I really felt like the crooks. It would take me a second to realize that "hey, he's one of us." People would flag me down and I'd just wave back and keep driving. They want a cop, not me. I'd find myself answering [radio] calls and flipping back to my old [street] vocabulary. It was very embarrassing. I'm still having problems.

. . . There may be interactive effects. If the agent has changed, colleagues may perceive this and act differently toward him, which may further encourage his paranoia and estrangement. Peers and supervisors may add to the problem should they not welcome the agent back with open arms. They may look skeptically on the recently submerged agent, wondering if he or she is (or always was) a bit strange. They may be ambivalent about what the agent has done. Perhaps they respect the agent's skill and courage, but also think that the agent was out having a good time and not doing much with an expense account, a fancy car, and an apartment while they were stuck in the office working regular hours. An agent who described this asked rhetorically: "If they think it's so much fun, why don't they volunteer then?". . .

25 The Pathology of Imprisonment

PHILIP G. ZIMBARDO

Why are our prisoners such powder kegs? To most persons, that is not a difficult queston and the answer is obvious—because of the kind of people who are locked up in prisons: They are criminals, antisocial, and disposed to violence. If not that, then they hate the guards, the food, or the restrictions of prison life (which is that they deserved in the first place!). Similarly, people have little difficulty explaining why prison guards are brutal: It is either the type of people with whom the guards must deal ("animals") or the type of people who are attracted to being prison guards in the first place ("sadistic types"). Such reasons are commonly cited to explain prison violence, but it turns out that much more fundamental social processes are involved. As Zimbardo's remarkable experiment uncovered, the structuring of relationships within the prison lays a firm foundation for prison brutality and violence.

While reading this fascinating account, you may begin to think about how prisons could be improved in order to minimize violence. To reach such a goal, what changes would you suggest that we make in the social structure of prisons?

I was recently released from solitary confinement after being held therein for 37 months [months!]. A silent system was imposed upon me and to even whisper to the man in the next cell resulted in being beaten by guards, sprayed with chemical mace, blackjacked, stomped and thrown into a strip-cell naked to sleep on a concrete floor without bedding, covering, wash basin or even a toilet. The floor served as toilet and bed, and even there the silent system was enforced. To let a moan escape your lips because of the pain and discomfort . . . resulted in another beating. I spent not days, but months there during my 37 months in solitary. . . . I have filed every writ possible against the administrative acts of brutality. The state courts have all denied the petitions. Because of my refusal to let the things die down and forget all that happened during my 37 months in solitary . . . I am the most hated prisoner in [this] penitentiary, and called a "hard-core incorrigible."

Maybe I am an incorrigible, but if true, it's because I would rather die

287

than to accept being treated as less than a human being. I have never complained of my prison sentence as being unjustified except through legal means of appeals. I have never put a knife on a guard's throat and demanded my release. I know that thieves must be punished and I don't justify stealing, even though I am a thief myself. But now I don't think I will be a thief when I am released. No, I'm not rehabilitated. It's just that I no longer think of becoming wealthy by stealing. I now only think of killing—killing those who have beaten me and treated me as if I were a dog. I hope and pray for the sake of my own soul and future life of freedom that I am able to overcome the bitterness and hatred which eats daily at my soul, but I know to overcome it will not be easy.

THIS ELOQUENT PLEA FOR PRISON REFORM—for humane treatment of human beings, for the basic dignity that is the right of every American—came to me secretly in a letter from a prisoner who cannot be identified because he is still in a state correctional institution. He sent it to me because he read of an experiment I recently conducted at Stanford University. In an attempt to understand just what it means psychologically to be a prisoner or a prison guard, Craig Haney, Curt Banks, Dave Jaffe and I created our own prison. We carefully screened over 70 volunteers who answered an ad in a Palo Alto city newspaper and ended up with about two dozen young men who were selected to be part of this study. They were mature, emotionally stable, normal, intelligent college students from middle-class homes throughout the United States and Canada. They appeared to represent the cream of the crop of this generation. None had any criminal record and all were relatively homogeneous on many dimensions initially.

Half were arbitrarily designated as prisoners by a flip of a coin, the others as guards. These were the roles they were to play in our simulated prison. The guards were made aware of the potential seriousness and danger of the situation and their own vulnerability. They made up their own formal rules for maintaining law, order and respect, and were generally free to improvise new ones during their eight-hour, three-man shifts. The prisoners were unexpectedly picked up at their homes by a city policeman in a squad car, searched, handcuffed, fingerprinted, booked at the Palo Alto station house and taken blindfolded to our jail. There they were stripped, deloused, put into a uniform, given a number and put into a cell with two other prisoners where they expected to live for the next two weeks. The pay was good ($15 a day) and their motivation was to make money.

We observed and recorded on videotape the events that occurred in the prison, and we interviewed and tested the prisoners and guards at various points throughout the study. Some of the videotapes of the actual encounters between the prisoners and guards were seen on the NBC News feature "Chronolog" on November 26, 1971.

At the end of only six days we had to close down our mock prison because what we saw was frightening. It was no longer apparent to most of the subjects (or to us) where reality ended and their roles began. The majority had indeed become prisoners or guards, no longer able to clearly differentiate between role playing and self. There were dramatic changes in virtually every aspect of their behavior, thinking and feeling. In less than a week the experience of imprisonment undid (temporarily) a lifetime of learning; human values were suspended, self-concepts were challenged, and the ugliest, most base, pathological side of human nature surfaced. We were horrified because we saw some boys (guards) treat others as if they were despicable animals, taking pleasure in cruelty, while other boys (prisoners) became servile, dehumanized robots who thought only of escape, of their own individual survival and of their mounting hatred for the guards.

We had to release three prisoners in the first four days because they had such acute situational traumatic reactions as hysterical crying, confusion in thinking and severe depression. Others begged to be paroled, and all but three were willing to forfeit all the money they had earned if they could be paroled. By then (the fifth day) they had been so programmed to think of themselves as prisoners that when their request for parole was denied, they returned docilely to their cells. Now, had they been thinking as college students acting in an oppressive experiment, they would have quit once they no longer wanted the $15 a day we used as our only incentive. However, the reality was not quitting an experiment but "being paroled by the parole board from the Stanford County Jail." By the last days, the earlier solidarity among the prisoners (systematically broken by the guards) dissolved into "each man for himself." Finally, when one of their fellows was put into solitary confinement (a small closet) for refusing to eat, the prisoners were given a choice by one of the guards: give up their blankets and the incorrigible prisoner would be let out, or keep their blankets and he would be kept in all night. They voted to keep their blankets and to abandon their brother.

About a third of the guards became tyrannical in their arbitrary use of power, in enjoying their control over other people. They were corrupted by the power of their roles and became quite inventive in their techniques of breaking the spirit of the prisoners and making them feel they were worthless. Some of the guards merely did their jobs as tough but fair correctional officers, and several were good guards from the prisoners' point of view since they did them small favors and were friendly. However, no good guards ever interfered with a command by any of the bad guards; they never intervened on the side of the prisoners, they never told the others to ease off because it was only an experiment, and they never even came to me as prison superintendent or experimenter in charge to complain. In part, they were good because the others were bad; they needed the others to help establish their own egos in a positive light. In a sense, the good guards perpetuated the prison more than the other guards because their own needs to be liked prevented them from disobeying or violating the implicit guards' code. At the same time, the act of befriending the prisoners created a social reality which made the prisoners less likely to rebel.

By the end of the week the experiment had become a reality, as if it were a Pirandello play directed by Kafka that just keeps going after the audience has left. The consultant for our prison, Carlo Prescott, an exconvict with 16 years of imprisonment in California's jails, would get so depressed and furious each time he visited our prison, because of its psychological similarity to his experiences, that he would have to leave. A Catholic priest who was a former prison chaplain in Washington, D.C., talked to our prisoners after four days and said they were just like the other first-timers he had seen.

But in the end, I called off the experiment not because of the horror I saw out there in the prison yard, but because of the horror of realizing that *I* could have easily traded places with the most brutal guard or become the weakest prisoner full of hatred at being so powerless that I could not eat, sleep, or go to the toilet without permission of the authorities. *I* could have become Calley at My Lai, George Jackson at San Quentin, one of the men at Attica or the prisoner quoted at the beginning of this article.

Individual behavior is largely under the control of social forces and environmental contingencies rather than personality traits, character, will power or other empirically unvalidated constructs. Thus we create an illusion of freedom by attributing more internal control to ourselves, to the individual, than actually exists. We thus underestimate the power and pervasiveness of situational controls over behavior because: (a) they are often nonobvious and subtle, (b) we can often avoid entering situations where we might be so controlled, (c) we label as "weak" or "deviant" people in those situations who do behave differently from how we believed we would.

Each of us carries around in our heads a favorable self-image in which we are essentially just, fair, humane, and understanding. For example, we could not imagine inflicting pain on others without much provocation or hurting people who had done nothing to us, who in fact were even liked by us. However, there is a growing body of social psychological research which underscores the conclusion derived from this prison study. Many people, perhaps the majority, can be made to do almost anything when put into psychologically compelling situations—regardless of their morals, ethics, values, attitudes, beliefs, or personal convictions. My colleague, Stanley Milgram, has shown that more than 60 percent of the population will deliver what they think is a series of painful electric shocks to another person even after the victim cries for mercy, begs them to stop, and then apparently passes out. The subjects complained that they did not want to inflict more pain but blindly obeyed the command of the authority figure (the experimenter) who said that they must go on. In my own research on violence, I have seen mild-mannered co-eds repeatedly give shocks (which they thought were causing pain) to another girl, a stranger whom they had rated very favorably, simply by being made to feel anonymous and put in a situation where they were expected to engage in this activity.

Observers of these and similar experimental situations never predict their outcomes and estimate that it is unlikely that they themselves would behave similarly. They can be so confident only when they are outside the situation. However, since the majority of people in these studies do act in nonrational, nonobvious ways, it follows that the majority of observers would also succumb to the social psychological forces in the situation.

With regard to prisons, we can state that the mere act of assigning labels to people and putting them into a situation where those labels acquire validity and meaning is sufficient to elicit pathological behavior. This pathology is not predictable from any available diagnostic indicators we have in the social sciences, and is extreme enough to modify in very significant ways fundamental attitudes and behavior. The prison situation, as presently arranged, is guaranteed to generate severe enough pathological reactions in both guards and prisoners as to debase their humanity, lower their feelings of self-worth, and make it difficult for them to be part of a society outside of their prison.

For years our national leaders have been pointing to the enemies of freedom, to the fascist or communist threat to the American way of life. In so doing they have overlooked the threat of social anarchy that is building within our own country without any outside agitation. As soon as a person comes to the realization that he is being imprisoned by his society or individuals in it, then, in the best American tradition, he demands liberty and rebels, accepting death as an alternative. The third alternative, however, is to allow oneself to become a good prisoner—docile, cooperative, uncomplaining, conforming in thought and complying in deed.

Our prison authorities now point to the militant agitators who are still vaguely referred to as part of some communist plot, as the irresponsible, incorrigible troublemakers. They imply that there would be no trouble, riots, hostages or deaths if it weren't for this small band of bad prisoners. In other words, then, everything would return to "normal" again in the life of our nation's prisons if they could break these men.

The riots in prison are coming from within—from within every man and woman who refuses to let the system turn them into an object, a number, a thing or a no-thing. It is not communist-inspired, but inspired by the spirit of American freedom. No man wants to be enslaved. To be powerless, to be subject to the arbitrary exercise of power, to not be recognized as a human being is to be a slave.

To be a militant prisoner is to become aware that the physical jails are but more blatant extensions of the forms of social and psychological oppression experienced daily in the nation's ghettos. They are trying to awaken the conscience of the nation to the ways in which the American ideals are being perverted, apparently in the name of justice but actually under the banner of apathy, fear, and hatred. If we do not listen to the pleas of the prisoners at Attica to be treated like human beings, then we have all become brutalized by our priorities for property rights over human rights. The consequence will not only be more prison riots but a loss of all those ideals on which this country was founded.

The public should be aware that they own the prisons and that their business is failing. The 70 percent recidivism rate and the escalation in severity of crimes committed by graduates of our prisons are evidence that current prisons fail to rehabilitate the inmates in any positive way. Rather, they are breeding grounds for hatred of the establishment, a hatred that makes every citizen a target of violent assault. Prisons are a bad investment for us taxpayers. Until now we have not cared, we have turned over to wardens and prison authorities the unpleasant job of keeping people who threaten us out of our sight. Now we are shocked to learn that their management practices have failed to improve the product and instead turn petty thieves into murderers. We must insist upon new management or improved operating procedures.

The cloak of secrecy should be removed from the prisons. Prisoners claim they are brutalized by the guards, guards say it is a lie. Where is the impartial test of the truth in such a situation? Prison officials have forgotten that they work for us, that they are only public servants whose salaries are paid by our taxes. They act as if it is their prison, like a child with a toy he won't share. Neither lawyers, judges, the legislature, nor the public is allowed into prisons to ascertain the truth unless the visit is sanctioned by authorities and until all is prepared for their visit. I was shocked to learn that my request to join a congressional investigating committee's tour of San Quentin and Soledad was refused, as was that of the news media.

There should be an ombudsman in every prison, not under the pay or control of the prison authority, and responsible only to the courts, the state legislature, and the public. Such a person could report on violations of constitutional and human rights.

Guards must be given better training than they now receive for the difficult job society imposes upon them. To be a prison guard as now constituted is to be put in a situation of constant threat from within the prison, with no social recognition from the society at large. As was shown graphically at Attica, prison guards are also prisoners of the system who can be sacrificed to the demands of the public to be punitive and the needs of politicians to preserve an image. Social scientists and business administrators should be called upon to design and help carry out this training.

The relationship between the individual (who is sentenced by the courts to a prison term) and his community must be maintained. How can a prisoner return to a dynamically changing society that most of us cannot cope with after being out of it for a number of years? There should be more community involvement in these rehabilitation centers, more ties encouraged and promoted between the trainees and family and friends, more educational opportunities to prepare them for returning to their communities as more valuable members of it than they were before they left.

Finally, the main ingredient necessary to effect any change at all in prison reform, in the rehabilitation of a single prisoner or even in the optimal development of a child is caring. Reform must start with people—especially people with power—caring about the well-being of others. Underneath the toughest, society-hating convict, rebel, or anarchist is a human being who wants his existence to be recognized by his fellows and who wants someone else to care about whether he lives or dies and to grieve if he lives imprisoned rather than lives free.

26 On Being Sane in Insane Places

DAVID L. ROSENHAN

On the one hand, it is not uncommon for people who violate *explicit* rules written into law to find themselves enmeshed in a formal system that involves passing judgment on their fitness to remain in society. As we have just seen with the preceding selection, removing people's freedom can thrust them into a highly volatile situation. On the other hand, people who violate *implicit* rules (the assumptions about what characterizes "normal" people) also can find themselves enmeshed in a formal system that involves passing judgment on their fitness to remain in society. "If found guilty of insanity," they, too, are institutionalized—placed in the care of keepers who oversee almost all aspects of their lives.

The fundamental taken-for-granted assumption in institutionalizing people who violate implicit rules is that we are able to tell the sane from the insane. If we cannot do so, the practice itself would be insane! In that case, we would have to explicitly question contemporary psychiatry as a mechanism of social control. But what kind of question is this? Even most of us non-psychiatrists can tell the difference between who is sane and who is not. However, in a fascinating experiment, Rosenhan put to the test whether or not even psychiatrists can differentiate between the sane and the insane. As detailed in this account, the results contain a few surprises.

IF SANITY AND INSANITY EXIST . . . how shall we know them? The question is neither capricious nor itself insane. However much we may be personally convinced that we can tell the normal from the abnormal, the evidence is simply not compelling. It is commonplace, for example, to read about murder trials wherein eminent psychiatrists for the defense are contradicted by equally eminent psychiatrists for the prosecution on the matter of the defendant's sanity. More generally, there are a great deal of conflicting data on the reliability, utility, and meaning of such terms as "sanity," "insanity," "mental illness," and "schizophrenia."[1] Finally, as early as 1934, Benedict suggested that normality and abnormality are not universal.[2] What is viewed as normal in one culture may be seen as quite aberrant in another. Thus, notions of normality and abnormality may not be quite as accurate as people believe they are.

To raise questions regarding normality and abnormality is in no way to question the fact that some behaviors are deviant or odd. Murder is deviant. So, too, are hallucinations. Nor does raising such questions deny the existence of the personal anguish that is often associated with "mental illness." Anxiety and depression exist. Psychological suffering exists. But normality and abnormality, sanity and insanity, and the diagnoses that flow from them may be less substantive than many believe them to be.

At its heart, the question of whether the sane can be distinguished from the insane (and whether degrees of insanity can be distinguished from each other) is a simple matter: Do the salient characteristics that lead to diagnoses reside in the patients themselves or in the environments and contexts in which observers find them? From Bleuler, through Kretchmer, through the formulators of the recently revised *Diagnostic and Statistical Manual* of the American Psychiatric Association, the belief has been strong that patients present symptoms, that those symptoms can be categorized, and, implicitly, that the sane are distinguishable from the insane. More recently, however, this belief has been questioned. Based in part on theoretical and anthropological considerations, but also on philosophical, legal, and therapeutic ones, the view has grown that psychological categorization of mental illness is useless at best and downright harmful, misleading, and pejorative at worst. Psychiatric diagnoses, in this view, are in the minds of the observers and are not valid summaries of characteristics displayed by the observed.[3,4,5]

Gains can be made in deciding which of these is more nearly accurate by getting normal people (that is, people who do not have, and have never suffered, symptoms of serious psychiatric disorders) admitted to psychiatric hospitals and then determining whether they were discovered to be sane and, if so, how. If the sanity of such pseudopatients were always detected, there would be *prima facie* evidence that a sane individual can be distinguished from the insane context in which he is found. Normality (and presumably abnormality) is distinct enough that it can be recognized wherever it occurs, for it is carried within the person. If, on the other hand, the sanity of the pseudopatients were never discovered, serious difficulties would arise for those who support traditional modes of psychiatric diagnosis. Given that the hospital staff was not incompetent, that the pseudopatient had been behaving as sanely as he had been outside of the hospital, and that it had never been previously suggested that he belonged in a psychiatric hospital, such an unlikely outcome would support the view that psychiatric diagnosis betrays little about the patient but much about the environment in which an observer finds him.

This article describes such an experiment. Eight sane people gained secret admission to twelve different hospitals.[6] Their diagnostic experiences constitute the data of the first part of this article; the remainder is devoted to a description of their experiences in psychiatric institutions. Too few psychiatrists and psychologists, even those who have worked in such hospitals, know what the experience is like. They rarely talk about it with former patients, perhaps because they distrust information coming from the previously insane. Those who have worked in psychiatric hospitals are likely to have adapted so thoroughly to the settings that they are insensitive to the impact of that experience. And while there have been occasional reports of researchers who submitted themselves to psychiatric hospitalization,[7] these researchers have commonly remained in the hospitals for short periods of time, often with the knowledge of the hospital staff. It is difficult to know the extent to which they were treated like patients or like research colleagues. Nevertheless, their reports about the inside of the psychiatric hospital have been valuable. This article extends those efforts.

Pseudopatients and Their Settings

The eight pseudopatients were a varied group. One was a psychology graduate student in his twenties. The remaining seven were older and "established." Among them were three psychologists, a pediatrician, a psychiatrist, a painter, and a housewife. Three pseudopatients were women, five were men. All of them employed pseudonyms, lest their alleged diagnoses embarrass them later. Those who were in mental health professions alleged another occupation in order to avoid the special attentions that might be accorded by staff, as a matter of courtesy or caution, to ailing colleagues.[8] With the exception of myself (I was the first pseudopatient and my presence was known to the hospital administrator and chief psychologist and, so far as I can tell, to them alone), the presence of pseudopatients and the nature of the research program were not known to the hospital staffs.[9]

The settings were similarly varied. In order to generalize the findings, admission into a variety of hospitals was sought. The twelve hospitals in the sample were located in five different states on the East and West coasts. Some were old and shabby, some were quite new. Some were research-oriented, others not. Some had good staff-patient ratios, others were quite understaffed. Only one was a strictly private hospital. All of the others were supported by state or federal funds, or in one instance, by university funds.

After calling the hospital for an appointment, the pseudopatient arrived at the admissions office complaining that he had been hearing voices. Asked what the voices said, he replied that they were often unclear, but as far as he could tell they said "empty," "hollow," and "thud." The voices were unfamiliar and were of the same sex as the pseudopatient. The choice of these symptoms was occasioned by their apparent similarity to existential symptoms. Such symptoms are alleged to arise from painful concerns about the perceived meaninglessness of one's life. It is as if the hallucinating person were saying, "My life is empty and hollow." The choice of these symptoms was also determined by the *absence* of a single report of existential psychoses in the literature.

Beyond alleging the symptoms and falsifying name, vocation, and employment, no further alterations of person, history, or circumstances were made. The significant events of the pseudopatient's life history were presented as they had actually occurred. Relationships with parents and siblings, with spouse and children, with people at work and in school, consistent with the aforementioned exceptions, were described as they were or had been. Frustrations and upsets were described along with joys and satisfactions. These facts are important to remember. If anything, they strongly biased the subsequent results in favor of detecting sanity, since none of their histories or current behaviors were seriously pathological in any way.

Immediately upon admission to the psychiatric ward, the pseudopatient ceased simulating *any* symptoms of abnormality. In some cases, there was a brief period of mild nervousness and anxiety, since none of the pseudopatients really believed that they would be admitted so easily. Indeed, their shared fear was that they would be immediately exposed as frauds and greatly embarrassed. Moreover, many of them had never visited a psychiatric ward; even those who had, nevertheless had some genuine fears about what might happen to them. Their nervousness, then, was quite appropriate to the novelty of the hospital setting, and it abated rapidly.

Apart from that short-lived nervousness, the pseudopatient behaved on the ward as he "normally" behaved. The pseudopatient spoke to patients and staff as he might ordinarily. Because there is uncommonly little to do on a psychiatric ward, he attempted to engage others in conversation. When asked by staff how he was feeling, he indicated that he was fine, that he no longer experienced symptoms. He responded to instructions from attendants, to calls for medication (which was not swallowed), and to dining-hall instructions. Beyond such activities as were available to him on the admissions ward, he spent his time writing down his observations about the ward, its patients, and the staff. Initially these notes were written "secretly," but as it soon became clear than no one much cared, they were subsequently written on standard tablets of paper in such public places as the dayroom. No secret was made of these activites.

The pseudopatient, very much as a true psychiatric patient, entered a hospital with no foreknowledge of when he would be discharged. Each was told that he would have to get out by his own devices, essentially by convincing the staff that he was sane. The psychological stresses associated with hospitalization were considerable, and all but one of the pseudopatients desired to be discharged almost immediately after being admitted. They were, therefore, motivated not only to behave sanely, but to be paragons of cooperation. That their behavior was in no way disruptive is confirmed by nursing reports, which have been obtained on most of the patients. These reports uniformly indicate that the patients were "friendly," "cooperative," and "exhibited no abnormal indications."

The Normal Are Not Detectably Sane

Despite their public "show" of sanity, the pseudopatients were never detected. Admitted, except in one case, with a diagnosis of schizophrenia,[10] each was discharged with a diagnosis of schizophrenia "in remission." The label "in remission" should in no way be dismissed as a formality, for at no time during any hospitalization had any question been raised about any pseudopatient's simulation. Nor are there any indications in the hospital records that the pseudopatient's status was suspect. Rather, the evidence is strong that, once labeled schizophrenic, the pseudopatient was stuck with that label. If the pseudopatient was to be discharged, he must naturally be "in remission"; but he was not sane, nor, in the institution's view, had he ever been sane.

The uniform failure to recognize sanity cannot be attributed to the quality of the hospitals, for, although there were considerable variations among them, several are considered excellent. Nor can it be alleged that there was simply not enough time to observe the pseudopatients. Length of hospitalization ranged from seven to fifty-two days, with an average of nineteen days. The pseudopatients were not, in fact, carefully observed, but this failure clearly speaks more to traditions within psychiatric hospitals than to lack of opportunity.

Finally, it cannot be said that the failure to recognize the pseudopatients' sanity was due to the fact that they were not behaving sanely. While there was clearly some tension present in all of them, their daily visitors could detect no serious behavioral consequences—nor, indeed, could other patients. It was quite common for the patients to "detect" the pseudopatients' sanity. During the first three hospitalizations, when accurate counts were kept, 35 of a total of 118 patients on the admissions ward voiced their suspicions, some vigorously. "You're not crazy. You're a journalist, or a professor [referring to the continual note-taking]. You're checking up on the hospital." While most of the patients were reassured by the pseudopatient's insistence that he had been sick before he came in but was fine now, some continued to believe that the pseudopatient was sane throughout his hospitalization.[11] The fact that the patients often recognized normality when staff did not raises important questions.

Failure to detect sanity during the course of hospitalization may be due to the fact that physicians operate with a strong bias toward what statisticians call the type 2 error.[5] This is to say that physicians are more inclined to call a healthy person sick (a false positive, type 2) than a sick person healthy (a false negative, type 1). The reasons for this are not hard to find: It is clearly more dangerous to misdiagnose illness that health. Better to err on the side of caution, to suspect illness even among the healthy.

But what holds for medicine does not hold equally well for psychiatry. Medical illnesses, while unfortunate, are not commonly pejorative. Psychiatric diagnoses, on the contrary, carry with them personal, legal, and social stigmas.[12] It was therefore important to see whether the tendency toward diagnosing the sane insane could be reversed. The following experiment was arranged at a research and teaching hospital whose staff had heard these findings but doubted that such an error could occur in their hospital. The staff was informed that at some time during the following three months, one or more pseudopatients would attempt to be admitted into the psychiatric hospital. Each staff member was asked to rate each patient who presented himself at admissions or on the ward according to the likelihood that the patient was a pseudopatient. A 10-point scale was used, with a 1 and 2 reflecting high confidence that the patient was a pseudopatient.

Judgments were obtained on 193 patients who were admitted for psychiatric treatment. All staff who had had sustained contact with or primary responsibility for the patient—attendants, nurses, psychiatrists, physicians, and psychologists—were asked to make judgments. Forty-one patients were alleged, with high confidence, to be pseudopatients by at least one member of the staff. Twenty-three were considered suspect by at least one psychiatrist. Nineteen were suspected by one psychiatrist and one other staff member. Actually, no genuine pseudopatient (at least from my group) presented himself during this period.

The experiment is instructive. It indicates that the tendency to designate sane people as insane can be reversed when the stakes (in this case, prestige and diagnostic acumen) are high. But what can be said of the nineteen people who were suspected by being "sane" by one psychiatrist and another staff member? Were these people truly "sane," or was it rather the case that in the course of avoiding the type 2 error the staff tended to make more errors of the first sort—calling the crazy "sane"? There is no way of knowing. But one thing is certain: Any diagnostic process that lends itself so readily to massive errors of this sort cannot be a very reliable one.

The Stickiness of Psychodiagnostic Labels

Beyond the tendency to call the healthy sick—a tendency that accounts better for diagnostic behavior on admission than it does for such behavior after a lengthy period of exposure—the data speak to the massive role of labeling in psychiatric assessment. Having once been labeled schizophrenic, there is nothing the pseudopatient can do to overcome the tag. The tag profoundly colors others' perceptions of him and his behavior.

From one viewpoint, these data are hardly surprising, for it has long been known that elements are given meaning by the context in which they occur. Gestalt psychology made this point vigorously, and Asch[13] demonstrated that there are "central" personality traits (such as "warm" versus "cold") which are so powerful that they markedly color the meaning of other information in forming an impression of a given personality.[14] "Insane," "schizophrenic," "manic-depressive," and "crazy" are probably among the most powerful of such central traits. Once a person is designated abnormal, all of his other behaviors and characteristics are colored by that label. Indeed, that label is so powerful that many of the pseudopatients' normal behaviors were overlooked entirely or profoundly misinterpreted. Some examples may clarify this issue.

Earlier I indicated that there were no changes in the pseudopatient's personal history and current status behond those of name, employment, and, where necessary, vocation. Otherwise, a veridical description of personal history and circumstances was offered. Those circumstances were not psychotic. How were they made consonant with the diagnosis of psychosis? Or were those diagnoses modified in such a way as to bring them into accord with the circumstances of the pseudopatient's life, as described by him?

As far as I can determine, diagnoses were in no way affected by the relative health of the circumstances of a pseudopatient's life. Rather, the reverse occurred: The perception of his circumstances was shaped entirely by the diagnosis. A clear example of such translation is found in the case of a pseudopatient who had had a close relationship with his mother but was rather remote from his father during his early childhood. During adolescence and beyond, however, his father became a close friend, while his relationship with his mother cooled. His present relationship with his wife was characteristically close and warm. Apart from occasional angry exchanges, friction was minimal. The children had rarely been spanked. Surely there is nothing especially pathological about such a history. Indeed, many readers may see a similar pattern in their own experiences, with no markedly deleterious consequences. Observe, however, how such a history was translated in the psychopathological context, this from the case summary prepared after the patient was discharged.

> This white 39-year-old male . . . manifests a long history of considerable ambivalence in close relationships, which begins in early childhood. A warm relationship with his mother cools during adolescence. A distant relationship to his father is described as becoming very intense. Affective stability is absent. His attempts to control emotionality with his wife and children are punctuated by angry outbursts and, in the case of the children, spankings. And while he says that

he has several good friends, one senses considerable ambivalence embedded in those relationships also. . . .

The facts of the case were unintentionally distorted by the staff to achieve consistency with a popular theory of the dynamics of schizophrenic reaction.[15] Nothing of an ambivalent nature had been described in relations with parents, spouse, or friends. To the extent that ambivalence could be inferred, it was probably not greater than is found in all human relationships. It is true the pseudopatient's relationships with his parents changed over time, but in the ordinary context that would hardly be remarkable—indeed, it might very well be expected. Clearly, the meaning ascribed to his verbalizations (that is, ambivalence, affective instability) was determined by the diagnosis: schizophrenia. An entirely different meaning would have been ascribed if it were known that the man was "normal."

All pseudopatients took extensive notes publicly. Under ordinary circumstances, such behavior would have raised questions in the minds of observers, as, in fact, it did among patients. Indeed, it seemed so certain that the notes would elicit suspicion that elaborate precautions were taken to remove them from the ward each day. But the precautions proved needless. The closest any staff member came to questioning these notes occurred when one pseudopatient asked his physician what kind of medication he was receiving and began to write down the response. "You needn't write it," he was told gently. "If you have trouble remembering, just ask me again."

If no questions were asked of the pseudopatients, how was their writing interpreted? Nursing records for three patients indicate that the writing was seen as an aspect of their pathological behavior. "Patient engages in writing behavior" was the daily nursing comment on one of the pseudopatients who was never questioned about his writing. Given that the patient is in the hospital, he must be psychologically disturbed. And given that he is disturbed, continuous writing must be a behavioral manifestation of that disturbance, perhaps a subset of the compulsive behaviors that are sometimes correlated with schizophrenia.

One tacit characteristic of psychiatric diagnosis is that it locates the sources of aberration within the individual and only rarely within the complex of stimuli that surrounds him. Consequently, behaviors that are stimulated by the environment are commonly misattributed to the patient's disorder. For example, one kindly nurse found a pseudopatient pacing the long hospital corridors. "Nervous, Mr. X?" she asked. "No, bored," he said.

The notes kept by pseudopatients are full of patient behaviors that were misinterpreted by well-intentioned staff. Often enough, a patient would go "berserk" because he had, wittingly or unwittingly, been mistreated by, say, an attendant. A nurse coming upon the scene would rarely inquire even cursorily into the environmental stimuli of the patient's behavior.

Rather, she assumed that his upset derived from his pathology, not from his present interactions with other staff members. Occasionally, the staff might assume that the patient's family (especially when they had recently visited) or other patients had stimulated the outburst. But never were the staff found to assume that one of themselves or the structure of the hospital had anything to do with a patient's behavior. One psychiatrist pointed to a group of patients who were sitting outside the cafeteria entrance half an hour before lunchtime. To a group of young residents he indicated that such behavior was characteristic of the oral-acquisitive nature of the syndrome. It seemed not to occur to him that there were very few things to anticipate in the psychiatric hospital besides eating.

A psychiatric label has a life and an influence of its own. Once the impression has been formed that the patient is schizophrenic, the expectation is that he will continue to be schizophrenic. When a sufficient amount of time has passed, during which the patient has done nothing bizarre, he is considered to be in remission and available for discharge. But the label endures beyond discharge, with the unconfirmed expectation that he will behave as a schizophrenic again. Such labels, conferred by mental health professionals, are as influential on the patient as they are on his relatives and friends, and it should not surprise anyone that the diagnosis acts on all of them as a self-fulfilling prophecy. Eventually, the patient himself accepts the diagnosis, with all of its surplus meanings and expectations, and behaves accordingly.[5]

The inferences to be made from these matters are quite simple. Much as Zigler and Phillips have demonstrated that there is enormous overlap in the symptoms presented by patients who have been variously diagnosed,[16] so there is enormous overlap in the behaviors of the sane and the insane. The sane are not "sane" all of the time. We lose our tempers "for no good reason." We are occasionally depressed or anxious, again for no good reason. And we may find it difficult to get along with one or another person— again for no reason that we can specify. Similarly, the insane are not always insane. Indeed, it was the impression of the pseudopatients while living with them that they were sane for long periods of time—that the bizarre behaviors upon which their diagnoses were allegedly predicated constituted only a small fraction of their total behavior. If it makes no sense to label ourselves permanently depressed on the basis of an occasional depression, then it takes evidence that is presently available to label all patients insane or schizophrenic on the basis of bizarre behaviors or cognitions. It seems more useful, as Mischel[17] has pointed out, to limit our discussions to *behaviors*, the stimuli that provoke them, and their correlates.

It is not known why powerful impressions of personality traits, such as "crazy" or "insane," arise. Conceivably, when the origins of and stimuli that give rise to a behavior are remote or unknown, or when the behavior strikes us as immutable, trait labels regarding the *behavior* arise. When, on the other hand, the origins and stimuli are known and available, discourse is limited to the behavior itself. Thus, I may hallucinate because I am sleeping, or I may hallucinate because I have ingested a peculiar drug. These are termed sleep-induced hallucinations, or dreams, and drug-induced hallucinations, respectively. But when the stimuli to my hallucinations are unknown, that is called craziness, or schizophrenia—as if that inference were somehow as illuminating as the others. . . .

The Consequences of Labeling and Depersonalization

Whenever the ratio of what is known to what needs to be known approaches zero, we tend to invent "knowledge" and assume that we understand more than we actually do. We seem unable to acknowledge that we simply don't know. The needs for diagnosis and remediation of behavioral and emotional problems are enormous. But rather than acknowledge that we are just embarking on understanding, we continue to label patients "schizophrenic," "manic-depressive," and "insane," as if in those words we had captured the essence of understanding. The facts of the matter are that we have known for a long time that diagnoses are often not useful or reliable, but we have nevertheless continued to use them. We now know that we cannot distinguish insanity from sanity. It is depressing to consider how that information will be used.

Not merely depressing, but frightening. How many people, one wonders, are sane but not recognized as such in our psychiatric institutions? How many have been needlessly stripped of their privileges of citizenship, from the right to vote and drive to that of handling their own accounts? How many have feigned insanity in order to avoid the criminal consequences of their behavior, and, conversely, how many would rather stand trial than live interminably in a psychiatric hospital—but are wrongly thought to be mentally ill? How many have been stigmatized by well-intentioned, but nevertheless erroneous, diagnoses? On the last point, recall again that a "type 2 error" in psychiatric diagnosis does not have the same consequences it does in medical diagnosis. A diagnosis of cancer that has been found to be in error is cause for celebration. But psychiatric diagnoses are rarely found to be in error. The label sticks, a mark of inadequacy forever.

Notes

1. P. Ash, *J. Abnorm. Soc. Psychol.* 44, 272 (1949); A. T. Beck, *Amer. J. Psychiat.* 119, 210 (1962); A. T. Boisen, *Psychiatry* 2, 233 (1938); N. Kreitman, *J. Ment. Sci.* 107, 876 (1961); N. Kreitman, P. Sainsbury, J. Morrisey, J. Towers, J. Scrivener, *ibid.*, p. 887; H. O. Schmitt and C. P. Fonda, *J. Abnorm. Soc. Psychol.*

52, 262 (1956); W. Seeman, *J. Nerv. Ment. Dis.* 118, 541 (1953). For an analysis of these artifacts and summaries of the disputes, see J. Zubin, *Annu. Rev. Psychol.* 18, 373 (1967); L. Phillips and J. G. Draguns, *ibid.* 22, 447 (1971).

2. R. Benedict. *J. Gen. Psychol.* 10, 59 (1934).

3. See in this regard H. Becker, *Outsiders: Studies in the Sociology of Deviance* (New York: Free Press, 1963); B. M. Braginsky, D. D. Braginsky, K. Ring, *Methods of Madness: The Mental Hospital as a Last Resort* (New York: Holt, Rinehart & Winston, 1969); G. M. Crocetti and P. V. Lemkau, *Amer. Sociol. Rev.* 30, 577 (1965); E. Goffman, *Behavior in Public Places* (New York: Free Press, 1964); R. D. Laing, *The Divided Self: A Study of Sanity and Madness* (Chicago: Quadrangle, 1960); D. L. Phillips, *Amer. Sociol. Rev.* 28, 963 (1963); T. R. Sarbin. *Psychol. Today* 6, 18 (1972); E. Schur, *Amer J. Sociol.* 75, 309 (1969); T. Szasz, *Law, Liberty and Psychiatry* (New York: Macmillan, 1963); *The Myth of Mental Illness: Foundations of a Theory of Mental Illness* (New York: Hoeber Harper, 1963). For a critique of some of these views, see W. R. Gove, *Amer. Sociol. Rev.* 35, 873 (1970).

4. E. Goffman. *Asylums* (Garden City, NY: Doubleday, 1961).

5. T. J. Scheff, *Being Mentally Ill: A Sociological Theory* (Chicago: Aldine, 1966).

6. Data from a ninth pseudopatient are not incorporated in this report because, although his sanity went undetected, he falsified aspects of his personal history, including his marital status and parental relationships. His experimental behaviors therefore were not identical to those of the other pseudopatients.

7. A. Barry, *Bellevue Is a State of Mind* (New York: Harcourt Brace Jovanovich, 1971); I. Belknap, *Human Problems of a State Mental Hospital* (New York: McGraw-Hill, 1956); W. Caudill, F. C. Redlich, H. R. Gilmore, E. B. Brody, *Amer J. Orthopsychiat.* 22, 314 (1952); A. R. Goldman, R. H. Bohr, T. A. Steinberg, *Prof. Psychol.* 1, 427 (1970); unauthored, *Roche Report 1* (No. 13), 8 (1971).

8. Beyond the personal difficulties that the pseudopatient is likely to experience in the hospital, there are legal and social ones that, combined, require considerable attention before entry. For example, once admitted to a psychiatric institution, it is difficult, if not impossible, to be discharged on short notice, state law to the contrary notwithstanding. I was not sensitive to these difficulties at the outset of the project, nor to the personal and situational emergencies that can arise, but later a writ of habeas corpus was prepared for each of the entering pseudopatients and an attorney was kept "on call" during every hospitalization. I am grateful to John Kaplan and Robert Bartels for legal advice and assistance in these matters.

9. However distasteful such concealment is, it was a necessary first step to examining these questions. Without concealment, there would have been no way to know how valid these experiences were; nor was there any way of knowing whether whatever detections occurred were a tribute to the diagnostic acumen of the staff or to the hospital's rumor network. Obviously, since my concerns are general ones that cut across individual hospitals and staffs, I have respected their anonymity and have eliminated clues that might lead to their identification.

10. Interestingly, of the twelve admissions, eleven were diagnosed as schizophrenic and one, with the identical symptomatology, as manic-depressive psychosis. This diagnosis has a more favorable prognosis, and it was given by the only private hospital in our sample. On the relations between social class and psychiatric diagnosis, see A. B. Hollingshead and F. C. Redlich, *Social Class and Mental Illness: A Community Study* (New York: Wiley, 1958).

11. It is possible, of course, that patients have quite broad latitudes in diagnosis and therefore are inclined to call many people sane, even those whose behavior is patently aberrant. However, although we have no hard data on this matter, it was our distinct impression that this was not the case. In many instances, patients not only singled us out for attention, but came to imitate our behaviors and styles.

12. J. Cumming and E. Cumming, *Community Ment. Health 1*, 135 (1965); A. Farina and K. Ring, *J. Abnorm. Psychol. 70*, 47 (1965); H. E. Freeman and O. G. Simmons, *The Mental Patient Comes Home* (New York: Wiley, 1963); W. J. Johannsen, *Mental Hygiene 53*, 218 (1969); A. S. Linsky, *Soc. Psychiat. 5*, 166 (1970).

13. S. E. Asch, *J. Abnorm. Soc. Psychol. 41*, 258 (1946); *Social Psychology* (New York: Prentice-Hall, 1952).

14. See also I. N. Mensh and J. Wishner, *J. Personality 16*, 188 (1947); J. Wishner, *Psychol. Rev. 67*, 96 (1960); J. S. Bruner and R. Tagiuri, in *Handbook of Social Psychology*, G. Lindzey, ed. (Cambridge, MA: Addison-Wesley, 1954), vol. 2, pp. 634–54; J. S. Bruner, D. Shapiro, R. Tagiuri, in *Person Perception and Interpersonal Behavior*, R. Tagiuri and L. Petrullo, eds. (Stanford, CA: Stanford Univ. Press, 1958), pp. 277–88.

15. For an example of a similar self-fulfilling prophecy, in this instance dealing with the "central" trait of intelligence, see R. Rosenthal and L. Jacobson, *Pygmalion in the Classroom* (New York: Holt, Rinehart & Winston, 1968).

16. E. Zigler and L. Phillips, *J. Abnorm. Soc. Psychol. 63*, 69 (1961). See also R. K. Freudenberg and J. P. Robertson, *A.M.A. Arch. Neurol. Psychiatr. 76*, 14 (1956).

17. W. Mischel, *Personality and Assessment* (New York: Wiley, 1968).

Social Inequality

I N ALL KNOWN PAST SOCIETIES and every contemporary society, the members are characterized by inequalities of some sort. Some people are stronger, learn more quickly, are swifter, shoot weapons more accurately, or have more of *whatever is considered important* in that particular society. Natural or biological inequalities are normal within human groups. Other inequalities, whatever form they take in a particular society, may appear more contrived—such as distinctions of social rank based on wealth. But, whether based on biological characteristics, social skills, or money, no system of dividing people into different groups is inevitable. Rather, each is arbitrary. Yet all societies rank their members in some way, and whatever arbitrary criteria they use appear quite reasonable to them.

The primary social division in small, preliterate groups is drawn along the line of gender. Sorted into highly distinctive groupings, men and women in these societies engage in separate activities—ones deemed "appropriate" for each sex. Indeed, in these small societies gender usually represents a cleavage that cuts across most of the group's endeavors. In addition, they also make finer distinctions on the much more individualistic levels of personality, skill, and reputation. Of the preliterate societies, hunting and gathering groups appear to have minimal stratification. These societies—where most activities revolve around subsistence and there is little or no material surplus— apparently also have the least *gender typing*, or division of activities by sex.

Perhaps the primary significance of a group's hierarchies and statuses is that they surround the individual with *boundaries*. Setting limits and circumscribing one's possibilities in life, these social divisions establish the framework of socialization. They launch the individual onto the social scene by presenting to him or her an already existing picture of what he or she ought to expect from life.

None of us escapes this fact of social life, which sociologists variously call *social inequality* and *social stratification*. No matter which our society, all of us are born into some system of social stratification, whose boundaries and limits affect almost all aspects of our lives—our relationships with others, our behaviors, beliefs, and attitudes, our goals and aspirations, even our perception of the social world and of the self.

In analyzing the social inequality of contemporary society, sociologists look at very large groupings of people. They call these groups *social classes*, which are determined by people's rankings on income, education, and occupation. The more income and education one has and the higher the prestige accorded one's work, the higher one's social class. Conversely, the lower one's income, education, and prestige of one's occupation, the lower one's social class.

On the basis of these three criteria, one can divide Americans into three principal social classes: upper, middle, and lower. The *upper* are the very rich (a million dollars wouldn't even begin to buy your way in); the *middle*—primarily professionals, managers, executives, and other business people—is heavily rewarded with the material goods our society has to offer; and the *lower*, to understate the matter, receives the least.

Some sociologists add an upper and a lower to each of these divisions and say there are *six* social classes in the United States: an upper-upper and lower-upper, an upper-middle and a lower-middle, and an upper-lower and a lower-lower. Membership in the *upper-upper* class is the most exclusive of all, accorded not only on the basis of huge wealth but also according to how long that money has been in the family. The longer, the better.

Somehow or other, it is difficult to make millions of dollars while remaining scrupulously honest in business dealings. It appears that most people who have entered the monied classes have found it necessary to cut moral corners, at least here and there. This "taint" to the money disappears with time, however, and the later generations of Vanderbilts, Rockefellers, Mellons, DuPonts, Chryslers, Kennedys, Morgans, Nashes, and so on are considered to have "clean" money simply by virtue of the passage of time. They can be philanthropic as well as rich. They have attended the best private schools and universities, the male heirs have probably entered law, and they protect their vast fortunes and economic empires with far-flung political connections and contributions.

And the *lower-upper* class? These people have money, but it is new, and therefore suspect. They have not gone to the right schools and cannot be depended on for adequate in-group loyalty. Unable themselves to make the leap into the upper-upper class, their hope for social supremacy lies in their children: If their children go to the right schools *and* marry into the upper-upper class, what has been denied the parents will be granted the children.

The *upper-middle* class consists primarily of people who have entered the professions or higher levels of management. They are doctors, professors, lawyers, dentists, pharmacists, and clergy. They are bank presidents and successful contractors and other business people. Their education is high, their income adequate for most of their needs.

The *lower-middle* class consists largely of lower-level managers, white-collar workers in the service industries, and the more highly paid and skilled blue-collar workers. Their education and income, and the prestige of their work, are correspondingly lower than those of their upper-middle class counterparts.

The *upper-lower* class is also known as the working class. (Americans find this term much more agreeable than the term "lower," as the latter brings negative connotations to mind, while "working" elicits more positive images.) This class consists primarily of blue-collar workers who work regularly, not seasonally, at their jobs. Their education is limited, and little prestige is attached to what they do. With the wage advances made by blue-collar workers during the past three decades, however, many have increased their income significantly, and the changes they have made in their life style make it more difficult to distinguish them from the lower-middle class.

At the bottom of the ladder of social inequality is the *lower-lower* class. This is the social class that gets the worst of everything society has to offer. Its members have the least education and the least income, and often their work is negatively valued, since they do share-cropping and other menial labor. The main difference between the lower-lower and the upper-lower classes is that the upper-lower class works the year round while the lower-lower class doesn't. Members of the lower-lower class are likely to be drawing welfare, and generally are considered the ne'er-do-wells of society.

We can use the example of the automotive industry to illustrate social class membership in American society. The Fords, for example, own and control a manufacturing and financial empire whose net worth is truly staggering. Their vast accumulation of money, not unlike their accrued power, is now several generations old. Their children definitely go to the "right" schools, know how to spend money in the "right" way, and can be trusted to make their family and class interests paramont in life. They are without question members of the upper-upper class.

Next in line come top Ford executives. Although they may have an income of several hundred thousand dollars a year (and some, with stock options and bonuses, earn well over a million dollars annually), they are new to wealth and power. Consequently, they remain on the rung below, and are considered members of the lower-upper class.

A husband and wife who own a successful Ford agency are members of the upper-middle class. Their income clearly sets them apart from the majority of Americans, and they have an enviable reputation in the community. More than likely they also exert greater-than-average influence in their community, but find their capacity to wield power highly limited.

A salesperson, as well as those who work in the office, would be considered members of the lower-middle class. Their income is less, their education is likely to be less, and people commonly assign less prestige to their work than to that of the owners of the agency.

A mechanic who repairs customers' cars would ordinarily be considered a member of the upper-lower class. High union wages, however, have blurred this distinction, and he or she might more properly be classified as a member of the lower-middle class. People who service Fords and are paid less, however, such as those who "detail" used cars (making them appear newer by washing and polishing the car, painting the tires and floor mats, and so on) would be members of the upper-lower class.

Window washers and janitors who are hired to clean the agency only during the busy season and then are laid off would be members of the lower-lower class. (If they are year-round employees of the agency, they would be members of the upper-lower class.) Their income would be the least, as would their education, while the prestige accorded their work would be minimal.

It is significant to note that children are automatically assigned the social class of their parents. It is for this reason that sociologists say that we are born into a social class. Sociologists call this *ascribed* membership, as compared with membership one earns on one's own, called *achieved* membership. If a child of a person doing "detail" work goes on to college, works as a salesperson in the agency part-time and during vacations, and then eventually buys the agency, he or she has upgraded his or her social class. Because of this *upward social mobility*, the new class membership is said to be achieved membership. Conversely, if a child of the agency owner becomes an alcoholic, fails to get through college, and takes a lower-status job, he or she experiences *downward social mobility*. The resulting change in social class membership is also achieved membership. ("Achieved" does not have to equal "achievement.")

You should note that this devision into six social classes is not the only way that sociologists look at our social class system. In fact, sociologists have no single standard, agreed-upon way of overviewing the American class system. Like others, the outline I have presented is both arbitrary and useful, but does not do justice to the nuances and complexities of our class system.

One view within sociology (generally called *conflict* or *Marxist*) holds that to understand social inequality one need focus only on income. What is the source of a person's income, and how much of it does he or she have? Know that, and you know the persons's social class. There are those with money and those without money. The monied own the means of production—the factories and machinery and buildings—and live off their investments, while those with little money exchange their labor to produce more money for the wealthy owners. In short, the monied (the capitalists) are in the controlling sector of society, while those with little money (the workers) find themselves controlled by the wealthy. With society divided into the haves and the have-nots, insist conflict theorists, it is misleading to pay attention to the fine distinctions among those with or without money.

Be that as it may (and this debate continues among sociologists), society certainly is stratified. And the significance of social inequality is that it determines people's *life chances*, the probabilities as to the fate one may expect in life. It is obvious that not everyone has the same chances in life, and the single most significant factor in determining a person's life chances in our society is money. Simply put, if you have money, you can do a lot of things you can't do if you haven't got it. And the more money you have, the more control over life you have, and the more likely you are to find life pleasant.

Beyond this obvious point, however, lies a connection between social inequality and life chances that is not so easily evident. It involves such things as one's chances of dying during infancy; being killed by accident, fire, or homicide; becoming a drug addict; getting arrested; ending up in prison; dropping out of school; getting divorced; becoming disabled; or trying to live only on Social Security payments after you reach retirement age. All vary indirectly with social class; that is, the lower a person's social class, the higher the chances that these things will happen to him or her. Conversely, the higher a person's social class, the smaller the risk that these events pose.

In this Part, as we present an overview of social inequality in American society, we examine some of its major dimensions and emphasize its severe and lifelong effects. G. William Domhoff sets the stage by focusing on the powerful wealthy in the United States, delineating some of the interconnections and associations that serve to maintain their class interests. We are fortunate to have this selection, because so little is known about the wealthy: one use they make of their wealth is to protect themselves from the prying eyes of sociologists!

Have you ever wondered why the poor continue in such vast numbers when we have the material capacity to eliminate poverty? Whereas one could attempt to explain this puzzle in a number of ways, Herbert J. Gans claims that it is because the poor are functional to society. That is, society benefits by keeping some segment in poverty. Following this provocative analysis, Nijole V. Benokraitis and Joe R. Feagin then examine subtle and covert forms of sex discrimination, in the workplace, adding the gender/occupational dimension to our analysis. Then Jonathan Kozol adds a racial/educational dimension in his analysis of social inequalities in American education. This emphasis on race and social inequality is maintained by Elliot Liebow's focus on lower-lower class men being hired for temporary employment one day at a time. Finally, Everett C. Hughes discusses "the final solution" used by one society to rid itself of those viewed as its undesirables; his article is indeed an appropriate closing to this Part on social inequality.

27 The Bohemian Grove and Other Retreats

G. WILLIAM DOMHOFF

Social inequality is a fact of life in all societies. Some people receive more of their society's goods and services, others far less. Although these divisions are much greater in some societies than they are in others, in no society on earth are all members equal. This is the way it has been in every known society of the past, is now, and—people's hopes to the contrary notwithstanding—probably always will be.

American society, much as many of us would wish it different, is no exception. On the one hand, in some ways we have much equality. That is especially true when we focus on our extensive middle class. Our society, indeed, holds open so many opportunities that millions of people try to enter our country each year, regardless of the obstacles they face and regardless of the legality of their entry.

On the other hand, we also are marked by vast divisions. Of those, wealth and power are among the greatest—in extent and in their effects on people's lives. Because the poor are the most accessible, in their studies of social inequality sociologists have concentrated on the poor. Domhoff, however, one of the exceptions, presents in this selection an analysis that ought to greatly expand your awareness of power and wealth in American society.

You might ask yourself in what ways life would be different if you had been born into one of the families on which this article focuses. Beyond the external differences of material surroundings, how do you suppose your ideas of the world and of your place in it would be different?

The Bohemian Grove

Picture yourself comfortably seated in a beautiful open-air dining hall in the midst of twenty-seven hundred acres of giant California redwoods. It is early evening and the clear July air is still pleasantly warm. Dusk has descended, you have finished a sumptuous dinner, and you are sitting quietly with your drink and your cigar, listening to nostalgic welcoming speeches and enjoying the gentle light and the eerie shadows that are cast by the two-stemmed gaslights flickering softly at each of the several hundred outdoor banquet tables.

You are part of an assemblage that has been meeting in this redwood grove sixty-five miles north of San Francisco for [over] a hundred years. It is not just any assemblage, for you are a captain of industry, a well-known television star, a banker, a famous artist, or maybe a member of the President's Cabinet. You are one of fifteen hundred men gathered together from all over the country for the annual encampment of the rich and the famous at the Bohemian Grove.

["Bohemians" of the 1970s and 1980s include such personages as President Ronald Reagan; Vice President George Bush; Attorney General William French Smith; Secretary of State George P. Schultz; former President Richard Nixon; former President Gerald Ford; Supreme Court Justice Potter Stewart; Herbert Hoover, Jr.; Herbert Hoover III; newspaperman William R. Hearst, Jr.; five members of the Dean Witter family of investment bankers; entertainers Art Linkletter and Edgar Bergen; presidents and chairmen of several oil companies such as Marathon Oil and Standard Oil; the president of Rockefeller University; officers of Anheuser-Busch breweries; the president of Kaiser Industries; bank presidents from California to New York; the president and chairman of Hewlett-Packard Co.; and many other representatives of American industry, finance, government, and entertainment. When these participants arrive for the annual "campout," an elaborate ritual called the Cremation of Care welcomes them and instructs them to leave all cares behind while they join together for two weeks of lavish entertainment, fellowship, and "communion with nature."]

The Cremation of Care is the most spectacular event of the midsummer retreat that members and guests of San Francisco's Bohemian Club have taken every year since 1878. However, there are several other entertainments in store. Before the Bohemians return to the everyday world, they will be treated to plays, variety shows, song fests, shooting contests, art exhibits, swimming, boating, and nature rides.

A cast for a typical Grove play easily runs to seventy-five or one hundred people. Add in the orchestra, the stagehands, the carpenters who make the sets, and other supporting personnel, and over three hundred people are involved in creating the High Jinks each year. Preparations begin a year in advance, with rehearsals occurring two or three times a week in the month before the encampment, and nightly in the week before the play.

Costs are on the order of $20,000 to $30,000 per High Jinks, a large amount of money for a one-night production which does not have to pay a penny for salaries (the highest cost in any commercial production). "And the costs are talked about, too," reports my . . . informant. "Hey, did you hear the High Jinks will cost $25,000 this year? one of them will say to another. The expense of the play is one way they can relate to its worth."

Entertainment is not the only activity at the Bohemian Grove. For a little change of pace, there is intellectual stimulation and political enlightenment every day at 12:30 P.M. Since 1932 the meadow from which people view the Cremation of Care also has been the setting for informal talks and briefings by people as varied as Dwight David Eisenhower (before he was President), Herman Wouk (author of *The Caine Mutiny*), Bobby Kennedy (while he was Attorney General), and Neil Armstrong (after he returned from the moon).

Cabinet officers, politicians, generals, and governmental advisers are the rule rather than the exception for Lakeside Talks, especially on weekends. Equally prominent figures from the worlds of art, literature, and science are more likely to make their appearance during the weekdays of the encampment, when Grove attendance may drop to four or five hundred (many of the members only come up for one week or for the weekends because they cannot stay away from their corporations and law firms for the full two weeks).

[T]he Grove is an ideal off-the-record atmosphere for sizing up politicians. "Well, of course when a politician comes here, we all get to see him, and his stock in trade is his personality and his ideas," a prominent Bohemian told a *New York Times* reporter who was trying to cover Nelson Rockefeller's 1963 visit to the Grove for a Lakeside Talk. The journalist went on to note that the midsummer encampments "have long been a major showcase where leaders of business, industry, education, the arts, and politics can come to examine each other."[1]

For 1971, [then] President Nixon was to be the featured Lakeside speaker. However, when newspaper reporters learned that the President planned to disappear into a redwood grove for an off-the-record speech to some of the most powerful men in America, they objected loudly and vowed to make every effort to cover the event. The flap caused the club considerable embarrassment, and after much hemming and hawing back and forth, the club leaders asked the President to cancel his scheduled appearance. A White House press secretary then announced that the President had decided not to appear at the Grove rather than risk the tradition that speeches there are strictly off the public record.[2]

However, the President was not left without a final word to his fellow Bohemians. In a telegram to the president of the club, which now hangs at the entrance to the reading room in the San Francisco clubhouse, he expressed his regrets at not being able to attend. He asked the club president to continue to lead people into the woods, adding that he in turn would redouble his efforts to lead people out of the woods. He also noted that, while anyone could aspire to be President of the United States, only a few could aspire to be president of the Bohemian Club.

Not all the entertainment at the Bohemian Grove takes place under the auspices of the committee in charge of special events. The Bohemians and their guests are divided into camps which evolved slowly over the years as the number of people on the retreat grew into the hundreds and then the thousands. These camps have become a significant center of enjoyment during the encampment.

At first the camps were merely a place in the woods where a half-dozen to a dozen friends would pitch their tents. Soon they added little amenities like their own special stove or a small permanent structure. Then there developed little camp "traditions" and endearing camp names like Cliff Dwellers, Moonshiners, Silverado Squatters, Woof, Zaca, Toyland, Sundodgers, and Land of Happiness. The next steps were special emblems, a handsome little lodge or specially constructed tepees, a permanent bar, and maybe a grand piano.[3] Today there are 129 camps of varying sizes, structures, and statuses. Most have between 10 and 30 members, but there are one or two with about 125 members and several with less than 10. A majority of the camps are strewn along what is called the River Road, but some are huddled in other areas within five or ten minutes of the center of the Grove.

The entertainment at the camps is mostly informal and impromptu. Someone will decide to bring together all the jazz musicians in the Grove for a special session. Or maybe all the artists or writers will be invited to a luncheon or a dinner at a camp. Many camps have their own amateur piano players and informal musical and singing groups which perform for the rest of the members.

But the joys of the camps are not primarily in watching or listening to performances. Other pleasures are created within them. Some camps become known for their gastronomical specialties, such as a particular drink or a particular meal. The Jungle Camp features mint juleps, Halcyon has a three-foot-high martini maker constructed out of chemical glassware. At the Owl's Nest [President Reagan's club] it's the gin-fizz breakfast—about a hundred people are invited over one morning during the encampment for eggs Benedict, gin fizzes, and all the trimmings.

The men of Bohemia are drawn in large measure from the corporate leadership of the United States. They include in their numbers directors from major corporations in every sector of the American economy. An indication of this fact is that one in every five resident members and one in every three nonresident members is found in Poor's *Register of Corporations, Executives, and Directors*, a huge volume which lists the leadership of tens of thousands of companies from every major business field except investment banking, real estate, and advertising.

Even better evidence for the economic prominence of the men under consideration is that at least one officer or director from 40 of the 50 largest industrial corporations in America was present, as a member or a guest, on the lists at our disposal. Only Ford Motor Company and Western Electric were missing among the top 25! Similarly, we found that officers and directors from 20 of the top 25 commercial banks (including all of the 15 largest) were on our lists. Men from 12 of the first 25 life insurance companies were in attendance (8 of these 12 were from the top 10). Other business sectors were represented somewhat less: 10 of 25 in transportation, 8 of 25 in utilities, 7 of 25 in conglomerates, and only 5 of 25 in retailing. More generally, of the top-level businesses ranked by *Fortune* for 1969 (the top 500 industrials, the top 50 commercial banks, the top 50 life insurance companies, the top 50 transportation companies, the top 50 utilities, the top 50 retailers, and the top 47 conglomerates), *29 percent of these 797 corporations were "represented" by at least 1 officer or director.*

Other Watering Holes

[Other camps and retreats were founded by wealthy and powerful men, based on the model provided by the Bohemian Grove. One example is the Rancheros Visitadores (Visiting Ranchers) who meet each May for horse-back rides through the California ranch land. These are accompanied by feasts, entertainment, and general merrymaking with a Spanish-ranch motif.]

[Among the Rancheros a] common interest in horses and horseplay provides a social setting in which men with different forms of wealth get to know each other better. *Sociologically speaking, the Rancheros Visitadores is an organization which serves the function (whether the originators planned it that way or not) of helping to integrate ranchers and businessmen from different parts of the country into a cohesive social class.*

[T]he Rancheros had to divide into camps because of a postwar increase in membership. There are seventeen camps, sporting such Spanish names as Los Amigos, Los Vigilantes, Los Tontos (bums), Los Bandidos, and Los Flojos (lazy ones). They range in size from fifteen to ninety-three, with the majority of them listing between twenty and sixty members. Most camps have members from a variety of geographical locations, although some are slightly specialized in that regard. Los Gringos, the largest camp, has the greatest number of members from out of state. Los Borrachos, Los Pisca-dores, and Los Chingadores, the next largest camps, have a predominance of people from the Los Angeles area. Los Vigilantes, with twenty members, began as a San Francisco group, but now incudes riders from Oregon, Washington, New York, and southern California.

In 1928 the Bohemian Grove provided John J. Mitchell with the inspira-tion for his retreat on horseback, the Rancheros Visitadores. Since 1930 the RVs have grown to the point where they are an impressive second best to the Grove in size, entertainment, and stature. Their combination of businessmen and ranchers is as unique as the Bohemian's amalgamation of businessmen and artists. It is hardly surprising that wealthy men from Los Angeles, San Francisco, Honolulu, Spokane, and Chicago would join Mitchell in wanting to be members of both.

[Another club, the Colorado-based Roundup Riders of the Rockies, imitates the RVs in its emphasis on "roughing it" and socializing.]

The riders do not carry their fine camp with them. Instead, twenty camp-hands are employed to move the camp in trucks to the next campsite. Thus, when the Roundup Riders arrive at their destination each evening they find fourteen large sleeping tents complete with cots, air mattresses, portable toilets, and showers. Also up and ready for service are a large green dining tent and an entertainment stage. A diesel-powered generator provides the camp with electricity.

Food service is provided by Martin Jetton of Fort Worth, Texas, a caterer advertised in the Southwest as "King of the Barbecue." Breakfasts and dinners are said to be veritable banquets. Lunch is not as elaborate, but it does arrive to the riders on the trail in a rather unusual fashion that only those of the higher circles could afford: "lunches in rugged country are often delivered by light plane or helicopter."[4] One year the men almost missed a meal because a wind came up and scattered the lunches, which were being parachuted from two Cessna 170s.

In addition to the twenty hired hands who take care of the camp, there are twenty wranglers to look after the horses. The horses on the ride—predominantly such fine breeds as Arabian, Quarter Horse, and Morgan—are estimated to be worth more than $200,000. Horses and riders compete in various contests of skill and horsemanship on a layover day in the middle of the week. Skeet shooting, trap shooting, and horseshoes also are a part of this event.

The Roundup Riders, who hold their trek at the same time the Bohemians hold their encampment, must be reckoned as a more regional organization. Although there are numerous millionaires and executives among them, the members are not of the national stature of most Bohemians and many Rancheros. They can afford to invest thousands of dollars in their horses and tack, to pay a $300 yearly ride fee, and to have their lunch brought to them by helicopter, but they cannot compete in business connections and prestige with those who assemble at the Bohemian Grove. Building from the Denver branch of the upper class, the Roundup Riders reach out primarily to Nebraska (six), Texas (five), Illinois (five), Nevada (three), California (three), and Arizona (three). There are no members from New York, Boston, Philadelphia, or other large Eastern cities.

Several other regional rides have been inspired by the Rancheros, rides such as the Desert Caballeros in Wickenburg, Arizona, and the Verde Vaqueros in Scottsdale, Arizona. These groups are similar in size and membership to the Roundup Riders of the Rockies. Like the Roundup Riders, they have a few overlapping members with the Rancheros. But none are of the status of the Rancheros Visitadores. They are minor legacies of the Bohemian Grove, unlikely even to be aware of their kinship ties to the retreat in the redwoods.

Do Bohemians, Rancheros, and Roundup Riders Rule America?

The foregoing material on upper-class retreats, which I have presented in as breezy a manner as possible, is relevant to highly emotional questions concerning the distribution of power in modern America. In this final [section] I will switch styles somewhat and discuss these charged questions in a sober, simple, and straightforward way. . . .

It is my hypothesis that there is a ruling social class in the United States. This class is made up of the owners and managers of large corporations, which means the members have many economic and political interests in common, and many conflicts with ordinary working people. Comprising at most 1 percent of the total population, members of this class own 25 to 30 percent of all privately held wealth in America, own 60 to 70 percent of the privately held corporate wealth, receive 20 to 25 percent of the yearly income, direct the large corporations and foundations, and dominate the federal government in Washington.

Most social scientists disagree with this view. Some dismiss it out of hand, others become quite vehement in disputing it. The overwhelming majority of them believe that the United States has a "pluralistic" power structure, in which a wide variety of "veto groups" (e.g., businessmen, farmers, unions, consumers) and "voluntary associations" (e.g., National Association of Manufacturers, Americans for Democratic Action, Common Cause) form shifting coalitions to influence decisions on different issues. These groups and associations are said to have differing amounts of interest and influence on various questions. Contrary to my view, pluralists assert that no one group, not even the owners and managers of large corporations, has the cohesiveness and ability to determine the outcome of a large variety of social, economic, and political issues.

As noted, I believe there is a national upper class in the United States. [T]his means that wealthy families from all over the country, and particularly from major cities like New York, San Francisco, Chicago, and Houston, are part of interlocking social circles which perceive each other as equals, belong to the same clubs, interact frequently, and freely intermarry.

Whether we call it a "social class" or a "status group," many pluralistic social scientists would deny that such a social group exists. They assert that there is no social "cohesiveness" among the various rich in different parts of the country. For them, social registers, blue books, and club membership lists are merely collections of names which imply nothing about group interaction.

There is a wealth of journalistic evidence which suggests the existence of a national upper class. It ranges from Cleveland Amory's *The Proper Bostonians* and *Who Killed Society?* to Lucy Kavaler's *The Private World of High Society* and Stephen Birmingham's *The Right People.* But what is the systematic evidence which I can present for my thesis? There is first of all the evidence that has been developed from the study of attendance at private schools. It has been shown that a few dozen prep schools bring together children of the upper class from all over the country. From this evidence it can be argued that young members of the upper class develop lifetime friendship ties with like-status age-mates in every section of the country.[5]

There is second the systematic evidence which comes from studying high-status summer resorts. Two such studies show that these resorts bring together upper-class families from several different large cities.[6] Third, there is the evidence of business interconnections. Several [studies] have demonstrated that interlocking directorships bring wealthy men from all over the country into face-to-face relationships at the board meetings of banks, insurance companies, and other corporations.[7]

And finally, there is the evidence developed from studying exclusive social clubs. Such studies have been made in the past, but the present investigation of the Bohemian Club, the Rancheros Visitadores, and the Roundup Riders of the Rockies is a more comprehensive effort. *In short, I believe the present [study] to be significant evidence for the existence of a cohesive American upper class.*

The Bohemian Grove, as well as other watering holes and social clubs, is relevant to the problem of class cohesiveness in two ways. First, the very fact that rich men from all over the country gather in such close circumstances as the Bohemian Grove is evidence for the existence of a socially cohesive upper class. It demonstrates that many of these men do know each other, that they have face-to-face communications, and that they are a social network. In this sense, we are looking at the Bohemian Grove and other social retreats as a *result* of social processes that lead to class cohesion. But such institutions also can be viewed as *facilitators* of social ties. Once formed, these groups become another avenue by which the cohesiveness of the upper class is maintained.

In claiming that clubs and retreats like the Bohemians and the Rancheros are evidence for my thesis of a national upper class, I am assuming that cohesion develops within the settings they provide. Perhaps some readers will find that assumption questionable. So let us pause to ask· Are there reasons to believe that the Bohemian Grove and its imitators lead to greater cohesion within the upper class?

For one thing, we have the testimony of members themselves. There are several accounts by leading members of these groups, past and present, which attest to the intimacy that develops among members. John J. Mitchell,

El Presidente of Los Rancheros Visitadores from 1930 to 1955, wrote as follows on the twenty-fifth anniversary of the group:

> All the pledges and secret oaths in the universe cannot tie men, our kind of men, together like the mutual appreciation of a beautiful horse, the moon behind a cloud, a song around the campfire or a ride down the Santa Ynez Valley. These are experiences common on our ride, but unknown to most of our daily lives. Our organization, to all appearances, is the most informal imaginable. Yet there are men here who see one another once a year, yet feel a bond closer than between those they have known all their lives.[8]

F. Burr Betts, chairman of the board of Security Life of Denver, says the following about the Roundup Riders:

> I think you find out about the Roundup Riders when you go to a Rider's funeral. Because there you'll find, no matter how many organizations the man belonged to, almost every pallbearer is a Roundup Rider. I always think of the Roundup Riders as the first affiliation. We have the closest knit fraternity in the world.[9]

A second reason for stressing the importance of retreats and clubs like the Bohemian Grove is a body of research within social psychology which deals with group cohesion. "Group dynamics" suggests the following about cohesiveness. (1) *Physical proximity is likely to lead to group solidarity.* Thus, the mere fact that these men gather together in such intimate physical settings implies that cohesiveness develops. (The same point can be made, of course, about exclusive neighborhoods, private schools, and expensive summer resorts.) (2) *The more people interact, the more they will be like each other.* This is hardly a profound discovery, but we can note that the Bohemian Grove and other watering holes maximize personal interactions. (3) *Groups seen as high in status are more cohesive.* The Bohemian Club fits the category of a high-status group. Further, its stringent membership requirements, long waiting lists, and high dues also serve to heighten its valuation in the eyes of its members. Members are likely to think of themselves as "special" people, which would heighten their attractiveness to each other and increase the likelihood of interaction and cohesiveness. (4) *The best atmosphere for increasing group cohesiveness is one that is relaxed and cooperative.* Again the Bohemian Grove, the Rancheros, and the Roundup Riders are ideal examples of this kind of climate. From a group-dynamics point of view, then, we could argue that one of the reasons for upper-class cohesiveness is the fact that the class is organized into a wide variety of small groups which encourage face-to-face interaction and ensure status and security for members.[10]

In summary, if we take these several common settings together—schools, resorts, corporation directorships, and social clubs—and assume on the basis of members' testimony and the evidence of small-group research that interaction in such settings leads to group cohesiveness, then I think we are justified in saying that wealthy families from all over the United States are linked together in a variety of ways into a national upper class.

Even if the evidence and arguments for the existence of a socially cohesive national upper class are accepted, there is still the question of whether or not this class has the means by which its members can reach policy consensus on issues of importance to them.

A five-year study based upon information obtained from confidential informants, interviews, and questionnaires has shown that social clubs such as the Bohemian Club are an important consensus-forming aspect of the upper class and big-business environment. According to sociologist Reed Powell, "the clubs are a repository of the values held by the upper-level prestige groups in the community and are a means by which these values are transferred to the business environment." Moreover, the clubs are places where problems are discussed:

> On the other hand, the clubs are places in which the beliefs, problems, and values of the industrial organization are discussed and related to other elements in the larger community. Clubs, therefore, are not only effective vehicles of informal communication, but also valuable centers where views are presented, ideas are modified, and new ideas emerge. Those in the interview sample were appreciative of this asset; in addition, they considered the club as a valuable place to combine social and business contacts.[11]

The revealing interview work of Floyd Hunter, an outstanding pioneer researcher on the American power structure, also provides evidence for the importance of social clubs as informal centers of policy making. Particularly striking for our purposes is a conversation he had with one of the several hundred top leaders that he identified in the 1950s. The person in question was a conservative industrialist who was ranked as a top-level leader by his peers:

> Hall [pseudonym] spoke very favorably of the Bohemian Grove group that met in California every year. He said that although over the entrance to the Bohemian Club there was a quotation, "Weaving spiders come not here," there was a good deal of informal policy made in this association. He said that he got to know Herbert Hoover in this connection and that he started work with Hoover in the food administration of World War I.[12]

Despite the evidence presented by Powell and Hunter that clubs are a setting for the development of policy consensus, I do not believe that such settings are the only, or even the primary, locus for developing policy on class-related issues. For policy questions, other organizations are far more important, organizations like the Council on Foreign Relations, the Committee for Economic Development, the Business Council, and the National Municipal League. These organizations, along with many others, are the "consensus-seeking" and "policy-planning" organizations of the upper class. Directed by the same men who manage the major corporations, and financed by corporation and foundation monies, these groups sponsor meetings and discussions wherein wealthy men from all over the country gather to iron out differences and formulate policies on pressing problems.

No one discussion group is *the* leadership council within the upper class. While some of the groups tend to specialize in certain issue areas, they overlap and interact to a great extent. Consensus slowly emerges from the interplay of people and the ideas within and among the groups.[13] This diversity of groups is made very clear in the following comments by Frazar B. Wilde, chairman emeritus of Connecticut General Life Insurance Company and a member of the Council on Foreign Relations and the Committee for Economic Development. Mr. Wilde was responding to a question about the Bilderbergers, a big-business meeting group which includes Western European leaders as well as American corporation and foundation directors:

> Business has had over the years many different seminars and discussion meetings. They run all the way from large public gatherings like NAM [National Association of Manufacturers] to special sessions such as those held frequently at Arden House. Bilderberg is in many respects one of the most important, if not the most important, but this is not to deny that other strictly off-the-record meetings and discussion groups such as those held by the Council on Foreign Relations are not in the front rank.[14]

Generally speaking, then, it is in these organizations that leaders within the upper class discuss the means by which to deal with problems of major concern. Here, in off-the-record settings, these leaders try to reach consensus on general issues that have been talked about more casually in corporate boardrooms and social clubs. These organizations, aided by funds from corporations and foundations, also serve several other functions:

1. They are a training ground for new leadership within the class. It is in these organizations, and through the publications of these organizations, that younger lawyers, bankers, and businessmen become acquainted with general issues in the areas of foreign, domestic, and municipal policy.
2. They are the place where leaders within the upper class hear the ideas and findings of their hired experts.
3. They are the setting wherein upper-class leaders "look over" young experts for possible service as corporation or governmental advisers.
4. They provide the framework for expert studies on important issues. Thus, the Council on Foreign Relations undertook a $1 million study of the "China question" in the first half of the 1960s. The Committee for Economic Development created a major study of money and credit about the same time. Most of the money for the studies was provided by the Ford, Rockefeller, and Carnegie foundations.[15]
5. Through such avenues as books, journals, policy statements, discussion groups, press releases, and speakers, the policy-planning organi-

zations greatly influence the "climate of opinion" within which major issues are considered. For example, *Foreign Affairs*, the journal of the Council on Foreign Relations, is considered the most influential journal in its field, and the periodic policy statements of the Committee for Economic Development are carefully attended to by major newspapers and local opinion leaders.

It is my belief, then, that the policy-planning groups are essential in developing policy positions which are satisfactory to the upper class as a whole. As such, I think they are a good part of the answer to any social scientist who denies that members of the upper class have institutions by which they deal with economic and political challenges.

However, the policy-planning groups could not function if there were not some common interests within the upper class in the first place. The most obvious, and most important, of these common interests have to do with the shared desire of the members to maintain the present monopolized and subsidized business system which so generously overrewards them and makes their jet setting, fox hunting, art collecting, and other extravagances possible. But it is not only shared economic and political concerns which make consensus possible. The Bohemian Grove and other upper-class social institutions also contribute to this process: *Group-dynamics research suggests that members of socially cohesive groups are more open to the opinions of other members, and more likely to change their views to those of fellow members.*[16] Social cohesion is a factor in policy consensus because it creates a desire on the part of group members to reconcile differences with other members of the group. It is not enough to say that members of the upper class are bankers, businessmen, and lawyers with a common interest in profit maximization and tax avoidance who meet together at the Council on Foreign Relations, the Committee for Economic Development, and other policy-planning organizations. We must add that they are Bohemians, Rancheros, and Roundup Riders.

Notes

1. Wallace Turner, "Rockefeller Faces Scrutiny of Top Californians: Governor to Spend Weekend at Bohemian Grove among State's Establishment," *New York Times*, July 26, 1963, p. 30. In 1964 Senator Barry Goldwater appeared at the Grove as a guest of retired General Albert C. Wedemeyer and Herbert Hoover, Jr. For that story see Wallace Turner, "Goldwater Spending Weekend in Camp at Bohemian Grove," *New York Times*, July 31, 1964, p. 10.

2. James M. Naughton, "Nixon Drops Plan for Coast Speech," *New York Times*, July 31, 1971, p. 11.

3. There is a special moisture-proof building at the Grove to hold the dozens of expensive Steinway pianos belonging to the club and various camps.

4. Robert Pattridge, "Closer to Heaven on Horseback," *Empire Magazine, Denver Post*, July 9, 1972, p. 12. I am grateful to sociologist Ford Cleere for bringing this article to my attention.

5. E. Digby Baltzell, *Philadelphia Gentlemen* (New York: Free Press, 1958), chapter 12, and G. William Domhoff, *The Higher Circles* (New York: Random House, 1970), p. 78.

6. Baltzell, *Philadelphia Gentleman*, pp. 248–51, and Domhoff, *The Higher Circles*, pp. 79–82. For recent anecdotal evidence on this point, see Stephen Birmingham, *The Right People* (Boston: Little, Brown, 1968), Part 3.

7. *Interlocks in Corporate Management* (Washington: U.S. Government Printing Office, 1965) summarizes much of this information and presents new evidence as well. See also Peter Dooley, "The Interlocking Directorate," *American Economic Review*, December, 1969.

8. Neill C. Wilson, *Los Rancheros Visitadores: Twenty-Fifth Anniversary* (Rancheros Visitadores, 1955), p. 2.

9. Pattridge, "Closer to Heaven on Horseback," p. 11.

10. Dorwin Cartwright and Alvin Zander, *Group Dynamics* (New York: Harper & Row, 1960), pp 74–82; Albert J. Lott and Bernice E. Lott, "Group Cohesiveness as Interpersonal Attraction," *Psychological Bulletin 64* (1965):259–309; Michael Argyle, *Social Interation* (Chicago: Aldine Publishing Company, 1969), pp. 220–23. I am grateful to sociologist John Sonquist of the University of California, Santa Barbara, for making me aware of how important the small-groups literature might be for studies of the upper class. Findings on influence processes, communication patterns, and the development of informal leadership also might be applicable to problems in the area of upper-class research.

11. Reed M. Powell, *Race, Religion, and the Promotion of the American Executive*, College of Administrative Science Monograph No. AA–3, Ohio State University, 1969, p. 50.

12. Floyd Hunter, *Top Leadership, U.S.A.* (Chapel Hill: University of North Carolina Press, 1959), p. 109. Hunter also reported (p. 199) that the most favored clubs of his top leaders were the Metropolitan, Links, Century, University (New York), Bohemian, and Pacific Union. He notes (p. 223 n.) that he found clubs to be less important in policy formation on the national level than they are in communities.

13. For a detailed case study of how the process works, see David Eakins, "Business Planners and America's Postwar Expansion," in David Horowitz (ed.), *Corporations and the Cold War* (New York: Monthly Review Press, 1969). For other examples and references, see Domhoff, *The Higher Circles*, chapters 5 and 6.

14. Carl Gilbert, personal communication, June 30, 1972. Mr. Gilbert has done extensive research on the Bilderberg group, and I am grateful to him for sharing his detailed information with me. For an excellent discussion of this group, whose role has been greatly distorted and exaggerated by ultraconservatives, see Eugene Pasymowski and Carl Gilbert, "Bilderberg, Rockefeller, and the CIA," *Temple Free Press*, No. 6, September 16, 1968. The article is most conveniently located in a slightly revised form in the *Congressional Record*, September 15, 1971, E9615, under the title "Bilderberg: The Cold War Internationale."

15. The recent work of arch-pluralist Nelson Polsby is bringing him dangerously

close to this formulation. Through studies of the initiation of a number of new policies, Polsby and his students have tentatively concluded that "innovators are typically professors or interest group experts." Where Polsby goes wrong is in failing to note that the professors are working on Ford Foundation grants and/or Council on Foreign Relations fellowships. If he would put his work in a sociological framework, people would not gain the false impression that professors are independent experts sitting in their ivory towers thinking up innovations for the greater good of humanity. See Nelson Polsby, "Policy Initiation in the American Political System," in Irving Louis Horowitz (ed.), *The Use and Abuse of Social Science* (New Brunswick, NJ: TransAction Books, 1971), p. 303.

16. Cartwright and Zander, *Group Dynamics*, p. 89; Lott and Lott, "Group Cohesiveness as Interpersonal Attraction," pp. 291–96.

28 The Uses of Poverty: The Poor Pay All

HERBERT J. GANS

Standing in sharp contrast to the preceding selection is this analysis of poverty, which helps us catch a glimpse of what it is like to live in American society with little money. Some people think that poverty simply means having to tighten your belt, but the meaning of poverty is much more profound. Sociologists have documented that the poor confront social conditions so damaging that their marriages are more likely to break up, they are sicker than others, their children are more likely to drop out of school and get in trouble with the law, they are more likely to be victimized by crime, and, on average, they die younger than most. It is difficult to romanticize poverty when one knows what its true conditions are.

In this selection, Gans does not document the degradation of the poor (although this is intrinsically present in his analysis), nor their failing health or troubled lives. Nor is his article a plea for social reform. Rather, from the observation that the poor are always present in society he concludes that this is because they perform vital services (functions) for society. (An essential assumption of *functionalism*, one of the theoretical schools in sociology, is that conditions persist in society only if they benefit—perform functions for—society or some of its parts.) In this selection, then, Gans tries to identify those functions.

Do you think the author has overlooked any "functions" of the poor? If his analysis, which many find startling, is not correct, what alternative explanation could you propose?

SOME YEARS AGO ROBERT K. MERTON applied the notion of functional analysis to explain the continuing though maligned existence of the urban political machine: If it continued to exist, perhaps it fulfilled latent—unintended or unrecognized—positive functions. Clearly it did. Merton pointed out how the political machine provided central authority to get things done when a decentralized local government could not act, humanized the services of the impersonal bureaucracy for fearful citizens, offered concrete help (rather than abstract law or justice) to the poor, and otherwise performed services needed or demanded by many people but considered unconventional or even illegal by formal public agencies.

Today, poverty is more maligned than the political machine ever was; yet it, too, is a persistent social phenomenon. Consequently, there may be some merit in applying functional analysis to poverty, in asking whether it also has positive functions that explain its persistence.

Merton defined functions as "those observed consequences [of a phenomenon] which make for the adaptation of adjustment of a given [social] system." I shall use a slightly different definition; instead of identifying functions for an entire social system, I shall identify them for the interest groups, socioeconomic classes, and other population aggregates with shared values that "inhabit" a social system. I suspect that in a modern heterogeneous society, few phenomena are functional or dysfunctional for the society as a whole, and that most result in benefits to some groups and costs to others. Nor are any phenomena indispensable; in most instances, one can suggest what Merton calls "functional alternatives" or equivalents for them, i.e., other social patterns or policies that achieve the same positive functions but avoid the dysfunction. [In the following discussion, positive functions will be abbreviated as functions and negative functions as dysfunctions. Functions and dysfunctions, in the planner's terminology, will be described as benefits and costs.]

Associating poverty with positive functions seems at first glance to be unimaginable. Of course, the slumlord and the loan shark are commonly known to profit from the existence of poverty, but they are viewed as evil men, so their activities are classified among the dysfunctions of poverty. However, what is less often recognized, at least by the conventional wisdom, is that poverty also makes possible the existence or expansion of respectable professions and occupations, for example, penology, criminology, social work, and public health. More recently, the poor have provided jobs for professional and para-professional "poverty warriors," and for journalists and social scientists, this author included, who have supplied the information demanded by the revival of public interest in poverty.

Clearly, then, poverty and the poor may well satisfy a number of positive functions for many nonpoor groups in American society. I shall describe 13 such functions—economic, social, and political—that seem to me most significant.

The Functions of Poverty

First, the existence of poverty ensures that society's "dirty work" will be done. Every society has such work: physically dirty or dangerous, temporary, dead-end and underpaid, undignified, and menial jobs. Society can fill these jobs by paying higher wages than for "clean" work, or it can force people who have no other choice to do the dirty work—and at low wages. In America, poverty functions to provide a low-wage labor pool that is willing— or, rather, unable to be *un*willing—to perform dirty work at low cost. Indeed, this function of the poor is so important that in some Southern states, welfare payments have been cut off during the summer months when the poor are needed to work in the fields. Moreover, much of the debate about the Negative Income Tax and the Family Assistance Plan has concerned their impact on the work incentive, by which is actually meant the incentive of the poor to do the needed dirty work if the wages therefrom are no larger than the income grant. Many economic activities that involve dirty work depend on the poor for their existence: restaurants, hospitals, parts of the garment industry, and "truck farming," among others, could not persist in their present form without the poor.

Second, because the poor are required to work at low wages, they subsidize a variety of economic activities that benefit the affluent. For example, domestics subsidize the upper-middle and upper classes, making life easier for their employers and freeing affluent women for a variety of professional, cultural, civic, and partying activities. Similarly, because the poor pay a higher proportion of their income in property and sales taxes, among others, they subsidize many state and local governmental services that benefit more affluent groups. In addition, the poor support innovation in medical practice as patients in teaching and research hospitals and as guinea pigs in medical experiments.

Third, poverty creates jobs for a number of occupations and professions that serve or "service" the poor, or protect the rest of society from them. As already noted, penology would be minuscule without the poor, as would the police. Other activities and groups that flourish because of the existence of poverty are the numbers game, the sale of heroin and cheap wines and liquors, pentecostal ministers, faith healers, prostitutes, pawn shops, and the peacetime army, which recruits its enlisted men mainly from among the poor.

Fourth, the poor buy goods others do not want and thus prolong the economic usefulness of such goods—day-old bread, fruit and vegetables that would otherwise have to be thrown out, secondhand clothes, and deteriorating automobiles and buildings. They also provide incomes for doctors, lawyers, teachers, and others who are too old, poorly trained, or incompetent to attract more affluent clients.

In addition to economic functions, the poor perform a number of social functions.

Fifth, the poor can be identified and punished as alleged or real deviants in order to uphold the legitimacy of conventional norms. To justify the desirability of hard work, thrift, honesty, and monogamy, for example, the defenders of these norms must be able to find people who can be accused of being lazy, spendthrift, dishonest, and promiscuous. Although there is some evidence that the poor are about as moral and law-abiding as anyone else, they are more likely than middle-class transgressors to be caught and punished when they participate in deviant acts. Moreover, they lack the political and cultural power to correct the stereotypes that other people hold of them and thus continue to be thought of as lazy, spendthrift, etc., by those who need living proof that moral deviance does not pay.

Sixth, and conversely, the poor offer vicarious participation to the rest of the population in the uninhibited sexual, alcoholic, and narcotic behavior in which they are alleged to participate and which, being freed from the constraints of affluence, they are often thought to enjoy more than the middle classes. Thus many people, some social scientists included, believe that the poor not only are more given to uninhibited behavior (which may be true, although it is often motivated by despair more than by lack of inhibition) but derive more pleasure from it than affluent people (which research by Lee Rainwater, Walter Miller, and others shows to be patently untrue). However, whether the poor actually have more sex and enjoy it more is irrelevant; so long as middle-class people believe this to be true, they can particpate in it vicariously when instances are reported in factual or fictional form.

Seventh, the poor also serve a direct cultural function when culture created by or for them is adopted by the more affluent. The rich often collect artifacts from extinct folk cultures of poor people; and almost all Americans listen to the blues, Negro spirituals, and country music, which originated among the Southern poor. Recently they have enjoyed the rock styles that were born, like the Beatles, in the slums; and in the last year, poetry written by ghetto children has become popular in literary circles. The poor also serve as culture heroes, particularly, of course, to the left; but the hobo, the cowboy, the hipster, and the mythical prostitute with a heart of gold have performed this function for a variety of groups.

Eighth, poverty helps to guarantee the status of those who are not poor. In every hierarchical society someone has to be at the bottom; but in American society, in which social mobility is an important goal for many and people need to know where they stand, the poor function as a reliable and relatively permanent measuring rod for status comparisons. This is particularly true for the working class, whose politics is influenced by the need to maintain status distinctions between themselves and the poor, much as the aristocracy must find ways of distinguishing itself from the *nouveaux riches*.

Ninth, the poor also aid the upward mobility of groups just above them in the class hierarchy. Thus a goodly number of Americans have entered the middle class through the profits earned from the provision of goods and services in the slums, including illegal or nonrespectable ones that upper-class and upper-middle-class businessmen shun because of their low prestige. As a result, members of almost every immigrant group have financed their upward mobility by providing slum housing, entertainment, gambling, narcotics, etc., to later arrivals—most recently to blacks and Puerto Ricans.

Tenth, the poor help to keep the aristocracy busy, thus justifying its continued existence. "Society" uses the poor as clients of settlement houses and beneficiaries of charity affairs; indeed, the aristocracy must have the poor to demonstrate its superiority over other elites who devote themselves to earning money.

Eleventh, the poor, being powerless, can be made to absorb the costs of change and growth in American society. During the nineteenth century, they did the backbreaking work that built the cities; today, they are pushed out of their neighborhoods to make room for "progress." Urban renewal projects to hold middle-class taxpayers in the city and expressways to enable suburbanites to commute downtown have typically been located in poor neighborhoods, since no other group will allow itself to be displaced. For the same reason, universities, hospitals, and civic centers also expand into land occupied by the poor. The major costs of the industrialization of agriculture have been borne by the poor, who are pushed off the land without recompense; and they have paid a large share of the human cost of the growth of American power overseas, for they have provided many of the foot soldiers for Vietnam and other wars.

Twelfth, the poor facilitate and stabilize the American political process. Because they vote and participate in politics less than other groups, the political system is often free to ignore them. Moreover, since they can rarely support Republicans, they often provide the Democrats with a captive constituency that has no other place to go. As a result, the Democrats can count on their votes, and be more responsive to voters—for example, the white working class—who might otherwise switch to the Republicans.

Thirteenth, the role of the poor in upholding conventional norms (see the *fifth* point, above) also has a significant political function. An economy based on the ideology of laissez-faire requires a deprived population that is allegedly unwilling to work or that can be considered inferior because it must accept charity or welfare in order to survive. Not only does the alleged moral deviancy of the poor reduce the moral pressure on the present political economy to eliminate poverty, but socialist alternatives can be made to look quite unattractive if those who will benefit most from them can be described as lazy, spendthrift, dishonest, and promiscuous.

The Alternatives

I have described 13 of the more important functions poverty and the poor satisfy in American society, enough to support the functionalist thesis that poverty, like any other social phenomenon, survives in part because it is useful to society or some of its parts. This analysis is not intended to suggest that because it is often functional, poverty *should* exist, or that it *must* exist. For one thing, poverty has many more dysfunctions than functions; for another, it is possible to suggest functional alternatives.

For example, society's dirty work could be done without poverty, either by automation or by paying "dirty workers" decent wages. Nor is it necessary for the poor to subsidize the many activities they support through their low-wage jobs. This would, however, drive up the costs of these activities, which would result in higher prices to their customers and clients. Similarly, many of the professionals who flourish because of the poor could be given other roles. Social workers could provide counseling to the affluent, as they prefer to do anyway; and the police could devote themselves to traffic and organized crime. Other roles would have to be found for badly trained or incompetent professionals now relegated to serving the poor, and someone else would have to pay their salaries. Fewer penologists would be employable, however. And pentecostal religion could probably not survive without the poor—nor would parts of the second- and third-hand-goods market. And in many cities, "used" housing that no one else wants would then have to be torn down at public expense.

Alternatives for the cultural functions of the poor could be found more easily and cheaply. Indeed, entertainers, hippies, and adolescents are already serving as the deviants needed to uphold traditional morality and as devotees of orgies to "staff" the fantasies of vicarious participation.

The status functions of the poor are another matter. In a hierarchical society, some people must be defined as inferior to everyone else with respect to a variety of attributes, but they need not be poor in the absolute sense. One could conceive of a society in which the "lower class," though last in the pecking order, received 75 percent of the median income, rather than 15–40 percent, as is now the case. Needless to say, this would require considerable income redistribution.

The contribution the poor make to the upward mobility of the groups that provide them with goods and services could also be maintained without the poor's having such low incomes. However, it is true that if the poor were more affluent, they would have access to enough capital to take over the provider role, thus competing with, and perhaps rejecting, the "outsiders." (Indeed, owing in part to antipoverty programs, this is already happening in a number of ghettos, where white storeowners are being replaced by blacks.) Similarly, if the poor were more affluent, they would make less willing clients for upper-class philanthropy, although some would still use settlement houses to achieve upward mobility, as they do now. Thus "Society" could continue to run its philanthropic activities.

The political functions of the poor would be more difficult to replace. With increased affluence the poor would probably obtain more political power and be more active politically. With higher incomes and more political power, the poor would be likely to resist paying the costs of growth and change. Of course, it is possible to imagine urban renewal and highway projects that properly reimbursed the displaced people, but such projects would then become considerably more expensive, and many might never be built. This, in turn, would reduce the comfort and convenience of those who now benefit from urban renewal and expressways. Finally, hippies could serve also as more deviants to justify the existing political economy—as they already do. Presumably, however, if poverty were eliminated, there would be fewer attacks on that economy.

In sum, then, many of the functions served by the poor could be replaced if poverty were eliminated, but almost always at higher costs to others, particularly more affluent others. Consequently, a functional analysis must conclude that poverty persists not only because it fulfills a number of positive functions but also because many of the functional alternatives to poverty would be quite dysfunctional for the affluent members of society. A functional analysis thus ultimately arrives at much the same conclusion as radical sociology, except that radical thinkers treat as manifest what I describe as latent: that social phenomena that are functional for affluent or powerful groups and dysfunctional for poor or powerless ones persist; that when the elimination of such phenomena through functional alternatives would generate dysfunctions for the affluent or powerful, they will continue to persist; and that phenomena like poverty can be eliminated only when they become dysfunctional for the affluent or powerful, or when the powerless can obtain enough power to change society.

Postscript[1]

Over the years, this article has been interpreted as either a direct attack on functionalism or a tongue-in-cheek satirical comment on it. Neither interpretation is true. I wrote the article for two reasons. First and foremost, I wanted to point out that there are, unfortunately, positive functions of poverty which have to be dealt with by antipoverty policy. Second, I was trying to show that functionalism is not the inherently conservative approach for which it has often been criticized, but that it can be employed in liberal and radical analyses.

---

1. The author added this clarifying postscript for this book.

29 Sex Discrimination— Subtle and Covert

NIJOLE V. BENOKRAITIS
JOE R. FEAGIN

A key aspect of social inequality in our society—indeed, around the world—is gender. Gender is so significant for social life that all of Part IV was devoted to it. There, we looked at how gender is our primary identifier or master trait; how our being sorted into one of two groups on the basis of sex has significance for everything we do in life. We also stressed how sexism is built into our basic communications.

In this article, we focus on other subtle and covert forms of sex discrimination. Benokraitis and Feagin examine a situation that many of you will soon face, if you haven't already. Looking at sexual discrimination in the world of work, they identify means by which women are discriminated against in the workplace, some so subtle that they exist beneath our level of immediate awareness. This article should sensitize you to forms of sexism that exist in your own corner of society.

How Subtle Sex Discrimination Works

BECAUSE MOST OF US are still almost exclusively concerned with documenting and identifying the more visible and widespread types of overt sex discrimination, we are inattentive to other forms of inequality. . . . Subtle sex discrimination is considerably more harmful than most of us realize. Subtle sex discrimination has the following characteristics: (1) It can be intentional or unintentional, (2) it is visible but often goes unnoticed (because it has been built into norms, values, and ideologies), (3) it is communicated both verbally and behaviorally, (4) it is usually informal rather than formal, and (5) it is most visible on individual (rather than organizational) levels. . . .

CONDESCENDING CHIVALRY

Condescending chivalry refers to superficially courteous behavior that is protective and paternalistic but treats women as subordinates. This behavior ranges from simple, generally accepted rules of etiquette regarding sex (for example, opening doors for women) to more deeply entrenched beliefs that women are generally helpless and require protection and close supervision.

Chivalrous behavior implies respect and affection. That is, many men assume that referring to women as "little girl," "young lady," "little lady," and "kiddo" is a compliment—especially if the woman is over thirty. Some women may be flattered by such terms of endearment. Yet, comparable references to men ("little boy," "little man") are considered insulting, demeaning, or disrespectful because they challenge men's adulthood and authority. Thus, it is acceptable to refer to women, but not men, as children.

Even when women are clearly in positions of authority, their power may be undercut through "gentlemanly" condescension. For example, one woman dean (who is responsible for, among other things, collecting, reviewing, and coordinating course schedules every semester) complained that some chairmen refuse to take her seriously. When chairs are late in submitting schedules and she calls them into her office, some emphasize her gender and ignore her administrative power: "They do things like put their arm around me, smile, and say, 'You're getting prettier every day' or 'You shouldn't worry your pretty little head about these things.'"

Chivalrous, paternalistic and "protective" behavior also limits women's employment opportunities. . . . A number of women we talked to said they were automatically excluded from some jobs because men still assume that women won't want to travel, will be unwilling to set up child-care arrangements, and "don't want to be in the public eye." Or, when women already have jobs, they will be excluded from important meetings or not considered for promotions because they should be "protected." Consider the experience of a thirty-three-year-old, unmarried store manager provided by one of our respondents:

> [Mary's] male counterparts in the company frequently were invited to out-of-town business meetings and social functions from which she was excluded. These occasions were a source for information on business trends and store promotions and were a rich source of potentially important business contacts. When [Mary] asked why she was not invited to these meetings and social gatherings, the response was that her employer thought it was "too dangerous for her to be driving out of town at night by herself. . . ."

In most cases, it is still assumed that women need, want, or should want protection "for their own good." During a recent lunch with colleagues, for example, one of the authors was discussing prospective faculty who could fill a dean's position that was about to be vacated. The comments, from both male and female faculty, were instructive:

Mary Ann is a very good administrator, but she plans to get married next year. I don't think she'll have time to be both a wife and a dean.

Well, Susan has the respect of both faculty and administration but hasn't she been talking about having children?

Tracy's been a great faculty leader and she's done an outstanding job on committees, but she's got kids. What if they get sick when important decisions have to be made in the dean's office?

Sara has been one of the best chairs in the college, a good researcher and can handle faculty. [A pause.] On the other hand, now that her kids are grown, she probably wants some peace and quiet and wouldn't want to take on the headaches of a dean's office. . . .

In effect, every prospective female candidate was disqualified from serious consideration because it is generally assumed that women should stay in presumably "safe" positions where their femininity, motherhood, and ability to fulfill wifely duties will remain intact.

Whether well-intentioned or malicious, chivalrous behavior is dysfunctional because it reinforces sex inequality in several ways. First, treating women as nonadults stunts their personal and professional growth. "There are problems harder to put a finger on: . . . suggestions initiated by a woman are listened to, but always a bit more reluctantly than those initiated by a man. People, sure, will listen, but we are not urged to suggest. Women, very simply, are not actively encouraged to develop." [1]

Second, chivalry justifies keeping women in low-paying jobs. Some have argued, for example, that because some women (for example, nurses and cleaning women) are encouraged to work long hours or late at night, state protective laws do not represent progressive reform but have been designed to reduce competiton from female workers and to save the premium overtime and better jobs for men. Finally, chivalrous behavior can limit women's opportunities. Men's belief that women should be protected may result, for example, in men's reluctance to criticize women:

A male boss will haul a guy aside and just kick ass if the subordinate performs badly in front of a client. But I heard about a woman here who gets nervous and tends to giggle in front of customers. She's unaware of it and her boss hasn't told her. But behind her back he downgrades her for not being smooth with customers. [2]

Thus, not receiving the type of constructive criticism that is exchanged much more freely and comfortably between men can lead to treating women like outsiders rather than colleagues.

BENEVOLENT EXPLOITATION

Women are often exploited. Much of the exploitation is carried off so gracefully, however, it often goes unnoticed.

Dumping. One of the most common forms of exploitation is dumping—getting someone else (i.e., a woman) to do a job you don't want to do and then taking credit for the results:

> Whenever my supervisor gets a boring, tedious job he doesn't want to do, he assigns it to me. He praises my work and promises it will pay off in his next evaluation. Then, he writes the cover letter and takes full credit for the project. . . . I've never been given any credit for any of the projects—and some were praised very highly by our executives. But, I suppose it's paid off because my boss has never given me negative evaluations. [Female engineer in aerospace industry]

Another form of dumping—much more elusive—is to segregate top workers by sex and depend on the women to get the work done while the men merely critique the work and implement the results in highly visible and prestigious ways. An aide in a highly placed political office said that one of the reasons her boss was extremely successful politically was because he recognized that his female aides were better, harder working, more committed, and more responsible than the male aides. Thus, he surrounds himself with such women, gives them fancy titles, and gets 60 to 70 hours of work out of them at much lower salaries than those of men. When the projects are finished, he gives a lunch for all his aides and praises the women's work. Even as the dessert is served, new projects for the women are announced. The men, however, publicize the projects and get widespread recognition.

Showcasing. "Showcasing" refers to placing women in visible and seemingly powerful positions in which their talents, abilities, and intelligence can be pulled out, whenever necessary, for the public's consumption and the institution's credibility.

One form of showcasing is to make sure that the institution's token women are present (though not participating) in the institution's meetings with "the outside." Thus, in higher education, a woman faculty member is often expected to serve on national committees (recruitment, articulation with high schools, community colleges, and colleges), grant proposals (to show the involvement of women), search committees (just in case affirmative action officers are lurking around), and a variety of external "women's-type" activities such as panels, commissions, and advisory boards. There is no compensation for these additional duties. Moreover, the women are not rewarded in later personnel reviews because this is "women's work" and because "women's work" has low status.

If an occasional committee is an important one, the women chosen are typically nonfeminists who won't "embarrass" the institution/agency/organization by taking women's issues seriously. Instead, they are Queen Bees,[3] naive neophytes, women who are either not powerful or are insensitive to sex discrimination.

Another form of showcasing is giving women directorships in dead-end jobs which are considered a "natural" for women:

> There's probably less discrimination in personnel offices because the job needs a person with traditionally female skills—being nice to people, having verbal abilities, and not being a threat to anyone because a director of personnel is a dead-end job. (Director of personnel in higher education) . . .

Technologically Based Abuses.   Americans place a high value on progress, product improvements, and technological advances. ("New," "improved," or "better than ever" detergents, toothpaste, and shampoos appear on the market annually, and many people go into debt purchasing such "necessities" as home computers, microwave ovens, electronic games, and VCRs. The profits generated by such "discoveries" are not translated into higher salaries for the many women who work in "high-tech" industries. In the case of new technologies, for example, employers often convince women that their newly developed skills are inadequate and should not be rewarded:

> While office technology creates opportunities for higher pay for some of us, for many others it is used as an excuse for keeping salary levels down. An employer may ignore the new skills you have learned in order to operate your machine and argue it's the machine itself that does all the work so that you are worthless.[4]

Employers/supervisors may discourage women from pursuing personal or professional development programs that might make them more dissatisfied with or question their current subordination:

> Under the negotiated rules, secretaries were entitled to take whatever courses they wanted at a state university, tuition reimbursed. We had . . . no application forms . . . although our immediate supervisors and the office supervisor knew and approved the tuition provision (after we educated them). The Queen Bee three places up on the hierarchy professed ignorance and had to be convinced anew when one of the secretaries wanted to take a history course . . . only in the last three years has anyone gone through the hassle and taken the courses. (Ex-secretary in higher education)

The implication here is that some groups of workers (especially office workers) are presumptuous in assuming that their professional development is significant enough to warrant the institution's attention or expenditures. Perhaps more importantly, college courses might lead to office workers wondering why they are performing high-tech jobs at low-tech salaries. . . .

Finally, "progress" has been a higher priority than the job hazards resulting from new technologies and automation. In most cases, the people using the new technologies are office workers—almost all of them women. The most commonly used new office equipment is the video-display terminal (VDT). There is evidence that long-term exposure to VDTs may be dangerous. Operators of VDTs experience eyestrain, neck and back pain, headaches, and blurred vision; the radiation and chemical fumes emitted by the terminals are believed to cause stress, cataracts, miscarriages, and birth defects.[5]

Yet, management has done little to improve work conditions even when many of the improvements are not costly. As one respondent put it, "Why save labor when it's cheap?"

Nudity in Advertising. One of the most widespread forms of exploitation is to use female nudity to sell everything from toothpaste to tractors. Such advertising may not be seen as exploitation because women are expected to be "decorative." The implicit message to men and women is that the primary role of women is to provide pleasure, sex, or sexual promise:

> A sexual relationship is . . . implied between the male product user and his female companion, such that the advertisement promises, in effect, that the product will increase his appeal to her. Not only will it give him a closer shave, it will also provide a sexually available woman.
>
> Often the advertisements imply that the product's main purpose is to improve the user's appeal to men, as the panty-hose advertisement which claims "gentlemen prefer Hanes." The underlying advertising message for a product advertised in the manner is that the ultimate benefit of product usage is to give men pleasure.[6]

The consistent and continuous message that advertisements send—to both men and women—is that women's roles in society are limited to two— that of housewife or sex partner. Other roles are not taken or presented seriously. Thus, women may dominate advertising space, but they are not dominant. . . .

How Covert Sex Discrimination Works

Covert sex discrimination refers to unequal and harmful treatment of women that is hidden, clandestine, and maliciously motivated. Unlike overt and subtle sex discrimination, covert sex discrimination is very difficult to document and prove because records are not kept or are inaccessible, the victim may not even be aware of being a "target," or the victim may be ignorant of how to secure, track, and record evidence of covert discrimination. . . .

TOKENISM

Despite its widespread usage since the 1970s, the term "tokenism" is rarely defined. For our purposes, tokenism refers to the unwritten and usually unspoken policy or practice of hiring, promoting, or otherwise including a minuscule number of individuals from underrepresented groups—women, minorities, the handicapped, the elderly. Through tokenism, organziations maintain the semblance of equality because no group is totally excluded. Placing a few tokens in strategically visible places precludes the necessity of practicing "real" equality—that is, hiring and promoting individuals regardless of their sex. . . .

How Tokenism Works.   There are three types of commonly practiced tokenism that limit women's equal participation in the labor force. A popular form is based on *numerical exclusion,* which uses quotas to maintain a predominantly male work force:

> As soon as they come into my office, a lot of recruiters tell me exactly how many women they plan to hire and in which departments. They say things like, "This year we need two women in accounting, one in marketing, and one in data processing." Some [of the recruiters] have fairly detailed data showing exactly how many women they should be hiring for their company.
> [What if the most qualified candidates are all women?]
> Most recruiters automatically assume that women are *not* the most qualified—they got high grades because they slept around, they're not serious about long-term job commitments, they don't understand the business world and so on. . . . They interview the [women] students we schedule, but rarely hire more than the one or two they're told to hire. (College job placement director)

Because male quotas are high—95 to 99 percent—it is not difficult to fill the low percentage of slots allocated to token women. . . .

SABOTAGE

Through sabotage, employers and employees purposely and consciously undermine or undercut a woman's position. Although sabotage can be contrived and carried out by individuals, it usually involves covert agreements between two or more persons. Because sabotage is difficult to prove, it is also easy to deny. In almost all cases, it comes down to "my word against yours" because saboteurs do not leave a "paper trail."

Sabotage strategies vary by degree of sophistication, which depends on whether the woman is in a traditionally female job, a traditionally male job, or a job in which boundaries are, in principle, nonexistent because they are, in practice, not job related.

Traditionally Female Jobs.   In traditionally female jobs (domestic, service, clerical), male sabotage is normative, because men at a comparable job level have higher status (owing to higher wages) or because men have supervisory positions. In terms of the latter, for example, there is a substantial literature documenting male supervisors' sexual harrassment of women subordinates because, among other things, men expect women to service all their (real or imagined) needs at all levels. Thus, office workers are the most common targets of sabotage if they don't "put out."

In comparable job levels, men can use sabotage because their job functions are less vulnerable to inspection and represent higher control than those of women:

> I was hassled by the bartender and the male kitchen staff. When you're a waitress, you have to keep in the good books of the guys backing you up. If the bartender takes a dislike to you, he can slow down on your orders to the point where you get no tips at all. The kitchen staff can sabotage you in other ways. The food can be cold, it can arrive late, and orders can be all mixed up.[7]

In traditionally female jobs, male sabotage is blatant, unmasked, raw, and unsophisticated. It is used openly to control and take advantage of women's inferior job status.

Traditionally Male Jobs. In traditionally male-dominated jobs, sabotage strategies are more sophisticated. In contrast to the "good ole boys" mentality, which literally and proudly espouses a "women-are-good-for-only-one-thing" rhetoric, traditionally male job occupants react to women negatively because women are seen as potentially threatening the "old gang" cohesion, camaraderie, and esprit de corps. . . .

In an effort to preserve long-accepted strongholds over men's jobs, men use a variety of sabotage techniques to discourage women's participation and success in traditionally male jobs:

> My co-workers would watch me talking to customers. When I went in to get the paperwork, they'd ridicule me to the customers. "She hasn't been here that long," "Women don't know much about cars." Then, they'd go over the same questions with the customers and get the sale. (Automobile salesperson)
>
> Every time there's a promotion [for corporal], I put my name in. I always get rejected even though I have seniority, have put in the same number of years on the street as the guys, and have the same firing range results as the men. When there's a temporary opening, a sergeant from another precinct is pulled into the temporary spot even when I request the assignment. . . . I think my supervisor is trying to mess up my work record purposely—I'm the last one to find out about special events and new cases, and I have been late for important meetings because I was told about them five or ten minutes before they start. (Female police sergeant)
>
> Ever since I became a meter reader, the guys have always teased me that I'd be attacked by dogs, raped, kidnapped, or not return. . . . That's scary, but I tried to ignore it. . . . What gets me is that sometimes I get to the customer's house and none of the keys I picked up fit. I have to go back to the company to get the right keys. I don't know who's doing it, but someone doesn't want me in this job. (Meter reader for a gas and electric company)

In contrast to women in female-dominated jobs, women in male-dominated jobs find that they are "set up" to fail but are not told, openly, that this is due to their gender.

Sex-neutral Jobs. The most sophisticated sabotage strategies occur in professional, technical, and administrative (and sometimes sales) jobs where sex is totally irrelevant to job performance. Because these occupations do not require physical strength but require professional or academic credentials (Ph.D., J.D., M.A., M.S.) and longer and more specialized training, there is presumably a greater objective reliance on sex-neutral qualifications. . . . One would expect, then, that sex-neutral jobs would be the least discriminatory. Such expectations have not proven to be true.

Quite to the contrary, sex-neutral jobs are often the most discriminatory because they are the most threatening to males dominating the higher echelons of the economy. The sabotage techniques are so subtle and covert that women see the sabotage long after it is too late to do anything about the discrimination:

> One mid-level manager [at a nationally known company] said she had gotten excellent ratings from her supervisors throughout her first year of employment. In the meantime, the company psychologist had called her in about once a month and inquired "how things were going." She was pleased by the company's interest in its employees. At the end of the year, one of her male peers (whose evaluations were known to be very mediocre) got the promotion and she didn't. When she pursued the reasons for her non-promotion, she was finally told, by one of the company's vice presidents, that "anyone who has to see the company psychologist once a month is clearly not management material." She had no way of proving she had been sabotaged.

In other examples, a female insurance agent is directed by the manager to nonelitist client accounts (in contrast to her male counterparts) and then not promoted because her clients take out only "policies for the poor"; and an urban renewal administrative assistant who is more qualified than her supervisor (and is frank about wanting his job) finds the information in her folders scrambled over a period of months and is told that her "administrative chaos" will lead to a demotion.

Notes

1. Ethel Strainchamps, Ed., *Rooms with No View: A Woman's Guide to the Man's World of the Media* (New York: Harper & Row, 1974), p. 146.

2. Susan Fraker, "Why Top Jobs Elude Female Executives," *Fortune*, Apr. 16, 1984, p. 46.

3. "Queen Bees" refer to women who are convinced that they have been successful solely because of their efforts and abilities rather than recognizing that their success could not have become a reality without the sacrifices, pioneering efforts, and achievements of their female predecessors. Because of their adamant "I'm-terrific-because-I-pulled-myself-up-by-*my*-bootstraps" beliefs, Queen Bees typically either ignore or resist helping women become upwardly mobile. Thus, Queen

Bees openly support men who reject sex equality and provide men (and other Queen Bees) with public rationalizations for keeping women in subordinate positions (in other words, as female drones).

4. Ellen Cassedy and Karen Nussbaum, *9 to 5: The Working Woman's Guide to Office Survival* (New York: Penguin Books, 1983), pp. 93–94.

5. Ibid., pp. 77–78.

6. Alice E. Courtney and Thomas W. Whipple, *Sex Stereotyping in Advertising* (Lexington, MA: Lexington Books, 1983), pp. 103–104.

7. Constance Backhouse and Leah Cohen, *Sexual Harrassment on the Job* (Englewood Cliffs, NJ: Prentice-Hall, 1981), p. 9.

30 Savage Inequalities

JONATHAN KOZOL

Social inequality so pervades American society that it leaves no area of life untouched. Consequently, because we are immersed in it, we usually take social inequality for granted. When social inequality does become visible to us, its *social* origins often disappear from sight. We tend to see social inequality as part of the *natural* ordering of life, often explaining it on the basis of people's individual characteristics. ("They" are lazier, dumber, less moral—or whatever—than others. That's the reason they have less than we do.) This selection, however, makes the *social* base of social inequality especially vivid.

To examine the American educational system, Kozol traveled around the country and observed schools in poor, middle-class, and rich communities. Because schools are financed largely by local property taxes, wealthier communities are able to offer higher salaries, purchase newer texts and equipment, and thereby provide their children better education. The extent of the disparities, however, is much greater than most people realize. As you read about the two schools contrasted in this selection, try to project yourself into each situation and see how these communities and schools would likely affect you—not only what you learn, but also your views on life, as well as your entire future.

"EAST OF ANYWHERE," writes a reporter for the *St. Louis Post-Dispatch*, "often evokes the other side of the tracks. But, for a first-time visitor suddenly deposited on its eerily empty streets, East St. Louis might suggest another world." The city, which is 98 percent black, has no obstetric services, no regular trash collection, and few jobs. Nearly a third of its families live on less than $7,500 a year; 75 percent of its population lives on welfare of some form. The U.S. Department of Housing and Urban Development describes it as "the most distressed small city in America."

Only three of the 13 buildings on Missouri Avenue, one of the city's major thoroughfares, are occupied. A 13-story office building, tallest in the city, has been boarded up. Outside, on the sidewalk, a pile of garbage fills a ten-foot crater.

The city, which by night and day is clouded by the fumes that pour from vents and smokestacks at the Pfizer and Monsanto chemical plants, has one of the highest rates of child asthma in America.

It is, according to a teacher at Southern Illinois University, "a repository for a nonwhite population that is now regarded as expendable." The *Post-Dispatch* describes it as "America's Soweto."

Fiscal shortages have forced the layoff of 1,170 of the city's 1,400 employees in the past 12 years. The city, which is often unable to buy heating fuel or toilet paper for the city hall, recently announced that it might have to cashier all but 10 percent of the remaining work force of 230. In 1989 the mayor announced that he might need to sell the city hall and all six fire stations to raise needed cash. Last year the plan had to be scrapped after the city lost its city hall in a court judgment to a creditor. East St. Louis is mortgaged into the next century but has the highest property-tax rate in the state. . . .

The dangers of exposure to raw sewage, which backs up repeatedly into the homes of residents in East St. Louis, were first noticed, in the spring of 1989, at a public housing project, Villa Griffin. Raw sewage, says the *Post-Dispatch*, overflowed into a playground just behind the housing project, which is home to 187 children, "forming an oozing lake of . . . tainted water." . . . A St. Louis health official voices her dismay that children live with waste in their backyards. "The development of working sewage systems made cities livable a hundred years ago," she notes. "Sewage systems separate us from the Third World." . . .

The sewage, which is flowing from collapsed pipes and dysfunctional pumping stations, has also flooded basements all over the city. The city's vacuum truck, which uses water and suction to unclog the city's sewers, cannot be used because it needs $5,000 in repairs. Even when it works, it sometimes can't be used because there isn't money to hire drivers. A single engineer now does the work that 14 others did before they were laid off. By April the pool of overflow behind the Villa Griffin project has expanded into a lagoon of sewage. Two million gallons of raw sewage lie outside the children's homes. . . .

. . . Sister Julia Huiskamp meets me on King Boulevard and drives me to the Griffin homes.

As we ride past blocks and blocks of skeletal structures, some of which are still inhabited, she slows the car repeatedly at railroad crossings. A seemingly endless railroad train rolls past us to the right. On the left: a blackened lot where garbage has been burning. Next to the burning garbage is a row of 12 white cabins, charred by fire. Next: a lot that holds a heap of auto tires and a mountain of tin cans. More burnt houses. More trash fires. The train moves almost imperceptibly across the flatness of the land.

Fifty years old, and wearing a blue suit, white blouse, and blue head-cover, Sister Julia points to the nicest house in sight. The sign on the front reads MOTEL. "It's a whorehouse," Sister Julia says.

When she slows the car beside a group of teen-age boys, one of them steps out toward the car, then backs away as she is recognized.

The 99 units of the Villa Griffin homes—two-story structures, brick on the first floor, yellow wood above—form one border of a recessed park and playground that were filled with fecal matter last year when the sewage mains exploded. The sewage is gone now and the grass is very green and looks inviting. When nine-year-old Serena and her seven-year-old brother take me for a walk, however, I discover that our shoes sink into what is still a sewage marsh. An inch-deep residue of fouled water still remains.

Serena's brother is a handsome, joyous little boy, but troublingly thin. Three other children join us as we walk along the marsh: Smokey, who is nine years old but cannot yet tell time; Mickey, who is seven; and a tiny child with a ponytail and big brown eyes who talks a constant stream of words that I can't always understand.

"Hush, Little Sister," says Serena. I ask for her name, but "Little Sister" is the only name the children seem to know.

"There go my cousins," Smokey says, pointing to two teen-age girls above us on the hill.

The day is warm, although we're only in the second week of March; several dogs and cats are playing by the edges of the marsh. "It's a lot of squirrels here," says Smokey. "There go one!"

"This here squirrel is a friend of mine," says Little Sister.

None of the children can tell me the approximate time that school begins. One says five o'clcok. One says six. Another says that school begins at noon.

When I ask what song they sing after the flag pledge, one says "Jingle Bells."

Smokey cannot decide if he is in the second or third grade.

Seven-year-old Mickey sucks his thumb during the walk.

The children regale me with a chilling story as we stand beside the marsh. Smokey says his sister was raped and murdered and then dumped behind his school. Other children add more details: Smokey's sister was 11 years old. She was beaten with a brick until she died. The murder was committed by a man who knew her mother.

The narrative begins when, without warning, Smokey says, "My sister has got killed."

"She was my best friend," Serena says.

"They had beat her in the head and raped her," Smokey says.

"She was hollering out loud," says Little Sister.

I ask them when it happened. Smokey says, "Last year." Serena then corrects him and she says, "Last week."

"It scared me because I had to cry," says Little Sister.

"The police arrested one man but they didn't catch the other," Smokey says.

Serena says, "He was some kin to her."

But Smokey objects, "He weren't no kin to me. He was my momma's friend."

"Her face was busted," Little Sister says.

Serena describes this sequence of events: "They told her go behind the school. They'll give her a quarter if she do. Then they knock her down and told her not to tell what they had did."

I ask, "Why did they kill her?"

"They was scared that she would tell," Serena says.

"One is in jail," says Smokey. "They cain't find the other."

"Instead of raping little bitty children, they should find themselves a wife," says Little Sister.

"I hope," Serena says, "her spirit will come back and get that man."

"And *kill* that man," says Little Sister.

"Give her another chance to live," Serena says.

"My teacher came to the funeral," says Smokey.

"When a little child dies, my momma say a star go straight to Heaven," says Serena.

"My grandma was murdered," Mickey says out of the blue. "Somebody shot two bullets in her head."

I ask him, "Is she really dead?"

"She dead all right," says Mickey. "She was layin' there, just dead."

"I love my friends," Serena says. "I don't care if they no kin to me. I *care* for them. I hope his mother have another baby. Name her for my friend that's dead."

"I have a cat with three legs," Smokey says.

"Snakes hate rabbits," Mickey says, again for no apparent reason.

"Cats hate fishes," Little Sister says.

"It's a lot of hate," says Smokey.

Later, at the mission, Sister Julia tells me this: "The Jefferson School, which they attend, is a decrepit hulk. Next to it is a modern school, erected two years ago, which was to have replaced the one that they attend. But the construction was not done correctly. The roof is too heavy for the walls, and the entire structure has begun to sink. It can't be occupied. Smokey's sister was raped and murdered and dumped between the old school and the new one." . . .

The problems of the streets in urban areas, as teachers often note, frequently spill over into public schools. In the public schools of East St. Louis this is literally the case.

"Martin Luther King Junior High School," notes the *Post-Dispatch* in a story published in the early spring of 1989, "was evacuated Friday afternoon after sewage flowed into the kitchen. . . . The kitchen was closed and students were sent home." On Monday, the paper continues, "East St. Louis Senior High School was awash in sewage for the second time this year." The school had to be shut because of "fumes and backed-up toilets." Sewage flowed into the basement, through the floor, then up into the kitchen and the students' bathrooms. The backup, we read, "occurred in the food preparation areas."

School is resumed the following morning at the high school, but a few days later the overflow recurs. This time the entire system is affected, since the meals distributed to every student in the city are prepared in the two schools that have been flooded. School is called off for all 16,500 students in the district. The sewage backup, caused by the failure of two pumping stations, forces officials at the high school to shut down the furnaces.

At Martin Luther King, the parking lot and gym are also flooded. "It's a disaster," says a legislator. "The streets are underwater; gaseous fumes are being emitted from the pipes under the schools," she says, "making people ill."

In the same week, the schools announce the layoff of 280 teachers, 166 cooks and cafeteria workers, 25 teacher aides, 16 custodians and 18 painters, electricians, engineers and plumbers. The president of the teachers' union says the cuts, which will bring the size of kindergarten and primary classes up to 30 students, and the size of fourth to twelfth grade classes up to 35, will have "an unimaginable impact" on the students. "If you have a high school teacher with five classes each day and between 150 and 175 students . . . , it's going to have a devastating effect." The school system, it is also noted, has been using more than 70 "permanent substitute teachers," who are paid only $10,000 yearly, as a way of saving money. . . .

East St. Louis, says the chairman of the state board, "is simply the worst possible place I can imagine to have a child brought up. . . . The community is in desperate circumstances." Sports and music, he observes, are, for many children here, "the only avenues of success." Sadly enough, no matter how it ratifies the stereotype, this is the truth; and there is a poignant aspect to the fact that, even with class size soaring and one quarter of the system's teachers being given their dismissal, the state board of education demonstrates its genuine but skewed compassion by attempting to leave sports and music untouched by the overall austerity.

Even sports facilities, however, are degrading by comparison with those found and expected at most high schools in America. The football field at East St. Louis High is missing almost everything—including goalposts. There are a couple of metal pipes—no crossbar, just the pipes. Bob Shannon, the football coach, who has to use his personal funds to purchase footballs and has had to cut and rake the football field himself, has dreams of having goalposts someday. He'd also like to let his students have new uniforms. The ones they wear are nine years old and held together somehow by a patchwork of repairs. Keeping them clean is a problem, too. The school cannot afford a washing machine. The uniforms are carted to a corner laundromat with fifteen dollars' worth of quarters. . . .

In the wing of the school that holds vocational classes, a damp, unpleasant odor fills the halls. The school has a machine shop, which cannot be used for lack of staff, and a woodworking shop. The only shop that's occupied this morning is the auto-body class. A man with long blond hair and wearing a white sweat suit swings a paddle to get children in their chairs. "What we need the most is new equipment," he reports. "I have equipment for alignment, for example, but we don't have money to install it. We also need a better form of egress. We bring the cars in through two other classes." Computerized equipment used in most repair shops, he reports, is far beyond the high school's budget. It looks like a very old gas station in an isolated rural town. . . .

The science labs at East St. Louis High are 30 to 50 years outdated. John McMillan, a soft-spoken man, teaches physics at the school. He shows me his lab. The six lab stations in the room have empty holes where pipes were once attached. "It would be great if we had water," says McMillan. . . .

Leaving the chemistry labs, I pass a double-sized classroom in which roughly 60 kids are sitting fairly still but doing nothing. "This is supervised study hall," a teacher tells me in the corridor. But when we step inside, he finds there is no teacher. "The teacher must be out today," he says.

Irl Solomon's history classes, which I visit next, have been described by journalists who cover East St. Louis as the highlight of the school. Solomon, a man of 54 whose reddish hair is turning white, has taught in urban schools for almost 30 years. A graduate of Brandeis University, he entered law school but was drawn away by a conern with civil rights. "After one semester, I decided that the law was not for me. I said, 'Go and find the toughest place there is to teach. See if you like it.' I'm still here. . . .

"I have four girls right now in my senior home room who are pregnant or have just had babies. When I ask them why this happens, I am told, 'Well, there's no reason not to have a baby. There's not much for me in public school.' The truth is, that's a pretty honest answer. A diploma from a ghetto high school doesn't count for much in the United States today. So, if this is really the last education that a person's going to get, she's probably perceptive in that statement. Ah, there's so much bitterness—unfairness—there, you know. Most of these pregnant girls are not the ones who have much self-esteem. . . .

"Very little education in the school would be considered academic in the suburbs. Maybe 10 to 15 percent of students are in truly academic programs. Of the 55 percent who graduate, 20 percent may go to four-year colleges: something like 10 percent of any entering class. Another 10 to 20 percent may get some other kind of higher education. An equal number join the military. . . .

"I don't go to physics class, because my lab has no equipment," says one student. "The typewriters in my typing class don't work. The women's toilets . . . " She makes a sour face. "I'll be honest," she says. "I just don't use the toilets. If I do, I come back into class and I feel dirty."

"I wanted to study Latin," says another student. "But we don't have Latin in this school."

"We lost our only Latin teacher," Solomon says.

A girl in a white jersey with the message DO THE RIGHT THING on the front raises her hand. "You visit other schools," she says. "Do you think the children in this school are getting what we'd get in a nice section of St. Louis?"

I note that we are in a different state and city.

"Are we citizens of East St. Louis or America?" she asks. . . .

In a seventh grade social studies class, the only book that bears some relevance to black concerns—its title is *The American Negro*—bears a publication date of 1967. The teacher invites me to ask the class some questions. Uncertain where to start, I ask the students what they've learned about the civil rights campaigns of recent decades.

A 14-year-old girl with short black curly hair says this: "Every year in February we are told to read the same old speech of Martin Luther King. We read it ever year. 'I have a dream. . . . ' It does begin to seem—what is the word?" She hesitates and then she finds the word: "perfunctory."

I ask her what she means.

"We have a school in East St. Louis named for Dr. King," she says. "The school is full of sewer water and the doors are locked with chains. Every student in that school is black. It's like a terrible joke on history."

It startles me to hear her words, but I am startled even more to think how seldom any press reporter has observed the irony of naming segregated schools for Martin Luther King. Children reach the heart of these hypocrisies much quicker than the grown-ups and the experts do. . . .

The train ride from Grand Central Station to suburban Rye, New York, takes 35 to 40 minutes. The high school is a short ride from the station. Built of handsome gray stone and set in a landscaped campus, it resembles a New England prep school. On a day in early June of 1990, I enter the school and am directed by a student to the office.

The principal, a relaxed, unhurried man who, unlike many urban principals, seems gratified to have me visit in his school, takes me in to see the auditorium, which, he says, was recently restored with private charitable funds ($400,000) raised by parents. The crenellated ceiling, which is white and spotless, and the polished dark-wood paneling contrast with the collapsing structure of the auditorium at [another school I visited]. The principal strikes his fist against the balcony: "They made this place extremely solid." Through a window, one can see the spreading branches of a beech tree in the central courtyard of the school.

In a student lounge, a dozen seniors are relaxing on a carpeted floor that is constructed with a number of tiers so that, as the principal explains, "they can stretch out and be comfortable while reading."

The library is wood-paneled, like the auditorium. Students, all of whom are white, are seated at private carrels, of which there are approximately 40. Some are doing homework; others are looking through the *New York Times*. Every student that I see during my visit to the school is white or Asian, though I later learn there are a number of Hispanic students and that 1 or 2 percent of students in the school are black.

According to the principal, the school has 96 computers for 546 children. The typical student, he says, studies a foreign language for four or five years, beginning in the junior high school, and a second foreign language (Latin is available) for two years. Of 140 seniors, 92 are now enrolled in AP [advanced placement] classes. Maximum teacher salary will soon reach $70,000. Per-pupil funding is above $12,000 at the time I visit.

The students I meet include eleventh and twelfth graders. The teacher tells me that the class is reading Robert Coles, Studs Terkel, Alice Walker. He tells me I will find them more than willing to engage me in debate, and this turns out to be correct. Primed for my visit, it appears, they arrow in directly on the dual questions of equality and race.

Three general positions soon emerge and seem to be accepted widely. The first is that the fiscal inequalities "do matter very much" in shaping what a school can offer ("That is obvious," one student says) and that any loss of funds in Rye, as a potential consequence of future equalizing, would be damaging to many things the town regards as quite essential.

The second position is that racial integration—for example, by the busing of black children from the city or a nonwhite suburb to this school—would meet with strong resistance, and the reason would not simply be the fear that certain standards might decline. The reason, several students say straightforwardly, is "racial" or, as others say it, "out-and-out racism" on the part of adults.

The third position voiced by many students, but not all, is that equity is basically a goal to be desired and should be pursued for moral reasons, but "will probably make no major difference" since poor children "still would lack the motivation" and "would probably fail in any case because of other problems."

At this point, I ask if they can truly say "it wouldn't make a difference" since it's never been attempted. Several students then seem to rethink their views and say that "it might work, but it would have to start with preschool and the elementary grades" and "it might be 20 years before we'd see a difference."

At this stage in the discussion, several students speak with some real feeling of the present inequalities, which, they say, are "obviously unfair," and one student goes a little further and proposes that "we need to change a lot more than the schools." Another says she'd favor racial integration "by whatever means—including busing—even if the parents disapprove." But a contradictory opinion also is expressed with a good deal of fervor and is stated by one student in a rather biting voice: "I don't see why we should do it. How could it be of benefit to us?"

Throughout the discussion, whatever the views the children voice, there is a degree of unreality about the whole exchange. The children are lucid and their language is well chosen and their arguments well made, but there is a sense that they are dealing with an issue that does not feel very vivid, and that nothing that we say about it to each other really matters since it's "just a theoretical discussion." To a certain degree, the skillfulness and cleverness that they display seem to derive precisely from this sense of unreality. Questions of unfairness feel more like a geometric problem than a matter of humanity or conscience. A few of the students do break through the note of unreality, but, when they do, they cease to be so agile in their use of words and speak more awkwardly. Ethical challenges seem to threaten their effectiveness. There is the sense that they were skating over ice and that the issues we addressed were safely frozen underneath. When they stop to look beneath the ice they start to stumble. The verbal competence they have acquired here may have been gained by building walls around some regions of the heart.

"I don't think that busing students from their ghetto to a different school would do much good," one student says. "You can take them out of the environment, but you can't take the environment out of *them*. If someone grows up in the South Bronx, he's not going to be prone to learn." His name is Max and he has short black hair and speaks with confidence. "Busing didn't work when it was tried," he says. I ask him how he knows this and he says he saw a television movie about Boston.

"I agree that it's unfair the way it is," another student says. "We have AP courses and they don't. Our classes are much smaller." But, she says, "putting them in schools like ours is not the answer. Why not put some AP classes into *their* school? Fix the roof and paint the halls so it will not be so depressing."

The students know the term "separate but equal," but seem unaware of its historical associations. "Keep them where they are but make it equal," says a girl in the front row.

A student named Jennifer, whose manner of speech is somewhat less refined and polished than that of the others, tells me that her parents came here from New York. "My family is originally from the Bronx. Schools are hell there. That's one reason that we moved. I don't think it's our responsibility to pay our taxes to provide for *them*. I mean, my parents used to live there and they wanted to get out. There's no point in coming to a place like this, where schools are good, and then your taxes go back to the place where you began."

I bait her a bit: "Do you mean that, now that you are not in hell, you have no feeling for the people that you left behind?"

"It has to be the people in the area who want an education. If your parents just don't care, it won't do any good to spend a lot of money. Someone else can't want a good life for you. You have got to want it for yourself." Then she adds, however, "I agree that everyone should have a chance at taking the same courses. . . ."

I ask her if she'd think it fair to pay more taxes so that this was possible.

"I don't see how that benefits me," she says.

31 Tally's Corner

ELLIOT LIEBOW

Liebow studied black streetcorner men, lower-lower class males whose chief activities and satisfactions take place "on the street." These men are materially poor because of the convergence of income, race, and education. Focusing on the adaptations these streetcorner men have made to their deprivation, Liebow analyzes their survival strategies.

In his analysis, Liebow applies the concept of the *self-fulfilling prophecy.* An example might help clarify this term. Let us suppose that reporters begin to discuss the possibility of a coming recession. They quote economists who see indicators that a recession might occur. These economists are not predicting a recession, however, and they carefully cover themselves with a lot of "ifs, ands, and buts." Some people who read the stories skip the disclaimers of the economists, however, and focus on the recession part of their statements. More and more, as they talk about the matter, people come to believe that a recession might be soon on its way. Consequently, business people cut down on their inventories "just in case." When enough people cut back, unsold goods build up, factory orders diminish, economic indexes begin to decline, and business people, more worried than ever, cut back on expansion plans—making ripples felt throughout the economy. The recession arrives, because it was predicted—and because people changed their behavior accordingly.

Although it oversimplifies economic matters, the above scenario illustrates a significant concept in social life. As Liebow applies the concept, it becomes apparent that self-fulfilling prophecies can create vicious cycles that drastically affect people's lives. The perceptions of the men he studied both predict failure at work and help cause the predicted failure (much as those that affected the Saints and the Roughnecks in Part VI).

Can you think of other self-fulfilling prophecies? Have you personally experienced any? What effect did they have on your life? How do you think the streetcorner men's cycle of self-fulfilling prophecies could be broken?

IN SUMMARY OF OBJECTIVE JOB CONSIDERATIONS [of streetcorner men], the most important fact is that a man who is able and willing to work cannot earn enough money to support himself, his wife, and one or more children. A man's chances for working regularly are good only if he is willing to work for less than he can live on, and sometimes not even then. On some jobs, the wage rate is deceptively higher than on others, but the higher the wage rate, the more difficult it is to get the job, and the less the job security. Higher-paying construction work tends to be seasonal and, during the season, the amount of work available is highly sensitive to business and weather conditions and to the changing requirements of individual projects.[1] Moreover, high-paying construction jobs are frequently beyond the physical capacity of some of the men, and some of the low-paying jobs are scaled down even lower in accordance with the self-fulfilling assumption that the man will steal part of his wages on the job.[2]

Bernard assesses the objective job situation dispassionately over a cup of coffee, sometimes poking at the coffee with his spoon, sometimes staring at it as if, like a crystal ball, it holds tomorrow's secrets. He is twenty-seven years old. He and the woman with whom he lives have a baby son, and she has another child by another man. Bernard does odd jobs—mostly painting—but here it is the end of January, and his last job was with the Post Office during the Christmas mail rush. He would like postal work as a steady job, he says. It pays well (about $2.00 an hour) but he has twice failed the Post Office examination (he graduated from a Washington high school) and has given up the idea as an impractical one. He is supposed to see a man tonight about a job as a parking attendant for a large apartment house. The man told him to bring his birth certificate and driver's license, but his license was suspended because of a backlog of unpaid traffic fines. A friend promised to lend him some money this evening. If he gets it, he will pay the fines tomorrow morning and have his license reinstated. He hopes the man with the job will wait till tomorrow night.

A "security job" is what he really wants, he said. He would like to save up money for a taxi cab. (But having twice failed the postal examination and having a bad driving record as well, it is highly doubtful that he could meet the qualifications or pass the written test.) That would be "a good life." He can always get a job in a restaurant or as a clerk in a drugstore but they don't pay enough, he said. He needs to take home at least $50 to $55 a week. He thinks he can get that much driving a truck somewhere. . . . Sometimes he wishes he had stayed in the army. . . . A security job, that's what he wants most of all, a real security job. . . .

When we look at what the men bring to the job rather than at what the job offers the men, it is essential to keep in mind that we are not looking at men who come to the job fresh, just out of school perhaps, and newly prepared to undertake the task of making a living, or from another job where they earned a living and are prepared to do the same on this job. Each man comes to the job with a long job history characterized by his not being able to support himself and his family. Each man carries this knowledge, born of his experience, with him. He comes to the job flat and stale, wearied by the sameness of it all, convinced of his own incompetence, terrified of responsibility—of being tested still again and found wanting. Possible exceptions are the younger men not yet, or just, married. They suspect all this but have yet to have it confirmed by repeated personal experience over time. But those who are or have been married know it well. It is the experience of the individual and the group; of their fathers and probably their sons. Convinced of their inadequacies, not only do they not seek out those few better-paying jobs which test their resources, but they actively avoid them, gravitating in a mass to the menial, routine jobs which offer no challenge—and therefore pose no threat—to the already diminished images they have of themselves.

Thus Richard does not follow through on the real estate agent's offer. He is afraid to do on his own—minor plastering, replacing broken windows, other minor repairs and painting—exactly what he had been doing for months on a piecework basis under someone else (and which provided him with a solid base from which to derive a cost estimate).

Richard once offered an important clue to what may have gone on in his mind when the job offer was made. We were in the Carry-out, at a time when he was looking for work. He was talking about the kind of jobs available to him.

> I graduated from high school [Baltimore] but I don't know anything. I'm dumb. Most of the time I don't even say I graduated, 'cause then somebody asks me a question and I can't answer it, and they think I was lying about graduating. . . . They graduated me but I didn't know anything. I had lousy grades but I guess they wanted to get rid of me.
>
> I was at Margaret's house the other night and her little sister asked me to help her with her homework. She showed me some fractions and I knew right away I couldn't do them. I was ashamed so I told her I had to go to the bathroom.

And so it must have been, surely, with the real estate agent's offer. Convinced that "I'm dumb . . . I don't know anything," he "knew right away" he couldn't do it, despite the fact that he had been doing just that sort of work all along.

Thus, the man's low self-esteem generates a fear of being tested and prevents him from accepting a job with responsibilities or, once on a job, from staying with it if responsibilities are thrust on him, even if the wages are commensurately higher. Richard refuses such a job, Leroy leaves one, and another man, given more responsibility and more pay, knows he will fail and proceeds to do so, proving he was right about himself all along. The self-fulfilling prophecy is everywhere at work. In a hallway, Stanton, Tonk, and Boley are passing a bottle around. Stanton recalls the time he was in the service. Everything was fine until he attained the rank of corporal.

He worried about everything he did then. Was he doing the right thing? Was he doing it well? When would they discover their mistake and take his stripes (and extra pay) away? When he finally lost his stripes, everything was all right again.

Lethargy, disinterest and general apathy on the job, so often reported by employers, has its streetcorner counterpart. The men do not ordinarily talk about their jobs or ask one another about them.[3] Although most of the men know who is or is not working at any given time, they may or may not know what particular job an individual man has. There is no overt interest in job specifics as they relate to this or that person, in large part perhaps because the specifics are not especially relevant. To know that a man is working is to know approximately how much he makes and to know as much as one needs or wants to know about how he makes it. After all, how much difference does it make to know whether a man is pushing a mop and pulling trash in an apartment house, a restaurant, or an office building, or delivering groceries, drugs, or liquor, or, if he's a laborer, whether he's pushing a wheelbarrow, mixing mortar, or digging a hole? So much does one job look like every other that there is little to choose between them. In large part, the job market consists of a narrow range of nondescript chores calling for nondistinctive, undifferentiated, unskilled labor. "A job is a job."

A crucial factor in the streetcorner man's lack of job commitment is the overall value he places on the job. *For his part, the streetcorner man puts no lower value on the job than does the larger society around him.* He knows the social value of the job by the amount of money the employer is willing to pay him for doing it. In a real sense, every pay day, he counts in dollars and cents the value placed on the job by society at large. He is no more (and frequently less) ready to quit and look for another job than his employer is ready to fire him and look for another man. Neither the streetcorner man who performs these jobs nor the society which requires him to perform them assesses the job as one "worth doing and worth doing well." Both employee and employer are contemptuous of the job. The employee shows his contempt by his reluctance to accept it or keep it, the employer by paying less than is required to support a family.[4] Nor does the low-wage job offer prestige, respect, interesting work, opportunity for learning or advancement, or any other compensation. With few exceptions, jobs filled by the streetcorner man are at the bottom of the employment ladder in every respect, from wage level to prestige. Typically, they are hard, dirty, uninteresting and underpaid. The rest of society (whatever its ideal values regarding the dignity of labor) holds the job of the dishwasher or janitor or unskilled laborer in low esteem if not outright contempt.[5] So does the streetcorner man. He cannot do otherwise. He cannot draw from a job those social values which other people do not put into it.[6]

Only occasionally does spontaneous conversation touch on these matters directly. Talk about jobs is usually limited to isolated statements of intention, such as "I think I'll get me another gig [job]," "I'm going to look for a construction job when the weather breaks," or "I'm going to quit. I can't take no more of this shit." Job assessments typically consist of nothing more than a noncommittal shrug and "It's O.K." or "It's a job."

One reason for the relative absence of talk about one's job is, as suggested earlier, that the sameness of job experiences does not bear reiteration. Another and more important reason is the emptiness of the job experience itself. The man sees middle-class occupations as a primary source of prestige, pride, and self-respect; his own job affords him none of these. To think about his job is to see himself as others see him, to remind him of just where he stands in this society.[7] And because society's criteria for placement are generally the same as his own, to talk about his job can trigger a flush of shame and a deep, almost physical ache to change places with someone, almost anyone, else.[8] The desire to be a person in his own right, to be noticed by the world he lives in, is shared by each of the men on the streetcorner. Whether they articulate this desire (as Tally does below) or not, one can see them position themselves to catch the attention of their fellows in much the same way as plants bend or stretch to catch the sunlight.[9]

Tally and I went in the Carry-out. It was summer, Tally's peak earning season as a cement finisher, a semiskilled job a cut or so above that of the unskilled laborer. His take-home pay during these weeks was well over a hundred dollars—"a lot of bread." But for Tally, who no longer had a family to support, bread was not enough.

"You know that boy came in last night? That Black Moozlem? That's what I ought to be doing. I ought to be in his place."

"What do you mean?"

"Dressed nice, going to [night] school, got a good job."

"He's no better off than you, Tally. You make more than he does."

"It's not the money. [Pause] It's position, I guess. He's got position. When he finish school he gonna be a supervisor. People respect him. . . . Thinking about people with position and education gives me a feeling right here [pressing his fingers into the pit of his stomach]."

"You're educated, too. You have a skill, a trade. You're a cement finisher. You can make a building, pour a sidewalk."

"That's different. Look, can anybody do what you're doing? Can anybody just come up and do your job? Well, in one week I can teach you cement finishing. You won't be as good as me 'cause you won't have the experience but you'll be a cement finisher. That's what I mean. Anybody can do what I'm doing and that's what gives me this feeling. [Long pause] Suppose I like this girl. I go over to her house and I meet her father. He starts talking about what he done today. He talks about operating on somebody and sewing them up and about surgery. I know he's a doctor 'cause of the way he talks. Then she starts talking about what she did. Maybe she's a boss or a supervisor. Maybe she's a lawyer and her father says to me, 'And what do you do, Mr.

Jackson?' [Pause] You remember at the courthouse, Lonny's trial? You and the lawyer was talking in the hall? You remember? I just stood there listening. I didn't say a word. You know why? 'Cause I didn't even know what you was talking about. That's happened to me a lot."

"Hell, you're nothing special. That happens to everybody. Nobody knows everything. One man is a doctor, so he talks about surgery. Another man is a teacher, so he talks about books. But doctors and teachers don't know anything about concrete. You're a cement finisher and that's your speciality."

"Maybe so, but when was the last time you saw anybody standing about talking about concrete?"

The streetcorner man wants to be a person in his own right, to be noticed, to be taken account of, but in this respect, as well as in meeting his money needs, his job fails him. The job and the man are even. The job fails the man and the man fails the job.

Furthermore, the man does not have any reasonable expectation that, however bad it is, his job will lead to better things. Menial jobs are not, by and large, the starting point of a track system which leads to even better jobs for those who are able and willing to do them. The busboy or dishwasher in a restaurant is not on a job track which, if negotiated skillfully, leads to chef or manager of the restaurant. The busboy or dishwasher who works hard becomes, simply, a hard-working busboy or dishwasher. Neither hard work nor perseverance can conceivably carry the janitor to a sitdown job in the office building he cleans up. And it is the apprentice who becomes the journeyman electrician, plumber, steam fitter or bricklayer, not the common unskilled Negro laborer.

Thus, the job is not a stepping stone to something better. It is a dead end. It promises to deliver no more tomorrow, next month or next year than it does today.

Delivering little, and promising no more, the job is "no big thing." The man appears to treat the job in a cavalier fashion, working and not working as the spirit moves him, as if all that matters is the immediate satisfaction of his present appetites, the surrender to present moods, and the indulgence of whims with no thought for the cost, consequences, the future. To the middle-class observer, this behavior reflects a "present-time orientation"—an "inability to defer gratification." It is this "present-time" orientation—as against the "future orientation" of the middle-class person— that "explains" to the outsider why Leroy chooses to spend the day at the Carry-out rather than report to work; why Richard, who was paid Friday, was drunk Saturday and Sunday and penniless Monday; why Sweets quits his job today because the boss looked at him "funny" yesterday.

But from the inside looking out, what appears as a "present-time" orientation to the outside observer is, to the man experiencing it, as much a future orientation as that of his middle-class counterpart.[10] The difference between the two men lies not so much in their different orientations to time as in their different orientations to future time or, more specifically, to their different futures.[11]

The future orientation of the middle-class person presumes, among other things, a surplus of resources to be invested in the future and a belief that the future will be sufficiently stable both to justify his investment (money in a bank, time and effort in a job, investment of himself in marriage and family, etc.) and to permit the consumption of his investment at a time, place and manner of his own choosing and to his greater satisfaction. But the streetcorner man lives in a sea of want. He does not, as a rule, have a surplus of resources, either economic or psychological. Gratification of hunger and the desire for simple creature comforts cannot be long deferred. Neither can support for one's flagging self-esteem. Living on the edge of both economic and psychological subsistence, the streetcorner man is obliged to expend all his resources on maintaining himself from moment to moment.[12]

As for the future, the young streetcorner man has a fairly good picture of it. In Richard or Sea Cat or Arthur he can see himself in his middle twenties; he can look at Tally to see himself at thirty, at Wee Tom to see himself in his middle thirties, and at Budder and Stanton to see himself in his forties. It is a future in which everything is uncertain except the ultimate destruction of his hopes and the eventual realization of his fears. The most he can reasonably look forward to is that these things do not come too soon. Thus, when Richard squanders a week's pay in two days it is not because, like an animal or a child, he is "present-time oriented," unaware of or unconcerned with his future. He does so precisely because he is aware of the future and the hopelessness of it all.

Sometimes this kind of response appears as a conscious, explicit choice. Richard had had a violent argument with his wife. He said he was going to leave her and the children, that he had had enough of everything and could not take any more, and he chased her out of the house. His chest still heaving, he leaned back against the wall in the hallway of his basement apartment.

> "I've been scuffling for five years," he said. "I've been scuffling for five years from morning till night. And my kids still don't have anything, my wife don't have anything, and I don't have anything."
>
> "There," he said, gesturing down the hall to a bed, a sofa, a couple of chairs and a television set, all shabby, some broken. "There's everything I have and I'm having trouble holding onto that."
>
> Leroy came in, presumably to petition Richard on behalf of Richard's wife, who was sitting outside on the steps, afraid to come in. Leroy started to say something but Richard cut him short.
>
> "Look, Leroy, don't give me any of that action. You and me are entirely different people. Maybe I look like a boy and maybe I act like a boy sometimes

but I got a man's mind. You and me don't want the same things out of life. Maybe some of the same, but you don't care how long you have to wait for yours and I—*want—mine—right—now*." [13]

Thus apparent present-time concerns with consumption and indulgences—material and emotional—reflect a future-time orientation. "I want mine right now" is ultimately a cry of despair, a direct response to the future as he sees it. [14]

In many instances, it is precisely the streetcorner man's orientation to the future—but to a future loaded with "trouble"—which not only leads to a greater emphasis on present concerns ("I want mine right now") but also contributes importantly to the instability of employment, family and friend relationships, and to the general transient quality of daily life.

Let me give some concrete examples. One day, after Tally had gotten paid, he gave me four twenty-dollar bills and asked me to keep them for him. Three days later he asked me for the money. I returned it and asked why he did not put his money in a bank. He said that the banks close at two o'clock. I argued that there were four or more banks within a two block radius of where he was working at the time and that he could easily get to any one of them on his lunch hour. "No, man," he said, "you don't understand. They close at two o'clock and they closed Saturday and Sunday. Suppose I get into trouble and I got to make it [leave]. Me get out of town, and everything I got in the world layin' up in that bank? No good! No good!"

In another instance, Leroy and his girl friend were discussing "trouble." Leroy was trying to decide how best to go about getting his hands on some "long green" (a lot of money), and his girl friend cautioned him about "trouble." Leroy sneered at this, saying he had had "trouble" all his life and wasn't afraid of a little more. "Anyway," he said, "I'm famous for leaving town." [15]

Thus, the constant awareness of a future loaded with "trouble" results in a constant readiness to leave, to "make it," to "get out ot town," and discourages the man from sinking roots into the world he lives in. [16] Just as it discourages him from putting money in the bank, so it discourages him from committing himself to a job, especially one whose payoff lies in the promise of future rewards rather than in the present. In the same way, it discourages him from deep and lasting commitments to family and friends or to any other persons, places, or things, since such commitments could hold him hostage, limiting his freedom of movement and thereby compromising his security which lies in that freedom.

What lies behind the response to the driver to the pickup truck [Liebow is referring to an example from earlier in his book], then, is a complex combination of attitudes and assessments. The streetcorner man is under continuous assault by his job experiences and job fears. His experiences and fears feed on one another. The kind of job he can get—and frequently only after fighting for it, if then—steadily confirms his fears, depresses his self-confidence and self-esteem until finally, terrified of an opportunity even if one presents itself, he stands defeated by his experiences, his belief in his own self-worth destroyed and his fears a confirmed reality.

Notes

1. The overall result is that, in the long run, a Negro laborer's earnings are not substantially greater—and may be less—than those of the busboy, janitor, or stock clerk. Herman P. Miller, for example, reports that in 1960, 40 percent of all jobs held by Negro men were as laborers or in the service trades. The average annual wage for nonwhite nonfarm laborers was $2,400. The average earning of nonwhite service workers was $2,500. *Rich Man, Poor Man*, (New York: Crowell-Collier Press, 1964), p. 90. Francis Greenfield estimates that in the Washington vicinity, the 1965 earnings of the union laborer who works whenever work is available will be about $3,200. Even this figure is high for the man on the streetcorner. Union men in heavy construction are the aristocrats of the laborers. Casual day labor and jobs with small firms in the building and construction trades, or with firms in other industries, pay considerably less.

2. For an excellent discussion of the self-fulfilling assumption (or prophecy) as a social force, see "The Self-Fulfilling Prophecy," Ch. XI in Robert K. Merton's *Social Theory and Social Structure*, Rev. ed. (Glencoe, IL.: The Free Press, 1957).

3. This stands in dramatic contrast to the leisure-time conversation of stable, working-class men. For the coal miners (of Ashton, England), for example, "the topic [of conversation] which surpasses all others in frequency is work—the difficulties which have been encountered in the day's shift, the way in which a particular task was accomplished, and so on." Josephine Klein, *Samples from English Cultures* (London: Routledge & Kegan Paul, 1965), I:88.

4. It is important to remember that the employer is not entirely a free agent. Subject to the constraints of the larger society, he acts for the larger society as well as for himself. Child labor laws, safety and sanitation regulations, minimum wage scales in some employment areas, and other constrains are already on the books; other control mechanisms, such as a guaranteed annual wage, are to be had for the voting.

5. See, for example, the U.S. Bureau of the Census, *Methodology and Scores of Socioeconomic Status*. The assignment of the lowest SES ratings to men who hold such jobs is not peculiar to our own society. A low SES rating for "the shoeshine boy or garbage man . . . seems to be true for all [industrial] countries." Alex Inkeles, "Industrial Man," *The American Journal of Sociology* 66 (1960):8.

6. That the streetcorner man downgrades manual labor should occasion no surprise. Merton points out that "the American stigmatization of manual labor . . . *has been found to hold rather uniformly in all social classes*" (emphasis in original). *Social Theory and Social Structure*, p. 145. That he finds no satisfaction in such work should also occasion no surprise: "[There is] a clear positive correlation between the over-all status of occupations and the experience of satisfaction in them." Inkeles, "Industrial Man," p. 12.

7. "[In our society] a man's work is one of the things by which he is judged, and certainly one of the more significant things by which he judges himself. . . . A man's work is one of the more important parts of his social identity, of his self; indeed, of his fate in the one life he has to live." Everett C. Hughes, *Men and Their Work* (Glencoe, IL.: The Free Press, 1958), pp. 42–43.

8. Noting that lower-class persons "are constantly exposed to evidence of their own irrelevance," Lee Rainwater spells out still another way in which the poor are poor: "The identity problems of lower class persons make the soul-searching of middle class adolescents and adults seem rather like a kind of conspicuous consumption of psychic riches." "Work and Identity in the Lower Class," paper prepared for Washington University Conference on Planning for the Quality of Urban Life, April 1965 (mimeographed), p. 3.

9. Sea Cat cuts his pants legs off at the calf and puts a fringe on the raggedy edges. Tony breaks his "shades" and continues to wear the horn-rimmed frames minus the lenses. Richard cultivates a distinctive manner of speech. Lonny gives himself a birthday party. And so on.

10. Taking a somewhat different point of view, S. M. Miller and Frank Riessman suggest that "the entire concept of deferred gratification may be inappropriate to understanding the essence of workers' lives." "The Working Class Subculture: A New View," *Social Problems* 9 (1961):87.

11. This sentence is a paraphrase of a statement made by Marvin Cline at a 1965 colloquium at the Mental Health Study Center, National Institute of Mental Health.

12. And if, for the moment, he does sometimes have more money than he chooses to spend or more food than he wants to eat, he is pressed to spend the money and eat the food anyway since his friends, neighbors, kinsmen, or acquaintances will beg or borrow whatever surplus he has or, failing this, they may steal it. In one extreme case, one of the men admitted taking the last of a woman's surplus food allotment after she had explained that, with four children, she could not spare any food. The prospect that consumer soft goods not consumed by oneself will be consumed by someone else may be related to the way in which portable consumer durable goods, such as watches, radios, television sets or phonographs, are sometimes looked at as a form of savings. When Shirley was on welfare, she regularly took her television set out of pawn when she got her monthly check. Not so much to watch it, she explained, as to have something to fall back on when her money runs out toward the end of the month. For her and others, the television set or the phonograph is her savings, and the pawn ticket is her bankbook.

13. This was no simple rationalization for irresponsibility. Richard had indeed "been scuffling for five years" trying to keep his family going. Until shortly after this episode, Richard was known and respected as one of the hardest-working men on the street. Richard had said, only a couple of months earlier, "I figure you got to get out there and try. You got to try before you can get anything." His wife Shirley confirmed that he had always tried. "If things get tough with me I'll get all worried. But Richard get worried, he don't want me to see him worried. . . . He *will* get out there. He's shoveled snow, picked beans, and he's done some of everything. . . . He's not ashamed to get out there and get us something to eat." At the time of the episode reported above, Leroy was just starting marriage and raising a family. He and Richard were not, as Richard thought, "entirely different

people." Leroy had just not learned, by personal experience over time, what Richard had learned. But within two years Leroy's marriage had broken up and he was talking and acting like Richard. "He just let go completely," said one of the men on the street.

14. There is no mystically intrinsic connection between "present-time" orientation and lower-class persons. Whenever people of whatever class have been uncertain, skeptical or downright pessimistic about the future, "I want mine right now" has been one of the characteristics responses, although it is usually couched in more delicate terms: e.g., Omar Khayyam's "Take the cash and let the credit go," or Horace's *"Carpe diem."* In wartime, especially, all classes tend to slough off conventional restraints on sexual and other behavior (i.e., become less able or less willing to defer gratification). And when inflation threatens, darkening the fiscal future, persons who formerly husbanded their resources with commendable restraint almost stampede one another rushing to spend their money. Similarly, it seems that future-time orientation tends to collapse toward the present when persons are in pain or under stress. The point here is that, the label notwithstanding, (what passes for) present-time orientation appears to be a situation-specific phenomenon rather than a part of the standard psychic equipment of Cognitive Lower Class Man.

15. And proceeded to do just that the following year when "trouble"—in this case, a grand jury indictment, a pile of debts, and a violent separation from his wife and children—appeared again.

16. For a discussion of "trouble" as a focal concern of lower-class culture, see Walter Miller, "Lower Class Culture as a Generating Milieu of Gang Delinquency," *Journal of Social Issues 14* (1958):7,8.

32 Good People and Dirty Work

EVERETT C. HUGHES

Assume that there is much hatred of some group; then assume that the people who are filled with that hatred take control of society; assume further that moving against the hated group seems to many to be in the best interests of the country. With these assumptions you have the makings of "the final solution," the use of state power to commit *genocide*, destroying an entire group of people on the basis of their presumed race or ethnicity. I use the word "presumed" because people around the world have intermarried and intermated to such a degree that there is serious doubt whether there is, on a genetic basis, any such thing as a race. For this reason, some researchers are now substituting for race the term "genetic pool." Because most sociological sources and people in our society use the term "race," however, we shall also use it.

Could a "final solution" happen in our country? Even the thought is abhorrent, and most people are inclined to answer immediately, "No! In no way could that happen here. The Holocaust was simply an aberration of history. We would not allow it." While such statements might be comforting, they beg the question: *Could* it happen here? To answer it, we need to deal with the issues raised above. Is there deep-seated hatred of groups on the basis of presumed racial characteristics? If so, is it possible for those with that hatred to gain control of society? If that happened, would it then be possible for them to use the bureaucratic machinery of the state to attempt to destroy the group they hate?

As you grapple with these issues, think about the fact that Germany had perhaps the most educated citizens in the world—with perhaps more Ph.D.s per square mile than any other place on the face of the earth. Remember also that Germany was a world leader in the arts, sciences, technology, and theology. Think also about the fact that about two generations ago the Nazis were but a small group of powerless fanatics who were not taken seriously.

That is enough to make me shiver. And where were the "regular" people, the ones who could have prevented it all? What were the "good" people doing while humans were being turned into soap and the stench of the crematoriums rose over towns and villages? That is what Hughes discusses.

THE NATIONAL SOCIALIST GOVERNMENT OF GERMANY, with the arm of its fanatical inner sect, the S.S., commonly known as the Brown Shirts or Elite Guard, perpetrated and boasted of the most colossal and dramatic piece of social dirty work the world has ever known. Perhaps there are other claimants to the title, but they could not match this one's combination of mass, speed, and perverse pride in the deed. Nearly all peoples have plenty of cruelty and death to account for. How many Negro Americans have died by the hand of lynching mobs? How many more from unnecessary disease and lack of food or of knowledge of nutrition? How many Russians died to bring about collectivization of land? And who is to blame if there be starving millions in some parts of the world while wheat molds in the fields of other parts?

I do not revive the case of the Nazi *Endlösung* (final solution) of the Jewish problem in order to condemn the Germans, or make them look worse than other peoples, but to recall to our attention dangers which lurk in our midst always. Most of what follows was written after my first post-war visit to Germany in 1948. The impressions were vivid. The facts have not diminished and disappeared with time, as did the stories of alleged German atrocities in Belgium in the first World War. The fuller the record, the worse it gets.

Several millions of people were delivered to the concentration camps, operated under the leadership of Heinrich Himmler with the help of Adolf Eichmann. A few hundred thousand survived in some fashion. Still fewer came out sound of mind and body. A pair of examples, well attested, will show the extreme of perverse cruelty reached by the S.S. guards in charge of the camps. Prisoners were ordered to climb trees; guards whipped them to make them climb faster. Once they were out of reach, other prisoners, also urged by the whip, were put to shaking the trees. When the victims fell, they were kicked to see whether they could rise to their feet. Those too badly injured to get up were shot to death, as useless for work. A not inconsiderable number of prisoners were drowned in pits full of human excrement. These examples are so horrible that your minds will run away from them. You will not, as when you read a slightly salacious novel, imagine the rest. I therefore thrust these examples upon you and insist that the people who thought them up could, and did, improvise others like them, and even worse, from day to day over several years. Many of the victims of the Camps gave up the ghost (this Biblical phrase is the most apt) from a combination of humiliation, starvation, fatigue, and physical abuse. In due time, a policy of mass liquidation in the gas chamber was added to individual virtuosity in cruelty.

This program—for it was a program—of cruelty and murder was carried out in the name of racial superiority and racial purity. It was directed mainly, although by no means exclusively, against Jews, Slavs, and Gypsies. It was thorough. There are few Jews in the territories which were under the control of the Third German Reich—the two Germanys, Holland, Czechoslovakia, Poland, Austria, Hungary. Many Jewish Frenchmen were destroyed. There were concentration camps even in Tunisia and Algeria under the German occupation.

When, during my 1948 visit to Germany, I became more aware of the reactions of ordianry Germans to the horrors of the concentration camps, I found myself asking not the usual question, "How did racial hatred rise to such a high level?" but this one, "How could such dirty work be done among and, in a sense, *by* the millions of ordinary, civilized German people?" Along with this came related questions. How could these millions of ordinary people live in the midst of such cruelty and murder without a general uprising against it and against the people who did it? How, once freed from the regime that did it, could they be apparently so little concerned about it, so toughly silent about it, not only in talking with outsiders— which is easy to understand—but among themselves? How and where could there be found in a modern civilized country the several hundred thousand men and women capable of such work? How were these people so far released from the inhibitions of civilized life as to be able to imagine, let alone perform, the ferocious, obscene, and perverse actions which they did imagine and perform? How could they be kept at such a height of fury through years of having to see daily at close range the human wrecks they made and being often literally spattered with the filth produced and accumulated by their own actions?

You will see that there are here two orders of questions. One set concerns the good people who did not themselves do this work. The other concerns those who did do it. But the two sets are not really separate; for the crucial question concerning the good people is their relation to the people who did the dirty work, with a related one which asks under what circumstances good people let the others get away with such actions.

An easy answer concerning the Germans is that they were not so good after all. We can attribute to them some special inborn or ingrained race consciousness, combined with a penchant for sadistic cruelty and unquestioning acceptance of whatever is done by those who happen to be in authority. Pushed to its extreme, this answer simply makes us, rather than the Germans, the superior race. It is the Nazi tune, put to words of our own.

Now there are deep and stubborn differences between peoples. Their history and culture may make the Germans especially susceptible to the doctrine of their own racial superiority and especially acquiescent to the actions of whoever is in power over them. These are matters deserving of the best study that can be given them. But to say that these things could happen in Germany simply because Germans are different—from us—buttresses their own excuses and lets us off too easily from blame for what happened there and from the question whether it could happen here.

Certainly in their daily practice and expression before the Hitler regime, the Germans showed no more, if as much, hatred of other racial or cultural groups than we did and do. Residential segregation was not marked. Intermarriage was common, and the families of such marriages had an easier social existence than they generally have in America. The racially exclusive club, school, and hotel were much less in evidence than here. And I well remember an evening in 1933 when a Montreal businessman—a very nice man, too—said in our living room, "Why don't we admit that Hitler is doing to the Jews just what we ought to be doing?" That was not an uncommon sentiment, although it may be said in defense of the people who expressed it that they probably did not know and would not have believed the full truth about the Nazi program of destroying Jews. The essential underlying sentiments on racial matters in Germany were not different in kind from those prevailing throughout the western, and especially the Anglo-Saxon, countries. But I do not wish to overemphasize this point. I only want to close one easy way out of serious consideration of the problem of good people and dirty work, by demonstrating that the Germans were and are about as good and about as bad as the rest of us on this matter of racial sentiments and, let us add, their notions of decent human behavior.

But what was the reaction of ordinary Germans to the persecution of the Jews and to the concentration camp mass torture and murder? A conversation between a German schoolteacher, a German architect, and myself gives the essentials in a vivid form. It was in the studio of the architect, and the occasion was a rather casual visit, in Frankfurt am Main in 1948.

The architect: "I am ashamed for my people whenever I think of it. But we didn't know about it. We only learned about all that later. You must remember the pressure we were under; we had to join the party. We had to keep our mouths shut and do as we were told. It was a terrible pressure. Still, I am ashamed. But you see, we had lost our colonies, and our national honor was hurt. And these Nazis exploited that feeling. And the Jews, they *were* a problem. They came from the east. You should see them in Poland; the lowest class of people, full of lice, dirty and poor, running about in their Ghettos in filthy caftans. They came here, and got rich by unbelievable methods after the first war. They occupied all the good places. Why, they were in the proportion of ten to one in medicine and law and government posts!"

At this point the architect hesitated and looked confused. He continued: "Where was I? It is the poor food. You see what misery we are in here, Herr Professor. It often happens that I forget what I was talking about. Where was I now? I have completely forgotten."

(His confusion was, I believe, not at all feigned. Many Germans said they suffered losses of memory such as this, and laid it to their lack of food.)

I said firmly: "You were talking about loss of national honor and how the Jews had got hold of everything."

The architect: "Oh, yes! That was it! Well, of course that was no way to settle the Jewish problem. But there *was* a problem and it had to be settled some way."

The schoolteacher: "Of course, they have Palestine now."

I protested that Palestine would hardly hold them.

The architect: "The professor is right. Palestine can't hold all the Jews. And it was a terrible thing to murder people. But we didn't know it at the time. But I am glad I am alive now. It is an interesting time in men's history. You know, when the Americans came it was like a great release. I really want to see a new ideal in Grmany. I like the freedom that lets me talk to you like this. But, unfortunately this is not the general opinion. Most of my friends really hang on to the old ideas. They can't see any hope, so they hang on to the old ideas."

This scrap of talk gives, I believe, the essential elements as well as the flavor of the German reaction. It checks well with formal studies which have been made, and it varies only in detail from other conversations which I myself recorded in 1948.

One of the most obvious points in it is unwillingness to think about the dirty work done. In this case—perhaps by chance, perhaps not—the good man suffered an actual lapse of memory in the middle of this statement. This seems a simple point. But the psychiatrists have shown that it is less simple than it looks. They have done a good deal of work on the complicated mechanisms by which the individual mind keeps unpleasant or intolerable knowledge from consciousness, and have shown how great may, in some cases, be the consequent loss of effectiveness of the personality. But we have taken collective unwillingness to know unpleasant facts more or less for granted. That people can and do keep a silence about things whose open discussion would threaten the group's conception of itself, and hence its solidarity, is common knowledge. It is a mechanism that operates in every family and in every group which has a sense of group reputation. To break such a silence is considered an attack against the group; a sort of treason, if it be a member of the group who breaks the silence. This common silence allows group fictions to grow up; such as, that grandpa was less a scoundrel and more romantic than he really was. And I think it demonstrable that it operates especially against any expression, except in ritual, of collective guilt. The remarkable thing in present day Germany is not that there is so little reference to something about which people do feel deeply guilty, but that it is talked about at all.

In order to understand this phenomenon we would have to find out who talks about the concentration camp atrocities, in what situations, in what mood, and with what stimulus. On these points I know only my own limited experiences. One of the most moving of these was my first postwar meeting with an elderly professor whom I had known before the Nazi time; he is an heroic soul who did not bow his head during the Nazi time and who keeps it erect now. His first words, spoken with tears in his eyes, were:

"How hard it is to believe that men will be as bad as they say they will. Hitler and his people said: 'Heads will roll,' but how many of us—

even of his bitterest opponents—could really believe that they would do it."

This man could and did speak, in 1948, not only to the likes of me, but to his students, his colleagues, and the public which read his articles, in the most natural way about the Nazi atrocities whenever there was occasion to do it in the course of his tireless effort to reorganize and to bring new life into the German universities. He had neither the compulsion to speak, so that he might excuse and defend himself, nor a conscious or unconscious need to keep silent. Such people were rare; how many there were in Germany I do not know.

Occasions of another kind in which the silence was broken were those where, in class, public lecture, or informal meetings with students, I myself had talked frankly of race relations in other parts of the world, including the lynchings which sometimes occur in my own country and the terrible cruelty visited upon natives in South Africa. This took off the lid of defensiveness, so that a few people would talk quite easily of what happened under the Nazi regime. More common were situations like that with the architect, where I threw in some remark about the atrocities in response to Germans' complaint that the world is abusing them. In such cases, there was usually an expression of shame, accompanied by a variety of excuses (including that of having been kept in ignorance) and followed by a quick turning away from the subject.

Somewhere in consideration of this problem of discussion versus silence we must ask what the good (that is, ordinary) people in Germany did know about these things. It is clear that the S.S kept the more gory details of the concentration camps a close secret. Even high officials of the government, the army, and the Nazi party itself were in some measure held in ignorance, although of course they kept the camps supplied with victims. The common people of Germany knew that the camps existed; most knew people who had disappeared into them; some saw the victims, walking skeletons in rags, being transported in trucks or trains or being herded on the road from station to camp or to work in fields or factories near the camps. Many knew people who had been released from concentration camps; such released persons kept their counsel on pain of death. But secrecy was cultivated and supported by fear and terror. In the absence of a determined and heroic will to know and publish the truth, and in the absence of all the instruments of opposition, the degree of knowledge was undoubtedly low, in spite of the fact that all knew that something both stupendous and horrible was going on; and in spite of the fact that Hitler's *Mein Kampf* and the utterances of his aides said that no fate was too horrible for the Jews and other wrong-headed or inferior people. This must make us ask under what conditions the will to know and to discuss is strong, determined, and effective; this, like most of the important questions I have raised, I leave unanswered except as answers may be contained in the statement of the case.

But to return to our moderately good man, the architect. He insisted over and over again that he did not know, and we may suppose that he knew as much and as little as most Germans. But he also made it quite clear that he wanted something done to the Jews. I have similar statements from people of whom I knew that they had had close Jewish friends before the Nazi time. This raises the whole problem of the extent to which those pariahs who do the dirty work of society are really acting as agents for the rest of us. To talk of this question one must note that, in building up his case, the architect pushed the Jews firmly into an out-group: they were dirty, lousy, and unscrupulous (an odd statement from a resident of Frankfurt, the home of old Jewish merchants and intellectual families long identified with those aspects of culture of which Germans are most proud). Having dissociated himself clearly from these people, and having declared them a problem, he apparently was willing to let someone else do to them the dirty work which he himself would not do, and for which he expressed shame. The case is perhaps analogous to our attitude toward those convicted of crime. From time to time, we get wind of cruelty practiced upon the prisoners in penitentiaries or jails; or, it may be, merely a report that they are ill-fed or that hygienic conditions are not good. Perhaps we do not wish that the prisoners should be cruelly treated or badly fed, but our reaction is probably tempered by a notion that they deserve something, because of some dissociation of them from the in-group of good people. If what they get is worse than what we like to think about, it is a little bit too bad. It is a point on which we are ambivalent. Campaigns for reform of prisons are often followed by counter-campaigns against a too high standard of living for prisoners and against having prisons run by softies. Now the people who run prisons are our agents. Just how far they do or could carry out our wishes is hard to say. The minor prison guard, in boastful justification of some of his more questionable practices, says, in effect: "If those reformers and those big shots upstairs had to live with these birds as I do, they would soon change their fool notions about running a prison." He is suggesting that the good people are either naive or hypocritical. Furthermore, he knows quite well that the wishes of his employers, the public, are by no means unmixed. They are quite as likely to put upon him for being too nice as for being too harsh. And if, as sometimes happens, he is a man disposed to cruelty, there may be some justice in his feeling that he is only doing what others would like to do, if they but dared; and what they would do, if they were in his place.

There are plenty of examples in our own world which I might have picked for comparison with the German attitude toward the concentration camps. For instance, a newspaper in Denver made a great scandal out of the allegation that our Japanese compatriots were too well fed in the camps where they were concentrated during the war. I might have mentioned some feature of the sorry history of the people of Japanese background in Canada. Or it might have been lynching, or some aspect of racial discrimination. But I purposely chose prisoners convicted of crime. For convicts are formally set aside for special handling. They constitute an out-group in all countries. This brings the issue clearly before us, since few people cherish the illusion that the problem of treating criminals can be settled by propaganda designed to prove that there aren't any criminals. Almost everyone agrees that something has to be done about them. The question concerns what is done, who does it, and the nature of the mandate given by the rest of us to those who do it. Perhaps we give them an unconscious mandate to go beyond anything we ourselves would care to do or even to acknowledge. I venture to suggest that the higher and more expert functionaries who act in our behalf represent something of a distillation of what we may consider our public wishes, while some of the others show a sort of concentrate of those impulses of which we are or wish to be less aware.

Now the choice of convicted prisoners brings up another crucial point in intergroup relations. All societies of any great size have in-groups and out-groups; in fact, one of the best ways of describing a society is to consider it a network of smaller and larger in-groups and out-groups. And an in-group is one only because there are out-groups. When I refer to *my* children I obviously imply that they are closer to me than other people's children and that I will make greater efforts to buy oranges and cod-liver oil for them than for others' children. In fact, it may mean that I will give them cod-liver oil if I have to choke them to get it down. We do our own dirty work on those closest to us. The very injunction that I love my neighbor as myself starts with me; if I don't love myself and my nearest, the phrase has a very sour meaning.

Each of us is a center of a network of in- and out-groups. Now the distinctions between *in* and *out* may be drawn in various ways, and nothing is more important for both the student of society and the educator than to discover how these lines are made and how they may be redrawn in more just and sensible ways. But to believe that we can do away with the distinction between *in* and *out*, *us* and *them* in social life is complete nonsense. On the positive side, we generally feel a greater obligation to in-groups; hence less obligation to out-groups; and in the case of such groups as convicted criminals, the out-group is definitely given over to the hands of our agents for punishment. That is the extreme case. But there are other out-groups toward which we may have aggressive feelings and dislike, although we give no formal mandate to anyone to deal with them on our behalf, and although we profess to believe that they should not suffer restrictions or disadvantages. The greater their social distance from us, the more we leave in the hands of others a sort of mandate by default to deal with them on our behalf. Whatever effort we put on reconstructing the lines which divide in- and out-groups, there remains the eternal problem of our treatment, direct or delegated, of whatever groups are considered somewhat outside. And here it is that the whole matter of our professed and possible deeper unprofessed wishes comes up for consideration; and the related problem of what we know, can know, and want to know about it. In Germany, the agents got out of hand and created such terror that it was best not to know. It is also clear that it was and is easier to the conscience of many Germans not to know. It is, finally, not unjust to say that the agents were at least working in the direction of the wishes of many people, although they may have gone beyond the wishes of most. The same questions can be asked about our own society, and with reference not only to prisoners but also to many other groups upon whom there is no legal or moral stigma. Again I have not the answers. I leave you to search for them.

In considering the question of dirty work we have eventually to think about the people who do it. In Germany, these were the members of the S.S. and of that inner group of the S.S. who operated the concentration camps. Many reports have been made on the social backgrounds and the personalities of these cruel fanatics. Those who have studied them say that a large proportion were "gescheiterte Existenzen," men and women with a history of failure, of poor adaptation to the demands of work and of the classes of society in which they had been bred. Germany between wars had large numbers of such people. Their adherence to a movement which proclaimed a doctrine of hatred was natural enough. The movement offered something more. It created an inner group which was to be superior to all others, even Germans, in their emancipation from the usual bourgeois morality; people above and beyond the ordinary morality. I dwell on this, not as a doctrine, but as an organizational device. For, as Eugen Kogon, author of the most penetrating analysis of the S.S. and their camps, has said, the Nazis came to power by creating a state within a state; a body with its own counter-morality, and its own counter-law, its courts and its own execution of sentence upon those who did not live up to its orders and standards. Even as a movement, it had inner circles within inner circles; each sworn to secrecy as against the next outer one. The struggle between these inner circles continued after Hitler came to power: Himmler eventually won the day. His S.S. became a state within the Nazi state, just as the Nazi movement had become a state within the Weimar state. One is reminded of the oft-quoted but neglected statement of Sighele: "At the center of a crowd look for the sect." He referred, of course, to the political sect; the fanatical inner group of a movement seeking power by revolutionary methods. Once the Nazis were in power, this inner sect, while becoming now the recognized agent of the state and, hence, of the masses of the people, could at the same time dissociate itself more completely from them in action, because of the very fact of having a mandate. It was now beyond all danger of interference and investigation. For it had the instruments of interference and investigation its own hands. These are also the instruments of secrecy. So the S.S. could and did build up a powerful system in which they had the resources of the state and of the economy of Germany and the conquered countries from which to steal all that was needed to carry out their orgy of cruelty luxuriously as well as with impunity.

Now let us ask, concerning the dirty workers, questions similar to those concerning the good people. Is there a supply of candidates for such work in other societies? It would be easy to say that only Germany could produce such a crop. The question is answered by being put. The problem of people who have run aground (gescheiterte Existenzen) is one of the most serious in our modern societies. Any psychiatrist will, I believe, testify that we have a sufficient pool or fund of personalities warped toward perverse punishment and cruelty to do any amount of dirty work that the good people may be inclined to countenance. It would not take a very great turn of events to increase the number of such people, and to bring their discontents to the surface. This is not to suggest that every movement based on discontent with the present state of things will be led by such people. That is obviously untrue; and I emphasize the point lest my remarks give comfort to those who would damn all who express militant discontent. But I think study of militant social movements does show that these warped people seek a place in them. Specifically, they are likely to become the plotting, secret police of the group. It is one of the problems of militant social movements to keep such people out. It is of course easier to do this if the spirit of the movement is positive, its conception of humanity high and inclusive, and its aims sound. This was not the case of the Nazi movement. As Kogon puts it: "The SS were but the arch-type of the Nazis in general." But such people are sometimes attracted, for want of something better, to movements whose aims are contrary to the spirit of cruelty and punishment. I would suggest that all of us look well at the leadership and entourage of movements to which we attach ourselves for signs of a negativistic, punishing attitude. For once such a spirit develops in a movement, punishment of the nearest and easiest victim is likely to become more attractive than striving for the essential goals. And, if the Nazi movement teaches us anything at all, it is that if any shadow of a mandate be given to such people, they will—having compromised us—make it larger and larger. The processes by which they do so are the development of the power and inward discipline of their own group, a progressive dissociation of themselves from the rules of human decency prevalent in their culture, and an ever growing contempt for the welfare of the masses of people.

The power and inward discipline of the S.S. became such that those who once became members could get out only by death; by suicide, murder, or mental breakdown. Orders from the central offices of the S.S. were couched in equivocal terms as a hedge against a possible day of judgment. When it became clear that such a day of judgment would come, the hedging and intrigue became greater; the urge to murder also became greater, because every prisoner became a potential witness.

Again we are dealing with a phenomenon common in all societies.

Almost every group which has a specialized social function to perform is in some measure a secret society, with a body of rules developed and enforced by the members and with some power to save its members from outside punishment. And here is one of the paradoxes of social order. A society without smaller rule-making and disciplining powers would be no society at all. There would be nothing but law and police; and this is what the Nazis strove for, at the expense of family, church, professional groups, parties, and other such nuclei of spontaneous control. But apparently the only way to do this, for good as well as for evil ends, is to give power into the hands of some fanatical small group which will have a far greater power of self-discipline and a far greater immunity from outside control than the traditional groups. The problem is, then, not of trying to get rid of all the self-disciplining, protecting groups within society, but one of keeping them integrated with one another and as sensitive as can be to a public opinion which transcends them all. It is a matter of checks and balances, of what we might call the social and moral constitution of society. . . .

PART VIII Social Institutions

$\mathbf{A}$ T FIRST GLANCE THE TERM "social institutions" appears far removed from everyday life. But in fact this term refers to concrete and highly relevant realities that profoundly affect our lives. Parents and their children, the basic family unit, constitute a social institution. So does the church, with its sacred books, clergy, and worship; and the law, with its police, lawyers, judges, courts, and prisons. Social institutions also means politics, the gamut of the American political process (including broken campaign promises), Congress, and the president and his Cabinet. Too, social institutions means the economic order, with new plants opening and old ones closing; working for a living; and drawing unemployment or welfare or a pension. Schools, colleges, and universities—places where people are socialized (as sociologists phrase the matter) or where they go to learn (as most other people put it)—also are examples of social institutions. Further, social institutions refers to science, with its test tubes and experiments, interviewers and questionnaires. It means doctors and nurses and hospitals, as well as the patients they treat, and the Medicare and Blue Cross and Blue Shield that people struggle to pay for in order to keep the American medical enterprise from destroying their present and future finances. And social institutions means the military, with its generals and privates and tanks and planes, and the whole war game that at times threatens to become too real. Far from being removed from life, then, social institutions means all these things—and more.

To understand social life it is necessary to understand the institutions of a society. It is not enough to understand what people do when they are in one another's presence. That certainly is significant, but it is only part of the picture. *Social institutions provide the structure within which people live their lives.*

377

The characteristics of a society's institutions, in fact, dictate much of that interaction. For example, because of the way our economic order is arranged, we normally work eight hours a day, are off 16, and repeat this pattern five days a week. There is nothing natural about such a pattern. Its regularity is but an arbitrarily imposed temporal arrangement for work, leisure, and personal concerns. Yet this one aspect of a single social institution has far-reaching effects on how we structure our own time and activities, how we deal with our family and friends, how we meet our personal needs and nonwork obligations, and indeed on how we view time and life.

Each social institution has similarly far-reaching effects on our lives and viewpoints. By shaping our society as a whole and establishing the context in which we live, these institutions give form to almost everything that is of concern to us. We can, in fact, say that if the social institutions of our society were different, we would be different people. We certainly could not be the same, for our ideas and attitudes and other orientations to the social world, and even to life itself, would be changed.

One of the most significant aspects of American social institutions is their arrangement into primary and secondary institutions. The *primary* social institutions are the economy, the political system, and the military establishment. According to *conflict theory,* it is these which dominate our society. The top leaders of these three social institutions make the major decisions that have the greatest impact on society. These three are far-reaching, not only for our society but also for the rest of the world.

The *secondary* social institutions are the others: education, religion, sports, medicine, and law. As the name implies, they are secondary in power, and, as conflict theorists stress, these secondary social institutions exist to serve the primary. According to conflict theory, the family produces workers (for the economy), voters and tax payers (for the political system), and soldiers (for the military); the religious institution instills patriotism and acceptance of the current arrangement of power; sports take people's minds off their problems so they can do better jobs in the work force; the medical institution produces wealth for people already wealthy and patches people up so they can continue working; and the law keeps the poor under its yoke so they don't rebel and upset current power arrangements.

To lead off this Part, Harry L. Gracey examines education from the conflict perspective. He focuses on kindergarten, analyzing it as the means by which children learn the student role—so they can become conformists in an educational system designed, in turn, to teach them to take a "proper" place in life. Arlie Hochschild and Anne Machung then turn to the family, examining the basic struggle of husbands and wives over housework.

Then, to turn the focus onto the religious institution, Lawrence K. Hong and Marion V. Dearman analyze streetcorner preachers, looking at their approaches, motives, views, and relationships. To represent the social institution of sports, Douglas E. Foley examines the role of football in a Texas school and community—uncovering its relationship to the reproduction of gender, race, and social class. Jack Haas and William Shaffir present an analysis of the medical institution, focusing on how medical students learn "the cloak of competence." Jennifer Hunt then examines the legal institution, looking at the how and why of police violence. Finally, C. Wright Mills concludes this Part with a penetrating and disturbing analysis of interrelationships among our military, economic, and political institutions, a partially subterranean intertwining that vitally affects the daily lives—and the future—of us all.

33 Learning the Student Role: Kindergarten as Academic Boot Camp

HARRY L. GRACEY

As we have seen in the preceding Parts, each society (and each group) maintains a vital interest in making people conform to expectations. A major social institution for which conformity is a primary goal is education. Educators want to graduate people who are acceptable to the community, not only in terms of marketable skills but also in terms of their ideas, attitudes, and behaviors. Whether it be grade school, high school, or college, educational administrators want instructors to teach standard ideas and facts, to steer clear of radical politics, and to not stir up trouble in the school or community. *Then* the social institution can go about its business—and that business, when you delve beyond offical utterances and uncover the "hidden curriculum," is producing conformists who fit well in society.

Although Gracey's focus is kindergarten, this article was chosen to represent the educational institution because it focuses on this essential nature of education, training in conformity. The primary goal of kindergarten is to teach children to be students—so they can participate in conformity. If this is what education really is about, where are intellectual stimulation, the excitement of discovery, and creativity—long associated in the public mind with education? The answer is that they may occur so long as they are noncontroversial. In other words they, too, are expected to reflect the conformist nature of the educational institution.

Basing your thinking on your own extensive experiences with education, how do you react to the idea that the essence of the educational institution is training into conformity?

EDUCATION MUST BE CONSIDERED one of the major institutions of social life today. Along with the family and organized religion, however, it is a "secondary institution," one in which people are prepared for life in society as it is presently organized. The main dimensions of modern life, that is, the nature of society as a whole, is determined principally by the "primary institutions," which today are the economy, the political system, and the military establishment. Education has been defined by sociologists, classical and contemporary, as an institution which serves society by socializing people into it through a formalized, standardized procedure. At the beginning of this century Emile Durkheim told student teachers at the University of Paris that education "consists of a methodical socialization of the younger generation." He went on to add:

> It is the influence exercised by adult generations on those that are not ready for social life. Its object is to arouse and to develop in the child a certain number of physical, intellectual, and moral states that are demanded of him by the political society as a whole and by the special milieu for which he is specifically destined. . . . To the egotistic and asocial being that has just been born, [society] must, as rapidly as possible, add another, capable of leading a moral and social life. Such is the work of education.[1]

The education process, Durkheim said, "is above all the means by which society perpetually recreates the conditions of its very existence."[2] The contemporary educational sociologist, Wilbur Brookover, offers a similar formulation in his recent textbook definition of education:

> Actually, therefore, in the broadest sense education is synonymous with socialization. It includes any social behavior that assists in the induction of the child into membership in the society or any behavior by which the society perpetuates itself through the next generation.[3]

The educational institution is, then, one of the ways in which society is perpetuated through the systematic socialization of the young, while the nature of the society which is being perpetuated—its organization and operation, its values, beliefs and ways of living—are determined by the primary institutions. The educational system, like other secondary institutions, *serves* the society which is *created* by the operation of the economy, the political system, and the military establishment.

Schools, the social organizations of the educational institution, are today for the most part large bureaucracies run by specially trained and certified people. There are few places left in modern societies where formal teaching and learning is carried on in small, isolated groups, like the rural, one-room schoolhouses of the last century. Schools are large, formal organizations which tend to be parts of larger organizations, local community School Districts. These School Districts are bureaucratically organized and their operations are supervised by state and local governments. In this context, as Brookover says:

> The term education is used . . . to refer to a system of schools, in which specifically designated persons are expected to teach children and youth certain types of acceptable behavior. The school system becomes a . . . unit in the

total social structure and is recognized by the members of the society as a separate social institution. Within this structure a portion of the total socialization process occurs.[4]

Education is the part of the socialization process which takes place in the schools; and these are, more and more today, bureaucracies within bureaucracies.

Kindergarten is generally conceived by educators as a year of preparation for school. It is thought of as a year in which small children, five or six years old, are prepared socially and emotionally for the academic learning which will take place over the next twelve years. It is expected that a foundation of behavior and attitudes will be laid in kindergarten on which the children can acquire the skills and knowledge they will be taught in the grades. A booklet prepared for parents by the staff of a suburban New York school system says that the kindergarten experience will stimulate the child's desire to learn and cultivate the skills he will need for learning in the rest of his school career. It claims that the child will find opportunities for physical growth, for satisfying his "need for self-expression," acquire some knowledge, and provide opportunities for creative activity. It concludes, "The most important benefit that your five-year-old will receive from kindergarten is the opportunity to live and grow happily and purposefully with others in a small society." The kindergarten teachers in one of the elementary schools in this community, one we shall call the Wilbur Wright School, said their goals were to see that the children "grew" in all ways: physically, of course, emotionally, socially, and academically. They said they wanted children to like school as a result of their kindergarten experiences and that they wanted them to learn to get along with others.

None of these goals, however, is unique to kindergarten; each of them is held to some extent by teachers in the other six grades at Wright School. And growth would occur, but differently, even if the child did not attend school. The children already know how to get along with others, in their families and their play groups. The unique job of the kindergarten in the educational division of labor seems rather to be teaching children the student role. The student role is the repertoire of behavior and attitudes regarded by educators as appropriate to children in school. Observation in the kindergartens of the Wilbur Wright School revealed a great variety of activities through which children are shown and then drilled in the behavior and attitudes defined as appropriate for school and thereby induced to learn the role of student. Observations of the kindergartens and interviews with the teachers both pointed to the teaching and learning of classroom routines as the main element of the student role. The teachers expended most of their efforts, for the first half of the year at least, in training the children to follow the routines which teachers created. The children were, in a very real sense, *drilled* in tasks and activities created by the teachers for their own purposes and beginning and ending quite arbitrarily (from the child's point of view) at the command of the teacher. One teacher remarked that she hated September, because during the first month "everything has to be done rigidly, and repeatedly, until they know exactly what they're supposed to do." However, "by January," she said, "they know exactly what to do [during the day] and I don't have to be after them all the time." Classroom routines were introduced gradually from the beginning of the year in all the kindergartens, and the children were drilled in them as long as was necessary to achieve regular compliance. By the end of the school year, the successful kindergarten teacher has a well-organized group of children. They follow classroom routines automatically, having learned all the command signals and the expected responses to them. They have, in our terms, learned the student role. The following observation shows one such classroom operating at optimum organization on an afternoon late in May. It is the class of an experienced and respected kindergarten teacher.

An Afternoon in Kindergarten

At about 12:20 in the afternoon on a day in the last week of May, Edith Kerr leaves the teachers' room where she has been having lunch and walks to her classroom at the far end of the primary wing of Wright School. A group of five- and six-year-olds peers at her through the glass doors leading from the hall cloakroom to the play area outside. Entering her room, she straightens some material in the "book corner" of the room, arranges music on the piano, takes colored paper from her closet and places it on one of the shelves under the window. Her room is divided into a number of activity areas through the arrangement of furniture and play equipment. Two easels and a paint table near the door create a kind of passageway inside the room. A wedge-shaped area just inside the front door is made into a teacher's area by the placing of "her" things there: her desk, file, and piano. To the left is the book corner, marked off from the rest of the room by a puppet stage and a movable chalkboard. In it are a display rack of picture books, a record player, and a stack of children's records. To the right of the entrance are the sink and clean-up area. Four large round tables with six chairs at each for the children are placed near the walls about halfway down the length of the room, two on each side, leaving a large open area in the center for group games, block building, and toy truck driving. Windows stretch down the length of both walls, starting about three feet from the floor and extending almost to the high ceilings. Under the windows are long shelves on which are kept all the toys, games, blocks, paper, paints and other equipment of the kindergarten. The left rear corner of the room is a play store with shelves, merchandise, and cash register; the right rear corner is a play kitchen with stove, sink, ironing board, and bassinette with baby dolls in it. This area is partly shielded from the rest of the room by a large standing display rack for posters and children's art work. A sandbox is found against the back wall between these two areas. The room is light, brightly colored and filled with things adults feel five- and six-year-olds will find interesting and pleasing.

At 12:25 Edith opens the outside door and admits the waiting children. They hang their sweaters on hooks outside the door and then go to the center of the room and arrange themselves in a semi-circle on the floor, facing the teacher's chair, which she has placed in the center of the floor. Edith follows them in and sits in her chair checking attendance while waiting for the bell to ring. When she has finished attendance, which she takes by sight, she asks the children what the date is, what day and month it is, how many children are enrolled in the class, how many are present, and how many are absent.

The bell rings at 12:30 and the teacher puts away her attendance book. She introduces a visitor, who is sitting against the wall taking notes, as someone who wants to learn about schools and children. She then goes to the back of the room and takes down a large chart labeled "Helping Hands." Bringing it to the center of the room, she tells the children it is time to change jobs. Each child is assigned some task on the chart by placing his name, lettered on a paper "hand," next to a picture signifying the task— e.g., a broom, a blackboard, a milk bottle, a flag, and a Bible. She asks the children who wants each of the jobs and rearranges their "hands" accordingly. Returning to her chair, Edith announces, "One person should tell us what happened to Mark." A girl raises her hand, and when called on says, "Mark fell and hit his head and had to go to the hospital." The teacher adds that Mark's mother had written saying he was in the hospital.

During this time the children have been interacting among themselves, in their semi-circle. Children have whispered to their neighbors, poked one another, made general comments to the group, waved to friends on the other side of the circle. None of this has been disruptive, and the teacher has ignored it for the most part. The children seem to know just how much of each kind of interaction is permitted—they may greet in a soft voice someone who sits next to them, for example, but may not shout greetings to a friend who sits across the circle, so they confine themselves to waving and remain well within understood limits.

At 12:35 two children arrive. Edith asks them why they are late and then sends them to join the circle on the floor. The other children vie with each other to tell the newcomers what happened to Mark. When this leads to a general disorder Edith asks, "Who has serious time?" The children become quiet and a girl raises her hand. Edith nods and the child gets a Bible and hands it to Edith. She reads the Twenty-third Psalm while the children sit quietly. Edith helps the child in charge begin reciting the Lord's Prayer; the other children follow along for the first unit of sounds, and then trail off as Edith finishes for them. Everyone stands and faces the American flag hung to the right of the door. Edith leads the pledge to the flag, with the children again following the familiar sounds as far as they remember them. Edith then asks the girl in charge what song she wants and the child replies, "My Country." Edith goes to the piano and plays "America," singing as the children follow her words.

Edith returns to her chair in the center of the room and the children sit again in the semi-circle on the floor. It is 12:40 when she tells the children, "Let's have boys' sharing time first." She calls the name of the first boy sitting on the end of the circle, and he comes up to her with a toy helicopter. He turns and holds it up for the other children to see. He says, "It's a helicopter." Edith asks, "What is it used for?" and he replies, "For the army. Carry men. For the war." Other children join in, "For shooting submarines." "To bring back men from space when they are in the ocean." Edith sends the boy back to the circle and asks the next boy if he has something. He replies "No" and she passes on to the next. He says "Yes" and brings a bird's nest to her. He holds it for the class to see, and the teacher asks, "What kind of bird made the nest?" The boy replies, "My friend says a rain bird made it." Edith asks what the nest is made of and different children reply, "mud," "leaves" and "sticks." There is also a bit of moss woven into the nest and Edith tries to describe it to the children. They, however, are more interested in seeing if anything is inside it, and Edith lets the boy carry it around the semi-cricle showing the children its insides. Edith tells the children of some baby robins in a nest in her yard, and some of the children tell about baby birds they have seen. Some children are asking about a small object in the nest which they say looks like an egg, but all have seen the nest now and Edith calls on the next boy. A number of children say, "I know what Michael has, but I'm not telling." Michael brings a book to the teacher and then goes back to his place in the circle of children. Edith reads the last page of the book to the class. Some children tell of books which they have at home. Edith calls the next boy, and three children call out, "I know what David has." "He always has the same thing." "It's a bang-bang." David goes to his table and gets a box which he brings to Edith. He opens it and shows the teacher a scale-model of an old-fashioned dueling pistol. When David does not turn around to the class, Edith tells him, "Show it to the children" and he does. One child says, "Mr. Johnson [the principal] said no guns." Edith replies, "Yes, how many of you know that?" Most of the children in the circle raise their hands. She continues, "That you aren't supposed to bring guns to school?" She calls the next boy on the circle and he brings two large toy soldiers to her which the children enthusiastically identify as being from "Babes in Toyland." The next boy brings an American flag to Edith and shows it to the class. She asks him what the stars and stripes stand for and admonishes him to treat it carefully. "Why should you treat it carefully?" she asks the boy. "Because it's our flag," he replies. She congratulates him, saying, "That's right."

"Show and Tell" lasted twenty minutes and during the last ten one girl in particular announced that she knew what each child called upon had to show. Edith asked her to be quiet each time she spoke out, but she was not content, continuing to offer her comment at each "show." Four children from other classes had come into the room to bring something from another teacher or to ask for something from Edith. Those with requests were asked to return later if the item wasn't readily available.

Edith now asks if any of the children told their mothers about their trip to the local zoo the previous day. Many children raise their hands. As Edith calls on them, they tell what they liked in the zoo. Some children cannot wait to be called on, and they call out things to the teacher, who asks them to be quiet. After a few of the animals are mentioned, one child says, "I liked the spooky house," and the others chime in to agree with him, some pantomiming fear and horror. Edith is puzzled, and asks what this was. When half the children try to tell her at once, she raises her hand for quiet, then calls on individual children. One says, "The house with nobody in it"; another, "The dark little house." Edith asks where it was in the zoo, but the children cannot describe its location in any way which she can understand. Edith makes some jokes but they involve adult abstractions which the children cannot grasp. The children have become quite noisy now, speaking out to make both relevant and irrelevant comments, and three little girls have become particularly assertive.

Edith gets up from her seat at 1:10 and goes to the book corner, where she puts a record on the player. As it begins a story about the trip to the zoo, she returns to the circle and asks the children to go sit at the tables. She divides them among the tables in such a way as to indicate that they don't have regular seats. When the children are all seated at the four tables, five or six to a table, the teacher asks, "Who wants to be the first one?" One of the noisy girls comes to the center of the room. The voice on the record is giving directions for imitating an ostrich and the girl follows them, walking around the center of the room holding her ankles with her hands. Edith replays the record, and all the children, table by table, imitate ostriches down the center of the room and back. Edith removes her shoes and shows that she can be an ostrich too. This is apparently a familiar game, for a number of children are calling out, "Can we have the crab?" Edith asks one of the children to do a crab "so we can all remember how," and then plays the part of the record with music for imitating crabs by. The children from the first table line up across the room, hands and feet on the floor and faces pointing toward the ceiling. After they have "walked" down the room and back in this posture they sit at their table and the children of the next table play "crab." The children love this; they run from their tables, dance about on the floor waiting for their turns and are generally exuberant. Children ask for the "inch worm" and the game is played again with the children squirming down the floor. As a conclusion Edith shows them a new animal imitation, the "lame dog." The children all hobble down the floor on three "legs," table by table to the accompaniment of the record.

At 1:30 Edith has the children line up in the center of the room: she says, "Table one, line up in front of me," and children ask, "What are we going to do?" Then she moves a few steps to the side and says, "Table two over here, line up next to table one," and more children ask, "What for?" She does this for table three and table four and each time the children ask, "Why, what are we going to do?" When the children are lined up in four lines of five each, spaced so that they are not touching one another, Edith puts on a new record and leads the class in calisthenics, to the accompaniment of the record. The children just jump around every which way in their places instead of doing the exercises, and by the time the record is finished, Edith, the only one following it, seems exhausted. She is apparently adopting the President's new "Physical Fitness" program for her classroom.

At 1:35 Edith pulls her chair to the easels and calls the children to sit on the floor in front of her, table by table. When they are all seated she asks, "What are you going to do for worktime today?" Different children raise their hands and tell Edith what they are going to draw. Most are going to make pictures of animals they saw in the zoo. Edith asks if they want to make pictures to send to Mark in the hospital, and the children agree to this. Edith gives drawing paper to the children, calling them to her one by one. After getting a piece of paper, the children go to the crayon box on the righthand shelves, select a number of colors, and go to the tables, where they begin drawing. Edith is again trying to quiet the perpetually talking girls. She keeps two of them standing by her so they won't disrupt the others. She asks them, "Why do you feel you have to talk all the time?" and then scolds them for not listening to her. Then she sends them to their tables to draw.

Most of the children are drawing at their tables, sitting or kneeling in their chairs. They are all working very industriously and, engrossed in their work, very quietly. Three girls have chosen to paint at the easels, and having donned their smocks, they are busily mixing colors and intently applying them to their pictures. If the children at the tables are primitives and neo-realists in their animal depictions, these girls at the easels are the class abstract-expressionists, with their broad-stroked, colorful paintings.

Edith asks of the children generally, "What color should I make the cover of Mark's book? Brown and green are suggested by some children "because Mark likes them." The other children are puzzled as to just what is going on and ask, "What book?" or "What does she mean?" Edith explains what she thought was clear to them already, that they are all going to put their pictures together in a "book" to be sent to Mark. She goes to a small table in the play-kitchen corner and tells the children to bring her their pictures when they are finished and she will write their message for Mark on them.

By 1:50 most children have finished their pictures and given them to Edith. She talks with some of them as she ties the bundle of pictures together—answering questions, listening, carrying on conversations. The children are playing in various parts of the room with toys, games and blocks which they have taken off the shelves. They also move from table to table examining each other's pictures, offering compliments and suggestions. Three girls at a table are cutting up colored paper for a collage. Another girl is walking about the room in a pair of high heels with a woman's purse over her arm. Three boys are playing in the center of the room with the large block set, with which they are building walk-ways and walking on them. Edith is very much concerned about their safety and comes over a number of times to fuss over then. Two or three other boys are pushing trucks around the center of the room, and mild altercations occur when they drive through the block constructions. Some boys and girls are playing at the toy store, two girls are serving "tea" in the play kitchen and one is washing a doll baby. Two boys have elected to clean the room, and with large sponges they wash the movable blackboard, the puppet stage, and then begin on the tables. They run into resistance from the children who are working with construction toys on the tables and do not want to dismantle their structures. The class is like a room full of bees, each intent on pursuing some activity, occasionally bumping into one another, but just veering off in another direction without serious altercation. At 2:05 the custodian arrives pushing a cart loaded with half-pint milk containers. He places a tray of cartons on the counter next to the sink, then leaves. His coming and going is unnoticed in the room (as, incidentally, is the presence of the observer, who is completely ignored by the children for the entire afternoon).

At 2:15 Edith walks to the entrance of the room, switches off the lights, and sits at the piano and plays. The children begin spontaneously singing the song, which is "Clean up, clean up. Everybody clean up." Edith walks around the room supervising the clean-up. Some children put their toys, the blocks, puzzles, games, and so on back on their shelves under the windows. The children making a collage keep right on working. A child from another class comes in to borrow the 45-rpm adaptor for the record player. At more urging from Edith the rest of the children shelve their toys and work. The children are sitting around their tables now and Edith asks, "What record would you like to hear while you have your milk?" There is some confusion and no general consensus, so Edith drops the subject and begins to call the children, table by table, to come get their milk. "Table one," she says, and the five children come to the sink, wash their hands and dry them, pick up a carton of milk and a straw, and take it back to their table. Two talking girls wander about the room interfering with the children getting their milk and Edith calls out to them to "settle down." As the children sit many of them call out to Edith the name of the record they want to hear. When all the children are seated at tables with milk, Edith plays one of these records called "Bozo and the Birds" and shows the children pictures in a book which go with the record. The record recites, and the book shows the adventures of a clown, Bozo, as he walks through a woods meeting many different kinds of birds who, of course, display the characteristics of many kinds of people or, more accurately, different sterotypes. As children finish their milk they take blankets or pads from the shelves under the windows and lie on them in the center of the room, where Edith sits on her chair showing the pictures. By 2:30 half the class is lying on the floor on their blankets, the record is still playing and the teacher is turning the pages of the book. The child who came in previously returns the 45-rpm adaptor, and one of the kindergartners tells Edith what the boy's name is and where he lives.

The record ends at 2:40. Edith says, "Children, down on your blankets." All the class is lying on blankets now, Edith refuses to answer the various questions individual children put to her because, she tells them, "it's rest time now." Instead she talks very softly about what they will do tomorrow. They are going to work with clay, she says. The children lie quietly and listen. One of the boys raises his hand and when called on tells Edith, "The animals in the zoo looked so hungry yesterday." Edith asks the children what they think about this and a number try to volunteer opinions, but Edith accepts only those offered in a "rest-time tone," that is, softly and quietly. After a brief discussion of animal feeding, Edith calls the names of the two children on milk detail and has them collect empty milk cartons from the tables and return them to the tray. She asks the two children on clean-up detail to clean up the room. Then she gets up from her chair and goes to the door to turn on the lights. At this signal the children all get up from the floor and return their blankets and pads to the shelf. It is raining (the reason for no outside play this afternoon) and cars driven by mothers clog the school drive and line up along the street. One of the talkative little girls comes over to Edith and pointing out the window says, "Mrs. Kerr, see my mother in the new Cadillac?"

At 2:50 Edith sits at the piano and plays. The children sit on the floor in the center of the room and sing. They have a repertoire of songs about animals, including one in which each child sings a refrain alone. They know these by heart and sing along through the ringing of the 2:55 bell. When the song is finished, Edith gets up and coming to the group says, "Okay, rhyming words to get your coats today." The children raise their hands and as Edith calls on them, they tell her two rhyming words, after which they are allowed to go into the hall to get their coats and sweaters. They return to the room with these and sit at their tables. At 2:59 Edith says. "When you have your coats on, you may line up at the door." Half of the children go to the door and stand in a long line.

When the three o'clock bell rings, Edith returns to the piano and plays. The children sing a song called "Goodbye," after which Edith sends them out.

Training for Learning and for Life

The day in kindergarten at Wright School illustrates both the content of the student role as it has been learned by these children and the processes by which the teacher has brought about this learning, or, "taught" them the student role. The children have learned to go through routines and to follow orders with unquestioning obedience, even when these make no sense to them. They have been disciplined to do as they are told by an authoritative person without significant protest. Edith has developed this discipline in the children by creating and enforcing a rigid social structure in the classroom through which she effectively controls the behavior of most of the children for most of the school day. The "living with others in a small society" which the school pamphlet tells parents is the most important thing the children will learn in kindergarten can be seen now in its operational meaning, which is learning to live by the routines imposed by the school. This learning appears to be the principal content of the student role.

Children who submit to school-imposed discipline and come to identify with it, so that being a "good student" comes to be an important part of their developing identities, *become* the good students by the school's definitions. Those who submit to the routines of the school but do not come to identify with them will be adequate students who find the more important part of their identities elsewhere, such as in the play group outside school. Children who refuse to submit to the school routines are rebels, who become known as "bad students" and often "problem children" in the school, for they do not learn the academic curriculum and their behavior is often disruptive in the classroom. Today schools engage clinical psychologists in part to help teachers deal with such children.

In looking at Edith's kindergarten at Wright School, it is interesting to ask how the children learn this role of student—come to accept school-imposed routines—and what, exactly, it involves in terms of behavior and attitudes. The most prominent features of the classroom are its physical and social structures. The room is carefully furnished and arranged in ways adults feel will interest children. The play store and play kitchen in the back of the room, for example, imply that children are interested in mimicking these activities of the adult world. The only space left for the children to create something of their own is the empty center of the room, and the materials at their disposal are the blocks, whose use causes anxiety on the part of the teacher. The room, being carefully organized physically by the adults, leaves little room for the creation of physical organization on the part of the children.

The social structure created by Edith is a far more powerful and subtle force for fitting the children to the student role. This structure is established by the very rigid and tightly controlled set of rituals and routines through which the children are put during the day. There is first the rigid "locating procedure" in which the children are asked to find themselves in terms of the month, date, day of the week, and the number of the class who are present and absent. This puts them solidly in the real world as defined by adults. The day is then divided into six periods whose activities are for the most part determined by the teacher. In Edith's kindergarten the children went through Serious Time, which opens the school day, Sharing Time, Play Time (which in clear weather would be spent outside), Work Time, Clean-up Time, after which they have their milk, and Rest Time, after which they go home. The teacher has programmed activities for each of these Times.

Occasionally the class is allowed limited discretion to choose between proffered activities, such as stories or records, but original ideas for activities are never solicited from them. Opportunity for free individual action is open only once in the day, during the part of Work Time left after the general class assignment has been completed (on the day reported the class assignment was drawing animal pictures for the absent Mark). Spontaneous interests or observations from the children are never developed by the teacher. It seems that her schedule just does not allow room for developing such unplanned events. During Sharing Time, for example, the child who brought a bird's nest told Edith, in reply to her question of what kind of bird made it, "My friend says it's a rain bird." Edith does not think to ask about this bird, probably because the answer is "childish," that is, not given in accepted adult categories of birds. The children then express great interest in an object in the nest, but the teacher ignores this interest, probably because the object is uninteresting to her. The soldiers from "Babes in Toyland" strike a responsive note in the children, but this is not used for a discussion of any kind. The soldiers are treated in the same way as objects which bring little interest from the children. Finally, at the end of Sharing Time the child-world of perception literally erupts in the class with the recollection of "the spooky house" at the zoo. Apparently this made more of an impression on the children than did any of the animals, but Edith is unable to make any sense of it for herself. The tightly imposed order of the class begins to break down as the children discover a universe of discourse of their own and begin talking excitedly with one another. The teacher is effectively excluded from this child's world of perception and for a moment she fails to dominate the classroom situation. She reasserts control, however, by taking the children to the next activity she has planned for the day. It seems never to have occurred to Edith that there might be a meaningful learning experience for the children in re-creating the "spooky house" in the classroom. It seems fair to say that this would have offered an exercise in spontaneous self-expression and an opportunity for real creativity on the part of the children. Instead, they are taken through a canned animal imitation procedure, an activity which they apparently enjoy, but which is also imposed upon them rather than created by them.

While children's perceptions of the world and opportunities for genuine spontaneity and creativity are being systematically eliminated from the kindergarten, unquestioned obedience to authority and rote learning of meaningless material are being encouraged. When the children are called to line up in the center of the room they ask "Why?" and "What for?" as they are in the very process of complying. They have learned to go smoothly through a programmed day, regardless of whether parts of the program make any sense to them or not. Here the student role involves what might be called "doing what you're told and never mind why." Activities which might "make sense" to the children are effectively ruled out and they are forced or induced to participate in activities which may be "senseless," such as the calisthenics.

At the same time the children are being taught by rote meaningless sounds in the ritual oaths and songs, such as the Lord's Prayer, the Pledge to the Flag, and "America." As they go through the grades children learn more and more of the sounds of these ritual oaths, but the fact that they have often learned meaningless sounds rather than meaningful statements is shown when they are asked to write these out in the sixth grade; they write them as groups of sounds rather than as a series of words, according to the sixth grade teachers at Wright School. Probably much learning in the elementary grades is of this character, that is, having no intrinsic meaning to the children, but rather being tasks inexplicably required of them by authoritative adults. Listening to sixth grade children read social studies reports, for example, in which they have copied material from encyclopedias about a particular country, an observer often gets the feeling that he is watching an activity which has no intrinsic meaning for the child. The child who reads, "Switzerland grows wheat and cows and grass and makes a lot of cheese" knows the dictionary meaning of each of these words but may very well have no conception at all of this "thing" called Switzerland. He is simply carrying out a task assigned by the teacher *because* it is assigned, and this may be its only "meaning" for him.

Another type of learning which takes place in kindergarten is seen in children who take advantage of the "holes" in the adult social structure to create activities of their own, during Work Time or out-of-doors during Play Time. Here the children are learning to carve out a small world of their own within the world created by adults. They very quickly learn that if they keep within permissible limits of noise and action they can play much as they please. Small groups of children formed during the year in Edith's kindergarten who played together at these times, developing semi-independent little groups in which they created their own worlds in the interstices of the adult-imposed physical and social world. These groups remind the sociological observer very much of the so-called "informal groups" which adults develop in factories and offices of large bureaucracies.[5] Here too, within authoritatively imposed social organizations people find "holes" to create little subworlds which support informal, friendly, unofficial behavior. Forming and participating in such groups seems to be as much part of the student role as it is of the role of bureaucrat.

The kindergarten has been conceived of here as the year in which children are prepared for their schooling by learning the role of student. In the classrooms of the rest of the school grades, the children will be asked to submit to systems and routines imposed by the teachers and the curriculum. The days will be much like those of kindergarten, except that academic subjects will be substituted for the activities of the kindergarten. Once out of the school system, young adults will more than likely find themselves working in large-scale bureaucratic organizations, perhaps on the assembly line in the factory, perhaps in the paper routines of the white collar occupations, where they will be required to submit to rigid routines imposed by "the company" which may make little sense to them. Those who can operate well in this situation will be successful bureaucratic functionaries. Kindergarten, therefore, can be seen as preparing children not only for participation in the bureaucratic organization of large modern school systems, but also for the large-scale occupational bureaucracies of modern society.

Notes

1. Emile Durkheim, *Sociology and Education* (New York: The Free Press, 1956), pp. 71–72.

2. *Ibid.*, p. 123.

3. Wilbur Brookover, *The Sociology of Education* (New York: American Book Company, 1957), p. 4.

4. *Ibid.*, p. 6.

5. See, for example, Peter M. Blau, *Bureaucracy in Modern Society* (New York: Random House, 1956), Chapter 3.

34 Men Who Share "The Second Shift"

ARLIE HOCHSCHILD
ANNE MACHUNG

The fast moving currents of social change have not left the American family untouched. We all are familiar with many of the consequences—later age at first marriage, smaller families, two paychecks, divorce, teenage pregnancy, illegitimacy, abortion, and cohabitation. Family violence may also be higher, but this is primarily speculation for we have no firm figures to measure the present, much less the past. Some of us come from broken homes; others of us have been divorced. Hardly any of us expects our marriage to be the way our grandparents' was, and many of us even anticipate that our approach to being a husband or wife will differ markedly from that of our own parents.

Although we can mentally project ourselves into anticipated roles, we have little idea of what we will really face. Certainly, with the rapid pace of change, many of our attitudes and ideas will be different in a few years. It seems certain, however, that increasing pressures will be brought to bear on husbands to share what Hochschild and Machung call the *second shift*, the housework and family and home duties that remain to be done after the day's work-for-pay is completed. To gather data for their study, Hochschild and her colleagues interviewed fifty families, following a dozen in depth. In these families, from different social classes and racial/ethnic groups, the wife was usually a "supermom," working the second shift herself with very little assistance from her husband. She averaged an extra *month* of work a year on the second shift than her husband. About 20 percent of the men, however, shared the second shift, and in this selection we examine differences between the men who did and those who did not and effects on the marriage and the children.

ONE OUT OF FIVE MEN in this study was as actively involved in the home as their wives—some were like Greg Alston, working the same hours as their wives but sharing in a more "male" way, doing such things as carpentry; others, like Art Winfield, shared the cooking and being a primary parent. In my study the men who shared the second shift had a happier family life, so I wanted to know what conditions produce such men. How do men who share *differ* from other men?

The men in this study who shared the work at home were no more likely than others to have "model" fathers who helped at home. Their parents were no more likely to have trained them to do chores when they were young. Michael Sherman and Seth Stein both had fathers who spent little time with them and did little work around the house. But Michael became extremely involved in raising his twin boys, whereas Seth said hello and goodbye to his children as he went to and from his absorbing law practice. Sharers were also as likely to have had mothers who were homemakers or who worked *and* tended the home as non-sharers. . . .

Did the men who shared the work at home love their wives more? Were they more considerate? It's true, egalitarian men had more harmonious marriages, but I would be reluctant to say that men like Peter Tanagawa or Ray Judson loved their wives less than men like Art Winfield or Michael Sherman, or were less considerate in other ways. One man who did very little at home said, "Just last week I suddenly realized that for the first time I feel like my wife's life is more valuable than mine, because my son needs her more than he needs me." Men who shared were very devoted to their wives; but, in a less helpful way, so were the men who didn't.

Two other, more external factors also did *not* distinguish men who did share from men who didn't: the number of hours they worked or how much they earned. Husbands usually work a longer "full-time" job than wives. But in the families I studied, men who worked fifty hours or more per week were just *slightly* less likely to share housework than men who worked forty-five, forty, or thirty-five hours a week. In addition, fifty-hour-a-week *women* did far *more* childcare and housework than men who worked the same hours. Other national studies also show that the number of hours a man works for pay has little to do with the number of hours he works at home.

Of all the factors that influence the relations between husbands and wives, I first assumed that money would loom the largest. The man who shared, I thought, would need his wife's salary more, would value her job more, and as a result also her time. . . .

I assumed that the man who shares would not earn more, and that the wage gap between other husbands and their wives might *cause* the leisure gap between them. Both spouses might agree that because his job came first, his leisure did too. Leaving childcare aside (since most men would want to do some of that), I assumed that men who earned *as much or less* than their wives would do more housework. I assumed that a woman who wanted fifty-fifty in the second shift but had married a high-earning man would reconcile herself to the family's greater need for her husband's work, set aside her desires, and work the extra month a year. By the same token, a traditional man married to a high-earning woman would swallow his traditional pride and pitch in at home. I assumed that money would talk louder than ideals, and invisibly shape each partner's gender strategy.

If money is the underlying principle behind men's and women's strategies, that would mean that no matter how much effort a woman put into her job, its lower pay would result in less help from her husband at home. Research about on-the-job stress suggests that jobs in the low-level service sector, where women are concentrated, cause more stress than blue-and white-collar jobs, where men are concentrated. Although working mothers don't work as long hours as working fathers, they devote as much *effort* to earning money as men, and many women earn less for work that's more stressful. Thus, by using his higher salary to "buy" more leisure at home, he inadvertently makes his wife pay indirectly for an inequity in the wider economy that causes her to get paid less. If money is the key organizing principle to the relations between men and women in marriage, it's a pity for men because it puts their role at home at the mercy of the blind fluctuations of the marketplace and for women because if money talks at home, it favors men. The extra month a year becomes an indirect way in which the woman pays *at home* for *economic* discrimination *outside* the home.

The Limits of Economic Logic

Money mattered in the marriages I studied, but it was not the powerful "invisible hand" behind the men who shared. For one thing, this is clear from the family portraits. Michael Sherman earned much more than Adrienne but his job didn't matter more, and he shared the work at home. For years Ann Myerson earned more than her husband but put her husband's job first anyway. John Livingston valued his wife's job as he did his own, but she took more responsibility at home.

A number of researchers have tried to discover a link between the *wage* gap between working parents and the *leisure* gap between them, and the results have been confusing. All but one study found no significant relation between the amount a man earns relative to his wife and how much housework or child care he does. Among couples in this study, these two factors were not related in a statistically significant way.

An intriguing clue appeared, however, when I divided all the men into three groups: men who earn more than their wives (most men), men who earn the same amount, and men who earn less. Of the men who earned more than their wives, 21 percent shared housework. Of the men who earned about the same, 30 percent. But among men who earned less than their wives, *none* shared.

If a logic of the pocketbook is only a logic of the *pocketbook*, it should operate the same whether a man earns more or a woman earns more. But this "logic of the pocketbook" didn't work that way. It only worked as long as men earned as much or more than their wives. Money frequently "worked" for men (it excused them from housework) but it didn't work for women (it didn't get them out of it).

Another principle—the principle of "balancing"—seems to be at work. According to this principle, if men lose power over women in one way, they make up for it in another way—by avoiding the second shift, for example. In this way they can maintain dominance over women. How much responsibility these men assumed at home was thus related to the deeper issue of male power. Men who earn much more than their wives already have a power over their wives in that they control a scarce and important resource. The more severely a man's financial identity is threatened—by his wife's higher salary, for example—the less he can afford to threaten it further by doing "women's work" at home.

Men who shared the second shift weren't trying to make up for losing power in other realms of their marriage; they didn't feel the need to "balance." Michael Sherman had given up the *idea* that he should have more power than Adrienne. Art Winfield talked playfully about men being "brought up to be kings."

But Peter Tanagawa felt a man *should* have more power, and felt he'd given a lot of it up when Nina's career rose so dramatically. He'd adjusted himself to earning much less, but to a man of his ideas, this had been a sacrifice. By making up for his sacrifice by doing more at home, Nina engaged in "balancing." Among other couples, too, it's not only men who "balance"; women do too.

Thus, more crucial than cultural beliefs about men's and women's *spheres*, were couples' beliefs about the right degree of men's and women's *power*. Women who "balanced" felt "too powerful." Sensing when their husbands got "touchy," sensing the fragility of their husbands' "male ego," not wanting them to get discouraged or depressed, such women restored their men's lost power by waiting on them at home.

Wives did this "balancing"—this restoring power to their husbands— for different reasons. One eccentric Englishman and father of three children, aged six, four, and one, took responsibility for about a third of the chores at home. A tenured member of the English department of a small college, he taught classes, and held obligatory office hours, but had abandoned research, minimized committee work, avoided corridor conversations, and had long since given up putting in for a raise. He claimed to "share" housework and childcare, but what he meant by housework was working on a new den, and what he meant by childcare was reflected in his remark, "The children do fine while I'm working on the house; they muck about by themselves." He was touchy about his accomplishments and covertly nervous, it seemed, about what he called the "limitless" ambitions of his workaholic wife. Without asking him to do more, perhaps his wife was making up for her "limitless ambitions" by carrying the load at home. In the meantime, she described herself as "crushed with work."

I looked again at other interviews I'd done with men who worked less than full time. One architect, the fourth of four highly successful brothers in a prosperous and rising black family, had lost his job in the recession of the late 1970s, become deeply discouraged, taken occasional contracting jobs, and otherwise settled into a life of semi-unemployment. His wife explained: "Eventually we're going to have to make it on my salary. But it's awfully hard on my husband right now, being trained as an architect and not being able to get a job. I take that into account." Her husband did no housework and spent time with his son only when the spirit moved him. "I do very little around the house," he said frankly, "but Beverly doesn't complain, bless her heart." Meanwhile, they lived in near-poverty, while Beverly worked part time, cared for their baby and home, and took courses in veterinary science at night, her overload the result of their economic need added to her attempt to restore a sense of power to her discouraged husband. As she let fall at the end of the interview, "Sometimes I wonder how long I can keep going."

Other men earned less and did less at home but weren't "balancing." They were going back to get a degree, and their wives were temporarily giving them the money and the time to do this. The husband's training for a job counted as much in their moral accounting system as it would if he already had that more important job. For example, one husband was unemployed while studying for a degree in pediatric nursing. His wife, a full-time administrator, cared for their home and their nine-month-old baby. The rhythm of their household life revolved around the dates of his exams. His wife explained: "My husband used to do a lot around here. He used to puree Stevy's carrots in the blender. He used to help shop, and weed the garden. Now he studies every evening until ten. His exams come first. Getting that "A' is important to him. He plays with the baby as a study break." She said she didn't mind doing the housework and caring for the baby and got upset when he complained the house was messy. She said, "I keep myself going by reminding myself this is *temporary*, until Jay gets his degree."

I heard of no women whose husbands both worked and cared for the family while the wives studied for a degree. For a woman, getting a degree was not so honored an act. There was no tradition of "putting your wife through college" analogous to the recent tradition of "putting your husband through college." A wife could imagine being supported or being better off when her husband got his degree. Husbands usually couldn't imagine either situation. One husband *had* shared the work at home fifty-fifty when his wife worked, but came to resent it terribly and finally stopped when his wife quit her job and went back to school to get a Ph.D. A job counted as legitimate recompense but working toward a degree did not. Feeling deprived of attention and service, one man shouted into my tape recorder—half in fun and half not: "You can't eat it. You can't talk to it. It doesn't buy a vacation or a new car. I *hate* my wife's dessertation!" Women who put their husbands through school may have resented the burden, but they didn't feel they had as much right to complain about it.

Taken as a whole, this group of men—semi-unemployed, hanging back at work, or in training—neither earned the bread nor cooked it. And of all the wives, theirs were the least happy. Yet, either because they sympathized with their husbands, or expected the situation to improve, or because they felt there was no way to change it, and because they were, I believe, unconsciously maintaining the "right" balance of power in their marriage, such women worked the extra month a year. Meanwhile, their lower-earning husbands often saw their wives as intelligent, strong, "a rock"; at the same time these men could enjoy the idea that, though not a king at work, a man still had a warm throne at home.

Some women had other ways of accumulating more power than they felt "comfortable" with. One woman I know, an M.D., not in this study, married a former patient, a musician who earned far less than she. Perhaps the feeling that her status was "too great" for their joint notion of the "right" balance, she—a feminist on every other issue—quietly did all the second shift and, as her husband put it, "She never asks." Another woman, a teacher, secretly upset the power balance by having a long-term extra-marital affair almost like another marriage. Life went on as usual at home, but she quietly made up for her secret life by being "wonderful" about all the chores at home.

In these marriages, money was not the main determinant of which men did or didn't share. Even men who earned much more than their wives didn't get out of housework *because* of it. One college professor and father of three, for example, explained why he committed himself to 50 percent of housework and childcare:

> My wife earns a third of what I earn. But as a public school teacher she's doing a job that's just as important as mine. She's an extraordinarily gifted teacher, and I happen to know she works just as hard at her teaching as I do at mine. So, when we come home, she's as tired as I am. We share the housework and childcare equally. But [in a tone of exasperation] if she were to take a job in insurance or real estate, she'd just be doing another job. She wouldn't be making the contribution she's making now. We haven't talked about it, but if that were the case, I probably wouldn't break my back like this. She would have to carry the load at home.

Ironically, had his wife earned *more* at a job he admired less—had she worked only for *money*—he would *not* have shared the second shift. . . .

That doesn't mean that money has nothing to do with sharing the second shift. In two different ways, it does. In the first place, couples do need to think about and plan around financial need. Most of the men who shared at home had wives who pretty much shared at work. The men earned some but not much more. And whatever their wives earned, working-class men like Art Winfield really needed their wives' wages to live. Second, future changes in the general economy may press more couples to do "balancing." Some experts predict that the American economy will split increasingly between an elite of highly paid, highly trained workers and an enlarging pool of poorly paid, unskilled workers. Jobs in the middle are being squeezed out as companies lose out to foreign competition or seek cheaper labor pools in the Third World. The personnel rosters of the so-called sunrise industries, the rapidly growing, high-technology companies, already reflect this split. Companies with many jobs in the middle are in the so-called sunset industries, such as car manufacturing. As the economist Bob Kuttner illustrates: "The fast food industry employs a small number of executives and hundreds of thousands of cashiers and kitchen help who make $3.50 an hour. With some variation, key punchers, chambermaids, and retail sales personnel confront the same short job ladder." In addition, unions in the sunrise industries often face companies' threats to move their plants to cheap labor markets overseas, and so these unions press less hard for better pay.

The decline in jobs in the middle mainly hits men in blue-collar union-protected jobs. Unless they can get training that allows them to compete for a small supply of highly skilled jobs, such men will be forced to choose between unemployment and a low-paid service job.

The "declining middle" is thus in the process of creating an economic crisis for many men. This crisis can lead to two very different results: As economic hardship means more women have to work, their husbands may feel it is "only fair" to share the work at home. Or, there may be a countervailing tendency for men and women to compensate for economically induced losses in male self-esteem by engaging in "balancing." If the logic of the pocketbook affects the way men and women divide the second shift, I think it will affect it in this way, through its indirect effect on male self-esteem.

All in all, men who shared were similar to men who didn't in that their fathers were just as unlikely to have been model helpers at home, and just as unlikely to have done housework as boys themselves. But the men who shared at home seemed to have more distant ties with their fathers, and closer ones with their mothers. They were similar to non-sharing men in the hours they worked, but they tended not to earn a great deal more or less than their wives.

Sharing men seemed to be randomly distributed across the class hierarchy. There were the Michael Shermans and the Art Winfields. In the working class, more men shared without believing it corresponded to the kind of man they wanted to be. In the middle class, more men didn't share even though they believed in it. Men who both shared the work at home and believed in it seemed to come from every social class. Everything else equal, men whose wives had advanced degrees and professional careers—who had what the sociologist Pierre Bourdieu calls "cultural capital"—were more likely to share than men whose wives lacked such capital. Men with career wives were more likely to share than men with wives in "jobs." All these factors were part of the social backdrop to the working man's gender strategy at home.

Added to these was also the strategy of his wife. Nearly every man who shared had a wife whose strategy was to urge—or at least welcome—his involvement at home. Such women did not emotionally hoard their children, as Nancy Holt came to do with Joey. When Evan had been about to leave to take Joey to the zoo for a father-son outing, Nancy had edged Evan out by deciding at the last minute to "help" them get along. At first awkward and unconfident with children, Michael Sherman could well have developed a "downstairs" retreat had it not been for Adrienne's showdown and continual invitation to join in the care of their twins. Often, something as simple as the way a mother holds her baby so he or she can "look at Dad" indicates her effort to share. Adrienne Sherman didn't just leave her twins with Daddy; she talked to them about what Daddy could do with them; consciously or not, she fostered a tie to him. She didn't play expert. She made room.

As a result, such men were—or became—sensitive to their children's needs. They were more realistic than other fathers about the limits of what their wives provide, and about what their children really need.

Limiting the Idea of Fatherhood

Involved fathers had a much fuller, more elaborate notion of what a father was than uninvolved fathers did. Involved fathers talked about fathering much as mothers talked about mothering. Uninvolved fathers held to a far more restricted mission—to discipline the child or to teach him about sports. For example, when asked what he thought was important about being a father, one black businessman and father of two said:

> Discipline. I don't put up with whining. It bothers me. I'm shorter tempered and my wife is longer tempered. I do a significant amount of paddling. I grew up with being paddled. When I got paddled I knew damn good and well that I deserved it. I don't whip them. One good pop on their bottom and I send them down to their room. I've scared them. I've never punched them. And I'll spank them in front of people as well as not in front of them.

To him, being a disciplinarian *was* being a father. As a result, his children gravitated to their mother. She had worked for an insurance company but, under the pressure of home and work, finally quit her job. In a strangely matter-of-fact way, she remarked that she didn't "feel comfortable" leaving the children with her husband for long periods. "If I go out to the hairdresser's on Saturday, I might come back and find he didn't fix them lunch; I don't leave them with him too much." If it wasn't a matter of discipline, he didn't think caring for children was his job.

Other fathers limited their notion of fathering mainly to teaching their children about the events in the newspaper, baseball, soccer. When I asked uninvolved fathers to define a "good mother" and "good father," they gave elaborate and detailed answers for "good mother," and short, hazy answers for "good father," sometimes with a specific mission attached to it, like "teach them about cars."

I asked one man, "What's a good mother?" and he answered: "A good mother is patient. That's the first thing. Someone who is warm, caring, who can see what the child needs, physically, who stimulates the child intellectually, and helps the child meet his emotional challenges."

"What is a good father?" I asked. "A good father is a man who spends time with his children." Another man said, "A good father is a man who is around."

It is not that men have an elaborate idea of fatherhood and then don't live up to it. Their idea of fatherhood is embryonic to being with. They often limit that idea by comparing themselves only to their own fathers and not, as more involved men did, to their mothers, sisters, or other fathers. As a Salvadoran delivery man put it, "I give my children everything my father gave me." But Michael Sherman gave his twins what his *mother* gave him.

Curtailing the Idea of What a Child Needs

Men who were greatly involved with their children react against two cultural ideas: one idea removes the actual care of children from the definition of *manhood,* and one curtails the notion of how much care a child needs. As to the first idea, involved fathers' biggest struggle was against the doubts they felt about not "giving everything to get ahead" in their jobs. But even when they conquered this fear, another cultural idea stood in the way—the idea that their child is "already grown-up," "advanced," and doesn't need much from him. A man's individual defense against seeing his children's need for him conspires with this larger social idea.

Just as the archetype of the supermom—the woman who can do it all—minimizes the real needs of women, so too the archetype of the "superkid" minimizes the real needs of children. It makes it all right to treat a young child as if he or she were older. Often uninvolved parents remarked with pride that their small children were "self-sufficient" or "very independent."

I asked the fifth-grade teacher in a private school how she thought her students from two-job families were doing. She began by saying that they did as well as the few children she had whose mothers stayed home. But having said that, her talk ran to the problems: "The good side of kids being on their own so much is that it makes them independent really early. But I think they pay a price for it. I can see them sealing off their feelings, as if they're saying, 'That's the last time I'll be vulnerable.' I can see it in their faces, especially the sixth-grade boys."

Throughout the second half of the nineteenth century, as women were increasingly excluded from the workplace, the cultural notion of what a child "needs" at home correspondingly grew to expand the woman's role at home. As Barbara Ehrenreich and Deirdre English point out in *For Her Own Good*, doctors and ministers argued strongly that a woman's place was at home. The child needed her there. As the economic winds have reversed, so has the idea of a woman's proper place—and the child's real needs. Nowadays, a child is increasingly imagined to need time with other children, to need "independence-training," not to need "quantity time" with a parent but only a small amount of "quality time." As one working father remarked: "Children need time to play with other children their age. It's stimulating for them. Nelson enjoyed it, I think, from when he was six months."

If in the earlier part of the century, middle-class children suffered from overattentive mothers, from being "mother's only accomplishment," today's children may suffer from an underestimation of their needs. Our idea of what a *child* needs in each case reflects what *parents* need. The child's needs are thus a cultural football in an economic and marital game.

An Orwellian "superkid" language has emerged to consolidate this sense of normality. In a September 1985 *New York Times* article entitled "New Programs Come to Aid of Latch Key Children," Janet Edder quotes a child-care professional as follows: "Like other child-care professionals, Mrs. Selgison prefers to use the phrase 'Children in Self Care' rather than 'Latch Key Children,' a term coined during the depression when many children who went home alone wore a key around their necks." "Children in Self Care" suggests that the children *are* being cared for, but by themselves, independently. Unlike the term "Latch Key Children," which suggests a child who is sad and deprived, the term "Children in Self Care" suggests a happy superkid.

Another article, in the August 1984 *Changing Times*, entitled "When You Can't Be Home, Teach Your Child What to Do," suggests that working parents do home-safety checkups so that a pipe won't burst, a circuit breaker won't blow, or an electrical fire won't start. Parents should advise children to keep house keys out of sight and to conceal from callers the fact that they're alone at home. It tells about "warm lines"—a telephone number a child can call for advice or simple comfort when he or she is alone. Earlier in the century, advice of this sort was offered to destitute widows or working wives of disabled or unemployed men while the middle class shook its head in sympathy. Now the middle class has "children in self-care" too.

The parents I talked to had younger chldren, none of whom were in "self-care." The children I visited seemed to me a fairly jolly and resilient lot. But parents I spoke to did not feel very supported in their parenthood; like Ann Myerson, many parents in the business world felt obligated to hide concerns that related to a child. Many female clerical workers were discouraged from making calls home. Many men felt that doing anything for family reasons—moving to another city, missing the office party, passing up a promotion—would be taken as a sign they lacked ambition or manliness. As for John Livingston's coworkers, the rule of thumb was: don't go home until your wife calls.

For all the talk about the importance of children, the cultural climate has become subtly less hospitable to parents who put children first. This is not because parents love children less, but because a "job culture" has expanded at the expense of a "family culture."

As motherhood as a "private enterprise" declines and more mothers rely on the work of lower-paid specialists, the value accorded the work of mothering (not the value of chidren) has declined for women, making it all the harder for men to take it up.

My Wife Is Doing It

Involved fathers are aware that their children depend on them. Every afternoon Art Winfield knew Adam was waiting for him at daycare. Michael Sherman knew that around six A.M. one of his twins could call out "Daddy." John Livingston knew that Cary relied on him to get around her mother's discipline. Such men were close enough to their children to know what they were and weren't getting from their mothers.

Uninvolved fathers were not. They *imagined* that their wives did more with the children than they did. For example, one thirty-two-year-old grocery clerk praised his wife for helping their daughter with reading on the weekends—something his wife complained he didn't make time for. But when I interviewed her, I discovered that her weekends were taken with housework, church, and visiting relatives.

Sometimes I had the feeling that fathers were passing the childcare buck to their wives while the wives passed it to the baby-sitter. Each person passing on the role wanted to feel good about it, and tended to deny the problems. Just as fathers often praised their wives as "wonderful mothers," so mothers often praised their baby-sitters as "wonderful." Even women who complain about daycare commonly end up describing the daycare worker as "great." So important to parents was the care of their child that they almost had to believe that "everything at daycare was fine." Sadly, not only was the role of caretaker transferred from parent to baby-sitter, but sometimes also the illusion that the child was "in good hands."

The reasons men gave for why their wives were wonderful—for example, that they were patient—were often reasons women gave for why the baby-sitters were wonderful. Just as uninvolved fathers who praised their wives often said they wouldn't want to trade places with their wives, so wives often said they wouldn't want to trade places with their daycare worker.

As one businesswoman and mother of a three-year-old boy commented: "Our baby-sitter is just fantastic. She's with the kids from seven o'clock in the morning until six o'clock at night. And some kids stay later. I don't know how she does it. *I* couldn't." Another working mother commented: "I couldn't be as patient as Elizabeth [the daycare worker] is. I love my child, but I'm not a baby person."

The daycare worker herself was often in a difficult spot. She depended economically on the parents, so she didn't want to say anything so offensive it might lead them to withdraw the child. On the other hand, sometimes she grew concerned about a child's behavior. Typical of many daycare workers, Katherine Wilson, who had cared for children for fifteen years, remarked:

> One out of five parents just drop their children off and run. Another three will come in and briefly talk with you. Then the last person will come in and talk to you quite a bit. Not too many call during the day. A lot of parents aren't too concerned with the day-to-day activities. They just trust we know what we're doing.

Some daycare centers even established a policy of check-in sheets that required parents to come inside the daycare center and sign their child in each morning, thus preventing the hurried few who might otherwise leave their children off at the sidewalk.

Pickup time was often hectic, and not a good time to talk. As one daycare worker observed:

> It's a hell of a life the parents lead. Every time I see them they're in a rush. It's rush in the morning and rush in the evening. They barely ask me what Danny had for lunch or how he seemed. I think they might feel bad when they see him around four o'clock in the afternoon. He gets kinds of restless then. He's waiting. He sees the parents of the other children come and each time the doorbell rings he hopes its his parents. But, see, they come in the last— six-thirty.

Sometimes a daycare worker becomes worried about a child. As Alicia Fernandez confided:

> I've had Emily for a year and a half now. She's never been real open with me and I don't think she is with her mother either. I think, in a way, Emily was hurt that her former sitter had to give her up. It was a hard adjustment coming in to me and in fact I don't think she has adjusted. One day she took the money out of my wallet—the money her mother had given me—and tore it up. I was so shocked. It was my pay. I slapped her across the knees. She didn't even

cry. I felt bad I'd done that, but even worse that she didn't even cry. I thought, hey, something's wrong.

Had she mentioned this to Emily's mother and father? I asked. She replied quickly and quietly: "Oh no. It's hard to talk about that. I feel badly about it but on the other hand if I told her mother, she might take Emily away."

The daycare worker, who could best judge how Emily's day had gone, felt afraid to confide her concerns to Emily's parents, who badly needed to hear them. Other daycare workers also kept their opinions to themselves. As another daycare worker noted: "You can feel sorry for them. I have Tim for nine hours. I have Jessica for ten and a half—now Jessie's mother is a single mother. Like I say, at the end of the day they cry." "Do you talk to their parents about the crying?" I asked. "They don't ask, and I don't bring it up." She continued, echoing a thought other daycare workers expressed as well:

> Don't get me wrong. These children are adaptable. They're pliant. As long as there's a sense of love here and as long as you feed them, they know I'm the one who satisfies their needs. That's all I am to them. The children love me and some little children, like Nelson, don't want to go home. He's three now, but I've had him since he was seven months old; Stephanie's three and I've had her since she was six weeks. But I do feel sorry for the children, I do. Because I know there are days when they probably don't feel like coming here, especially Mondays.

When daycare workers feel sorry for the children they care for something is wrong. This women, a thirty-year-old black mother of three, was gentle and kindly, a lovely person to care for children. What seemed wrong to me was the overly long hours, the blocked channels of communication, and the fathers who imagined their wives were "handling it all."

A Father's Influence

In a time of stalled revolution—when women have gone to work, but the workplace, the culture, and most of all, the men, have not adjusted themselves to this new reality—children can be the victims. Most working mothers are already doing all they can, doing that extra month a year. It is men who can do more.

Fathers can make a difference that shows in the child. I didn't administer tests to the children in the homes I visited nor gather systematic information on child development. I did ask the baby-sitters and daycare workers for their general impressions of differences between the children of single parents, two-job families in which the father was uninvolved, and two-job families in which the father was actively involved. All of them said that the children of fathers who were actively involved seemed to them "more secure" and "less anxious." Their lives were less rushed. On Monday, they had more to report about Sunday's events: "Guess what I did with my dad. . . ."

But curiously little attention has been paid to the effect of fathers on children. Current-research focuses almost exclusively on the influence on children of the working *mother*. A panel of distinguished social scientists chosen by the National Academy of Sciences to review the previous research on children of working mothers concluded in 1982 that a mother's employment has no consistent ill effects on a child's school achievement, IQ, or social and emotional development. Other summary reviews offer similar but more complex findings. For example, in charting fifty years of research on children of working mothers, Lois Hoffman, a social psychologist at the University of Michigan, has concluded that most girls of all social classes and boys from working-class families, whose mothers worked, were more self-confident and earned better grades than children whose mothers were housewives. But she also found that compared to the sons of housewives, middle-class boys raised by working mothers were less confident and did less well in school. But what about the influence of the fathers?

Apart from my study, other systematic research has documented a fact one might intuitively suspect: the more involved the father, the better developed the child intellectually and socially. Professor Norma Radin and her students at the University of Michigan have conducted a number of studies that show that, all else being equal, the children of highly involved fathers are better socially and emotionally adjusted than children of noninvolved fathers and score higher on academic tests. In Professor Radin's research, "highly involved" fathers are those who score in the top third on an index comprised of questions concerning responsibility for physical care (e.g. feeding the children), responsibility for socializing the child (e.g., setting limits), power in decision-making regarding the child, availability to the child, and an overall estimate of his involvement in raising his preschooler. In one study of fifty-nine middle-class families with children between the ages of three and six, Professor Radin found that highly involved fathers had sons who were better adjusted and more socially competent, more likely to perceive themselves as masters of their fate, and had a higher mental age on verbal intelligence tests. A 1985 study by Abraham Sagi found Israeli children of highly involved fathers to be more empathetic than other children.

A 1985 comprehensive and careful study by Carolyn and Phil Cowan, two psychologists at the University of California, Berkeley, found that three-and-a-half-year-old children of involved fathers achieved higher scores on certain playroom tasks (classifying objects, putting things in a series, role-taking tasks) than other children. When fathers worked longer hours outside the home, the Cowans found in their observation sessions, the three-and-a-half-year-olds showed more anxiety. The daughters of long-hours men were, in addition, less warm and less task oriented at playroom tasks, although they had fewer behavior problems. When fathers worked long hours, mothers tended to "compensate" by establishing warm relations with their sons. But when mothers worked long hours, husbands did not "compensate" with their daughters. In spite of this, the girls did well in playroom tasks. When fathers *or* mothers worked more outside the home, the parent established a closer bond with the *boy*.

Finally, the results of active fatherhood seem to last. In one study, two psychologists asked male undergraduates at the University of Massachusetts, Amherst, to respond to such statements as "My father understood my problems and worries and helps with them, hugged or kissed me goodnight when I was small, was able to make me feel better when I was upset, gave me a lot of care and attention." They were also asked to describe his availability ("away from home for days at a time, . . . out in the evening at least two nights a week, . . . home afternoons when children came home from school" and so on). The young men who ranked their fathers highly—or even moderately—nurturant and available were far more likely to describe themselves as "trusting, friendly, loyal, and dependable, industrious and honest."

In the end, caring for children is the most important part of the second shift, and the effects of a man's care or his neglect will show up again and again through time—in the child as a child, in the child as an adult, and probably also in the child's own approach to fatherhood, and in generations of fathers to come. Active fathers are often in reaction against a passive, detached father, a father like Seth Stein. But an exceptionally warmhearted man, like the step-father of Art Winfield, could light the way still better. In the last forty years, many women have made a historic shift, into the economy. Now it is time for a whole generation of men to make a second historic shift—into work at home.

35 The Streetcorner Preacher

LAWRENCE K. HONG
MARION V. DEARMAN

Religion is vital to Americans, and anyone who misses this point fails to understand American society adequately. Although in previous years some professionals predicted that with the rise of science and the general secularization of American culture religion would quietly fade into the background, that has not happened. Americans repeatedly go through periods of decreased religious involvement—and to some it then looks as though religion is on its way out—only to enter an inevitable subsequent period of increased religious participation. Although church and synagogue membership and attendance ebb and flow, in American society there always remains a strong current of genuine religiosity based on sincere convictions.

It is no exaggeration, then, to say that religion is one of the principal social institutions in American society. In it Americans find solace and courage, as well as the answers to many of the perplexing questions that contemporary social life poses. Those who have religious convictions grasp the meaning of what I am writing, while those with few or none must remain "outsiders," somewhat perplexed by all the activities of which they are not a part.

While most Americans are at least "somewhat" religious, most of us also think that religion should remain primarily a private matter. "We all believe what we believe, and it is no one else's business" is likely to be the attitude most of us take. Consequently, few of us are likely to preach on streetcorners or to accost people on the sidewalk with a religious message—or to approve those who do. Streetcorner preaching strikes most of us as somewhat humorous, somehow unseemly, and "pushy," if not as an invasion of our privacy.

In spite of such common negative reactions, however, some people persist in preaching on streetcorners. Focusing on just this one aspect of the fascinatingly multifaceted social institution we call religion, Hong and Dearman's analysis helps the unfamiliar take on just a little more familiarity. From the lens of these sociologists, then, we gain greater understanding of another aspect of our social world.

Alleluia, alleluia, Lord, I glorify your name. Thank you, Jesus, Heaven come to your heart, heaven come to your heart. Amen, amen. Devil is here, but Jesus is right here. Alleluia, alleulia. Praise the Lord. Thank you, Jesus.

On a busy downtown street corner a black man in his late fifties, clapping his hands, striking his arms, striding back and forth, preaches at the top of his voice to the ceaseless streams of pedestrians. Adults avert their eyes in apparent embarrassment for the preacher; children stare at him while being jerked forward by their mothers who admonish them to pay no attention. Police walk or drive by, glance at him indifferently, and go their way. These sights and sounds are part of the permanent landscape of most major cities from New York to Los Angeles. The experienced city dweller apparently takes the streetcorner preachers for granted, along with slow traffic, stale air, sleazy movies, and monotonous neon signs. But to the novice or newcomer, they add excitement and color to the kaleidoscopic, carnival atmosphere which inner city life presents to him.

Who are these streetcorner preachers? Where do they come from? What do they try to accomplish? These and other questions have brought the authors of this paper to the streets of downtown Los Angeles. Over a period of three months, we observed and interviewed the preachers, a spokesman of the church of which many were members, different types of pedestrians, and the police in an attempt to search for the answers. . . .

One Situation, Multiple Definitions

With few exceptions, all the passers-by whom we interviewed regard the streetcorner preachers as "crazy," "insane," or "mentally disturbed." The following comment from a regular downtown shopper is typical:

I think he is crazy. Mentally unbalanced, you know. There are many of them. They always stand over in that corner, making a lot of noise. Nobody ever listens to them. I think they are nuts.

Policemen agreed with this opinion, although a desk sergeant confided to us that "some of them [the preachers] are righteous but most of them are squirrels, nuts, kooks." Another policeman told us that "they are definitely a nuisance but, you know, free speech and all that jazz" makes it impossible to eliminate them.

The preachers, in turn, define the passers-by as sinners—heathens, drunkards, thieves, and worse; the policemen are seen as would-be persecutors of God's spokesmen, the preachers. By thus defining themselves as the representatives of God, the creator and master of the universe, the preachers perceive themselves as the "winners" while the others become poor, pitiful "losers" who are going to Hell if they fail to heed their warnings.

Very much contrary to the definitions of the police and pedestrians, we soon discovered that these preachers are quite rational, intelligent people and sincere, dedicated Christians. Our basis for this definition will emerge in the remaining pages of this paper.

Organization of "Frenetic" Behavior

It did not take us long to discover that just beneath the surface of their seemingly erratic behavior was a close group of people who share many of the system characteristics—mutual obligations, common goals, status hierarchy, and territoriality—of the streetcorner society that Whyte (1943) has described. The permanent cadre, or nucleus, of the street preachers are members of a major Pentecostal denomination—the Church of God in Christ (CGC)—that claims national membership of around three million.[1] Although these preachers are neither licensed to preach, nor ordained by their church, they are well organized and follow a schedule almost are regular as that of suburban churches in conducting their religious services. They begin their preaching around noon every day and finish around five. During this five-hour interval, three or four preachers will take turns preaching, each having a time slot of about half an hour. Other preachers may also stand by, but only a few will have a chance to preach on the same day.

The street preachers feel very close to one another, and frequently have lunch or coffee breaks together in a cafeteria in the immediate area. In the cafeteria, they will also meet with other "brothers" and "sisters" who perform other religious services in the vicinity such as passing out religious tracts and mini-bibles. Their interactions are characterized by warmth and rapport. This observation is also confirmed by an ordained minister of their church (who does not preach in the street but has a regular pastoral appointment):

> They have a way to be aware of each other's needs. They preach by turns and help one another out. They get to know each other very well. Sometimes, they even live together. Some of them share the same apartment. They are very close.

When a preacher is preaching, his voice may appear to be emotional and his utterances disjunct, but the whole presentation is delivered with a deliberate effort and what appears to be a carefully considered style. He fully understands that very few individuals will stop and listen to his preaching and, therefore, it is not necessary to deliver a coherent, logical discourse on Christianity and salvation. . . . Hence, in contrast to other downtown religious groups such as the Skid Row Missions (Bibby and Mauss, 1974), the goal of the street preacher is not concerned with immediate conversion; his goal, rather, is to "sow the seeds" by scattering discrete words and phrases of virtue and holiness to the downtown crowds, hoping that someone will pick up a word or two here and there.[2] As one of the preachers explains their technique:

What we try to accomplish here is to sow the seeds. What we do out here is like spreading the germs. They get into the air and someone may pick them up. They may not know it now, but one of these days when he is in trouble, he may remember what he has heard here today. It may turn him to the Lord. All it takes is one word, and he may be saved.

. . . The organization of the streetcorner preachers is also manifested in their informal status hierarchy. This status differentiation is determined by the style of delivery and paraphernalia. On the top of the hierarchy is "Brother James," who is a black man in his late forties. Brother James is a recognized virtuoso of streetcorner preachers. His voice is firm and forceful. He does not rattle like many of the other preachers in the lower hierarchy. He always preaches with a high degree of confidence and considerable skill. He also has a charismatic quality which holds the attention of his listeners. Furthermore, he dresses differently than the other streetcorner preachers. His suit is well tailored and his shirt well pressed, while many of the other preachers wear old clothes which desperately need a thorough cleaning. . . .

The preaching style and dress of the other preachers are visibly inferior. Accordingly, their status in the eyes of their peers is also lower. This is evident in the magnitude of support and the size of the gathering accorded to them by their colleagues while they are preaching. Brother James has the largest gathering. When he preaches, all the other preachers gather along the opposite edge of the sidewalk and respond to his utterances enthusiastically. They repeat after him, clap their hands rhythmically, and fix their attention on him intensively:

BROTHER JAMES: Alleluia, alleluia
OTHER PREACHERS: Alleluia
BROTHER JAMES: Lord, I glorify your name
OTHER PREACHERS: I glorify your name
BROTHER JAMES: Thank you Jesus
OTHER PREACHERS: Thank you Jesus
BROTHER JAMES: Lord, give us strength through this journey
OTHER PREACHERS: Through this journey

But, when a lower-status preacher preaches, at most one or two of his colleagues give him support. The type of support is also less enthusiastic. Instead of repeating in full or partially what he actually says, they tend to use standard responses such as "Praise the Lord" and "Alleluia." Furthermore, they rarely clap their hands. Sometimes, they even suspend their support by engaging in social talks. Brother James also occupies an interstitial role between the regular Church of God in Christ and the streetcorner preachers. He is an evangelist who travels from city to city preaching the gospel to down-and-outers and street people. He represents the church and his role allows church members to feel comfortable that their group is both ministering to the lost ones on the downtown streets as well as assisting the streetcorner preachers in their humble and, at first glance, unrewarding task. . . .

Another manifestation of the organization of the street preachers is their concern over territoriality. The corners where they preach are located on certain of the busiest intersections of downtown Los Angeles. The street preachers have more or less occupied these intersections as their own; other downtown religious groups such as the Salvation Army, Jesus People, and Hare Krishna respect, perhaps reluctantly, their "right" to be there and seldom conduct their activities on those corners. . . .

We have observed only one territorial violation during the period of study. The violator was a Hare Krishna who was giving out his sect's newspapers to the passers-by in the exact location where the preachers usually conduct their activities. He took over the area while the preachers were taking their coffee break inside a cafeteria. Upon discovering their spot had been occupied by an intruder (after their coffee break), the immediate response of the preachers was motionless silence. They stood across from the Hare Krishna, stared at him in silence and remained almost motionless. But the Hare Krishna ignored their "silent treatment." After waiting for a couple of minutes in futility, the preachers tried a different technique; they flooded the area with their own people and tried to crowd the Hare Krishna out.

One of the preachers walked over to the Hare Krishna, positioned next to him, and started to preach in the highest decibel. His audio output was matched by the ferocity of his bodily movement. The Hare Krishna adjusted his distance, moving a few feet away from the preacher. The preacher readjusted his position to keep close to the Hare Krishna. Standing across from the couple, the "brothers" and "sisters" of the preacher clapped their hands and responded "alleluia" and "thank you Jesus" to the beat of the preacher's delivery. Finally, the Hare Krishna left the location and moved to a new area about a block away. Although we have observed only one episode, the spontaneity of the preachers' actions and the effortlessness of their coordination in defending their territory strongly suggest that they have employed these techniques before.

Rebirth of the Evangelist

Who are these street preachers? What are their backgrounds? These are some of the most difficult questions that we encountered in our research. As a group, the street preachers are below average in education—most of them have not finished high school. We have met only one preacher who has some college experience, a geography major who dropped out from college after the second year. In spite of their lack of education, the preachers are intelligent, knowledgeable persons who have a good grasp of themselves and happenings in society. In great contrast to the style they preach in the street, they speak conventionally and coherently when they engage in social talks.

They are gregarious and interesting to talk to. Not unlike people in other walks of life, during a typical coffee break they comment on a wide variety of subjects, ranging from politics to personal events. However, there is one topic that is almost a taboo—their past life, that is, their life before their religious conversion. In a way, the street preachers are very much like the streetcorner men in Tally's corner (Liebow, 1967): They do not like to talk about their past, and not even their best friends know about the details of their past. When asked, they speak in generality. One of the preachers speaks of his past in this way:

> Before I became a Christian, I was in sin. Drink, women, and all kinds of troubles. But, I don't do that anymore. One day, I talked to myself. I didn't want to do that anymore. Jesus came into my heart. Now, I am as happy as I can be.

Another preacher relates a similar story:

> I was born in Texas, and then I moved to Tennessee. I came out here 10 years ago. I have been to many places, seen all kinds of people. I did almost everything. I have worked all kinds of jobs. I always had troubles with the laws, nothing serious, you know. Traffic tickets and things like that. Nothing big. And then the Lord spoke to me in my heart. He asked me to come out here. This is where He wants me to be. I follow Him. Jesus cannot be wrong.

To the best of our reconstruction of their past, all the street preachers have gone through an experience of "rebirth."[3] Throughout their early adulthood, they worked on low-paying jobs in various cities. They were the drifters, moving from one city to another. Like many other people in similar circumstances, they had a long history of minor infractions with the law. However, unlike many of their peers, they did not get deeper into trouble. At some moments in their middle years, they decided that they could not live like that anymore and resolved to do something that they considered to be meaningful. Perhaps, through the influence of a friend, or the contact with a preacher, or the experience in a revival meeting, they concluded that ministry was their vocation.

Preaching in Church

Why don't they become regular ministers? Why don't they preach in a church? In our conversation with the street preachers, it is evident that they are interested in conducting religious service in a church. When asked, they usually become somewhat defensive; one of the preachers retorted:

> I can preach in a church. Sometimes, I do. I'm a minister of Jesus Christ just like all other ministers. I am doing the same work. Jesus sent me here just like the others. If I want to preach in a church, I can.

However, they are also quick to point out that they see street preaching as their vocation, and they are satisfied with it. As one preacher puts it:

> Yeah, I preach in the church sometimes. I like to preach in a church. But, this is my calling, out here in the street. This is where the Lord sent me. There is no difference where you preach, in the street, on TV, or in the church. They are all the same. The Lord has many ways to reach people. This is the way He wants me to do. And I am doing as He says.

But, according to a pastor in their church, the street preachers never preach in the church. However, he did point out that it is common practice for members of his congregation to "testify" during religious service. In view of the fact that these testimonials are quite long—sometimes so long that the leader of the testimony service will discreetly terminate the "testimonial" by singing a hymn, joined by the congregation, lest the testifier intrude too far into the prerogatives of the pastor—it is unclear where they end and preaching *per se* begins. Furthermore, according to the same pastor, no street preacher has ever been appointed as a regular minister in a church, and therefore street preaching cannot be viewed as a stepping stone for advancing toward a pastoral appointment. He explains:

> The street preachers are lay preachers. They are not ordained ministers. Our church believes that every Christian has the right to witness. It is a personal thing. Many of them feel the call to witness in the street. Witnessing in the street is just as significant as witnessing in the church. They are just different forms of evangelism. There might be more effective ways to preach, but I don't discourage them because I do not want to lessen their intensity, feeling and freedom. To the best of my knowledge, no street preacher has ever become a pastor in our church.

When pressed as to why their church does not ordain at least some of the preachers, he replies:

> To be ordained, you have to have education. Most of these people have very little education. It also takes time to gather your congregation. You have to have a congregation before you can have a pastoral appointment. As I said before, what they are doing in the street is very significant. It is as significant as witnessing in the church. I do not want to discourage them.

It is obvious that there is a paradox here. The street preachers view themselves as regular ministers and want to preach in a church, but their church encourages them to preach in the street and does not accept them as ordained ministers. While their lack of education may be one of the reasons that has kept them from being ordained, other factors apparently are also involved. Possibly, another factor is their church's lack of confidence in the street preachers' ability to attract and maintain a congregation. As their pastor mentioned earlier: "You have to have a congregation before you can have a pastoral appointment." This appears to be a major factor that keeps the street preachers away from the mainstream of the ministry. . . .

Summary and Conclusion

In this paper, we have attempted to demonstrate that the seemingly frenetic streetcorner preachers are actually rational, intelligent, dedicated Christians. Furthermore, their activities on the street corner display many organizational characteristics such as goals, status hierarchy, and territoriality. Thus, in a way, our findings give support to the highly publicized observation that Whyte (1943) made more than [forty] years ago—i.e., an ostensibly disorganized street corner may have a complex and well-established organization of its own. . . .

Notes

1. This figure, provided by a spokesman of the church, is most likely too high. A yearbook of churches (Jacquet, 1973) gives the Church of God in Christ membership as 501,000 in 1971. This figure, however, is only an estimate; the last census was taken in the late 1960s. At the time of our research, the spokesman informed us that a new census is at the planning stage. Three things are certain regarding the CGC: as with all pentecostals, it is very difficult to determine their membership precisely; they are a very large and fast-growing pentecostal group and one of the largest black pentecostal sects.

2. It should be noted this method is somewhat similar to that used by the sophisticated advertising agencies on their billboard and spot radio and television messages.

3. "Rebirth" for pentecostals usually requires some kind of proof of genuine repentance of their sins, baptism in water as a sign of this repentance, and baptism "in the Spirit," the initial sign of which is "speaking in tongues" (glossolalia).

References

Bibby, R. W., and A. L. Mauss (1974). "Skidders and their servants; variable goals and functions of the skid road rescue mission." *J. for the Scientific Study of Religion* 13: 421–36.

Jacquet, C. H. (1973). *Yearbook of American and Canadian Churches, 1973*. New York: Abingdon.

Liebow, E. (1967). *Tally's Corner*. Boston: Little, Brown.

Whyte, W. F. (1943). *Street Corner Society*. Chicago: University of Chicago Press.

36 The Great American Football Ritual

DOUGLAS E. FOLEY

Any visitor to the United States soon notices how important sports are to Americans. Baseball, football, basketball, hockey, softball, soccer, tennis, golf, swimming, gymnastics, track and field, auto racing, bowling, polo, horseshoes, bass fishing, skateboarding, and sky diving do not begin to exhaust the list. Some sports are taken more seriously than others, and a few have even become almost national obsessions—notably baseball, football, golf, basketball, and hockey. Although most sports are played "for fun," professional sports have become part of America's mass entertainment business enterprise—yielding vast profits for players, managers, owners, and the companies that use them to sell a wide variety of products.

It would not take much of a trained sociological eye for a visitor to American society to notice that many professional sports open with the singing of the national anthem, and to conclude from this that sports are vitally linked to patriotism. Besides this vital function of engendering national, regional, and local loyalties, sociologists have also analyzed how sports reproduce social class, gender, and race. As analyzed in this article, high school football serves as a means by which the adult generation reproduces its version of society—its status hierarchy, or customary divisions, between gender, race, and social classes. Following the "first wisdom" of sociology—that things are not what they seem, that there is a deeper layer of reality than appearances would indicate—sociologists conclude that high school football is much more than a game, that it is one of the ways of maintaining social inequalities across the generations.

. . . THE SETTING OF THIS FIELD STUDY was "North Town," a small (8,000 population) South Texas farming/ranching community with limited industry, considerable local poverty, and a population that was 80% Mexican-American. "North Town High" had an enrollment of 600 students, and its sports teams played at the Triple-A level in a five-level state ranking system.

During the football season described here, I attended a number of practices, rode on the players' bus, and hung out with the coaches at the fieldhouse and with players during extensive classroom and lunchtime observations. I also participated in basketball and tennis practices and interviewed students extensively about student status groups, friendship, dating, and race relations. The participant observation and interviewing in the sports scene involved hundreds of hours of fieldwork over a 12-month period. . . .

The Weekly Pep Rally

Shortly after arriving in North Town I attended my first pep rally. Students, whether they liked football or not, looked forward to Friday afternoons. Regular 7th-period classes were let out early to hold a mass pep rally to support the team. Most students attended these events but a few used it to slip away from school early. During the day of this pep rally I overheard a number of students planning their trip to the game. Those in the school marching band (80) and in the pep club (50) were the most enthusiastic. . . .

The Friday afternoon pep rally was age-graded. The older, most prominent students took the center seats, thus signaling their status and loyalty. Younger first- and second-year students sat next to the leaders of the school activities if they were protégés of those leaders. In sharp contrast, knots and clusters of the more socially marginal students, the "druggers," and the "punks and greasers," usually claimed the seats nearest the exits, thus signaling their indifference to all the rah-rah speeches they had to endure. The "nobodies" or "nerds," those dutiful, conforming students who were followers, tended to sit in the back of the center regions. Irrespective of the general territory, students usually sat with friends from their age group. Teachers strategically placed themselves at the margins and down in front to assist in crowd control.

The pep rally itself was dominated by the coaches and players, who were introduced to the audience to reflect upon the coming contest. In this particular pep rally the team captains led the team onto the stage. All the Anglo players entered first, followed by all the Mexicano players. Coach Trujillo started out with the classic pep talk that introduced the team captains, who in turn stepped forward and spoke in an awkward and self-effacing manner, thus enacting the ideal of a sportsman—a man of deeds, not words. They all stuttered through several "uhs" and "ers," then quickly said, "I hope y'all come support us. Thanks." Generally students expected their jocks to be inarticulate and, as the cliché goes, strong but silent types. . . .

The Marching Band

The quality of the marching band was as carefully scrutinized as the football team by some community members. The band director, Dante Aguila, was keenly aware of maintaining an excellent winning band. Like sport teams, marching bands competed in local, district, and statewide contests and won rankings. The ultimate goal was winning a top rating at the state level. In addition, each band sent its best players of various instruments to district contests to compete for individual rankings. Individual band members could also achieve top rankings at the state level.

A certain segment of the student body began training for the high school marching band during their grade-school years. Band members had a much more positive view of their participation in band than the players did. The band was filled with students who tended to have better grades and came from the more affluent families. The more marginal, deviant students perceived band members as "goodie goodies," "richies," and "brains." This characterization was not entirely true because the band boosters club did make an effort to raise money to help low-income students join the band. Not all band students were top students, but many were in the advanced or academic tracks. Band members were generally the students with school spirit who were proud to promote loyalty to the school and community. The marching band was also a major symbolic expression of the community's unity and its future generation of good citizens and leaders.

The view that band members were the cream of the crop was not widely shared by the football players. Many female band members were socially prominent and "cool," but some were also studious homebodies. On the other hand, "real men" supposedly did not sign up for the North Town band. According to the football players, the physically weaker, more effeminate males tended to be in the band. Males in the band were called "band fags." The only exceptions were "cool guys" who did drugs, or had their own rock and roll band, or came from musical families and planned to become professional musicians. . . .

The main masculinity test for "band fags" was to punch their biceps as hard as possible. If the victim returned this aggression with a defiant smile or smirk, he was a real man; if he winced and whined, he was a wimp or a fag. The other variations on punching biceps were pinching the forearm and rapping the knuckles. North Town boys generally punched and pinched each other, but this kind of male play toward those considered fags was a daily ritual degradation. These were moments when physically dominant males picked on allegedly more effeminate males and reaffirmed their place in the male pecking order. Ironically, however, the players themselves rarely picked on those they called "band fags." Males who emulated jocks and hoped to hang out with them were usually the hit men. The jocks signaled their real power and prestige by showing restraint toward obviously weaker males.

Cheerleaders and Pep Squads

As in most pep rallies, on the Friday I am describing, the cheerleaders were in front of the crowd on the gym floor doing dance and jumping routines in unison and shouting patriotic cheers to whip up enthusiasm for the team. The cheerleaders were acknowledged as some of the prettiest young women in the school and they aroused the envy of nobodies and nerds. Male students incessantly gossiped and fantasized about these young women and their reputations. . . . Students invariably had their favorites to adore and/or ridicule. Yet they told contradictory stories about the cheerleaders. When privately reflecting on their physical attributes and social status, males saw going with a cheerleader as guaranteeing their coolness and masculinity. Particularly the less attractive males plotted the seduction of these young women and reveled in the idea of having them as girlfriends. When expressing their views of these young women to other males, however, they often accused the cheerleaders of being stuck-up or sluts.

This sharp contradiction in males' discourse about cheerleaders makes perfect sense, however, when seen as males talking about females as objects to possess and dominate and through which to gain status. Conversations among males about cheerleaders were rhetorical performances that bonded males together and established their rank in this patriarchal order. In public conversations, males often expressed bravado about conquest of these "easy lays." In private conversations with intimate friends, they expressed their unabashed longing for, hence vulnerable emotional need for, these fantasized sexual objects. Hence, cheerleaders as highly prized females were dangerous, status-confirming creatures who were easier to relate to in rhetorical performances than in real life. Only those males with very high social status could actually risk relating to and being rejected by a cheerleader. The rest of the stories the young men told were simply male talk and fantasy.

Many young women were not athletic or attractive enough to be cheerleaders; nevertheless they wanted to be cheerleaders. Such young women often joined the pep squad as an alternative, and a strong esprit de corps developed among the pep squad members. They were a group of 50 young women in costume who came to the games and helped the cheerleaders arouse crowd enthusiasm. The pep squad also helped publicize and decorate the school and town with catchy team-spirit slogans such as "Smash the Seahawks" and "Spear the Javelinos." In addition, they helped organize after-the-game school dances. Their uniforms expressed loyalty to the team, and pep squad members were given a number of small status privileges in the school. They were sometimes released early for pep rallies and away games. . . .

Homecoming: A Rite of Community Solidarity and Status

Ideally, North Town graduates would return to the homecoming bonfire and dance to reaffirm their support and commitment to the school and team. They would come back to be honored and to honor the new generation presently upholding the name and tradition of the community. In reality, however, few ex-graduates actually attended the pregame bonfire rally or postgame school dance. Typically, the game itself drew a larger crowd and the local paper played up the homecoming game more. College-bound youth were noticeably present at the informal beer party after the game. Some townspeople were also at the pregame bonfire rally, something that rarely happened during an ordinary school pep rally. . . .

Three groups of boys with pickup trucks . . . created a huge pile of scrap wood and burnable objects that had been donated. The cheerleaders, band, and pep squad members then conducted the bonfire ceremonies. Several hundred persons, approximately an equal number of Anglo and Mexicano students, showed up at the rally along with a fair sprinkling of older people and others who were not in high school. Nearly all of the leaders were Anglos and they were complaining that not enough students supported the school or them. The cheerleaders led cheers and sang the school fight song after brief inspirational speeches from the coaches and players. . . .

The huge blazing fire in the school parking lot . . . added to the festive mood, which seemed partly adolescent high jinks and partly serious communion with the town's traditions. The collective energy of the youth had broken a property law or two to stage this event. Adults laughed about the "borrowed" packing crates and were pleased that others "donated" things from their stores and houses to feed the fire. The adults expressed no elaborate rationale for having a homecoming bonfire, which they considered nice, hot, and a good way to fire up the team. Gathering around the bonfire reunited all North Towners, past and present, for the special homecoming reunion and gridiron battle. . . .

After the homecoming game, a school dance was held featuring a homecoming court complete with king and queen. The queen and her court and the king and his attendants, typically the most popular and attractive students, were elected by the student body. Ideally they represented the most attractive, popular, and successful youth. They were considered the best of a future generation of North Towners. Following tradition, the queen was crowned during halftime at midfield as the band played and the crowd cheered. According to tradition, the lovely queen and her court, dressed in formal gowns, were ceremoniously transported to the crowning in convertibles. The king and his attendants, who were often football players and dirty and sweaty at that, then came running from their halftime break to escort the young women from the convertibles and to their crowning. The king and his court lingered rather uneasily until the ceremony was over and then quickly returned to their team to rest and prepare for the second half. . . .

The Powder-Puff Football Game:
Another Rite of Gender Reproduction

A powder-puff football game was traditionally held in North Town on a Friday afternoon before the seniors' final game. A number of the senior football players dressed up as girls and acted as cheerleaders for the game. A number of the senior girls dressed up as football players and formed a touch football team that played the junior girls. The male football players served as coaches and referees and comprised much of the audience as well. Perhaps a quarter of the student body, mainly the active, popular, successful students, drifted in and out to have a laugh over this event. More boys than girls, both Anglo and Mexicano, attended the game.

The striking thing about this ritual was the gender difference in expressive manner. Males took the opportunity to act in silly and outrageous ways. They pranced around in high heels, smeared their faces with lipstick, and flaunted their padded breasts and posteriors in a sexually provocative manner. Everything, including the cheers they led, was done in a very playful, exaggerated, and burlesque manner.

In sharp contrast, the females donned the football jerseys and helmets of the players, sometimes those of their boyfriends, and proceeded to huff and puff soberly up and down the field under the watchful eyes of the boys. They played their part in the game as seriously as possible, blocking and shoving with considerable gusto. This farce went on for several scores, until one team was the clear winner and until the females were physically exhausted and the males were satiated with acting in a ridiculous manner.

. . . Anthropologists . . . call such curious practices "rituals of inversion," specially marked moments when people radically reverse everyday cultural roles and practices. During these events people break, or humorously play with, their own cultural rules. Such reversals are possible without suffering any sanctions or loss of face. These moments are clearly marked so that no one familiar with the culture will misread such reversals as anything more than a momentary break in daily life.

Males of North Town High used this moment of symbolic inversion to parody females in a burlesque and ridiculous manner. They took great liberties with the female role through this humorous form of expression. The power of these young males to appropriate and play with female symbols of sexuality was a statement about males' social and physical dominance. Conversely, the females took few liberties with their expression of the male role. They tried to play a serious game of football. The females tried earnestly to prove they were equal. Their lack of playfulness was a poignant testimony to their subordinate status in this small town. . . .

Prominent Citizens and Their Booster Club: Reproducing Class Privileges

North Town was the type of community in which male teachers who had athletic or coaching backgrounds were more respected than other teachers. For their part, the other teachers often told "dumb coach" jokes and expressed resentment toward the school board's view of coaches. North Town school board members, many of them farmers and ranchers—rugged men of action—generally preferred that their school leaders be ex-coaches. Consequently a disproportionate number of ex-coaches became school principals and superintendents. . . . School board members invariably emphasized an ex-coach's ability to deal with the public and to discipline the youth.

Once gridiron warriors, coaches in small towns are ultimately forced to become organization men, budget administrators, and public relations experts. . . . Ultimately they must appease local factions, school boards, administrators, booster clubs, angry parents, and rebellious teenagers. The successful North Town coaches invariably become excellent public relations men who live a "down home" rural lifestyle; they like to hunt and fish and join local coffee klatches or Saturday morning quarterback groups. They must be real men who like fraternizing with the entrepreneurs, politicians, and good ole' boys who actually run the town. This role as a local male leader creates a web of alliances and obligations that put most coaches in the debt of the prominent citizens and their booster club.

North Town's booster club, composed mainly of local merchants, farmers, and ranchers, had the all-important function of raising supplementary funds for improving the sports program and for holding a postseason awards banquet. The club was the most direct and formal link that coaches had with the principal North Town civic leaders. North Town had a long history of booster club and school board interference in coaching the team. One coach characterized North Town as follows: "One of the toughest towns around to keep a job. Folks here take their football seriously. They are used to winning, not everything, not the state, but conference and maybe bidistrict, and someday even regional. They put a lot of pressure on you to win here." . . .

The pattern of community pressures observed in North Town was not particularly exceptional. A good deal of the public criticism and grumbling about choices of players had racial overtones. The debate over which Anglo varsity quarterback to play also reflected community class differences among Anglos. North Town students and adults often expressed their fears and suspicion that racial and class prejudices were operating. It would be an exaggeration, however, to portray the North Town football team as rife with racial conflict and disunity. Nor was it filled with class prejudice. On a day-to-day basis there was considerable harmony and unity. Mexicanos and Anglos played side by side with few incidents. A number of working-class Mexicano youths and a few low-income Anglos were also members of the football program. At least in a general way, a surface harmony and equality seemed to prevail. . . .

Local sports enthusiasts are fond of arguing that coaches select players objectively, without class or racial prejudices, because their personal interest, and that of the team, is served by winning. Unfortunately, this free-market view glosses over how sport actually functions in local communities. Small-town coaches are generally subjected to enormous pressures to play everyone's child, regardless of social class and race. Success in sport is an important symbolic representation of familial social position. Men can reaffirm their claim to leadership and prominence through the success of their offspring. A son's athletic exploits relive and display the past physical and present social dominance of the father. In displaying past and present familial prominence, the son lays claim to his future potential. Every North Town coach lived and died by his ability to win games *and* his social competence to handle the competing status claims of the parents and their children.

Socially prominent families, who want to maintain their social position, promote their interests through booster clubs. The fathers of future community leaders spend much time talking about and criticizing coaches in local coffee shops. These fathers are more likely to talk to the coaches privately. Coaches who have ambitions to be socially prominent are more likely to "network" with these sportsminded community leaders. A symbiotic relationship develops between coaches, especially native ones, and the traditional community leaders. Preferential treatment of the sons of prominent community leaders flows from this web of friendships, hunting privileges, Saturday morning joking, and other such exchanges.

The booster club that coach Trujillo had to deal with was run by a small clique of Anglos, . . . "good ole' boys and redneck types." They became outspoken early in the season against their "weak Mexican coach." They fanned the fires of criticism in the coffee-drinking sessions over which of the two freshman quarterbacks should start, the "strong-armed Mexican boy" or the "all-around, smart Anglo boy." The Anglo boy was the son of a prominent car dealer and . . . booster club activist. The Mexican boy was the son of a migrant worker and small grocery store manager. The freshman coach, Jim Ryan, chose the Anglo boy. . . . In a similar vein, conflict also surfaced over the selection of the varsity quarterback. Coach Trujillo chose the son of an Anglo businessman, an underclassman, over a senior, the son of a less prominent Anglo. The less educated Anglo faction lambasted the coach for this decision, claiming he showed his preference for the children of the more socially and politically prominent [families].

Moreover, considerable pressure to favor the sons of prominent citizens comes from within the school as well. The school and its classrooms are also a primary social stage upon which students enact their social privilege. These youths establish themselves as leaders in academic, political, and social affairs, and teachers grant them a variety of privileges. This reinforces the influence of their parents in the PTA, the sports and band booster clubs, and the school board. Both generations, in their own way, advance the interests of the family on many fronts.

The Spectators: Male Socialization Through Ex-players

Another major aspect of the football ritual is how the spectators, the men in the community, socialize each new generation of players. In North Town, groups of middle-aged males with families and businesses were influential in socializing the new generation of males. These men congregated in various restaurants for their morning coffee and conversation about business, politics, the weather, and sports. Those leading citizens particularly interested in sports could be heard praising and criticizing "the boys" in almost a fatherly way. Some hired the players for part-time or summer jobs and were inclined to give them special privileges. Athletes were more like to get well-paying jobs as road-gang workers, machine operators, and crew leaders. Most players denied that they got any favors, but they clearly had more prestige than other high school students who worked. Nonplayers complained that jocks got the good jobs. On the job site the men regaled players with stories of male conquests in sports, romance, and business.

Many players reported these conversations, and I observed several during Saturday morning quarterback sessions in a local restaurant and gas station. One Saturday morning after the all-important Harris game, two starters and their good buddies came into the Cactus Bowl Café. One local rancher-businessman shouted, "Hey, Chuck, Jimmie, get over here! I want to talk to you boys about the Harris game!" He then launched into a litany of mistakes each boy and the team had made. Others in the group chimed in and hurled jokes at the boys about "wearing skirts" and being "wimps." Meanwhile the players stood slope-shouldered and "uh-huhed" their tormentors. One thing they had learned was never to argue back too vociferously. The players ridiculed such confrontations with "old-timers" privately, but the proper response from a good kid was tongue-biting deference. . . .

Some ex-players led the romanticized life of tough, brawling, womanizing young bachelors. These young men seemed suspended in a state of adolescence while avoiding becoming responsible family men. They could openly do things that the players had to control or hide because of training rules. Many of these ex-players were also able to physically dominate the younger high school players. But ex-players no longer had a stage upon which to perform heroics for the town. Consequently they often reminded current players of their past exploits and the superiority of players and teams in their era. Current players had to "learn" from these tormentors and take their place in local sports history.

Players Talking About Their Sport: The Meaning of Football

The preceding portrayal of the community sports scene has already suggested several major reasons why young males play football. Many of them are willing to endure considerable physical pain and sacrifice to achieve social prominence in their community. Only a very small percentage are skilled enough to play college football, and only one North Towner has ever made a living playing professional football. The social rewards from playing football are therefore mainly local and cultural.

However, there are other more immediate psychological rewards for playing football. When asked why they play football and why they like it, young North Town males gave a variety of answers. A few openly admitted that football was a way for them to achieve some social status and prominence, to "become somebody in this town." Many said football was fun, or "makes a man out of you," or "helps you get a cute chick." Others parroted a chamber of commerce view that it built character and trained them to have discipline, thus helping them be successful in life. Finally, many evoked patriotic motives—to beat rival towns and to "show others that South Texas plays as good a football as East Texas."

These explicit statements do not reveal the deeper . . . lessons learned in sports combat, however. In casual conversations, players used phrases that were particularly revealing. What they talked most about was "hitting" or "sticking" or "popping" someone. These were all things that coaches exhorted the players to do in practice. After a hard game, the supreme compliment was having a particular "lick" or "hit" singled out. Folkloric immortality, endless stories about that one great hit in the big game, was what players secretly strove for. For most coaches and players, really "laying a lick on" or "knocking somebody's can off" or "taking a real lick" was that quintessential football moment. Somebody who could "take it" was someone who could bounce up off the ground as if he had hardly been hit. The supreme compliment, however, was to be called a hitter or head-hunter. A hitter made bone-crushing tackles that knocked out or hurt his opponent.

Players who consistently inflicted outstanding hits were called animals, studs, bulls, horses, or gorillas. A stud was a superior physical specimen who fearlessly dished out and took hits, who liked the physical contact, who could dominate other players physically. Other players idolized a "real stud," because he seemed fearless and indomitable on the field. Off the field a stud was also cool, or at least imagined to be cool, with girls. Most players expected and wanted strong coaches and some studs to lead them into battle.

They talked endlessly about who was a real stud and whether the coach "really kicks butt."

The point of being a hitter and stud is proving that you have enough courage to inflict and take physical pain. Pain is a badge of honor. Playing with pain proves you are a man. In conventional society, pain is a warning to protect your body, but the opposite ethic rules in football. In North Town bandages and stitches and casts became medals worn proudly into battle. Players constantly told stories about overcoming injuries and "playing hurt." A truly brave man was one who could fight on; his pain and wounds were simply greater obstacles to overcome. Scars were permanent traces of past battles won, or at the very least fought well. They became stories told to girlfriends and relatives. . . .

Many players, particularly the skilled ones, described what might be called their aesthetic moments as the most rewarding thing about football. Players sitting around reviewing a game always talked about themselves or others as "making a good cut" and "running a good route," or "trapping" and "blindsiding" someone. All these specific acts involved executing a particular type of body control and skill with perfection and excellence. Running backs made quick turns or cuts that left would-be tacklers grasping for thin air. Ends "ran routes" or a clever change of direction that freed them to leap into the air and catch a pass. Guards lay in wait for big opposing linemen or aggressive linebackers to enter their territory recklessly, only to be trapped or blindsided by them. Each position had a variety of assignments or moments when players used their strength and intelligence to defeat their opponents. The way this was done was beautiful to a player who had spent years perfecting the body control and timing to execute the play. Players talked about "feeling" the game and the ball and the pressure from an opponent.

Team sports, and especially American football, generally socialize males to be warriors. The young men of North Town were being socialized to measure themselves by their animal instincts and aggressiveness. Physicality, searching for pain, enduring pain, inflicting pain, and knowing one's pain threshold emphasizes the biological, animal side of human beings. These are the instincts needed to work together and survive in military combat and, in capitalist ideology, in corporate, academic, and industrial combat. The language used—head-hunter, stick 'em, and various aggressive animal symbols—conjures up visions of Wall Street stockbrokers and real estate sharks chewing up their competition.

Other Males: Brains, Farm Kids, and Nobodies

What of those males who do not play high school football? Does this pervasive community ritual require the participation of all young males? Do all nonathletes end up in the category of effeminate "band fags"? To the contrary, several types of male students did not lose gender status for being unathletic. There were a small number of "brains" who were obviously not physically capable of being gridiron warriors. Some of them played other sports with less physical contact such as basketball, tennis, track, or baseball. In this way they still upheld the ideal of being involved in some form of sport. Others, who were slight of physique, wore thick glasses, lacked hand-eye coordination, or ran and threw poorly, sometimes ended up hanging around jocks or helping them with their schoolwork. Others were loners who were labeled nerds and weirdos.

In addition, there were many farm kids or poor kids who did not participate in sports. They were generally homebodies who did not participate in many extracurricular activities. Some of them had to work to help support their families. Others had no transportation to attend practices. In the student peer groups they were often part of the great silent majority called "the nobodies."

Resistance to the Football Ritual: The Working-Class Chicano Rebels

There were also a number of Mexicano males who formed anti-school oriented peer groups. They were into a "hip" drug-oriented lifestyle. These males, often called "vatos" (cool dudes), made it a point to be anti-sports, an activity they considered straight. Although some were quite physically capable of playing, they rarely tried out for any type of team sports. They made excuses for not playing such as needing a job to support their car or van or pickup. They considered sports "kids' stuff," and their hip lifestyle as more adult, cool, and fun.

Even for the vatos, however, sports events were important moments when they could publicly display their lifestyle and establish their reputation. A number of vatos always came to the games and even followed the team to other towns. They went to games to be tough guys and "enforcers" and to establish "reps" as fighters. The vatos also went to games to "hit on chicks from other towns." During one road game, after smoking several joints, they swaggered in with cocky smiles plastered on their faces. The idea was to attract attention from young women and hopefully provoke a fight while stealing another town's women. Unlike stealing watermelons or apples from a neighbor, stealing women was done openly and was a test of courage. A man faced this danger in front of his buddies and under the eyes of the enemy.

. . . [A]fter the game the vatos told many tales about their foray into enemy territory. With great bravado they recounted every unanswered slight and insult they hurled at those "geeks." They also gloried in their mythical conquests of local young women. . . . As the players battled on the field, the vatos battled on the sidelines. They were another kind of warrior that established North Town's community identity and territoriality through the sport of fighting over and chasing young women.

The Contradiction of Being "In Training"

In other ways, even the straight young men who played football also resisted certain aspects of the game. Young athletes were thrust into a real dilemma when their coaches sought to rationalize training techniques and forbade various pleasures of the flesh. Being in training meant no drugs, alcohol, or tobacco. It also meant eating well-balanced meals, getting at least 8 hours of sleep, and not wasting one's emotional and physical energy chasing women. These dictates were extremely difficult to follow in a culture where drugs are used regularly and where sexual conquest and/or romantic love are popular cultural ideals. Add a combination of male adolescence and the overwhelming use of sex and women's bodies to sell commodities, and you have an environment not particularly conducive to making sacrifices for the coach and the team. North Town athletes envied the young bachelors who drank, smoked pot, and chased women late into the night. If they wanted to be males, American culture dictated that they break the rigid, unnatural training rules set for them.

. . . [M]any North Town football players . . . broke their training rules. They often drank and smoked pot at private teen parties. Unlike the rebellious vatos, who publicly flaunted their drinking and drugs, jocks avoided drinking in public. By acting like all-American boys, jocks won praise from adults for their conformity. Many of them publicly pretended to be sacrificing and denying themselves pleasure. They told the old-timers stories about their "rough practices" and "commitment to conditioning." Consequently, if jocks got caught breaking traiing, the men tended to overlook these infractions as slips or temptations. In short, cool jocks knew how to manage their public image as conformists and hide their private nonconformity. . . .

Fathers who had experienced this training contradiction themselves . . . gave their sons and other players stern lectures about keeping in shape, *but* they were the first to chuckle at the heroic stories of playing with a hangover. They told these same stories about teammates or about themselves over a cup of coffee or a beer. As a result, unless their youth were outrageously indiscreet—for example passing out drunk on the main street or in class, getting a "trashy girl" pregnant—a "little drinking and screwing around" was overlooked. They simply wanted the school board to stop being hypocritical and acknowledge that drinking was all part of growing up to be a prominent male.

In the small sports world of North Town, a real jock actually enhances his public image of being in shape by occasionally being a "boozer" or "doper." Indeed, one of the most common genres of stories that jocks told was the "I played while drunk/stoned," or the "I got drunk/stoned the night before the game" tale. Olmo, a big bruising guard who is now a hard-living, hard-drinking bachelor, told me a classic version of this tale before the homecoming game:

> Last night we really went out and hung one on. Me and Jaime and Arturo drank a six-pack apiece in a couple of hours. We were cruising around Daly City checking out the action. It was real dead. We didn't see nobody we knew except Arturo's cousin. We stopped at his place and drank some more and listened to some music. We stayed there till his old lady [mom] told us to go home. We got home pretty late, but before the sun come up, 'cause we're in training, ha ha.

[*Conclusion*]

. . . [T]he football ritual remains a powerful metaphor of American capitalist culture. In North Town, football is still a popular cultural practice deeply implicated in the reproduction of the local ruling class of white males, hence class, patriarchal, and racial forms of dominance. Local sports, especially football, are still central to the socialization of each new generation of youth and to the maintenance of the adolescent society's status system. In addition, this ritual is also central to the preservation of the community's adult status hierarchy. The local politics of the booster club, adult male peer groups, and Saturday morning coffee klatches ensnare coaches and turn a son's participation in the football ritual into an important symbolic reenactment of the father's social class and gender prominence. . . .

37 The Cloak of Competence

JACK HAAS
WILLIAM SHAFFIR

No one wants to entrust himself or herself to a professional (or to someone in the trades) who is incompetent. Yet we know that there are varying degrees of competence among the members of every profession. This knowledge presents a dilemma for someone who wants to select a professional. How do you know you will get a competent physician, lawyer, teacher, or member of the clergy? An old joke centers on the doctor who couldn't help a patient who complained about a mole (skin cancer, toenail, etc.). The reason was that, when a medical student, the doctor overslept and missed class the morning an instructor lectured on moles (skin cancer, toenails, etc.).

If the problematic question for the client is not knowing whether the professional is competent in some area, the counterpart issue for the professional is to convince the client that he or she *is* competent. Without that conviction, the professional cannot succeed. And, yet, the professional simply *cannot* be competent in *all* aspects of his or her profession. Because the dilemma is deep and recurring, the solutions have become embedded in the learning of the profession itself, as Haas and Shaffir indicate in their analysis of the socialization of medical students at McMaster University.

[*Methodology*]

[This study of the socialization of medical students] is based on data that were collected . . . on the socialization of medical students at a medical school in Ontario, Canada. The data were collected by means of participant observation and interviews. We observed students during the full range of their educational and informal activities.

Unlike most medical schools, the school we are studying has a three-year program where long summer vacations are eliminated. Admission is not restricted to individuals within strong premedical or science backgrounds. The school deemphasizes lectures and has no formal tests or grades. Students are introduced to clinical settings from the very beginning of their studies. Learning revolves around a "problem-solving" approach as students meet in six-person tutorial groups.[*]

[Expectations of Competence]

Though managing impressions and role-playing are basic parts of the sociological drama, they may be more obvious where participants perceive a potentially critical and condemning audience. This is obvious when the audience has high expectations of competence for others and expect, if not demand, displays of competence, particularly when those assumed to be competent control the situation and act or make decisions affecting the well-being of others. The affected parties then look for cues and indications of personal and/or collective (institutional) competence and practitioners organize a carefully managed presentation of self to create and sustain a reality of competence.

    This concern about the competence of those granted rights and responsibilities affecting others is very obvious in the case of patient relationships with medical professionals. Patients look for competent advice and assistance and want to believe they will get it. Conversely, medical professionals, particularly doctors, want to convince those they treat that they are indeed competent and trustworthy, and that the patient can confidently allow them to diagnose, prescribe, and intervene to affect the patient's condition. . . .

The Symbols of Professionalism

The professionalization of medical students is facilitated by symbols the neophytes take on which serve to announce to insiders and outsiders how they are to be identified. During the first weeks of their studies students begin wearing white lab jackets with plastic name tags identifying them as medical students. . . . Along with their newly acquired identity kit, students begin to learn and express themselves in the medical vernacular. Distinctive dress, badges, tools, and language provide the student with symbols which announce their role and activity. They are identified as students learning to be doctors.

    The significance of these symbols to the professionalization process is

---

[*]The two paragraphs under "[Methodology]" have been repositioned from elsewhere in the authors' text.

critical. The symbols serve, on the one hand, to identify and unite the bearers as members of a community of shared interests, purposes, and identification (Roth, 1957). Simultaneously, the symbols distinguish and separate their possessors from lay people, making their role seem more mysterious, shrouded, and priest-like (Bramson, 1973). The early possession of these symbols serves to hasten their identification and commitment to the profession, while at the same time facilitating their separation from the lay world.

At this point, their very selection of medicine as a career has produced a set of reactions by friends, family, and others which reinforce in the students' minds the idea that they are becoming very special people. Immediately upon acceptance into medical school, students perceive themselves being related to, in typified fashion, as medical students and future physicians. This reaction of others intensifies as students enter training and immerse themselves in it. At the same time, students see that they must devote more and more time and energy to their studies, and less time to past relationships and interests. They find themselves increasingly separated from social worlds outside of medicine; more and more they find themselves either alone or with other medical people. The socialization experience is intense, extensive, anguishing, and exhausting.

One of the first difficult tasks that faces students is to begin to learn and communicate in the symbolic system that defines medical work and workers. Immediately in tutorials, readings, demonstrations, and rounds, students are inundated with a language they know they are expected to become facile in. Their task is even more difficult because this exotic language is used to describe very complex processes and understandings. Students are taken aback at the difficulty of learning to communicate in their new language. They begin carrying medical dictionaries to help them translate and define terms and phrases. They complain about the problems of simultaneously translating readings with understanding, and committing to memory such elusive material.

The separation between "we" and "they" becomes clearer to students as they are absorbed into the medical culture. As they move through the culture, they learn how the symbols are used to communicate and enforce certain definitions of the situation. Students learn how practicing physicians use these symbols of the profession to shape and control the definition of the situation.

The ability to use the language symbols of medicine defines members of the profession and creates a boundary that is only occasionally erased. Reflecting on the significance of this technical terminology, a student remarks:

> [Y]ou just can't survive if you don't learn the jargon. It's not so much an effort to identify as it is an effort to survive. People in medicine have a world

unto themselves and a language unto themselves. It's a world with a vocabulary . . . and a vocabulary that, no question about it, creates a fraternity that excludes the rest of the world and it's a real tyranny to lay persons who don't understand it. . . .

Turning Off Your Feelings

[A]s students move through school and develop a professional self-image, and thus begin to take on the identity of a doctor, their views on medicine become transformed. . . . Students become less vocal in their questioning and criticisms of the medical profession. They attribute many of their earlier concerns to naïveté, and argue for a more sympathetic view of doctors and the profession as a whole:

> I think I went through a phase, as I went from knowing very little about medicine to a little bit. . . . You go through a sort of stage of disillusion in which you sort of expect doctors to be perfect, and the medical profession and treatment and everything else to be perfect. And you find out that it's not. So you sort of react to that. I think now, after about two years, I'm starting to get to the phase now where I'm quite pleased with it really. . . . [K]nowing doctors the way you do, and I've seen them operate, if other professions were as self-critical as doctors were and had a good sense of responsibility to duty, then I think a lot of the professions would be a lot better off. Part of the flack that you hear about medical doctors and malpractice suits, and about things that go wrong, are partly due to the fact that doctors tend to look after themselves and examine their own profession very carefully.

. . . Although they are often initially dismayed by how physicians and other hospital staff treat patients, they come to accept that the objectification of patients is a routine feature of doctor-patient relationships. It is the "professional" way to deal with medical situations. In time they accept the view that patients must be objectified and depersonalized or the doctor will be unable to maintain clinical objectivity (Coombs and Powers, 1975; Emerson, 1970). While initially bothered, even offended, by this detachment, they come to see it as part of the professional situation over which they have little control. They believe it is, at least, temporarily necessary if they are to learn clinical symptoms and pathology, thus adding to their medical knowledge and competence.

> I think you realize that there is a structural problem, and there are a lot of demands made on you and you are forced to act in certain ways just to accomplish your work. But right now in the training phase, I find if the clinical preceptor takes me around to listen to six patients with heart murmurs and I only have five minutes with each patient, I don't get concerned that I'm not getting it on with the patient, because I'm trying to learn about heart murmurs.

Striving for competence is the primary student rationale to explain avoiding or shutting off emotional reactions. As they progress through the program students come to express the belief that their relationship with the patient should be governed strictly by the patient's medical problem; emotional feelings are a hindrance. They believe that they do not have time for both learning and caring, and learn to stifle their feelings because of the higher value they and others place on competence. . . .

The dominant concern with learning medicine leads students to maintain their learning efficiency and productivity. Students come to believe that they have no time for the frills of emotional involvement and quickly learn to close off feelings that interfere with their work (Lief and Fox, 1963). The following statement by a student emphasizes the idea of productivity:

> You can't function if you think about things like that [death and dying]. Every-thing you see sort of gets in there and turns about in your mind and you aren't productive. The reason you have to shut it off is because you won't be productive. . . . I think that my prime objective is to learn the pathology and just to know it and then, understanding that, I can go back to these other things and worry about the personal part of it.

. . . As they are gradually introduced to the content and "core" of medicine, they begin to realize that there is too much to know and little time in which to learn it all. Like the religious or political convert who becomes fanatically observant and committed, students devote themselves to the task of learning medicine. Time becomes a commodity that must be spent wisely. They become very concerned about not misusing or wasting their time studying certain topics deemed unproductive. In this context, the psychosocial component becomes less important:

> One thing you have to do at medical school is pick up all the pathophysiology and to pick up all of the anatomy and pick up the clinical histories, the presenta-tions, the clinical skills and so on. So psychosocial time is really a luxury, it can't really be afforded sometimes. Not that it gets pushed out of the way. It's just that in a tutorial group if you are given two weeks and two hours per tutorial group, how do you most profitably spend that time in terms of the task at hand? Do you want to learn a lot of what we call the core material . . . or do you want to rehash a lot of arguments that are of fundamental human importance but really can't be resolved within a reasonable time limit.

Although they put them aside, students continue to recognize that psychosocial matters are important. They believe this area must be neglected, however, in the interests of acquiring as much medical knowledge and competence as possible. They believe that if they feel for their patients and become involved with them they will not become professionally compe-tent:

> When you see someone who is going to die, especially when you're still learning, you're really cut off from that personal level. You just clue into the pathology. You really shut off. You sort of turn it out of your mind that this person is going to die. You just look at the pathology, all of the symptoms, and you

have one train of thought. You don't really think, "What about the family?" what they must be going through. . . . You can't fall to pieces because you find your patient is going to die in three months or is rapidly going downhill. You have a role to play here. You can't come apart and cry in the patient's room for half an hour every time you see him.

. . . Students alter their understanding of how medicine should be practiced. Unable to feel as deeply concerned about the patient's total condition as they believe they should, they discover an approach that justifies concentrating only on the person's medical problem. As a student remarks:

Somebody will say "Listen to Mrs. Jones's heart. It's just a little thing flubbing on the table." And you forget about the rest of her. Part of that is the objectivity and it helps in learning in the sense that you can go in to a patient, put your stethoscope on the heart, listen to it and walk out. . . . The advantage is that you can go in a short time and see a patient, get the important things out of the patient, and leave.

As students learn to objectify patients they lose their sensitivity for them. When they can concentrate on the interesting pathology of the patient's condition, students' feelings for the patient's total situation are eroded:

In the neuro unit you can define exactly where the lesion is by deciding on how well you know the conducting system and, of course, if there is a lesion closer to the cortex than to the midbrain, then you will see all kinds of behavioral problems. But then you won't think they are a psychiatric case. They are a neurological case showing an interesting effect. . . . And you get that kind of approach and you really lose your sensitivity in terms of what's happening in terms of the anxiety of the patient.

. . . Students learn to become objective during their clinical skills sessions in hospital settings. They are introduced to striking examples of how patients' needs, rights, and dignities are submerged to the clinical task at hand. The following [example indicates] the kind of objectivity the students are exposed to and affected by:

. . . [T]hat really got me when I did go to a cancer clinic at the Fensteran and I saw the way they were just herding in ladies that had hysterectomies and cancer, and just the way the doctors would walk right in and wouldn't even introduce us as students, and just open them up and just look and say a lot of heavy jargon. And the ladies would be saying, "How is it?", "Am I better, worse?" And they say in this phony assuring tone, "Yes, you're fine," and take you into the hallway and say how bad the person was.

. . . Students discover that such experiences are a routine feature of the hospital setting, regularly accepted by the medical profession. More importantly, however, they learn and accept the rationales usually given. They heed their teachers' reminders that their primary object at this stage of their career is to absorb as much pathology as possible. This end, they are told, is best achieved by examining patients. They are made to realize that the physician's high case load precludes attending to anything but the patient's medical condition.

Students use the pressures of learning medicine and developing competence to rationalize their growing alienation from patients and their willingness to ignore the more extreme examples of objectivity:

> You sort of go in and you don't know the people that are under anesthesia. Just practice putting the tube in, and the person wakes up with a sore throat, and well, it's just sort of a part of the procedure kind of thing. "How do you feel about intubating dead on arrivals?" Someone comes in who has croaked, "Well come on, here is a chance to practice your intubation." It seems awfully barbaric.

Though not entirely pleased with how they see medicine practiced, and how they practice it themselves, they elect to put their idealism in abeyance. Their solution to the problem of protecting themselves from becoming emotionally involved with patients is to present themselves as they believe they are expected to behave. Their assessment of the situation is that they are to act professionally (competently and objectively) and they organize their self-presentation to coincide with this expectation.

Acting the Professional Role

Students believe they are expected to act as if they are in the know, not in ways which might put their developing competence into question. The pressure to be seen as competent by faculty, fellow students, hospital personnel, and patients narrows the range of alternative roles students can assume. Students recognize their low status in the hospital hierarchy and on hospital rotations. They realize that the extent of their medical knowledge can easily be called into question by fellow students, tutors, interns, residents, and faculty. To reduce the possibility of embarrassment and humiliation which, at this stage in their medical career, is easily their fate, students attempt to reduce the unpredictability of their situation by manipulating an impression of themselves as enthusiastic, interested, and eager to learn. At the same time, students seize opportunities which allow them to impress others, particularly faculty and fellow students, with their growing competence and confidence.

. . . A perspective shared by students to manage an appearance of competence is to limit their initiatives to those situations which will be convincing demonstrations of their competence. Some students decide, for example, to ask questions in areas with which they are already familiar, to cultivate an impression of competence.

> The best way of impressing others with your competence is asking questions you know the answers to. Because if they ever put it back on you: "Well

what do you think?" then you tell them what you think and you'd give a very intelligent answer because you knew it. You didn't ask it to find out information. You ask it to impress people.

The general strategy that the students adopt is to mask their uncertainty and anxiety with an image of self-confidence. Image making becomes recognized as being as important as technical competence. As one student remarks: "We have to be good actors, put across the image of self-confidence, that you know it all. . . ."

[R]eferring to the importance of creating the right impression, [a student said]: . . .

> Dr. Jones who was my adviser or boss for medicine, he always came and did rounds on Wednesday mornings. Well he didn't have very many patients on the service, but we always knew that his interest was in endocrinology, and he knew . . . if he had an endocrine patient . . . and . . . we knew . . . that he was going to pick that endocrine patient to talk about. And so, of course, Tuesday night, any dummy can read up Tuesday night like hell on the new American Diabetic Association standards for diabetes or hyperglycemia and you can read up like hell on it, or read it over twice, and you can handle general medicine. So the next day you seem fairly knowledgeable. . . . that afternoon you forget about it because you figure Thursday morning hematology people make their rounds and, of course, you have to read up on hematology. . . .

. . . Students realize that to be a good student-physician is either to be or appear to be competent. They observe that others react to their role-playing. A student describes the self-fulfilling nature of this process when he says:

> To be a good GP, you've got to be a good actor, you've got to respond to a situation. You have to be quick, pick up the dynamics of what is going on at the time and try to make the person leave the office thinking that you know something. And a lot of people, the way they handle that is by letting the patient know that they know it all, and only letting out a little bit at a time, and as little as possible. I think that they eventually reach a plateau where they start thinking themselves they are really great and they know it all, because they have these people who are worshiping at their feet.

The process of adopting the cloak of competence is justified by students as helpful to the patient. A student summarizes the relationship between acting competently and patients responding to such a performance by getting well when he says:

> You know the patients put pressure on you to act as if you are in the know. If you know anything about the placebo effect, you know that a lot of the healing and curing of patients does not involve doing anything that will really help them, but rather creating confidence in the patient that things are being done and will be done. We know that the placebo effect for example has

even cured cancer patients. If they have the confidence in the doctor and what doctor and what treatment they are undergoing, they are much more likely to get well, irrespective of the objective effects of the treatment. . . .

Conclusion

Everett Hughes provides all students of occupations with a sound sociological maxim when he says:

> I think it a good rule to assume that a feature of work behavior found in one occupation, even a minor or odd one, will be found in others. The fact that it is denied at first by the people in some occupations, or that it has not been revealed by previous research, should not be considered sufficient evidence it is not there (1952:425).

Hughes's principle makes sociological research both exciting and mundane. The basic processes of social life operate throughout the social structure. All social groups create boundaries and differences, view themselves ethnocentrically, and create and manipulate symbols to present themselves in the most favorable ways. All individuals and groups strive to protect themselves from ridicule and charges of incompetence. In this sense, our paper only describes what has been a "taken-for-granted" understanding of social life: Much behavior is performance designed to elicit certain reactions. Professional behavior is, or can be, understood as performance. . . .

Medical students learn a new symbol system that not only distinguishes them as neophyte members of a distinctive and powerful community but creates an imagery of authoritativeness and competence. At the same time, students learn that the student role requires an objectification of patients and a covering of personal feelings and reactions. Students initially adopt this professional-scientific posture to help them increase their learning efficiency. They believe they do not have enough time to deal with psychosocial problems because of the dominant concern with learning the "core" of medicine. With more clinical experiences the rationale for objectifying patients and closing off feelings comes to be reinterpreted as professionally appropriate and, even, helpful to patients. . . .

Students observe, particularly in clinical situations, the physician–patient relationship. They come to realize that an important part of becoming a doctor is learning a role or roles that project an image of competence and reduce threats or charges of incompetence. In a situation where too much is expected, professionalism provides a protective shield helping students and practitioners define and exert control over medical situations.

Our findings should be analogous to other professions and their socialization processes. The process of making some expert and more competent separates professionals from those they are presumed to help and serves to create a situation where the exaggerated expectations of competence are managed by symbolically defining and controlling the situation to display the imagery of competence. Impression management is basic and fundamental in those occupations and professions which profess competence in matters seriously affecting others. . . .

The development of a cloak of competence is, perhaps, most apparent for those who must meet exaggerated expectations. . . . For those required to perform beyond their capacities, in order to be successful, there is the constant threat of breakdown or exposure. . . . Expectations of competence are dealt with by strategies of impression management, specifically manipulation and concealment. Interactional competencies depend on convincing presentations, and much of professionalism requires the masking of insecurity and incompetence with the symbolic-interactional cloak of competence.

References

Bramson, Roy (1973). "The Secularization of American Medicine." *Hastings Center Studies*, pp. 17–28.

Coombs, Robert H., and Pauline S. Powers (1975). "Socialization for Death: The Physician's Role." *Urban Life 4*: 250–71.

Emerson, Joan P. (1970). "Behavior in Private Places: Sustaining Definitions of Reality in Gynecological Examinations." Pp. 73–97 in Hans Peter Dreitzel (ed.), *Recent Sociology*. New York: Macmillan.

Hughes, Everett C. (1952). "The Sociological Study of Work: An Editoral Foreword." *American Journal of Sociology* 57: 423–26.

Lief, Harold I., and Renée Fox (1963). "Training for 'Detached Concern' in Medical Students." Pp. 12–35 in H. I. Lief, V. Lief, and N. R. Lief (eds.), *The Psychological Basis of Medical Practice*. New York: Harper & Row.

Roth, Julius A. (1957). "Ritual and Magic in the Control of Contagion." *American Sociological Review* 22: 310–14.

38 Police Accounts of Normal Force

JENNIFER HUNT

My personal contacts with the police have been infrequent and brief. Nevertheless, I have seen a policeman handcuff a rape suspect to a tree and then slap him in the face in front of a group of citizen-witnesses. I have heard another threaten the life of a suspect he was escorting near a stream, saying he wished the suspect would attempt to flee so he "could shoot her and watch her body float down the river." And in Mexico, after recovering my billfold and apprehending the two men who had picked my pocket, the secret police offered to hold the culprits while I beat them. They felt that I ought to beat them because, as they said, the men had caused me (and presumably them) so much trouble.

Those random events have convinced me that police violence is no random matter but is a regular part of the occupation. Why should that be so? Is it because the police recruit certain personality types? As a sociologist, Hunt does not look for explanations lodged within something called "personality." Rather, she examines the occupational culture, especially the constraints of the occupation and the effects of norms on recruits.

If you were a social reformer and you wanted to decrease police violence, where would you start? Keep in mind the virtual absence of differences by gender, the distinction between formal and informal expectations, and the strong support for "normal" violence that is built into this occupation—and the lessons from the Zimbardo experiment in Part VI.

THE POLICE ARE REQUIRED to handle a variety of peacekeeping and law enforcement tasks including settling disputes, removing drunks from the street, aiding the sick, controlling crowds, and pursuing criminals. What unifies these diverse activities is the possibility that their resolution might require the use of force. Indeed, the capacity to use force stands at the core of the police mandate (Bittner, 1980). . . . The following research . . . explores how police themselves classify and evaluate acts of force as either legal, normal, or excessive. Legal force is that coercion necessary to subdue, control, and restrain a suspect in order to take him into custody. Although force not accountable in legal terms is technically labeled excessive by the courts and the public, the police perceive many forms of illegal force as normal. Normal force involves coercive acts that specific "cops" on specific occasions formulate as necessary, appropriate, reasonable, or understandable. Although not always legitimated or admired, normal force is depicted as a necessary or natural response of normal police to particular situational exigencies. . . . Brutality is viewed as illegal, illegitimate, and often immoral violence, but the police draw the lines in extremely different ways and at different points [from] either the court system or the public. . . .

The article is based on approximately eighteen months of participant observation in a major urban police department referred to as the Metro City P.D. I attended the police academy with male and female recruits and later rode with individual officers in one-person cars on evening and night shifts in high crime districts.[1] The female officers described in this research were among the first 100 women assigned to the ranks of uniformed patrol as a result of a discrimination suit filed by the Justice Department and a policewoman plaintiff.

Learning to Use Normal Force

The police phrase "it's not done on the street the way that it's taught at the academy" underscores the perceived contradiction between the formal world of the police academy and the informal world of the street. This contradiction permeates the police officer's construction of his world, particularly his view of the rational and moral use of force.

In the formal world of the police academy, the recruit learns to account for force by reference to legality. He or she is issued the regulation instruments and trained to use them to subdue, control, and restrain a suspect. If threatened with great bodily harm, the officer learns that he can justifiably use deadly force and fire his revolver. Yet the recruit is taught that he cannot use his baton, jack, or gun unnecessarily to torture, maim, or kill a suspect.

When recruits leave the formal world of the academy and are assigned to patrol a district, they are introduced to an informal world in which police recognize normal as well as legal and brutal force. Through observation and instruction, rookies gradually learn to apply force and account for its use in terms familiar to the street cop. First, rookies learn to adjust their arsenals to conform to street standards. They are encouraged to buy the more powerful weapons worn by veteran colleagues as these colleagues point out the inadequacy of a wooden baton or compare their convoy jacks to vibrators. They quickly discover that their department-issued equipment marks them as new recruits. At any rate, within a few weeks, most rookies have dispensed with the wooden baton and convoy jack and substituted . . . the more powerful plastic nightstick and flat-headed slapjack.[2]

Through experience and informal instruction, the rookie also learns the street use of these weapons. In school, for example, recruits are taught to avoid hitting a person on the head or neck because it could cause lethal damage. On the street, in contrast, police conclude that they must hit wherever it causes the most damage in order to incapacitate the suspect before they themselves are harmed. New officers also learn that they will earn the respect of their veteran co-workers not by observing legal niceties in using force, but by being "aggressive" and using whatever force is necessary in a given situation.

Peer approval helps neutralize the guilt and confusion that rookies often experience when they begin to use force to assert their authority. One female officer, for example, learned she was the object of a brutality suit while listening to the news on television. At first, she felt so mortified that she hesitated to go to work and face her peers. In fact, male colleagues greeted her with a standing ovation and commented, "You can use our urinal now." In their view, any aggressive police officer regularly using normal force might eventually face a brutality suit or civilian complaint. Such accusations confirm the officer's status as a "street cop" rather than an "inside man" who doesn't engage in "real police work."

Whereas male rookies are assumed to be competent dispensers of force unless proven otherwise, women are believed to be physically weak, naturally passive, and emotionally vulnerable.[3] Women officers are assumed to be reluctant to use physical force and are viewed as incompetent "street cops" until they prove otherwise. As a result, women rookies encounter special problems in learning to use normal force in the process of becoming recognized as "real street cops." It becomes crucial for women officers to create or exploit opportunities to display their physical abilities in order to overcome sexual bias and obtain full acceptance from co-workers. As a result, women rookies are encouraged informally to act more aggressively and to display more machismo than male rookies. . . .

For a street cop, it is often a graver error to use too little force and develop a "shaky" reputation than it is to use too much force and be told to calm down. Thus officers, particularly rookies, who do not back up their partners in appropriate ways or who hesitate to use force in circumstances where it is deemed necessary are informally instructed regarding their aberrant ways. If the problematic incident is relatively insignificant and his general reputation is good, a rookie who "freezes" one time is given a second chance before becoming generally known as an untrustworthy partner. However, such incidents become the subject of degrading gossip, gossip that pressures the officer either to use force as expected or risk isolation.

Such talk also informs rookies about the general boundaries of legal and normal force.

For example, a female rookie was accused of "freezing" in an incident that came to be referred to as a "Mexican standoff." A pedestrian had complained that "something funny is going on in the drugstore." The officer walked into the pharmacy where she found an armed man committing a robbery. Although he turned his weapon on her when she entered the premises, she still pulled out her gun and pointed it at him. When he ordered her to drop it, claiming that his partner was behind her with a revolver at her head, she refused and told him to drop his.[4] He refused, and the stalemate continued until a sergeant entered the drugstore and ordered the suspect to drop his gun.

Initially, the female officer thought she had acted appropriately and even heroically. She soon discovered, however, that her hesitation to shoot had brought into question her competence with some of her fellow officers. Although many veterans claimed that "she had a lot a balls" to take her gun out at all when the suspect already had a gun on her, most contended "she shoulda shot him." Other policemen confirmed that she committed a "rookie mistake"; she had failed to notice a "lookout" standing outside the store and hence had been unprepared for an armed confrontation. Her sergeant and lieutenant, moreover, even insisted that she had acted in a cowardly manner, despite her reputation as a "gung-ho cop," and cited the incident as evidence of the general inadequacy of policewomen.

In the weeks that followed, this officer became increasingly depressed and angry. She was particularly outraged when she learned that she would not receive a commendation, although such awards were commonly made for "gun pinches" of this nature. Several months later, the officer vehemently expressed the wish that she had killed the suspect and vowed that next time she would "shoot first and ask questions later." The negative sanctions of supervisors and colleagues clearly encouraged her to adopt an attitude favorable to using force with less restraint in future situations. . . .

At the same time that male and female rookies are commended for using force under appropriate circumstances, they are reprimanded if their participation in force is viewed as excessive or inappropriate. In this way, rookies are instructed that although many acts of coercion are accepted and even demanded, not everything goes. They thereby learn to distinguish between normal and brutal force. . . .

Accounting for Normal Force

Police routinely normalize the use of force by two types of accounts: excuses and justifications. . . .

EXCUSES AND NORMAL FORCE

Excuses are accounts in which police deny full responsibility for an act but recognize its inappropriateness. Excuses therefore constitute socially approved vocabularies for relieving responsibility when conduct is questionable. Police most often excuse morally problematic force by referring to emotional or physiological states that are precipitated by some circumstances of routine patrol work. These circumstances include shootouts, violent fights, pursuits, and instances in which a police officer mistakenly comes close to killing an unarmed person.

Police work in these circumstances can generate intense excitement in which the officer experiences the "combat high" and "adrenaline rush" familiar to the combat soldier.[5] Foot and car pursuits not only bring on feelings of danger and excitement from the chase, but also a challenge to official authority. As one patrolman commented about a suspect: "Yeh, he got tuned up [beaten] . . . you always tune them up after a car chase." Another officer normalized the use of force after a pursuit in these terms:

> It's my feeling that violence inevitably occurs after a pursuit. . . . The adrenaline . . . and the insult involved when someone flees increases with every foot of the pursuit. I know the two or three times that I felt I lost control of myself . . . was when someone would run on me. The further I had to chase the guy the madder I got. . . . The funny thing is the reason for the pursuit could have been something as minor as a traffic violation or a kid you're chasing who just turned on a fire hydrant. It always ends in violence. You feel obligated to hit or kick the guy just for running.

Police officers also excuse force when it follows an experience of helplessness and confusion that has culminated in a temporary loss of emotional control. This emotional combination occurs most frequently when an officer comes to the brink of using lethal force, drawing a gun and perhaps firing, only to learn there were no "real" grounds for this action. The officer may then "snap out" and hit the suspect.[6] In one such incident, for example, two policemen picked up a complainant who positively identified a suspect as a man who just tried to shoot him. Just as the officers approached the suspect, he suddenly reached for his back pocket for what the officers assumed to be a gun. One officer was close enough to jump the suspect before he pulled his hand from his pocket. As it turned out, the suspect had no weapon, having dropped it several feet away. Although he was unarmed and under control, the suspect was punched and kicked out of anger and frustration by the officer who had almost shot him.

Note that in both these circumstances—pursuit and near-miss mistaken shootings—officers would concede that the ensuing force is inappropriate and unjustifiable when considered abstractly. But although abstractly wrong, the use of force on such occasions is presented as a normal, human reaction to an extreme situation. Although not every officer might react violently in such circumstances, it is understandable and expected that some will.

Officers also justify force as normal by reference to interactional situations in which an officer's authority is physically or symbolically threatened. [In contrast to excuses, which deny responsibility for the act but recognize that the act is blameworthy, justifications accept responsibility for the act but deny that the act is blameworthy.—Ed.] In such accounts, the use of force is justified instrumentally—as a means of regaining immediate control in a situation where that control has become tenuous. Here, the officer depicts his primary intent for using force as a need to reestablish immediate control in a problematic encounter, and only incidentally as hurting or punishing the offender.

Few officers will hesitate to assault a suspect who physically threatens or attacks them. In one case, an officer was punched in the face by a prisoner he had just apprehended for allegedly attempting to shoot a friend. The incident occurred in the stationhouse, and several policemen observed the exchange. Immediately, one officer hit the prisoner in the jaw and the rest immediately joined the brawl.

Violations of an officer's property such as his car or hat may signify a more symbolic assault on the officer's authority and self, thus justifying a forceful response to maintain control. Indeed, in the police view, almost any person who verbally challenges a police officer is appropriately subject to force. . . .

On rare occasions, women officers encounter special problems in these regards. Although most suspects view women in the same way as policemen, some seem less inclined to accord female officers *de facto* and symbolic control in street encounters, and on a few occasions seem determined to provoke direct confrontations with such officers, explicitly denying their formal authority and attempting none too subtly to sexualize the encounter. Women officers, then, might use force as a resource for rectifying such insults and for establishing control over such partially sexualized interactions. Consider the following woman officer's extended account providing such situational justifications for the use of force:

> . . . I'm sitting at Second Street, Second and Nassau, writing curfews up. And this silver Thunderbird . . . blows right by a stop sign where I'm sitting. And I look up and think to myself, "Now, do I want to get involved." And I figure, it was really belligerent doing in right it front of me. So I take off after him, put my lights on and he immediately pulls over. So he jumps out of the car. I jump out of the car right away and I say, "I'm stopping you for that stop sign you just blew through. . . . Let me see your cards please."

Then he starts making these lip smacking noises at me everytime he begins to talk. He said, (smack) "The only way you're seeing my cards is if you lock me up and the only way you're gonna lock me up is if you chase me." And I said to him, "Well, look, I will satisfy you on one account. Now go to your car because I will lock you up. . . . And just sit in your car. I'll be right with you." He smacks his lips, turns around and goes to his car and he sits. And I call a wagon at Second and Nassau. They ask me what I have. I say, "I've got one to go." So as the wagon acknowledges, the car all of a sudden tears out of its spot. And I get on the air and say, "I'm in pursuit." And I give them a description of the car and the direction I'm going. . . . And all of a sudden he pulls over about a block and a half after I started the pursuit. So I got on the air and I said, "I got him at Second and Washington." I jumped out of my car and as I jumped out he tears away again. Now I'm ready to die of embarrassment. I have to get back on the air and say no I don't have him. So I got on the air and said, "Look, he's playing games with me now. He took off again." I said, "I'm still heading South on Second street." He gets down to Lexington. He pulls over again. Well, this time I pulled the police car in front of him. . . . I go over to the car and I hear him lock the doors. I pull out my gun and I put it right in his window. I say, "Unlock that door." Well, he looked at the gun. He nearly like to shit himself. He unlocked the door. I holster my gun. I go to grab his arms to pull him out and all of a sudden I realize Anne's got him. So we keep pulling him out of the car. Throw him on the trunk of his car and kept pounding him back down on the trunk. She's punching his head. I'm kicking him. Then I take out my blackjack. I jack him across the shoulder. Then I go to jack him in the head and I jack Anne's fingers. . . . The next thing they know is we're throwing him bodily into the wagon. And they said, "Did you search him?" We go to the wagon, drag him out again. Now we're tearing through his pockets throwing everything on the ground. Pick him up bodily again, threw him in. . . . So I straightened it out with the sergeant. . . . I said, "What did you want me to do? Let any citizen on the street get stopped and pull away and that's the end of it?"

In this instance, a male suspect manages to convey a series of affronts to the officer's authority. These affronts become explicitly and insultingly sexual, turning the challenge from the claim that "no cop will stop me" to the more gender specific one, "no woman cop will stop me." Resistance ups the ante until the suspect backs down in the face of the officer's drawn revolver. The force to which the culprit was then subjected is normalized through all the accounts considered to this point—it is situationally justified as a means to reestablish and maintain immediate and symbolic control in a highly problematic encounter and it is excused as a natural, collective outburst following resolution of a dangerous, tension-filled incident. And finally, it is more implicitly justified as appropriate punishment, an account building upon standard police practices for abstract justification, to which I now turn.

ABSTRACT JUSTIFICATIONS

Police also justify the use of extreme force against certain categories of morally reprehensible persons. In this case, force is not presented as an instrumental means to regain control that has been symbolically or physically threatened. Instead, it is justified as an appropriate response to particularly heinous offenders. Categories of such offenders include: cop haters who have gained notoriety as persistent police antagonizers; cop killers or any person who has attempted seriously to harm a police officer (Westley, 1970:131); sexual deviants who prey on children and "moral women"; child abusers; and junkies and other "scum" who inhabit the street. The more morally reprehensible the act is judged, the more likely the police are to depict any violence directed toward its perpetrator as justifiable. Thus a man who exposes himself to children in a playground is less likely to experience police assault than one who rapes or sexually molests a child.

"Clean" criminals, such as high-level mafiosi, white-collar criminals, and professional burglars, are rarely subject to abstract force. Nor are perpetrators of violent and nonviolent street crimes who prey on adult males, prostitutes, and other categories of persons who belong on the street.[7] Similarly, the "psycho" or demented person is perceived as so mentally deranged that he is not responsible for his acts and hence does not merit abstract, punitive force (Van Maanen, 1978:233–34).

Police justify abstract force by invoking a higher moral purpose that legitimates the violation of commonly recognized standards. In one case, for example, a nun was raped by a seventeen-year-old male adolescent. When the police apprehended the suspect, he was severely beaten and his penis put in an electrical outlet to teach him a lesson. The story of the event was told to me by a police officer who, despite the fact that he rarely supported the use of extralegal force, depicted this treatment as legitimate. Indeed, when I asked if he would have participated had he been present, he responded, "I'm Catholic. I would have participated."

Excessive Force and Peer Responses

Although police routinely excuse and justify many incidents where they or their co-workers have used extreme force against a citizen or suspect, this does not mean that on any and every occasion the officer using such force is exonerated. Indeed, the concept of normal force is useful because it suggests that there are specific circumstances under which police officers will not condone the use of force by themselves or colleagues as reasonable and acceptable. Thus, officer-recognized conceptions of normal force are subject to restrictions of the following kinds:

1. Police recognize and honor some rough equation between the behavior of the suspect and the harmfulness of the force to which it is subject. There are limits, therefore, to the degree of force that is acceptable in particular circumstances. In the following incident, for example, an officer reflects on a situation in which a "symbolic assailant" (Skolnick, 1975:45) was mistakenly subject to more force than he "deserved" and almost killed:

> One time Bill Johnson and I . . . had a particularly rude drunk one day. He was really rude and spit on you and he did all this stuff and we even had to cuff him lying down on the hard stretcher, like you would do an epileptic. . . . So we were really mad. We said let's just give him one or two shots . . . slamming on the brakes and having him roll. But we didn't use our heads . . . we heard the stretcher go nnnnnBam and then nothing. We heard nothing and we realized we had put this man in with his head to the front so when we slammed on the brakes his stretcher. . . . I guess it can roll four foot. Well, it was his head that had hit the front. . . . So, we went to Madison Street and parked. It's a really lonely area. And we unlocked the wagon and peeked in. We know he's in there. We were so scared and we look in and there's not a sound and we see blood coming in front of the wagon and think ". . . we killed this man. What am I gonna do? What am I gonna tell my family?" And to make a long story short, he was just knocked out. But boy was I scared. From then on we learned, feet first.

2. Similarly, even in cases where suspects are seen as deserving some violent punishment, this force should not be used randomly and without control. Thus, in the following incident, an officer who "snapped out" and began to beat a child abuser clearly regarded his partner's attempt to stop the beating as reasonable.

> . . . I knock on the door and a lady answers just completely hysterical. And I say, "Listen, I don't know what's going on in here," but then I hear this, just this screeching. You know. And I figure well I'm just going to find out what's going on so I just go past the lady and what's happening is that the husband had. . . . The kid was being potty trained and the way they were potty training this kid, this two-year-old boy, was that the boyfriend of this girl would pick up this kid and he would sit him down on top of the stove. It was their method of potty training. Well, first of all you think of your own kids. I mean afterwards you do. I mean I've never been this mad in my whole life. You see this little two-year-old boy seated on top of the stove with rings around it being absolutely scalding hot. And he's saying "I'll teach you to go. . . ." It just triggered something. An uncontrollable. . . . It's just probably the most violent I ever got. Well you just grab that guy. You hit him ten, fifteen times . . . you don't know how many. You just get so mad. And I remember my partner eventually came in and grabbed me and said, "Don't worry about it. We got him. We got him." And we cuffed him and we took him down. Yeah that was bad.

Learning these sorts of restrictions on the use of normal force and these informal practices of peer control are important processes in the socialization of newcomers. This socialization proceeds both through ongoing observation and experience and, on occasion, through explicit instruction. For example, one veteran officer advised a rookie, "The only reason to go in on a pursuit is not to get the perpetrator but to pull the cop who gets there first offa the guy before he kills him."

Conclusion

The organization of police work reflects a poignant moral dilemma: For a variety of reasons, society mandates to the police the right to use force but provides little direction as to its proper use in specific, "real life" situations. Thus, the police, as officers of the law, must be prepared to use force under circumstances in which its rationale is often morally, legally, and practically ambiguous. This fact explains some otherwise puzzling aspects of police training and socialization.

The police academy provides a semblance of socialization for its recruits by teaching formal rules for using force. . . . [T]he full socialization of a police officer takes place outside the academy as the officer moves from its idealizations to the practicalities of the street. . . .

. . . [J]ustifications and excuses . . . conventionalize but do not reform situations that are inherently charged and morally ambiguous. In this way they simultaneously preserve the self-image of police as agents of the conventional order, provide ways in which individual officers can resolve their personal doubts as to the moral status of their action and those of their colleagues, and reinforce the solidarity of the police community.

Notes

1. Nonetheless masculine pronouns are generally used to refer to the police in this article, because the Metro P.D. remained dominated by men numerically, in style, and in tone. . . .

2. Some officers also substitute a large heavy duty flashlight for the nightstick. If used correctly, the flashlight can inflict more damage than the baton and is less likely to break when applied to the head or other parts of the body.

3. As the Metro City Police Commissioner commented in an interview: "In general, they [women] are physically weaker than males. . . . I believe they would be inclined to let their emotions all too frequently overrule their good judgment . . . there are periods in their life when they are psychologically unbalanced because of physical problems that are occurring within them."

4. The woman officer later explained that she did not obey the suspect's command because she saw no reflection of the partner in the suspect's glasses and therefore assumed he was lying.

5. The combat high is a state of controlled exhilaration in which the officer

experiences a heightened awareness of the world around him. Officers report that perception, smell, and hearing seem acute; one seems to stand outside oneself, and the world appears extraordinarily vivid and clear. At the same time, officers insist that they are able to think rationally and instantly translate thoughts into action; when experienced, fear is not incapacitating but instead enhances the ability to act.

6. This police experience of fear and helplessness, leading to a violent outburst, may be analogized to a parent's reaction on seeing his child almost die in an accident. Imagine a scene in which a father is walking with his six-year-old son. Suddenly, the boy runs into the street to get a red ball on the pavement. The father watches a car slam on the brakes and miss the boy by two inches. He grabs his son and smacks him on the face before he takes him in his arms and holds him. . . .

7. The categories of persons who merit violence are not unique to the police. Prisoners, criminals, and hospital personnel appear to draw similar distinctions between morally unworthy persons; on the latter, see Sudnow (1967:105).

References

Bittner, E. (1980). *The Functions of the Police in Modern Society*. Cambridge, MA: Oelgeschlager, Gunn & Hain.

Hunt, J. (forthcoming). "The development of rapport through the negotiation of gender in field work among police." *Human Organization*.

Skolnick, J. (1975). *Justice Without Trial*. New York: John Wiley.

Sudnow, D. (1967). *Passing On: The Social Organization of Dying*. Englewood Cliffs, NJ: Prentice-Hall.

Van Maanen, J. (1978). "The asshole." In P. K. Manning and J. Van Maanen (eds.), *Policing: A View from the Street*. Santa Monica, CA. Goodyear.

Westley, W. A. (1970). *Violence and the Police: A Sociological Study of Law, Custom and Morality*. Cambridge, MA: MIT Press.

39 The Structure of Power in American Society

C. WRIGHT MILLS

". . . we must understand the elite today in connection with . . .
the development of a permanent war-establishment, alongside a
privately incorporated economy, inside a virtual political vacuum."
—C. Wright Mills

The preceding articles in this Part have focused on six American
social institutions. We now return to the question we dealt with in
Domhoff's article on the Bohemian Grove (in Part VII), probably
the most critical question concerning our social institutions: Who
has the power? Just who is it who makes those "big" decisions that
drastically affect our lives and influence the course of world events?

Mills says that in order to understand modern society, we must
take as our starting point the enlargement and centralization of the
means of power. Our political, military, and economic institutions
are not only large, but also are centralized and powerfully interconnected. Consequently, their significance has outstripped our other
social institutions. There is no longer a separation of politics, the
economy, and the military. Rather, we now have a *"triangle of power"*
built on overlapping leadership with mutuality of interests. The electorate (the "public") finds itself at the bottom of the hierarchy while,
at best, most politicians, labor leaders, and business heads reach
only to the middle of the hierarchy. They are secondary when it
comes to making the crucial policy decisions that critically affect
the nation, for it is a *power elite,* those top persons in the political,
economic, and military sectors, that makes the significant decisions
that so vitally affect our welfare.

I

Power has to do with whatever decisions men make about the arrangements
under which they live, and about the events which make up the history of
their times. Events that are beyond human decision do happen; social ar-

rangements do change without benefit of explicit decision. But in so far as such decisions are made, the problem of who is involved in making them is the basic problem of power. In so far as they could be made but are not, the problem becomes who fails to make them?

We cannot today merely assume that in the last resort men must always be governed by their own consent. For among the means of power which now prevail is the power to manage and to manipulate the consent of men. That we do not know the limits of such power, and that we hope it does have limits, does not remove the fact that much power today is successfully employed without the sanction of the reason or the conscience of the obedient.

Surely nowadays we need not argue that, in the last resort, coercion is the "final" form of power. But then, we are by no means constantly at the last resort. Authority (power that is justified by the beliefs of the voluntary obedient) and manipulation (power that is wielded unbeknown to the powerless) must also be considered, along with coercion. In fact, the three types must be sorted out whenever we think about power.

In the modern world, we must bear in mind, power is often not so authoritative as it seemed to be in the medieval epoch: Ideas which justify rulers no longer seem so necessary to their exercise of power. At least for many of the great decisions of our time—especially those of an international sort—mass "persuasion" has not been "necessary"; the fact is simply accomplished. Furthermore, such ideas as are available to the powerful are often neither taken up nor used by them. Such ideologies usually arise as a response to an effective debunking of power; in the United States such opposition has not been effective enough recently to create the felt need for new ideologies of rule.

There has, in fact, come about a situation in which many who have lost faith in prevailing loyalties have not acquired new ones, and so pay no attention to politics of any kind. They are not radical, not liberal, not conservative, not reactionary. They are inactionary. They are out of it. If we accept the Greek's definition of the idiot as an altogether private man, then we must conclude that many American citizens are now idiots. And I should not be surprised, although I do not know, if there were not some such idiots even in Germany. This—and I use the word with care—this spiritual condition seems to me the key to many modern troubles of political intellectuals, as well as the key to much political bewilderment in modern society. Intellectual "conviction" and moral "belief" are not necessary, in either the rulers or the ruled, for a ruling power to persist and even to flourish. So far as the role of ideologies is concerned, their frequent absences and the prevalence of mass indifference are surely two of the major political facts about the western societies today.

How large a role any explicit decisions do play in the making of history is itself an historical problem. For how large that role may be depends very much upon the means of power that are available at any given time in any given society. In some societies, the innumerable actions of innumerable men modify their milieux, and so gradually modify the structure itself. These modifications—the course of history—go on behind the backs of men. History is drift, although in total "men make it." Thus innumerable entrepreneurs and innumerable consumers by ten-thousand decisions per minute may shape and reshape the free-market economy. Perhaps this was the chief kind of limitation Marx had in mind when he wrote, in *The 18th Brumaire* that; "Men make their own history, but they do not make it just as they please; they do not make it under circumstances chosen by themselves. . . ."

But in other societies—certainly in the United States and in the Soviet Union today—a few men may be so placed within the structure that by their decisions they modify the milieux of many other men, and in fact nowadays the structural conditions under which most men live. Such elites of power also make history under circumstances not chosen altogether by themselves, yet compared with other men, and compared with other periods of world history, these circumstances do indeed seem less limiting.

I should contend that "men are free to make history," but that some men are indeed much freer than others. For such freedom requires access to the means of decision and of power by which history can now be made. It has not always been so made; but in the later phases of the modern epoch it is. It is with reference to this epoch that I am contending that if men do not make history, they tend increasingly to become the utensils of history-makers as well as the mere objects of history.

The history of modern society may readily be understood as the story of the enlargement and the centralization of the means of power—in economic, in political, and in military institutions. The rise of industrial society has involved these developments in the means of economic production. The rise of the nation-state has involved similar developments in the means of violence and in those of political administration.

In the western societies, such transformations have generally occurred gradually, and many cultural traditions have restrained and shaped them. In most of the Soviet societies, they are happening very rapidly indeed and without the great discourse of western civilization, without the Renaissance and without the Reformation, which so greatly strengthened and gave political focus to the idea of freedom. In those societies, the enlargement and the coordination of all the means of power has occurred more brutally, and from the beginning under tightly centralized authority. But in both types, the means of power have now become international in scope and similar in form. To be sure, each of them has its own ups and downs; neither is as yet absolute; how they are run differs quite sharply.

Yet so great is the reach of the means of violence, and so great the economy required to produce and support them, that we have in the immediate past witnessed the consolidation of these two world centers, either of which dwarfs the power of Ancient Rome. As we pay attention to the awesome means of power now available to quite small groups of men we come to realize that Caesar could do less with Rome than Napoleon with France; Napoleon less with France than Lenin with Russia. But what was Caesar's power at its height compared with the power of the changing inner circles of Soviet Russia and the temporary administrations of the United States? We come to realize—indeed they continually remind us—how a few men have access to the means by which in a few days continents can be turned into thermonuclear wastelands. That the facilities of power are so enormously enlarged and so decisively centralized surely means that the powers of quite small groups of men, which we may call elites, are now of literally inhuman consequence.

My concern here is not with the international scene but with the United States in the middle of the twentieth century. I must emphasize "in the middle of the twentieth century" because in our attempt to understand any society we come upon images which have been drawn from its past and which often confuse our attempt to confront its present reality. That is one minor reason why history is the shank of any social science: we must study it if only to rid ourselves of it. In the United States, there are indeed many such images and usually they have to do with the first half of the nineteenth century. At that time the economic facilities of the United States were very widely dispersed and subject to little or to no central authority. The state watched in the night but was without decisive voice in the day. One man meant one rifle and the militia were without centralized orders.

Any American, as old-fashioned as I, can only agree with R. H. Tawney that "Whatever the future may contain, the past has shown no more excellent social order than that in which the mass of the people were the masters of the holdings which they ploughed and the tools with which they worked, and could boast . . . 'It is a quietness to a man's mind to live upon his own and to know his heir certain.'"

But then we must immediately add: all that is of the past and of little relevance to our understanding of the United States today. Within this society three broad levels of power may now be distinguished. I shall begin at the top and move downward.

II

The power to make decisions of national and international consequence is now so clearly seated in political, military, and economic institutions that other areas of society seem off to the side and, on occasion, readily subordinated to these. The scattered institutions of religion, education, and family are increasingly shaped by the big three, in which history-making decisions now regularly occur. Behind this fact there is all the push and drive of a fabulous technology; for these three institutional orders have incorporated this technology and now guide it, even as it shapes and paces their development.

As each has assumed its modern shape, its effects upon the other two have become greater, and the traffic between the three has increased. There is no longer, on the one hand, an economy, and, on the other, a political order, containing a military establishment unimportant to politics and to money-making. There is a political economy numerously linked with military order and decision. This triangle of power is now a structural fact, and it is the key to any understanding of the higher circles in America today. For as each of these domains has coincided with the others, as decisions in each have become broader, the leading men of each—the high military, the corporation executives, the political directorate—have tended to come together to form the power elite of America.

The political order, once composed of several dozen states with a weak federal center, has become an executive apparatus which has taken up into itself many powers previously scattered, legislative as well as administrative, and which now reaches into all parts of the social structure. The longtime tendency of business and government to become more closely connected has, since World War II, reached a new point of explicitness. Neither can now be seen clearly as a distinct world. The growth of executive government does not mean merely the "enlargement of government" as some kind of autonomous bureaucracy; under American conditions, it has meant the ascendancy of the corporation man into political eminence. Already during the New Deal, such men had joined the political directorate; as of World War II, they came to dominate it. Long involved with government, now they have moved into quite full direction of the economy of the war effort and of the postwar era.

The economy, once a great scatter of small productive units in somewhat automatic balance, has become internally dominated by a few hundred corporations, administratively and politically interrelated, which together hold the keys to economic decision. This economy is at once a permanent-war economy and a private-corporation economy. The most important relations of the corporation to the state now rest on the coincidence between military and corporate interests, as defined by the military and the corporate rich, and accepted by politicians and public. Within the elite as a whole, this coincidence of military domain and corporate realm strengthens both of them and further subordinates the merely political man. Not the party politician but the corporation executive, is now more likely to sit with the military to answer the question: what is to be done?

The military order, once a slim establishment in a context of civilian distrust, has become the largest and most expensive feature of government;

behind smiling public relations, it has all the grim and clumsy efficiency of a great and sprawling bureaucracy. The high military have gained decisive political and economic relevance. The seemingly permanent military threat places a premium upon them and virtually all political and economic actions are now judged in terms of military definitions of reality; the higher military have ascended to a firm position within the power elite of our time.

In part, at least, this is a result of an historical fact, pivotal for the years since 1939: the attention of the elite has shifted from domestic problems—centered in the thirties around slump—to international problems—centered in the forties and fifties around war. By long historical usage, the government of the United States has been shaped by domestic clash and balance; it does not have suitable agencies and traditions for the democratic handling of international affairs. In considerable part, it is in this vacuum that the power elite has grown.

1. To understand the unity of this power elite, we must pay attention to the psychology of its several members in their perspective milieux. In so far as the power elite is composed of men of similar origin and education, of similar career and style of life, their unity may be said to rest upon the fact that they are of similar social type, and to lead to the fact of their easy intermingling. This kind of unity reaches its frothier apex in the sharing of that prestige which is to be had in the world of the celebrity. It achieves a more solid culmination in the fact of the interchangeability of positions between the three dominant institutional orders. It is revealed by considerable traffic of personnel within and between these three, as well as by the rise of specialized go-betweens as in the new-style high-level lobbying.

2. Behind such psychological and social unity are the structure and the mechanics of those institutional hierarchies over which the political directorate, the corporate rich, and the high military now preside. How each of these hierarchies is shaped and what relations it has with the others determine in large part the relations of their rulers. Were these hierarchies scattered and disjointed, then their respective elites might tend to be scattered and disjointed; but if they have many interconnections and points of coinciding interest, then their elites tend to form a coherent kind of grouping. The unity of the elite is not a simple reflection of the unity of institutions, but men and institutions are always related; that is why we must understand the elite today in connection with such institutional trends as the development of a permanent war-establishment, alongside a privately incorporated economy, inside a virtual political vacuum. For the men at the top have been selected and formed by such institutional trends.

3. Their unity however, does not rest solely upon psychological similarity and social intermingling, nor entirely upon the structural blending of commanding positions and common interests. At times it is the unity of a more explicit coordination.

To say that these higher circles are increasingly coordinated, that this is *one* basis of their unity, and that at times—as during open war—such coordination is quite willful, is not to say that the coordination is total or continuous, or even that it is very sure-footed. Much less is it to say that the power elite has emerged as the realization of a plot. Its rise cannot be adequately explained in any psychological terms.

Yet we must remember that institutional trends may be defined as opportunities by those who occupy the command posts. Once such opportunities are recognized, men may avail themselves of them. Certain types of men from each of these three areas, more far-sighted than others, have actively promoted the liaison even before it took its truly modern shape. Now more have come to see that their several interests can more easily be realized if they work together, in informal as well as in formal ways, and accordingly they have done so.

The idea of the power elite is of course an interpretation. It rests upon and it enables us to make sense of major institutional trends, the social similarities and psychological affinities of the men at the top. But the idea is also based upon what has been happening on the middle and lower levels of power, to which I now turn.

III

There are of course other interpretations of the American system of power. The most usual is that it is a moving balance of many competing interests. The image of balance, at least in America, is derived from the idea of the economic market: in the nineteenth century, the balance was thought to occur between a great scatter of individuals and enterprises; in the twentieth century, it is throught to occur between great interest blocs. In both views, the politician is the key man of power because he is the broker of many conflicting powers.

I believe that the balance and the compromise in American society— the "countervailing powers" and the "veto groups," of parties and associations, of strata and unions—must now be seen as having mainly to do with the middle levels of power. It is these middle levels that the political journalist and the scholar of politics are most likely to understand and to write about— if only because, being mainly middle class themselves, they are closer to them. Moreover these levels provide the noisy content of most "political" news and gossip; the images of these levels are more or less in accord with the folklore of how democracy works; and, if the master-image of balance is accepted, many intellectuals, especially in their current patrioteering, are readily able to satisfy such political optimism as they wish. Accordingly, liberal interpretations of what is happening in the United States are now virtually the only interpretations that are widely distributed.

But to believe that the power system reflects a balancing society is, I think, to confuse the present era with earlier times, and to confuse its top and bottom with its middle levels.

By the top levels, as distinguished from the middle, I intend to refer, first of all, to the scope of the decisions that are made. At the top today, these decisions have to do with all the issues of war and peace. They have also to do with slump and poverty which are now so very much problems of international scope. I intend also to refer to whether or not the groups that struggle politically have a chance to gain the positions from which such top decisions are made, and indeed whether their members do usually hope for such top national command. Most of the competing interests which make up the clang and clash of American politics are strictly concerned with their slice of the existing pie. Labor unions, for example, certainly have no policies of an international sort other than those which given unions adopt for the strict economic protection of their members; neither do farm organizations. The actions of such middle-level powers may indeed have consequence for top-level policy; certainly at times they hamper these policies. But they are not truly concerned with them, which means of course that their influence tends to be quite irresponsible.

The facts of the middle levels may in part be understood in terms of the rise of the power elite. The expanded and centralized and interlocked hierarchies over which the power elite preside have encroached upon the old balance and relegated it to the middle level. But there are also independent developments of the middle levels. These, it seems to me, are better understood as an affair of entrenched and provincial demands than as a center of national decision. As such, the middle level often seems much more of a stalemate than a moving balance.

1. The middle level of politics is not a forum in which there are debated the big decisions of national and international life. Such debate is not carried on by nationally responsible parties representing and clarifying alternative policies. There are no such parties in the United States. More and more, fundamental issues never come to any point of decision before the Congress, much less before the electorate in party campaigns. In the case of Formosa, in the spring of 1955 the Congress abdicated all debate concerning events and decisions which surely bordered on war. The same is largely true of the 1957 crisis in the Middle East. Such decisions now regularly bypass the Congress, and are never clearly focused issues for public decision.

The American political campaign distracts attention from national and international issues but that is not to say that there are no issues in these campaigns. In each district and state, issues are set up and watched by organized interests of sovereign local importance. The professional politician is of course a party politician, and the two parties are semifeudal organizations: they trade patronage and other favors for votes and for protection. The differences between them, so far as national issues are concerned, are very narrow and very mixed up. Often each seems to be fifty parties, one for each state; and accordingly, the politician as campaigner and as Congressman is not concerned with national party lines, if any are discernible. Often he is not subject to any effective national party discipline. He speaks for the interests of his own constituency, and he is concerned with national issues only in so far as they affect the interests effectively organized there, and hence his chances of re-election. That is why, when he does speak of national matters, the result is so often such an empty rhetoric. Seated in his sovereign locality, the politician is not at the national summit. He is on and of the middle levels of power.

2. Politics is not an arena in which free and independent orgnaizations truly connect the lower and middle levels of society with the top levels of decision. Such organizations are not an effective and major part of American life today. As more people are drawn into the political arena, their associations become mass in scale, and the power of the individual becomes dependent upon them; to the extent that they are effective, they have become larger, and to that extent they have become less accessible to the influence of the individual. This is a central fact about associations in any mass society; it is of most consequence for political parties and for trade unions.

In the thirties, it often seemed that labor would become an insurgent power independent of corporation and state. Organized labor was then emerging for the first time on an American scale, and the only political sense of direction it needed was the slogan, "organize the unorganized." Now without the mandate of slump, labor remains without political direction. Instead of economic and political struggles it has become deeply entangled in administrative routines with both corporation and state. One of its major functions, as a vested interest of the new society, is the regulation of such irregular tendencies as may occur among the rank and file.

There is nothing, it seems to me, in the make-up of the current labor leadership to allow us to expect that it can or that it will lead, rather than merely react. In so far as it fights at all, it fights over a share of the goods of a single way of life and not over that way of life itself. The typical labor leader in the U.S.A. today is better understood as an adaptive creative creature of the main business drift than as an independent actor in a truly national context.

3. The idea that this society is a balance of powers requires us to assume that the units in balance are of more or less equal power and that they are truly independent of one another. These assumptions have rested, it seems clear, upon the historical importance of a large and independent middle class. In the latter nineteenth century and during the Progressive Era, such a class of farmers and small businessmen fought politically—and lost—their struggle for a paramount role in national decision. Even then, their aspirations seemed bound to their own imagined past.

This old, independent middle class has of course declined. On the most generous count, it is now 40 percent of the total middle class (at most 20 percent of the total labor force). Moreover, it has become politically as well as economically dependent upon the state, most notably in the case of the subsidized farmer.

The *new* middle class of white-collar employees is certainly not the political pivot of any balancing society. It is in no way politically unified. Its unions, such as they are, often serve merely to incorporate it as hanger-on of the labor interest. For a considerable period, the old middle class *was* an independent base of power; the new middle class cannot be. Political freedom and economic society *were* anchored in small and independent properties; they are not anchored in the worlds of the white-collar job. Scattered property holders were economically united by more or less free markets; the jobs of the new middle class are integrated by corporate authority. Economically, the white-collar classes are in the same condition as wage workers; politically, they are in a worse condition, for they are not organized. They are no vanguard of historic change; they are at best a rear-guard of the welfare state.

The agrarian revolt of the nineties, the small-business revolt that has been more or less continuous since the eighties, the labor revolt of the thirties—each of these has failed as an independent movement which could countervail against the powers that be; they have failed as politically autonomous third parties. But they have succeeded, in varying degrees, as interests vested in the expanded corporation and state; they have succeeded as parochial interests seated in particular districts, in local divisions of the two parties, and in the Congress. What they would become, in short, are well-established features of the *middle* levels of balancing power, on which we may now observe all those strata and interests which in the course of American history have been defeated in their bids for top power or which have never made such bids.

Fifty years ago many observers thought of the American state as a mask behind which an invisible government operated. But nowadays, much of what was called the old lobby, visible or invisible, is part of the quite visible government. The "governmentalization of the lobby" has proceeded in both the legislative and the executive domain, as well as between them. The executive bureaucracy becomes not only the center of decision but also the arena within which major conflicts of power are resolved or denied resolution. "Administration" replaces electoral politics; the maneuvering of cliques (which include leading Senators as well as civil servants) replaces the open clash of parties.

The shift of corporation men into the political directorate has accelerated the decline of the politicians in the Congress to the middle levels of power; the formation of the power elite rests in part upon this relegation. It rests also upon the semiorganized stalemate of the interests of sovereign localities, into which the legislative function has so largely fallen; upon the virtually complete absence of a civil service that is a politically neutral but politically relevant depository of brainpower and executive skill; and it rests upon the increased official secrecy behind which great decisions are made without benefit of public or even of Congressional debate.

IV

There is one last belief upon which liberal observers everywhere base their interpretations and rest their hopes. That is the idea of the public and the associated idea of public opinion. Conservative thinkers, since the French Revolution, have of course Viewed With Alarm the rise of the public, which they have usually called the masses, or something to that effect. "The populace is sovereign," wrote Gustave LeBon, "and the tide of barbarism mounts." But surely those who have supposed the masses to be well on their way to triumph are mistaken. In our time, the influence of publics or of masses within political life is in fact decreasing, and such influence as on occasion they do have tends, to an unknown but increasing degree, to be guided by the means of mass communication.

In a society of publics, discussion is the ascendant means of communication, and the mass media, if they exist, simply enlarge and animate this discussion, linking one face-to-face public with the discussions of another. In a mass society, the dominant type of communication is the formal media, and publics become mere markets for these media: the "public" of a radio program consists of all those exposed to it. When we try to look upon the United States today as a society of publics, we realize that it has moved a considerable distance along the road to the mass society.

In official circles, the very term, "the public," has come to have a phantom meaning, which dramatically reveals its eclipse. The deciding elite can identify some of those who clamor publicly as "Labor," others as "Business," still others as "Farmer." But these are not the public. "The public" consists of the unidentified and the nonpartisan in a world of defined and partisan interests. In this faint echo of the classic notion, the public is composed of these remnants of the old and new middle classes whose interests are not explicitly defined, organized, or clamorous. In a curious adaptation, "the public" often becomes, in administrative fact, "the disengaged expert," who, although never so well informed, has never taken a clear-cut and public stand on controversial issues. He is the "public" member of the board, the commission, the committee. What "the public" stands for, accordingly, is often a vagueness of policy (called "openmindedness"), a lack of involvement in public affairs (known as "reasonableness"), and a professional disinterest (known as "tolerance").

All this is indeed far removed from the eighteenth century idea of the public of public opinion. The idea parallels the economic idea of the magical market. Here is the market composed for freely competing entrepreneurs; there is the public composed of circles of people in discussion. As price is the result of anonymous, equally weighted, bargaining individuals, so public opinion is the result of each man's having thought things out for himself and then contributing his voice to the great chorus. To be sure, some may have more influence on the state of opinion than others, but no one group monopolizes the discussion, or by itself determines the opinions that prevail.

In this classic image, the people are presented with problems. They discuss them. They formulate viewpoints. These viewpoints are organized, and they compete. One viewpoint "wins out." Then the people act on this view, or their representatives are instructed to act it out, and this they promptly do.

Such are the images of democracy which are still used as working justifications of power in America. We must now recognize this description as more a fairy tale than a useful approximation. The issues that now shape man's fate are neither raised nor decided by any public at large. The idea of a society that is at bottom composed of publics is not a matter of fact; it is the proclamation of an ideal, and as well the assertion of a legitimation masquerading as fact.

I cannot here describe the several great forces within American society as well as elsewhere which have been at work in the debilitation of the public. I want only to remind you that publics, like free associations, can be deliberately and suddenly smashed, or they can more slowly wither away. But whether smashed in a week or withered in a generation, the demise of the public must be seen in connection with the rise of centralized organizations, with all their new means of power, including those of the mass media of distraction. These, we now know, often seem to expropriate the rationality and the will of the terrorized or—as the case may be—the voluntarily indifferent society of masses. In the more democratic process of indifference, the remnants of such publics as remain may only occasionally be intimidated by fanatics in search of "disloyalty." But regardless of that, they lose their will for decision because they do not possess the instruments for decision; they lose their sense of political belonging because they do not belong; they lose their political will because they see no way to realize it.

The political structure of a modern democratic state requires that such a public as is projected by democratic theorists not only exist but that it be the very forum within which a politics of real issues is enacted.

It requires a civil service that is firmly linked with the world of knowledge and sensibility, and which is composed of skilled men who, in their careers and in their aspirations, are truly independent of any private, which is to say, corporation, interests.

It requires nationally responsible parties which debate openly and clearly the issues which the nation, and indeed the world, now so rigidly confronts.

It requires an intelligentsia, inside as well as outside the universities, who carry on the big discourse of the Western world, and whose work is relevant to and influential among parties and movements and publics.

And it certainly requires, as a fact of power, that there be free associations standing between families and smaller communities and publics, on the one hand, and the state, the military, the corporation, on the other. For unless these do exist, there are no vehicles for reasoned opinion, no instruments for the rational exertion of public will.

Such democratic formations are not now ascendant in the power structure of the United States, and accordingly the men of decision are not selected and formed by careers within such associations and by their performance before such publics. The top of modern American society is increasingly unified, and often seems willfully coordinated: at the top there has emerged an elite whose power probably exceeds that of any small group of men in world history. The middle levels are often a drifting set of stalemated forces: the middle does not link the bottom with the top. The bottom of this society is politically fragmented, and even as a passive fact, increasingly powerless: at the bottom there is emerging a mass society.

These developments, I believe, can be correctly understood neither in terms of the liberal nor the Marxian interpretation of politics and history. Both these ways of thought arose as guidelines to reflection about a type of society which does not now exist in the United States. We confront there a new kind of social structure, which embodies elements and tendencies of all modern society, but in which they have assumed a more naked and flamboyant prominence.

That does not mean that we must give up the ideals of these classic political expectations. I believe that both have been concerned with the problem of rationality and of freedom: liberalism, with freedom and rationality as supreme facts about the individual; Marxism, as supreme facts about man's role in the political making of history. What I have said here, I suppose, may be taken as an attempt to make evident why the ideas of freedom and of rationality now so often seem so ambiguous in the new society of the United States of America.

PART IX Social Change

$\mathcal{S}$HIFTING EVENTS SWIRL AROUND US, at times seeming to engulf us in a sea of social change. Nothing seems to remain the same. Familiar landmarks are torn down and replaced, seemingly overnight, by a supermarket or fast-food outlet, while farm fields and woods are paved over and turned into malls and shopping centers. Ideas of proper relations between the sexes become outmoded so fast that the guidelines of only a few years ago no longer apply. Drugs move into middle-class homes. Divorce rates soar while marriage rates decline, increase, and again decline. Clothing styles of the 1940s, cars of the 1950s, furniture of the 1930s come back into fashion.

Debit cards and notebook computers. A plane propelled by human muscle-power, and another that goes around the world without refueling. Price scanners in the supermarkets, and "smart cards" to control access and security. Video games and video recorders. Talking wristwatches and talking automobiles. Interactive television and "virtual reality."

Although change is an essential part of modern society, it is anything but new. Twenty-five hundred years ago, Heraclitus said, "Everything flows; nothing stands still." Six hundred years later, Marcus Aurelius Antoninus wrote, "The universe is change." A more recent observer of the social scene put it this way: "The only thing constant is the certainty of change."

While social change was indeed a part of past civilizations, there is an essential difference between those changes and what we are experiencing today. Barring catastrophe in the form of human or natural disaster, change in ancient times was slow and orderly. Change sometimes was so slow that even over generations the effects were barely perceptible. In all societies of the world, in fact, it was routinely the case that the father passed his occupation down to his son, who in turn passed it on to his son, and so on. Mothers, too, passed their occupation to their daughters. Thus the society the son or daughter lived in was identical to that of his or her parents. Although the players had changed, the basic social institutions, with their routine ways of handling things, remained the same over generations.

The contrast with our situation is stark. Most children today take it for granted that they are different from their parents—some even being amazed if they notice similarities with them. Adolescents routinely assume that their parents will not understand, for each represents a different world. With worlds so different, it is not uncommon for a grown child visiting his or her parents, following an absence of months or years, to find that after the first hour or so they have little or nothing left to talk about. Social change has sorted them into different worlds, their differing experiences imparting contrasting orientations to life.

"Adapt or die" may be the maxim under which living creatures exist. Only the organisms that adapt to changing circumstances survive, and humans are no exception. Confronted with challenge, humans adapt. They change their social institutions to match changing circumstances. The effects are highly visible as people change their outward behaviors. But the consequences are hardly limited to the external, for they penetrate within people, changing their ideas, attitudes, and beliefs, their basic orientations to the world.

It is with discussions of this vital aspect of social life that we conclude this book. Marlise Simons opens this Part with a focus on the Kaiapo Indians of Brazil, whose traditional way of life is being challenged by television and other contacts with the industrialized world. Robin Wagner-Pacifici's and Barry Schwartz's analysis of the Vietnam War Memorial brings us face to face with changing and conflicting views of reality. Douglas L. Murray analyzes how social change brought about widespread use of a little hoe, *el cortito*—which abolition, in turn, led to extensive changes in labor relations. William Ouchi examines how decisions are made in Japanese organizations, a process that, because of its competitive success, is being defensively adopted (and modified) by many of our business firms. We end this Part with a first-person account of the effects of social change on an individual's life, as Richard Rodriguez tells us about the profound alterations in his personal identity as he underwent life-transforming experiences in the educational institution.

In conclusion, I would like to add that you, the reader, are the future. Certainly you cannot escape being shaped by your experiences of the vast changes occurring in society. For you to make better sense of your transforming experiences, however, I highly recommend the sociological imagination—the idea with which we began this book.

40 The Amazon's Savvy Indians

MARLISE SIMONS

Social change comes about when different groups come in contact with one another—through conquest, travel, trade, migration, and electronic communication. Sociologist William F. Ogburn identified three processes of social change: *Invention* (think of the changes ushered in by the automobile and computer), *discovery* (such as the discovery of gold in California and Alaska), and *diffusion* (the spread of an invention or discovery from one area to another). Invention, which changes our technology, is an especially powerful source of social change. Because *technology* (tools, items used to accomplish tasks) is integrated into a group's way of life, to change technology means that at least some aspects of the group's usual way of life must also change.

In contrast to the rapid change in industrialized societies, the way of life of preliterate groups usually changes so slowly that even in hundred-year intervals little is noticeably different. If a group's environment stays constant, then the adjustments that a people has worked out remain viable. Contact with groups that have a sharply contrasting way of life, however—as is happening with the Kaiapo Indians of Brazil featured in this selection—can rapidly undermine a traditional way of life. Note how the diffusion of industrialized technology to the Kaiapo is not simply a matter of changes in housing, diet, and tools—it alters their traditional relationships and, ultimately, transforms their values, leading to a different way of viewing life itself.

IT IS GETTING DARK WHEN Chief Kanhonk sits down in the yard outside his home, ready for a long evening of conversation. Night birds are calling from the bush that sparkles with fireflies. Whooping frogs make a racket by the river. No one seems worried by the squadron of bats sweeping low overhead.

It is that important moment of the day when Indians of the Amazon, who use no written language, meet to talk, pass on information and tell stories. The night is when they recall ancestral customs, interpret dreams and comment on changes in nature and other events of the day. But from

469

a nearby home come the sounds of a powerful rival: a television set is screeching cartoons at a group of children. I understand now why, that morning, by way of saying hello, these naked children of the rain forest had shouted things like "He-Man" and "Flintstones."

Three years ago, when money from the sale of gold nuggets and mahogany trees was pouring into Gorotire, Chief Kanhonk agreed to bring in television, or the "big ghost," as it is called here. A shiny satellite dish now stands on the earthen plaza like an alien sculpture, signaling that Gorotire—a small settlement of some 800 people on the Fresco River, a tributary of the Amazon—has become one of the wealthiest Indian villages in Brazil.

Yet Chief Kanhonk appears to regret his decision. "I have been saying that people must buy useful things like knives or fishing hooks," he says darkly. "Television does not fill the stomach. It only shows our children and grandchildren white people's things."

The "big ghost" is just one of the changes that have been sweeping over Gorotire, but it seems to be worrying the elders the most. Some believe it is powerful enough to rob them of their culture. Bebtopup, the oldest medicine man in the village, explains his misgivings: "The night is the time the old people teach the young people. Television has stolen the night."

When I discuss this with Eduardo Viveiros, a Brazilian anthropologist who works with a more isolated Amazonian tribe, he seems less worried. "At least they quickly understood the consequences of watching television," he says. "Many people never discover. Now Gorotire can make a choice."

It was the issue of choice that first drew me to the Kaiapo Indians of the lower Amazon Basin. They seemed to be challenging the widely held notion that forest Indians are defenseless in face of the pressures of the competitive and predatory Western world around them. Unlike most of Brazil's 230,000 Indians, they go out into the white world to defend their interests, and it is no longer unusual to see Kaiapo men—in their stunning body paint and feathered headdresses—showing up in Congress in Brasilia, the nation's capital, or lobbying by doing a war dance outside a Government office. They have even bought Western gadgets to record and film their festivals.

Once the masters of immense stretches of forest and savannas, the Kaiapo were for hundreds of years among the most skillful farmers and hunters and fiercest warriors of central Brazil. They terrified other tribes with their raids. From the 17th to the 19th centuries, they not only resisted the slaving raids of the Portuguese invaders but they also attacked white traders and gold prospectors with such a vengeance that royal orders came from Portugal to destroy the Kaiapo. The white man's wrath and his diseases killed many, yet there are still close to 3,600 Kaiapo in more than a dozen different villages near the Xingu River. They have quarreled and regrouped, but their lands, several vast reservations, are more secure than those of many other tribes.

After many years of isolation to the forest, the Kaiapo now have to deal with the growing encroachments of white society. "They are going through a great transition," says Darrell Posey, an American anthropologist who has worked in Gorotire for more than a decade. "Their survival is a miracle in itself. But I worry whether they can go on making the changes on their own terms."

Colombia, Ecuador, Peru and Venezuela—four of nine nations in the Amazon Basin, which harbors some 800,000 Indians—each have large numbers of tropical-forest Indians. But nowhere are pressures on Indian land as great as they are in Brazil. As the Amazon is opened up, developers bring in highways, settlers, cattle ranchers, mines and hydroelectric dams. In Brazil alone, more than 90 tribes have disappeared since the beginning of this century.

The clearing of large areas of the rain forest and the fate of the Indians are also rapidly becoming an issue of international concern. Interest in the region has risen as ecological concerns, such as ozone depletion, the greenhouse effect and other changes in the global environment become political issues. More attention is paid to scientists who are alarmed at the destruction of the rain forest—a vital flywheel in the world's climate and the nursery of at least half of the world's plant and animal species.

This has also prompted an increasing interest in the highly structured world of the forest Indians and their ancient and intricate knowledge of nature that permits them to survive in the tropical jungle without destroying it. . . .

As Indians find greater support among environmentalists, they also get more organized in their fight to protect their habitat. The Kaiapo held their first international congress last week in Altamira, in central Brazil, protesting Government plans to build several massive dams that would flood Indian land.

In Brazil, Indian tribes occupy 10 percent of the nation's territory, although much of their land has not been demarcated. Brazil's past military regimes elevated Indian affairs to a national-security issue, because many tribes live in large areas of border land. It is official policy to integrate Indians into the larger society, and the National Indian Foundation, with its 4,900 employees, is in charge of implementing this.

In my 18 years in Latin America, I have heard many politicians and anthropologists discuss what is usually called "the Indian problem," what to "do" about cultures that have changed little in thousands of years. One school of thought holds that the remote tribes should be kept isolated and protected until they can slowly make their own choices. Another school accepts that the Indian world is on the wane, and talks about "guiding" the Indians toward inevitable change—a process that should take several generations.

But some anthropologists and politicians, including the Brazilian Government, believe in still more rapid integration. When Romeo Jucá was head of the Indian Foundation, he said that it was only right for Indians to exploit their wealth, even if it meant acculturation. "We have to be careful how fast we go," he said, "but being Indian does not mean you have to be poor."

Gerardo Reichel-Dolmatoff is one of Latin America's most respected anthropologists. He insists that the Indians are their own best guides into Western society. An Austrian-born Colombian, Reichel-Dolmatoff has worked in Colombia's forests, at the Amazon's headwaters, for almost fifty years. "We cannot choose for them," he insists. "And we cannot put them into reserves, ghettos, ashokas. They are not museum exhibits. . . . If Indians choose the negative aspects of our civilization, we cannot control that. If there is one basic truth in anthropology, it is that cultures change. Static cultures do not exist."

The Indians themselves are pleading for more protection and respect for their cultures. Conrad Gorinsky, son of a Guyana Indian mother and himself a chemist in London, recently said: "We don't want the Indians to change because we have them comfortably in the back of our mind like a kind of ShangriLa, something we can turn to even if we work ourselves to death in New York. But we are hounding and maligning them instead of recognizing them as the guardians of the forests, of the world's genetic banks, of our germ plasm and lifelines."

The aboriginal peoples we call Indians are as different from one another as, say, Europeans are. Even the most isolated groups remain separate fiefdoms with widely varying experiences, beliefs and histories. The degree of contact they have with the outside world is just as varied.

I first met Kaiapo tribesmen three years ago in Belém, a large city at the mouth of the Amazon. I saw them again in Brasilia, the capital. In both places, they demonstrated their political skills and capacity to mobilize, showing up in large numbers to protest measures by the Government. They seemed particularly adept at commanding the attention of the press. Their body paint, feathers and other paraphernalia made them appear warlike, exotic and photogenic.

Back in Gorotire, as it turns out, they are more "ordinary." Wearing feathers and beads, explains Kubei, a chief's son, is for special occasions. "It's our suit and tie." Besides the satellite dish, the Kaiapo also have their own small airplane. Their new wealth has also given them the luxury of hiring non-Indians to help plant new fields. But they remain ready to attack white intruders; some of the adult men have markings on their chests that record the number of outsiders they have killed.

Two roads fan out from the center of Gorotire. A new sand track leads east on a five-hour drive to the town of Redenção. The other road goes south and, in a sense, it leads into the past. Dipping into the forest, it becomes a path that meanders through open patches where the Kaiapo women grow corn, sweet potatoes, bananas, manioc. On the plain ahead, it joins an ancient trail system that once reached for hundreds of miles into northern and western Brazil.

One morning, Bebtopup (medicine man, shaman, connoisseur of nature), the anthropologist Darrell Posey (who speaks the Kaiapo language) and I wander into the bush. Bebtopup walks past the plants the way you go down a street where you know everyone. Stopping, nodding, his face lighting up with happy recognition, he sometimes goes into a song—a soft, high-pitch chant for a particular plant.

He picks leaves, each one familiar, each one useful. One serves to remove body hair. Another, he says, can prevent pregnancy. The underside of one leaf is so rough it is used to sandpaper wood and file fingernails. Bebtopup collects his plants in the morning, he says, because "that is when they have the most strength."

Stopping at a shrub, we look at the large circle around its stem, where nothing grows. "This and other plants have been sent to a laboratory for analysis," says Posey. "We think this one has a natural weedkiller."

Beptopup holds up a branch of what he calls the "eye of the jaguar." "This was our flashlight," he says, showing how to set it afire and swing it gently so its strong glow will light one's path.

One afternoon, when the heat has crept into everything, the women and children come back from the fields to their village. They stop and sit in a creek to escape the swirling gnats and buzzing bees. Others sit outside their homes, going about their age-old business. One woman plucks the radiant feathers of a dead macaw. Another removes her eyebrows and eyelashes, because the Kaiapo women think they are ugly. (A nurse once told me that this custom might have a hygienic origin—to ward off parasites, for instance.) Kaiapo women also deepen their foreheads by shaving the top of their head in a triangle that reaches the crown—a fearsome sight to the unaccustomed eye.

I envy a mother who is clearly enjoying herself fingerpainting her three children. She draws black designs with genipap juice. On the face and the feet she puts red dye from the "urucu," or annatto, plant; Indians say it keeps away chiggers and ticks.

Change has come to Gorotire along the other road, the one leading east to Redenção. Recent Kaiapo history is full of "firsts," but a notable turning point came when prospectors struck gold on Gorotire land in 1980. The Kaiapo raided the camp, 20 miles from the village, but failed to drive away the trespassers. Then they made a deal.

Last fall, when I was visiting Gorotire, about 2,000 gold diggers were stripping the land to the bone farther upstream, and the River Fresco passed the village the color of mud, its water contaminated with oil and mercury. I heard no one complain about that. Gorotire gets 7 percent of the mine's profits—several pounds of gold a week.

In 1984, a lumber company completed the first road. It signed a contract with the Indian Foundation for Gorotire's mahogany (the Indians are wards of the Brazilian Government). Most of the mahogany is gone now, and the Government agency split the profits with the Kaiapo. Gorotire chose to spend its gold and timber profits on new water and electricity lines and rows of brick houses. Only about half of the inahbitants now live in traditional palm-frond huts.

The young Kaiapo who earn a salary as supervisors at the gold camp have bought their own gas stoves, radios, sofas and mattresses. For the community, the four tribal chiefs ordered several boats, trucks and a small plane that ferries people and goods among nearby Kaiapo villages.

One evening, a truck arriving from Redenção—bringing rice, sugar, bottled gas, oil for the generator—is another reminder of how fast Gorotire is adapting to a Western economy. From being a largely self-sufficient community of hunters and farmers, it is now increasingly dependent on outside goods. In Gorotire, it is clearly money, no longer disease or violence, that has become the greatest catalyst for change. Money has given the Kaiapo the means and the confidence to travel and lobby for their rights. At the same time, it is making them more vulnerable.

I have seen other villages where Indians have received large sums of money—for the passage of a railroad or a powerline, or from a mining company. Such money is usually released in installments, through banks, but its arrival has put new strains on the role of the chiefs. Money and goods have introduced a new, materialistic expression of power in societies that have been egalitarian. Among most Indians, a man's prestige has always depended not on what he acquires but on what he gives away.

In Gorotire, some of the young men complain that the chiefs are not distributing community money and goods equally, that the chiefs' relatives and favorites are getting a bigger share and more privileges.

Darrell Posey, the anthropologist, believes the greatest political change came with the road. With it, he says, "the Kaiapo chiefs lost control of which people and what goods would come in." Previously, the chiefs had been the sole distributors. They had also played the vital roles of keeping the peace and leading the ceremonies. Now, the chiefs hardly know the liturgy of the ceremonies; their main task seems to be to deal with the outside world.

The transition is also changing the role of the medicine man. Bebtopup, for example, has an arsenal of remedies for the common ailments—fevers, diarrheas, snake bites, wounds. But he and his colleagues have lost prestige because they do not know how to deal with the diseases brought to Gorotire by white men, such as the pneumonia that strikes the children and the malaria spreading from the gold miners' camp.

Anthropologists sometimes say that when outsiders visit the Indian world, they often focus on themes central not to Indians but to themselves. This might explain why I was so bothered by the garbage, the flotsam of Western civilization.

Gorotire's setting is Arcadian. It lies on a bluff overlooking the River Fresco, with views of the forests across and the mountains behind. Spring rains bring waterfalls and blossoms. But these days the village is awash with rusting cans, plastic wrappers, tapes sprung from their cassettes, discarded mattresses and clothes. New domestic animals such as dogs, pigs and ducks have left a carpet of droppings. And giant rats, which suddenly appeared some years ago, seem to be everywhere; some have bitten small children.

"Indians have never had garbage that was not blodegradable," says Sandra Machado, a Brazilian researching Kaiapo farming techniques here. "No one wants to take care of it."

It is a mild moonlit evening, and in the men's house many Kaiapo are watching soccer on television. The bank of the river is a quieter place to talk.

"If you look beyond the garbage and the stone houses, this is still a strong and coherent indigenous culture," says Darrell Posey, speaking of the mixed feelings he has about a decade of developments in Gorotire. "Despite everything, the language is alive, the festivals and initiation rights are observed."

Posey says that the Kaiapo in Gorotire and in other villages continue with their age-old natural farming techniques, using plants to fix nitrogen in the soil, chunks of termite nests instead of chemical fertilizers, plant infusions to kill pests, the nests of ferocious ants to protect fruit trees from other ant predators.

Biologists often complain that there have been many studies of exotic rituals, paraphernalia and kinships of Indians, but that Western science has paid scant attention to the Indians' use of animals and plants.

Like others working in the Amazon region, Posey worries about the gap between the old and the young. "The old chiefs are turning over decisions to the young because they can drive a truck or operate a video machine or go to the bank," he says, "But the young people don't see the relevance of learning the tribal knowledge and its being lost."

"You can afford to lose one generation," he adds, "because grandparents do the teaching of their grandchildren. But you cannot afford to lose two generations."

Gorotire has a small Government school, designed to help Indians integrate into the national society. The teacher, who speaks only Portuguese, has started organizing annual Independence Day parades. On the blackboard is a list of patriotic holidays, including Independence Day and the Day of the Soldier. I ask the children later what a soldier is, "Something of white people," one of them says.

Chief Poropot agrees that everyone must learn Portuguese. "The language of the Kaiapo is very ancient and it will never end," he says. "But the women and the children need to learn Portuguese to defend themselves."

Defend themselves?

"If they go to shop in Redenção, they have to talk," he says. "If they get sick, they cannot tell the doctor what they have."

Thirty miles from Gorotire, in the village of Aukre, another Kaiapo tribe is choosing a different strategy for change. Its best-known member is Paiakan, 37 years old, the son of Chief Tikiri.

Calm and articulate, Paiakan has been named to "keep an eye on the whites" in the state capital of Belém. He acts as a kind of roving ambassador for the Kaiapo, even though each village is autonomous. When Kaiapo interests are threatened, he sends out warnings to the communities.

Paiakan's contacts with the outside world and the many pitfalls it holds for Indians have made him more conservative, he says, more so than in the early days, in the 1970's, when he first left home to work on the Trans-Amazonian Highway. As his father's main adviser, he has insisted that Aukre remain a traditional village.

It is built in the age-old circle of mud-and-thatch huts. There is no television, running water, pigs or piles of garbage. Paiakan and his father have also banned logging and gold digging. This appears to have saved Aukre from the consumerism—and widespread influenza and malaria—of Gorotire.

"The lumber men have come to us with their bags of money," he says. "And we know we have a lot of gold. But we do not want to bring a lot of money in. The Indian still does not know the value of white man's objects or how to treat them." Paiakon cites clothing as an example. "The Indian wears something until it is stiff with dirt, then he throws it out."

But people now want things from the "world of the whites," he continues. "Pressure from the white society is so strong, there is no wall that can stop it." It is the task of the chief to measure the change, provide explanations, he says. "If someone wants to get a radio or a tape recorder, the chiefs cannot stop it."

In Aukre where two aging chiefs are still in charge of buying goods for the community, they say that they will not buy gadgets. "We explain we cannot buy this thing for you because we do not have the batteries you need and we cannot repair it," Paiakan says.

Of late, Paiakan has been invited abroad to campaign for the protection of the rain forest. He knows the problem only too well. Ranchers have moved almost to the reservation's doorstep, felled trees and set massive forest fires. Because of deforestation, there have been unusual changes in the water level of the Fresco River.

"Our people are getting very disoriented," says Paiakan. "It would be as if people from another planet came to your cities and started to tear down your houses. The forest is our home." With all the destruction going on, he continues, "the breath of life is drifting up and away from us."

At the age of 78 and retired from teaching at the University of California at Los Angeles, the anthropologist Gerardo Reichel-Dolmatoff lives in Bogotá, Colombia, and is still writing. After studying changes in the Amazon for five decades, he is not optimistic about the prospects for the Indians.

"In Colombia, I don't know of a single case where an aboriginal culture has found a strong adaptive mechanism," he says. "Physical survival is possible. But I have not seen the ancient values replaced by a workable value system. I wish I could be more positive. But in 50 years I have seen too many traditions being lost, too many tribes disappear.

"For 500 years we have witnessed the destruction of the Indians. Now we are witnessing the destruction of the habitat. I suggest more field work, and immediate field work, because soon it will be too late."

At a conference on ethnobiology last fall, Reichel-Dolmatoff urged scientists to insist on spreading the message that Western science has much to learn from Indians, from their well-adapted lives and deeply-felt beliefs, their view that whatever man subtracts he must restore by other means.

What suggestions has he made to Indians?

"Indians have to stay in touch with their language—that is absolutely essential," he says. "It embodies their thought patterns, their values, their philosophy." Moreover, he says, talented young Indians should be given a modern academic education, but also the chance to keep in touch with their people. "They come from cultures based on extraordinary realism and imagery. They should not be forced to enter at the lowest level of our society."

One night, I ask the chiefs in Gorotire: What happens if the gold runs out? After all, most of the mahogany is already gone. Young tribesmen have wanted to invest some of the income, and the chiefs have accepted the idea. Gorotire has bought a home in Belém for Kaiapo who travel there, as well as three houses in Redenção. There is talk of buying a farm, a curious thought, perhaps for a community that lives on eight million acres of land. But the Kaiapo, so they say, want it so that white farmers can grow rice for them.

And there is talk of planting new mahogany trees. Soon the conversation turns to a bird that a tribesman explains is very important. It is the bird, he says, that spreads the mahogany seeds.

41 The Vietnam War Memorial

ROBIN WAGNER-PACIFICI
BARRY SCHWARTZ

As has been noted in several previous selections, meaning is not contained in objects and events. Rather, meaning is socially constructed; that is, people jointly decide that such aspects of social life as "events" have particular meanings. One consequence is that speaking about an "event" then arouses common sentiments. One of the major needs of each society, then, is to establish meanings that unify its people, so its members can think similarly about its "significant events." Monuments of the Revolutionary War and World War II, for example, elicit a collective response; that is, most Americans attach similar meanings to these wars, which helps to provide a common identity, partially overcoming the many factors that divide them.

The war in Vietnam, however, divided the nation as it had not been split since the Civil War. With their intense feelings for and against the war, Americans were confused, emotional, defensive, and ready to fight one another. Many people across the land protested the war, especially on university campuses, and Ohio and Mississippi national guards even shot student protesters at Kent State and Jackson State. The loss of the war and the withdrawal of American troops brought shame to some, relief to others. But it did not bring common, unifying meaning about the war. What, then, does a country do about erecting a memorial to such a wrenching, devisive event? That is the focus of this article, which examines how meaning is established in a shifting context.

Dedication of the War Memorial

On November 11, 1982, seven years after the last American died in Vietnam, the Vietnam Veterans Memorial was dedicated. Immediately before the dedication ceremony, 150,000 spectators watched and applauded as 15,000

478

veterans passed before them. Elaborate floats and flyovers by fighter planes and helicopters embellished the three-hour parade. The more solemn aspects of this colorful Veterans Day had been established by the reading out of the names of all 57,939 Americans killed in Vietnam in an earlier 56-hour candlelight vigil at the National Cathedral. The president of the United States participated in the observance, lighting a candle for the dead and listening to part of the long roster of names.

From the very beginning of these commemorative rites, the themes of recovery and solidarity were repeated. The motto of the Veterans Day parade, "Marching along Together," reflected these themes and prefaced the dedication day invocation: "Let the Memorial begin the healing process and forever stand as a symbol of our national unity." The rhetoric, however, expressed an ideal, not a reality. If official spokesmen defined the Memorial as a way "to unite our beloved America with her bravest and best," the bravest and best were inclined to ask what took so long. As one veteran put it: "They should have had this when we first came back in 1971." Secretary of Defense Caspar Weinberger conceded the delay, but added, "We have finally come to appreciate your sacrifice." . . .

Dilemmas of Commemoration

. . . One of the most influential perspectives on the social functions of commemoration is Émile Durkheim's. Commemorative rites and symbols, Durkheim tells us (1965, p. 420), preserve and celebrate traditional beliefs; they "serve to sustain the vitality of these beliefs, to keep them from being effaced from memory and, in sum, to revivify the most essential elements of the collective consciousness. Through [commemoration] the group periodically renews the sentiment which it has of itself and of its unity." . . . But suppose a society is divided over the very event it selects for commemoration. Suppose that event constitutes a painful moment for society, such as a military defeat or an era of domestic oppression. What kinds of "traditional beliefs" and "essential elements," and what kind of monuments, if any, can crystallize these moments and unify the society around them? How is commemoration without consensus, or without pride, possible?

The Vietnam Veterans Memorial provides a good case to use in thinking about these issues. The succession of events that led to the Memorial's creation and public reception was a culture-producing process. In that process, contrasting moral evaluations of the Vietnam War and its participants were affirmed. . . .

From a comparative perspective, the moral evaluations reflected in the Vietnam Memorial derive from a formula common to all societies that seek to commemorate controversial military ventures. When the cause of a lost war is widely held to be immoral or at best needless, then, in James Mayo's (1988, p. 170) words, "defeat . . . cannot be forgotten and a nation's people must find ways to redeem those who died for their country to make defeat honorable. This can be done by honoring the individuals who fought rather than the country's lost cause." This commemorative formula, as will be shown, has been expressly invoked to justify the marking of the Vietnam War. . . . The dualism of cause and participant is . . . dramatized in the American South. Confederate Memorial Day ceremonies throughout the South vary from one place to the next, but one thread unites them all, and that is the determination to honor the gallantry of the Confederate soldier, without mention of secession and slavery. It was this same principle—the separation of the men from their cause—that President Ronald Reagan's supporters invoked to justify his visit to Bitberg to honor Nazi Germany's war dead. The Soviet Union, after its evacuation of Afghanistan, also faces questions on how to recognize men who fought and lost a war. In an unprecedented gesture of kindness toward its own prisoners of war, the Soviet government not only accorded the benefit of doubt to those whose conduct during imprisonment was uncertain, but also declared that "forgiveness toward POWs who succumbed to enemy pressure [is] a necessary part of the national healing process" (*New York Times*, June 14, 1988). "National healing"—precisely the need invoked in America to justify the honoring of the Vietnam soldiers. . . .

Data Collection

. . . [We] examined the discourses of such relevant institutions and individuals as Congress, the Commission of Fine Arts, the mass media, the Memorial's designers and visitors, among others. We found much of this discourse in the *Congressional Record*, dedication speeches, Veterans Day oratory, and commentaries appearing in newspapers and magazines. In addition, many written messages addressed to the dead soldiers are being left at the Memorial by friends and relatives. A sample of 250 of these documents includes statements about the significance of the Memorial itself. A different layer of the Memorial's meaning was the object of observations we made at the site and of similar observations reported by informants. Also, we obtained from the Department of the Interior a partial inventory of objects left at the Memorial since its completion. Typically presented in memory of the dead by family and friends, these objects range from national symbols, like flags, to private possessions, like toys or articles of clothing that once belonged to the deceased. All such tokens are gathered up from the Memorial site by the National Park Service at the end of each day and, along with the written correspondence, are cataloged and stored at the Museum and Archaeological Regional Storage Facility in Lanham, Maryland, where we inspected them.

No one segment of this material provides much useful information. It takes the total body of material, duly combined and arrayed in proper sequence, to reveal the unfolding of commemorative meaning.

A Nation's Gratitude: Search for a Genre

The first official recognition of the Vietnam veteran was not bestowed until 1978, three years after the last American was flown out of Saigon. The recognition itself was hesitant and uncertain. A Vietnam War crypt had already been prepared in the Tomb of the Unknown Soldier, but the Army determined that neither of its two unidentified bodies (only 30% of the remains in either case) made for a decent corpse. Instead of honoring its Vietnam battle dead by symbolically joining them, through entombment of unknown soldiers' remains, with men fallen in earlier wars, the army recommended that a plaque and display of medals be set apart behind the tomb, along with the following inscription: "Let all know that the United States of America pays tribute to the members of the Armed Forces who answered their country's call." This strange declaration bears no reference at all to the Vietnam War, and it required an act of the Veterans Affairs subcommittee to make it more specific: "Let all people know that the United States pays tribute to those members of the Armed Forces who served honorably in Southeast Asia during the Vietnam era" (*The Nation*, April 8, 1978, p. 389). In even this second, stronger statement, three things are noteworthy: (1) although revised in Congress, the statement was initiated by the military; (2) it received little publicity; and (3) it designated the conflict in Vietnam by the word "era" rather than "war." Thus the recognition came from only a small part of the society for whose interests and values the war was fought; it was communicated to that society without conspicuous ceremony; and it betrayed confusion about the meaning of the war by its failure to find a word to describe it. This last point is the most noteworthy of all. Although a war had not been officially declared, many congressional resolutions during the 1980s referred to the hostilities in Vietnam as "the Vietnam war." Touchiness during the late 1970s about what to call the conflict stemmed from social, not legal, concerns. To name an event is to categorize it morally and to provide an identity for its participants. Anomalous names betray ambiguity about an event's nature and uncertainty about how to react to the men who take part in it. . . .

Official ambivalence toward the Vietnam War showed up next in the activities of Congress. It was in Congress, in fall 1978, that the work culminating in the Veterans Memorial began. The plan then discussed, however, was not to commemorate those who had died in the war, but to set aside a special "Vietnam Veterans Week" for its survivors. Thus evolved a second solution to the problem of finding a genre to commemorate the

Vietnam War. Time, rather than granite, the dedication of a week rather than the dedication of a tangible monument, sufficed to honor the Vietnam fighting man. This plan's principal entrepreneurs were the members of the Vietnam-Era Caucus, 19 U.S. representatives and senators who had served in the military during the Vietnam War years. They meant to achieve two goals: to unify a nation divided by war and to induce Congress to recognize that many war veterans were suffering from unmet needs. . . .

. . . During the time that the Vietnam-Era Caucus worked on its legislation, a former army corporal from a working-class family, Jan Scruggs, had independently decided on a plan of his own. As noted above, one of the premises of Vietnam Veterans Week was that the soldier must be separated from the cause. This separation is precisely what Scruggs aimed to celebrate publicly. At first, his idea attracted little notice, but it eventually overshadowed Vietnam Veterans Week in commemorative significance. He would build a memorial to the men who served in Vietnam and would inscribe on it the names of all the war dead. The plan represented a different solution to the commemorative genre problem than those previously proposed. It was different in that it combined the traditional idea of a stone monument to the war dead with the radical idea of excluding from it any prominent symbol of national honor and glory. In place of such a symbol would appear a list of the dead soldiers' names—58,000 of them. On May 28, 1979, Scruggs announced the formation of the Vietnam Veterans Memorial Fund to raise money to build the monument. . . .

The memorial chosen by the Commission of Fine Arts from the more than 1,400 designs submitted was, indeed, the simplest and least imposing: two unadorned black walls, each about 250 feet in length, composed of 70 granite panels increasing in height from several inches at the end of each wall to 10 feet where they come together at a 125 degree angle. Although this angle aligns the two walls with the Lincoln Memorial and Washington Monument, the walls themselves are placed below ground level, invisible from most vantage points on or near the Mall. The Vietnam War is thus defined as a national event, but in a spatial context that brackets off that event from those commemorated by neighboring monuments. The walls add to this sense of detachment by their internal format, which draws the viewer into a separate warp of time and space. As one moves from the edge of one wall to the point where it joins the other, one experiences a descending movement in space and a circular movement in time, for the 57,939 soldiers' names appear in the chronological order of the dates of their deaths, such that the war's first and last fatalities are joined at the walls' conjunction.

The commission's preference for this design was unanimous. However, for every layman who approved that choice, another seemed to be enraged by it. Those who shared the designer's goals were inclined to believe she had achieved them. Maya Ying Lin declared that her design was not meant to convey a particular political message but to evoke "feelings, thoughts, and emotions" of a variant and private nature: "What people see or don't see is their own projection." . . .

Uses of Genre: The Enshrinement Process

The meaning of the Vietnam Veterans Memorial is defined by the way people behave in reference to it. Some monuments are rarely talked about or visited and never put to ceremonial use. Other monuments, like the Tomb of the Unknown Soldier, are used often as formal ceremonial sites and visited year after year by large numbers of people. Between the Vietnam Veterans Memorial and its visitors, a very different relationship obtains. Not only is the Memorial an object of frequent ceremony and frequent visitation (more than 2.5 million visitors and 1,100–1,500 reunions per year), it is also an object with which visitors enter into active and affective relationships. These relationships have thwarted all original intentions as to what the Memorial should be and represent.

Conceived as something to be passively looked at and contemplated, the Vietnam Memorial has become an object of emotion. This is not the case for the Memorial site as a whole, just the wall and its names. The names on the wall are touched, their letters traced by the moving finger. The names are caressed. The names are reproduced on paper by pencil rubbing and taken home. And something is left from home itself—a material object bearing special significance to the deceased or a written statement by the visitor or mourner. . . .

Uses of Genre: The Representation of Ambivalence

All nonperishable articles left at the Vietnam Veterans Memorial are collected each day and kept at the Museum and Archeological Regional Storage Facility. Row after row of airtight shelters preserve these "gifts" for the future, thus extending the Memorial in space and in time. This part of the Veterans Memorial complex is the most populist, for its contents, in accordance with Interior Department policy, are determined by the people who visit the Memorial and not by professional curators. . . .

The most colorful objects left by visitors are flowers, taped to the wall or placed on the ground beneath a loved one's name. Nothing of a political nature is embodied in these floral displays; however, the Park Service's inventory of other (nonperishable) items does convey a coherent political message. This inventory shows that the one object most frequently left by the wall is a small American flag attached to a stick and set in the ground below the name that the visitor desired to mark. Through this offering, visitors uttered a political statement that was not supposed to be made. They asserted their patriotism, their loyalty to a nation. Whether they got the idea themselves or copied it from one another, they could think of no better way to dignify their loved one's memory than to associate his name with his country's emblem.

These assertions are amplified by other objects. The largest category of objects, almost a third of everything that has been deposited by the visitors, consists of military items, mostly patches and insignias marking military-unit membership, as well as parts of uniforms, dog tags, identification bracelets, medals, awards, and certificates. The memorial site was thus decorated by symbols of the roles through which living veterans once enacted their commitment to the nation. These symbols began to appear in great profusion as soon as the Memorial was dedicated and continued to appear two years later when the statue of the three soldiers was unveiled. Designed to draw attention to the individual and away from the nation and its cause, the Memorial's wall turns out to be a most dramatic locus of patriotic feeling. The wall's use moved it toward that traditional war monument genre that opponents and supporters alike once believed it deviated from. . . .

From its very inception, the Memorial's sponsors insisted that it would make no statement about the war—a promise predicated on the assumption that political silence could somehow be ensured by the Memorial's design. An ordinance that expressly prohibits political demonstrations on Memorial grounds supplemented this assumption. Thus deprived of a traditional public forum, political opinions were, instead, inserted into many of the written statements brought to the wall. Letters, poems, and memos, often accompanied by photographs, can be viewed analytically as publicly accessible private sentiments or as privatized public opinion. Either way, they articulate the public's diverse visions of Vietnam. Not all these written statements included opinions about the war itself. Among the opinions that were expressed in the letters, however, more than half were ambivalent or negative. And the wall is the site where these opinions were displayed. One poem declares: "And in that time / When men decide and feel safe / To call the war insane / Take one moment to embrace / Those gentle heroes / You left behind." Another correspondent laments the soldiers who went "So far from home and the land of their own / To fight in a war the reason unknown." . . .

The intensive, emotional reaction to the Memorial has superimposed itself upon, but has never replaced other reactions. The Memorial as it is presently constituted by wall, flag, and statue remains a multifocal version of the war monument genre, a version ambiguous enough to accommodate a wide span of commemorative meanings. By interacting with it and interpreting it, different constituencies make this multivocal quality operative. For politicians, the Memorial helps to acquit the nation's overdue debt to its veterans; for artists, it represents a novel combination of symbols and forms; for the veterans, it is an emblem of their rightful place in the nation's political and moral heritage; for families of the dead, it is a shrine linking home and nation; for those who supported the war and defined it as honorable, it is a vindication; for those who opposed the war and defined it as dishonorable, also a vindication. . . .

[*Conclusion*]

. . . [T]o a large extent, we read the Vietnam Veterans Memorial through its uses. Ironically, the memorial designed to be least visible has become the most visible because its users have opened up its spaces and extended them outward. They have done this by the depositing of items at the wall, by the creation of a vast facility for their storage and their display, by the addition to the original site of a flag and statue, by the devising of a Moving Wall, and by the establishment in cities across the land of Vietnam War Memorials that resemble the Washington prototype. . . .

. . . The rituals that take place [at the Vietnam Memorial] are not the kind Durkheim would have understood. These are not rituals that strengthen common sentiments by bringing together those who hold them and putting them into closer and more active relations with one another (1965, p. 241). We are dealing with ritual assemblies that are intense even though, or perhaps because, the volume of common thoughts and sentiments about their object is so sparse. In studying the Vietnam Memorial, we have come to believe that people may need more ritual to face a painful and controversial part of the past than to deal with a painful part of the past about whose cause and meaning there is agreement. Rituals, however, do not resolve historical controversies; they only articulate them, making their memory public and dramatic. Unable to convince one another about what went wrong in Vietnam, therefore, the men and women who assemble at the Vietnam Memorial do so with more gravity than is displayed at shrines commemorating any other war.

In the end, contexts and meanings change. A day will come when the names that appear on the Vietnam Memorial's wall are known to few living persons. On this day, the intensity of feeling evoked by the wall will be less acute; the flags and objects that decorate the wall will be less dense; the solemnity that now grips those who enter the Memorial site will be diluted by an air of casualness; the ritual relation that now links shrine and pilgrim will become a mundane relation that links attraction and tourist. On this day, the Vietnam War will have become a less fitful part of American history. But the Vietnam Veterans Memorial, its several parts continuing to reflect different aspects of and beliefs about the war, will echo the ambivalence with which that war was first commemorated.

References

Durkheim, Emile. 1965. *The Elementary Forms of the Religious Life*. New York: Free Press.

Mayo, James M. 1988. *War Memorials as Political Landscape: The American Experience and Beyond*. New York: Praeger.

42 The Abolition of *El Cortito*

DOUGLAS L. MURRAY

When a problem is experienced by an individual, it is a *personal problem*. When many people experience the same problem, *and* they perceive the potential of being able to do something about it, it is a *social problem*. At the basis of the change from a personal to a social problem is perception—first the perception that many others are experiencing similar things, and second, the perception that people don't have to put up with conditions the way they are but can take action to change matters.

This change from a personal to a social problem happens every now and then in our society. Sexual harassment and environmental pollution are two well-known examples. The problem that Murray examines in this selection went through this change, but it is a problem practically unknown outside the Hispanic community. *El cortito*, a simple, short-handled hoe, became a source of controversy, and even violence. This little tool, enmeshed in racism, health hazards, and the oppression of workers, became a rallying point for worker discontent, union organizing, and, ultimately, significant social change.

As you read this article, note how the success of the struggle around *el cortito* depended on wide-scale change that had taken place in American society.

LATE ONE AFTERNOON IN THE SPRING OF 1973, farm workers leaving the fields of the fertile Salinas Valley in central California gathered beside the buses which would take them to the nearby labor camps for the night. They moved nervously about a large pile of short-handled hoes which they had been using that day to thin and weed long rows of lettuce. One farm worker quickly doused the hoes with gasoline; another tossed a match, setting them ablaze. Cries of protest swept through the crowd as the farm workers served their bosses with a defiant notice: no longer would they work with *el cortito*, the short-handled hoe.

Farm workers have protested in the California fields throughout the

20th century, yet most of their attempts to improve agricultural working conditions have met with little success. Often their protests have unleashed repressive measures from growers or local governments. But the struggle over the short-handled hoe was an unusual event in farm worker history. *El cortito* became the focus of California government hearings, a California Supreme Court ruling (*Sebastian Carmona et al. v. Division of Industrial Safety.* January 13, 1975), and ultimately a California administrative edict (Administrative Interpretation No. 62, Division of Industrial Safety, April 7, 1975) banning the tool from further use in the California fields.

The abolition of *el cortito* is an example of the reliance upon administrative and legal institutions by groups challenging specific social conditions, a political phenomenon that has increased significantly in the United States since the 1950s. The civil rights, anti-Vietnam war, and environmental movements have all relied heavily on legal action to force social change or generate popular support for legislative reform. . . . Whereas movements in the 19th and early 20th centuries mainly used cultural, community, occupational and other traditional resources (Tilly, 1978), contemporary social movements have relied increasingly upon access to, and mobilization of, state institutions to bring about social change. Legal institutions have played a particularly important role (Black, 1973; Lipsky, 1968). Litigation has attacked social issues ranging from school desegregation (Greenberg, 1959) to environmental degradation (Dunlap, 1981). . . .

This emphasis in contemporary research on the role legal institutions play in bringing about social change neglects the important role legal institutions play in structuring and redefining the very issues involved. The way a social problem is defined by the government institutions and legal statutes used to resolve it, and the relationship between the original problem and its resolution through state policy, remain relatively unexplored questions.

The abolition of *el cortito* is an example of how social problems are solved within the state arena and how state policy affects the sources of social conflict. . . .

The Origin of El Cortito

The short-handled hoe has not always been an integral part of agricultural production in California. Its introduction and the subsequent conflict it generated are rooted in the early organization of corporate farming. The combination of large land holdings inherited from the Mexican colonial period and the shift to labor-intensive farming transformed California agriculture in the late 19th century. The resulting agribusiness which emerged from this era was characterized by the cultivation of single crops on large tracts of land and the dependence upon a large supply of cheap labor.

The emphasis on labor-intensive farming was accompanied by a need to maintain control over the workers in an effort to assure a profitable return. Direct involvement in the work process to achieve this end was largely unnecessary, however, since most immigrant workers used on the California farms were fleeing extreme economic or political hardships and had no option but to work under whatever terms of employment they were offered.

With such externally imposed discipline, more direct control of the farm workers was unnecessary, and the workers retained a degree of autonomy. Growers relied heavily upon the self-organization of these immigrant workers and the skills they provided. . . .

It was from this self-organized labor process that the short-handled hoe first emerged. California growers began cultivating sugar beets intensively near the end of the 19th century. Most farm workers on the west coast at this time came from Japan. Like the Chinese farm workers before them (Saxton, 1971), the Japanese were valued for their skills in the intensive cultivation of row crops. Among the techniques the Japanese relied upon was a traditional tool used in Japanese gardening, the short-handled hoe.

Japanese farm workers used the short-handled hoe in conjunction with a variety of tools and techniques over which they had a significant degree of control. They worked in closely knit units called clubs or associations, selecting a secretary from among the group to contract and direct the work (McWilliams, 1971). These farm workers used both short- and long-handled hoes, rotating tasks among themselves to alleviate the strain of using the short-handled hoe.

At first, the Japanese farm workers' knowledge of intensive cultivation and their ability to organize and supervise themselves were prized by growers. But once established as an integral part of production, the farm workers began to demand better wages. Their wages rose 50 percent over a 15-year period and by 1907 they were the highest-paid group of workers in California agriculture (McWilliams, 1971:111). Growers faced the same dilemma as employers in other industries at this time. The degree of autonomy maintained by skilled immigrant workers became the source of leverage in labor's confrontation with capital.

The Japanese farm workers posed a serious threat to California agriculture: they could stop production, often during the crucial harvest period, and drive up the cost of labor. The solution adopted by the growers over the second decade of the 20th century was similar to that used by industrialists in the eastern United States; they recruited a new labor force, one which did not have a history of organization and conflict in California agriculture. To ensure that no such organization developed, the growers increased their control over the labor process.

The new labor force to which the growers turned had been arriving from Mexico as early as the Japanese. They came at first to work on the railroads, and subsequently moved into agriculture as the demand for labor grew. By the end of the 19th century, with the railroads connecting much of Mexico and the United States, the northward migration of workers was increasing (Galarza, 1964). The strategy of economic development pursued in Mexico under the regime of president Porfirio Diaz (1876–1911), of which the railroads were a major part, created not only the vehicle for the northward migration, but the motivation as well. The economic stagnation that grew from this period and the subsequent turmoil of the Mexican Revolution (Goldfrank, 1975) led large numbers of *campesinos* to come north in search of work or to escape political persecution (Hoffman, 1974). The Mexican farm workers, unlike their predecessors, came mainly from regions in Mexico that did not farm intensively. The skills and knowledge of intensive farming, including the use of the short-handled hoe, were not a part of their culture. But the California growers had a greater need for a controllable labor supply than for skilled laborers, and to achieve this control they reorganized the agricultural labor process.

Transformation of the Labor Process

The shift in control of the labor process took subtle forms, often with unseen effects. But the seemingly incremental changes in the first decades of the 20th century had a profound effect on the lives of the farm workers. During this period of transformation, the use of the short-handled hoe emerged as one of the most difficult and oppressive conditions of California farm labor.

Growing resistance and organization by farm workers prompted the growers to form organizations such as the California Farm Bureau Federation to foster "the rational recruitment of seasonal labor" (Chambers, 1952:23). Where Japanese farm workers had selected a secretary from their own ranks to contract work for their crew, the growers began to rely on their own contractors to find workers. The Spanish-speaking farm workers referred to the contractors as *el coyote*. The contractor and his "crew pushers" were responsible for getting maximum productivity out of the labor force; herein lies the beginning of the health hazard posed by the short-handled hoe. Thinning and weeding became specialized tasks done by gangs of farm workers over larger and larger plots of land. The short-handled hoe began to be used exclusively for thinning and weeding, as the long-handled hoe gradually disappeared from the fields. Growers claimed they preferred the short-handled hoe for its greater accuracy and efficiency, but farm workers and contractors saw a more sinister motive behind the choice of the short-handled hoe. Farm worker Sebastian Carmona recalled a supervisor's response to his objection to the short-handled hoe:

> With the long-handled hoe I can't tell whether they are working or just leaning on their hoes. With the short-handled hoe I know when they are not working by how often they stand up (Personal interview, March 1, 1979).

The short-handled hoe was no longer an implement in the repertoire of farm worker tools and techniques for cultivation of row crops. It had become part of the growers' and contractors' repertoire of techniques for the supervision and control of the workers. Hector de la Rosa, another farm worker, described the effects of using this tool:

> When I used the short-handled hoe my head would ache and my eyes hurt because of the pressure of bending down so long. My back would hurt whenever I stood up or bent over. I moved down the rows as fast as I could so I could get to the end and rest my back for a moment (Personal interview, March 1, 1979).

Thus, the short-handled hoe also became a means of increasing productivity. Workers moved faster down the rows, in the knowledge that only at the end could they stand up momentarily to rest their backs.

During the 1920s and the Depression years that followed, growers tried to increase productivity and cut costs to maintain a viable profit margin. With the high level of fixed capital and subsequent financing costs, labor became the main target for cost-cutting schemes. The short-handled hoe was seized upon by growers and contractors throughout the region. Its usefulness to growers, and hardship to farm workers, spread as competition standardized agricultural practices in California.

Vivid evidence of changes in the use of the short-handled hoe in California can be found in various written and photographic accounts. References to hoeing activities at the beginning of the 20th century describe it as "squat labor" (Chambers, 1952). Photographs of the pre-1920s period show workers with their head up and hips to the ground. Accounts of later periods describe such work as "stoop labor" (McWilliams, 1971). Photographs show workers with legs nearly straight, head lowered and upper torso parallel to the ground. This position allowed for a faster pace of work, but placed much greater stress on the back.

Use of the short-handled hoe in the stoop position over prolonged periods of time results in a degeneration of the spine, leading to permanent disabilities. This condition was attested to by numerous physicians and medical specialists in hearings on the short-handled hoe held by California's Industrial Safety Board (ISB). The testimony of one physician is indicative of the conclusions reached by the medical experts:

> Anybody that's been using the [short-handled hoe] extensively in the field over a ten-year period has got back trouble. Whether or not you're seeing him for tonsilitis or something like that, he still has back problems. He may not be absolutely symptomatic, but that spine is wearing out. He's not going to make it to any retirement age of sixty-five (ISB hearing, May 3, 1973).

The use of the short-handled hoe to increase productivity, and to control labor generally, depends upon an abundance of available workers to replace those who could not keep up the pace. Growers not only expected a high turnover in this work, they actually preferred it. One grower testified during an Industrial Safety Board hearing that the daily turnover in short-handled hoe gangs was "hopefully" 75 to 80 percent (ISB hearing, May 3, 1973). With a steady supply of cheap labor from Mexico, supplemented by a growing population of Mexican-Americans in California, the growers could disregard the destructiveness of the short-handled hoe by relying upon the steady turnover of a transient labor force.

Resistance to El Cortito

The farm workers were quick to recognize work with the short-handled hoe as the most difficult and least desirable task. The tool came to be known as *el cortito*, "the short one," a symbol of the oppressive nature of stoop labor. One farm worker, reflecting on the conditions during the 1920s and 1930s, attributed the failing health and premature death of many farm workers indirectly to the short-handled hoe:

> In the Sacramento Valley, many of the farm workers would drink wine before going to work to kill the pain in their backs. They would grow old fast, or become sick. When they died people would say it was because they drank. But we knew it was from *el cortito* (Personal interview: Salvatore Gutierrez, March 1, 1979).

Growers and politicians who defended use of the short-handled hoe often argued that farm workers were better equipped physically and culturally to do this kind of work. The testimony of Mervyn Bailey is indicative:

> My father ran a crew of Hindus in 1911 in the Salinas Valley in thinning and hoeing beets. Then Japanese. Then we followed with Filipinos. And then the Mexicans. The stoop [laborers], most of them are small or more agile than the ordinary anglo due to their build and the fact that they seem to have a stronger body for the job (*Sebastian Carmona et al. v. Division of Industrial Safety:* Reply to Amicus Brief of Bud Antle, Inc., July 29, 1974:12).

. . . Use of the short-handled hoe and other working conditions were the focus of many spontaneous and organized protests and strikes by farm workers, particularly in the late 1920s (Galarza, 1970; Hoffman, 1974). Growers and labor contractors reported instances when temporary labor shortages were followed by protests and work stoppages by farm workers over the use of the short-handled hoe (ISB hearing, May 3, 1973:16). That these protests did not spread was more the result of the repressive and often violent response of growers, supported by the police and government agencies, than the result of any cultural heritage or proclivity for stoop labor among the farm workers. Under these conditions, the efforts of farm workers to challenge the use of the short-handled hoe were futile. With the subsequent migration to California of several hundred thousand Dustbowl refugees during the Depression came further exploitation of the farm workers. The

"Okies" and "Arkies" became the major source of farm labor during the Depression until the Second World War drew many of them into military service or war-industry jobs. These newly arrived migrants were willing to do any work, including using the short-handled hoe—and for lower wages. Their arrival doomed early union organizing efforts which were developing during the late 1920s among the Mexican farm workers. The Dustbowl migrants refused to cooperate with non-white organizers and workers, and remained unorganizable themselves (Stein, 1973). . . .

The Rise of Farm Worker Power in the 1960s

. . . After the war, Congress passed Public Law 78, known as the Bracero Program, to provide access to temporary workers from Mexico whenever labor shortages occurred. With government policies such as the Bracero Program assuring an abundant immigrant labor force, the growers saw little need to negotiate with farm workers (Majka, 1978). . . .

Yet, in spite of grower resistance and the barrier posed by the *braceros*, a farm worker union movement was developing. An unsuccessful strike against DiGiorgio vineyards in California's Central Valley in 1947 broke the AFL-affiliated National Farm Laborers' Union, in large part due to the availability of *bracero* labor. As organizers from this strike scattered throughout the state, they began to organize again (Galarza, 1970). During the 1950s these organizers began to build a base for a successful union throughout California. But the DiGiorgio lesson was clear: the *braceros* had to be overcome if a successful organizing drive was to be sustained.

In the early 1960s the challenge to the Bracero Program was gaining momentum. Congressman Adam Clayton Powell led a campaign on Capitol Hill to end Public Law 78 with the backing of some of the major unions. The use of *braceros* to break strikes and undermine organizing had become well known among organized labor, fueling the opposition to the Bracero Program and support for farm worker organizing. The AFL-CIO and the United Auto Workers provided funds for the union organizing drive. The campaign finally succeeded in November, 1964, when Congress ended the Bracero Program. This set the stage for the changes in California farm labor which would occur over the ensuing decade.

The changing political climate in the fields was not only the result of continuing struggles by farm workers and organized labor. The civil rights movement was changing political institutions and popular consciousness throughout the United States. The middle class was awakened from its post-war somnambulism by the sight of blacks and whites staging sit-ins, demonstrations for equal education and employment, snarling police dogs and the violent reactions of southern bigots. Inner city riots and the rise of the black power movement provided further testimony that a spirit had gripped the oppressed. Students and the clergy became active supporters of movements for social change. The farm workers in California found support coming not only from trade unions, but from urban liberals and students as well. Civil rights activists from the Student Non-Violent Coordinating Committee (SNCC) and the Congress of Racial Equality (CORE) came to the aid of the farm worker union movement.

Less than six months after the end of the Bracero Program, Coachella Valley in southern California was hit by farm worker strikes. In 1965, cries of *viva la huelga* ("long live the strike") drew national attention to the strike against grape growers in Delano, California. In 1966, two farm worker groups merged into the United Farm Workers (UFW) union, led by Cesar Chavez. The Delano strike gained momentum as a nation-wide boycott of table grapes, which by 1970 "had seriously eroded regular market outlets and substantially reduced grape sales" (Majka, 1978:150), demonstrated that the UFW and California farm workers had gained widespread support across the nation, signaling a significant shift in the historical confrontation between agribusiness and farm laborers.

It was against this background that the short-handled hoe became a focus of farm worker protest. A key factor in the eventual abolition of *el cortito* was the emergence of government institutions as advocates of the farm worker cause, and the state as an arena for the resolution of farm worker demands.

President Lyndon Johnson, in his State of the Union address of January 8, 1964, declared "unconditional war on poverty in America" as part of his campaign to build the "Great Society." Congress quickly passed Johnson's Economic Opportunities Bill of 1964, which he signed in August of that year and which led to creation of the Office of Economic Opportunity (OEO). This agency became a significant component of federal government efforts to both meet and channel the demands of social unrest. The legislation setting up the OEO contained a provision for legal service agencies for the disadvantaged. California Rural Legal Assistance (CRLA) was one of these agencies. The program was created and staffed primarily by young activist attorneys with close links to the civil rights and farm worker union movements. They believed legal action could significantly change the conditions of the oppressed. One CRLA attorney said:

> For legal service attorneys, law reform means using the law, either through litigation, legislative or administrative rule-making, to attack the root causes of poverty to enhance the power of the poor (Heistand, 1970:178).

With the belief that a legal solution could reach the "root causes of poverty," together with the CRLA links to the farm workers and a social and political climate receptive to farm worker demands, the conditions were right for the short-handled hoe to become a public issue within the state arena.

El Cortito *and the State*

In 1969, CRLA attorney Maurice Jourdane and community worker Henry Cantú visited a labor camp for farm workers near Salinas. While taking testimony on housing complaints within the camp, they were challenged by a group of farm workers. As Jourdane recalled:

> They had become frustrated over the lengthy process of questioning and checking details. One of them finally said: "This is bullshit! There are real problems for you to deal with, like *el cortito*." The entire group supported his demand. When we left the camp that night we talked and even joked about it some. But several more visits to the camp convinced us that the farm workers were serious, the short-handled hoe was the issue that concerned them (Personal interview, November 28, 1978).

An avenue was sought which would allow the case to be made quickly and provide a legal appeal. Jourdane chose as his vehicle for change a health and safety standard within Title 8 of the California Administrative Code (Section 3316) which prohibited the use of unsafe hand tools. Jourdane knew this section had traditionally applied to the use of faulty or broken tools, but felt an effort to push for an expanded interpretation was promising since an adverse ruling by the administrative agency could immediately be appealed in the state courts. The choice of strategy reflected not only Jourdane's assessment of the political terrain, but also the principal function and assumption of the OEO mandate—to improve conditions for the oppressed through the courts. Wrote CRLA attorney Fred Heistand:

> CRLA . . . has merely tried to implement what the judiciary, at least the Supreme Court, has been saying since the late 1930s: that the courts, not the legislatures, are the branch of government least responsive to immediate pressures, the branch with the greatest flexibility and opportunity, and thereby the greatest responsibility to safeguard and vindicate the rights of the poor (1970:179).

While the judiciary may be the most insulated branch of government, it is also the most selective. Interpretative action is premised upon a historically evolved structure of law and judicial precedence which selects from the array of possible issues, explanations and resolutions, those conditions and interpretations which most nearly approximate the existing legal and social relations (Offe, 1975). The courts can be flexible in their interpretations, and thereby responsive to social problems. But the task remained for the CRLA to develop the issue of *el cortito* in a manner that made the case viable within the established legal parameters. In so doing, the CRLA was redefining the farm workers' issue within the constraints of state policy.

Jourdane petitioned the Industrial Safety Board (ISB) of California's Division of Industrial Safety (DIS) on September 20, 1972, seeking prohibition of the use of *el cortito*. . . . The ISB held public hearings on the CRLA petition in El Centro, California, on May 1, 1973, and in Salinas, California, on May 3, 1973. the CRLA came to the hearings with a strong case, built on four years of research and the efforts of a national network of legal aid attorneys, civil rights and farm worker activists, doctors, and the UFW. The attorneys argued that *el cortito* was a health hazard to farm workers. They presented the testimony of 11 doctors familiar with farm worker health problems to support this claim. The declaration of Dr. David Brooks demonstrates the position held by all the doctors.

> I can unequivocally say that the use of this hoe will often cause tissue injury and severe back pain, and later may result in degeneration of the intervertebral discs and other supporting elements of the spine, thereby causing pain, limitation of motion, increased vulnerability to severe injury, and in many cases, complete physical disability (Petition for hearing before the ISB, September 20, 1972: Exhibit M).

The demonstration of an occupational hazard is only part of the process by which a complainant can successfully eliminate a tool or practice under the occupational health and safety codes. A complainant must also meet the requirements of Section 6306 (a) of the California Labor Code, which provides that workers have a right to "such freedom from danger to the life, safety, or health of employees as the nature of the employment reasonably permits." The traditional interpretation of this section has required that not only must a hazard be demonstrated, but it must be shown that a viable alternative also exists, to meet the criteria of "reasonably permits."

The CRLA argued that long-handled hoes were as efficient as short-handled hoes. They presented as evidence the results of a national survey conducted by legal aid agencies in 1971 and 1972 (Petition for hearing before ISB, September 20, 1972:6–10); it showed that the long-handled hoe was used to cultivate the same crops in all other regions of the United States. A representative from a California farm workers' cooperative testified that they had found that workers using long-handled hoes could sustain a productive pace over an entire day and work each day at this pace, while workers using short-handled hoes had fewer productive hours on subsequent days.

It became clear from the CRLA case against *el cortito* that the tool was a symbol to farm workers of the oppressive nature of farm labor. Repeated reference to contractors' and growers' preference for the short-handled hoe as a means of control served to heighten the image of brutality and oppression. Farm workers saw this case as a statement of changing power relations in agriculture.

> They felt threatened when the people at the bottom said, "Heh, we're not going to be on our knees no more, we're gonna stand up." They didn't want the farm worker to stand up. Psychologically, that gives them some dignity.

. . . When you are kneeling, it's showing humility. The majority of us are Catholics. We've been kneeling for years. It was time for us to overcome these things. We weren't going to be on our knees anymore (Personal interview: Hector de la Rosa, March 1, 1979).

The conflict over the short-handled hoe was symbolic to the growers as well. They saw the CRLA case as part of a growing threat to their power over the workers and the labor process. . . . The case challenged the grower's prerogatives over labor, as did the union movement, and the two were often indistinguishable to the growers in the overall conflict with farm workers.

. . . Medical evidence of the health hazard of the short-handled hoe was countered with disbelief or claims that sore and tired backs are part of hard work. The testimony of Robert Grainger, a grower in the Salinas Valley, is indicative:

> People always complain about back problems. I've thinned and hoed and I'm a great big man. I've thinned lettuce along with workers when I was a younger fellow and I was starting out in the farming business, and it hurts and it hurts badly for about three or four days. Then after that you're in shape (ISB hearing, May 3, 1973:16).

The growers claimed that the short-handled hoe was the traditional tool for thinning and weeding and had not been the subject of complaint prior to the CRLA's intervention. Grainger's testimony again indicates the growers line of argument:

> The people that work for me, and have worked for me, take a great deal of pride in their work that they do, and they want to do it with the short-handled hoe, and we have a wonderful relationship. I have a crew right now. These people are all happy to be there. They're happy to do their work. They want the work done correctly and they do it with the short-handled hoe (ISB hearing, May 3, 1973:15).

Growers made further arguments that the farm workers must stoop to avoid damaging the plants while thinning and weeding, but were unable to provide evidence to support these claims. . . .

After deliberating for two months, the ISB denied the CRLA petition to ban the short-handled hoe on July 13, 1973, claiming the tool had not been demonstrated to be a hazard under Section 3316 of the California Administrative Code, Title 8. The board said a hazardous tool was one that was damaged or improperly maintained, not a tool that was a hazard due to its normal use. The ISB avoided the issues raised by the CRLA case and retreated into the traditionally narrow interpretation of the legal statute applying to unsafe hand tools (Section 3316). The board reiterated the traditional view of worker health and safety in a letter conveying its decision to the CRLA:

There are, in fact, many work operations that hasten aging of various body parts at varying rates according to individual resistance. . . . Very few of these conditions are logically controllable by safety orders, because such orders have few ways of adjusting to the fact that some people are quite resistant to the related aging process (*Sebastian Carmona et al. v. Division of Industrial Safety:* Petition for Writ of Review, October 11, 1973: Exhibit B).

In effect, the ISB placed the blame for injuries resulting from use of the hoe upon the farm workers. In so doing it located the source of the problem in the weakness of the individual worker, the traditional interpretation of occupational hazards (Berman, 1978; Cobb and Sennett, 1973).

The relationship between agricultural interests and the board was further demonstrated by an in-house memorandum, written by board member H. Howard White, which was brought to light by CRLA attorney Maurice Jourdane:

On May 3, 1973, three members of the Board visited a field owned by the largest lettuce grower in the Salinas Valley, wherein workers were using the short hoe. They visited the field with representatives of Interharvest. Mr. White noted in a memo that "We were all watching carefully for any evidence of discomfiture or even low morale, such as expressions or actions, or whatever. I observed literally none. Note that I visited two fields and the same situation existed in both."

Jourdane observed:

It is incredible that board members would go to a field with grower representatives and expect to see any complaint or indication of low morale by a worker. Obviously, the board has failed to consider how long a worker could expect to retain his job should he indicate dissatisfaction with his work in the presence of grower representatives (Petition for Rehearing, August 3, 1973:17).

On October 11, 1973, the CRLA filed a Petition for Writ of Review with the California Supreme Court. The petition maintained that the ISB had erred in its application of state occupational health and safety standards to the case of the short-handled hoe. The evidence from the original petition to the ISB, along with evidence from the public hearings, was submitted to the court for consideration. But Jourdane introduced one additional argument to the evidence. He stressed the burden to the taxpayer of unemployed farm workers injured by the short-handled hoe. While such an argument had little relevance to the legal code in question, it had a great deal to do with the agenda prepared by CRLA. In anticipating an appeal to the legislative arena and a public which had elected a conservative governor committed to cutting the cost of welfare, this argument successfully linked the case with a broader constituency by appealing not only to their moral sensibilities but their economic interests.

Agribusiness interests filed a brief in support of the ISB ruling. Attorneys for the Bud Antle Corporation, the largest lettuce grower in the world, argued in the brief that banning the short-handled hoe would be disastrous for the industry and consequently the consumer. But the productivity argument had not fared well in the hearings and did not convince the Supreme Court Justices either. On January 13, 1975, the California Supreme Court ruled that the ISB had interpreted its mandate too narrowly. . . . (*Sebastian Carmona et al. v. Division of Industrial Safety . . .*).

The case came before the California Supreme Court during Jerry Brown's successful campaign for the governorship, based in large part upon a coalition sympathetic to the plight of the farm workers. . . . Following the California Supreme Court ruling . . . Richard Wilkins, the Reagan-appointed Chief of the Division of Industrial Safety, took swift action. On April 7, 1975, he issued Administrative Interpretation Number 62, which stated: "the use of the short-handled hoe shall be deemed a violation of safety order Section 8 CAC 3316."

As DIS personnel later observed:

> Wilkins could recognize, like everyone else, the political climate had changed. Jerry Brown was coming in, and the UFW had become an important influence in the new administration (Personal interview: William Becker and Michael Schneider, March 15, 1979).

. . . The administrative interpretation effectively marked the end of the short-handled hoe. Grower efforts to retain its use soon subsided. Bob Antle, head of Bud Antle Inc. and a leader in the fight against the ban of *el cortito*, admitted he was wrong in his opposition to the abolition of the short-handled hoe. Antle compared the use of the short-handled hoe with the long-handled hoe and found the long-handled hoe could be substituted without loss of productivity (*San Francisco Chronicle*, 1975). A few growers have been cited for violation of Section 3316 and have received fines ranging from $100 for first offenses to $500 for second violations. No grower has yet been cited for a third violation, which would receive a fine of thousands of dollars. . . .

El Cortito: *The Problem and The Solution*

What have the farm workers gained by state intervention into the agricultural labor process? The CRLA case must be evaluated for what it did not accomplish as well as its success. The development of the case in relation to particular government codes, the identification of the problem as a hazardous tool as defined by Title 8, California Administrative Code, Section 3316, and the demonstration of a viable alternative consistent with the requirements of California Labor Code Section 6306 (a) were all part of a process of selective development within the legal arena (Offe, 1975). This arena limits the kind of problems and solutions it will examine. The precondition to protecting the health of the farm worker was the protection of the grower, through the requirement of an alternative means to maintain the existing productive activities and the labor/management relations they sustain. By identifying the problem as the hazardous use of a tool, the statutes deflected the attention away from the hazardous nature of production organized, directed and controlled by a corporation. Lawyers must present their cases with the selective criteria of this legal system in mind. While a changing political environment lends itself to new and more flexible interpretations, as this case demonstrates, there are nevertheless definite limits. The CRLA case did not, and could not, confront the questions of autonomy and control inherent in existing worker/management relations. Nor could the case challenge the organization of corporate agriculture, even though the hazards of *el cortito* are rooted in these conditions.

Clearly, the switch to the long-handled hoe has been an improvement in the conditions of the farm workers. Some growers have reported a significant decrease in Workers Compensation claims for farm worker back injuries since the ban (Personal interview: Maurice Jourdane, November 28, 1978). Conditions for farm worker organizing have also been affected by the ban of *el cortito*. With healthier workers and less turnover, union organizers can work with the same farm workers over entire seasons to build a base for union elections. . . . Current cutbacks in state programs and spending may seriously alter future opportunities for this kind of mobilization around social change in the state arena.

The success of this case has also encouraged worker resistance to other conditions in the agricultural labor process. One farm worker indicated that lessons from the short-handled hoe case are being applied to challenging the hazards of farm worker pesticide exposure (Personal interview: Hector de la Rosa, March 1, 1979). This challenge involves a much more powerful array of interests and political institutions. Thus the case of *el cortito* has not only raised farm worker awareness of worker health issues, but has opened up questions of technology which implicitly question control of the labor process as well. A challenge to pesticide technology could reach much deeper into the organization of agricultural production than the case of *el cortito*.

The example of the CRLA attorneys and the farm workers who campaigned against the short-handled hoe is evidence of the on-going contribution people are making toward improving the conditions under which farm workers and many others must live and work. But the task remains to develop effective strategies and institutions which place more fundamental questions of control and autonomy at the center of these struggles for social change.

References

Berman, Daniel (1978). "Death on the job: occupational health and safety struggles in the United States." New York: Monthly Review.

Black, Donald (1973). "The mobilization of law." *Journal of Legal Studies* 2:125–49.

Chambers, Clarke (1952). *California Farm Organizations*. Berkeley: University of California Press.

Cobb, Jonathan, and Richard Sennett (1973). *Hidden Injuries of Class*. New York: Random House.

Dunlap, Thomas R. (1981). *DDT: Scientists, Citizens, and Public Policy*. Princeton: Princeton University Press.

Galarza, Ernesto (1964). *Merchants of Labor: A Study of the Managed Migration of Farm Workers in California, 1942–1960*. Santa Barbara: McNally and Loftin.

———— (1970). *Spiders in the House and Workers in the Fields*. Notre Dame: University of Notre Dame Press.

Goldfrank, Walter J. (1975). "World system, state structure, and the onset of the Mexican revolution." *Politics and Society* 5(4): 417–39.

Greenberg, Jack (1959). *Race Relations and American Law*. New York: Columbia University Press.

Heistand, Fred J. (1970). "The politics of poverty law." Pp. 160–189 in Bruce Wasserstein and Mark J. Green (eds.), *With Justice for Some: An Indictment of the Law by Young Advocates*. Boston: Beacon Press.

Hoffman, Abraham (1974). *Unwanted Mexicans in the Great Depression*. Tucson: University of Arizona Press.

Lipsky, Michael (1968). "Protest as a political resource." *American Political Science Review* 62: 1144–58.

McWilliams, Carey (1971). *Factories in the Fields: The Story of Migratory Farm Labor in California*. Santa Barbara: Peregrine.

Majka, Theo (1978). "Regulating farmworkers: the state and the agricultural labor supply in California." *Contemporary Crises* 2: 141–55.

Offe, Claus (1975). "The theory of the capitalist state and the problem of policy formation." Pp. 168–85 in Leon Lindberg, Robert Alford, Colin Crouch, and Claus Offe (eds.), *Stress and Contradiction in Modern Capitalism*. Lexington, MA: D.C. Heath.

San Francisco Chronicle (1975). "Praise for long hoes." April 15:20.

Saxton, Alexander (1971). *The Indispensable Enemy; Labor and the Anti-Chinese Movement in California*. Berkeley: University of California Press.

Stein, Walter J. (1973). *California and the Dustbowl Migration*. Westport, CT: Greenwood.

Tilly, Charles (1978). *From Mobilization to Revolution*. Reading, MA: Addison Wesley.

Case Cited

Sebastian Carmona et al. v. Division of Industrial Safety. 13 C. 3d 313, January 13, 1975. California Supreme Court Number: S.F. 23053.

Codes Cited

Title 8 California Administrative Code, Section 3556 (b). Register 75, No. 13:March 29, 1975. Formerly 8 CAC 3316 (a).
California Labor Code, Section 6306 (a). (West, 1981:343).

43 Decision Making in Japanese Organizations

WILLIAM OUCHI

"No man is an island, entire of itself" wrote the poet John Donne in about 1600. Apart from what is today considered sexist language, Donne's sentiment is that we all are interconnected with one another: What each of us does has consequences for others. Sociologists use the term *social system* to refer to the interconnections that make people and organizations part of the same network.

It is obvious that all Americans are interconnected within the same social system. But today our interconnections do more than just span a continent. They have grown so extensively in recent years that we now are part of a global social system, and what happens in some far part of the earth has ramifications for us. A major indication of this change is that the world's nations have become part of a global system of economic exchange and competition.

Until recently, the United States was the undisputed economic leader of the world. In recent years, however, our country has been severely challenged, the most notable challenge coming from Japan. As a consequence of how serious this challenge is, many of our leaders have reluctantly concluded that we should examine the Japanese system of organization to see what we can learn that might help make us more competitive. In this selection, Ouchi analyzes essential aspects of the Japanese decision-making process, focusing on their consensual or "participative decision making." This process, if adopted here, will represent fundamental change—perhaps even forcing basic adjustment in our culture itself.

PROBABLY THE BEST KNOWN FEATURE of Japanese organizations is their participative approach to decision making. In the typical American organization the department head, division manager, and president typically each feel that "the buck stops here"—that they alone should take the responsibility for making decisions. Recently, some organizations have adopted explicitly participative modes of decision making in which all of the members of a department reach consensus on what decision to adopt. Decision making by consensus has been the subject of a great deal of research in Europe and the United States over the past twenty years, and the evidence strongly suggests that a consensus approach yields more creative decisions and more effective implementation than does individual decision making.

Western style participative decision making is by now a fairly standardized process. Typically, a small group of not more than eight or ten people will gather around a table, discuss the problem and suggest alternative solutions. During this process, the group should have one or more leaders skilled at managing relationships between people so that underlying disagreements can be dealt with constructively. The group can be said to have achieved a consensus when it finally agrees upon a single alternative and each member of the group can honestly say to each other member three things:

1. I believe that you understand my point of view.
2. I believe that I understand your point of view.
3. Whether or not I prefer this decision, I will support it, because it was arrived at in an open and fair manner.

At least a few managers instinctively follow this approach in every company, government office, and church meeting, but the vast majority do not. some companies have officially instituted this consensual approach throughout, because of its superiority in many cases to individual decision making. However, what occurs in a Japanese organization is a great deal more far reaching and subtle than even this participative approach.

When an important decision needs to be made in a Japanese organization, everyone who will feel its impact is involved in making it. In the case of a decision where to put a new plant, whether to change a production process, or some other major event, that will often mean sixty to eighty people directly involved in making the decision. A team of three will be assigned the duty of talking to all sixty to eighty people and, each time a significant modification arises, contacting all the people involved again. The team will repeat this process until a true consensus has been achieved. Making a decision this way takes a very long time, but once a decision is reached, everyone affected by it will be likely to support it. Understanding and support may supersede the actual content of the decision, since the five or six competing alternatives may be equally good or bad. What is important is not the decision itself but rather how committed and informed people are. The "best" decisions can be bungled just as "worst" decisions can work just fine.

A friend in one of the major Japanese banks described their process:

When a major decision is to be made, a written proposal lays out one 'best' alternative for consideration. The task of writing the proposal goes to the youngest and newest member of the department involved. Of course, the president or vice-president knows the acceptable alternatives, and the young person tries like heck to figure out what those are. He talks to everyone, soliciting their opinions, paying special attention to those who know the top man best. In so doing he is seeking a common ground. Fortunately, the young person cannot completely figure out from others what the boss wants, and must add his own thoughts. This is how variety enters the decision process in a Japanese company. The company relies so heavily on socializing employees with a common set of values and beliefs that all experienced employees would be likely to come up with similar ideas. Too much homogeneity would lead to a loss of vitality and change, so the youngest person gets the assignment.

Frequently, according to my informant, this young person will in the process make a number of errors. He will suggest things that are technically impossible or politically unacceptable, and will leave things out. Experienced managers never over-direct the young man, never sit him down and tell him what the proposal should say. Even though errors consume time, effort, and expense, many will turn out to be good ideas. Letting a young person make one error of his own is believed to be worth more than one hundred lectures in his education as a manager and worker.

Ultimately, a formal proposal is written and then circulated from the bottom of the organization to the top. At each stage, the manager in question signifies his agreement by affixing his seal to the document. At the end of this *ringi* process, the proposal is literally covered with the stamps of approval of sixty to eighty people.

American managers are fond of chiding the Japanese by observing that, "If you're going to Japan to make a sale or close a deal and you think it will take two days, allow two weeks and if you're lucky you'll get a 'maybe.' It takes the Japanese forever to make a decision." True enough, but Japanese businesspeople who have experience dealing in the United States will often say, "Americans are quick to sign a contract or make a decision. But try to get them to implement it—it takes them forever!"

Remember that this apparently cumbersome decision process takes place within the framework of an underlying agreement on philosophy, values, and beliefs. These form the basis for common decision premises that make it possible to include a very large number of people in each decision. If, as in some Western organizations, each of the sixty people had a fundamentally different view of goals and procedures, then the participative process would fail. Because the Japanese only debate the suitability of a particular alternative to reach the agreed-upon values, the process can be broadly participatory yet efficient. In Western-style consensual processes, by comparison, often underlying values and beliefs need to be worked out, and for that reason decision making teams are deliberately kept small.

Another key feature of decision making in Japan is the intentional ambiguity of who is responsible for what decisions. In the United States we have job descriptions and negotiations between employees for the purpose of setting crystal clear boundaries on where my decision authority ends and yours begins. Americans expect others to behave just as we do. Many are the unhappy and frustrated American businessmen or lawyers returning from Japan with the complaint that, "If only they would tell me who is really in charge, we could make some progress." The complaint displays a lack of understanding that, in Japan, no one individual carries responsibility for a particular turf. Rather, a group or team of employees assumes joint responsibility for a set of tasks. While we wonder at their comfortableness in not knowing who is responsible for what, they know quite clearly that each of them is completely responsible for all tasks, and they share that responsibility jointly. Obviously this approach sometimes lets things "fall through the cracks" because everyone may think that someone else has a task under control. When working well, however, this approach leads to a naturally participative decision making and problem solving process. But there is another important reason for the collective assignment of decision responsibility.

Many Americans object to the idea of lifetime employment because they fear the consequences of keeping on an ineffective worker. Won't that create bottlenecks and inefficiency? Clearly the Japanese have somehow solved that problem or they couldn't have achieved their great economic success. A partial answer comes from the collective assignment of decision responsibility. In a typical American firm, Jim is assigned sole responsibility for purchasing decisions for office supplies, Mary has sole responsibility for purchasing maintenance services and Fred is solely responsible for purchasing office machines. If Fred develops serious problems of a personal nature, or if he becomes ill or has some other problem that seriously impedes his ability to function at work, a bottleneck will develop. Office machine orders will not be properly processed or perhaps will not be processed at all. The whole company will suffer, and Fred will have to be let go.

In a Japanese company, by comparison, Mitsuo, Yoshito, and Nori will comprise a team collectively responsible for purchasing office supplies, maintenance services, and office machines. Each of them participates in all significant decisions in purchasing any of those goods or services. If Nori is unable to work, it is perfectly natural and efficient for Mitsuo and Yoshito to take up his share of the load. When Nori returns to work again, he can step right back in and do his share. This does mean that Mitsuo and Yoshito probably will have to work harder than usual for perhaps six months or a year, and they may also have to draw on Masao, who used to work in purchasing but has now been transferred to the computer section. This flow of people can be accomplished only if Mitsuo and Yoshito are confident that the organization has a memory and know that their extra efforts now will be repaid later. Fairness and equity will be achieved over the long run. It also depends upon the practice of job rotation, so that short-run labor needs can be filled internally without having to hire and fire people as such needs come and go. As with all other characteristics of the Japanese management system, decision making is embedded in a complex of parts that hang together and rely upon trust and subtlety developed through intimacy.

44 Searching for Roots in a Changing World

RICHARD RODRIGUEZ

Americans are certainly among the most geographically mobile of all people. Approximately 17 percent of our population moves each year, that is, in every six-year period, a number equal to our entire population changes residence. One of the basic reasons for this American restlessness is the attempt to better oneself, to climb another rung on the social class ladder. Yet the personal costs of social mobility are high—especially the severing of roots, a breaking with family and friends and their orientations. This tearing away can lead to personal disorientation, to a questioning of who one is. In our final selection, Richard Rodriguez relates how he realized that he had cut himself off from his roots, that the costs of this rupture were extremely difficult to bear, and how he felt the need to embark on a search to rediscover himself by examining his past.

If you are strongly rooted (and, in the extreme case, a few of you probably have lived in the same house from childhood, and you intend your college education to be a means to maintain your social class membership), you can contrast your experiences with those analyzed in this article. Some of you, however—like Rodriguez—are using the educational institution to take huge leaps in social mobility. As you identify with this author's experiences, you might ask yourself, as he does, how much of your roots you are willing to give up.

TODAY I AM ONLY TECHNICALLY the person I once felt myself to be—a Mexican-American, a Chicano. Partly because I had no way of comprehending my racial identity except in this technical sense, I gave up long ago the cultural consequences of being a Chicano.

The change came gradually but early. When I was beginning grade school, I noted to myself the fact that the classroom environment was so different in its styles and assumptions from my own family environment that survival would essentially entail a choice between both worlds. When I became a student, I was literally "remade"; neither I nor my teachers considered anything I had known before as relevant. I had to forget most of what my culture had provided, because to remember it was a disadvantage. The past and its cultural values became detachable, like a piece of clothing grown heavy on a warm day and finally put away.

Strangely, the discovery that I have been inattentive to my cultural past has arisen because others—students colleagues and faculty members—have started to assume that I am a Chicano. The ease with which the assumption is made forces me to suspect that the label is not meant to suggest cutural, but racial, identity. Nonetheless, as a graduate student and a prospective university faculty member, I am routinely expected to assume intellectual leadership *as a member of a racial minority.* Recently, for example, I heard the moderator of a panel discussion introduce me as "Richard Rodriguez, a Chicano intellectual." I wanted to correct the speaker—because I felt guilty representing a nonacademic cultural tradition that I had willingly abandoned. So I can only guess what it would have meant to have retained my culture as I entered the classroom, what it would mean for me to be today a *Chicano intellectual.* (The two words juxtaposed excite me; for years I thought a Chicano had to decide between being one or the other.)

Does the fact that I barely spoke any English until I was nine, or that as a child I felt a surge of *self*-hatred whenever a passing teenager would yell a racial slur, or that I saw my skin darken each summer—do any of these facts shape the ideas which I have or am capable of having? Today, I suspect they do—in ways I doubt the moderator who referred to me as a "Chicano intellectual" intended. The peculiar status of being a "Chicano intellectual" makes me grow restless at the thought that I have lost at least as much as I have gained through education.

I remember when, 20 years ago, two grammar-school nuns visited my childhood home. They had come to suggest—with more tact than was necessary, because my parents accepted without question the church's authority—that we make a greater effort to speak as much English around the house as possible. The nuns realized that my brothers and I led solitary lives largely because we were barely able to comprehend English in a school where we were the only Spanish-speaking students. My mother and father complied as best they could. Heroically, they gave up speaking to us in Spanish—the language that formed so much of the family's sense of intimacy in an alien world—and began to speak a broken English. Instead of Spanish sounds, I began hearing sounds that were new, harder, less friendly. More important, I was encouraged to respond in English.

The change in language was the most dramatic and obvious indication that I would become very much like the "gringo"—a term which was used descriptively rather than pejoratively in my home—and unlike the Spanish-speaking relatives who largely constituted my preschool world. Gradually, Spanish became a sound freighted with only a kind of sentimental significance, like the sound of the bedroom clock I listened to in my aunt's house when I spent the night. Just as gradually, English became the language I came not to *hear* because it was the language I used every day, as I gained access to a new, larger society. But the memory of Spanish persisted as a reminder of the society I had left. I can remember occasions when I entered a room and my parents were speaking to one another in Spanish, seeing me, they shifted into their more formalized English. Hearing them speak to me in English troubled me. The bonds their voices once secured were loosened by the new tongue.

This is not to suggest that I was being *forced* to give up my Chicano past. After the initial awkwardness of transition, I committed myself, fully and freely, to the culture of the classroom. Soon what I was learning in school was so antithetical to what my parents knew and did that I was careful about the way I talked about myself at the evening dinner table. Occasionally, there were moments of childish cruelty: a son's condescending to instruct either one of his parents about a "simple" point of English pronunciation or grammar.

Social scientists often remark, about situations such as mine, that children feel a sense of loss as they move away from their working-class identifications and models. Certainly, what I experienced, others have also—whatever their race. Like other generations of, say, Polish-American or Irish-American children coming home from college, I was to know the silence that ensues so quickly after the quick exchange of news and the dwindling of common interests.

In addition, however, education seemed to mean not only a gradual dissolving of familial and class ties but also a change of racial identity. The new language I spoke was only the most obvious reason for my associating the classroom with "gringo" society. The society I knew as Chicano was barely literate—in English *or* Spanish—and so impatient with either prolonged reflection or abstraction that I found the academic environment a sharp contrast. Sharpening the contrast was the stereotype of the Mexican as a mental inferior. (The fear of this stereotype has been so deep that only recently have I been willing to listen to those, like D. H. Lawrence, who celebrate the "noncerebral" Mexican as an alternative to the rational and scientific European man.) Because I did not know how to distinguish the healthy nonrationality of Chicano culture from the mental incompetency of which Chicanos were unjustly accused, I was willing to abandon my nonmental skills in order to disprove the racist's stereotype.

I was wise enough not to feel proud of the person education had helped me to become. I knew that education had led me to repudiate my race. I was frequently labeled a *pocho*, a Mexican with gringo pretensions, not only because I could not speak Spanish but also because I would respond in English with precise and careful sentences. Uncles would laugh good-naturedly, but I detected scorn in their voices. For my grandmother, the least assimilated of my relations, the changes in her grandson since entering school were especially troubling. She remains today a dark and silently critical figure in my memory, a reminder of the Mexican-Indian ancestry that somehow my educational success has violated.

Nonetheless, I became more comfortable reading or writing careful prose than talking to a kitchen filled with listeners, withdrawing from situations to reflect on their significance rather than grasping for meaning at the scene. I remember, one August evening, slipping away from a gathering of aunts and uncles in the backyard, going into a bedroom tenderly lighted by a late sun, and opening a novel about life in nineteenth-century England. There, by an open window, reading, I was barely conscious of the sounds of laughter outside.

With so few fellow Chicanos in the university, I had no chance to develop an alternative consciousness. When I spent occasional weekends tutoring lower-class Chicano teenagers or when I talked with Mexican-American janitors and maids around the campus, there was a kind of sympathy—a sense, however privately held—that we knew something about one another. But I regarded them all primarily as people from my past. The maids reminded me of my aunts (similarly employed); the students I tutored reminded me of my cousins (who also spoke English with barrio accents).

When I was young, I was taught to refer to my ancestry as Mexican-American. *Chicano* was a word used among friends or relatives. It implied a familiarity based on shared experience. Spoken casually, the term easily became an insult. In 1968 the word *Chicano* was about to become a political term. I heard it shouted into microphones as Third World groups agitated for increased student and faculty representation in higher education. It was not long before I *became* a Chicano in the eyes of students and faculty members. My racial identity was assumed for only the simplest reasons: my skin color and last name.

On occasion I was asked to account for my interests in Renaissance English literature. When I explained them, declaring a need for cultural assimilation on the campus, my listener would disagree. I sensed suspicion on the part of a number of my fellow minority students. When I could not imitate Spanish pronunciations of the dialect of the barrio, when I was plainly uninterested in wearing ethnic costumes and could not master a special handshake the minority students often used with one another, they knew I was different. And I was. I was assimilated into the culture of a graduate department of English. As a result, I watched how in less than five years nearly every minority graduate student I knew dropped out of school, largely for cultural reasons. Often they didn't understand the value of analyzing literature in professional jargon, which others around them readily adopted. Nor did they move as readily to lofty heights of abstraction. They became easily depressed by the seeming uselessness of the talk they heard around them. "It's not for real," I still hear a minority student murmur to herself and perhaps to me, shaking her head slowly, as we sat together in a class listening to a discussion on punctuation in a Renaissance epic.

I survived—thanks to the accommodation I had made long before. In fact, I prospered, partly as a result of the political movement designed to increase the enrollment of minority students less assimilated than I in higher education. Suddenly grants, fellowships, and teaching offers became abundant.

In 1972 I went to England on a Fulbright scholarship. I hoped the months of brooding about racial identity were behind me. I wanted to concentrate on my dissertation, which the distractions of an American campus had not permitted. But the freedom I anticipated did not last for long. Barely a month after I had begun working regularly in the reading room of the British Museum, I was surprised, and even frightened, to have to acknowledge that I was not at ease living the rarefied life of the academic. With my pile of research file cards growing taller, the mass of secondary materials and opinions was making it harder for me to say anything original about my subject. Every sentence I wrote, every thought I had, became so loaded with qualifications and footnotes, that it said very little. My scholarship became little more than an exercise in caution. I had an accompanying suspicion that whatever I did manage to write and call my dissertation would be of little use. Opening books so dusty that they must not have been used in decades, I began to doubt the value of writing what only a few people would read.

Obviously, I was going through the fairly typical crisis of the American graduate student. But with one difference: After four years of involvement with questions of racial identity, I now saw my problems as a scholar in the context of the cultural issues that had been raised by my racial situation. So much of what my work in the British Museum lacked, my parents' culture possessed. They were people not afraid to generalize or to find insights in their generalities. More important, they had the capacity to make passionate statements, something I was beginning to doubt my dissertation would ever allow me to do. I needed to learn how to trust the use of "I" in my writing the way they trusted its use in their speech. Thus developed a persistent yearning for the very Chicano culture that I had abandoned as useless.

Feelings of depression came occasionally but forcefully. Some days I found my work so oppressive that I had to leave the reading room and stroll through the museum. One afternoon, appropriately enough, I found myself in an upstairs gallery containing Mayan and Aztec sculptures. Even there the sudden yearning for a Chicano past seemed available to me only as nostalgia. One morning, as I was reading a book about Puritan autobiography, I overheard two Spaniards whispering to one another. I did not hear what they said, but I did hear the sound of their Spanish—and it embraced me, filling my mind with swirling images of a past long abandoned.

I returned from England, disheartened, a few months later. My dissertation was coming along well, but I did not know whether I wanted to submit it. Worse, I did not know whether I wanted a career in higher education. I detested the prospect of spending the rest of my life in libraries and classrooms, in touch with my past only through the binoculars nostalgia makes available. I knew that I could not simply re-create a version of what I would have been like had I not become an academic. There was no possibility of going back. But if the culture of my birth was to survive, it would have to animate my academic work. That was the lesson of the British Museum.

I frankly do not know how my academic autobiography will end. Sometimes I think I will have to leave the campus, in order to reconcile my past and present. Other times, more optimistically, I think that a kind of negative reconciliation is already in progress, that I can make creative use of my sense of loss. For instance, with my sense of the cleavage between past and present, I can, as a literary critic, identify issues in Renaissance pastoral—a literature which records the feelings of the courtly when confronted by the alternatives of rural and rustic life. And perhaps I can speak with unusual feeling about the price we must pay, or have paid, as a rational society for confessing seventeenth-century Cartesian faiths. Likewise, because of my sense of cultural loss, I may be able to identify more readily than another the ways in which language has meaning simply as sound and what the printed word can and cannot give us. At the very least, I can point up the academy's tendency to ignore the cultures beyond its own horizons.

February 1974

On my job interview the department chairman has been listening to an oral version of what I have just written. I tell him he should be very clear about the fact that I am not, at the moment, confident enough to call myself a Chicano. Perhaps I never will be. But as I say all this, I look at the interviewer. He smiles softly. Has he heard what I have been trying to say? I wonder. I repeat: I have lost the ability to bring my past into my present; I do not know how to be a Chicano reader of Spenser or Shakespeare. All that remains is a desire for the past. He sighs, preoccupied, looking at my records. Would I be interested in teaching a course on the Mexican novel in translation? Do I understand that part of my duties would require that I become a counselor of minority students? What was the subject of that dissertation I did in England? Have I read the book on the same subject that was published this month?

Behind the questioner, a figure forms in my imagination: my grandmother, her face solemn and still.

Glossary

Account One's version of an incident; often an excuse or justification for unexpected or inappropriate behavior. See *Excuse* and *Justification*.

Achieved status A person's position or ranking achieved at least partly through personal efforts (such as becoming a college student) or failings (such as becoming a skid row alcoholic).

Aggregate People grouped together for the purpose of social research because of characteristics they have in common. An example is American females between the ages of 18 and 23 who wear contact lenses.

Alienation A sense of separation, of not belonging, of being estranged. Includes the idea that one has little control over the social world. May include a sense that one's world is meaningless.

Anomie Normlessness; conflict between norms, weakened respect for norms, or absence of norms.

Anticipatory socialization Learning the perspectives of a role before entering it. See *Role* and *Socialization*.

Ascribed status A person's position or ranking assigned on the basis of arbitrary standards over which the individual has little or no control, such as age, race, or sex.

Authority Power that is regarded as legitimate or proper by those over whom it is exercised.

Background expectancies The taken-for-granted assumptions people have about the way the world is. See *Social construction of reality*.

Belief An idea about some part of the natural or social world; a view of reality.

Body language   Giving and receiving messages through the movement and positioning of the body.

Bureaucracy   A form of organization characterized by multiple "layerings" of authority, usually depicted by a pyramid. Decisions flow downward, accountability for fulfilling orders goes upward, rules are explicit, emphasis is placed on written records, resources are directed toward efficiently reaching the goals of the organization, the "bottom line" is of utmost concern, and the personal is kept strictly separate from that which belongs to the organization. The reality does not necessarily match this *Ideal type*.

Case study   An in-depth investigation of a single event, experience, organization, or situation in order to better understand that case or to abstract principles of human behavior.

Charisma   Extraordinary personal qualities which make it relatively easy for their possessors to (for example) achieve normally hard-to-come-by goals, such as coveted positions of leadership or authority. It varies from simply a "magnetic" personality to qualities so extraordinary that they are assumed to be supernatural.

Charismatic authority   Leadership exercised on the basis of charisma. See *Charisma* and *Traditional authority*.

Class   See *Social class*.

Class conflict   The struggle between social classes; generally thought of as the struggle between the rich (and powerful) and the poor (and powerless), or those who own the means of economic production and those who do not.

Collective behavior   Relatively spontaneous, unstructured, and transitory ways of thinking, feeling, and acting that develop among a large number of people.

Community   Its primary meaning is that of people inhabiting the same geographical area who share common interests and feel a sense of "belonging." From this sense comes a derived meaning of people who share common interests and have a sense of "belonging" but who do not inhabit the same geographical area, such as in the phrase "a community of scholars."

Conflict theory   The theoretical view (or school) which emphasizes conflict as the inevitable outcome in society due to its various groups competing for limited resources. See *Functionalism* and *Symbolic interactionism*.

Conformity   Following social norms or expectations.

Control Group   The subjects in an experiment who are not exposed to the independent variable, as opposed to the experimental group who are subjected to the variable. See *Experiment, Experimental group, Independent variable* and *Variable*.

Covert participant observation   See *Participant observation*.

Crime   An act prohibited by law.

Cultural diffusion   The process by which the characteristics of one culture are adopted by members of another culture.

Cultural relativity The view that one cannot judge the characteristics of any culture to be morally superior to those of another. See its opposite, *Ethnocentrism.*

Culture A way of life, or shared ways of doing things; includes nonmaterial culture (such as norms, beliefs, values, and language) and material culture (such as art, tools, weapons, and buildings). See *Ideal culture* and *Real culture.*

Culture lag (Cultural lag) A term developed by William F. Ogburn to refer to a dislocation or imbalance due to the material culture changing more rapidly than the nonmaterial culture. Thought by some to be a primary factor in social change.

Culture of poverty The distinctive culture said to exist among the poor of industrialized societies, some of whose central features are defeatism, dependence, and a present time orientation; thought to help perpetuate poverty.

Culture shock The disorienting effect that immersion in a strange culture has on a visitor as he or she encounters markedly different norms, values, beliefs, practices, and other basic expectations of social life. One no longer is able to rely on the basics of one's socialization.

Data The information scientists gather in their studies.

Definition of reality A view of what the world or some part of the world is like. See *Social construction of reality.*

Demography The study of the size, distribution, composition, and change in human populations.

Dependent variable That which is being explained as the result of other factors; a variable or social phenomenon thought to be changed or influenced by another variable. See *Independent variable.*

Deviance Violation of social norms or expectations.

Deviant One who violates social norms or expectations. As used by sociologists, a neutrally descriptive rather than a negative term.

Deviant career The main course of events during one's involvement in deviance; generally refers to those who are habitually, or at least for a period of time heavily, involved in some deviant activity.

Differential association If a person associates with one group of people, he or she will learn one set of attitudes, ideas, and norms; associating with a different group teaches a different approach to life. Thus such differential association is highly significant in influencing people either to conform or to deviate.

Diffusion The spread of an invention or discovery from one area to another.

Disclaimer An excuse or justification for inappropriate behavior that is *about* to take place. Examples are: "Now don't get me wrong, but . . . ;" and "Let me be the devil's advocate for a minute."

Discrimination The denial of rights, privileges, or opportunities to others on the basis of their group membership. See *Minority group, Racism,* and *Sexism.*

Division of labor A concept developed by the French sociologist Emile Durkheim to refer to the work specializations in a society (the various ways in which work is divided, with some people specializing in produciton, others in advertising and distribution, and so on).

Double standard More stringent expectations being applied to one group than to another. *The* double standard refers to attitudes and ideas more favorable to males than to females—often to more lax standards of sexuality being allowed males.

Downward social mobility Movement from a higher to a lower social position. See *Social class.*

Dramaturgical analysis Developed by Erving Goffman, this terms refers to viewing human interaction as theatrical performances. People are seen as actors, their clothing as costumes, what they do as parts they play, what they say as delivery of lines, where they interact as a stage, and so on.

Dramaturgy Refers to theatrical performances. The same as *Dramaturgical analysis.*

Ecology The study of reciprocal relationships between organisms and their environment.

Education One of the primary institutions of society whose teaching of values, skills, and knowledge are designed to help maintain the stability of society.

Ego Commonly used as a term to refer to the self; technically, Freud's term for the conscious, rational part of an individual.

Endogamy A cultural pattern of marrying *within* one's own social group. See *Exogamy.*

Ethnic group A group of people with a sense of common ancestry, who generally share similar cultural traits and regard themselves as distinct from others.

Ethnic stratification Hierarchical arrangements based on ethnic group membership. See *Social stratification.*

Ethnocentrism Using the standards of one's own culture or subculture to evaluate the characteristics of other cultures or subcultures, generally from the point of view that one's own are superior. See its opposite, *Cultural relativity.*

Ethnography A report or study that details the major characteristics of the way of life of a group of people; can be of an entire preliterate tribe, an entire village, or a smaller group within a large society, such as a study of urban cabdrivers.

Ethnomethodology Developed by Harold Garfinkel, the term refers to the study of the worlds of reality that people construct, their taken-for-granted background assumptions, and the ways by which different people make sense out of their experiences.

Excuse An account of an event in which one acknowledges that an act is blameworthy, but denies responsibility for the act. See *Account* and *Justification.*

Exogamy A cultural pattern of marrying *outside* one's social group. See *Endogamy.*

Experiment A study in which the researcher manipulates one or more variables (independent variables) in order to measure the results on other variables (dependent variables). See *Variable*.

Experimental group The subjects in an experiment who are exposed to the independent variable, as opposed to the control group who do not experience this variable. See *Experiment*.

Extended family A family consisting of two or more generations (extended beyond the nuclear family), usually living together. See *Nuclear family*.

False consciousness A person's understanding of his or her social class membership that does not square with objective facts; often used to refer to people identifying with social classes higher than the one to which they belong.

Family People related by ancestry, marriage, or adoption who generally live together and form an economic unit, and whose adult members assume responsibility for the young. The form of the family varies remarkably from one culture to another.

Family of orientation The family into which one is born. See *Family* and *Family of procreation*.

Family of procreation The family created by marriage. See *Family* and *Family of orientation*.

Femininity Our behaviors and orientations as females. Assumed in sociology to be an expression not of biology but of cultural or social learning.

Feral children Children who have been found in the wilderness, supposedly raised by animals. Not only do they possess no language, but they also exhibit few behaviors that we ordinarily associate with humans.

Field research Another term for *Participant observation*.

Field study Another term for *Participant observation*.

Folk society A term developed by Robert Redfield to refer to small, traditional societies in which there is little social change.

Folkways Developed by William G. Sumner, this term refers to norms people are expected or encouraged to follow, but whose violation is not considered immoral; the ordinary rules, usages, conventions, and expectations of everyday life, such as, in American society, the use of deodorant. See *Mores*.

Formal organization A social group brought into existence to reach specific goals; often utilizes a bureaucratic mode of operation to achieve those objectives. See *Bureaucracy*.

Formal sanction A social reward or punishment that is formally applied, often a part of ritual recognition for achievement (such as receiving a passing grade in school, or being promoted at work) or failure (such as receiving a failing grade in school, or being fired from one's job). See *Sanction*.

Functionalism The theoretical view (or school) that stresses how the parts of a society or social group are interrelated. Emphasis is placed on the contributions (functions) that one part makes for the adjustment or well-being of other parts. Each part, working properly, is seen as contributing to the stability of the whole. See *Symbolic interactionism* and *Conflict theory.*

Future shock   A term developed by Alvin Toffler to refer to the dizzying disorientation brought on by the rapid arrival of the future.

Gender   The social expectations attached to a person on account of that person's sex. Sex is biological, while gender is social.

Gender socialization   Learning one's gender. See *Gender.*

Generalized other   An internalized idea of the expectations of a major reference group or of society in general.

Genocide   Killing an entire population, usually because of the group's biological and cultural traits.

Gentrification   The process by which the relatively affluent move to decaying urban neighborhoods, renovate buildings, and displace the poor.

Gestures   Symbols under the purposeful control of the actor that involve the movement and positioning of the body. See *Body language.*

Heterosexuality   Sexual acts or feelings toward members of the opposite sex.

Holocaust   The Nazi destruction, in death camps and by means of death squads, of Jews, gypsies, Slavs, homosexuals, the mentally retarded, and others considered threats to the purity of the so-called Aryan race.

Homosexuality   Sexual acts or feelings toward members of the same sex.

Horizontal mobility   Movement from one social position to another that is approximately equivalent.

Human ecology   Study of the reciprocal relationships between people and their environment.

Hypothesis   A prediction about the relation between variables. See *Variable.*

Ideal culture   The way of life represented in people's values and norms, rather than by their actual practices. See *Real culture.*

Ideal type   Developed by Max Weber, this term refers to a model or description of something that is derived from examining a number of real cases and abstracting what appear to be the essential characteristics of those cases.

Identity formation   The process by which we develop a personal identity; our internalization of social expectations. The end result is that we come to think of ourselves in a certain way; that is, we apply select concepts to ourselves. By this process we develop a "self."

Ideology   Statements or beliefs (especially of reasons and purposes) that justify a group's actions or interests; they buttress, uphold, or legitimate the existing social order.

Incest   Socially forbidden sexual intercourse with specific categories of kinfolk.

Incest taboo The social prohibition against sexual intercourse with specific categories of kinfolk.

Independent variable That which is thought to affect or to cause change in some other factor; the variable thought to influence another variable. See *Dependent variable*.

Informal sanction A social reward or punishment informally applied, often being a spontaneous gesture of approval or disapproval. Examples include staring, smiling, and gossip.

Ingroup The group to which an individual belongs, identifies, and feels loyalty. See *Outgroup*.

Institution See *Social institution*.

Institutional(ized) racism The use of social institutions to discriminate, exploit, or oppress a racial (or ethnic) group. See *Discrimination* and *Racism*.

Institutional(ized) sexism The use of social institutions to discriminate, exploit, or oppress either males or females as a group. See *Discrimination* and *Sexism*.

Interaction See *Social interaction*.

Interactional sociology The emphasis is on the study of social interaction. See *Qualitative sociology, Participant observation*, and *Structural sociology*.

Internalization Experiences becoming part of one's "internal" consciousness.

Interview A face-to-face meeting with a respondent for the purpose of gathering data. See *Respondent*.

Involuntary associations Groups to which people belong, but about which they have little or no choice. Examples include grade school for youngsters and military service during periods of conscription. See *Voluntary associations*.

Justification An account of an event in which one accepts responsibility for an act, while denying that the act is blameworthy. See *Account* and *Excuse*.

Kin People who are related by birth, adoption, or marriage.

Kinfolk See *Kin*.

Kinship The network of people who are related to one another by birth, adoption, or marriage.

Labeling theory or perspective The focus on the effects of labels (or terms) on people. This perspective stresses that acts are not inherently deviant (or criminal) but are such only because those acts have been so labeled (or defined). Deviants are those on whom the label of deviant has been successfully applied.

Life chances The likelihood that an individual or group will benefit from their society's opportunities, goods and services, and other satisfactions in life.

Life cycle The biological and social sequencing through which individuals pass; those cluster around birth, childhood, maturity, old age, and death.

Life expectancy The average number of years a person can expect to live.

Life style The general patterns that characterize an individual or group, including their clothing, manners, recreation, mating, and childraising practices.

Looking-glass self Charles Horton Cooley's term for the process by which people see themselves through the eyes of others. As people act, others react. In those reactions people see themselves reflected. Perceiving this, they interpret its meaning, which yields a particular self-image.

Masculinity Our behaviors and orientations as males. Generally assumed in sociology to be an expression not of biology but of cultural or social learning.

Mass media Forms of communication that reach a large audience, with no personal contact between the senders and receivers of the message. Examples are movies, radio, television, newspaper, magazines, plays, and books.

Master status (or trait) A social role (or achieved or ascribed status) that cuts across most other social roles and provides a major basis for personal and public identity.

Material culture See *Culture.*

Meanings The significance that something has to someone. Also called symbols, mental constructs, ideas, and stereotypes. See *Qualitative sociology.*

Methodology, Methods The procedures scientists use to conduct their studies.

Military-industrial complex The relationships between top leaders of the Pentagon and American coprorations by which they reciprocally support one another and thereby influence political decisions on their behalf.

Minority group A group of people who are treated unequally because of their physical or cultural characteristics. See *Discrimination.*

Mores (Pronounced more-rays) Developed by William G. Sumner, this term refers to norms whose violation is considered a moral transgression. Examples are the norms against murder and theft. See *Folkways.*

Negative sanction. Punishment for disapproved behavior. See *Sanction.*

Neutralization Deflecting social norms, allowing one to continue activities for which there is social condemnation; the means of doing this are called *Techniques of Neutralization.* An example is saying, "The circumstances required it" or, "I didn't know what I was doing."

Nonmaterial culture See *Culture.*

Nonverbal communication Communication by the use of symbols other than language. Examples are *Body language* and traffic lights.

Norms Rules concerning appropriate and inappropriate behavior by which people are judged and sanctions applied. See *Sanction.*

Nuclear family A family consisting of a husband, wife, and their children. See *Extended family.*

Organization A social unit established for the purpose of attaining some agreed-upon goals.

Outgroup A group to which an individual does not belong and with which he or she does not identify. See *Ingroup.*

Overt participant observation. see *Participant observation.*

Participant observation A method of studying social groups in which the researcher participates in the group being studied. If the people being studied know the researcher is in their midst, this method is called *overt participant observation;* if they do not know they are being studied, it is called *covert participant observation.*

Particular other An internalized idea of the expectations of specific individuals.

Peer group Associates of similar social status who are usually close in age. Examples are one's playmates as a child and workmates as an adult.

Personal identity Our ideas of who we are. Roughly equivalent to self concept. See *Public identity* and *Self.*

Personality An individual's tendency over time to act (and think and feel) in ways similar to those he or she did in the past; the stable behavior patterns we come to expect of people.

Positive sanction A reward for approved behavior. See *Sanction.*

Power The ability to control others, even over their objections.

Power elite C. Wright Mills's term to refer to a small group of people with interlocking interests who appear to make the most important political decisions.

Prejudice Negative attitudes, ideas, and feelings, usually about people one does not know. See *Discrimination* and *Ethnocentrism.*

Prestige Favorable evaluation, respect, or social recognition.

Primary group People whose relationship is intimate, face-to-face, expressive, and extended over time. Examples are one's family and close friends.

Prostitution The relatively indiscriminate exchange of sexual favors for economic gain.

Public identity The ideas that others have of what we ought to be like. Roughly equivalent to the publc social roles we play. See *Personal identity* and *Self.*

Qualitative sociology An emphasis on the *meanings* of people's experiences. The goal is to determine how people construct their worlds, develop their ideas and attitudes, communciate these with one another, and how their meanings affect their ideas about the self and their relationships to one another. See *Meanings* and *Quantitative sociology.*

Quantitative sociology An emphasis on precise measurement, or numbers, in the study of people. Sociologists with this orientation stress that proper measurement by the use of statistical techniques is necessary if one is to undertand human behavior. See *Qualitative sociology.*

Questionnaire   An interview taking a written form.

Race   A large number of people who share visible physical characteristics on the basis of which they regard themselves as a biological unit and are similarly regarded by others.

Racism   One racial or ethnic group dominating or exploiting another, generally based on seeing those they exploit as inferior. See *Discrimination* and *Ethnocentrism*.

Rapport   A feeling of trust and communication between people.

Real culture   A people's actual way of life, as contrasted with the way of life expressed by their ideals. See *Ideal culture*.

Reference groups   The groups to which people refer when they evaluate themselves, their behavior, or actions they are considering.

Relative deprivation   Feeling deprived relative to what others have; the sense that the gap between the resources or rewards that one actually has and what others have is unjust.

Research methods   See *Methodology*.

Resocialization   Learning norms, values, and behaviors that contrast with one's previous experiences.

Respondent   A person who has been interviewed or who has filled out a questionnaire. (He or she has *responded* to the request for data.)

Rising expectations   A situation in which people who have accepted existing conditions in the past now feel they have a right to better conditions.

Rites of passage   Formal, customary rituals marking someone's transition from one social status to another. Examples include bar mitzvahs, confirmations, first communions, weddings, graduation ceremonies, and funerals.

Role   The part played by a person who occupies a particular status. See *Status*.

Role conflict   If a person playing two or more roles finds himself or herself torn between their conflicting demands, that person is said to be experiencing role conflict. Examples include a student wanting to date on the same night he or she is supposed to study for a final examination.

Role taking   Figuratively putting yourself in the shoes of someone else and speaking, seeing how things look from that perspective.

Sanction   A social reward for approved behavior, or punishment for disapproved behavior.

Secondary group   The more formal, impersonal, and transitory groups to which people belong, such as a college class in introductory sociology.

Self   The sense of identity that individuals have of themselves as a distinct person; this sense, idea, or conception is acquired through social interaction.

Self-fulfilling prophecy   A false definition of a situation ("The bank is in trouble") that causes people to change their behavior ("People rush to the bank to withdraw their savings") and makes the originally false statement come true ("The bank is now in trouble as it does not have enough cash on hand to meet the unexpected demand for immediate withdrawals").

Sex role   The behaviors and characteristics a male or female is expected to demonstrate, based on stereotypical cultural concepts of masculinity or femininity; assigned on the basis of one's sex organs.

Sex role socialization   Learning one's sex role. *See Sex role.*

Sexism   Males or females dominating or exploiting the other, with the exploitation generally based on seeing the other as inferior; usually used to refer to males dominating females. See *Discrimination* and *Ethnocentrism.*

Social change   Alteration in society, in its patterns of social structure, social institutions (or some small part of them), culture, and people's behavior.

Social class   A number of people having about the same amount of social power; based on different characteristics in different societies. In ours, some sociologists see the primary bases as the amount of one's income and education and the prestige of one's occupation. Other sociologists see the essential difference in terms of one's relationship to the means of production—whether one is a capitalist (owns the means of production) or a worker (works for capitalists).

Social class mobility   Changing one's social class, usually in relationship to that of one's parents. See *Social mobility.*

Social construction of reality   The process by which definitions of reality (views of what some part of the world is like) are socially created, objectified, internalized, and then taken for granted.

Social control   The techniques used to keep people in line or, if they step out, to bring them back into line. Examples include persuasion, coercion, education, and punishment. See *Sanction.*

Social group   Any human group.

Social inequality   Another term for *Social stratification.*

Social institution   Standardized practices (clustered around a set of norms, values, beliefs, statuses, and roles) that develop around the attempt to meet a basic need of society. Examples include government and politics (for social order), education (for training in conformity and the transmission of skills and knowledge), and the military (for protection from external enemies and the implementation of foreign policy).

Social interaction   People acting in anticipation of the reactions of others; people influencing each other's feelings, attitudes, and actions.

Social mobility   Movement from one social position to another. See *Downward, Horizontal,* and *Upward social mobility.*

Social stratification   Large groups of people ranked in a hierarchy that yields different access to the rewards their society has to offer.

Social structure   The ways in which the basic components of a group or society are related to one another.

Socialization   Refers to learning; the process of social interaction by which people learn the way of life of their society, or learn to play specific roles.

Society   A group of interacting individuals who share the same territory and participate in a common culture.

Sociobiology   The study of the biological bases of social behavior.

Sociology   The scientific study of human society and social behavior.

Status   One's position in a group or society, such as woman, mother, and plumber.

Stereotypes   A generalization (or idea) about people (or even animals and objects); a mental image that summarizes what is believed to be typical about these people.

Stigma   A mark of social disgrace.

Stratification   See *Social stratification.*

Structural sociology   The emphasis is on the influence of social structure on human behavior, with a focus on social institutions and other group memberships. See *Aggregates, Qualitative sociology,* and *Social structure.*

Subculture   A group that shares in the overall culture of a society but also has its own distinctive values, norms, beliefs, and life-style. Examples include cabdrivers, singles, prostitutes, muggers, and physicians.

Subjective interpretation   See *Verstehen.*

Symbol   Any act, object, or event that represents something, such as a traffic light, a gesture, or this definition. See *Symbolic interactionism.*

Symbolic interaction   People's interaction based on symbols. See *Symbolic interactionism.*

Symbolic interactionism   Developed by Herbert Blumer, this term refers to the school of thought (or theoretical perspective) that focuses on symbols as the basis of human behavior—the signs, gestures, and language by which people communicate with one another and change or refine their courses of action in anticipation of what others might do. See *Conflict theory* and *Functionalism.*

Techniques of neutralization   See *Neutralization.*

Technology   Tools or items used to accomplish tasks.

Theory   A statement that organizes a set of concepts in a meaningful way by explaining the relationship between them.

Total institution   Erving Goffman's term to refer to a place in which people are confined, cut off from the rest of society, and under the almost absolute control of the people in charge. Examples include prisons, the military, and convents.

Traditional authority   Authority that is legitimated by custom and practice. The explanation for something is, "We have always done it that way." See *Charismatic authority.*

Trust   The willingness to accept the definition someone offers of oneself and to play a corresponding role based on that definition.

Upward social mobility   Movement from a lower to a higher social position.

Value conflict   Basic disagreement over goals, ideals, policies, or other expressions of values.

Value judgment   A personal, subjective opinion based on one's own set of values.

Values   An idea about what is worthwhile.

Variable   Any condition or characteristic that varies from one situation or person or group to another. Examples include age, occupation, beliefs, and attitudes. See *Dependent variable, Experiment,* and *Independent variable.*

Verstehen   A term used by the German sociologist Max Weber to refer to subjective interpretation of human behavior; that is, because one is a member of a group or culture, one gains insight and understanding into what others are experiencing, allowing one to interpret those experiences. See *Qualitative sociology.*

Vertical social mobility   Movement to a higher or a lower social position.

Voluntary associations   Groups that people join voluntarily, often because they wish to promote some goal or be with like-minded people. Examples include a church, a college class, and a bowling league. See *Involuntary associations.*

White-collar crime   Crimes committed by "respectable" persons of high status, frequently during the course of their occupation.

Appendix: Correlation Chart

THIRTY BASIC SOCIOLOGY TEXTS are listed alphabetically across the top of the correlation chart. The chapters of those texts are located in the column to the left of the boxes. The numbers within the boxes refer to the articles in *Down to Earth Sociology*.

For this edition, I have listed an article only once. The attempt, of course, has been to match the emphases of the article in this anthology with those of the chapters in the basic texts. In order to make certain that the articles in *Down to Earth Sociology* are distributed throughout the chapters, I have occasionally placed an article according to its subemphases. Because there are so many different ways of classifying these articles and each of us may see different ways of teaching them, you may prefer a different order than the one I have worked out. The *Instructor's Manual* contains a topical classification of articles that may be of value in this endeavor.

Actually, when I use a basic textbook in conjunction with *Down to Earth* (and I prefer to use *Down to Earth* by itself), I do things just the opposite. I build the course around the selections of *Down to Earth* and then supplement those readings with only a few chapters from the basic text. In that way, students are concentrating on *primary* sociological materials, rather than secondary analyses. Moreover, I find that because of the inherent interest of most of these readings, as well as the engaging class activities one can build around them (see the *Instuctor's Manual*), students are given a much more pleasing introduction to sociology.

The numbers within the boxes refer to selection numbers in **Down to Earth Sociology**.

The numbers directly below refer to chapters in the basic texts:	Henslin, 1st Edition, 1993	Giddens, 1st Edition, 1991	Farley, 2nd Edition, 1992	Eshleman, 4th Edition, 1993	Eitzen and Zinn, 5th Edition, 1991	Doob, 3rd Edition, 1991	Coser, Nock, Steffan, and Spain, 3rd Edition, 1991	Bryjak and Soroka, 1st Edition, 1992	Broom, Bonjean, and Broom, 1st Edition, 1990	Brinkerhoff and White, 3rd Edition, 1991
1	1, 2, 3	1, 2, 3	1, 2, 3	1, 2	1, 2, 3, 4	1, 2, 3	1, 2, 3	1, 2, 3, 4	1, 2, 3, 4, 5	1, 2, 3
2	5, 9, 21	6, 7	4, 5	3	8, 9	4	4	6, 7, 8, 9, 19, 21, 41, 42	6, 7, 8, 9	4
3	6, 7, 8	10, 11	7, 8, 9, 19, 21	4, 19	17	6, 7, 19	6, 7, 8, 9, 19	14, 15, 17, 20	10, 11, 12, 22	6, 7, 8
4	10, 11	8, 9, 14, 17, 19, 21	6	6, 7, 10, 11, 14, 38		15, 20	14, 15, 17	10, 11, 12	14, 17, 19, 24, 41	14, 15, 20
5	4	22, 23, 24, 38	10, 11, 14	15	6, 7	8, 9, 14, 16, 17, 21	10, 11, 38	18, 27, 28	15, 25, 26, 37, 38, 43	19, 21
6	14, 15, 19	5, 12, 13	12, 13, 29	8, 9	5, 10, 11, 21	10, 11, 38	25, 26	31, 32	30, 33, 34, 35, 36, 39, 44	9, 10, 11, 12
7	43	18, 27, 28, 29	15	22, 23, 24, 25, 26	14, 15, 24, 25, 26, 38	12, 13	18, 27, 28	13, 29, 30	18, 20, 21, 23, 27, 28	18
8	22, 24, 25, 26, 38	31, 32	22, 23, 24, 25, 26, 38	18, 27, 28	19, 22	5, 22, 23, 24, 25, 26	5, 22, 23, 24, 38	5, 22, 23, 24, 25, 26, 43	31, 32, 42	22, 23, 24, 25, 26, 38
9	27	15, 25, 26	18, 20, 28	31, 32	23, 27, 28	18, 27, 28	31, 32	33, 34, 35, 36, 37, 38, 39, 44	13, 16, 29	27, 28
10	18, 23, 28		27	5, 12, 13, 29	16, 18	31, 32	13, 29		40	31, 32
11	12, 13, 29	39, 41	31, 32		31, 32	29	34	16		5, 13, 29

530

	31, 32, 44	34	39, 43	34	12, 13, 29	34	20	40	
12		40							
13	34		30, 33, 36, 44	30, 33, 35, 36, 44	20, 40, 43	35	34	30, 33, 36, 44	
14	30, 33, 44		37	39, 42, 43	39, 41, 42	30, 33, 36, 44	30, 33, 36, 44	35	34
15	39		35	37	34	39	35	20, 43	30, 33, 36
16	36, 42, 43		39	40	30, 33, 36, 37, 44	20, 42, 43	37	40	35
17	35		41, 42	41	35	21, 37		16	37
18	37		40			41	16, 17	37	20
19			43				41		39
20	16, 17		16			16, 17	40, 42	42	16, 17
21	41					40		4	41
22	40								40, 42
23									

The numbers within the boxes refer to selection numbers in **Down to Earth Sociology**.

The numbers directly below refer to chapters in the basic texts:

Chapter	Hess, Markson, and Stein, 4th Edition, 1991, update 1993	Hess, Markson, and Stein, Brief Edition, 1992	Hunt and Colander, 7th Edition, 1990	Incardi and Rothman, 1st Edition, 1990	Johnson, 3rd Edition, 1992	Kammeyer, Ritzer, and Yetman, 4th Edition, 1990	Kornblum, 2nd Edition, 1991	Levin and Spates, 4th Edition, 1990	Luhman, 3rd Edition, 1992	Macionis, 3rd Edition, 1991
1	1, 2, 3	1, 2, 3, 4	2, 4	1, 2, 3	1, 2	1, 2, 3	1, 2, 3	1, 2, 3, 4	1, 2, 3	1, 2, 3, 36
2	4, 5	6, 7, 36, 40	1, 3	4, 5	5, 19	4, 5, 6	4, 5, 6	6, 7, 8, 9, 19	4	4
3	6, 7, 8	8, 9, 15, 16, 17, 19, 20, 21		6, 7, 8	15	7		10, 11, 12, 13, 14	6, 7, 8, 19	6, 7, 19
4	9, 19	10, 11, 44	6, 7, 8, 9	9, 14, 19, 21	40	8, 9, 14, 19	7, 8, 19	15, 16, 17, 20, 21	9, 10, 11, 14, 25, 26, 38	
5	10	5, 22, 23, 24, 25, 26	17, 19, 22	15, 25, 26	3	10, 11	16, 17	18, 27, 28, 29, 30, 31	5, 22, 23, 24,	10, 11, 12
6	14, 15, 18, 22, 24, 25, 26	18, 27, 28	21	10, 11	4	15, 22, 24, 25, 26, 38	10, 11	33, 34, 35, 36, 37, 38, 39	12, 13, 15, 20, 21, 29	8, 9, 14, 17, 21
7	12	12, 13, 14, 29, 37	40	22, 23, 24	10, 11, 38	12	9, 12, 14	5, 22, 23, 24, 25, 26, 32	18, 27, 28	15, 20
8	23, 27, 28	31, 32	10, 11, 12, 13, 14, 38	18, 20, 27, 28	7, 8, 9, 14, 17, 21	18, 23, 27, 28	18	41	31, 32	5, 22, 23, 24, 25, 26, 38
9	11, 13, 29	34	5, 15, 23, 24, 25, 26	31, 32	20	31, 32	15, 22, 24, 25, 26, 38	40, 42, 43, 44	34, 42, 44	
10		38, 39, 43	34	12, 13, 29	16	13, 29			30, 33, 36, 37	18, 27, 28
11	31, 32	30, 33, 35		34	6, 22, 23, 24, 25, 26				35, 39, 43	40

	12	13	14	15	16	17	18	19	20	21	22	23
31, 32		13, 29		34	30, 33	35	39	43	37	16	41	42, 44
16, 17, 40		41										
21, 23, 27, 28		31, 32	13, 29	34	35	30, 33, 36, 37, 44	20, 43	39, 41	40, 42			
30, 33, 36, 44		20, 43	21, 37	35	39, 42	16, 17	40, 41					
18, 27, 28		31, 32	12, 13, 29		34	30, 33, 36, 42	37	42, 43	39	35		41
35		30, 33, 36, 44	39	38	41	16, 17	40	37, 42, 43				
35		30, 33, 36, 37, 44	18, 20, 27, 28	16, 31, 32	39	41		29, 42, 43				
41, 42												
35												
34		20, 21	39	30, 33	35	38	37	40, 42, 43		16, 17	36	41

The numbers within the boxes refer to selection numbers in **Down to Earth Sociology**.

The numbers directly below refer to chapters in the basic texts:	McNall and McNall, 1st Edition, 1992	Persell, 3rd Edition, 1990	Robertson, 3rd Edition, 1987	Sanderson, 1st Edition, 1991	Schaefer, 4th Edition, 1993	Stark, 4th Edition, 1992	Sullivan and Thompson, 2nd Edition, 1990	Thio, 1st Edition, 1991	Thio, 3rd Edition, 1992	Tischler, 4th Edition, 1993
1	1, 2, 3	1, 2, 3	1, 2, 3	1, 2, 3, 4	1, 2, 3	15	1, 2, 3, 4	1, 2, 3, 4	1, 2, 3	1, 2, 3
2	4, 5	4	4	7, 8, 9, 19, 21	4	1, 2, 3, 6, 14	6, 7, 8, 9, 19, 21, 40	6, 7, 19	4	4
3	6, 7, 8	6, 7	7		6, 7, 8, 19	4, 5	10, 11, 12	8, 9, 14, 17, 21	6, 7, 8	6, 7, 8, 19
4	10	8, 9, 14, 15, 21	6, 19, 25, 36	6	9, 10, 11, 21, 38		15, 20	15, 20	9, 17, 19	10, 11, 38
5	11, 12, 13, 29, 38	10, 11	10, 11, 38		14, 15, 16, 17	7, 8	5, 22, 23, 24, 25, 26, 38	10, 11, 12	15, 20	9, 14, 15, 16, 17, 21
6	9, 14, 21	19	8, 9, 14, 17, 21	18		9, 10, 17, 20, 21, 37	18, 27, 28	5, 22, 23, 24, 25, 26, 38	10, 11, 14	5, 22, 23, 24, 25, 26
7	15, 17, 20	22, 23, 24, 25, 26	15		5, 22, 23, 24, 25, 26	19, 22, 23	13, 14, 29, 31, 32	18, 27, 28	5, 22, 23, 24, 25, 26	27, 28
8	19	27	22, 23, 24, 26	40, 42	18, 20, 27, 28	24, 25, 26	34, 37	31, 32	21	20, 31
9		18, 28	5	15, 20, 23, 28, 43	31, 32	18, 27	30, 33, 35, 36	13, 29	18, 27, 28	32
10	18, 27, 28	31, 32	18, 28, 39		12, 13, 29	28, 39	39, 43	34	31, 32	12, 13, 29
11	22, 23, 24, 25, 26	12, 13, 29	31, 32			31, 32, 36	16, 17	33, 36, 44	12, 13, 29	34

12	16, 31, 32	34	12, 13, 29	24, 25, 26, 27, 38, 39	34	11, 12, 13, 29, 38	41, 42, 44	35	35	30, 33, 36, 44
13	34	20, 38, 43	34	16, 17, 31, 32	35	34		39, 42, 43	34	39
14	30, 33, 44	39	30, 33, 44	5, 10, 11, 12, 13, 14, 22, 29	39	35		37	30, 33, 44	
15	35, 36	30, 33, 44	35		42, 43	39		16	35	18
16	37	35	37	34	30, 33, 36, 44	30, 33, 44		40, 41	39	37
17	39	42	20, 43	30, 33, 36, 37, 44	37	40			38, 43	41
18	43	37	27, 40	35	16				37	40, 42, 43
19		40, 41	42			16			42	
20	41	16, 17		41	41	43			36	
21	40, 42	5	16		40	41, 42			40	
22		36							16	
23			41						41	

Name Index